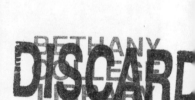

THE NEUROPSYCHOLOGY HANDBOOK: BEHAVIORAL AND CLINICAL PERSPECTIVES

Danny Wedding, Ph.D., received his doctorate from the University of Hawaii in 1979. He spent a postdoctoral year studying behavioral medicine and clinical neuropsychology at the University of Mississippi Medical Center and spent the following four years teaching at East Tennessee State University. He came to Marshall University in 1984 where he currently directs the neuropsychology and biofeedback service for the School of Medicine. He co-authored *Clinical and Behavioral Neuropsychology* (1984).

Arthur MacNeill Horton, Jr., Ed.D., received his doctorate from the University of Virginia and has earned a Diplomate in Clinical Psychology from the American Board of Professional Psychology. He is coordinator of the Alcoholism Section, Medical Service, and Staff Psychologist, Neurology Service, Veterans Administration Center, Baltimore, MD. The founder of the Behavioral Neuropsychology Special Interest Group of the Association for the Advancement of Behavior Therapy, Dr. Horton has published over ninety scientific papers and edited *Mental Health Interventions for the Aging* (1982) and co-authored *Clinical and Behavioral Neuropsychology* (1984).

Jeffrey S. Webster, Ph.D., received his doctorate in psychology from the University of Georgia in 1980 with a major in clinical and minor in biopsychology. He is currently Coordinator of the Neuropsychology Service at the Veterans Administration Medical Center in Long Beach, California. Dr. Webster has published over thirty scientific papers as well as several book chapters.

The
NEUROPSYCHOLOGY
Handbook

Behavioral and Clinical Perspectives

Danny Wedding, Ph.D.
Arthur MacNeill Horton, Jr., Ed.D.
Jeffrey Webster, Ph.D.

Editors

SPRINGER PUBLISHING COMPANY
New York

To our wives
Cynthia, Mary, and Reda
with love

86 87 88 89 90 / 5 4 3 2 1

Library of Congress Cataloging-in-Publication Data

The Neuropsychology handbook.

  Includes bibliographies and index.
  1. Neuropsychology. 2. Neuropsychological tests.
3. Neuropsychiatry. I. Wedding, Danny. II. Horton,
Arthur MacNeill, 1947–   . III. Webster, Jeffrey.
[DNLM: 1. Nervous System Diseases. 2. Neuropsychological
Tests. 3. Neuropsychology. WL 103 N49355]
QP360.N4945 1986   152   86-17764
ISBN 0-8261-4650-3

Contents

Preface

The past decade has witnessed phenomenal growth in clinical neuropsychology. A new specialty division (# 40) of the American Psychological Association testifies to this growth as does the rapidly increasing membership of the International Neuropsychological Society (INS) and the National Academy of Neuropsychologists (NAN). New journals have appeared devoted exclusively to clinical neuropsychology and neuropsychology is being increasingly represented in established and respected journals like the *Journal of Consulting and Clinical Psychology* and *Archives of General Psychiatry*. New psychological assessment instruments have been developed and advances in medical neurodiagnostics such as computerized tomography, positron emission tomography, and nuclear magnetic resonance offer unparalleled information about both brain structure and function. Moreover, new graduate training programs in clinical neuropsychology are becoming increasingly popular and the number of internship and postdoctoral training options is steadily rising.

It is probable, however, that neurodiagnostic evaluation by neuropsychologists will prove to be less important than the ability to specify precisely behavioral deficits and strengths. Perhaps most important will be the neuropsychologist's ability to propose precise training programs for motor, sensory, and cognitive deficits. While considerable work has been done by other disciplines (e.g., physical and occupational therapy) in retraining motor and sensory function, only minimal progress has been made in cognitive rehabilitation. This is not an easy challenge for clinical neuropsychology; however, it will be a critical one.

The techniques, methods, and tools of behavioral psychology hold great promise for both assessment and treatment of the brain-impaired individual. Colleagues in the Association for the Advancement of Behavior Therapy (AABT), historically quick to eschew psychological testing, are becoming interested in the behavioral sampling of clinical neuropsychology, while neuropsychology colleagues, moving beyond assessment, are looking for behavioral methods to apply to the rehabilitation of the patients they assess.

These considerations are reflected in the planning and design of this volume. Considerable effort was devoted to providing a balanced presentation of human neuropsychology with special emphasis on remediation of behavioral deficits secondary to brain damage. Leading figures in contemporary clinical and behavioral neuropsychology have been recruited as contributors.

This Handbook is primarily designed to serve as a basic reference for the practicing clinical and behavioral neuropsychologist and as a text for graduate study. In Part I the contributors present an overview of human neuropsychology and focus attention on internal and cross-discipline issues. Also presented are a discussion of the neurological foundations of human neuropsychology including theories of brain functioning, selected neurological disorders, and the lateralization of cerebral functions. Part II is devoted to assessment procedures and includes discussion of the physical neurological examination, the Halstead-Reitan Neuropsychological Battery, the Luria-Nebraska Neuropsychology Battery, and the Kaufman Assessment Battery for children. Part III describes treatment approaches and includes single-case design, behavioral neuropsychology, cognitive retraining, and family therapy. Part IV presents a variety of special populations, such as the head injured, alcoholics, the aged, pediatric patients, and school-aged children, in which human neuropsychology is making its greatest impact. Part V provides a discussion of some emerging areas of clinical practice such as prediction of everyday behavior, legal issues, and computer applications.

We hope the Handbook will also be found useful by a wide variety of professionals beyond the neuropsychologist. Among them are behavioral neurologists, pediatric neurologists, family practitioners, general and child psychiatrists, clinical and child psychologists, school psychologists, behavior therapists, special educators, learning disabilities specialists, speech pathologists, nurses, occupational therapists, rehabilitation counselors, and other professionals working with the brain-impaired, who may find it of value. It is clear that the complexity of brain impairment is such that only if individuals from many different professional orientations contribute their enthusiasm, encouragement, and expertise will it be possible to even begin to cope with the plethora of problems these patients face. The expectation and hope is that delineation of these concerns will be of some value in meeting the challenge of alleviating human distress and promoting social well-being for the brain-impaired population.

The Editors

Acknowledgments

A number of people contributed indirectly by their teaching, to the present volume. These include neuropsychologists such as Howard Gudeman, Richard J. Browne, James Craine, Thomas J. Boll, Walter Issacs, William Tsushima, Daniel Hallahan, and behavior therapists such as Len Ullmann, Carl Johnson, Roland Tharp, James M. Kaufman, Scott MacDonald, Julian Libet, Terence Keane, Dean Kilpatrick, and Marion MacDonald and personal mentors such as Donald Medley, Virgil S. Ward, Paul B. Walter, R. Dean Taylor, Elisabeth D. Decker, Kashmiri Parakh, Francis R. O'Brien, Hillel Panish, Len Epstein, Asha Badour, Robert Varapapa, Daniel Druback, and Henry Adams. Other colleagues took time to discuss ideas and issues in human neuropsychology which contributed greatly to the Handbook. These include Hugh Criswell, Eddythe Carr, Pat Sloan, Bruce Becker, Manfried Meier, Gerald Goldstein, Richard Berg, Peggy Michaelis, Michelle Timmons, Greta Wilkening, Cathy Tetzrow, Robert Elliott, Andrew Phay, James Fozzard, and Jason Brandt. They were willing to share ideas and to provide encouragement and their support was appreciated. Betty Eichmiller was the perfect secretary and returned typed copy with the English much improved. Most of all we owe thanks to our wives who were patient and long suffering through the length of this project's preparation.

Contributors

Ronald H. Baisden, Ph.D.
Department of Anatomy
Quillen-Dishner College of Medicine
East Tennessee State University
Johnson City, Tennessee

Mary Gail Becker, M.S.
Department of Educational Psychology
University of Georgia
Athens, Georgia

Erin D. Bigler, Ph.D.
Department of Psychology
University of Texas at Austin
Austin, Texas

Paul D. Blanton, M.S.
Medical Psychology Program
University of Alabma at Birmingham
Birmingham, Alabama

Nelson Butters, Ph.D.
Department of Psychiatry
University of California School of
    Medicine at San Diego
San Diego, California

Gordon J. Chelune, Ph.D.
Department of Psychiatry
The Cleveland Clinic Foundation
Cleveland, Ohio

Raymond S. Dean, Ph.D.
Department of Psychology
Ball State University
Muncie, Indiana

Cheri L. Geckler, Ph.D.
Department of Rehabilitation Medicine
New England Medical Center
Boston, Massachusetts

Charles J. Golden, Ph.D.
Department of Medical Psychology
University of Nebraska Medical
    Center
Omaha, Nebraska

William Drew Gouvier, Ph.D.
Department of Psychology
Louisiana State University
Baton Rouge, Louisiana

Lawrence C. Hartlage, Ph.D.
Department of Psychology
University of Arkansas
Little Rock, Arkansas

Frusanna B. Hayes, Ed.D.
Division of Exceptional Children
University of Georgia
Athens, Georgia

Arthur MacNeill Horton, Jr., Ed.D.
Alcoholism Section, Medical Service
Veterans Administration Medical
    Center
Baltimore, Maryland

George W. Hynd, Ed.D.
Department of Educational Psychology
University of Georgia
Athens, Georgia

Randy W. Kamphaus, Ph.D.
Department of Psychology
Eastern Kentucky University
Richmond, Kentucky

Charles J. Long, Ph.D.
Department of Psychology
Memphis State University
Memphis, Tennessee

Paul F. Malloy, Ph.D.
Department of Psychiatry & Human
 Behavior
Brown University School of Medicine
Providence, Rhode Island

Mark Maruish, Ph.D.
Professional Assessment Services
National Computer Systems
Minneapolis, Minnesota

Robert J. McCaffrey, Ph.D.
Department of Psychology
State University of New York at Albany
Albany, New York

William Gene Miller, Ph.D.
Department of Psychology and
 Psychobiology
Western Maryland College
Westminster, Maryland

Kurt A. Moehle, Ph.D.
Department of Psychology
Purdue University
Bloomington, Indiana

Stephen E. Nadeau, M.D.
Department of Neurology
University of Mississippi Medical School
Jackson, Mississippi

Roberta Nolan, M.A.
The Neuropsychology Service
Baylor College of Medicine
Houston, Texas

John E. Obrzut, Ph.D.
Department of Educational Psychology
University of Arizona
Tucson, Arizona

Francis J. Pirozzolo, Ph.D.
The Neuropsychology Service
Baylor College of Medicine
Houston, Texas

Antonio E. Puente, Ph.D.
Department of Psychology
University of North Carolina at
 Wilmington
Wilmington, North Carolina

Ralph M. Reitan, Ph.D.
Reitan Neuropsychology Laboratories
 Inc.
Tucson, Arizona

Cecil R. Reynolds, Ph.D.
Department of Educational Psychology
Texas A&M University
College Station, Texas

Mitchell Rosenthal, Ph.D.
Department of Physical Medicine
Rush Medical College
Chicago, Illinois

Christopher Ryan, Ph.D.
Department of Psychiatry
University of Pittsburgh School of
 Medicine
Pittsburgh, Pennsylvania

Scott W. Sautter, M.A.
Department of Psychology and Human
 Development
Vanderbilt University
Nashville, Tennessee

Reda R. Scott, Ph.D.
Geropsychology Service
Veterans Administration Medical
 Center
Long Beach, California

Andrew A. Swihart, Ph.D.
Department of Neurology
University of Pittsburgh Medical Center
Pittsburgh, Pennsylvania

Mark Wagner, Ph.D.
Department of Rehabilitation Medicine
University of Rochester
Rochester, New York

Jeffrey S. Webster, Ph.D.
Neuropsychology Service
Veterans Administration Medical
  Center
Long Beach, California

Danny Wedding, Ph.D.
Neuropsychology and Biofeedback
  Service
Marshall University School of Medicine
Huntington, West Virginia

Deborah Wolfson, Ph.D.
Reitan Neuropsychology Laboratories
  Inc.
Tucson, Arizona

Michael L. Woodruff, Ph.D.
Department of Anatomy
Quillen-Dishner College of
  Medicine
East Tennessee State University
Johnson City, Tennessee

PART I
Neurological Foundations

1

Human Neuropsychology: An Overview*

Arthur MacNeill Horton, Jr. and
Antonio E. Puente

HISTORICAL CONTEXT

Ebbinghaus stated a hundred years ago that "psychology has a long past but a short history." The same could be said of neuropsychology. Although its history can be traced to the Greeks, it was not until the last half of this century that the discipline became organized and widely accepted.

Euroasian Contributions

The earliest written records of attempts to localize neural function are dated between 2500 and 3000 B.C. (Walsh, 1978). These records contain descriptions of 48 case histories involving brain trauma. In more recent history, individuals such as Andreas Vesalius (1514–1564) began to analyze neural anatomy and function more systematically. Nevertheless, it was Rene Descartes (1569–1650) who is credited with first popularizing the notion of mind–body dualism, as well as the localization of function. The localization of the "seat of the soul" to the centrally located, single pineal gland remains classic. Continuing the French tradition, Paul Broca (1824–1880) followed the progress of an aphasic placed under his care at the Bicetre, an asylum near Paris. By meticulous observation and an eventual autopsy in 1874, Broca was

---

*Dr. Horton's contribution to this chapter was made in his capacity as a private citizen and without support or endorsement by the Veterans Administration.

able to conclude that aphasia was neither a loss of memory nor a muscular dysfunction. Instead, loss of speech could be directly attributed to trauma (in this case, a tumor) to the base of the third frontal convolution of the left cerebral hemisphere.

Pierre Flourens (1794–1867), a powerful opponent of the phrenology movement as espoused by Gall and Spurzheim, could be considered a forerunner to modern experimental neuropsychology. By developing ablation (i.e., lesion) techniques, Flourens proposed one of the first viable nonlocalization theories of brain functioning. During the twentieth century numerous neuropsychologists have contributed to the development of the field in Europe. Most notable of this group is Kurt Goldstein (1878–1965), who evaluated the effects of missile wounds in soldiers and military veterans in Germany. Using the case history approach popular with European neuropsychologists, the Russian A. R. Luria (1902–1977) systematically observed and interacted with numerous brain-injured individuals prior to formulating a functional theory of brain functioning. Luria cogently argued for the importance of individual brain systems in the organization of complex psychological activity.

North American Contributions

Although the development of neuropsychology has a more time-limited tradition in North America, the field has benefited from the contributions of numerous eminent psychologists. One of the first to contribute significantly was Karl Lashley (1890–1958), who performed numerous ablation studies (mainly of the visual cortex) while at the University of Minnesota, the University of Chicago, and Harvard. In contrast to the localization theories of the day, Lashley proposed the radical concept of equipotentiality of neural structures. Roger Sperry, associated with California Technological University, pioneered the split-brain studies in humans. In these studies, Sperry and colleagues (most notably Gazzaniga) examined the hemispheric function of individuals who had undergone a commissurotomy. In 1982, Sperry was recognized for his pioneering efforts in brain research by being awarded the Nobel Prize.

Applied neuropsychology in North America is often traced to Ward Halstead who, while at the University of Chicago Medical School, administered psychometric tests to individuals with frontal lobe damage. His results, the basis of his theory of biological intelligence, suggest that damage to the frontal lobes results in general reduction of adaptive abilities. One of Halstead's students, Ralph Reitan, was instrumental in furthering Halstead's concepts and translating these ideas into a psychometric battery of tests still widely used today. Hartlage and Telzrow (1982) recently reported the results of a survey of 158 neuropsychologists, who indicated that Reitan ranks as the individual who has made the most significant contribution to the field of clinical neuropsychology since 1940. The entire Reitan battery (e.g., the Halstead–

Reitan Neuropsychological Battery) was reported to be the fourth most frequently used neuropsychological assessment tool by this sample. Many other living neuropsychologists, too numerous to mention, are continuing to make significant contributions to the field and shaping the course of its history.

CONCEPTUALIZING HUMAN NEUROPSYCHOLOGY

In pursuit of conceptual clarity, the following brief definitions are provided. The terms to be discussed have been used in idiosyncratic fashion by numerous authors. This practice has undoubtedly diminished the conceptual clarity of the issues. To date, satisfactory methods of correcting this situation have not been developed.

Neuropsychology Defined

While different authors have advanced multiple definitions of neuropsychology, in the context of this chapter the following definition was selected: "Neuropsychology is the scientific study of brain-behavior relationships" (Meier, 1974).

Some limitations of this definition will be noted. It fails adequately to address the many fields of neuropsychology that have developed over the years (Davison, 1974; Horton, Wedding, & Phay, 1981). Also, the collateral areas of speech pathology and physiological psychology could easily have been included in this definition, although they will not be addressed (Meier, 1974). In order to provide further clarification, the following section will offer a brief survey of some selected subfields of neuropsychology: clinical neuropsychology, experimental neuropsychology, behavioral neurology, and behavioral neuropsychology.

Clinical neuropsychology is the "application of our understanding of human brain-behavior relationships to clinical problems" (Horton, Wedding, & Phay, 1981, p. 59). Similar to the development of the clinical psychologist as a professional psychologist with special psychometric and psychotherapeutic expertise in the general area of psychopathology, the clinical neuropsychologist is a professional psychologist with diagnostic skills and psychometric expertise applicable to behavioral dysfunction associated with central nervous system dysfunction. Just as carefully validated and rigorously standardized psychometric instruments such as the Wechsler Intelligence Scales (WAIS, WAIS-R, etc.) and Minnesota Multiphasic Personality Inventory (MMPI) are strongly associated with clinical psychology, the Halstead–Reitan Neuropsychology Battery and Luria–Nebraska Neuropsychology Battery are identified with clinical neuropsychology. The emphasis on psychometrics is in large part the result of the contribution of Ralph M. Reitan.

Experimental neuropsychology is the "elucidation of basic brain-behavior relationships" (Horton, Wedding, & Phay, 1981, p. 59). Like experimental psychology, experimental neuropsychology has a primary focus on theoretical questions rather than practical applications. Due to the nature of the questions most often addressed, experimental neuropsychologists often use nonhuman subjects. The degree of generality of basic neurobehavioral relationships depends upon the species and area of psychology under study. For example, since the higher cortical function of language only achieves its full expression in human beings, it is difficult to conceptualize a truly appropriate nonhuman model for study (see Terrace, Petitto, Sanders, & Bever, 1979, for further elucidation on this issue).

Behavioral neurology is the third subfield of neuropsychology. Like clinical neuropsychology, behavioral neurology is concerned with clinical applications of scientific knowledge. However, unlike clinical neuropsychology, behavioral neurology utilizes a qualitative, intuitive approach; by contrast, clinical neuropsychology is seen as more psychometric and quantitatively based. Moreover, behavioral neurology utilizes a more traditional medical case study approach, such as that espoused by A. R. Luria (1973), to the conceptualization of neurobehavioral phenomena. This approach, of course, assumes that the practitioner has considerable clinical expertise as well as a thorough understanding of neural structure and function.

Behavioral neuropsychology is a recent addition to the principal subfields of neuropsychology. Horton (1979) has offered the following definition of behavioral neuropsychology:

> Essentially, behavioral neuropsychology may be defined as the application of behavior therapy techniques to problems of organically impaired individuals while using a neuropsychological assessment and intervention perspective. This treatment philosophy asserts that inclusion of data from neuropsychological assessment strategies would be helpful in the formulation of hypotheses regarding antecedent conditions (external or internal) for observed phenomena of psychopathology. (p. 20)

This new area of research and clinical interest combines segments of both neuropsychology and behavior therapy. Despite a focus upon applied aspects of neuropsychology, behavioral neuropsychology may be easily discriminated from these related subfields of neuropsychology by its reliance upon behavior therapy research for its treatment techniques. The major emphasis of behavioral neuropsychology is upon the problems of management, retraining, and rehabilitation. In contrast, the subfields of clinical neuropsychology and behavioral neurology are both strongly associated with the problems of differential diagnosis. Furthermore, it should be clear that experimental neuropsychology can be easily separated from clinical neuropsychology, behavioral neurology, and behavioral neuropsychology by the "pure" research aims of the former and the more clinical focus of the latter.

Examinations of some trends in behavioral therapy can help delineate the scope of behavioral neuropsychology. Behavior therapy can be seen as having developed three salient trends. These are, in order of importance, behavioral, cognitive, and affective. Based on the work of Watson (1913), Skinner (1938), and others, behavior therapy is based upon the principle that behavior is a function of consequences and utilizes reinforcement as a major concept. In contrast, the cognitive trend in behavior therapy is of more recent vintage (Mahoney, 1974). The cognitive trend postulates that inferred variables, such as thoughts and images, should be seen as legitimate concepts in the functional analysis of human behavior (Mahoney, 1974). The cognitive trend in behavior therapy has been a subject of continuing controversy (Beck & Mahoney, 1979; Ellis, 1979; Lazarus, 1979; Wolpe, 1978).

The affective trend in behavior therapy has a most curious history. Some would date these trends from the early work of Joseph Wolpe, M.D. (1978), the South African psychiatrist who is credited with the establishment of clinical behavior therapy. His techniques of systematic desensitization and assertiveness training have, in large part, sparked the clinical behavior therapy movement. Despite Wolpe's contribution, the affective nature of his work has remained unappreciated. More recently, however, there have been indications of increasing interest in affect by behavior therapists.

Brain Damage/Cerebral Dysfunction

A critical starting point in this volume would be to distinguish the terms *brain damage* and *cerebral dysfunction*. As is well known, a brain lesion is a pathological alteration of brain tissue. In almost all cases neurodiagnostic methods can identify these incidences of structural change brain lesions. However, classification of changes in brain physiology that are not reflected in structural modification is a more complex issue. For example, an open head injury caused by a gunshot wound clearly results in structural brain damage; yet obvious structural brain changes caused by toxic conditions would escape verification by many neurobiomedical diagnostic procedures (Horton & Wedding, 1984). Sometimes the term *cerebral dysfunction* is preferred to describe situations in which functional changes are clear, but the issue of structural changes is not yet clarified.

Organicity

In the context of addressing the proper usage of *brain damage* and *cerebral dysfunction,* some comments regarding the term *organicity* are appropriate. Davison (1974) has suggested the following:

> The concept includes the assumption that any and all kinds of brain damage lead to similar behavioral effects, and that behavioral differences among the brain damaged are due primarily to severity of damage and to premorbid personality characteristics. (p. 14)

Historically, the concept had roots in the equipotentiality/localization debate and is perhaps most associated, at least in the United States, with Karl Lashley (1929). As observed by Horton and Wedding (1984):

> ... to understand brain damage as existing on a single dimension is as realistic and useful as the assertion that human beings vary on the dimension of height. To be sure, the assertion is true in a general sense, and, in special situations, could be quite useful (e.g. college basketball) but in many circumstances there could be a need for additional data with regard to sources of variation. (p. 12)

Despite the limitations of the concept of organicity, it has developed as a two-category (organic vs. functional) diagnostic paradigm for decades. The only positive development has been a clear trend toward the differentiation of the concept of organicity into various subtypes.

DSM III Categories of Organic Mental Disorders

With the development of the *Diagnostic and Statistical Manual* (DSM) by the American Psychiatric Association in 1962 came the growing acceptance by the mental health community and insurance industry of the need for diagnostic systems. The DSM has, of course, been subjected to critical review and extensive revisions (first in 1966 and, most recently, under the direction of Robert Spitzer in 1980). Regardless of the psychological community's skepticism and continued search for alternative diagnostic systems (cf. Miller, Bergstrom, Cross, & Grube, 1981; Smith & Kraft, 1983), the DSM-III continues to be the most widely used diagnostic system for clinical and research activities in North America.

Organic brain syndromes (OBS) were relatively easy to diagnose with the early versions of the DSM. Basic distinctions were predicated essentially on whether the syndrome was acute or chronic, thus resulting in only two major diagnostic categories. In the DSM II classification was accomplished with the variable of psychosis. The primary symptoms associated with OBS, according to the DSM II, were impairment of orientation, memory, intellectual functions, judgment, and affect.

The DSM III provides a more extensive array of classifications. Significantly different from the DSM II, the most recent version makes a clear distinction between syndrome and etiology. Organic syndromes refer to the resulting behavior without regard to the etiology, while organic mental disorder (OMD) directly reflects an etiology of brain dysfunction. The most common syndromes listed include delirium, dementia, intoxication, and withdrawal. The DSM III allows the development of a diagnosis according to either symptomology or etiology. If the etiology is known, then it should be used to diagnose. Otherwise, one simply focuses on the syndrome.

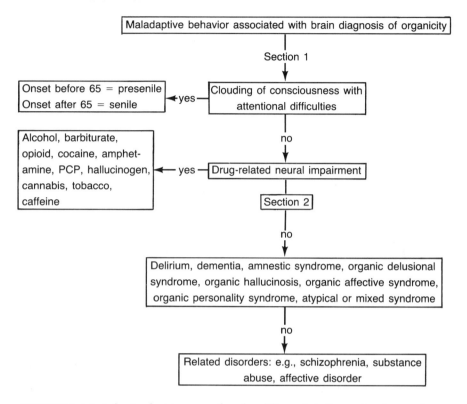

FIGURE 1.1 A basic decision tree for the differential diagnosis of organic mental disorders according to the DSM III.

As Figure 1.1 indicates, the most recent version of the DSM is divided into two sections based on whether the behavior or etiology of the behavior is found in the mental disorder section of the World Health Organization's *International Classification of Diseases—Ninth Revision—Clinical Modification* (ICD-9-CM, 1978). The largest number of diagnoses fall under section 1, those behaviors or etiologies listed in the ICD-9-CM. This section is subdivided into two main categories. First, dementia covers disorders related to "a loss of intellectual abilities of sufficient severity to interfere with social or occupational functioning." Dementias develop (1) prior to the age of 65, presenile, (2) after the age of 65, senile, or (3) because of an infarct (i.e., necrosis due to circulatory obstruction). Secondly, a category exists for substance use disorders that affect central nervous system functioning.

Section 2 contains diagnoses for which syndromes or etiologies are not noted in the prenatal disorder section of ICD-9-CM or are unknown. Additionally, this section is often used when the syndrome's etiology is directly traceable to a physical disorder already listed in Axis III of the diagnosis. The main diagnoses are delirium and dementia.

HUMAN NEUROPSYCHOLOGY AND TRADITIONAL
MEDICAL SPECIALTIES

Like other fields of psychology, neuropsychology is related to and often confused with medical disciplines. A strong working relationship and an understanding of these related disciplines are critical to the development of neuropsychology as a science and as a profession. The confusion between neuropsychology and these disciplines arises from a misunderstanding of the training and scope of these medical specialties. This misunderstanding can, in large part, be attributed to the limited understanding of neuropsychology by the general medical community (cf. Anchor, 1983).

Neurology

The historical view of psychology, in general, and neuropsychology, in particular, traditionally held by neurologists is similar to that outlined by Greenberg (1983): while the brain is involved with behavior, it is not the source of behavior. This appears to have been especially true for higher-order behaviors. As a consequence, a specialist in the science of behavior could only offer limited contributions to the care of the neurologically impaired patient.

This limited perspective is rapidly vanishing as inroads are being made between these closely related professions. Indeed, it is not uncommon for psychologists to have clinical appointments in departments or clinics of neurology. This development has occurred in part as a function of the need for expert opinion on issues of behavior related to central nervous system functioning, especially higher cortical functions. This has become critical during the last several decades since neurology has moved away from its original (and once inseparable) partner, psychiatry. Strub and Black (1982) suggest that neurology has shifted its emphasis to the peripheral nervous system effectively, ignoring behavioral abnormalities. As neurology continues to deemphasize complex central nervous system behaviors, the neuropsychologist will continue playing a critical role for the neurologist.

Neurosurgery

Although the neuropsychologist is basically interested in the quantification, description, and remediation of behavior associated with brain damage, an implicit interest has been the anatomical localization of behavioral dysfunction. The current state of empirical knowledge indicates that while numerous advances have been made in the psychometric localization, further investigation needs to be performed with well-documented cases before acceptable levels of confidence can be attained in this endeavor. Until then, it is critical that the neuropsychologist work closely with neurosurgeons and neuroradiologists in an effort to develop more sophisticated tests and scales for cerebral localization.

From the standpoint of service to the neurosurgeon, a neuropsychologist can provide valuable assistance in the documentation of psychological dysfunction due to neural impairment (Freeman, 1981). Specifically, neuropsychologists can provide documentation of behavioral deficits both presurgery and postsurgery as a means to (a) determine changes linked to surgical intervention, (b) chart the course of neural dysfunction over time (e.g., tumor growth), (c) arrive at a prognosis of behavioral deficiencies, and (d) evaluate the risks and benefits to be derived from surgical intervention. Often overlooked by both disciplines is the role of the neuropsychologist in the rehabilitative process. Considering the invasive, nonpersonal nature of surgery, coupled with the limitations of the neurosurgeon in nonsurgical rehabilitation, behavioral neuropsychology plays an important role in the recovery process. Beyond dealing with primary issues resulting from the actual neural impairment, the neuropsychologist can assist in dealing with the secondary symptoms (e.g., depression, surgical recuperation, treatment compliance) as well as with family issues (e.g., readjustment, support) (see Chapter 12). Finally, an emerging role of the neuropsychologist within neurosurgery is the assessment and treatment of pain.

Psychiatry

One of the most important roles of the neuropsychologist in psychiatry has been the differential diagnosis of organic and functional disorders and of the existence of neural impairment in functional disorders (cf. Puente, Heidelberg-Sanders, & Lund, 1982; Ross & Rush, 1981). Considering that the psychiatrist is inevitably interested in behavioral dysfunction, the neuropsychologist comes as close as any professional to being able to provide pertinent information in the diagnosis and treatment of the neurologically impaired patient. There are several areas that warrant attention, including psychiatric manifestation of neural impairment and psychiatric basis for neural impairment. Of increasing importance to the psychiatrist working with neuroleptics is the assessment of neurobehavioral functioning associated with drug metabolism.

Behavioral intervention with brain-damaged individuals manifesting a combination of neural and behavioral deficiencies (e.g., dementia) is an area in which the neuropsychologist can effectively collaborate with the psychiatrist. This is especially important when the neuropsychologist has training in a particular subspecialty such as vocational retraining.

Rehabilitation Medicine

Although rehabilitation medicine has only recently been linked to neuropsychology, analysis of the function and purpose of this medical specialty provides suggestions for interaction. The primary function of the specialist in rehabilitation medicine is to help the patient return to normal functioning after an illness or injury. While this function seemingly suggests dealing with a wide variety of physical problems, the specialty has tended to focus on chronic diseases. The two diseases that have received considerable attention have been movement and cardiovascular disorders. In the former, the neuropsychologist can assist in diagnosing and following the course of treatment for general motor dysfunction, including fine motor control. In the latter, the neuropsychologist provides differential diagnosis of stroke and related disorders and functional problems.

The neuropsychologist can play a significant role in relating neurobehavioral findings to the prediction of vocational performance. A problem that has long been neglected by neuropsychologists is the determination of disability in workmen's compensation and Social Security cases (Puente, 1982; Puente, in press).

HUMAN NEUROPSYCHOLOGY AND SELECTED NONMEDICAL SPECIALTIES

In this section, attention will be devoted to four nonmedical specialties: clinical psychology, health psychology, educational evaluation, and vocational evaluation. It is of course acknowledged that other nonmedical specialties could have been selected for discussion. Unfortunately, space limitation dictated that difficult choices had to be made and, in the opinion of the authors, the nonmedical specialties selected were most relevant to the practice and study of neuropsychology at present.

Clinical Psychology

Just as clinical psychology emerged from the interface of psychology with psychiatry, clinical neuropsychology emerged from the interface of psychology and neurology. That is to say, the particular problems that were encountered by psychiatrists in clinical practice were often those posed to the clinical psychologist. To a degree, the assessment devices that evolved and prospered in clinical psychology were devoted to diagnostic issues of vital importance to psychiatrists. For example, the Rorschach, Thematic Apperception Test, Wechsler Intelligence Scales, Minnesota Multiphasic Personality Inventory, and Bender–Gestalt Test are perhaps a classical selection (Lubin, Wallis, & Paine, 1971). As a battery these tests had both positive and negative consequences. On the positive side, the tests did an admirable job of selecting appropriate candidates for psychoanalytic therapy. Since for many years the majority of psychiatrists have been analytically oriented, the provision of a valid and reliable prediction of a patient's likelihood to engage profitably in this type of therapy was clearly of great value (Horton & Wedding, 1984).

On the negative side, the emphasis on suitability for psychoanalytic psychotherapy had deleterious effects on the development of comprehensive assessment procedures for other varieties of patients such as the brain damaged. In simple terms, brain-damaged or "organic" patients were *not* seen as appropriate for individual analytically oriented therapy; they were identified as a class to be excluded without careful attention to relevant parameters or conceptual paradigms to explain facets of brain injury.

Health Psychology

Formal definitions aside (Stone, Cohen, & Adler, 1979), one might construct a working definition of health psychology as "psychology applied to medical complications and specialties." Within this working definition one sees that neuropsychology emerges as the branch of psychology that attends to the problems of neurology.

To be sure, all health psychologists are not neuropsychologists. Conversely, the proposition that all neuropsychologists are health psychologists is one that will engender spirited debate. If one accepts the aforementioned definition of health psychology as psychology (science and professional knowledge and skills) applied to medical specialties (including public health as a medical specialty), then the conclusion evolves that health psychology encompasses neuropsychology.

It is, of course, acknowledged that such a conclusion is not endorsed by all, but still the conclusion raises some crucial points. For example, a major focus in health care is cost containment and medical care utilization. At present the implications of such issues for neuropsychology are relatively unexamined. Similarly, more attention to the emerging paradigm of psychosocial intervention by health psychologists in the realm of medical specialties, such as cardiology, pediatrics, and oncology, would yield a different perspective on the role of the neuropsychologist. Moreover, recent data on neuropsychological sequelae of medical conditions not previously thought to produce neurological deficits (Ryan et al., 1984) are demonstrating some robust potential for the health/neuropsychology interface.

Education

One of the first to suggest that neuropsychological knowledge would be helpful in understanding childhood learning disorders was William Gaddes (1968). Many have advocated such a position (Hynd & Obrzut, 1981; Rourke, 1975); indeed, some have gone so far as to suggest that the interface of education and human neuropsychology has been so productive that a subdiscipline has evolved. Various terms advocated to describe this new subdiscipline have included *school neuropsychology* (Hynd & Obrzut, 1981), *developmental neuropsychology* (van der Vlugt, 1979), and *educational neuropsychology* (Gaddes, 1981). Factors which have contributed to the current enthusiasm regarding the educational relevance of neuropsychological data include the wealth of reliable clinical findings correlating localized brain lesions and academic performance.

Of even more immediate value to the notion of promoting an interface between education and human neuropsychology has been research demonstrating the value of neuropsychological data in treatment planning for educational deficiencies. Perhaps some of the most interesting results were obtained by Hartlage (1975). In this early study, first-grade children were placed in reading programs based upon neuropsychological assessment data. The experimental group was 1.5 standard deviations above the control group in reading after one year. Similar results have been obtained by others (Kaufman & Kaufman, 1983). It should be noted that these studies utilized a strengths approach to treatment planning (Reynolds, 1981). Expectations are that a strengths approach will be of great value and that more effective use of behavior modification techniques can be made with this approach (Horton et al., 1981).

Vocational Evaluation

Although the evaluation of neural impairment by neuropsychologists is becoming increasingly accepted, the evaluation of vocational performance in brain-damaged individuals by the neuropsychologist remains a relatively little-explored professional and academic pursuit. Dennerll, Rodin, Gonzales, Schwartz, and Lin (1969) were among the first to investigate employed brain-damaged individuals. In a later study (Schwartz, Dennerll, & Lin, 1966), the use of prediction models for this population was reported. Similarly, Heaton, Chelune, and Lehman (1978) found significant differences between employed and nonemployed patients referred for neuropsychological evaluations. Employed referrals performed significantly better on a variety of neuropsychological tests. In a more recent effort, Cole and Long (in press) reported the relationship between neuropsychological and vocational performance in neurologically-impaired patients. These findings suggest that a high degree of correlation exists between both types of assessment. The authors conclude that duplication of services in the evaluation of neurological patients frequently occurs, indirectly giving greater credence to psychometrically-oriented evaluation. For a more complete review of the literature, the reader is referred to Heaton and Pendleton (1981).

Until recently, little scientific evidence had been reported to support clinical practice in the disability evaluation of brain impairment cases. Nevertheless, the importance of adequate evaluation and prediction for individuals with brain damage takes on an urgent nature in light of the August 1982 report by the Subcommittee on the Oversight of Government Management. This report indicated that while 75% of all disability determination reviews use at least one consultative exam, 68% of these consultations were deemed "not useful" by state disability determination services. Anecdotal evidence also suggests that state agencies are being required to give greater weight to these examinations for reasons of accountability. It is assumed that neuropsychological evaluations of proven worth for determining vocational ability would be most helpful in this regard.

EMERGING TRENDS IN HUMAN NEUROPSYCHOLOGY

As observed by Costa (1983), it is a commonly held assumption that human beings demonstrate an ability to utilize the past and make projections of the future in order to govern present behavior. Thus, some speculations are offered regarding the possible future direction in which human neuropsychology will evolve in the coming years. The areas considered include education, clinical training, certification, new concepts, new technology, and new populations.

Education and Training

To a large extent, the recent history of education and training in human neuropsychology has been dominated by Manfred J. Meier of the University of Minnesota Medical School. Dr. Meier, through his writings (1981a) and his chairmanship of the International Neuropsychology Society Task Force on education, accreditation, and credentialing (1981b), has profoundly influenced events relative to the education and training of neuropsychologists. The task force outlined four models for education and training for neuropsychologists. Essentially, Model I casts neuropsychology as a subspecialty area in a traditionally applied curriculum. At a slightly more advanced level, Model II posits an interdisciplinary program between a department of psychology and a medical school. Model III is a Boulder Model scientific/practitioner, while Model IV is a combined scientific Ph.D. and professional Psy.D. program that requires a minimum of six years of training.

In terms of the future, one can anticipate a progressive increase of Model II programs, which currently exist in only a few universities. At present only a single university offers a Ph.D. in neuropsychology that follows the Boulder scientific/practitioner Model. One wonders if, rather than Model IV (Ph.D./Psy.D. programs), one might be more likely to see professional Psy.D. programs in neuropsychology. In terms of political and economic realities, it is likely that strong preexisting applied programs will not be the most fertile ground for neuropsychology programs and that very few students will have the financial resources to complete the six or more years of graduate work deemed necessary to pursue a combined Ph.D./Psy.D. program.

Certification

At present, the clinical practice of neuropsychology falls under the generic licensure umbrella of psychology in the United States and Canada. While the aforementioned International Neuropsychology Society Task Force on education, accreditation, and credentialing promulgated specific criteria for the clinical practice of neuropsychology, these guidelines are without the force of law. In the past, neuropsychological practice has been based largely on a measure of self-identification. In response to this situation, two diplomate-level granting boards have arisen to identify skilled practitioners of neuropsychology. The American Board of Clinical Neuropsychology (ABCN) is comprised largely of current International Neuropsychology Society members and has recently become affiliated with the American Board of Professional Psychology (ABPP). In contrast, the American Board of Professional Neuropsychology (ABPN) is comprised largely of individuals who are members of both the International Neuropsychology Society and the National Academy of Neuropsychologists. While some efforts have been made to combine these boards, at present both are operating separately. There is speculation that as more individuals are credentialed at the diplomate level, laws will be modified to restrict the practice of neuropsychology to designated individuals.

A related but separate development of importance is the concurrent development by the American Psychological Association (APA) of specific criteria for the recognition of new professional psychological specialties other than the traditional ones (i.e., clinical, counseling, school and industrial/organizational). New standards will be developed by APA relative to the practice of new specialties.

RECENT DEVELOPMENTS

New Concepts

Subcortical Brain Damage

Historically, high-order functions delineated by the cerebral cortex have been emphasized by the neuropsychologist to the exclusion of the examination of subcortical integrity. Considering the relatively large volume of noncortical area, the complexity of the behavior that it regulates, and the number of common neural disorders with subcortical origins, the importance of the subcortex should not be minimized. As a consequence, there is no substitute for a thorough understanding of subcortical anatomy and function.

Numerous behavioral changes are regularly observed as a function of subcortical damage. Typical subcortical damage often involves sensory systems, most notably the visual and auditory systems. However, the lower brain stem, as well as thalamic lesions, may affect pain and temperature sensations (Soffine, Feldman, & Bender, 1968). Disruption of extensive motor pathways, originating in the cortex and extending to the spinal cord via the basal ganglia and midbrain, may lead to either fine or gross motor disturbance. Generally, basal ganglia dysfunction produces problems with slower and more precise skilled movements, while lesions of the lower structures affect faster and more automatic movements such as posturing (Brodal, 1969). Limbic and basal ganglia structures have also been experimentally implicated in learning. Specifically, lesions of these areas result in overresponsiveness and an inability to learn behavioral tasks or to generalize learned behavior (Ellen & Powell, 1962). Recall of learned information appears to be regulated by many of the same structures as learning (Barbizet, 1963; Ojemann, 1966). While limbic nuclei have historically been implicated in the regulation of affective behavior (Papez, 1937), in some cases damage to this area may result in increases in reactivity or in placidity, depending on the location of the lesion. Of the numerous structures associated with the limbic system, hypothalamic damage appears to play an important role in producing significant and permanent increases in emotional reactivity (Flynn, 1967). The role of cognition has typically been delegated to the frontal lobe. However, there is recent evidence to suggest that perceptual and cognitive behaviors, such as hallucinations and delusions, are directly linked to subcortical structure dysfunction (Fredrickson & Richelson, 1979).

In summary, numerous important behaviors often observed in neuropsychological settings are mediated by subcortical structures. One might consider the concept of subcortical brain damage as a new, emerging trend within neuropsychology; note, however, that the average date of the references included in this brief section is 1964. Clearly, research in subcortical behavioral pathology is not a new concept. Instead, what is new is the developing interest in and understanding of this important area of the brain.

Rehabilitation and Behavior Management

As noted by Satz and Fletcher (1981), the therapeutic role of the neuropsychologists is emerging. A major and salient trend in human neuropsychology is the move away from the classic diagnostic role toward that of intervention/therapy (Diller & Gordon, 1981; Horton & Miller, 1984; Horton & Wedding, 1984).

One strong trend in the therapy of the brain-impaired is the use of behavior modification with the brain-injured (Horton, 1979; Horton & Wedding, 1984). Recent research documents excellent results (Horton & Wedding, 1984). Another exciting trend is the use of computers in rehabilitation. Lynch (1981) at the Palo Alto Veterans Administration Medical Center, for example, has adapted video games for retraining purposes. In a similar trend, Seron, Deloche, Moulard, and Rovsller (1980) have devised a computer-based therapy for the treatment of aphasic patients with writing problems. Still another potentially rich treatment option is the combination of behavioral and pharmacological agents (Pirozzolo, Campenella, Christensen, & Lawson-Kerr, 1981). Similarly, the use of acetylcholine precursors (e.g., lecithin) to improve cognitive skills in the aged has produced some positive findings (Davis & Berger, 1979). The potential of combining behavior modification and appropriate pharmacological agents is untapped and clearly in need of careful study.

New Technology

Over the last twenty years more accurate diagnostic techniques have been developed. The EEG can now be analyzed using averaged evoked potentials. While the advances in metabolic monitoring have been useful, the traditional radiographic techniques need additional improvement in detection of mass lesions. The first and still most commonly used of the new generation techniques is computerized axial tomography (CAT), in which a device rotates around the patient's head emitting x-ray beams later deciphered by x-ray sensitive detectors (instead of the traditional x-ray film). As a rule, multiple horizontal slices extending from the base of the skull to the vertex are photographed several millimeters apart. More recent developments include dynamic spatial reconstruction (DSR) techniques, which provide a three-dimensional perspective (rather than the two-dimensional one provided by CAT scan) of the brain. Positron-emission transaxial tomography (PETT) combines mass localization and metabolic detection methods by providing a phasic (rather than the usual static) presentation of metabolic activity of the brain. The most promising and newest of these scan methods is nuclear magnetic resonance (NMR), which uses radiation to provide a proton-base developed image of the brain. As exciting as these new diagnostic techniques are, they still fail (because of the inherent aspects of the technology) to provide an adequate presentation of human behavior. Since the neuropsychologist is beginning to use these methods as adjuncts to both research and clinical activities, further developments hinge on a close relationship between these two approaches (e.g., Swiercinsky & Leigh, 1979; Wedding, 1980).

New Populations

Numerous disorders that have traditionally been considered as functional in origin appear to have at least a limited neural basis. This has been the case not only for disorders such as schizophrenia, but for disorders for which, in the past, neural involvement was considered unimportant, such as depression (e.g., Ross & Rush, 1981). As a consequence, neuropsychological inquiry into the neural basis for psychopathology in general should be extended much further than its current boundaries.

According to Costa (1983), increasing interest should also be shown to patients from various fields of clinical medicine, especially those involving systemic disease. Neuropsychology can provide valuable understanding in the treatment of such chronic diseases as lupus, chronic obstructive lung disease (emphysema), cardiovascular disorders, and certain types of oncological disorders. The assessment of the effects of administration of pharmaceuticals for general medical disorders (e.g., high blood pressure) also warrants further attention. In this respect, any medical complication or treatment having a direct or indirect impact on neural integrity should be considered within the scope of neuropsychology.

CONCLUSIONS

In the preceeding discussion, efforts were devoted to conceptualizing human neuropsychology and the historical context of neuropsychology was summarized. Current relations with traditional medical and selected nonmedical specialties were also examined, albeit quickly. Finally, attention was devoted to emerging trends in human neuropsychology and some exciting possibilities for the future were described.

From the aforementioned discussion a few conclusions naturally follow. First, human neuropsychology is a promising discipline with the potential for service to humanity. Second, change in terms of role functioning, techniques, concepts, patients served, and technology is a fact of life that is more salient with each passing day. Third, the degree to which human neuropsychology realizes its potential to be of service will be in large measure due to its ability to adapt to the previously mentioned changes.

REFERENCES

Anchor, K. N. (1983). Availability and awareness of neuropsychological assessment in the community hospital: A survey. *Clinical Neuropsychology, 5,* 7–8.

Barbizet, J. (1963). Defect of memorizing of hippocampal mamillary origin: A review. *Journal of Neurology, Neurosurgery, and Psychiatry, 26,* 127–135.

Beck, A., & Mahoney, M. J. (1979). Schools of thought. *American Psychologist, 34,* 93–98.

Brodal, A. (1969). *Neurological anatomy* (2nd ed.). New York: Oxford University Press.

Cole, J. C., & Long, C. J. (in press). Interrelationships of neuropsychological and vocational assessments in neurologically-impaired patients. *International Journal of Clinical Neuropsychology.*

Costa, L. (1983). Clinical neuropsychology: A discipline in evolution. *Journal of Clinical Neuropsychology, 5,* 1–11.

Davis, K. L., & Berger, P. A. (Eds.). (1979). *Brain acetylcholine and neuropsychiatric disease.* New York: Plenum Press.

Davison, L. A. (1974). Introduction. In R. M. Reitan and L. A. Davison, *Clinical neuropsychology: Current status and applications.* New York: Wiley.

Dennerll, R. D., Rodin, E. A., Gonzales, S., Schwartz, M. C., & Lin, Y. (1969). Neurological and psychological factors related to employability of persons with epilepsy. *Epilepsia, 7,* 318–329.

Diller, L., & Gordon, W. A. (1981). Interventions for cognitive deficits in brain injured adults. *Journal of Consulting and Clinical Psychology, 49,* 822–834.

Ellen, P., & Powell, E. W. (1962). Effects of septal lesions on behavior generated by positive reinforcement. *Experimental Neurology, 6,* 1–11.

Ellis, A. (1979). On Joseph Wolpe's espousal of cognitive-behavior therapy. *American Psychologist, 34,* 98–99.

Flynn, J. P. (1967). The neural basis of aggression in cats. In D. C. Glass (Ed.), *Neurophysiology and emotion* (pp. 40–60). New York: Rockefeller University Press.

Fredrickson, P., & Richelson, E. (1979). Mayo seminars in psychiatry. Dopamine and schizophrenia—a review. *Journal of Clinical Psychiatry, 6,* 399–405.

Freeman, F. R. (1981). *Organic mental disorders*. New York: S. P. Medical and Scientific Books.

Gaddes, W. H. (1968). A neuropsychological approach to learning disorders. *Journal of Learning Disabilities, 1,* 523–534.

Gaddes, W. H. (1981). An examination of the validity of neuropsychological knowledge in educational diagnosis and remediation. In G. W. Hynd and J. E. Obrzut (Eds.), *Neuropsychological assessment and the school-aged child: Issues and procedures* (pp. 27–84). New York: Grune & Stratton.

Greenberg, G. (1983). Psychology without the brain. *The Psychological Record, 33,* 49–58.

Hartlage, L. C. (1975). Neuropsychological approaches to predicting outcome of remedial education strategies for learning disabled children. *Pediatric Psychology, 3,* 23–28.

Hartlage, L. C., & Telzrow, C. F. (1982). The practice of clinical neuropsychology in the US. *Clinical Neuropsychology, 2,* 200–202.

Heaton, R. K., Chelune, C. J., & Lehman, R. A. (1978). Using neuropsychological and personality tests to assess the likelihood of patient employment. *Journal of Nervous and Mental Disease, 166,* 408–416.

Heaton, R. K., & Pendleton, M. G. (1981). Use of neuropsychological tests to predict adult patient's everyday functioning. *Journal of Consulting and Clinical Psychology, 49,* 807–821.

Horton, A. M., Jr. (1979). Behavioral neuropsychology: Rationale and presence. *Clinical Neuropsychology, 1,* 20–23.

Horton, A. M., Jr, & Miller, W. G. (1984). Brain damage and rehabilitation. In C. J. Golden (Ed.), *Current topics in rehabilitation psychology* (pp. 77–105). New York: Grune & Stratton.

Horton, A. M., Jr., & Wedding, D. (1984). *Clinical and behavioral neuropsychology*. New York: Praeger Press.

Horton, A. M., Jr., Wedding, D., & Phay, A. (1981). Current perspective on assessment of a therapy for brain-damaged individuals. In C. J. Golden, S. E. Alcaparras, F. Stredes, & B. Graber (Eds.), *Applied technique in behavioral medicine* (pp. 59–85). New York: Grune & Stratton.

Hynd, G. W., & Obrzut, J. E. (1981). School neuropsychology. *Journal of School Psychology, 19,* 45–50.

Kaufman, A. S., and Kaufman, N. L. (1983). *Kaufman Assessment Battery for Children*. Circle Pines, MN: American Guidance Services.

Lashley, K. S. (1929). *Brain mechanisms and intelligence*. Chicago: University of Chicago Press.

Lazarus, A. A. (1979). A matter of emphasis. *American Psychologist, 34,* 100.

Lubin, B., Wallis, R. R., & Paine, C. (1971). Patterns of psychological test usage in the United States: 1935–1969. *Professional Psychology, 2,* 70–74.

Luria, A. R. (1973). *The working brain*. New York: Basic Books.

Lynch, W. (1981, January). The use of video games in rehabilitation. Paper presented at a conference on Models and Techniques of Cognitive Rehabilitation. Indianapolis, IN.

Mahoney, M. J. (1974). *Cognition and behavior modification*. Cambridge, MA: Ballinger.

Meier, M. J. (1974). Some challenges for clinical neuropsychology. In R. M. Reitan & L. A. Davison (Eds.), *Clinical neuropsychology: Current status and application* (pp. 289–323). New York: Wiley.

Meier, M. J. (1981a). Education for competency assurance in human neuropsychology: Antecedents, models, and directions. In S. B. Filskov & T. J. Boll (Eds.), *Handbook of clinical neuropsychology* (pp. 754–781). New York: Wiley.

Meier, M. J. (Ed.). (1981b). Report of International Neuropsychological Society Task Force on education, accreditation, and credentialing. *INS Bulletin,* September, 5–10.

Miller, L. S., Bergstrom, D. A., Cross, H. J., & Grube, J. W. (1981). Opinions and use of the DSM system. *Professional Psychology, 12,* 385–390.

Obrish, M. E. (1984). Personal communication.

Ojemann, R. G. (1966). Correlation between specific human brain lesions and memory change: A critical survey of the literature. *Neuroscience Research Program Bulletin, 4,* 110.

Papez, J. W. (1937). A proposed mechanism of emotion. *Archives of Neurology and Psychiatry, 38,* 725–743.

Pirozzolo, F. J., Campenella, D. J., Christensen K., & Lawson-Kerr, K. (1981). Effects of cerebral dysfunction on neurolinguistic performance in children. *Journal of Consulting and Clinical Psychology, 49,* 791–806.

Puente, A. E. (1982). The role of clinical neuropsychology in disability determinations. *Social Security Forum,* 10–11.

Puente, A. (in press). Psychological determination of disability. In M. Glancy (Ed.), *Social security law practice guide* (Vol. 4). New York: Matthew Bender.

Puente, A. E., Heidelberg-Sanders, C., & Lund, N. (1982). Discrimination of schizophrenics with and without nervous system damage using the Luria-Nebraska Neuropsychological Battery. *International Journal of Neuroscience, 16,* 59–62.

Reynolds, C. R. (1981). Neuropsychological assessment and the habilitation of learning: Consideration in the search for the aptitude treatment interaction. *School Psychology Review, 10,* 342–349.

Ross, E. P., & Rush, A. J. (1981). Diagnosis and neuroanatomical correlates of depression in brain-damaged patients. *Archives of General Psychiatry, 38,* 1344–1345.

Rourke, B. P. (1975). Brain-behavior relationships in children with learning disabilities: A research program. *American Psychologist, 30,* 911–920.

Ryan, C., Vega, A., Longstreet, C., & Drash, A. (1984). Neuropsychological changes in adolescents with insulin-dependent diabetes. *Journal of Clinical Psychology, 3,* 335–342.

Satz, P., & Fletcher, J. M. (1981). Emergent trends in neuropsychology: An overview. *Journal of Consulting and Clinical Psychology, 49(6),* 851–865.

Schwartz, M. C., Dennerll, R. D., & Lin, Y. (1966). Neuropsychological and psychosocial predictors of employability in epilepsy. *Journal of Clinical Psychology, 24,* 174–177.

Seron, X., Deloche, G., Moulard, G., & Rovsller, M. (1980). A computer-based therapy for the treatment of aphasic subjects with writing disorders. *Journal of Speech and Hearing Disorders, 4,* 45–58.

Skinner, B. F. (1938). *The behavior of organisms.* New York: Appleton-Century-Crofts.

Smith, D., & Kraft, W. A. (1983). DSM III: Do psychologists really want an alternative? *American Psychologist, 38,* 777–785.

Soffine, G., Feldman, M., & Bender, M. R. (1968). Alteration of sensory levels in vascular lesions of the lateral medulla. *Archives of Neurology, 8,* 178–190.

Stone, G. C., Cohen, F., & Adler, N. E. (Eds.). (1979). *Health Psychology—a handbook: Theories, applications, and challenges of a psychological approach to the health care system.* San Francisco: Jossey-Bass.

Strub, R. L., & Black, F. W. (1982). *Organic brain syndrome: An introduction to neurobehavioral disorders.* Philadelphia: F. A. Davis.

Swiercinsky, D., & Leigh, G. (1979). Comparison of neuropsychological data in the diagnosis of brain impairment with computerized tomography and other neurological procedures. *Journal of Clinical Psychology, 35,* 242–246.

Terrace, H. S., Petitto, C. A., Sanders, R. M., & Bever, J. G. (1979). Can an ape create a sentence? *Science, 206,* 891–902.

van der Vlugt, H. (1979). Aspects of normal and abnormal neuropsychological development. In M. S. Gazzaniga (Ed.), *Handbook of behavioral neurobiology* (Vol. 2) (pp. 754–781). New York: Plenum Press.

Walsh, K. W. (1978). *Neuropsychology: A clinical approach.* New York: Churchill Livingston.

Watson, J. B. (1913). Psychology as the behaviorist views it. *Psychological Review, 20,* 158–177.

Wedding, D. (1980). Implication of computerized axial tomography for clinical neuropsychology. *Professional Psychology,* February, 31–38.

Wolpe, J. (1958). *Psychotherapy by reciprocal inhibition.* Stanford, CA: Stanford University Press.

Wolpe, J. (1978). Cognition and causation in human behavior and its therapy. *American Psychologist, 33,* 437–446.

World Health Organization (1978). *International classification of disease-clinical modification* (9th ed.). Geneva: author.

2

Theories of Brain Functioning: A Brief Introduction to the Study of the Brain and Behavior*

*Michael L. Woodruff
and Ronald H. Baisden*

The brain is certainly the most structurally complex organ found within the human body. Its activity and the products of its activity, mentation and behavior, are equally complex. The number of approaches to the study of the brain and behavior reflects this complexity. Indeed, probably no other branch of human inquiry involves the variety of disciplines that have contributed to the understanding of brain function. The ultimate phenomena of concern are the behavioral and mental output of human beings. The nature of these phenomena, the relations among them, and their meaning, have been described, analyzed, and discussed by philosophers, psychologists, anthropologists, sociologists, physicians, and theologians. Equal attention has been given to the biological correlates and substrates of these phenomena by anatomists, physiologists, biochemists, biophysicists, pharmacologists, neurologists, and neuropsychologists. Despite, or perhaps even because of, these myriad perspectives, the complexity of the subject has masked coherence, and no single, commonly accepted theory exists concerning the specific manner in which the brain produces mentation and behavior.

*We would like to thank Professor A. Hunt Ewell, Department of Psychology, Middlebury College (VT) for his helpful comments concerning the first draft of this chapter. Preparation of this chapter was supported, in part, by a grant from the Research Foundation of East Tennessee State University to MLW.

PRINCIPLES OF ORGANIZATION OF BRAIN FUNCTION

Certain general conceptual principles of the organization of brain function have emerged, at least at the "molar" or "phrenological" level of analysis. The first principle is that of hierarchical organization of neural functioning. This principle states first that the more rostral, or cephalic, structures (e.g., the neocortex) of the nervous system are the most structurally and functionally complex. Second, the more rostral structures are the last to develop fully, both in phylogenetic and ontogenetic progression. This process of encephalization of complexity of the nervous system parallels increased complexity in the behavioral capacity of the organism. Finally, more rostral structures modulate the activity of more caudally dwelling structures in which basic behavioral responses to the environment are "hard-wired."

The second principle involves the separation of sensory and motor systems. For example, the dorsal (posterior) roots of the spinal cord carry sensory input, while motor outflow exits via the ventral (anterior) roots. The dorsolateral medulla and pons contain nuclei concerned with sensory mechanisms, while the more ventromedial portion of these structures contains nuclei concerned with motor activity of the head, neck, and viscera. Moreover, the neocortex can be divided along its sagittal axis into an anterior part devoted more to expressive, or motor, activity, and a posterior part concerned with receptive, or sensory, functions. This admittedly gross division pertains not only to the classical motor and sensory cortical areas (e.g., the precentral gyrus, or Brodmann's area 4, and the postcentral gyrus, or Brodmann's areas 3, 1, 2), but has also, as will be discussed below, been applied to the so-called association cortices.

The third principle is that of laterality of function. This principle differs from the first two in that, rather than including the entire central nervous system, discussion of laterality of function generally includes only neocortical and, on occasion, limbic structures. Moreover, sources for construction of this concept have come essentially from observation of humans, while a comparative approach to neurological function has provided crucial data and impetus for development of the first two principles.

Laterality of human cerebral function is an accepted postulate, as is the separation of primary motor and sensory functions in the central nervous system. However, the more general corollary of these two principles, localization of all brain functions, has not been as universally accepted. Resolution of the debate concerning whether or not relatively restricted parts of the brain control equally restricted behavioral or cognitive modes, such as eating or mnemonic processing, would have obvious impact upon both experimental and clinical approaches to neuroscience. Unfortunately the data to resolve this debate will probably never be produced. Therefore, a fourth and overriding principle of brain function, which would incorporate this resolution and state that the brain exhibits either strict localization of function or equipotentiality (after Lashley, 1929), can never be formulated. Resolution will not be achieved for the simple reason that the brain functions neither as a set of strictly localizable functional centers nor as an amorphous aggregate field, but rather as a grouping of distributed systems. The concept of distributed systems represents a formulation of how the brain functions, which lies somewhere in between the idea of brain function as an aggregate field and a strict localizationist interpretation. It becomes, then, the fourth, albeit tentative, principle. The brain functions as a cluster of "unit modules" that join one another in function as appropriately linked distributed systems (Mountcastle, 1979).

Hierarchical Organization of Brain Function

Caudal to Rostral Organization

Current concepts regarding encephalization of function and the hierarchical organization of the neuraxis owe much to the prescient formulations of John Hughlings Jackson. Based upon clinical observation and an astute analysis of the available literature concerning ontogenetic neurodevelopment and comparative neuroethology, Jackson (1958) proposed that the neuraxis could be divided into three parts. These parts represent stages of motoric development, and it is important, when considering Jackson's theories, to realize that he viewed the production of movement as the chief function of the nervous system. As such it is the role of the nervous system in motor output that determines both its organization and essentially all of its other activities. Sensory processing, within this context, is a secondary activity.

The brainstem and spinal cord constitute the most caudal of these divisions. This level is also anatomically and functionally the simplest level, involving only reflexive integration of sensory input leading to motor output via the lower motor neurons of the somatic and visceral (autonomic) efferent systems. The perirolandic cortex (pre- and postcentral gyri) and its associated long tracts, as well as the basal ganglia, compose the second level in Jackson's organizational scheme. Sensorimotor integration is much more complete at this level, and if this level and the more caudal lower-motor level are both intact, relatively discrete control of movement and of autonomic function is possible.

Although Jackson also included the cerebellum at this level, he procrastinated as to the most appropriate placement of this structure within his scheme. He concluded that, while it was associated with the middle level of his hierarchy, the cerebellum also participated as a component of the other two levels. This observation is of particular interest because, even when divided as the neo-, archi-, and paleocerebellum, this portion of the brain resists convenient classification and has several complex, higher-order nonmotoric functions (Fish, Baisden, & Woodruff, 1979; McCormick, Guyer, & Thompson, 1982; Watson, 1978).

The third level is composed entirely of components of the neocortex. The non-Rolandic frontal and prefrontal areas, as well as the parietal lobe posterior to the postcentral gyrus, make up the highest level of the neuraxis. In Jackson's scheme these areas are capable of complete sensorimotor integration, representing the entire body in complex combinations. Moreover, their functioning produces the conscious state of mind, as well as the intellect, thought, and emotions.

The data gathered through both experimental and clinical approaches to research in neurobiology have rendered the specifics of Jackson's theory untenable. However, his broad conceptual framework regarding the hierarchical organization of the nervous system is very much a part of the *Weltanschauung* of modern neuropsychology. For example, Jackson proposed that destruction of various amounts of tissue composing the higher levels of the nervous system would lead to a correspondingly severe reduction of behavioral capacity and flexibility. In essence an animal, or human, suffering such destruction would be reduced to a more "primitive" ontogenetic or phylogenetic stage of behavioral development. An important assumption implicitly contained within this idea is that although the behavioral repertoire of an animal with its telencephalon removed would be reduced, the preserved responses to the environment would not be fragmented movements unrelated to eliciting stimuli, but would be appropriate, albeit simplified, acts proceeding in an integrated pattern.

Motoric Capabilities of the Isolated Spinal Cord These predictions have been confirmed through systemic experiments in which the effects of sequential rostral-caudal separation from the spinal cord of all of, or parts of, the brain have been studied. Following a period of trauma-induced shock the spinal cord isolated from the entire brain is capable of supporting such reflexive responses as withdrawal from an aversive stimulus to the distal part of the limb, appropriately directed scratching of the trunk when cutaneous irritation is presented, and muscle stretch reflexes that allow the rudiments of postural support (Kuhn, 1950; Kuhn & Macht, 1949; Liddell & Sherrington, 1924; Riddoch, 1917). Reciprocal inhibition and the flexion-crossed extension reflex are also retained (Sherrington, 1906). This permits coordinated movements of all four limbs that, if the weight of the animal, or human, is supported, resemble normal walking (Grillner, 1973).

Behavior Following Low Decerebration Preservation of the pons, medulla, and cerebellum allows a substantial enhancement of behavioral responsiveness. A cat in which all structures rostral to the pons have been removed (Bard, 1928; Bard & Macht, 1958; Bazett & Penfield, 1922) is still capable of swallowing food or water placed in the mouth. Because the fifth through the twelfth cranial nerve nuclei remain integrated with the spinal cord by means of long ascending and descending tracts, as well as by means of the intact caudal portion of the reticular formation, such low decerebrate animals can also react to aversive stimuli not only with limb withdrawal, but also by growling, hissing, and biting. Moreover, although such a cat cannot stand or support its weight, if it is placed on its side and a strong cutaneous stimulus (tail pinch) is applied, or if a loud noise is produced, the cat will pull its upper body and head into an upright position by means of a series of appropriately coordinated flexion-extension movements of the upper limbs combined with rotation of the head and neck. This response is possible despite the characteristic rigidity exhibited by the hindlimbs of such preparations (decerebrate rigidity).

Concurrent Behavioral States Following High Decerebration The chronic low decerebrate animal cannot walk, or even right itself completely. However, if the midbrain is preserved the animal will recover function (over a period of from 7 to 10 days) to the point where it not only rights itself, but will locomote spontaneously. In fact, if the level of destruction in such a high decerebrate preparation is just caudal to the posterior edge of the mammillary bodies, thereby leaving essentially the entire midbrain and more caudal structures of the neuraxis intact, the animal can walk, run, and even climb almost as well as a cat with only its neocortex removed. Locomotor activity and crouching in these animals occur as phasic activities that temporarily supplant the tonic decerebrate rigidity exhibited by animals (and humans) suffering from destruction of the forebrain, but having the mid- and hindbrains intact.

Decerebrate rigidity is the result of enhanced activity in the muscle spindle reflex system, primarily of the extensors. This rigidity is not a consequence of local spinal cord activity because, although myotatic extensor reflexes are enhanced in "spinal" animals, including humans, with cord transections in the upper cervical region, the pronounced rigidity characteristic of the decerebrate state does not occur. This observation suggests that a downplay of supraspinal excitatory influence upon spinal reflex mechanisms involved in the stretch reflex of the limb extensors is responsible. The brainstem sites usually thought to be responsible for this unabated excitation are the nuclei of origin of the vestibulospinal system, especially Deiter's nucleus (Bach & Magoun, 1947), and of the reticulospinal system (Lindsley, Schreiner, & Magoun, 1949). The anterior cerebellum is also in part responsible for the state but exerts its influence through the reticular system (Lindsley, 1952). It should come as no surprise that the vestibular nuclei and cerebellum (which receives direct input from the muscle stretch receptors and tendon organs via the spinocerebellar pathways), structures customarily associated with unconscious maintenance of posture, appear to make significant contributions to a reflexively based, tonic antigravity state.

Study of the decerebrate preparations and of decerebrate rigidity makes several contributions to conceptualizations of the hierarchical nature of the control of behavior by the brain. First, it indicates that production of an antigravity posture is a primary function of the lower anatomic levels of a neuraxis viewed as being hierarchically organized. Second, forebrain structures in the intact animal act to inhibit brainstem areas that are released from inhibition in decerebrate animals. However, the third thing that these studies demonstrate is that "programs" for behaviors involving complex sensorimotor integration are contained within the pons, medulla, and, especially, the midbrain. The neural substrates of these "programs" are capable of overriding the tonic postural rigidity associated with these decerebrated preparations in order to exert their influence and permit performance of quite sophisticated stereotyped, or automatic, behaviors including walking, running, climbing, grooming, and assumption of species-typical postures for sexual activity and defecation. The existence of these behaviors in the same surgical preparations in which decerebrate rigidity occurs as a basic behavior indicates that functional hierarchical complexity within the central nervous system does not have to be organized according to some simplified scheme diagramed in a serial manner from caudal to rostral along the spinal cord-telencephalic axis (e.g., MacLean, 1970, 1978; Isaacson, 1982), but can exist in parallel within the same structural level. This observation is certainly not incompatible with John Hughlings Jackson's original formulations and is of substantial importance when considering the function of the neocortex (e.g., Luria, 1966, 1970; Mountcastle, 1979).

The Diencephalon Enhances Both Somatic and Autonomic Coordination Animals with high decerebrations are indeed capable of a surprising variety of apparently integrated behavioral patterns, including components of emotional display such as growling, hissing, and clawing. However, such behaviors are short-lived, fragmented, and not accompanied by autonomic signs of emotion. Preservation of the diencephalon (thalamus and hypothalamus) markedly alters this picture. Such animals are not only capable of sustained episodes of attack behavior, but this behavior differs little from the normal species-typical patterns exhibited by intact members of the same species (Bard, 1928; Bard & Mountcastle, 1948). Autonomic correlates of emotion, such as piloerection, pupillary dilation, and increased cardiovascular activity, are present, as well as appropriate endocrine responses. However, these ragelike episodes appear, as Bard and Mountcastle note, to be rather more easily elicited than in intact animals and the attack behavior is not directed toward the offending stimulus. For these reasons the behavioral pattern is usually called, after Cannon and Britton (1924), "sham rage." Episodes of sham rage can last for hours and may be instigated by something as innocuous as a fly landing upon the animal's nose.

The diencephalon, then, adds a significant element of visceromotor and somatomotor integration to the elementary neural "programs" of the hindbrain. This enhanced ability to produce complex patterns of autonomic activity allows for temperature regulation. In addition, the hormonal system, linked to the nervous system via the hypothalamus, becomes coupled to behavior.

Sensorimotor integration is enhanced, probably because of the presence of the thalamus, and fragmented movements become linked into organized, apparently motivated behavioral sequences. Organized somatic response sequences appear to couple easily with visceral responses to produce emotional behavior that, although called "sham," would certainly appear genuine to the naive observer.

As has been argued for the presence of rigidity in decerebrate animals, the behavior of "diencephalic" animals supports the proposition that the cortex acts generally to inhibit patterns of activity generated by brainstem areas. Not only do diencephalic preparations tend to demonstrate rage reactions at lower thresholds than normals; they also tend to be spontaneously hyperactive (e.g. Grill & Norgren, 1978a,b; Grillner, 1973). In sum, then, the behavior of diencephalic animals seems to indicate a release from inhibition. This inhibition is presumably imposed in the intact animal by the next, and highest, level of the hierarchy, the cortex. Both the proposition that sham rage and hyperactivity represent release from inhibition, and the idea that a level above the diencephalon is responsible for inhibition in the intact animal, are very much in accord with the early concepts of John Hughlings Jackson.

Recapitulation of the Contributions of Brainstem Levels of the Hierarchy to Behavior and a Sketch of the Role of the Telencephalon Generally, an animal (or human) with just an intact spinal cord is capable of making limited responses to discrete stimulation. No spontaneous, volitional behavior is emitted by the limbs. However, within the inflexible limitations of the stimulus-bound (reflexive) nature of the available response repertoire, the responses are very refined and accurate. For example, an irritated spot on the back is accurately scratched by the paw of a "spinal" dog. Both the accuracy of response and the limited repertoire are the consequence of a very precise, but completely determined, set of neural connections linking the input of the dorsal root ganglia to the output of the ventral roots.

Addition of the medulla, pons, cerebellum, and midbrain allows significantly more integration of behavior. The restricted neural circuitry of the spinal cord is subject to descending input, and postural support is provided. Coordination of the limbs is sufficient to allow rudimentary locomotion. Some motor patterns that might be interpreted as fragments of emotion are present. However, while the accuracy of the cord reflexes remains, responses of the entire animal to stimuli are far from accurate or complete. The movement of the limbs, relying on supraspinal influence essentially from the reticular formation, lacks precision. As Riss (1968) emphasizes in his version of a neural hierarchical theory, the reticular formation exerts its influence on movement primarily by biasing reflexes. The anatomical structure of the input to the cord from the reticular formation is diffuse and this contributes to the lack of precision in stimulus-response relationships exhibited by the decerebrate. The relationships between stimulus and response that do exist are probably related to integrity of the cerebellum and the midbrain tectum (Riss, 1968). The cerebellum receives a topographically-ordered projection from the spinal cord, and the tectum can coordinate head and neck movements with those of the body.

Preservation of the diencephalon releases locomotion, exacerbates emotional reactivity, and allows basic autonomic regulation, but adds little to the animal's ability to react in a directed manner to irritating stimuli other than to withdraw a limb reflexively or scratch at a maintained irritation on the body surface. In fact, although the limbs are coordinated, locomotor patterns are near normal, and the animal manifests some behaviors, such as lapping of water and chewing food if these items are placed in its way, that might be interpreted as reflecting the functioning of motivational systems, the "diencephalic" animal is not much better off than the "spinal" animal in its ability to relate accurately to stimuli with appropriately oriented and integrated behavior.

The basal ganglia, subcortical limbic structures, and especially the neocortex give to the entire animal the ability to respond appropriately to a vast array of external stimuli through extended periods of time and to act on the environment in order to satisfy demands imposed by the *milieu interieur*. This requires the ability to chain appropriate movements together into maintained sequences of adaptive behavior. The basal ganglia (Kornhuber, 1974) and limbic cortex (Thomas, Hostetter, & Barker, 1968) appear to contribute markedly to this ability. In addition, parts of the limbic system presumably contribute to the relationship of ongoing behavioral sequences to previous experiences of the animal and to its current biological needs. Finally, the neocortex allows precise interpretation of multimodal sensory input and prediction of the consequences of behavior. Its ability, as suggested by the hierarchical model, to inhibit brainstem motor "programs" takes on added importance within this context.

The Triune Brain: A Metaphorical Approach to Hierarchical Analysis

The view of the hierarchical organization of the central nervous system presented in the first part of this chapter reflected not only the theoretical underpinnings of Jackson, but also the experimental tradition exemplified by Sherrington and Bard. This tradition has maintained a relatively strict description of the behavior of animals and humans with damage to various parts of the neuraxis along its rostral-caudal extent and a correspondingly close theoretical interpretation of the data. The use of metaphors to construct theoretical interpretations is not the typical trend. The theoretical expositions of Paul MacLean (e.g., 1970, 1972, 1975, 1978) are an exception to this tradition and deserve comment for three reasons. First, MacLean develops the role of the limbic system in behavior within a hierarchical context. These forebrain regions are not typically discussed at any length in such formulations. Second, as indicated above, most hierarchical expositions of brain function deal primarily with descriptions of motor capacity. MacLean considers sensory mechanisms much more thoroughly. Finally, MacLean's ideas are oriented toward an hierarchical explanation of central nervous system control of complex emotional, motivational, and cognitive functions, not only the exposition of patterns of motor expression.

MacLean divides the brain into three functional levels, which he names according to their presumed place in evolutionary development. The reptilian brain forms the lowest level and includes all structures from spinal cord through basal ganglia. The paleomammalian brain is the middle level and is equated with the limbic system. The neomammalian brain is at the top of the hierarchy and corresponds to the neocortex.

MacLean tends to present the three levels as almost autonomous units, each responsible for certain classes of behavioral acts and mental states. His choice of the designation *brain* for each of his divisions emphasizes such an autonomy. The reptilian brain, for example, produces stereotype behaviors and mental correlates of such stereotypes. The modifiability of the reptilian brain is limited, and once a behavioral pattern or belief structure is established at this level, it is not easily changed. Thus, in mammals, including humans, the reptilian brain is presumably responsible for formation and maintenance of social groupings, territorial defense, imprinting, breeding patterns, and the like. Corresponding attitudes, such as adament nationalism or religious fanaticism, would also be related to activity of the reptilian brain.

The paleomammalian brain first appears in primitive mammals. Its presence allows far greater flexibility, linking the animal's response more closely to present conditions and overriding preexisting, or ancestral, programs (MacLean, 1970). At the same time the paleomammalian brain produces immediate emotional feelings, which need not be related to knowledge (MacLean, 1975). MacLean supports this last supposition in part with reports concerning the clinical effects of focal epileptiform seizures, which begin in some part of the limbic system (e.g., the hippocampus), and, while irradiating to include essentially all structures of the limbus, do not involve neocortical areas. Such seizures, usually classified as psychomotor, produce symptoms including automatic behaviors, affectual feelings, and perceptual disturbances. Amnesia for the period of the ictus is also a part of psychomotor epilepsy. The afflicted individual, therefore, may execute complex acts with accompanying emotional tone, but have no recollection of the behavior when the seizure is finished. MacLean interprets such observations to indicate the existence of a large degree of functional autonomy for the paleomammalian brain. He also presents considerable anatomical and electrophysiological data indicating that the limbic system receives convergent sensory input from both exteroceptive and interoceptive sources. MacLean argues that such convergence of input from both outside and inside the body is virtually unique to the limbic system. Furthermore, because of this unique convergence, the paleomammalian division not only produces emotional tone, but also is responsible for rudimentary formulation of a person's sense of individuality.

The neomammalian brain is the final division of the triune brain. It is composed essentially of the neocortex but also includes subcortical structures primarily connected to the neocortex. The neomammalian brain is related to the external environment. Its structure allows fine discriminations to be made among incoming exteroceptive signals, and it has a propensity for dividing things into smaller and smaller units of analysis. As a result it is at the level of the neocortex that true conscious perception occurs. Because of its ability to analyze the elements of sensation and combine, and recombine, these elements into perceptions, the neomammalian brain becomes the most modifiable of the three brains. Intellectual activity, creativity, and the ability to plan are all derivatives of the basic flexibility of the actions of the neomammalian brain.

In summary, MacLean develops his theory from the point of view of the evolution of both brain and behavior. He makes the point that once acquired, a given brain system is never lost; rather, "newer" systems are laid on top of it. Moreover, the older systems continue to function in "ancestral" fashion and can dramatically influence the behavioral and mental expressions of the higher neural levels. He emphasizes the importance of changing patterns of sensory input and the increasing sophistication of more rostral brain structures in sensory processing. He also attempts to correlate brain anatomy with physiological function and with behavioral and mental capacity as deduced from clinical neurological disorders and experimental neurophysiology.

One final point needs to be made concerning MacLean's theoretical constructs. His presentations emphasize the independent functioning of his three levels to the extent that the fact that they interact to produce behavior is obscured. Therefore, it is easy to interpret MacLean's position as being one in which phylogenetically more recent structures perform newly created functions and do not assume functions from the older structures. This is not entirely an accurate interpretation of MacLean's conceptualizations. In fact, probably because his views are based to a great degree upon a perspective derived from the study of sensory systems, he (MacLean, 1975) emphasizes the concept of encephalization.

Encephalization is the process whereby higher structures, particularly the neocortex, assume the functions of lower structures. This is reflected in the effects on behavioral capacity of damage to the neocortex in different species having differing complexities of cortical development. For example, even after complete removal of its visual cortex the tree shrew, a mammal considered to be a direct antecedant to primates, retains the ability to make form and pattern discriminations and to localize objects in space utilizing the remainder of its visual system (Snyder & Diamond, 1968). These residual capacities appear to be mediated in the tree shrew by a collicular-pulvinar-temporal pathway (Harting, Hall, Diamond, & Martin, 1973). This pathway is not sufficient to allow any degree of sophisticated visual function in higher primates deprived of their geniculo-striate system. The general interpretation of these data is that in higher primates, especially as represented by humans, the sensory areas of the neocortex, with their specific thalamic nuclei, "take over" the specific functions to such an extent that if these areas, or thalamic nuclei, are destroyed the particular function is irrevocably lost.

Psychosomatic Disorders and Brain Hierarchy Malmo (1975), using data from many clinical and experimental studies, has based a theory concerning the etiology of psychosomatic emotional disturbances upon concepts very like those of MacLean. Malmo's ideas are similar to those of MacLean in that he believes that the phylogenetically more primitive levels of the brain contain emotional response systems that can function quite independently of the neocortex. He does differ somewhat from MacLean in that his theory, after the lead of John Hughlings Jackson, is very much a motor theory. He maintains that the response patterns controlled by the archaic levels of the brain (essentially the paleomammalian and reptilian brains of MacLean) were appropriate both in intensity and in relation to the environment when they were manifested in more primitive environments and, for this reason, the neural circuits that produce these behavioral patterns became a permanent part of the brain. Malmo then maintains that these response patterns, such as vascular and cardiac changes, are no longer appropriate for survival in their magnitude and duration. He argues that these inappropriate visceral and somatic changes may not be attenuated as they should be because the neocortex does not have sufficiently tight anatomical linkage to the lower brain levels to produce appropriate modulation. Malmo's employment of a hierarchical model of central nervous system function to provide a physical neurological basis for psychosomatic illnesses such as hypertension, Reynaud's syndrome, and tension headaches extends the use of the explanatory power of such theories into the realm of clinical psychology and represents a final interesting use of a hierarchical model of brain functioning.

How Useful Are Hierarchical Theories of Brain Functioning?

Hierarchical theories of brain function have provided the only hypotheses regarding the manner in which the central nervous system as a whole (as opposed to only its neocortical division) functions to produce behavior. They have provided the background against which much of our present understanding of brain function in behavior has been obtained. They have been useful in providing a framework within which to explain some of the effects of brain damage (e.g., the release phenomenon). They have even provided, as demonstrated by the formulations of MacLean and Malmo, theoretical explanations for emotional disorders that have bridged the gap between neurological and psychological concepts. Moreover, as will be discussed later, Luria (1966, 1970) has also used a hierarchical model to integrate cognitive and neural processes. However, these theories have definite limitations that need to be mentioned. Some of these limitations are shared by the theories of cortical functioning discussed later in this chapter.

A danger in hierarchical theories of brain function is that their use can easily lead to reification. This is exemplified by the use of metaphors such as "reptilian" and "paleomammalian." It must be kept in mind that such words are linguistic symbols with their associated connotations. These symbols should not be mistaken for the phenomenon they are intended to represent. As should be obvious from the discussion of the effects of separation of the forebrain from the hindbrain, the isolated brainstem of a mammal produces very little that resembles reptilian behavior. Its similarity lies in a vague structural homology and the fact that the behavior it supports is very rigidly defined and unmodifiable.

In addition, hierarchical models offer very little in the way of explanation. Those that describe the "behavioral" ability of animals, or humans, with truncated nervous systems provide some idea concerning the organization of neural input—output systems, but offer little in the way of integrative theory. Those that choose a metaphorical approach may provide a theoretical integration, but, because of the problems noted in the previous paragraph, the terms chosen do little to elucidate the neural mechanisms involved in the production of the behavioral constellations they attempt to describe and may even be detrimental if the metaphors lead to psychologisms that turn attention from the problem under consideration (i.e., brain function). As Weiss (1967) has remarked, although it may be productive to characterize neural anatomical collectives with new terms, these terms " . . . must come from rigorous scientific procedure rather than from anthropomorphic translocutions and allegorical allusions to mythology" (p. 802).

Finally, hierarchical theories have had less and less heuristic impact in neuroscience through the past two decades. The reason for this appears to lie in their inability to answer satisfactorily the question: How does the brain produce behavior x? Technical advances have begun to make the possibility of supplying an answer to this question seem feasible, and successes using these techniques, particularly those taken from physiology and anatomy, have shaped both experimental paradigms and hypotheses regarding brain function to a great degree in recent years. Examples of such techniques and hypotheses are best found in the study of sensory and motor systems, the segregation of which was specified as our second putative principle of neural functioning.

Sensory-Motor Dichotomy Within the Central Nervous System

In the vertebrate phyla the division of the central nervous system into sensory and motor portions occurs very early during embryogenesis and provides the substrate for all subsequent neural development. For example, the early neural tube becomes divided into dorsal and ventral condensations of nerve cells that are anatomically separated by a ventricular groove, the sulcus limitans. The ventral condensation, or basal plate, develops quickly and gives rise to the principal effector element of the central nervous system, the ventral, or anterior, horn cell. With the appearance of these cells the potential for reflexively organized motor activity exists. This occurs at about the eighth week of intrauterine life in the human. The dorsal part of the neural tube becomes the alar plate. Neurons within the alar plate receive processes of bipolar cells located in the peripheral sensory ganglia (e.g., dorsal root ganglia, spiral cochlear ganglia). The more distal processess of these bipolar cells are in direct contact with peripheral receptors. Ultimately, neurons of the alar plate will connect to both more cephalic areas of the brain and complete the local neural circuitry of the spinal cord that allows integrated reflexive responses to specific and localized stimuli to be effected.

In adults the dorsal-sensory, ventral-motor dichotomy of the spinal cord gray matter persists along the entire length of the cord. Although the alar and basal columns break up into condensations of nerve cells that become the component nuclei of the cranial nerves, this general organization is maintained in the brainstem. That is, the sensory nuclei originate in the alar plate, while the motor nuclei are basal in origin. In the brainstem, however, another region, which cannot be designated as either entirely sensory or entirely motor in function, obtains prominence. This is the reticular formation. The reticular formation functions in both the motor and sensory spheres. It relays rather nonspecific aspects of sensory information to more rostral structures, but also acts as a primary component of the extrapyramidal motor pathway.

At the level of the cerebral cortex the sensory-motor dichotomy is evident in those areas that receive input from specific thalamic nuclei. The primary motor area (Brodmann's area 4), the premotor cortex (area 6), and the frontal eye fields (area 8), which compose the motor portion of the neocortex, are found in the frontal lobe. In gyrencephalic brains the principal sensory areas are found posterior to the primary fissure, with the somatosensory area in the parietal lobe, the auditory area in the temporal lobe, and the visual area in the occipital lobe. In addition to differences in location, motor and sensory areas can be differentiated histologically according to the distribution of their dominant neuronal types across the cortical lamina. A larger number of small neurons (stellate or granule cells), which are presumably involved in the local interactions necessary for sensory processing, are evident in sensory cortex. For this reason sensory cortex is referred to as "granular" cortex. There is a relative paucity of granule cells in the motor regions. Hence motor cortex is referred to as "agranular" cortex.

In addition to differences in gross location and cytological appearance, motor and sensory cortices may be differentiated according to criteria of principal extrinsic connections, electrophysiological activity, and the effects of localized destruction. For example, cortical areas 4, 6, and 8 have a preponderance of large pyramidal neurons, with area 4 (primary motor cortex) containing the Betz cells, some of which are sufficiently large to be visible to the unaided eye in Nissl-stained tissue. The primary branch of the axons of these neurons may project all the way to the ventral horn of the spinal cord. Input to these neurons is derived from other cortical regions, but principally from the ventral lateral nucleus of the thalamus. This thalamic element is considered to be motoric in function and relays information from subcortical motor structures, such as the cerebellum and basal ganglia, to the motor cortex.

These observations concerning the obvious extrinsic connections of the sensory and motor cortices certainly distinguish agranular cortex from granular cortex. However, the motor cortex does receive topographically organized somesthetic input from the dorsal column system by way of the oral subdivision of the ventral posterior lateral thalamic nucleus (Asanuma, 1981). This input primarily conveys proprioceptive information and appears to act as a short-loop feedback system regarding limb and body movement as load on muscles changes.

The results of experiments using electrophysiological techniques have indicated that the basic functional organization of the motor cortex is the radially oriented column, or module (Scheibel & Scheibel, 1970; Shepherd, 1979). These columns are in turn organized into larger units called "projection areas," which contribute a topographically arranged, systematic input to the spinal motor neuron pool. Neuronal activity in this larger radially oriented organizational unit relates to action of synergistic and antagonistic muscles such that movements around joints are programed.

Outputs from the cells of the sensory cortices (somesthetic; Brodmann's areas 3, 1, 2; visual, area 17; auditory, areas 41 and 42) are primarily restricted to local circuit interactions and short intracortical connections. The projection neurons of the sensory areas send axons to terminate upon thalamic elements. Neurons of the visual cortex, for example, project upon the lateral geniculate nucleus.

Inputs to sensory cortex come from other cortical areas, as well as several subcortical sites, but especially from the modality-appropriate specific thalamic nuclei. The projections from the specific thalamic nuclei not only define the modality of the innervated sensory area (e.g., lateral geniculate projections to area 17 of visual cortex), but also are in part responsible for the functional columnar organization of the cortex.

However, although the columnar organization of sensory cortex is more apparent anatomically and more readily appreciated physiologically, than that of motor cortex, it is the presence of large numbers of granule, or stellate, cells, and of unique thalamic inputs, not the columnar organization, that defines sensory cortex physiologically as well as anatomically. Stellate cells are especially involved in processing information in local circuits, and it is such processing that is responsible for encoding sensory information.

Sensory processing by local neuronal circuits has been extensively studied in the primary visual cortex, where various cells within a column can be observed to respond to different aspects of peripheral stimulation (Hubel & Wiesel, 1977). All neurons within a specific column will respond to stimuli presented in only one eye. These stimuli may include a spot of light, a bar oriented in a particular direction, or movement of a particularly oriented bar in either one or both directions parallel to the surface of the retina. All neurons in a column respond to the same orientation, and only that orientation. If neuronal responses are recorded from the adjacent column, responses may be found to stimuli presented to the same eye at the same point in the visual field. However, in this adjacent column the orientation of the stimulus that is effective in eliciting a response from the neurons will be slightly different.

If neuronal responses to stimuli in the visual field are studied in a column lying orthogonal to the first column described, the responses would be identical to those of neurons located within the original column in terms of adequate orientation of the bar and direction of movement, but would be obtained only from such stimuli presented to the opposite eye. A collection of adjacent columns taken from the two dimensions of the cortical surface within a restricted region of area 17 will, thence, produce a unit, the hypercolumn (Figure 2.1), cells of which will respond to all stimulus parameters at one spot in the visual field presented to both eyes. This arrangement allows perception not only of characteristics inherent in the stimulus, but also of depth of field. Adjacent hypercolumns will respond to adjacent points in the visual field and a visuotopic map of the entire visual field is reconstructed in this manner.

As illustrated in some detail by this example of the response to sensory stimulation by elements of the visual cortex, the cortical column is an input–output processing unit. Similar units, functioning in a modality-appropriate manner, have been described for primary somesthetic (Carli, LaMotte, & Mountcastle, 1971) and auditory (Imig & Adrian, 1977) cortices. As indicated above, the motor cortex is also organized functionally in a columnar manner. Moreover, Mountcastle (1979) has presented electrophysiological evidence for such organization within parietal association cortex. There is even evidence that language function is organized in the human cortex according to a columnar pattern (Ojemann, 1983). The cortical column, then, appears to be the true, basic information processing unit of the cerebrum.

Early Localizationist Views of Sensory-Motor Dichotomies in Association Cortices

Although the apparent ubiquity of the cortical column entails that neurons are organized in many, or all, areas of the neocortex to process information in a similar manner, this ubiquity does not entail lack of separation of function. As noted above, both the extrinsic connections and intrinsic structure of the various cortical areas suggest functional, as well as structural, parcellation. That this is the case is obvious in primary motor and sensory cortices. In addition at least gross functional division is evident in association areas, and

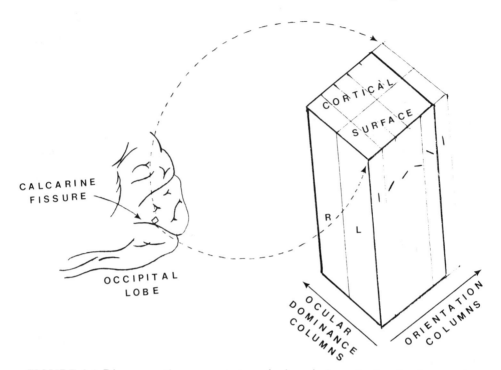

FIGURE 2.1 Diagrammatic representation of a hypercolumn in the visual cortex in which all cells respond to stimuli at one point in the visual field. The hypercolumn consists of a group of orientation and ocular dominance columns such that all orientations of stimuli presented to each eye are represented within the hypercolumn.

such a division may also be made along the lines of a sensory-motor dichotomy. The typical division of the aphasias into an anterior motor type and a posterior sensory type illustrates this dichotomy.

Broca (1865) is sometimes hailed as the founder of the school of functional cerebral localization because of the impact of his clinical case reports and his interpretation of these reports. Broca emphasized the prevalence of a syndrome in which right-sided hemiplegia was combined with the inability to speak. Further, he reported that upon autopsy the lesion responsible for this syndrome consistently involved the posterior portion of the left frontal lobe which is solely involved in speech production.

The speech disorder described by Broca is typically referred to as motor, or expressive, aphasia. It may also be called afluent, or anterior, aphasia. As indicated by these terms, the disorder lies in the production of speech and is characterized by difficulty in articulation and by a paucity of speech. The aphasia described by Wernicke (1874) is generally called a sensory, or receptive, aphasia, although it may be called fluent aphasia or posterior aphasia. It is characterized by severe disturbance in comprehension, which is very apparent when the patient is asked to repeat words. Verbal output is fluent, and language sounds are readily produced, but speech is paraphasic and jargonistic, often to the point of being nonsensical. The lesion responsible for a "pure" Wernicke's aphasia lies in the left posterior superior temporal gyrus and may be accompanied by a right homonomous hemianopsia.

Antilocalizationist Views of Brain-Damage-Induced Language Dysfunction

The separation of speech functions into motor and sensory components, and the localization of each of these components in a different area of the left hemisphere, allows the postulate that language and, by inference, other mental functions are physically dissectable and therefore localizable at the cortical level. Although this position, as exemplified by the constructions of Geschwind (1965, 1979), is presently widely accepted, the localizationist position, even in the restricted case of the relationship between brain damage and language dysfunction, has not been accepted by all those working in the neurological sciences.

Head (1921, 1926) took specific exception to the division of aphasia into motor and sensory subtypes based upon localized damage to different brain regions. Rather, while he described four subtypes of aphasia (verbal, syntactical, nominal, semantic), he believed that all aphasias were due to the inability to formulate and use symbols. Head attributed apparent clinical differences produced by brain lesions of varying location to the degree, rather than the location, of the destruction and, importantly, to the remote effects produced by the lesion.

Goldstein (1948) also took issue with the Broca-Wernicke localizationist position. He attributed aphasia to "disturbance of abstract attitude" and protested that the aphasia-producing effects of cortical lesions were due not only to removal of certain specific parts of the cortex, but also to both the physical and psychological reactions of the organism to the loss of this tissue. Unfortunately, Goldstein's conceptualization of the aphasias appears to be primarily a naive reaction to overinterpretation of lesion data by the advocates of a localizationist position. It is not especially useful in determining the role of brain damage in production of speech deficits or, conversely, in the determination of the mechanism whereby the intact brain produces speech.

Lesion-Induced Remote Changes May Lead to Behavioral Change The antilocalizationist arguments of Head and of Goldstein necessitate an important caution regarding theoretical interpretation of the effects of damage to a circumscribed region of the brain. Destruction of a given brain area is not necessarily equivalent to simple removal of that region. Positive and negative changes take place in many other regions previously connected to the damaged area. Loss of input and even transsynaptic degeneration are two examples of changes that lead to tissue loss in brain areas remote from the lesion. The effects of these negative changes are further complicated by the

potential effects of lesion-induced axonal sprouting and reactive syn-
aptogenesis, which occurs in partially denervated sites. These positive changes
may lead to recovery of behavioral function (Loesche & Steward, 1977;
Steward, Loesche, & Horton, 1977) but may also lead to loss of behavioral
function not attributable to actual removal of tissue, but rather to lesion-
induced remote collateral sprouting (Baisden & Woodruff, 1980).

Sensory-Motor Dichotomy of Language Function Enjoys Current Support

Geschwind (1965, 1971, 1975, 1979) has been the most influential modern
proponent of the positions of Broca and Wernicke. He has used a localizationist position to explain aphasias and apraxias, concentrating his analysis on the
effects of disconnection of various regions of the cortex. Geschwind begins
with the assumption, based upon the clinical effects of cortical lesions and
certain anatomical asymmetries between the cerebral hemispheres, that there
exists a posterior receptive area for speech and an anterior expressive area. The
clinical effects of lesions of the anterior and posterior speech regions were
described above. The most notable anatomical asymmetry is the enhanced size
of the left planum temporale, a portion of cortex just posterior to primary
auditory cortex (Geschwind & Levitsky, 1968). The planum temporale corresponds to Wernicke's posterior speech area, and Geschwind argues that its
enhanced size on one side of the brain in humans indicates a physical basis for
language specialization. The report of Wada, Clarke, and Hamm (1975) that
this area is larger in the language hemisphere of a fetus by about the fifth
month of gestation supports Geschwind's interpretation.

According to Geschwind's model, language is understood in the region of
the posterior superior temporal gyrus classically defined as Wernicke's area.
Therefore, for example, in order for written language to be interpreted pathways between the visual cortices and Wernicke's area must be intact. For
spoken language to be understood pathways between the auditory areas and
Wernicke's area must be intact. Disruption of the former pathways, then, leads
to alexia, while destruction of the latter leads to word deafness. Furthermore,
transmission of information from the receptive region of Wernicke proceeds
forward over the arcuate fasciculus to Broca's area, thereby allowing vocal
repetition of language that is heard or read.

If what is heard or read is a command for motor action, this information is
transferred via the arcuate fasciculus to the ipsilateral premotor region and
subsequently to either the ipsilateral precentral gyrus or transcallosally to the
contralateral premotor cortex. Disruption of any portion of this pathway will
produce apraxia, a disorder of learned movement. For example, destruction of
the arcuate fasciculus will cause, in addition to a conduction aphasia, a
bilateral apraxia, while destruction of the lateral posterior inferior frontal lobe
may cause afluent aphasia, paralysis of the contralateral face and upper

extremity, and an ipsilateral apraxia. Transection of the anterior two-thirds of the corpus callosum by means of a vascular accident involving the anterior cerebral artery or by surgical intervention often results in an apraxia of the limbs ipsilateral to the language hemisphere. Loss of either the lateral posterior frontal lobe or the anterior callosum prevents the transfer of linguistic information to the nonlanguage hemisphere and, in this manner, causes the apraxia. It should be noted, however, that surgical separation of the callosum does not produce as profound, or long-lasting, an apraxia as vascular trauma. This suggests that the apraxia caused by vascular damage to the anterior callosum is due to destruction that involves neural structures other than the corpus callosum.

Geschwind's theory represents a localizationist viewpoint. He proposes that information taking the form of the symbols of language is encoded from relevant sensory modalities in the region of the posterior superior temporal gyrus and that the ability to perform such encoding in anything resembling a sophisticated, normal manner is restricted in the majority of people to this area. This information is then passed along a long intrahemispheric pathway (the arcuate fasciculus) to access motor programs for both verbal and nonverbal expression that are stored only in frontal regions. In most people these programs are stored in only one hemisphere and any physical disruption of brain pathways that segregates these motor programs from the language centers results in an apraxia.

Moreover, Geschwind proposes a further separation of function in that motor program storage may be localized in the hemisphere opposite the dominant language hemisphere. Case reports by Heilman, Coyle, Gonyea, and Geschwind (1973) and by Margolin (1980) emphasize this point. Heilman and colleagues describe a left-handed man who suffered a stroke that destroyed the right lateral cortex, including areas 4 and 6. As expected, he developed a paralysis of his dominant left side. However, although he did not manifest difficulties with language, as would be expected if he had language dominance in the right hemisphere, he did suffer from an apraxia in his unparalyzed right arm. These observations were interpreted to indicate that language programs were stored in this patient's left hemisphere, but that motor programs were stored in the right. Although the sensorimotor connections for language were intact, the motor programs for skilled movements had been destroyed when the right motor and premotor areas were compromised.

Geschwind's disconnection theory is, then, explicitly one in which integration of sensory input with language takes place in restricted parts of the posterior cerebrum, while motor programs are usually stored in one side of the frontal lobe. Communication among these modular centers takes place over long intrahemispheric and commissural pathways. The data supporting this theory also support an anterior-posterior dichotomy of motor-sensory function, laterality of cerebral function, and a strong localizationist position.

Sensorimotor Hierarchy and the Neocortex: Luria's View of Cortical Function

Luria's (1966, 1970) view of the functional organization of the brain is also one of information flow from sensory to motor areas; but, in addition, it explicitly incorporates the hierarchical principle of brain function. Luria concentrates upon the function of the cerebral cortex but includes the reticular formation in his model, stressing its ability to activate the cortex. Because of its polysensory input, the reticular formation has the role of arousing the cerebral cortex to set the stage for specific sensory processing. Although Luria does not dwell upon this function, it should be kept in mind that the reticular system also biases spinal cord reflexes in such a way as to modulate cortical and peripheral sensory influences on the motor neurons of the anterior horn.

Luria divides the neocortex into a sensory unit and a motor unit. Each of these units is, in turn, subdivided into primary, secondary, and tertiary units. All functional units are correlated with anatomical divisions of the cortex. The primary sensory zones correspond to the traditional primary sensory cortical areas, which process unimodal sensory input with precise representation of peripheral receptive field characteristics and secure synaptic linkage. The secondary areas bound the primary (e.g., visual association cortex—areas 18 and 19) and are within one or two synapses of the specific sensory cortical regions. The tertiary sensory zones essentially represent the traditional association areas of the temporal, occipital, and parietal lobes. It is within the tertiary sensory zones that polymodal sensory input is coded for symbolic and abstract features.

The motor zone lies entirely within the pre-Rolandic portion of the neocortex. According to Luria's scheme symbolic information from the tertiary sensory areas is passed forward to the tertiary motor areas located in the prefrontal granular cortex, where it is evaluated and translated into intention. The prefrontal cortex is, therefore, viewed as an executive processor that passes its output to the premotor strip. The premotor strip selects appropriate motor programs from area 4 to represent intention in behavioral action.

In addition to demonstrating more complexity in the processing of information and, therefore, less specific sensorimotor function, the tertiary zones are also proposed to exhibit laterality of function, whereas the primary zones do not. That this is the case is obvious for language and spatial representation, even for patients with unilateral frontal lobe damage (Milner, 1971). However, the tertiary zones of the prefrontal cortex, the very place where, according to Luria's model, one would expect the greatest degree of lateralization, do not appear to be more lateralized, or even as lateralized, in function as are the secondary and primary motor zones that subserve dominance for handedness. The report of Heilman and colleagues (1973) serves to illustrate this point. In this report motor programs for dominance are lost subsequent to an unilateral lesion, although language function has been preserved. These motor programs are presumably found in the secondary and primary motor regions, not the tertiary association zones of the prefrontal cortex. This observation, combined with the apparent lack of laterality of several functions associated with the tertiary zones of the prefrontal cortex (Deutsch, Kling, & Steklis, 1979), supports the proposition that lateralization of function is not necessarily predictable from knowledge of position in the cortical hierarchy.

Furthermore, although Luria's model is useful as a framework for the evaluation of neuropsychological disorders, as a general theory of brain function it falls short in that it does not lead from the molar level of analysis to the more cellular. It shares this weakness with the hierarchical theories discussed previously and with Geschwind's disconnection theory. The ideal theory of brain function has not yet, of course, been developed. However, when and if it is, it will link neuronal activity to cognitive function. Luria's theory not only fails to do this, but is not cast in a way that is especially useful as a heuristic guide for investigations that might lead in such a direction.

Evaluation of the Sensory-Motor Dichotomy Within Association Neocortex

Clearly areas of association cortex cannot be classified as being either sensory or motor with the same facility as can the primary cortices lying along the Rolandic fissure. The posterior, superior temporal gyrus is "sensory" only inasmuch as destruction of this area compromises the person's ability to understand language. On the other hand, the cortex of Broca's area is motor only in as much as its destruction results in a reduction in the ability to produce language. Moreover, the effects of lesions of these two cortical areas would seem to be more easily classified as sensory and motor than are the clinical effects of damage to other cortical association areas. This would appear to be especially true of the prefrontal cortex. Although Luria (1966), using neuro-psychological testing, has found that a tendency to perseveration and disruption of sequential ordering in motor tasks are among the chief behavioral sequelae of frontal lobe damage, study of such patients also reveals attentional deficits that are not clearly motor in character (Hecaen & Albert, 1975). Furthermore, such patients also demonstrate difficulties in the ability to reverse standpoint when dealing with mirror images of their own bodies (Teuber, 1964). These reports, as well as the spatial response impairments long associated with frontal lobe damage in monkeys (Jacobsen, 1936), lend support to the contention that the prefrontal cortex participates in several processess more closely related to the sensory than the motor sphere.

The prefrontal cortex may not, therefore, fall clearly into either the motor or the sensory domain. However, other portions of the frontal lobe outside of the language areas, the frontal eye fields, and the premotor cortex may have interesting relationships both to motor functioning and to sensory function of postcentral association areas. The medial frontal cortex may best exemplify this point. Unilateral destruction of the medial frontal cortex has been reported to produce a syndrome referred to as the "alien hand sign." A patient presenting this syndrome will complain that one hand and arm behave as if they were not under the patient's volitional control, acting, in effect, as if they did not belong to the patient. This syndrome is often associated with enhanced grasp reflexes and motor perseveration. The condition may lead to intermanual conflict as the patient uses the unaffected hand to stop the action of the "alien" hand. The alien hand sign has been associated with commissurotomy (Bogen, 1979), but Goldberg, Mayer, and Toglia (1981) have provided convincing evidence that the disorder is due to destruction of the medial frontal cortex.

The alien hand sign appears to be a motor disorder. It also would seem to qualify as a release phenomenon in that the affected hand produces behavior that is both uninhibitable and unwanted by the patient. However, the patient recognizes that the misbehaving hand is indeed his or her own hand. Neglect, a disorder most often associated with damage to the parietal lobe, especially of the nonlanguage hemisphere, appears in some ways to be the sensory equivalent of the alien hand sign. A discussion of the theoretical issues involved in classifying this syndrome and discerning whether it is the result of, for example, inattention or some more fundamental change in the patient's perceptual world, is beyond this chapter. (The interested reader is directed to Heilman (1979) for a thorough discussion of neglect.) However, the disorder does appear to fall more within the sensory than the motor domain. Patients exhibiting neglect often fail to respond to stimuli presented to the surface of the body opposite the lesion. They may not read part of a sentence and may even fail to dress and groom one half of their body. However, once they do respond to stimuli, they are capable of controlling the action of either hand.

It would seem, then, that, as might be expected from the mixed nature of the intrinsic structure and extrinsic connectivity of the association areas, a complete dichotomy does not exist between sensory and motor functions within the association cortices. However, it appears to be far more accurate to segregate posterior cortical areas from anterior cortical areas along the sensorimotor dimension than it does to classify these areas as possessing any substantial degree of equipotentiality of sensory-motor function. As will be observed in the following section, a similar statement may also be made regarding laterality of function of the cerebral hemispheres. While some functions are indeed shared by each hemisphere, it is more accurate to view each half of the cerebral mantle as having its own functions.

Laterality of Function

That the human neocortex exhibits laterality of function has been demonstrated using data from at least six different sources and cannot be doubted as a principle of cerebral organization. Lateralization of function has been revealed by comparison of the behavioral deficits and, importantly, the remaining behavioral capacities of patients with cortical damage restricted to one hemisphere or the other and by comparison of the behavioral effects produced by anesthetization of each hemisphere individually with intracarotid sodium amytal (Wada & Rasmussen, 1960). Electrical stimulation of the cortical surface in humans prior to surgical excision of regions involved in generation of focal epilepsy (Penfield & Roberts, 1959) and, to some extent, study of speech-correlated electrical potentials (Fried, Ojemann, & Fetz, 1981) have also revealed lateralization of function. Left–right differences in cerebral blood flow may also be related to laterality of cognitive function (Dabbs, 1980; Dabbs & Choo, 1980). Finally, the study of patients having suffered surgical transection of the cerebral commissures (Sperry, 1961, 1974; Sperry, Gazzaniga, & Bogen, 1969) has provided the most valuable information regarding the separate capacities of the two hemispheres.

Asymmetry of Structure and Function in the Human Brain

The human brain presents a number of structural asymmetries. As indicated above, the left planum temporale is significantly larger than the right and a longer Sylvian fissure accompanies this asymmetry (Geschwind & Levitsky, 1968). It is also known that the left occipital region is usually longer than the right (Chui & Damasio, 1980; Hadziselimovic & Cus, 1966; LeMay, 1976). This pattern appears to be reflected in an asymmetrical distribution of the posterior Sylvian branches of the middle cerebral artery (Ratcliff, Dila, Taylor, & Milner, 1980).

It is, of course, tempting to assume some type of causative connection between these asymmetries and left hemispheric dominance for language. However, at least one difficulty is associated with uncritical acceptance of such an assumption. Wada, Clarke, and Hamm (1975) have reported that the area of the left frontal operculum is less than that of the right. However, as indicated by Wada and colleagues, this observation may be an artifact introduced by the presence of interindividual differences in gyral pattern within the frontal opercular area and the resulting difficulty in obtaining consistent measurement of total surface area within this cortical region. The left frontal opercular area could actually be larger than that of the right in the majority of left-dominant individuals (Ratcliff et al., 1980). This supposition is supported by the finding of Gur et al. (1980) that there is a higher ratio of gray matter to white matter in the left hemisphere compared to the right, especially in the frontal and precentral regions.

Incentive for conducting the research just summarized has come from clinical and experimental observations that indicate that the left hemisphere is preferentially involved in integration and production of language. Data typically cited (Milner, Branch, & Rasmussen, 1964, 1966) indicate that some 92% of right handers and 69% of left handers have language localized to the left hemisphere. In addition, it is recognized that the right hemisphere in left-language-dominant individuals possesses the advantage over the left hemisphere in performance of several unique and complex functions.

For example, when the right hemisphere is tested in commissurotomized patients (Bogen, 1969; Bogen & Gazzaniga, 1965), it is found to be better than the left hemisphere in construction of block designs and in copying geometrical figures. This observation is compatible with the occurrence of constructional apraxia subsequent to right parietal lobe damage (Arrigoni & DeRenzi, 1964; Critchely, 1953). Moreover, as long as the required response is manual (i.e. pointing), not verbal, the right hemisphere is superior to the left in recognition of shapes, especially those that cannot easily be described in words (Milner & Taylor, 1972). These observations lead to the conclusion that the right hemisphere functions in a mode that employs direct synthetic perceptual processing and a similar sort of memory. It is superior to the left analytic-language hemisphere in tasks, such as facial recognition, that require synthesis of complex sensory patterns and may also be involved in the production of dream imagery (Kerr & Foulkes, 1981). As might be expected, the left hemisphere appears responsible for the narrative aspects of dreaming (Kerr & Foulkes, 1981).

However, although hemispheric specialization is marked, it is well to make the point that the functions of the hemispheres are generally coordinated in performance of any particular type of activity. For example, the right hemisphere participates in its own way both in normal comprehension and production of language. Its integrity appears necessary for the understanding and expression of emotional tone in speech (prosody), and damage to the right hemisphere may produce an aprosodic patient (Heilman, Scholes, & Watson, 1975; Ross, 1981; Ross & Mesulam, 1979). In addition, Wapner, Hamby, and Gardner (1981) have found that right-hemisphere-damaged patients have difficulty in assessing the emotional content of a story. They also have difficulty in such tasks as picking the appropriate punch line for a joke or assessing a story's plausibility. Wapner and colleagues interpret these data to indicate that persons with damage to the nonlanguage-dominant hemisphere have difficulties in interpreting the more subtle aspects of complex linguistic material, especially that which depends upon utilization of context.

As was discussed earlier in this chapter, the anatomic separation of sensory and motor functions within the central nervous system extends to the neocortex and to the physical parcellation of propositional language function into a posterior receptive area and an anterior expressive area. Moreover, substantial evidence has also been reported supporting this dichotomy for the structural-functional organization of the affective aspects of language within the nondominant hemisphere. For example, individuals suffering damage restricted to the inferior one-half to two-thirds of the nondominant frontal lobe often show an inability to express emotion in speech, but are capable of correctly interpreting emotional tone in the speech and gestures of others. On the other hand, individuals with damage to the inferior parietal and superior temporal regions surrounding the posterior one-half of the Sylvian fissure may often have difficulty in understanding the emotional tone of others (Ross, 1981; Ross & Mesulam, 1979). The parallel to the dichotomy of relationships found in the language-dominant hemisphere is obvious and serves to reinforce the concept that posterior-anterior segregation of sensorimotor functions is a primary anatomic/functional relationship within neocortical tissue.

The nonlanguage-dominant hemisphere, then, appears to be involved not only in spatio-constructional functions, but in interpretation and production of emotional tone in language. However, this observation does not mean that the left hemisphere is not involved in emotional behaviors. Several reports indicate that there exists a laterality of emotional processess within the cortex, as damage to the left hemisphere appears to produce a dysphoric mood state, whereas damage to the right hemisphere can be associated with euphoria (Gainotti, 1972; Hall, Hall, & Lavoie, 1968; Sackeim, Greenberg, Weiman, Gur, Hungerbuhler, & Geschwind, 1982). It appears, therefore, that, although each hemisphere contributes its own unique input, hemispheric interaction is necessary for normal complete manifestation of both expressive and receptive language function, as well as for the normal manifestation of emotion. In addition, the interaction of the two hemispheres also appears to be necessary for the control of musical ability, with neither hemisphere being clearly dominant for recognition of complex musical patterns. Rather, the right hemisphere appears to be dominant for melody recognition, while the left participates in determination of time and rhythm factors (Gates & Bradshaw, 1977).

Two points emerge from the preceding. First, in most individuals the cerebral hemispheres demonstrate laterality of dominant function. Second, lateral dominance is not absolute. The individual hemispheres share functions, and both hemispheres normally interact to produce integrated behavior. These facts make it difficult to develop a theory that explains the biological basis of hemispheric dominance. However, it does appear that laterality of function is in some way related to motor function and vocalization. Moreover, recent reports have indicated anatomical and biochemical asymmetries in the brains of animals that appear to be related to the functions of locomotion and species-specific patterns of vocalization. These observations may be important because, if hemispheric asymmetries exist in infrahuman species, their study may provide a basis for the development of an explanation for the existence of laterality in humans. For example, such study might be used to resolve the issue of whether lateralization and cerebral dominance are related specifically to the development of language (Walker, 1980), or whether they are related to the more general processess of encephalization, specialization, and differentiation of function implicit in hierarchical theories of brain function (e.g., Luria, 1970).

Asymmetries in Infrahuman Brains

It is clear that anatomic cerebral asymmetries are found in some infrahuman species. For example, the right hemisphere of rats, mice, rabbits, and cats is larger in terms of brain weight and surface area than the left hemisphere (Kolb, Sutherland, Nonneman, & Whishaw, 1982). In rats this size difference appears to be a consequence of a relative increase in thickness of the neocortex and may be related to the observations made by Sherman, Garbanati, Rosen, Yutzey, and Denenberg (1980) indicating that the right hemisphere of the rat controls preference of movement direction. In addition, ligation of the middle cerebral artery of the right hemisphere in rats is followed by spontaneous hyperactivity and decreases in norepinephrine in cortical and subcortical areas (Robinson, 1979; Robinson & Coyle, 1980). These changes do not occur following ligation of the left middle cerebral artery. It is difficult to generalize from these data, as the observations are limited to rats, but the observations of Robinson and of Sherman et al. suggest that the right hemisphere may be dominant for initiation of movement of the entire body through space. It is tempting to speculate that this may be related phylogenetically to the superior ability of the nonlanguage hemisphere of humans in the coding of spatial relationships.

It is also tempting to relate asymmetries observed in the brains of primates to asymmetries seen in the language-dominant hemisphere in humans and, therefore, to attribute the development of such specializations to a progressive evolutionary development of cognitive capacity to communicate to cospecifics. The left Sylvian fissure in orangutans, chimpanzees, and gorillas has been reported in many instances to be longer than the right Sylvian fissure, a feature that is also found in human brains (Galaburda, LeMay, Kemper, & Geschwind, 1978; Yeni-Komshian & Benson, 1976). A similar asymmetry may also have existed in several human ancestral species (Galaburda et al., 1978). However, while these differences might indicate functional asymmetries in apes, evidence as to what these functions might be is not readily available. It is possible that, at least in Japanese macaques, the left hemisphere is responsible for analysis of species-typical calls (Petersen, Beecher, Zoloth, Moody, & Stebbins, 1978), but the experiment purporting to demonstrate this phenomenon can be criticized for substantial methodological flaws (Walker, 1980). Moreover, production of species-typical vocalization in monkeys appears primarily to be controlled by the midline cortex, especially that of the cingulate gyrus (Jurgens & Pratt, 1979), and not by lateral cortical areas. It is, therefore, difficult to use comparative data, at least from the study of infraprimate monkeys, to understand the development of cerebral dominance in humans.

Another model for laterality of vocal expression has supported the proposition that hemispheric dominance is either the cause or the consequence of development of sophisticated intraspecific communication. Lesions in the left cerebrum of male canaries severely disrupt their ability to produce song, while right hemispheric lesions are much less disruptive (Nottebohm, 1971; Nottebohm, Stokes, & Leonard, 1976). The most effective lesion is placed just posterior to the auditory receptive areas. The parallel to the close spatial relationship between primary auditory cortex and Wernicke's area in humans is interesting. It is also interesting that the canary's song recovers if the damage is done before maturity. Similar recovery is often seen in human children with left hemispheric damage (Lenneberg, 1967) and, as with humans (Kinsbourne, 1971), the right cerebrum appears to assume the production of the canary "language" if song does recover subsequent to left hemispheric damage.

The Place of Laterality in Structural-Functional Relationships within the Brain

Several conclusions may be drawn from the foregoing. First, asymmetries exist in the brains of infrahuman species. (Several asymmetries have been found that were not discussed. The interested reader may consult the papers by Galaburda et al., 1978; Kolb et al., 1982; and Walker, 1980, for references.) Second, these asymmetries can be related to function. For example, the right hemisphere of the rat may be dominant for control of movement through space, although not for control of movement of individual limbs. Third, the behavioral functions controlled by lateralized asymmetries seem to be relatively complex in nature and of marked importance to the species. In particular, the abilities to relate movement of self to the environment and to produce and understand sophisticated species-typical vocal patterns tend to be lateralized functions.

Finally, within the context of a theory of brain function, there is nothing special about lateralization. Rather, lateralization represents a special case of localization of functions. Within this context lateralization of language to one hemisphere and nonlanguage spatio-temporal functions to the other represents usage of the second plane along the two-dimensional cortical surface. As discussed above, many individually defineable functions are dichotomized in the sensorimotor sphere along the anterior-posterior axis of the cerebrum. Lateralization simply represents a dichotomization of two other variables, language-analytical in one hemisphere, spatial-intuitive in the other. There is, therefore, nothing new or extraordinary about the lateralization of these functions. As language developed it was simply parcelled into one hemisphere, rather than being segregated from other functions along the anterior-posterior axis. A general corollary to this position would be that the more discrete and specialized a function becomes, the more localized it is likely to be. Encephalization of sensorimotor function represents another example of this postulate.

Theories of Brain Functioning: Localized Microstructure But Distributed Processing

The material presented in this chapter represents a condensed amalgam of theories generated by many neuroscientists. With the exception of the work discussed above of Hubel and Wiesel and of Mountcastle, the dominant theoretical trends have portrayed the central nervous system as made up of a series of hierarchically arranged units of increasing complexity that allow for ever-increasing sophistication of input-output processing. Such theories usually link functional hierarchy to physical placement of a structure along the caudal-rostral axis of the central nervous system. They also usually include, either implicitly or explicitly, the concept of encephalization of function. That is, as rostral, or cephalic, structures develop either in phylogeny or ontogeny, they assume functions once delegated to more caudal structures of the neuraxis. The more caudal structures remain necessary, but are often relegated to the position of simple relay stations.

A complete hierarchical theory of brain function would include structures from spinal cord to cortex and would emphasize motor capability and the ability to process information. MacLean's theory of the triune brain probably best approximates such a theory. However, global hierarchical theories usually do not elaborate the individual functions of the cerebral neocortex. Other theories that arise from a hierarchical approach to brain function generally discuss cortical function in detail, but are not true hierarchical theories in the sense of detailed incorporation of subcortical levels of the central nervous system within their scope. Such theories are exemplified by the work of Geschwind and Luria. These theories are hierarchical only in the sense that they typically discuss information flow from the relatively simple responses of the primary cortices through the complex associations performed in homotypical areas of the parietal and temporal lobes to motor outflow from the cortex of the precentral gyrus. This approach represents, as Pribram (1974) has stated, the classical view that the cerebral cortex functions as a series of transcortical reflex arcs.

The theories discussed thus far have, for the most part, been based upon data collected from humans and infrahumans with damage to one or another part of the central nervous system. These data and the resultant theories have significantly advanced our understanding of brain function. However, new theoretical directions are rapidly emerging within neuroscience generally and within neuropsychology specifically. Many of these theories rely upon data from neurophysiological procedures to construct hypotheses regarding the manner in which the central nervous system actually processess information. The writings of Pribram (1971, 1974) are an example especially pertinent to neuropsychology. Pribram's theory incorporates the function of subcortical and cortical structures in the production of behavior and mental life. However, his view of neural processing of sensory information, especially within the visual system, will serve as a good illustrative example of his general view of brain functioning.

Pribram recognizes the cortical column as the basic functional unit of the cortex. His interest lies in how columns come to encode information and, moreover, how columns that are removed from one another on the cortical surface come to possess the same informational content.

The latter issue is of particular interest and may be taken as an anti-localizationist position. Such an interpretation would appear warranted based upon Pribram's prior association with Lashley. However, Pribram obviously recognizes the differences in function of the large divisions of the neocortex, and he should not be accused of taking the extreme position that all neocortical areas are equipotential in function. In fact, he clearly denies the idea that the brain functions as a network of randomly associated elements upon which order is imposed by current sensory input.

Pribram (1971) proposes that repeated stimulation produces changes in local neuronal circuitry, especially in the pattern of junctional contacts, by means of axonal sprouting. Changes in local neuronal circuitry are reflected in changes in local junctional slow potentials. The slow potentials represent the actual workings of the local neuronal circuitry and are an expression of the information code. Pribram neglects only one possibility in this part of his theory. That is, he does not include the possibility of postsynaptic morphological change. For example, repeated input along a particular pathway could cause physical expansion of dendritic spines, which, in turn, might result in facilitated transmission of information from one neuron to the next. This mechanism would utilize modification of transmission through existing synaptic contacts to produce new information transfer patterns without the presynaptic growth and formation of new synapses postulated by Pribram.

Regardless of the physical substrate, Pribram's emphasis on the organization of slow potentials as localized signs of changes in cortical function is important because it relates precise electrical activation of the cortex to modular information processing. It is important to recognize that, while part of Pribram's thesis is that information-processing modules are replicated in many places, the electrical activity of any single module is restricted in space by the lateral inhibitory network that surrounds each active cortical element. Pribram (1971, 1974) emphasizes the importance of the ability of excited neurons to inhibit the activity of neurons that surround them in allowing feature extraction and discusses this ability as a function of short, localized intracortical connections. Such "surround inhibition" is an example of a neural "signal-to-noise" improvement mechanism. Enhancement of signal-to-noise relationships appears to be such an important aspect of neural functioning that, in addition to the actions of intracortical circuitry, the diffuse projections from the noradrenergic locus coeruleus also appear to produce a relative enhancement of neuronal responses to sensory stimulation (Waterhouse & Woodward, 1980).

Lateral inhibition serves, then, to organize information, the basis of which is a "microstructure of slow potentials" (Pribram, 1974). This microstructure is replicated many times throughout a particular cortical area. Therefore, for example, evoked potentials associated with one special visual sensory pattern may be recorded from several discontinuous points within the striate cortex of the monkey, but neural activity at each point is very restricted in space (Pribram, 1974). Because the information is replicated, destruction of any one part, or even large parts, of the striate cortex does not eliminate the appreciation of visual pattern. Pribram refers to the effect of such replication as the production of a holographic representation of experience within the brain.

Because of the holographic rendering of information a small part of the sensory system may access an entire sensory image. Pribram uses a clinical example to illustrate this point, stating that "When a patient suffers a stroke that wipes out half or more of his visual system, he does not go home to recognize only half of his family. With whatever visual field he has left he is able to recognize all that he ever recognized" (1974, p. 251). He then extends the holographic model developed for sensory cortices to account for memory formation throughout the brain.

It is, of course, obvious that information is not replicated endlessly throughout the brain. While a patient may not require his or her entire striate cortex to recognize everything that he or she may have been able to recognize before a stroke, lesions to certain cortical structures assuredly produce, for example, very specific agnosias. This type of clinical observation limits the generalizability of the holographic concept and may point out the importance of separating memory storage mechanisms from information retrieval mechanisms.

To this point one might assume that Pribram's theory is also a hierarchical "cortical reflex" theory. However, he clearly does not believe that information flows strictly from primary sensory cortex to secondary sensory association cortex to tertiary areas. For example, he emphasizes the role of the inferotemporal cortex in visual pattern recognition, including its ability to modify responses in both striate cortex and the lateral geniculate nucleus. This is a very important concept and is not included explicitly in any of the previously discussed theories. Pribram incorporates into his theory the ability of tertiary association areas to alter sensory input even before it reaches primary sensory cortex. This clearly separates his theories from those which present a hierarchically organized flow of information.

CONCLUSION

Pribram's theory is unique in that it represents an attempt to use data from a variety of disciplines within neuroscience to construct a hypothesis concerning brain function. If any global theory of brain functioning in behavior can be constructed to exceed those which have been discussed above, the data to construct this theory must be derived from more than the study of the effects of brain damage on behavior. Such a theory must incorporate information from anatomy, biochemistry, physiology, pharmacology, and psychology in order to produce a product that addresses the issue of how the brain with its units and subunits actually works to produce behavior. Such a theory must also be cast in a manner that permits testable hypotheses to be generated from it. At present a theory of this sort does not appear to be forthcoming. In fact, neuroscience and its subdisciplines appear to be in a very atheoretical period devoted to much raw empiricism. The alternative to this problem will not be found in perusal of the theories outlined above. The alternative is to begin with a different point of view and to synthesize material of an amazingly diverse nature. The question becomes not whether this should be done, but rather, whether it can be done. However, rather than forsake the enterprise it is better to attend to the words of Sir Charles Sherrington. In 1933 Sherrington said: "To the question of the relation between brain and mind the answer given by a physiologist 60 years ago was 'Ignorabimus'. . . . The problem today has one virtue at least, it will longer offer to those who pursue it the comfort that to journey is better than to arrive; but that comfort assumes arrival. Some of us—perhaps because we are too old—or is it, too young—think that there may be arrival at last." (Quoted in Penfield, 1960, p. 1441.)

REFERENCES

Arrigoni, G., & DeRenzi, E. (1964). Constructional apraxia and hemispheric locus of lesion. *Cortex, 1,* 170–179.

Asanuma, H. (1981). Functional role of sensory inputs to the motor cortex. *Progress in Neurobiology, 16,* 242–262.

Bach, L. M. N., & Magoun, H. W. (1947). The vestibular nuclei as an excitatory mechanism for the cord. *Journal of Neurophysiology, 10,* 331–337.

Baisden, R. H., & Woodruff, M. L. (1980). Behavioral effects of hippocampal lesions with prior intraseptal injections of 6-hydroxydopamine. *Physiological Psychology, 8,* 33–39.

Bard, P. (1928). A diencephalic mechanism for the expression of rage, with special reference to the sympathetic nervous system. *American Journal of Physiology, 84,* 490–515.

Bard, P., & Macht, M. B. (1958). The behavior of chronically decerebrate cats. In G. E. W. Wolstenholme & C. M. O'Conner (Eds.), *Ciba Foundation symposium on neurological basis of behavior* (pp. 55–75). London: J. & A. Churchill.

Bard, P., & Mountcastle, V. B. (1948). Some forebrain mechanisms involved in expression of rage with special reference to suppression of angry behavior. *Research Publications of the Association for Research in Nervous and Mental Disease, 27,* 362–404.

Bazett, H. C., & Penfield, W. G. (1922). A study of the Sherrington decerebrate animal in the chronic as well as the acute condition. *Brain, 45,* 185–265.

Bogen, J. E. (1969). The other side of the brain. I: Dysgraphia and dyscopia following cerebral commissurotomy. *Bulletin of the Los Angeles Neurological Society, 34,* 73–105.

Bogen, J. E. (1979). The callosal syndrome. In K. E. Heilman & E. Valenstein (Eds.), *Clinical neuropsychology* (pp. 308–359). New York: Oxford University Press.

Bogen, J. E., & Gazzaniga, M. S. (1965). Cerebral commissurotomy in man: Minor hemisphere dominance for certain visuospatial functions. *Journal of Neurosurgery, 23,* 394–399

Broca, P. (1865). Remarques sur le siege de la faculte du language articule. *Bulletin de la Societe d'Anthropologie, 6,* 18–28.

Cannon, W. B., & Britton, S. W. (1924). Pseudoaffective medulliadrenal secretion. *American Journal of Physiology, 72,* 283–294.

Carli, G., LaMotte, R. H., & Mountcastle, V. B. (1971). A simultaneous study of somatic sensory behavior and the activity of somatic sensory cortical neurons. *Federation Proceedings, 30,* 664.

Chui, H. C., & Damasio, A. R. (1980). Human cerebral asymmetries evaluated by computed tomography. *Journal of Neurology, Neurosurgery, and Psychiatry, 43,* 873–878.

Critchley, M. (1953). *The parietal lobes.* London: Edward Arnold.

Dabbs, J. M. (1980). Left-right differences in carotid blood flow and cognition. *Psychophysiology, 17,* 548–551.

Dabbs, J. M., & Choo, G. (1980). Left-right carotid blood flow predicts specialized mental ability. *Neuropsychologia, 18,* 548–551.

Deutsch, R. D., Kling, A., & Steklis, H. D. (1979). Influence of frontal lobe lesions on behavioral interactions in man. *Research Communications in Psychology, Psychiatry and Behavior, 4,* 415–431.

Fish, B. S., Baisden, R. H., & Woodruff, M. L. (1979). Cerebellar nuclear lesions in rats: Subsequent avoidance behavior and ascending anatomical connections. *Brain Research, 166,* 27–38.

Fried, I., Ojemann, G., & Fetz, E. (1981). Language related potentials specific to human language cortex. *Science, 199,* 852–856.

Gainotti, G. (1972). Emotional behavior and hemispheric side of the lesion. *Cortex, 8,* 41–55.

Galaburda, A. M., LeMay, M., Kemper, T. L., & Geshwind, N. (1978). Right-left asymmetries in the brain. *Science, 199,* 852–856.

Gates, A., & Bradshaw, J. L. (1977). The role of the cerebral hemispheres in music. *Brain and Language, 6,* 403–441.

Geshwind, N. (1965). Disconnexion syndromes in animals and man. *Brain, 88,* 237–294.

Geshwind, N. (1971). Current concepts: Aphasia. *New England Journal of Medicine, 284,* 654–656.

Geshwind, N. (1975). The apraxias. Neural mechanisms of disorders of learned movement. *American Scientist, 63,* 188–195.

Geshwind, N. (1979). Specializations of the human brain. *Scientific American, 241,* 180–199.

Geshwind, N., & Levitsky, W. (1968). Human brain: Left-right asymmetries in temporal speech region. *Science, 161,* 186–187.

Goldberg, G., Mayer, N. H., & Toglia, J. U. (1981). Medial frontal cortex infarction and the alien hand sign. *Archives of Neurology, 38,* 683–686.

Goldstein, K. (1948). *Language and language disturbances.* New York: Grune & Stratton.

Grill, H. J., & Norgren, R. (1978a). Chronically decerebrate rats demonstrate satiation but not baitshyness. *Science, 201,* 267–269.

Grill, H. J., & Norgren, R. (1978b). Neurological tests and behavioral deficits in chronic thalamic and chronic decerebrate rats. *Brain Research, 143,* 299–312.

Grillner, S. (1973). Locomotion in the spinal cat. In R. B. Stein, K. G. Pearson, R. S. Smith, & J. B. Redford (Eds.), *Control of posture and locomotion* (pp. 515–535). New York: Plenum Press.

Gur, R. C., Packer, I. K., Hungerbuhler, J. P., Reivich, M., Obrist, W. E., Amarnek, W. S., & Sackheim, H. A. (1980). Differences in the distribution of gray and white matter in human cerebral hemispheres. *Science, 207,* 1226–1228.

Hadziselimovic, H., & Cus, M. (1966). The appearance of the internal structures of the brain in relation to the configuration of the human skull. *Acta Anatomica, 63,* 289–299.

Hall, M. M., Hall, G. C., & Lavoie, P. (1968). Ideation in patients with unilateral or bilateral midline brain lesions. *Journal of Abnormal Psychology, 73,* 526–531.

Harting, J. K., Hall, W. C., Diamond, I. T., & Martin, G. F. (1973). Anterograde degeneration study of the superior colliculus in Tupaia glis: Evidence for a subdivision between superficial and deep layers. *Journal of Comparative Neurology, 148,* 361–386.

Head, H. (1921). Disorders of symbolic thinking and expression. *British Journal of Psychology, 11,* 179–193.

Head, H. (1926). *Aphasia and kindred disorders of speech* (2 Vols.). London: Cambridge University Press.

Heath, R. G., Franklin, D. E., & Shraberg, D. (1979). Gross pathology of the cerebellum in patients diagnosed and treated as functional psychiatric disorders. *Journal of Nervous and Mental Disease, 167,* 585–592.

Hecaen, H., & Albert, M. L. (1975). Disorders of mental functioning related to frontal lobe pathology. In D. F. Benson & D. Blumer (Eds.), *Psychiatric aspects of neurologic disease* (pp. 137–159). New York: Grune & Stratton.

Heilman, K. M. (1979). Neglect and related disorders. In K. M. Heilman & E. Valenstein (Eds.), *Clinical neuropsychology* (pp. 268–307). New York: Oxford University Press.

Heilman, K. M., Coyle, J. M., Gonyea, E. F., & Geshwind, N. (1973). Apraxia and agraphia in a left-hander. *Brain, 96,* 21–28.

Heilman, K. M., Scholes, R., & Watson, R. T. (1975). Auditory affective agnosia: Disturbed comprehension of affective speech. *Journal of Neurology, Neurosurgery and Psychiatry, 38,* 69–72.

Hubel, D. H., & Wiesel, T. N. (1977). Functional architecture of macaque monkey cortex. *Proceedings of the Royal Society of London, B198,* 1–59.

Imig, T. J., & Adrian, H. O. (1977). Binaural columns in the primary field (A1) of cat auditory cortex. *Brain Research, 138,* 245–257.

Isaacson, R. L. (1982). *The limbic system* (2nd ed.). New York: Plenum Press.

Jackson, J. H. (1958). *Selected writings of John Hughlings Jackson.* J. Taylor (Ed.), New York: Basic Books.

Jacobson, C. F. (1936). Studies of cerebral function in primates. *Comparative Psychology Monographs, 13,* 1–68.

Jurgens, U., & Pratt, R. (1979). The cingular vocalization pathway in the squirrel monkey. *Experimental Brain Research, 34,* 490–510.

Kerr, N. H., & Foulkes, D. (1981). Right hemispheric mediation of dream visualization: A case study. *Cortex, 17,* 603–610.

Kinsbourne, M. (1971). The minor cerebral hemisphere as a source of aphasic speech. *Archives of Neurology, 25,* 302–306.

Kolb, B., Sutherland, R. J., Nonneman, A. J., & Whishaw, I. Q. (1982). Asymmetry in the cerebral hemispheres of the rat, mouse, rabbit and cat: The right hemisphere is larger. *Experimental Neurology, 78,* 348–359.

Kornhuber, H. H. (1974). Cerebral cortex, cerebellum and basal ganglia: An introduction to their motor functions. In F. O. Schmitt & F. G. Worden (Eds.), *The neurosciences: Third study program* (pp. 267–280). Cambridge, MA: The MIT Press.

Kuhn, R. A. (1950). Functional capacity of the isolated human spinal cord. *Brain, 73,* 1–51.

Kuhn, R. A., & Macht, M. B. (1949). Some manifestations of reflex activity in spinal man with particular reference to the occurrence of extensor spasm. *Bulletin of the Johns Hopkins Hospital, 84,* 43–75.

Lashley, K. S. (1929). *Brain mechanisms and intelligence.* Chicago, IL: University of Chicago Press.

LeMay, M. (1976). Morphological cerebral asymmetries of modern man, fossil man, and non-human primates. *Annals of the New York Academy of Sciences, 280,* 349–366.

Lenneberg, E. (1967). *Biological foundations of language.* New York: Wiley.

Liddell, E. G. T., & Sherrington, C. S. (1924). Reflexes in response to stretch (myotatic) reflexes. *Proceedings of the Royal Society of London (Biology)*, 96, 212–249.

Lindsley, D. B. (1952). Brain stem influences on spinal motor ability. *Research Publications of the Association of Nervous and Mental Diseases*, 30, 174–195.

Lindsley, D. B., Schreiner, L. H., & Magoun, H. W. (1949). An electromyographic study of spasticity. *Journal of Neurophysiology*, 12, 197–205.

Loesche, J., & Steward, O. (1977). Behavioral correlates of denervation and reinnervation of the hippocampal formation of the rat: Recovery of alternation performance following unilateral entorhinal cortex lesions. *Brain Research Bulletin*, 2, 31–39.

Luria, A. R. (1966). *Higher cortical functions in man.* New York: Basic Books.

Luria, A. R. (1970). The functional organization of the brain. *Scientific American, 222,* 66–78.

MacLean, P. D. (1970). The triune brain, emotion and scientific bias. In F. O. Schmitt (Ed.), *The neurosciences: Second study program* (pp. 336–348). New York: Rockefeller University Press.

MacLean, P. D. (1972). Cerebral evolution and emotional processes. *Annals of the New York Academy of Sciences, 193,* 137–149.

MacLean, P. D. (1975). Sensory and perspective factors in emotional functions of the triune brain. In L. Levi (Ed.), *Emotions: Their parameters and measurement* (pp. 71–92). New York: Raven Press.

MacLean, P. D. (1978). A mind of three minds: Educating the triune brain. *Seventy-seventh yearbook of the National Society for the Study of Education* (pp. 308–342). Chicago, IL: University of Chicago Press.

Malmo, R. B. (1975). *On emotions, needs and our archaic brain.* New York: Holt, Rinehart & Winston.

Margolin, D. I. (1980). Right hemisphere dominance for praxis and left hemisphere dominance for speech in a left-hander. *Neuropsychologia, 18,* 715–719.

McCormick, D. A., Guyer, P. E., & Thompson, R. F. (1982). Superior cerebellar peduncle lesions selectively abolish the ipsilateral classically conditioned nictitating membrane response of the rabbit. *Brain Research, 244,* 347–350.

Milner, B. (1971). Interhemispheric differences in the localization of psychological processes in man. *British Medical Bulletin, 27,* 272–277.

Milner, B., Branch, C., & Rasmussen, T. (1964). Observations on cerebral dominance. In A. V. S. deReuck & M. O'Connor (Eds.), *Ciba Foundation symposium on disorders of language.* (pp. 122–145). London: J. A. Churchill.

Milner, B., Branch, C., & Rasmussen, T. (1966). Evidence for bilateral speech representation in some non-right-handers. *Transactions of the American Neurological Association, 91,* 306–308.

Milner, B., & Taylor, L. (1972). Right hemisphere superiority in tactile pattern recognition after cerebral commissurotomy: Evidence for nonverbal memory. *Neuropsychologia, 10,* 1–15.

Mountcastle, V. B. (1979). An organizing principle for cerebral function: The unit module and the distributed system. In F. O. Schmitt & F. O. Worden (Eds.), *The neurosciences: Fourth study program* (pp. 21–42). Cambridge, MA: The MIT Press.

Nottebohm, F. (1971). Neural lateralization of vocal control in a passerine bird. I. Song. *Journal of Experimental Zoology, 177,* 229–262.

Nottebohm, F., Stokes, M. M. Q., & Leonard, C. M. (1976). Central control of song in the canary, Sennus canaria. *Journal of Comparative Neurology, 165,* 457–486.

Ojemann, G. A. (1983). Brain organization for language from the perspective of electrical stimulation mapping. *The Behavioral Brain Sciences, 6,* 457–486.

Penfield, W. (1960). Neurophysiological basis of the higher functions of the nervous system—Introduction. In J. Field, H. W. Magoun, & V. Hall (Eds.), *Handbook of physiology, section I: Neurophysiology* (Vol. 3) (pp. 1441–1445). Washington, DC: American Physiological Society.

Penfield, W., & Roberts, L. (1959). *Speech and brain mechanisms.* Princeton, NJ: Princeton University Press.

Petersen, M. R., Beecher, M. D., Zoloth, S. R., Moody, D., & Stebbins, W. L. (1978). Neural lateralization of species-specific vocalizations by Japanese macaques (Macaca fuscata). *Science, 202,* 324–327.

Pribram, K. H. (1971). *Languages of the brain.* Englewood Cliffs, NJ: Prentice-Hall.

Pribram, K. H. (1974). How is it that sensing so much we can do so little? In F. O. Schmitt & F. G. Worden (Eds.), *The neurosciences: Third study program* (pp. 249–261). Cambridge, MA: The MIT Press.

Ratcliff, G., Dila, C., Taylor, L., & Milner, B. (1980). The morphological asymmetry of the hemispheres and cerebral dominance for speech: A possible relationship. *Brain and Language, 11,* 87–89.

Riddoch, G. (1917). The reflex functions of the completely divided spinal cord in man compared with those associated with less severe lesions. *Brain, 40,* 264–402.

Riss, W. (1968). Overview of the design of the central nervous system and the problem of natural units of behavior. *Brain, Behavior and Evolution, 1,* 124–131.

Robinson, R. G. (1979). Differential behavioral and biochemical effects of right and left hemisphere cerebral infarction in the rat. *Science, 205,* 707–710.

Robinson, R. G., & Coyle, J. T. (1980). The differential effect of right versus left hemispheric cerebral infarction on catecholamines and behavior in the rat. *Brain Research, 188,* 63–78.

Ross, E. D. (1981). The aprosodias: Functional-anatomic organization of the affective components of language in the right hemisphere. *Archives of Neurology, 38,* 561–569.

Ross, E. D., & Mesulam, M.-M. (1979). Dominant language functions of the right hemisphere? Prosody and emotional gesturing. *Archives of Neurology, 36,* 144–148.

Sackeim, H. A., Greenberg, M. S., Weiman, A. L., Gur, R. C., Hungerbuhler, J. P., & Geshwind, N. (1982). Hemispheric asymmetry in the expression of positive and negative emotions: Neurologic evidence. *Archives of Neurology, 39,* 210–218.

Scheibel, M. E., & Scheibel, A. B. (1970). Elementary processes in selected thalamic and cortical subsystems—The structural substrates. In F. O. Schmitt (Ed.), *The neurosciences: Second study program* (pp. 443–447). New York: Rockefeller University Press.

Shepherd, G. M. (1979). *The synaptic organization of the brain* (2nd ed.). New York: Oxford University Press.

Sherman, G. F., Garbanati, J. A., Rosen, G. D., Yutzey, D. A., & Denenberg, V. H. (1980). Brain and behavioral asymmetries for spatial preference in rats. *Brain Research, 192,* 61–67.

Sherrington, C. S. (1906). *The integrative action of the nervous system.* New Haven, CT: Yale University Press.

Snyder, M., & Diamond, I. T. (1968). The organization and function of the visual cortex in the tree shrew. *Brain, Behavior and Evolution, 1,* 244–288.

Sperry, R. W. (1961). Cerebral organization and behavior. *Science, 133,* 1749–1757.

Sperry, R. W. (1974). Lateral specialization in the surgically separated hemispheres. In F. O. Schmitt and F. G. Worden (Eds.), *The neurosciences: Third study program* (pp. 5–20). Cambridge, MA: MIT Press.

Sperry, R. W., Gazzaniga, M. S., & Rogen, J. E. (1969). Interhemispheric relationships: The neocortical commissures; syndromes of hemispheric disconnection. *Handbook of Clinical Neurology, 4,* 273–290.

Steward, O., Loesche, J., & Horton, W. C. (1977). Behavioral correlates of denervation and reinnervation of the hippocampal formation of the rat: Open field activity and cue utilization following bilateral entorhinal cortex lesions. *Brain Research Bulletin, 2,* 41–48.

Teuber, H.-L. (1964). The riddle of frontal-lobe function in man. In J. M. Warren & K. Akert (Eds.), *The frontal granular cortex and behavior* (pp. 410–444). New York: McGraw-Hill.

Thomas, G. J., Hostetter, G., & Barker, D. J. (1968). Behavior functions of the limbic system. In E. Stellar & J. M. Sprague (Eds.), *Progress in physiological psychology* (Vol. 2) (pp. 229–311). New York: Academic Press.

Wada, J. A., Clarke, R., & Hamm, A. (1975). Cerebral hemispheric asymmetry in humans. *Archives of Neurology, 32,* 239–246.

Wada, F., & Rasmussen, T. (1960). Intracarotid injection of sodium amytal for the lateralization of cerebral speech dominance: Experimental and clinical observations. *Journal of Neurosurgery, 17,* 266–282.

Walker, S. F. (1980). Lateralization of functions in the vertebrate brain: A review. *British Journal of Psychology, 71,* 329–367.

Wapner, W., Hamby, S., & Gardner, H. (1981). The role of the right hemisphere in the apprehension of complex linguistic materials. *Brain and Language, 14,* 15–33.

Waterhouse, B. D., & Woodward, D. J. (1980). Interaction of norepinephrine with cerebro-cortical activity evoked by stimulation of somatosensory afferent pathways. *Experimental Neurology, 67,* 11–34.

Watson, P. J. (1978). Nonmotor functions of the cerebellum. *Psychological Bulletin, 85,* 944–967.

Weiss, P. (1967). One plus one does not equal two. In G. C. Quarton, T. Melnechuk, & F. O. Schmitt (Eds.), *The neurosciences: A study program* (pp. 801–821). New York: Rockefeller University Press.

Wernicke, C. (1874). *Der aphasische symptomenkomplex.* Breslau, Poland: Cohn & Weigert.

Yeni-Komshian, G. H., & Benson, D. A. (1976). Anatomical study of cerebral asymmetry in the temporal lobe of humans, chimpanzees and rhesus monkeys. *Science, 192,* 387–389.

3

Neurological Disorders

Danny Wedding

An understanding of neuropathology and the pathophysiology of central nervous system disorders is essential for the neuropsychologist. Without it, the psychologist working with neurologists or in a medical context is at best patronized and at worst considered an interloper, intruding in an area without adequate understanding of either the landmarks or the language of the realm. Unfortunately, many training programs in neuropsychology, and especially in clinical psychology, leave the student ill prepared and inexperienced in this area, and the neophyte neuropsychologist is apt to be dismayed by both the number and complexity of central nervous system disorders that may first manifest themselves through aberrant behavior.

This chapter will survey the major neurological disorders that are apt to be encountered by the neuropsychologist. For a more comprehensive review, the reader can consult any recognized text on neurology (e.g., Matthews, 1982) or the very scholarly book *Organic Psychiatry* (Lishman, 1978).

For convenience and ease of reference, each disorder is discussed under a convenient rubric; however, it is important to realize that oftentimes neurological disorders coexist and that the patient with Alzheimer's disease, for example, may also suffer from multi-infarct dementia; the alcoholic patient may also have experienced multiple episodes of trauma secondary to falls while intoxicated. This overlap confounds simple interpretation of behavioral data; however, it also provides much of the challenge of neuropsychology.

NEOPLASMS

Brain tumors present a fluctuating clinical picture that varies with lesion location, size, type, and rate of growth. The clinician is frequently amazed by huge lesions that produce minimal behavioral manifestations because they are relatively slow growing and in the so-called "silent" areas of the cortex. In contrast, very small lesions in strategic locations can have devastating and sometimes fatal consequences.

Seizures and headaches are commonly part of the clinical picture in the patient with an intracranial neoplasm. Seizures occur in 20% to 30% of all tumor cases and require immediate surgical evaluation; likewise, headaches of recent origin are suspect, especially in those cases where posture and movement are affected.

Approximately half of all patients with brain tumors present with psychiatric symptoms; this is especially common with tumors involving the limbic portions of the frontal and temporal lobes. Hallucinations resembling those found in schizophrenia may occur along with other "psychiatric" problems such as depression, apathy, euphoria, social impropriety, and personality change (Strub & Black, 1981). Hallucinations, however, will often be visual or olfactory and will less often be of the auditory type so commonly noted in schizophrenia. In addition, the auditory hallucinations found in cases of brain damage will lack the bizarre quality present in the hallucinations of the schizophrenic patient.

Tumors are typically graded with a scale of 1 to 4, on which the least life threatening are classed as grade 1 and the most malignant as grade 4. Tumors are also classified by the type of cell from which the neoplasm originated. Gliomas arise from glial cells, the supportive tissue of the brain, and are among the most common types of brain tumor. One type of glioma, the glioglastoma multiforme, is especially lethal because of its rapid growth and because its branching tendrils elude complete surgical extirpation. John Gunther, in the autobiographical *Death Be Not Proud,* has described his son's battle with glioblastoma multiforme. These lesions typically have pronounced behavioral consequences and result in considerable disruption of performance on neuro-psychological measures. (For example, suppressions on the sensory-perceptual examination are common with gliomas.) Astrocytomas are somewhat slower growing, infiltrative lesions with an equally poor prognosis. Other types of gliomas include ependymomas, medulloblastomas, and oligodendrogliomas.

Metastatic lesions, another common form of brain tumor, arise from primary carcinomas in other body parts, most typically from the lungs and breast. These are also rapidly growing tumors with an extremely bleak prognosis. Cerebral edema is common, resulting in a diffuse pattern of dysfunction with pockets of marked impairment. Metastatic lesions comprise as much as 40% of all tumors seen in the elderly (Golden, 1981).

Meningiomas develop in the meningial layer between the brain and the skull. They are typically rather slow-growing lesions with a good surgical prognosis. They include about 15% to 20% of all brain tumors, produce much of their damage by pressure effects, and rarely cause suppressions. Benign meningiomas often produce chronic psychiatric symptoms and have been found in disproportionate numbers of long-term institutionalized patients in

TABLE 3.1 Frequency of Major Types of Brain Tumors

Intracranial Tumors		Frequency of Occurrence
Gliomas		50%
Glioblastoma multiforme	50%	
Astrocytoma	20%	
Ependymoma	10%	
Medulloblastoma	10%	
Oligodendroglioma	5%	
Mixed	5%	
Meningiomas		20%
Nerve sheath tumors		10%
Metastatic tumors		10%
Congenital tumors		5%
Miscellaneous tumors		5%

Adapted from Chusid, J. G. (1982). *Correlative neuroanatomy and functional neurology.* Los Altos, CA: Lange.

psychiatric hospitals (Lishman, 1978). The frequencies for the major classes of intercranial neoplasm are listed in Table 3.1.

Lesion effects will vary across cerebral geography as well as across lesion type. Frontal lobe lesions are apt to manifest themselves in lack of spontaneity, slowing, inertia, irritability, and apathy. Depression may also be present, and frontal tumor symptoms will often mimic psychiatric illness. Urinary incontinence is common. Posterior frontal lobe involvement will result in contralateral motor dysfunction; weakness or damage in the region of the third convolution in the dominant hemisphere will typically result in expressive language problems. Slow-growing extrinsic frontal tumors often spare mental abilities (especially as measured with standard psychometric instruments such as the Wechsler Adult Intelligence Scale), and their only sign may be subtle behavioral changes. These patients, if improperly evaluated, are commonly misdiagnosed as presenting with a primary dementing illness.

The patient with a parietal lobe tumor is less apt to display psychiatric symptomatology but will be more likely to manifest sensory and motor symptoms that lead to earlier diagnosis. Astereognosis and impairment of two point discrimination are common with parietal lesions. Suppressions are frequently noted with parietal tumors, and damage to this region will often result in construction and dressing apraxias. Dyscalculia and right-left confusion may result. Nondominant parietal tumors will also frequently affect body sense, and denial of illness (anosognosia) and unilateral neglect are common.

In contrast, occipital lobe tumors produce few lateralizing or localizing signs except for visual field defects. Prosopagnosia (failure to recognize familiar faces) is common with nondominant occipital lesions (Lishman, 1978).

Temporal lobe tumors are those most likely to mimic psychiatric disorders.

Receptive language deficits are frequently found with posterior dominant hemisphere temporal lobe neoplasms; affective disturbances are common with temporal lesions on either side. Epilepsy occurs in approximately 50% of cases of temporal lobe tumor, and complex hallucinations may be present with or without other manifestations of a seizure. Visual hallucinations restricted to a single half field are almost always diagnostic of a temporal lobe disturbance (Golden, Moses, Coffman, Miller, & Strider, 1983). Perhaps the most reliable behavioral sign of a temporal lobe lesion is a contralateral homonymous upper quadrant visual field defect.

VASCULAR DISORDERS

A cerebrovascular accident (CVA) or stroke occurs when there is an inadequate supply of blood and oxygen to some area of the brain. The CVA is a focal neurological disorder characterized by sudden onset. The two major classes of stroke are infarctions and hemorrhages. Infarctions typically result from occlusions of cerebral blood flow. Infarctions are three times as common as hemorrhages but are far less lethal. Specifically, 75% of patients with cerebral infarction survive the event, while only 20% of patients survive cerebral hemorrhages (Lishman, 1978). Necrosis of the surrounding neural tissue typically occurs after 10 to 20 minutes following cessation of blood flow (Wiederholt, 1982); however, an occlusion may occur without disruption of function if collateral blood flow is adequate to maintain oxygen supplies for the brain areas involved.

Occlusions can be either thrombotic or embolic. A thrombus develops following the buildup of atherosclerotic plaques on the arterial wall, typically at the bifurcation of a vessel. Thrombi usually develop more slowly than emboli and are often preceded by transient ischemic attacks (TIAs). The thrombotic stroke frequently occurs during sleep, perhaps precipitated by the mild state of hypotension present while supine.

The embolus, less common that the thrombus, occurs when a particle of fat or some other substance, or a fragment of a thrombotic lesion that has broken loose, becomes lodged in a narrow blood vessel. The resulting stroke is sudden and without warning. Embolic strokes tend to occur at earlier ages than thrombotic strokes and are more likely to involve the anterior areas of the brain (therefore patients with Broca's aphasia secondary to vascular disease tend to be younger than those patients with Wernicke's aphasia following a CVA) (Lezak, 1983).

A cerebral hemorrhage results when neural tissue is compromised by blood spilling from a vessel. The hemorrhage is most often precipitated by exertion and, unlike the thrombus, rarely occurs during sleep. The lesion typically produces a highly lateralized neurological and neuropsychological picture, and suppressions are common. Treatment consists of the administration of steroids to reduce swelling and possible surgical evacuation of the clot.

The symptoms of major vessel occlusions have been clearly delineated by Lechtenberg (1982). Disruption of blood flow in the middle cerebral artery, which serves the lateral portions of the brain and the major motor and sensory areas, produces contralateral weakness and sensory loss (with the arm and face more affected than the leg), homonymous hemianopsias, dementia, and, with dominant hemisphere lesions, expressive, receptive, or global aphasias. Body image disturbance may occur with nondominant lesions. The middle cerebral artery is the most common site for cerebrovascular accidents.

Occlusion of the anterior cerebral artery may result in contralateral weakness, with the leg weaker than the arm, contralateral sensory loss, urinary incontinence, dementia, and occasionally paralysis of the opposite side of the face.

Lesions affecting the blood supply of the posterior cerebral artery can produce contralateral visual field cuts due to damage in the region of the calcarine cortex. Posterior cerebral artery damage to the dominant hemisphere can produce reading difficulties and alexia without agraphia. Memory disorders may result if there is temporal lobe involvement. Bilateral infarctions may lead to cortical blindness with denial of disability (Anton's syndrome). However, infarctions of the posterior cerebral artery are relatively rare.

An aneurysm occurs when part of a vessel, most commonly an artery, enlarges ("balloons") and creates a space-occupying lesion. Most aneurysms occur in the region of the Circle of Willis and produce mild but localized neuropsychological deficits. Signs of a ruptured aneurysm include extremely painful headaches, nausea, and vomiting.

Multi-infarct dementia is a vascular disorder that frequently initially appears to be a primary degenerative dementia. The disorder results from a series of small strokes and is more common in men than in women. The diagnosis can usually be made when there is a history of hypertension, a picture of stepwise deterioration in neurologic and mental functioning, and more dramatic neurological signs than those typically found with the primary degenerative dementias.

Transient ischemic attacks (TIAs) are focal neurological events with effects that last, by definition, for less than 24 hours (if the signs are present for more than a day, the condition is defined as a stroke). At least 25% of patients who experience TIAs eventually sustain a major stroke (Lechtenberg, 1982). Behavioral and clinical signs of TIAs can include transient aphasia, agraphia, amusia, geographical disorientation, and confusion (Strub & Black, 1981). Contrary to popular belief, TIAs have been shown to produce mild cognitive impairment (Delaney, Wallace, & Egelko, 1980).

Although the incidence of stroke appears to be decreasing, it is still the third leading cause of death in the United States, with approximately half a million people in this country suffering a stroke each year. Of these, 10% will die immediately and 20% to 40% will die in the months just after their strokes. Of the survivors, 10% will be disabled to the extent that they will require permanent institutional care, 40% will require special care, 40% will have a persistent, mild neurological defect, and 10% will return to normal premorbid levels of functioning (Wiederholt, 1982). For those patients who do survive, improvement typically follows a decelerating learning curve, with the most improvement noted in the first six months. Physical disabilities tend to have a shorter resolution period than mental disabilities such as aphasia and visuospatial deficits (Lishman, 1978). However, these are general trends only, and wide individual differences exist across different patients.

The major risk factors for stroke include a prior history of cerebrovascular disease, diabetes, heart disease, atherosclerosis in other parts of the body, and hypertension. While the incidence for stroke is greater for males than for females, some subgroups of women are especially high-risk candidates (e.g., women who both smoke and use oral contraceptives).

DEMENTIAS

The dementias are defined as clinical syndromes that result from loss of brain function due to diffuse organic brain disease (Wells & Duncan, 1980). The term is often loosely and imprecisely used; however, most authorities would agree that the following characteristics apply: (1) onset is insidious, (2) brain dysfunction is localized predominantly in the cerebral cortex, and (3) there are demonstrable pathological changes in cerebral tissue (often seen only at autopsy or with brain biopsy). Some neurologists would restrict the use of the term to those conditions that are ultimately irreversible. Others point out that a wide variety of clinical disorders can first present as a dementing illness and that it is critical that the examiner be sensitive to the panoply of conditions that are in fact reversible. Normal pressure hydrocephalus, collagen-vascular disorders, and infections are especially likely to be misdiagnosed. A number of possible "reversible dementias" are listed in Table 3.2.

In an elderly population (65 or older), 4% to 5% of the population will display a moderate to severe dementia; the cause will be Alzheimer's disease in 65% of these cases (Lechtenberg, 1982). Dementias occurring before the age of 65 have traditionally been referred to as presenile dementias; however, most contemporary authorities find little utility in the distinction between presenile and senile dementias, since the two appear to be identical clinical entities.

Lechtenberg (1982) lists dementia as the fifth leading cause of death in the United States; Glenner (1982) maintains that Alzheimer's disease alone is the fourth most common cause of death. Whatever its rank, it is clear that dementia tends to be underrepresented in mortality statistics, since secondary causes of death (e.g., pneumonia) are frequently listed on death certificates. Over half of the patients over the age of 65 institutionalized in nursing homes

TABLE 3.2 Causes of Reversible Dementia

Intracranial conditions
  Meningiomas
  Subdural hematomas
  Hydrocephalus
    Communicating
    Noncommunicating
  Epilepsy
  Multiple sclerosis
  Wilson's disease
Systemic illness
  Pulmonary insufficiency
  Cardiac arrythmia
  Severe anemia
  Polycythemia vera
  Uremia
  Hyponatremia
  Portosystemic encephalopathy
  Porphyria
  Hyperlipidemia
Deficiency states
  B12 deficiency
  Pellagra
  Folate deficiency
Endocrinopathies
  Addison's disease
  Panhypopituitarism
  Myxedema
  Hypoparathyroidism
  Hyperparathyroidism
  Recurrent hypoglycemia
  Cushing's disease and steroid therapy
  Hyperthyroidism
Drugs
  Methyldopa and haloperidol
  Clonidine and fluphenazine
  Disulfiram
  Lithium carbonate
  Phenothiazines
  Haloperidol and lithium carbonate
  Bromides
  Phenytoin

Drugs *cont.*
  Mephenytoin
  Barbiturates
  Clonidine
  Methyldopa
  Propranolol hydrochloride
  Atropine and related compounds
Heavy metals
  Mercury
  Arsenic
  Lead
  Thallium
Exogenous toxins and industrial agents
  Trichloroethylene
  Toluene
  Carbon disulfide
  Organophosphates
  Carbon disulfide
  Alcohol
Infections
  General paresis
  Chronic meningitis
  Cerebral abscess
  Cysticercosis
  Whipple's disease
  Progressive multifocal leukoencephal-
    opathy
Collagen-vascular and vascular disor-
  ders
  Systemic lupus erythematosus
  Temporal arteritis
  Sarcoidosis
  Cogan's syndrome
  Bechcet's syndrome
  Carotid artery stenosis (?)
"Potentially recoverable dementia"
  Cerebral anoxia
  Trauma
  Excessive Electroconvulsive Drugs/
    Therapy
  Encephalitis

Adapted from Cummings, J., Benson, F., & LoVerma, S. (1980). Reversible dementia: Illustrative cases, definition, and review. *JAMA, 243,* 2434–2439.

carry the diagnosis of dementia, and it is clear that dementia is becoming a public health problem of astonishing dimensions as our population ages. Currently, half of the population of the United States reaches age 75 and one-fourth will live to age 85 (Mortimer, Schuman, & French, 1981); because of our increasing life span, all of us are at greater risk for developing these dementing diseases associated with old age. At age 70, our risk for developing dementia is 1.2%; by age 80, our risk increases to 5.2% (Wiederholt, 1982).

Wells and Duncan (1980) have delineated three identifiable stages in the progression of dementia. The early phase is characterized by vague complaints, multiple and diffuse somatic concerns, and mild memory impairment. Depression, anxiety, apathy, or irritability are often present and may be the presenting symptoms. In this stage, patients will struggle hard to accomplish previously easy tasks and may use an inordinant number of lists, schedules, notes, and so forth. The neurological exam is almost always normal during this phase, making clinical acumen and a detailed history all the more critical. It is also essential that family and friends be available to discuss subtle but significant behavioral changes that might well be precursors of the more blatant behavioral changes associated with the disease.

During the middle phase of the illness, one finds clear evidence of impairment in orientation, memory, judgment, and intellectual function. Mood is apt to be labile and shallow, and personality and behavioral changes are obvious to the casual observer. By this time, family and friends have recognized that the patient is ill and that his behavior cannot be merely described as eccentric or idiosyncratic.

In the last phase of the dementing illness, one finds increasing and profound apathy, marked neurological impairment, and urinary and fecal incontinence. Expressive or global aphasias and visual agnosias are common. Brain mass and weight are typically reduced, and snout, root, and grasp reflexes may emerge (see Malloy & Nadau, Chapter 5 of this volume).

Alzheimer's disease is the most frequent cause of dementia. It currently affects 1.5 million Americans at an annual cost of $20 billion (Glenner, 1982). The disorder affects about twice as many women as men; 96% of the cases are over the age of 40. Although not a simple genetic disorder, there are evident genetic influences in its etiology. For example, Kallmann's data demonstrated that 43% of monozygotic twins are concordant for senile dementia in contrast to only 8% of dizygotic twins (Lishman, 1978).

In the past, Alzheimer's disease was often thought to be a manifestation of vascular disease; it is still often confused with multiinfarct dementia. However, more abrupt onset, stepwise progression, and history of hypertension should help identify the less common disorder of multiinfarct dementia.

Eighty percent of patients who develop Alzheimer's will display initial symptoms before the age of 65 (Lechtenberg, 1982); this becomes significant insofar as early onset is associated with more severe and more rapid deterioration (Lezak, 1983).

In Alzheimer's patients, it is typical for the EEG to show diffuse slowing and for the results of computerized tomography to show ventricular enlargement and widening of the cortical sulci. In addition, one finds decreasing cerebral oxygen uptake and blood flow. However, it is important to emphasize that the EEG and CT can both be normal in patients with pronounced dementia (likewise, marked atrophy of the cerebral hemispheres may be evident on CT evaluation in a patient functioning adequately). In general, there is only a minimal correlation between cerebral atrophy, as estimated by computed tomography, and mortality (Lechtenberg, 1982).

The prognosis for Alzheimer's patients is decidedly poor, markedly so for those patients who present with expressive language deficits as an early clinical sign. Many patients will require institutionalization within a year after diagnosis. The average life span from diagnosis to death is slightly over seven years, with functional impairment serving as a better predictor of longevity than cerebral atrophy per se (Strub & Black, 1981). Various approaches to treatment have been proposed, including administration of choline (or lecithin, a more palatable substance degraded in the body to choline) and vasodilators. To date, there is no strong evidence for the efficacy of any of these approaches; however, a number of major laboratories in this country and abroad are presently investigating pharmacological approaches to the treatment of Alzheimer's disease, and this renewed interest holds considerable promise for the future. In the meantime, those programs emphasizing reality orientation appear to offer the optimal available treatment.

Strub and Black (1981) have detailed the neuropsychological changes most commonly noted with Alzheimer's. These include the following: a memory quotient markedly lower than the Full-Scale IQ, Performance IQs that are lower than Verbal IQs, poorer performance on WAIS-R tests of fluid intelligence (e.g., Comprehension) than on tests of crystallized intelligence (e.g., Vocabulary and Information), considerable scatter across subtests, Bender drawings more impaired than predicted, and especially poor performance on the Category Test and Part B of the Trail Making Test from the Halstead–Reitan Battery.

Pick's disease is clinically very similar to Alzheimer's, and final diagnostic determination must usually await histological confirmation. Pick's is one-fifth as common as Alzheimer's and occurs in males and females with about equal frequency. Cortical atrophy is often restricted to the frontal and temporal lobes, and these patients tend not to show the strong parietal signs (e.g., construction dyspraxia) so common in Alzheimer's. Probably because of the strong frontal focus, the patient with Pick's disease tends to lose social graces much earlier in the disease process (Wiederholt, 1982). Most of these patients will present with impaired speech, and about one-third of them will develop echolalia (Strub & Black, 1981). A strong genetic relationship is present, with the disease probably transmitted by an autosomal dominant gene (Roth, 1981).

Huntington's disease is another autosomal-dominant disease characterized by marked motor disturbance, including choreiform movements, facial grimacing, swaying, and lurching of gait. Unfortunately, onset of symptoms typically occurs after the childbearing years, with offspring facing a 50% chance of developing the disorder. The disease has been clearly linked to degeneration of those GABA-ergic neurons that project to the substantia nigra.

The usual onset is between the ages of 45 and 55, with cognitive and personality changes typically preceding the development of a movement disorder. The suicide rate is high for these patients; in the absence of suicide, death usually occurs within 15 years after the onset of the disease.

Parkinson's disease is another relatively common neurological disorder characterized by rigidity, tremor, bradykinesia, loss of balance, and masked fascies. The disorder has been clearly linked with loss of dopamine from the substantia nigra and can be treated very effectively with replacement dopamine (e.g., L-dopa). Although James Parkinson, for whom the disease is named, initially thought there was no intellectual deterioration concomitant with the disease, more contemporary thinking suggests that as many as 55% of these patients will develop an unquestionable dementia (Lechtenberg, 1982). This is usually milder than the other forms of dementia and is reflected in deficits in orientation, construction, and memory. Micrographia is common. Social skills, appropriate interpersonal behavior, and language tend to be spared.

Normal pressure hydrocephalus is a disorder of obscure pathophysiology that results in enlarged ventricles secondary to accumulation of cerebrospinal fluid (CSF). When the cause is unknown, as is generally the case, the disorder is frequently referred to as occult hydrocephalus. The peak age of onset is in the late fifties. Computed tomography reveals massively enlarged ventricles with little cortical atrophy. Behaviorally, these patients present with gait disturbance, dementia, and incontinence. Treatment involves surgical shunting of the CSF from the lateral ventricles to the general circulation.

Depression can also present with all the classic signs of an early dementia, and one of the major diagnostic dilemmas facing either the neurologist or the neuropsychologist is the differentiation between true dementias and pseudodementias secondary to depression. Unfortunately, major depressions can almost perfectly mimic the clinical signs and neuropsychological results of true dementia, extending across the motor, cognitive, and sensory-perceptual domains. It is especially tragic when the depressed patient is diagnosed as having Alzheimer's disease or another nontreatable dementia, since depression itself responds so readily to pharmacological intervention. In the case of pseudodementias, negative findings on neuropsychological testing are frequently more valuable than positive (since test results can be used to rule out a true dementia but are of less value when attempting to rule in the presence of dementing illness).

TRAUMATIC HEAD INJURIES

Head trauma is the leading cause of brain damage for children and for young adults up to the age of 42 (Lezak, 1983). It is a critical problem for the neuropsychologist, since neuropsychological testing can often reveal subtle defects not seen with formal neurological evaluation. The behavioral manifestations of head injuries are variegated and, as with other forms of cerebral damage, depend in large part on the site of the lesion and the extent of the injury. In general, however, intellectual deficits are most likely to be noted with traumatic injuries involving the parietal and temporal areas.

Lacerations or open head injuries refer to those cases in which the skull is penetrated and obvious neural damage has occurred. Although open head injuries typically produce focal effects, edema and bleeding may result in a diffuse pattern of damage upon which focal effects are superimposed. Much of the existing knowledge base in neuropsychology can be attributed to the study of the effects of open head injuries in combat casualties; Teuber (1960) and Luria (1980) were particularly influenced by their experience with brain-injured soldiers.

Those patients who survive open head injuries tend to make rapid gains during the first year or two, especially in language skills and construction abilities. The majority of these patients return to work following their injury; low pretraumatic intellectual ability and the presence of frontotemporal injury are the best predictors of an inability to return to work following open head trauma (Lezak, 1983). The most devastating consequences of lacerations occur following hemorrhage by one of the major arteries of the cerebral hemispheres.

Somewhat more common are closed head injuries, characterized by *coup,* the blow at the point of impact, and *contrecoup,* damage to tissue opposite the site of impact. Contrecoup is more frequent in cases of occipital injury. It is least likely to result from injuries in which the head is at rest (e.g., simple assault) and occurs most often in those cases when the head itself is in motion (e.g., falls, motorcycle accidents) (Lishman, 1978). Direct effects of trauma are most likely to damage the tips of the temporal lobes and the frontal areas of the brain that protrude into the fossa of the skull; this may result in the well-known frontal lobe syndrome characterized by decreased inhibition, declining social graces, and lack of moral restraint. Increased apathy or labile affect may be noted with little overall decline in intellectual ability.

Closed head injuries are conveniently classified into three major groups: concussions, contusions, and hematomas. The concussion is defined as "an acute impairment of cerebral function secondary to an impact injury to the head in which the following are usually, but not invariably, present: amnesia, loss of consciousness, and complete recovery" (Strub & Black, 1981, p. 271). Both anterograde and retrograde amnesia are common; in themselves, they do not indicate significant brain damage (Lechtenberg, 1982). However, the duration of posttraumatic amnesia (i.e., anterograde amnesia) is a better predictor of the extent of brain damage present that is either retrograde amnesia or the total duration of unconsciousness. (In attempting to measure the total duration of posttraumatic amnesia, it is important to assess the time from the injury to restoration of *continuous* awareness, since memory for posttraumatic events may wax and wane) (Matthews, 1982). Concussions producing posttraumatic amnesia of less than one hour are considered mild, those lasting for several hours are considered moderate, and any concussion resulting in a posttraumatic amnesia of a day or more is considered severe.

Considerable controversy exists concerning the utility of the concept of the postconcussion syndrome, which is said to be characterized by headaches, intellectual and physical fatigue, pervasive anxiety, impotence, irritability, dizziness, sensitivity to noise, and an inability to concentrate. These symptoms last for weeks or months after the accident, and the neurological examination is almost always normal. Critics of the syndrome point to the frequency of these complaints in cases involving litigation. While issues of secondary gain complicate assessment, it is clear that problems with memory and concentration are common following traumatic insult to the cerebral hemispheres and that headaches are reported by the vast preponderance of head trauma cases. A comprehensive neuropsychological examination, which is quite difficult for the patient to fake in a consistent and neurologically meaningful fashion, can prove invaluable in assessing the sequelae of a head injury; in addition, it can assist in ruling out the ever-present threat of a subdural hematoma.

With repeated concussions, chronic traumatic encephalopathy *(dementia pugilistica)* may occur. Also known as the punch-drunk syndrome, because of its common occurrence in aging boxers, the disorder is characterized by dysarthric speech, mixed pyramidal and extrapyramidal signs, slowness of thought, emotional lability, paranoia, and temper outbursts. Memory and concentration problems are frequent complaints, and the disorder appears to increase sensitivity to the effects of alcohol (Strub & Black, 1981). The severity of the symptoms correlates well with the severity and frequency of head trauma. Cortical atrophy is marked, and perforation of the septum pallucidum is common. Neurofibrillary degeneration is usually present but without the senile plaques found in Alzheimer's disease (Lishman, 1978). A recent study, published in the *Journal of the American Medical Association,* revealed that 87% of professional boxers displayed definite evidence of brain damage when they were assessed with neurological examinations, computerized tomographic scanning of the brain, electroencephalograms, and neuropsychological tests. The neuropsychological tests proved to be the most sensitive index of brain damage, and every subject had at least one abnormal test score. An ad hoc impairment index was computed for each boxer, reflecting the percentage of test scores that fell in the impaired range. This index correlated significantly with the number of professional fights and with age. Impairment was most notable on tests of short-term memory, suggesting that deep midline structures of the brain bear the brunt of damage in boxers. The authors of this study recommend periodic administration of neuropsychological tests in order to detect early signs of potentially reversible encephalopathy (Casson et al., 1984).

The contusion is a somewhat more serious consequence of head injury caused by the impact between the skull and the brain during an accident. Contusions result from minor hemorrhages under the site of impact or from the tearing of blood vessels connecting the brain and meninges. Neuropsychologically, one finds strong focal effects in the area of the contusion and more lasting deficits than are present with concussions (Golden, 1981). Basal frontotemporal contusions are the most common type and may produce emotional lability and personality change.

An especially serious consequence of head trauma is the subdural hematoma. The hematoma is almost always the result of trauma and occurs when blood and cerebrospinal fluid fill the subdural (or sometimes the epidural) space. This produces pressure effects and compromise of function similar to that found with meningiomas. The elderly are especially susceptible because of their fragile vascular systems and the increasing number of accidents in which they are involved; however, they may be unable to isolate a specific traumatic event that preceded the development of symptoms. Frequently the lesion will be too small to be observed on the initial CT scan. The patient will often be comatose at the time of evaluation; over 10% of all patients admitted in coma after severe head injuries have subdural hematomas, and the mortality rate for these patients is in the range of 60% to 90% (Lechtenberg, 1982).

The consequences of head injury are somewhat less severe in children than in adults, and there is better potential for recovery, especially in those cases involving language disorders. One of the major challenges facing neuropsychology in the coming decade will be the need to develop realistic training programs for rehabilitation of cognitive functions in the traumatically brain impaired. Initial efforts in this area suggest that there is considerably more promise for cognitive rehabilitation following head trauma than was initially believed.

EPILEPSY

Epilepsy is a general term used loosely to refer to a variety of disorders characterized by recurrent paroxysmal, uncontrolled discharge of cerebral neurons that interferes with normal activity. It is important to stress that epilepsy is best considered as a symptom of some cerebral insult rather than as a disease entity per se. Some major causes of epilepsy include perinatal insults, genetic disorders (e.g., Tay-Sachs disease), trauma, anoxia, infections, metabolic disorders (e.g., Reye's syndrome), exposure to environmental toxins, degenerative diseases, tumors, and vascular disorders. When the presumed cause of the seizure disorder cannot be found, the patient is said to have idiopathic epilepsy. Cerebral trauma is the single most frequent identifiable cause of epilepsy; it develops in about 5% of cases of closed head injury and in 45% of cases of penetrating head wounds (Lishman, 1978).

The incidence of epilepsy in the United States is about 0.5%. The disorder occurs somewhat more frequently in males, possibly due to the greater likelihood of traumatic head injury in men. Thirty-three percent of seizure injuries occur before the age of 4; 75% begin before the age of 20. Less than 2% of seizure disorders have their onset after the age of 50 (Trauner, 1982). Seizures that occur before 6 months of age almost always reflect birth injury, congenital defects, or infectious disease. Seizures occurring between the ages of 2 and 20 are usually idiopathic, while those with onset after age 35 suggest vascular disease or a tumor (Pincus & Tucker, 1978).

Although not universally accepted, the International Classification of Epileptic Seizures (see Table 3.3) used by the World Federation of Neurology is becoming the standard nosology for categorizing seizure disorders. It replaces antiquated and loosely used terms like *grand mal* and *petit mal,* with rubrics reflecting degree of cortical involvement (e.g., generalized vs. partial) and degree of behavioral complexity (e.g., complex vs. elementary).

Generalized seizures involve both cerebral hemispheres and produce bilaterally symmetrical EEG patterns. The origin of the disturbance is pre-

TABLE 3.3 International Classification of Epileptic Seizures

I. Partial Seizures (seizures beginning locally)
   A. Partial seizures with elementary symptomatology (generally without impairment of consciousness)
      1. With motor symptoms
         a. Focal motor
         b. Jacksonian
         c. Versive (generally contraversive)
         d. Postural
         e. Somatic inhibitory (?)
         f. Aphasic
         g. Phonatory (vocalization and arrest of speech)
      2. With special sensory or somatosensory symptoms
         a. Somatosensory
         b. Visual
         c. Auditory
         d. Olfactory
         e. Gustatory
         f. Vertiginous
      3. With autonomic symptoms
      4. Compound forms
   B. Partial seizures with complex symptomatology (generally with impairment of consciousness)
      1. With impaired consciousness only
      2. With cognitive symptomatology
         a. With dysmnesic disturbances
         b. With ideational disturbances
      3. With affective symptomatology
      4. With "psychosensory" symptomatology
         a. Illusions
         b. Hallucinations
      5. With "psychomotor" symptomatology (automatisms)
      6. Compound forms
   C. Partial seizures secondarily generalized

TABLE 3.3 (*continued*)

II. Generalized Seizures (bilaterally symmetrical and without local onset)
  A. Absences (petit mal)
    1. Simple absences, with impairment of consciousness only
    2. Complex absences with other associated phenomena
      a. With mild clonic components (myoclonic)
      b. With increase of postural tone (retropulsive)
      c. With diminution or abolition of postural tone (atonic)
      d. With automatisms
      e. With automatic phenomena (e.g., enuresis)
      f. Mixed forms
  B. Bilateral massive epileptic myoclonus (myoclonic jerks)
  C. Infantile spasms
  D. Clonic seizures
  E. Tonic seizures
  F. Tonic-clonic seizures ("grand mal" seizures)
  G. Atonic seizures
    1. Of very brief duration (drop attacks)
    2. Of longer duration (including atonic absences)
  H. Akinetic seizures (loss of movement without atonia)
III. Unilateral or Predominantly Unilateral Seizures
IV. Unclassified Epileptic Seizures (includes all seizures that cannot be classified because of inadequate or incomplete data)

Adapted from H. Gastaut (1970). Clinical and electroencephalographical classification of epileptic seizures. *Epilepsia, II,* 102, 102–113.

sumed to lie in midbrain structures, with rapid spread to the cortex. Tonic-clonic (grand mal) seizures are a dramatic form of generalized seizures in which there is sudden loss of consciousness with tonic ridigity followed by clonic jerking. The patient will typically fall to the ground and may bite his tongue. Fecal and urinary incontinence are common. The seizure lasts for one to two minutes and is followed by a postictal period of confusion, headache, and fatigue. The individual will frequently sleep for several hours following a seizure, and there is total amnesia for the events of the ictal period.

Auras and prodromata may precede the actual occurrence of a seizure. The prodrome is a behavioral or mood change that serves as a harbinger of the impending seizure, often persisting for several days before the actual event. The prodrome phenomenon is not fully understood but typically is not reflected in abnormal EEG activity. The aura occurs somewhat more frequently (in about half of tonic-clonic seizure patients) and signals the imminent arrival of a seizure. The aura is often an unpleasant olfactory or gustatory sensation accompanied by a feeling of apprehension; however, the sensation may be perceived as pleasant and exciting. Dostoyevski, who was epileptic, described his auras as pleasant and highly rewarding experiences.

Another common form of generalized epilepsy is the absence (petit mal) seizure. Typical absence seizures occur almost exclusively in young children and are characterized by brief altered states of consciousness without loss of muscle tone. There is a vacant stare and occasional eye-blinking during the seizure episode. An EEG taken at this time will reveal a characteristic wave and spike discharge occurring at the rate of about 3 per second. Hyperventilation is sometimes useful in eliciting the seizure response for recording purposes. The absences typically occur randomly throughout the day; if the frequency is less than 5 per day, the diagnosis should be questioned (Lishman, 1978). The disorder is only rarely associated with decrements in intellectual ability.

Partial seizures occur in focal areas of the hemisphere without callosal transfer to the adjacent side of the brain. Partial elementary seizures do not involve any alteration in consciousness but are instead characterized by sudden jerking of muscle groups on one side of the body. This jerking often begins distally and moves in a proximal direction, resulting in what is sometimes called a Jacksonian march (after the neurologist John Hughlings Jackson). During a seizure of this sort, abnormal twitching might begin in the fingers, move to the hand and arm, and then spread to include the entire side of the body contralateral to the affected hemisphere.

Complex partial seizures are considerably more interesting for the psychologist. Also referred to as psychomotor seizures, these disorders most commonly originate in the temporal lobes and may produce hallucinations, stereotyped motor behavior, feelings of unreality, and intense fear. The sensations of *déjà vu* and, somewhat less commonly, *jamais vu* may be reported. (*Jamais vu* refers to the situation in which one feels that there is something very strange and unusual about very ordinary events or settings.) Abnormalities in the region of the anterior tip of the temporal lobe is a characteristic EEG sign, but the waking electroencephalogram will be normal in at least half of the patients evaluated (Pincus & Tucker, 1978).

Hallucinations are reported by about 18% of patients with complex partial seizures; these are commonly visual or auditory. Visual hallucinations originating in the temporal lobes will appear as complex and detailed; if occipital foci are present, the hallucinations will be simpler and will appear as colored lines, stars, and circles in the contralateral visual field. Unlike the hallucinations of the patient with a functional psychosis, the auditory hallucinations of the patient with complex partial seizures are uniform, come from inside the head rather than outside the body, and rarely contain bizarre, threatening, or accusatory material (Kilpatrick & Hall, 1980).

Although rage reactions can occur, the actual incidence of violence is quite low for patients with psychomotor seizures. It is interesting that Jack Ruby's attorneys argued that Ruby was experiencing a complex partial seizure when he assassinated Lee Harvey Oswald; this appears unlikely, for it is very difficult for an individual to maintain a series of complex coordinated activities during the actual seizure episode.

There has been considerable interest in characterizing the "temporal lobe personality" of the patient with complex partial seizures. Descriptors have traditionally included circumstantiality, fascination with philosophical issues, emotional lability, and decreased frustration tolerance. While this constellation of personality traits is not consistently found, there is evidence that seizure patients with right temporal foci are emotionally labile and prone to affective disorders, while those with left temporal foci experience paranoid or grandiose delusions and are more likely to develop schizophreniform symptoms (Flor-Henry, 1974; Kilpatrick & Hall, 1980).

Across classes of epilepsy, some degree of psychiatric disturbance is found in about 30% to 50% of patients (Golden et al., 1983). Global hyposexuality is one of the most frequent disturbances noted; this is more common in cases of complex partial seizures and is almost always due to a lack of sexual desire rather than the result of erectile dysfunction in males. Although most noninstitutionalized epileptics have normal IQs, their scores will generally cluster around the lower end of this range (Strub & Black, 1981). Of course, severity, age of onset, type of seizure, and frequency will mediate both the psychiatric and the cognitive sequelae of epilepsy.

Status epilepticus refers to an emergency situation in which the patient has multiple seizures without regaining consciousness between seizure episodes. It affects 5% of all epileptics at some time (Pryse-Phillips & Murray, 1982). The longer the status episode, the greater the likelihood of serious brain damage or death. This condition requires immediate medical attention; contrary to clinical lore and some previous practice, one should not attempt to insert any type of object in the mouth of the patient experiencing a major seizure. Instead, primary efforts should be directed toward protecting the head from trauma and providing whatever emotional support is necessary following the incident.

Dramatic improvements have occurred in the treatment of seizure disorders over the past two decades. Medication is the treatment of choice, and typically phenytoin (Dilantin), phenobarbital, primidone, carbamazepine, valproic acid, or clomazepam will be prescribed; these drugs are believed to have direct effects in the region of the motor cortex. (It is important to remember that all of these drugs may affect the results of neuropsychological testing.) Surgical approaches in cases of intractable epilepsy have included the removal of epileptic brain tissue, commissurotomy, and cerebellar stimulation with implanted electrodes. Finally, one of the most innovative approaches to the treatment of epilepsy involves the use of EEG biofeedback to teach patients to regulate brain wave activity (Lubar, 1981).

SCHIZOPHRENIA

A decade ago, schizophrenia would never have been included under the rubric of neurological disorders. However, recent evidence suggests that there is at least a subgroup of schizophrenics with pronounced neurological abnormalities. These findings help to explain the well-documented tendency for schizophrenic patients to perform in the brain-damaged range on neuropsychological tests (Heaton, Baade, & Johnson, 1978; Malec, 1978) and the disproportionate number of neurological soft signs and EEG abnormalities found in systematic studies comparing schizophrenics with the general population.

Although a variety of cerebral anomalies have been documented in schizophrenic groups, the most interesting data have pointed to the presence and prominence of cerebral atrophy and ventricular enlargement in these patients. Ventricular enlargement had been noted in earlier studies using pneumoencephalography (e.g., Haug, 1962); however, the invasiveness and danger of the technique limited extensive investigation or the use of appropriate controls. The recent development of computerized tomography has made systematic investigation of the morphological features of the human brain both convenient and safe, and a wealth of data has accrued suggesting that ventricular enlargement is commonplace in schizophrenics. Johnstone, Crow, Frith, Husband, and Kreel (1976) were the first to use the new technology to document enlarged cerebral ventricles in schizophrenics; their findings have been replicated by Weinberger and his colleagues (1979, 1980) and by Golden and Moses and colleagues (1980) using inpatients, and by Carr and Wedding (1984) using a group of outpatients treated at community mental health centers. In addition to increased ventricular size, a number of studies have documented schizophrenic sucal enlargement, increased width of the interhemispheric fissure, cerebellar atrophy, and reversal of the usual brain asymmetry (i.e., most right-handed people have wider right frontal and left occipital lobes; a reverse pattern is found in many schizophrenic patients). Golden, Graber, Coffman, Berg, Newlin, and Bloch (1981) have extended the CT studies to demonstrate differences in tissue density, with lower densities noted in schizophrenics. These differences are especially pronounced in the left hemisphere. These anomalies are not correlated with age, length of institutionalization, or medication use. Those patients who demonstrate morphological changes are also those most apt to perform poorly on neuropsychological tests and least likely to respond to neuroleptic medication (Weinberger et al., 1980).

Converging data suggesting the presence of neurological underpinnings for what has traditionally been considered a functional disorder come from studies of regional cerebral blood flow (rCBF) (demonstrating decreased blood flow to the left frontal area in schizophrenics), from studies of conjugate lateral eye movements (demonstrating a tendency for schizophrenic patients to glance to the right when responding to reflective questions), from the increased incidence of sinistrality in schizophrenics, and from the fact that in monozygotic twins discordant for schizophrenia, the schizophrenic sibling is far more likely to be left handed. Other supportive data include an increased number of right ear omissions made by schizophrenics performing temporal discrimination tasks and the increased incidence of left-sided epileptic foci in schizophrenics with epilepsy. Finally, psychophysiological studies have demonstrated electrodermal hyporesponsiveness in the left hand of schizophrenics (electrodermal responsivity is presumed to be mediated by the ipsilateral hemisphere). These studies, reviewed in detail in Newlin (1983) and Henn and Nasrallah (1982), converge to suggest that (1) both structural and functional differences exist between the brains of schizophrenics and normal controls and (2) these differences are most pronounced in the left hemisphere.

It is important that one not overrespond to the findings reported above by viewing schizophrenia as "simply" a brain disease. Clearly a host of factors may be involved in the etiology of those disorders we label as schizophrenia; these may range from double-binding schizophrenogenic mothers to genetic factors to structural abnormalities in the cerebral hemispheres. Crow (1982) has proposed that there are essentially two basic types of schizophrenia. Type I is characterized by positive symptoms, the absence of intellectual deterioration, and dopaminergic hyperactivity. Type II schizophrenics are characterized by negative symptoms, asocial behavior, a relatively chronic course, and enlarged cerebral ventricles. It is likely that attempts like this, which more clearly delineate the subclasses of schizophrenia, will result in greater understanding of what increasingly appears to be a multitude of heterogeneous disorders with differing etiologies.

CONCLUSIONS

Space limitations preclude a more detailed or extensive survey of neurological disorders; however, the disorders discussed above will comprise at least 95% of the professional time of the clinical neuropsychologist, and the references cited will provide detailed data concerning the remaining 5%. It is clearly an exciting time for the neuroscientist of any sort. Major advances are being made almost daily in our understanding of both the behavioral geography and the mechanics of brain functioning; many of these advances are made possible by recent innovations in imaging technology, which will be discussed in detail in subsequent chapters. The research neuropsychologist who works to delineate and measure the precise relationships between brain structure and function and the clinical neuropsychologist who attempts to apply these findings to provide relevant information and to ameliorate human suffering are both operating at the cutting edge of what is rapidly becoming one of the more important subfields of psychology. However, it is equally clear that additional training in neuropathology and a greater appreciation of CNS disorders (versus traditional psychiatric diseases) are crucial if the clinical neuropsychologist is to be truly useful in helping to diagnose, describe, and treat neurological disease.

REFERENCES

Carr, E., & Wedding, D. (1984). Neuropsychological assessment of cerebral ventricular size in chronic schizophrenics. *The International Journal of Clinical Neuropsychology, 6,* 106–110.

Casson, I. R., Siegel, O., Sham, R., Campbell, E. A., Tarlau, M., & DiDomenico, A. (1984). Brain damage in modern boxers. *The Journal of the American Medical Association, 251,* 2663–2667.

Chusid, J. G. (1982). *Correlative neuroanatomy and functional neurology* (16th ed.). Los Altos, CA: Lange.

Crow, R. R. (1982). Recent genetic research in schizophrenia. In F.A. Henn & H.A. Nasrallah (Eds.), *Schizophrenia as a brain disease* (pp. 40–55). New York: Oxford University Press.

Delaney, R. C., Wallace, J. D., & Egelko, S. (1980). Transient cerebral ischemic attacks and neuropsychological deficit. *Journal of Clinical Neuropsychology, 2,* 107–114.

Flor-Henry, P. (1974). Psychosis, neurosis, and epilepsy: Developmental and gender-related effects and their aetiological contribution. *British Journal of Psychiatry, 124,* 144–150.

Glenner, G. (1982). Alzheimer's disease (senile dementia): A research update and critique with recommendations. *Journal of American Geriatric Society, 30,* 58–62.

Golden, C. J. (1981). *Diagnosis and rehabilitation in clinical neuropsychology.* Springfield, IL: Charles C. Thomas.

Golden, C. J., Graber, B., Coffman, J., Berg, R. A., Newlin, D. B., & Bloch, S. (1981). Structural brain deficits in schizophrenia: As identified by CT scan density parameters. *Archives of General Psychiatry, 38,* 1014–1017.

Golden, C. J., Moses, J. A., Coffman, J. A., Miller, W. R., & Strider, F. D. (1983). *Clinical neuropsychology: Interface with neurologic and psychiatric disorders.* New York: Grune & Stratton.

Golden, C. J., Moses, J. A., Zelazowski, R., Graber, B., Zata, L. M., Horvath, T. B., & Berger, P. A. (1980). Cerebral ventricular size and neuropsychological impairment in young chronic schizophrenics: Measurement by the standard Luria-Nebraska Neuropsychological Battery. *Archives of General Psychiatry, 37,* 619–623.

Haug, J. O. (1962). Pneumoencephalographic studies in mental disease. *Acta Psychiatrica Scandiavica, 44* (Suppl. 203), 135–143.

Heaton, R. K., Baade, L. E., & Johnson, K. L. (1978). Neuropsychological test results associated with psychiatric disorders in adults. *Psychological Bulletin, 85,* 141–162.

Henn, P. A., & Nasrallah, H. A. (1982). *Schizophrenia as a brain disease.* New York: Oxford University Press.

Johnstone, E. C., Crow, T. J., Frith, C. D., Husband, J., & Kreel, J. (1976). Cerebral ventricular size and cognitive impairment in chronic schizophrenia. *Lancet, 2,* 924–926.

Kilpatrick, B., & Hall, R. C. W. (1980). Seizure disorders. In R. C. W. Hall (Ed.), *Psychiatric presentations of medical illness: Somatopsychic disorders* (pp. 243–258). New York: Spectrum Publications.

Lechtenberg, R. (1982). *The psychiatrist's guide to diseases of the nervous system.* New York: Wiley.

Lezak, M. D. (1983). *Neuropsychological assessment* (2nd ed.). New York: Oxford University Press.

Lishman, W. A. (1978). *Organic psychiatry: The psychological consequences of cerebral disorder.* Oxford, England: Blackwell.

Lubar, J. (1981). *Behavioral approaches to neurology.* New York: Academic Press.

Luria, A. (1980). *Higher cortical functions in man* (2nd ed.). New York: Basic.

Malec, J. (1978). Neuropsychological assessment of schizophrenia versus brain damage: A review. *Journal of Nervous and Mental Disease, 166,* 507–516.

Matthews, W. B. (1982). *Diseases of the nervous system* (4th ed.). Oxford, England: Blackwell.

Mortimer, J. A., Schuman, L. M., & French, L. R. (1981). Epidemiology of dementing illness. In J. A. Mortimer & L. M. Schuman (Eds.), *The epidemiology of dementia* (pp. 3–23). New York: Oxford University Press.

Newlin, D. (1983). Assessing brain damage in schizophrenia. In C. J. Golden, J. A. Moses, J. A. Coffman, W. R. Miller, & F. D. Strider (Eds.), *Clinical neuropsychology: Interface with neurologic and psychiatric disorders* (pp. 197–271). New York: Grune & Stratton.

Pincus, J. D., & Tucker, G. (1978). *Behavioral neurology* (2nd ed.). New York: Oxford University Press.

Pryse-Phillips, W., & Murray, T. J. (1982). *Essential neurology* (2nd ed.). Garden City, NJ: Medical Examination Publishing Company.

Roth, M. (1981). The diagnosis of dementia in late and middle life. In J. A. Mortimer & L. M. Schuman (Eds.), *The epidemiology of dementia* (pp. 24–61). New York: Oxford University Press.

Strub, R. L., & Black, F. W. (1981). *Organic brain syndromes: An introduction to neurobehavioral disorders.* Philadelphia: F. A. Davis.

Teuber, H. L. (1960). *Visual field defects after penetrating missile wounds of the brain.* Cambridge: Harvard University Press.

Trauner, D. A. (1982). Seizure disorder. In W. G. Wiederholt (Ed.), *Neurology for non-neurologists* (pp. 283–297). New York: Academic Press.

Weinberger, D. R., Bigelow, L. B., Kleinman, J. E., Klein, S. T., Rosenblatt, J. E., & Wyatt, R. J. (1980). Cerebral ventricular enlargement in chronic schizophrenia: An association with poor response to treatment. *Archives of General Psychiatry, 37,* 11–13.

Weinberger, D. R., Torrey, E. F., Neophytides, A. N., & Wyatt, R. J. (1979). Lateral cerebral ventricular enlargement in chronic schizophrenia. *Archives of General Psychiatry, 36,* 735–739.

Wells, C. E., & Duncan, G. W. (1980). *Neurology for psychiatrists.* Philadelphia: F. A. Davis.

Wiederholt, W. C. (1982). Dementias. In W. C. Wiederholt (Ed.), *Neurology for non-neurologists* (pp. 191–204). New York: Academic Press.

4

Lateralization of Cerebral Functions

Raymond S. Dean

The human brain is clearly divided into hemispheres by a deep longitudinal fissure. Although these hemispheres are similar from a gross anatomical point of view, research over the past century suggests that they have specialized functions. In fact, microanatomical and psychophysiological differences in hemispheres of the brain have been observed as early as the thirtieth week in gestation (Molfese, Freeman, & Palermo, 1975; Wada, Clarke, & Hamm, 1975). While elementary lateralization is measurable in the neonate, more complex patterns of hemispheric specialization continue to develop during childhood (e.g., Satz, Bakker, Teunissen, Goebel, & van der Vlugt, 1975). This chapter examines aspects of hemispheric lateralization of functions that may hold clinical insights. Following a review of a number of critical issues in the assessment and understanding of hemispheric differences, the clinical significance of a lack of secure hemispheric lateralization will be examined for language disorders.

HISTORICAL ANTECEDENTS

Early in the nineteenth century a number of papers were published that began to link complex psychological functions to specific areas of the brain. Although efforts in the specific localization of functions to microstructures of the brain have not fared well, broad organizational principles of the relationship between automical features of the brain and behavior remain the focus of neuropsychology (Dean, 1985a). It is now well recognized that an individual's developmental history and normal differences in both the structure and chemistry of the brain interact such that highly specific structural localization of functions is a tenuous pursuit. Thus, while hemispheric differences are acknowledged, highly specific localization of function does not appear as robust as once portrayed.

Serious consideration of functional asymmetry of hemispheres may be traced to Broca's (1861) and Dax's (1865) clinical observations of brain-damaged subjects. Moreover, patients with damage to the left hemisphere were reported to have compromised linguistic processes. Specifically, Broca (1861) concluded that with damage to the third convolution of the left cerebral cortex, many aspects of the patient's speech were impaired. Jackson's (1874) seminal work in the late nineteenth century began to articulate more fully the idea of two different, yet coexisting, modes of cognitive processing that followed hemispheric lines of the brain. Summarizing his clinical observations, Jackson (1874) argued that "in most people, the left side of the brain is the leading side—the side of the so-called will, and the right is the automatic side" (p. 141). While describing the left hemisphere as dominant for expression, Jackson (1874) posited that the right hemisphere served functions of sensation and perception. These conclusions extended Dax's (1865) and Broca's (1861) observations and provided the underpinnings of what has been referred to as the bimodal theory of hemispheric processing. The evolving notion of hemispheric dominance was originally articulated to distinguish that hemisphere which most clearly served language functions and has only recently taken on more global connotations associated with control functions. The luxury of retrospect allows criticisms of reports that offered conclusions on normal function based on the study of diseased brains. However, these early papers are the antecedents of the renewed research efforts in the past 30 years.

Congruent with increased experimental sophistication of recent investigations has come debate as to the nature of the lateralization process. Thus, while consistent hemispheric differences are acknowledged by most neuroscientists, debate continues as to whether hemispheric differences in processing (e.g., Geschwind & Levitsky, 1968), attention (e.g., Kinsbourne, 1975), or storage (e.g., Hardyck, Tzeng, & Wang, 1978) are responsible. Although most investigators have found the arguments favoring processing differences to be more heuristic, Hardyck and colleagues' (1978) data concerning hemispheric lateralization in memory storage and Kinsbourne's (1970) reports regarding the direction of attention between hemispheres need to be seriously addressed when attempting conclusions concerning the underlying neurological mechanism.

LATERALIZATION OF FUNCTIONS

The notion that hemispheres of the brain selectively serve rather different psychological functions has gained scientific credence during the last two decades (Dean, 1985b). While acknowledging interhemispheric communication, laboratory and clinical researchers portray distinct hemispheric differences for more complex cognitive functions. As may be gathered from Table 4.1, investigations of patients who have undergone surgical section of the corpus callosum and those with localized brain damage to one hemisphere indicate rather clear differences in the functional efficiency between hemispheres. As suggested early on by Dax, Broca, and Jackson, the left hemisphere has been more closely linked to processing involving speech, language, and calculation (Sperry, 1969; Reitan, 1955) than the right. These differences seem more heuristically attributed to the mode in which information is processed than to the specific stimuli or modality of presentation (Brown & Hecaen, 1976). That is to say, the left hemisphere has been shown to be better prepared to process information in a more analytical, logical, or sequential fashion; as such, language is an excellent tool for such processing (Kimura, 1961). Research that has examined the electrical activity of the brain (electroencephalographic studies) and that which relies on perceptual asymmetries reinforce the duality of cerebral processing (Gordon, 1978; Kimura, 1967; Morgan, McDonald, & McDonald, 1971).

Generally, the linguistic dependence of the left hemisphere is not seen in tasks shown to be typically served by the right hemisphere. As shown in Table 4.1, the right hemisphere is more closely linked to a direct representation of visual-spatial reality. Indeed, the right hemisphere is shown to be prepotent (Sperry, 1969) in the presence of nonverbal-spatial task requirements. The frequent inference that this verbal–nonverbal distinction follows hemispheric lines seems something of an overstatement (Dean, 1985b). Moreover, the recent research indicates one must closely examine the requirements of the individual task before assuming hemispheric differences.

Research with clinical populations who have suffered right hemispheric damage contrasts with the findings for patients with damage to the left hemisphere. In general, it seems that the right hemisphere more efficiently serves tasks that require the holistic, or simultaneous, processing of nonverbal gestalts and the complex transformations of complex visual patterns (e.g., Milner, 1962). As such, incoming information of a parallel or spatial nature that requires cognitive manipulation has been shown to be closely linked to processing of the right hemisphere (e.g., Gordon, 1970). It also seems that information that does not lend itself to verbal mediation, such as diffuse representation of the environment, is most efficiently served by the right cortical hemisphere (Levy, Trevarthen, & Sperry, 1972). Recent research has expanded the commonly assumed nonverbal functions of the right hemisphere to include aspects of memory, depth perception, and motor integration (see Table 4.1).

Apparently, individuals have some control over the mode of processing that will be utilized and thus the specific hemisphere. Recently, Dean and Hua (1982) have offered data portraying hemispheric specialization as an active constructive process, with the specific form of encoding dependent on con-

TABLE 4.1 Lateralized Functions of the Right and Left Hemispheres

Right Hemisphere

Processing Modes	Reference
Simultaneous	Sperry (1974)
Holistic	Sperry (1969)
	Dimond & Beaumont (1974)
Visual/nonverbal	Sperry (1974)
Imagery	Seamon & Gazzaniga (1973)
Spatial reasoning	Sperry (1974)

Nonverbal Functions	Reference
Depth perception	Carmon & Bechtoldt (1969)
Melodic perception	Shankweiler (1966)
Tactile perception (integration)	Boll (1974)
Haptic perception	Witelson (1974)
Nonverbal sound recognition	Milner (1962)
Motor integration	Kimura (1967)
Visual constructive performance	Parsons, Vega, & Burn (1969)
Pattern recognition	Eccles (1973)

Memory/Learning	Reference
Nonverbal memory	Stark (1961)
Face recognition	Milner (1967)
	Hecaen & Angelergues (1962)

Left Hemisphere

Processing Modes	Reference
Sequential	Sperry, Gazzaniga, Bogen (1969)
	Mills (1977) Efron (1963)
Temporal	Morgan, McDonald, & McDonald (1971)
Analytic	Eccles (1973)

Verbal Functions	Reference
Speech	Wada (1949) Reitan (1955)
General language/verbal abilities	Gazzaniga (1970)
	Smith (1974)
Calculation/arithmetic	Reitan (1955)
	Gerstmann (1957)
	Eccles (1973)
Abstract verbal thought	Gazzaniga & Sperry (1962)
Writing (composition)	Sperry (1974)
	Hecaen & Marcie (1974)
Complex motor functions	Dimond & Beaumont (1974)
Body orientation	Gerstmann (1957)
Vigilance	Dimond & Beaumont (1974)

Learning Memory	Reference
Verbal paired-associates	Dimond & Beaumont (1974)
Short-term verbal recall	Kimura (1961)
Abstract and concrete words	McFarland, McFarland, Bain, & Ashton (1978)
	Seamon & Gazzaniga (1975)
	Dean (1983)
Verbal mediation/rehearsal	Seamon & Gazzaniga (1973)
Learning complex motor functions	Dimond & Beaumont (1974)

straints of attention and individual differences in the lateralization of functions. Evidence for this position also comes from investigations showing that visual spatial stimuli may be encoded semantically (Conrad, 1964) and verbal material can be represented as visual traces (Paivio, 1971). Apparently, individuals can process and encode information in at least two qualitatively distinct but interconnected systems (see Bower, 1970; Paivio, 1971). Important to the present discussion, these processing modes have been shown in part to follow the left–right functional distinction. In essence, learners can readily generate nonverbal or verbal processing strategies regardless of the form of the original stimulus. These rather different modes of processing correspond to function ordinarily seen as hemispheric specific (Bower, 1970; Dean, 1985a; Paivio, 1971). A corollary view, in concert with Luria's theory (1966), has been articulated by Das (1973). These researchers have characterized differences in hemispheric processes as complementary and coexisting modes. Research here seems consistent with cortical functions of the right and left cerebral hemispheres (e.g., Luria, 1966), spoken of as simultaneous and successive modes of information processing.

Hemispheric Functional Similarities

Despite compelling evidence favoring hemispheric lateralization of functions, a good deal of symmetrical processing occurs. Research with normal individuals and patients who have suffered unilateral lesions indicates equal proficiency of hemispheres in registering and storing "low level sensory features" (Milner, 1962). The magnitude of functional lateralization would seem to increase in direct proportion to the amount of conceptual reformulation, or, if you will, cognitive processing, necessary for interpretation and encoding (Gordon, 1974).

Patients with unilateral lesions to either hemisphere generally show deficit performance in the extraction of stimulus features (e.g., brightness, color, pitch, and elements of somatosensory perception) when compared with normal controls (e.g., Scotti & Spinnler, 1970; Milner, 1962; Gordon, 1974). In contrast to higher-order differences in function between groups of patients with unilateral left and right hemispheric lesions, lower-level sensory discrimination differences between patients with localized lesions lack robustness (e.g., McKeever & Gill, 1972; Gordon, 1974). Apparently, specific performance deficits that correspond to the hemisphere in which the patient has suffered damage occur only when patients are required to reorder, categorize, integrate, or abstract stimulus elements. It would seem that as the degree of cognitive processing necessary for a task increases, so too does the extent to which that function is asymmetrically lateralized.

Using split visual field (e.g., McKeever & Gill, 1972), auditory evoke potentials (Gordon, 1974), and dichotic listening (Darwin, 1974 & 1975) techniques with normal subjects, a number of investigators have shown hemispheric symmetry in the extraction of low-order visual, auditory, and tactile elements with normal adults. Such findings seem robust and have been found even in cases in which the target stimuli are embedded in a verbal or nonverbal context (e.g., Rabinowicz, 1976; Wood, 1975). Apparently, then, when normal subjects must discriminate simple sensory elements such as brightness, pitch, color, pressure, sensitivity, sharpness, or contour, few hemispheric differences in processing are evident. However, when the task requires higher-order cognitive processing beyond that found in such simple discrimination, rather clear hemispheric differences become evident.

Recent evidence indicates that hemispheric asymmetries are also related to the amount of previously encoded information that must be used to interpret incoming sensory information (e.g., Moscovitch, 1976; Goodglass & Peck, 1972). Moscovitch (1979) argues elegantly that accentuated hemispheric asymmetries occur after a delay in the recognition or recall of incoming stimuli (e.g., Milner, 1968; Goodglass & Peck, 1972). Functional lateralization varies in proportion to the degree of transformation that has occurred prior to encoding. In sum, then, it appears that hemispheric asymmetries in function are more clearly evidenced in tasks requiring higher-order processing or when incoming information must be interpreted in light of prior knowledge.

Developmental Aspects

Structural differences in the hemispheres of the brain exist prior to birth (Geschwind & Levitsky, 1968). Left hemispheric structures (left temporal planum), most often considered to serve speech functions, are significantly larger than temporal structures of the right hemisphere early in gestation (Geschwind & Levitsky, 1968; Witelson & Pallie, 1973). Rather clear structural differences have also been noted in the rate at which the pyramidal tract develops projections to hemispheres of the brain. Yakovlev and Rakic (1966) have shown consistently earlier crossing of projections from the left hemisphere than that seen for the right hemisphere. Such research has begun to outline early structural differences between hemispheres that may be the precursor of functional differences in cerebral hemispheres.

Equipotentiality, most clearly attributed to Lenneberg (1967), portrays the cerebral hemispheres of the brain as having equal potential in the development of functional specialization for language. Although this is an appealing notion, neurophysiological differences between hemispheres (Molfese, Freeman, & Palermo, 1975; Wada, Clarke, & Hamm, 1975) and early neuroanatomical differences limit its explanatory power. Of course, the rejection of early equal potential of hemispheres does not rule out the possibility that functional lateralization is a progressive, developmental process.

The extent to which functions are progressively lateralized to cerebral hemispheres is still a matter of controversy (Kinsbourne, 1975; Satz, 1976). Cerebral lateralization has been portrayed by many to follow patterns similar to that for the development of numerous psychological functions (Bruner, 1974; Piaget, 1952). From this point of view, the functional lateralization of hemispheres is seen to follow a progressive pattern of consolidation of functions corresponding to the child's neurological development (e.g., Dean, 1985a; Satz, Bakker, Teunissen, Goebel, & van der Vlugt, 1975). Although arguments favoring early specific specialization continue (Kinsbourne, 1975), a large corpus of data exists favoring developmental progression in the lateralization of functions (see Dean, 1985a). The lateralization of language to the left hemisphere has been argued to correspond to the continuing maturation of secondary association areas, which begins some time after the fifth year of life (Peiper, 1963). Indeed, we find a decrease in the role played by the right hemisphere in language, which covaries with the child's neurological development (see Krashen, 1973). Sperry (1968, 1969) has suggested that this progressive lateralization of function may well relate to the rather slow maturation of the commissure-associative cortex. In this regard, numerous reports suggest that the rate of lateralization varies with the specific function being examined (Molfese, 1977; Waber, 1977). Clearly, it would seem that although hemispheric asymmetries for certain functions are observable in the neonate, patterns of functional lateralization continue to develop in an orderly fashion throughout the early childhood years (see Satz, Bakker, Teunissen, Goebel, & van der Vlugt, 1975).

Related to developmental aspects of hemispheric specialization is the notion of functional plasticity. Plasticity here refers to the degree to which functions of a damaged hemisphere are preempted by the other. As early as the nineteenth century, clinical reports suggested that the effects of damage to the left hemisphere before adolescence were less severe and language disturbances more transient than those from similar lesions occurring in adults (Dax, 1865). Since these early reports, numerous investigators have presented data favoring what amounts to a "critical period," occurring from five to seven years of age. Prior to this critical period, functions normally served by the left hemisphere may more completely be subserved by the right cerebral hemisphere following damage to the language centers (Chelune & Edwards, 1981; Dikman, Matthews, & Harley, 1975; Pirozzolo, Campanella, Christensen, & Lawson-Kerr, 1981). In contrast, damage to similar areas occurring after this critical period are more severe and less transient (e.g., Dikman et al., 1975). These conclusions are consistent with Krashen's (1973) data suggesting a decreasing role of the right hemisphere for language with age.

The completeness of the transfer of functions between hemispheres is also positively related to the severity with which the brain is damaged (e.g., Pirozzolo et al., 1981). This conclusion is evidenced in patients who have undergone a left hemispherectomy before this critical period. In such cases, the behavioral effects are less devastating in terms of later language function than disabilities that occur with relatively minor damage to the left hemisphere (Pirozzolo et al., 1981; Dikman et al., 1975). Smith and Sugar (1975) have hypothesized that with the removal of the left hemisphere "competition for language" functions are less likely to occur than is true when more localized damage occurs. The heuristic value of plasticity as an explanatory term has recently begun to be questioned. The interested reader is directed to Fletcher and Satz (1983) for the subtleties of the counterargument.

Sex Differences in Lateralization

Subtle structural neurological differences have been observed between males and females (see McLusky & Naftolin, 1981). However, neuropsychological dissimilarity between adult males and females are more heuristically attributed to functional–organizational factors than an obvious central nervous system disparity (Dean, 1985a; Kolata, 1979). Although genetic and morphological differences exist from conception between males and females, sex hormones have been shown to have more striking effects on the structure and function of the central nervous system (Baum, 1979; McLusky & Naftolin, 1981; Weintraub, 1981). These sex steroids have a dramatic effect on the function and development of the nervous system because these chemicals are permeable to the blood-brain barrier. Hence, rapid changes in some sex-related brain functions may be due in part to the structure of androgens, which enable rapid access to the brain (Schmeck, 1980). Importantly, these sex hormones have privileged access to the brain early in gestation when rates of development heighten their sensitivity (Baum, 1979).

The extent to which genetic-hormonal sex differences are responsible for hemispheric lateralization remains in dispute (see Maccoby, 1966). Of course, one must be careful not to attribute differences in neuropsychological functioning to gender when behavior could heuristically be attributed to social-cultural variables. With this caveat in mind, numerous neuropsychological differences between normal males and females have been reported that relate directly to an appreciation of the lateralization of brain functions. For example, the superior spatial ability of males and relatively greater verbal facility of females have been attributed to sex differences in hemispheric specialization arising from sex-specific steroids (Levy & Levy, 1978; Dean, 1985a). In this regard, Witelson (1976) offers data favoring earlier right hemispheric specialization for spatial processing in males than that found for females, who more often exhibit bilateral representation of these functions until early adolescent years. Hemispheric specialization for language has also been observed earlier in males than in females, who show less consistent lateralization throughout the life span (Levy, 1973). MacLusky and Naftolin (1981) argue convincingly that such findings may more heuristically be attributed to genetic-hormonal differences than to developmental rates in general. Goy and McEwen (1980) have presented data suggesting that sex hormonal differences also result in a proclivity to rely upon specific cues (e.g., verbal, spatial) in learning and differences in the rate of acquisition for verbal and spatial stimuli.

Findings of less secure hemispheric specialization for females stand in contrast to the consistent report of more coherent lateral preference (handedness, earedness, and so forth) for females (Dean, 1986; Levy, 1973; Annett, 1976). With the frequently drawn association between lateral preference and the functional lateralization of hemispheres, such findings seem rather paradoxical. Although lateral preference will be examined more in depth later in this chapter, it suffices to say at this point that the one-to-one relationship between hand preference and hemispheric specialization for language may be rather naive.

Although males evidence more consistent hemispheric lateralization of verbal and nonverbal functions, this consistency does not seem to come without a cost (Dean, 1985a; Nottebohm, 1979). The cost here seems exacted in a higher risk of specific expressive and receptive language disorders for males (Benton, 1975; Brain, 1965; Dean, 1981). Benton (1975) has reported a ten times greater risk of language disorders for males when compared with that for female cohorts.

INFERRING FUNCTIONAL LATERALIZATION

Undoubtedly the most predominant difficulty in the measurement and study of functional lateralization is the inaccessibility of the human brain. Indeed, the vast majority of our knowledge of human neuropsychology generally and the study of functional lateralization specifically has come about as the result of inferential methods. Neuropsychological assessment grew out of a need to describe objectively the behavioral effects of known brain damage. Thus, until quite recently functions of specific areas of the brain were inferred from behavioral deficits that corresponded to localized lesions. Correlational in nature, these data have been the basis of the quantitative-actuarial approach that has dominated neuropsychology in North America. Clearly, attempts to link structure and function from this data base often become a tautological pursuit.

With this limitation in mind, one can state that damage to the left hemisphere of the brain in most right-handed individuals corresponds to deficits in speech, language, and calculation (Boll, 1974; Reed & Reitan, 1963; Reitan, 1955), whereas damage to the right hemisphere correlates with functional deficits of a more nonverbal nature (Reitan, 1955). Although handedness will be examined in greater detail below, it suffices to say that language disturbances for left-handed individuals after left hemispheric damage are less severe and more transient than those for right handers (Hecaen, 1962). These results are often cited as the basis for inferring less secure left hemispheric lateralization of language for most left-handed individuals. Such data have been cited as the basis for making inferences from scores on neuropsychological test batteries (Reitan, 1969).

Sperry and his associates (Gazzaniga & Sperry, 1962; Sperry, Gazzaniga, & Bogen, 1969; Sperry, 1968) have confirmed and extended the neuropsychological findings for patients with localized lesions in research involving surgical section of the corpus callosum as a treatment for intractable seizures. The amount of communication between hemispheres is drastically reduced with this procedure, and functions of individual hemispheres can be more completely examined. Although difficulties exist in drawing conclusions about normal hemispheric functioning from such patients, the contribution of Sperry and his associates to our understanding of hemispheric function has been seminal. In general, research with split-brain subjects has refined our understanding of functional lateralization and confirmed that, in most right-handed and many left-handed individuals, complex linguistic functions are served by the left hemisphere (Dean & Hua, 1982; Kimura, 1961; Sperry, 1968) and visual-spatial reality is more closely linked to the right hemisphere (Milner, 1962).

In addition to the data base concerning functions that are compromised with lateralized lesions, most neuropsychological batteries utilize tasks that allow comparison of right-side with left-side performance. This is possible, of course, because simple unimanual performance and sensory perception to one side of the body are served by the contralateral hemisphere. Thus, left versus right differences in strength of grip, finger tapping, and finger localization are compared against normal values. With larger than expected differences come inferences concerning lateralized impairment. In turn, these results are interpreted in conjunction with functions (e.g., language) most often associated with either the left or right hemisphere impairment. Although less useful in making diagnostic statements, most neuropsychology batteries include a measure of lateral preference for motor tasks (e.g., Halstead–Reitan Lateral Dominance Examination) as an indicator of the degree to which functions ordinarily ascribed to one hemisphere or the other can be applied to a given patient.

Normal Perceptual Asymmetry

The Wada Test (Wada, 1949), which involves the intracarotid injection of amytal to one hemisphere or the other, is considered to be the most emphatic measure of hemispheric functional specialization. Obviously, the use of this methodology with basically normal subjects is questionable. Short of this technique, the use of perceptual asymmetry techniques to infer functional lateralization based on a left–right difference in performance has been the most extensively used procedure with normal subjects (Dean, 1983).

In the dichotic listening technique, which was first introduced by Broadbent (1954) and refined by Kimura (1961), auditory asymmetries for various verbal and nonverbal stimuli are assessed. Specifically, the ear advantage is measured when different stimuli are presented simultaneously to each ear. In this way, hemispheric differences are inferred because there are a greater number of contralateral than ipsilateral ear-to-hemisphere "nerve connections"; and ipsilateral input from one ear is "blocked" by simultaneous stimuli presented to the contralateral ear. Thus, the dominant hemisphere for a particular stimuli (e.g., consonant–vowel letter groups) is inferred from more consistent recall and/or recognition of specific stimuli presented to the ear opposite that hemisphere. Therefore, if a given subject reports more correctly or reacts more quickly for a specific signal to one ear than the other (ear advantage), the contralateral hemisphere to that ear is considered to be specialized for that function (Kimura, 1961). Although any simple comparison of individual studies is difficult due to differences in specific stimuli and subtleties in procedures, it may safely be concluded that for normal adults (Dean & Hua, 1982; Kimura, 1961) and children (Dean, 1983; Hynd & Obrzut, 1977; Summers & Taylor, 1972) a right ear advantage exists for linguistic stimuli when presented in a dichotic fashion. Thus, these data with normals support a left hemisphere specialization for language often inferred from clinical studies of brain-damaged patients (e.g., Reitan, 1955). In contrast, dichotic presentation of nonverbal tones most often has been shown to produce a left-ear advantage for most normal right-handed subjects (Kimura, 1967). Although distinct methodological difficulties exist (Berlin & Cullen, 1977; Birkett, 1977; Bryden, 1978; Satz, 1976), the dichotic listening technique is considered by many to be the most valid noninvasive indicator for inferring functional hemispheric lateralization for language.

The split visual field technique is similar to the dichotic listening paradigm in terms of neurological assumptions. Because the visual half fields in humans are contralaterally served by the hemispheres of the brain, stimuli presented to one visual field (e.g., right) have privileged access to the opposite hemisphere (e.g., left). The presentation of stimuli is most often accomplished with a tachistoscope, which allows exposure to different stimuli by both visual fields simultaneously. Very brief exposure periods reduce the methodological difficulties that would be attributed to the possibility of eye movements during presentation. Early on, research utilizing the visual half field technique employed unilateral presentations (e.g., Heron, 1957). Recent research has been more sensitive to the methodological difficulties associated with unilateral presentations and has focused on simultaneous bilateral exposures. In this research we would expect, and indeed we find, a right visual half advantage (left hemispheric) for linguistically related material (Marcel & Rajan, 1975; Kershner, 1977). Because of the possibility of postexposure attentional scanning (Witelson, 1977) and other difficulties related to the visual mode of presentation (Dean, 1981), methodological difficulties continue in the use of this technique with linguistic stimuli. A left-field advantage has consistently been reported when tasks involve more nonverbal spatial stimuli (Kimura & Durnford, 1974).

Kinsbourne and Cook (1971) have reported data favoring hemispheric lateralization when subjects are required to perform different tasks, both of which are lateralized in a single hemisphere, simultaneously. The consistent finding using this paradigm has been significantly greater interference for verbal tasks in the right-hand performance of motor tasks than that found for the left hand. Comparing left- and right-hand performance on dowel-balancing and finger-tapping tasks, researchers have inferred greater lateralization of language functions in the left hemisphere because of greater interference in the performance of the right hand (e.g., Kinsbourne & Cook, 1971).

Research that has examined the electrical activity of the brain also reinforces the hemispheric lateralization of functions. When utilizing electroencephalographic (EEG) leads, decreased activity is inferred from the presence of alpha waves. The majority of studies that employ this technique have shown increased alpha activity in the right hemisphere (postcentral area) when normal right-handed subjects are involved in verbal analytic tasks (Morgan, McDonald & McDonald, 1971). Conversely, greater alpha activity has been noted in the left hemisphere of normal individuals when they have been required to perform spatial or musical tasks (Morgan, McDonald & McDonald, 1971; Davidson & Schwartz, 1977). Thus, in concert with research involving other research paradigms, EEG studies indicate a verbal–analytical versus spatial–holistic processing difference that corresponds to the left and right hemispheres of the brain.

Lateral Preference

The performance of unimanual activities on one side of the body is served by the contralateral hemisphere of the brain. Consistent with the rather antiquated notion of cerebral dominance, it has long been inferred that lateral preference may be a behavioral expression of the degree of functional specialization of the left hemisphere for language and other control functions. Indeed, most clinical examinations and neuropsychological batteries have incorporated some measure of lateral preference (handedness, eyedness, and the like) as an indicator of the underlying functional organization of cortical hemispheres. A corollary to the notion of hemispheric dominance is the long held hypothesis that anomalous preference patterns may underlie many functional disorders (e.g., Orton, 1937). The relationship between atypical patterns of lateral preference and cortical functioning remains one of the most studied and controversial issues in neuropsychology (Dean, 1985a).

The implicit assumption has been that observable patterns of preference would reflect functional lateralization of cortical hemispheres (Harris, 1947).

Although measures have varied from direction of eye gaze (Reynolds, 1978) to the left or right turning of the individual's hair whorl (Tjossen, Hansen, & Ripley, 1961), research has concentrated on hand preference (Dean, 1983). This concentration probably relates to the deceptive ease in assessment and various reports of a higher incidence rate of mixed-hand preference for individuals with a number of expressive and receptive language disorders (e.g., Orton, 1937).

Population estimates based on large samples suggest that some 90% of normal individuals could be considered as right-handed. The remaining 10% consist of individuals who are either consistently left-handed or without a clear hand preference (Annett, 1976; Oldfield, 1971). Although a number of clinical reports have stressed the importance of assessing hand preference, it has become obvious that simple handedness does not relate directly to functional lateralization for language (Dean, 1982; Kinsbourne & Hiscock, 1977).

Inconsistent findings in the study of lateral preference seem understandable when in many cases simple hand preference for writing is the only measure of laterality. Dean (1982) has argued that confusion in past research that has used lateral preference as a measure of hemispheric lateralization may well be related to the specific index of preference used. Indeed, it seems that the relationship between simple hand preference and cerebral lateralization is less than robust (Dean, 1979, 1982). In fact, conclusions concerning hemispheric specialization based on hand preference are more likely to be in error than if the assumption is made that language is served by the left hemisphere in all subjects regardless of handedness. (Dean, 1986). This conclusion is reflected in research showing that for most right- and left-handed individuals, complex linguistic functions are served by the left hemisphere (Lake & Bryden, 1976). Milner (1974) reports that some 95% of right-handed and 70% of left-handed individuals have secure left hemispheric specialization for language. For some 30% of left-handed individuals, language has been shown to be served by the right hemisphere, or symmetrically organized. These data stand in contrast to early speculations of right hemispheric language dominance for all left-handed individuals. Other than the social learning that occurs, differences between left handers in language lateralization may be attributed to differences in the etiology of left-hand preference (Satz, 1976). Moreover, although there has been shown to be a distinct genetic factor in left handedness (Levy & Nagylaki, 1972), a number of researchers have argued in favor of a form of left handedness which arises out of pathological factors relating to early brain damage and/or a developmental anomaly in the left hemisphere.

Satz (1976) has argued convincingly against measures of lateral preference based on simple handedness as an index of cerebral dominance for language. This seems reasonable when the degree of social learning and environmental constraints are considered in the establishment of hand preference. Clearly, early theoretical notions that offered handedness as a definitive indicator of cortical specialization appear naive in light of our present research base (Dean,

1981). It seems, then, that while preference for peripheral activities may reflect cortical organization, the relationship is not a simple one.

Measures of lateral preference have often been used to classify respondents in a rather arbitrary, nominal fashion (left, right, mixed) (e.g., Annett, 1976; Harris, 1947; Jasper & Raney, 1937; Oldfield, 1971). Like other individual difference variables, lateral preference seems more heuristically considered as a continuous variable; and, as such, one would expect individuals to show various degrees of preference (see Whitaker & Ojemann, 1977; Shankweiler & Studdert-Kennedy, 1975; Dean, 1978). From this point of view, it is not surprising to find confusion between studies that have relied on methodologies that portray lateral preference as an all-or-nothing variable.

Dunlop, Dunlop, and Fenelon (1973) have presented data showing little reliable variance associated with simple hand preference as a predictor of language. However, these authors showed a clear association between inconsistent eye/hand use and confused hemispheric lateralization for language. This finding seems consistent with other research showing discrepancies in ear/hand preference (e.g., Bryden, 1967) and more confused hand preference for fine motor activities requiring visual guidance, (Dean, Schwartz, & Smith, 1981; Kaufman, Zalma, & Kaufman, 1978) which may be more sensitive indicators of language confusion. Examining preference for a large number of items in a continuous fashion, Dean (1982) offered data favoring lateral preference as a factorial complex variable that is best represented on a continuum from entirely right to entirely left. Dean (1982) argues that the neurological significance of lateral preference may well have been masked in methodologies that summed across subjects' preferences for individual activities with little more than intuitive support.

Dean et al. (1981) hypothesized that much of the inconsistency in the results in studies of lateral preference may well vary as a function of the specific tasks chosen to infer lateral dominance. Using factor analysis, Dean (1982) isolated six distinct dimensions that accounted for some 90% of the variability in subjects' preferences for activities involving the hands, arms, eyes, ears, and feet. Research comparing individual factors with sophisticated measures of hemispheric language lateralization indicates a more robust relationship with that factor, which involves preference for visually guided motor tasks (Dean, 1985b). These data suggest that the choice of preference items (writing, etc.) in past research may have played an interactive role with other neuropsychological variables (Dean, in press 1986c). Thus, lateral preference patterns would seem not only to vary from individual to individual but, more important to the present discussion, for each individual as a function of the cerebral system under study.

Using a multifactor measure of lateral preference, Dean (1981) has offered data favoring a greater mixed tendency for males than for females. Although these results are consistent with Oldfield's (1971) data, sex differences in lateral preference are not as simplistic as once proposed (Oldfield, 1971).

Moreover, Dean (1979, 1982) showed males to present a significantly more mixed pattern in lateralization for factors involving strength and those requiring visual guidance in their performance. Although genetic factors that would predict such differences have been proposed (Levy & Levy, 1978), sex steroids and specific social learning cannot be dismissed (see McGlone, 1980).

ATYPICAL LATERALIZATION AND LANGUAGE DISORDERS

Incomplete hemispheric lateralization of language has long been hypothesized as a predisposing factor for a number of disorders. The most often articulated view speculates that language-related disorders may result from the bilateral representation of language functions in the brain and thus some form of competition between hemispheres (e.g., Orton, 1937; Zangwill, 1962). Orton's (1937) early hypothesis of confused lateralization for severe reading disorders was based on his clinical observations of a higher incidence of confused lateral preference (hand and/or hand/eye preference) for children referred for reading problems. As outlined above, because purposeful unimanual activities are served by the contralateral hemisphere of the brain, observed confusion for such behaviors was seen to reflect confused lateralization of cortical functions (Annett, 1976; Orton, 1937; Zangwill, 1962). In support of this notion, Zangwill (1960) offers data showing that some 88% of "congenital dyslexics" present with some form of confused lateral preference. Although nearly a half century has passed since Orton's (1937) hypothesis, cerebral dominance as an etiological factor in reading disorders remains one of the most controversial issues in neuropsychology.

As mentioned above, measures of hemispheric specialization based on simple handedness do not relate to language lateralization in a one-to-one fashion. In the Dunlop, Dunlop, and Fenelon (1973) study, little relationship between handedness in isolation and language-related disorders was found. However, when crossed eye-hand preference was examined, this index was shown to be clearly associated with such disorders. Similarly, Dean, Schwartz, and Smith (1981) have recently offered data favoring less coherently lateralized systems of lateral preference for children diagnosed as learning disabled. Interestingly, when summed across systems of lateral preference, learning-disabled children differed little from normal controls.

Inconsistencies in this area exist not only in how lateral preference is measured but also in a lack of a consistent rationale for inclusion of individuals in nosological categories. Moreover, classifications such as reading disabilities, dyslexia, and the like are both overlapping and confounded. Using a more descriptive approach to reading disorders, Dean (1978, 1979) has reported significantly greater mixed systems of lateralization for children with adequate decoding skills who experience problems in reading comprehension. However, in the same investigation, poor readers deficient in decoding also were similar to good readers in their lateral preference patterns. Thus, refined diagnostic specificity in considering language disorders is as important as the measure of lateralization used. A good deal of recent research indicates a consistent right-ear advantage for language-disabled patients when verbal stimuli are presented in a dichotic fashion (Dean & Hua, 1982; Hynd, Obrzut, Weed, & Hynd, 1979; Satz, Bakker, Teunissen, Goebel, & van der Vlugt, 1975), a pattern similar to that found for normals. Thus, these data would suggest that language lateralization for language-disabled patients when measured in an auditory fashion is similar to that reported for normals (Dean & Hua, 1982). However, when language lateralization is inferred from a visual presentation (split visual field), the majority of studies show a smaller right visual field superiority for linguistic material in language-disabled patients than that found for normal controls (Kershner, 1977; Marcel, Katz, & Smith, 1974; Marcel & Rajan, 1975). Interestingly then, it appears that while evidence of normal language lateralization exists when measured in an auditory fashion, many language-disabled individuals show less secure visual language lateralization. The etiology of such deficits has been attributed to developmental aberrations (Satz, 1976), early insult (Geschwind, 1974), genetic factors (Levy & Reid, 1976), and the interaction of these factors. Indeed, professional controversy persists concerning neuropsychological aspects of reading disorders in general and the heuristic value of Orton's (1937) original hypothesis of inconsistent cerebral dominance for many linguistically disabled children.

Beaumont and Rugg (1978) have offered an interesting hypothesis that attempts to reconcile findings of normal auditory (right-ear advantage) and less secure visual (split visual field) language asymmetries for patients who present with severe reading disorders. In concert with Pizzamiglio's (1976) and Geschwind's (1974) conceptualizations, Beaumont and Rugg (1978) have hypothesized a functional disassociation in the lateralization of auditory and visual language systems. The deficit here is seen as integration of visual–verbal systems in the presence of normal auditory-verbal functioning. From this point of view, functional lateralization for language may vary for an individual as a function of the specific system (i.e., visual–verbal) examined (Beaumont & Rugg, 1978; Dean & Rothlisberg, 1983; Luria, 1966).

Although empirical attempts to subtype linguistic disorders in the selection of subjects is encouraging (Boder, 1970; Pirozzolo, 1979), the lack of relevant diagnostic criteria represents a major difficulty in drawing conclusions in this area of research (Dean, 1986). The reader needs to be particularly alert to the myriad of practical assessment and complex theoretical issues when drawing clinical inferences of functional lateralization as part of a comprehensive neuropsychological evaluation. Moreover, although inconsistent patterns of functional lateralization may be viewed as having potential clinical implications, there is little robust evidence that atypical lateralization should be considered pathogenic in isolation.

REFERENCES

Annett, M. (1976). Hand preference and the laterality of cerebral speech. *Cortex, 11,* 305–329.

Baum, M. J. (1979). Differentiation of coital behavior in mammals: A comparative analysis. *Neuroscience and Biobehavioral Reviews, 3,* 265–284.

Beaumont, J. G., & Rugg, M. D. (1978). Neuropsychological laterality of function and dyslexia: A new hypothesis. *Dyslexia Review, 1,* 18–21.

Benton, A. L. (1975). Development dyslexia: Neurological aspects. In W. J. Friedlander (Ed.), *Advances in neurology* (Vol. 7). New York: Raven Press.

Berlin, C. I., & Cullen, J. K. (1977). Acoustic problems in dichotic listening tasks. In S. J. Segalowitz & F. A. Gruber (Eds.), *Language development and neurological theory.* New York: Academic Press.

Birkett, P. (1977). Measures of laterality and theories of hemispheric process. *Neuropsychologia, 15,* 693–696.

Boder, E. (1970). Developmental dyslexia: A new diagnostic approach based on the identification of three subtypes. *Journal of School Health, 40,* 289–290.

Boll, T. J. (1974). Behavioral correlates of cerebral damage in children aged 9 through 14. In R. M. Reitan & L. A. Davison (Eds.), *Clinical neuropsychology: Current status and applications.* New York: Wiley.

Boll, T. J. (1974). Right and left cerebral hemisphere damage and tactile perception: Performance of the ipsilateral and contralateral sides of the body. *Neuropsychologia, 12,* 235–238.

Bower, G. H. (1970). Analysis of a mnemonic device. *American Scientist, 58,* 496–510.

Brain, L. (1965). *Speech disorders.* London: Butterworths.

Broadbent, P. E. (1954). The role of auditory localization in attention and memory span. *Journal of Experimental Psychology, 47,* 191–196.

Broca, P. (1861). Nouvelle observation d'aphemie produite par une lesion de la moite posterieure des deuxieme et troiseme circonvolutions frontales. *Bulletin de la Societé Anatomique de Paris, 36,* 398–407.

Brown, J. W., & Hecaen, H. (1976). Lateralization and language representation. *Neurology, 26,* 183–189.

Bruner, J. S. (1974). *Beyond the information given.* London: George Allen & Unwin.

Bryden, M. P. (1967). An evaluation of some models of laterality effects in dichotic listening. *Acta-otolaryngol, 63,* 595–604.

Bryden, M. P. (1978). Strategy effects in the assessment of hemispheric asymmetry. In G. Underwood (Ed.), *Strategies of information processing.* London: Academic Press.

Carmon, A., & Bechtoldt, H. (1969). Dominance of the right cerebral hemisphere for stereopsis. *Neuropsychologia, 7,* 29–39.

Chelune, G. J., & Edwards, P. (1981). Early brain lesions: Ontogenic-environmental considerations. *Journal of Consulting and Clinical Psychology, 39,* 777–790.

Conrad, R. (1964). Acoustic confusions in immediate memory. *British Journal of Psychology, 55,* 75–83.

Darwin, C. J. (1974). Ear differences and hemispheric specialization. In F. O. Schmitt and F. G. Worden (Eds.), *The Neurosciences: Third study program.* Cambridge, MA: The MIT Press, 57–63.

Darwin, C. J. (1975). Speech perception. In E. C. Carterette and M. P. Freedman (Eds.), *Handbook of Perception* (Vol. 7). New York: Academic Press.

Das, J. P. (1973). Structure of cognitive abilities: Evidence for simultaneous and successive processing. *Journal of Educational Psychology, 65,* 103–108.

Davidson, R. J., & Schwartz, G. (1977). The influence of musical training on patterns of EEG asymmetry during musical and nonmusical self-generation tasks. *Psychophysiology, 14,* 58–63.

Dax, G. (1865). Lesions de la moitie gauche de l'encephale coincident avec l'oubli des signes de la pensee. *Gaz. Hebdom. Med. Chir, 2,* 259–262.

Dean, R. S. (1978). Cerebral laterality and reading comprehension. *Neuropsychologia, 16,* 633–636.

Dean, R. S. (1979, September). *Lateral preference and reading comprehension.* Paper presented at the Annual Meeting of the American Psychological Association, New York, NY.

Dean, R. S. (1981). Cerebral dominance and childhood learning disorders: Theoretical perspectives. *School Psychology Review, 10,* 373–380.

Dean, R. S. (1982). Assessing patterns of lateral preference. *Journal of Clinical Neuropsychology, 4,* 124–128.

Dean, R. S. (1983, February). *Dual processing of prose and cerebral laterality.* Paper presented at the Annual Meeting of the International Neuropsychological Society, Mexico City, Mexico.

Dean, R. S. (1985a) Foundation and rationale for neuropsychological bases of individual differences. In L. C. Hartlage & C. F. Telzrow (Eds.), *The neuropsychology of individual differences: A developmental perspective.* New York: Plenum Publishing.

Dean, R. S. (1985b) Neuropsychological assessment. In J. D. Cavenar, R. Michels, H. K. H. Brodie, A. M. Cooper, S. B. Guze, L. L. Judd, G. L. Klerman, & A. J. Solnit (Eds.), *Psychiatry.* Philadelphia: J. B. Lippincott.

Dean, R. S. (1986). Perspectives on the future of neuropsychological assessment. In B. S. Plake and J. C. Witt (Eds.), *Buros-Nebraska series on measurement and testing.* New York: Lawrence Erlbaum.

Dean, R. S., & Hua, M. S. (1982). Laterality effects in cued auditory asymmetries. *Neuropsychologia, 20,* 685–690.

Dean, R. S., & Rothlisberg, B. A. (1983). Lateral preference patterns and cross-modal sensory integration. *Journal of Pediatric Psychology, 8,* 285–292.

Dean, R. S., Schwartz, N. H., & Smith, L. S. (1981). Lateral preference patterns as a discriminator of learning difficulties. *Journal of Consulting and Clinical Psychology, 49,* 227–235.

Dikman, S., Matthews, C. G., & Harley, J. P. (1975). The effect of early versus late onset of major motor epilepsy upon cognitive intellectual performance. *Epilepsia, 16,* 73–77.

Dimond, S., & Beaumont, J. (1974). *Hemisphere function in the human brain.* London: Elek Scientific Books.

Dunlop, D. B., Dunlop, P., & Fenelon, B. (1973). Vision laterality analysis in children with reading disability: The results of new techniques of examination. *Cortex, 9,* 227–236.

Eccles, J. C. (1973). *The understanding of the brain.* New York: McGraw-Hill.

Efron, R. (1963). The effect of handedness on the perception of simultaneity and temporal order. *Brain, 86,* 261–284.

Fletcher, J. M., & Satz, P. (1983). Age, plasticity, and equipotentiality: A reply to Smith. *Journal of Consulting and Clinical Psychology, 31,* 763–767.

Gazzaniga, M. S. (1970). *The bisected brain.* New York: Appleton-Century-Crofts.

Gazzaniga, M. S., & Sperry, R. W. (1962). Language after section of the cerebral commissures. *Brain, 90,* 131–148.

Gerstmann, J. (1957). Some notes on the Gerstmann syndrome. *Neurology, 7,* 866–869.

Geschwind, N. (1974). *Selected papers on language and the brain.* The Netherlands: D. Reidel Publishing Company.

Geschwind, N., & Levitsky, W. (1968). Human brain: Left-right asymmetries in temporal speech region. *Science, 161,* 186–187.

Goodglass, H., & Peck, E. A. (1972). Dichotic ear order effects in Korsakoff and normal subjects. *Neuropsychologia, 10,* 211–217.

Gordon, H. W. (1970). Hemispheric asymmetries in the perception of musical chords. *Cortex, 6,* 387–398.

Gordon, H. W. (1974). Auditory specialization of the right and left hemispheres. In M. Kinsbourne and W. L. Smith (Eds.)., *Hemispheric disconnection and cerebral function.* Springfield, IL: Thomas.

Gordon, H. W. (1978). Left hemisphere dominance for rhythmic elements in dichotically-presented melodies. *Cortex, 14,* 58–70.

Goy, R. W., & McEwen, B. S. (1980). *Sexual differentiation of the brain.* Cambridge, MA: The MIT Press.

Hardyck, C., Tzeng, O. J. L., & Wang, W. S-Y. (1978). Lateralization of function and bilingual judgements: I. Thinking lateralized. *Brain and Language, 5,* 56–71.

Harris, A. J. (1947). *Harris tests of lateral dominance.* New York: Psychological Corporation.

Hecaen, H. (1962). Clinical symptomatology in right and left hemisphere lesions. In V. B. Mountcastle (Ed.), *Interhemispheric relations and cerebral dominance.* Baltimore: Johns Hopkins University Press.

Hecaen, H., & Angelergues, R. (1962). Agnosia for faces (prosopagnosia). *Archives of Neurology, 7,* 24–32.

Hecaen, H., & Marcie, P. (1974). Disorders of written language following right hemisphere lesions: Spatial dysgraphia. In S. J. Dimond & J. G. Beaumont (Eds.), *Hemisphere function in the human brain.* New York: Wiley, 345–366.

Heron, W. (1957). Perception as a function of retinal locus and attention. *American Journal of Psychology, 70,* 38–48.

Hynd, G. W., & Obrzut, J. E. (1977). Effects of grade level and sex on the magnitude of the dichotic ear advantage. *Neuropsychologia, 15,* 689–692.

Hynd, G. W., Obrzut, J. E., Weed, W., & Hynd, C. R. (1979). Development of cerebral dominance: Dichotic listening asymmetry in normal and learning disabled children. *Journal of Experimental Child Psychology, 28,* 445–454.

Jackson, J. H. (1874/1932). On the duality of the brain. Medical Press, 1:19. Reprinted in J. Taylor (Ed.), *Selected writings of John Hughlings Jackson* (Vol. II). Hodder and Stoughton: London.

Jasper, H. H., & Raney, E. T. (1937). The phi-test of lateral dominance. *American Journal of Psychology, 49,* 450–457.

Kaufman, A. S., Zalma, R., & Kaufman, N. L. (1978). The relationship of right hand dominance to motor coordination, mental ability, and right-left advantages of young normal children. *Child Development, 49,* 885–888.

Kershner, J. B. (1977). Cerebral dominance in disabled readers, good readers, and gifted children: Search for a valid model. *Child Development, 48,* 61–67.

Kimura, D. (1961). Cerebral dominance and the perception of verbal stimuli. *Canadian Journal of Psychology, 15,* 166–171.

Kimura, D. (1963). Right temporal lobe damage. *Archives of Neurology, 8,* 264–271.

Kimura, D. (1967). Functional asymmetry of the brain in dichotic listening. *Cortex, 3,* 163–178.

Kimura, D., & Durnford, M. (1974). Normal studies on the function of the right hemisphere in vision. In S. J. Dimond and J. G. Beaumont (Eds.), *Hemisphere function in the human brain.* London: Elek Scientific Books.

Kinsbourne, M. (1970). The cerebral basis of lateral asymmetries in attention. *Acta Psychologica, 33,* 193–201.

Kinsbourne, M. (1975). Cerebral dominance, learning, and cognition. In H. R. Myklebust (Ed.), *Progress in learning disabilities.* New York: Grune & Stratton.

Kinsbourne, M., & Cook, J. (1971). Generalized and lateralized effects of concurrent verbalization on a unimanual skill. *Quarterly Journal of Experimental Psychology, 23,* 341–345.

Kinsbourne, M., & Hiscock, M. (1977). Does cerebral dominance develop? In S. J. Segalowitz & F. A. Gruber (Eds.), *Language development and neurological theory.* New York: Academic Press.

Kolata, G. B. (1979). Sex hormones and brain development. *Science, 205,* 985–987.

Krashen, S. D. (1973). Lateralization, language learning, and the critical period: Some new evidence. *Language Learning, 23,* 63–74.

Lake, D., & Bryden, M. (1976). Handedness and sex differences in hemispheric asymmetry. *Brain and Language, 3,* 266–282.

Lenneberg, E. H. (1967). *Biological foundations of language.* New York: Wiley.

Levy, J. (1973). Lateral specialization of the human brain: Behavioral manifestations and possible evolutionary basis. In J. Kriger (Ed.), *The biology of behavior.* Corvallis: Oregon State University Press.

Levy, J., & Levy, J. M. (1978). Human lateralization from head to foot: Sex-related factors. *Science, 200,* 1291–1292.

Levy, J., & Nagylaki, T. (1972). A model for the genetics of handedness. *Genetics, 72,* 117–128.

Levy, J., & Reid, M. (1976). Variations in writing posture and cerebral organization. *Science, 194,* 337–339.

Levy, J., Trevarthen, C., & Sperry, R. W. (1972). Perception of bilateral chimeric figures following hemispheric deconnection. *Brain, 95,* 61–78.

Luria, A. R. (1966). *Human brain and psychological processes.* New York: Harper & Row.

Maccoby, E. E. (1966). *The development of sex differences.* Stanford, CA: Stanford University Press.

McLusky, N. J., & Naftolin, F. (1981). Sexual differentiation of the central nervous system. *Science, 211,* 1294–1302.

Marcel, T., Katz, L., & Smith, M. (1974). Laterality and reading proficiency. *Neuropsychologia, 12,* 133–139.

Marcel, T., & Rajan, P. (1975). Lateral specialization for recognition of words and faces in good and poor readers. *Neuropsychologia, 13,* 489–497.

McFarland, K., McFarland, M. L., Bain, J. D., & Ashton, R. (1978). Ear differences of abstract and concrete word recognition. *Neuropsychologia, 16,* 555–561.

McGlone, J. (1980). Sex differences in human brain asymmetry: A critical review. *The Behavioral and Brain Sciences, 3,* 215–263.

McKeever, W. F., & Gill, K. M. (1972). Interhemispheric transfer time for visual stimulus information varies as a function of the retinal locus of stimulation. *Psychonomic Science, 26,* 308–310.

Mills, L. (1977). *Left-hemispheric specialization in normal subjects for judgements of successive order and duration of nonverbal stimuli.* Unpublished doctoral thesis, University of Western Ontario.

Milner, B. (1962). Laterality effects in audition. In V. B. Mountcastle (Ed.), *Interhemispheric relations and cerebral dominance.* Baltimore: Johns Hopkins University Press.

Milner, B. (1967). Brain mechanisms suggested by studies of temporal lobes. In C. H. Millikan and F. L. Darley (Eds.), *Brain mechanisms underlying speech and language.* New York: Grune & Stratton.

Milner, B. (1968). Visual recognition and recall after right temporal-lobe excision in man. *Neuropsychologia, 6,* 191–209.

Milner, B. (1974). Hemispheric specialization: Scope and limits. In F. O. Schmitt and F. G. Warden (Eds.), *The neurosciences: Third study programme.* Cambridge, MA: The MIT Press.

Molfese, D. L. (1977). Infant cerebral asymmetry. In S. J. Segalowitz and F. A. Gruber (Eds.), *Language development and neurological theory.* New York: Academic Press.

Molfese, D. L., Freeman, R. B., & Palermo, D. S. (1975). The ontogeny of brain lateralization for speech and non-speech stimuli. *Brain and Language, 2,* 356–368.

Morgan, A., McDonald, P. J., & McDonald, H. (1971). Differences in bilateral alpha activity as a function of experimental tasks, with a note on lateral eye movements and hypnotizability. *Neuropsychologia, 9,* 459–469.

Moscovitch, M. (1976, September). *Verbal and spatial clustering in free recall of drawings following left or right temporal lobectomy: Evidence for dual encoding.* Paper presented at the Canadian Psychological Association Meeting, Toronto.

Moscovitch, M. (1979). Information processing and the cerebral hemispheres. In M. S. Gazzaniga (Ed.), *Handbook of behavioral neurobiology (Vol. 2: Neuropsychology).* New York: Plenum Press.

Nottebohm, F. (1979). Origins and mechanisms in the establishment of cerebral dominance. In M. S. Gazzaniga (Ed.), *Handbook of behavioral neurobiology* (Vol. 2: Neuropsychology). New York: Plenum Press.

Oldfield, R. C. (1971). The assessment and analysis of handedness: The Edinburgh inventory. *Neuropsychologia, 9,* 97–113.

Orton, S. T. (1937). Specific reading disability—strephosymbolia. *Journal of the American Medical Association, 90,* 1095–1099.

Paivio, A. (1971). *Imagery and verbal processes.* New York: Holt, Rinehart and Winston.

Parsons, O. A., Vega, A., Jr., & Burn, J. (1969). Different psychological effects of lateralized brain damage. *Journal of Consulting and Clinical Psychology, 33,* 551–557.

Peiper, A. (1963). *Cerebral function in infancy and childhood.* Translation by B. and M. Nagler of 3rd rev. ed. (German). New York: Consultants Bureau.

Piaget, J. (1952). *The origins of intelligence in children.* New York: International Universities Press.

Pirozzolo, F. J. (1979). *The neuropsychology of developmental reading disorders.* New York: Praeger Press.

Pirozzolo, F. J., Campanella, D. J., Christensen, K., & Lawson-Kerr, K. (1981). Effects of cerebral dysfunction on neurolinguistic performance in children. *Journal of Consulting and Clinical Psychology, 49,* 791–806.

Pizzamiglio, L. (1976). Cognitive approach to hemispheric dominance. In R. M. Knights and D. Bakker (Eds.), *The neuropsychology of learning disorders.* Baltimore: University Park Press.

Rabinowicz, B. H. (1976). *A non-lateralized auditory process in speech perception.* Unpublished M. A. thesis, University of Toronto.

Reed, H., & Reitan, R. (1963). Intelligence test performances in brain damaged subjects with lateralized motor deficits. *Journal of Consulting Psychology, 27*(2), 101–106.

Reitan, R. M. (1955). Certain differential effects of left and right cerebral lesions in human adults. *Journal of Comparative and Physiological Psychology, 48,* 474–477.

Reitan, R. M. (1969). *Manual for administration of neuropsychological test batteries for adults and children.* Indianapolis: Author.

Reynolds, C. R. (1978). Latency to respond and conjugate lateral eye movements: A methodological and theoretical note. *Perceptual and Motor Skills, 47,* 843–847.

Satz, P. (1976). Cerebral dominance and reading disability: An old problem revisited. In

R. M. Knights & D. Bakker (Eds.), *The neuropsychology of learning disorders*. Baltimore: University Park Press.

Satz, P., Bakker, D. J., Teunissen, J., Goebel, R., & van der Vlugt, H. (1975). Developmental parameters of the ear asymmetry: A multivariate approach. *Brain and Language, 2,* 71–85.

Schmeck, H. H., Jr. (1980). His brain, her brain. *Science and Living Tomorrow, 15,* 23–24.

Scotti, G., & Spinnler, H. (1970). Colour imperception in unilateral hemisphere-damaged patients. *Journal of Neurology, Neurosurgery, and Psychiatry, 33,* 22–28.

Seamon, J. G., & Gazzaniga, M. D. (1973). Coding strategies and cerebral laterality effects. *Cognitive Psychology, 5,* 249–256.

Shankweiler, D. (1966). Effects of temporal-lobe damage on perception of dichotically presented melodies. *Journal of Comparative Psychology, 62,* 115–119.

Shankweiler, D., & Studdert-Kennedy, M. (1975). A continuum of lateralization for speech perception. *Brain and Language, 2,* 212–225.

Smith, A. (1974). Dominant and nondominant hemispherectomy. In M. Kinsbourne and W. L. Smith (Eds.), *Hemispheric deconnection and cerebral function*. Springfield, IL: Thomas.

Smith, A., & Sugar, O. (1975). Development of above normal language and intelligence 21 years after left hemispherectomy. *Neurology, 25,* 813–818.

Sperry, R. W. (1968). Hemispheric deconnection and unity in conscious awareness. *American Psychologist, 23,* 723–733.

Sperry, R. W. (1969). A modified concept of consciousness. *Psychological Review, 76,* 532–536.

Sperry, R. W. (1974). Lateral specialization in the surgically separated hemispheres. In F. O. Schmitt and F. G. Worden (Eds.), *The neurosciences: Third study program*. New York: Wiley.

Sperry, R. W., Gazzaniga, M. S., & Bogen, J. H. (1969). Interhemispheric relationships: The neocortical commissures: Syndromes of hemisphere disconnection. In P. Vinken & G. W. Bruyn (Eds.), *Handbook of clinical neurology* (Vol. 4). New York: Wiley.

Stark, R. (1961). An investigation of unilateral cerebral pathology with equated verbal and visual-spatial tasks. *Journal of Abnormal and Social Psychology, 62,* 282–287.

Summers, R. K., & Taylor, M. L. (1972). Cerebral speech dominance in language-disordered and normal children. *Cortex, 8,* 224–232.

Taylor, M. A., Greenspan, B., & Abrams, R. (1979). Lateralized neuropsychological dysfunction in affective disorder and schizophrenia. *American Journal of Psychiatry, 136,* 1031–1034.

Tjossen, T. D., Hansen, T. J., & Ripley, H. S., (1961, August). *An investigation of reading difficulty in young children*. Paper presented at the 117th Annual Meeting of the American Psychological Association, Chicago, IL.

Waber, D. P. (1977). Sex differences in mental abilities, hemispheric lateralization, and rate of physical growth at adolescence. *Developmental Psychology, 13,* 29–38.

Wada, J. (1949). A new method for the determination of the side of cerebral speech dominance: A preliminary report on the intra-carotid injection of sodium amytal in man. *Medical Biology, 14,* 221.

Wada, J. A., Clarke, R., & Hamm, A. (1975). Cerebral hemispheric asymmetry in humans. *Archives of Neurology, 32,* 239–246.

Weintraub, P. (1981). The brain: His and hers. *Discover, 2,* 14–20.

Whitaker, H. A., & Ojemann, G. A. (1977). Lateralization of higher cortical functions: A critique. In S. J. Dimond & D. A. Blizard (Eds.), *Evaluation and lateralization of the brain*. New York: New York Academy of Sciences, 299, 459–473.

Witelson, S. F. (1974). Hemispheric specialization for linguistic and nonlinguistic tactual perception using a dichotomous stimulation technique. *Cortex, 10,* 1–17.

Witelson, S. F. (1976). Early hemisphere specialization and interhemisphere plasticity: An empirical and theoretical review. In S. Segalowitz and F. Gruber (Eds.), *Language and development and neurological theory.* New York: Academic Press.

Witelson, S. F. (1977). Developmental dyslexia: Two right hemispheres and none left. *Science, 195,* 309–311.

Witelson, S. F., & Pallie, W. (1973). Left hemisphere specialization for language in the newborn: Neuroanatomical evidence of asymmetry. *Brain, 96,* 641–646.

Wood, C. C. (1975). Auditory and phonetic levels of processing in speech perception: Neurophysiological and information processing analyses. *Journal of Experimental Psychology: Human Perception and Performance, 104,* 3–20.

Yakovlev, P. I., & Rakic, P. (1966). Patterns of decussation of bulbar pyramids and distribution of pyramidal tracts on two sides of the spinal cord. *Transactions of the American Neurology Association, 91,* 366–367.

Zangwill, O. L. (1960). *Cerebral dominance and its relationship to psychological function.* London: Oliver & Boyd.

Zangwill, O. L. (1962). Dyslexia in relation to cerebral dominance. In J. Money (Ed.), *Reading disability.* Baltimore: Johns Hopkins University Press.

PART II
Assessment

5

The Neurological Examination and Related Diagnostic Procedures in Behavioral Neurology and Neuropsychology

Paul F. Malloy and
Stephen E. Nadeau

This chapter is intended to acquaint nonspecialists with the essentials of the neurological examination, and to clarify its relationship to other diagnostic methods from psychology, electrophysiology, and radiology. For the novice, the chapter should make the components of the exam and the medical short-hand used to record results more understandable. The more experienced reader may gain a better understanding of the meaning of common abnormalities in clinical neurology.

The purpose of the neurological exam is to localize the site of pathology within the nervous system. Localization provides valuable information regarding the nature of the disease process, vastly narrows the differential diagnosis, and provides the basis for intelligent selection of diagnostic tests. This process is never a simple clerical task of tabulating the results of various maneuvers. The patient's history should enable the examiner to formulate hypotheses regarding the locus and nature of the disease process. The examination then consists of an organized assessment to test the validity of these hypotheses and serves as a basis for the formulation of further hypotheses. For this reason, the pattern of abnormalities detected in a given patient is far more meaningful than results of any single diagnostic maneuver. Experienced neurologists are often expert at pattern recognition and may arrive at the appropriate diagnosis with the most abbreviated of exams, but development of this pattern-oriented approach is frequently a source of considerable difficulty to physicians, especially early in their training. It is fair to say that trying to interpret an exam in a patient's chart is likely to be a futile exercise unless the examiner is able to organize the clinical findings into a coherent picture.

Given variations in the completeness and accuracy of the exam, the clinician is well advised to consider the training and expertise of the examiner when reviewing exam results. One should not assume, for example, that because a physician has noted no language deficits that the patient is not dysphasic. Many physicians embed only a very cursory neurological exam within the general physical exam, and they may have limited experience in interpretation of abnormal neurological findings. It is not unusual for a nonneurologist to miss significant deficits, and even neurologists often give too little attention to higher cortical functions in their examinations.

Behavioral neurologists, in contrast, have special training and interest in higher functions and perform many of the same maneuvers during bedside assessment as do neuropsychologists. The two approaches differ primarily in the degree of quantification of results. Whereas the behavioral neurologist depends mainly on qualitative measures of performance, the neuropsychologist utilizes standardized tests and normative comparisons. During language assessment, for example, the behavioral neurologist would typically sample repetition ability by having the patient repeat a few difficult phrases, such as "no ifs, ands, or buts." The neuropsychologist would typically administer an aphasia battery that would include numerous high- and low-difficulty repetition tasks yielding a standardized error score. The behavioral neurology approach has the advantages of flexibility and brevity, while the neuropsychological approach adds reliability and comprehensiveness. Neuropsychology is likely to continue to complement the behavioral neurological exam in the assessment of mild brain impairment (Malloy & Webster, 1981), the assessment of right hemisphere and frontal functions that are difficult to assess at the bedside (Ben-Yishay, Gertsman, Diller, & Haas, 1970; Milner, 1964), and the quantification of longitudinal changes in chronic disease (Golden, Strider, Strider, Moore, & Gust, 1979). In addition, since behavioral neurologists are not available in many settings and their techniques are not firmly entrenched in neurology training programs, the assessment of higher functions is likely to remain primarily the responsibility of neuropsychologists for some time to come.

COMPONENTS OF THE NEUROLOGICAL EXAM

The exam begins with taking a history of the presenting complaint from the patient and his family. This is supplemented by relevant medical, family, and social history. The skilled examiner then inquires about the presence or absence of various neurological and systemic symptoms in an effort to confirm or reject hypotheses formed during history taking.

The general physical exam includes the measurement of vital signs and assessment of specific signs of organ dysfunction. The nervous system is commonly involved in systemic disease, and neurological signs and symptoms often provide valuable clues to the nature of the systemic process. Conversely, the general history and physical exam may be crucial to understanding the nature of the neurological disease. For example, a history of sudden changes in abilities coupled with evidence from the physical examination of widespread vascular disease suggests the strong possibility of a multiple infarct etiology in a case of dementia.

The neurological exam itself is comprised of the evaluation of mental status, cranial nerves, and sensory and motor functions. The pattern of neurological signs associated with various disease loci and the basis of this pattern in neuroanatomy and neurophysiology will be stressed below. The discussion here will of necessity be abbreviated, and the interested reader is referred to standard textbooks for more detailed information (DeJong, 1979; Cummings & Benson, 1983; Van Allen & Rodnitzky, 1981; Demeyer, 1980).

Mental Status

The traditional psychiatric mental status examination (MSE) usually includes assessment of orientation, appearance and behavior, mood and affect, speech and thought content, insight and judgment. While the areas assessed are reasonably standard, the methods are quite variable and depend considerably on impressionistic observations in the context of an interview. Psychiatric MSEs are ill suited for use with patients with neurologic disease because they fail to assess many higher cortical functions with sufficient precision to permit judgments of localization and etiology. A detailed neurological MSE can be essential to accurate diagnosis, particularly in evaluating any patient with dementia, in differentiating between cortical and subcortical disease (a crucial distinction in the evaluation of the stroke patient), and in assessing the clinical relevance of abnormalities demonstrated on radiological or laboratory tests.

Many behavioral neurologists (e.g. Heilman & Watson, 1977) conceive of the MSE as an assessment of four general systems subserving attention, memory, cognition, and intention. Although any division of cerebral function is somewhat arbitrary, this scheme is based upon major anatomical and physiological subsystems of the brain, each of which are particularly susceptible to certain disease processes.

Attention

The attentional system makes it possible to screen irrelevant sensory input from the myriad incoming stimuli, attend to meaningful stimuli, and maintain the flexibility to switch to alternative stimuli when conditions demand it. The core of the attentional system is the midbrain reticular activating system (RAS), which maintains tonic arousal and provides for phasic arousal via direct brainstem pathways and a thalamocortical gating system (Watson, Valenstein, & Heilman, 1981). The thalamocortical gating system includes multimodal association cortex (superior temporal sulcus, medial parietal lobe, frontal eye fields) and supramodal association cortex (such as the angular gyrus region), which enable the direction of attention based upon a complex cortical analysis of incoming sensory data. Posterior cortical regions probably manipulate attention on the basis of the relationship of the intrinsic value of incoming data to prior experience (long-term memory). To a large extent, however, attention is directed to stimuli that are directly related to plans for ongoing behavior. It is in this aspect of attention that the frontal lobes are crucial, particularly the frontal eyefields.

Lesions of the RAS and the thalamus result in generalized disorders of attention and arousal, ranging from mild lethargy to delirium and coma. Mild deficits in attention may be difficult to detect and may even be misinterpreted as lack of cooperation. The patient may appear slightly out of touch, fail to notice important environmental stimuli, or require frequent redirection to the task at hand. More structured assessments of generalized attentional deficits include digit repetition forward and vigilance tasks requiring the patient to signal or cancel out a designated letter in a random array presented visually or verbally (Diller et al., 1974; Strub & Black, 1977).

Lesions to cortical attentional zones result in neglect, or the failure to respond to unilateral sensory stimuli. In clinical practice, significant neglect is caused almost exclusively by right parietal or frontal eye field lesions and is therefore a valuable sign of nondominant cortical damage (Heilman, 1979). Neglect has been reported with RAS, thalamic, and cingulate gyrus lesions as well (Heilman & Valenstein, 1979), but these are less common. Extreme neglect is easily assessed by simply observing that the patient denies that the side of the body in neglected hemispace exists and fails to direct behavior to the neglected side. Patients with neglect may insist that their left arms belong to the examiner, turn the head or trunk constantly to the right, or eat only the food on the right side of the plate. Milder forms of neglect can be assessed by observation of extinction on simultaneous bilateral stimulation, omissions or distortions on the left side of drawings, and use of only the right half of the page in writing and cancellation tasks.

Memory

Memory is one of the most complex and poorly understood neuropsychological functions. It is usually divided clinically into recent and remote memory. Recent memory refers to the storage and retrieval of new information over a brief period, whereas remote memory refers to retrieval of previously learned information over a relatively long time span.

Structures that have been found to be essential in memory processing include mesial temporal cortex, hippocampus, amygdala, fornix, mammillary bodies, anterior and dorsomedial thalamic nuclei, and posteromedial orbitofrontal cortex (Hecaen & Albert, 1978). Left temporal lesions produce relatively poor recall of verbal material, while right temporal lesions predominantly affect nonverbal memory. Bilateral temporal lesions have been shown to produce severe impairment in new learning of both verbal and nonverbal information. Verbal recent memory is usually assessed in the neurological MSE by giving the patient three unrelated words (e.g., "Boston," "Cadillac," "elephant"), distracting him or her with an unrelated task for three minutes, and then requesting recall. Nonverbal recent memory can be assessed similarly by substituting three shapes not readily labeled verbally or by placing three objects around the room and asking the patient to find them after a delay. In interpreting results, care must be taken to differentiate deficits in attention, planning, and motor programming that might disrupt performance on memory tasks (e.g., drawing the same shape repeatedly during recall).

Remote memories are probably encoded in association cortex throughout the brain, and therefore in practice remote memory is significantly impaired only by diffuse cerebral disease. Remote memory is usually assessed by having the patient recall personal and historical events from the distant past (e.g., birthplace, date of marriage, recent presidents, last war).

Cognition

Cognition is used here to denote language, calculation, praxis, spatial, and constructional functions. These cognitive abilities are subserved mainly by frontoparietal cortex in both hemispheres. Although there are important exceptions, in clinical practice it will be observed that the left hemisphere controls most language, calculation, and praxis abilities, while the right hemisphere controls most spatial and constructional functions (Springer & Deutsch, 1981). Cognitive assessment can be very useful in discriminating cortical from subcortical, right from left hemisphere, and focal from diffuse lesions, as well as in classifying dementia.

Present knowledge indicates that left hemisphere language functions are quite clearly localized in perisylvian and surrounding convexity regions. The perisylvian area represents the language cortex proper and can be viewed as a phonemic processor. It is interfaced via the angular and supramarginal gyri with association areas throughout the brain that are responsible for concept formation. The language cortex is most susceptible to focal lesions, whereas the concept system is most susceptible to diffuse cerebral disease affecting association cortex and to focal lesions of the angular and supramarginal gyri, which disrupt the interconnections noted above. Thus, perisylvian lesions produce a variety of language disorders including pure word deafness and Wernicke's, Broca's, and conduction aphasias, which are characterized by deficient phonemic processing, including repetition deficit, and usually by the presence of literal paraphasic errors (e.g., "bog" for "dog"). Lesions of the surrounding associational system produce transcortical sensory, transcortical motor, and anomic aphasias, which generally are characterized by disorders of semantic content, comprehension, and naming; verbal (e.g., "coat" for "shirt") but not literal paraphasias; and relative sparing of repetition (Benson & Geschwind, 1971). These aphasias are commonly overlooked by clinicians or misinterpreted as a confusional state. The commonly used dichotomies of anterior and posterior or expressive and receptive aphasias are clinically irrelevant in terms of neurological treatment. Discriminating the perisylvian from the anomic and transcortical aphasias has great clinical significance, however. The former are usually caused by infarction in the middle cerebral artery distributions, while the latter most commonly result from infarction in the posterior cerebral artery distribution, cortical dementias such as Alzheimer's disease or carbon monoxide poisoning, or disruption of the border zone circulation between the middle and anterior or middle and posterior cerebral artery distributions.

Bedside language testing should include assessment of spontaneous language, repetition, comprehension, naming, reading, and writing. Spontaneous language should be scrutinized for paraphasic errors, word-finding difficulty and circumlocutions, meaningful content, presence of major lexical items, and the degree to which language is organized and goal directed. The patient should be asked to repeat simple sentences dominated by major lexical items arranged in a logical way, such as "The President lives in Washington," as well as sentences with little meaning composed of largely arbitrary arrangements of nonsubstantive words, such as "No ifs, ands, or buts." He should be asked both to point to and to name high- and low-frequency items. Comprehension of both simple and compound commands should be tested. Commands can be made more difficult by using unusual syntactic arrangements. "With the pen, point to the book" may be easier for certain patients than "Point to the book with the pen" because of the primacy of the active object in the first sentence. "Point to the pen with the dollar bill" is an example of an unusual command that stresses syntactic comprehension.

Calculation can be tested by asking the patient to add one- and two-digit numbers and to subtract 7 from 100 serially. Performance is critically dependent not just upon the integrity of the dominant frontoparietal cortex but upon attention and education.

Assessment of praxis should include samples of responses to commands for buccofacial and whole body movements (e.g., show how you whistle, walk across the room) and transitive and intransitive limb movements performed with each hand (e.g., show me how you comb your hair, show me how you salute). Bilateral limb apraxias are most commonly found with posterior left hemisphere lesions, while left-limb apraxias reflect callosal or right frontal disease (Geschwind, 1975). The examiner must be careful to distinguish basic motor weakness or comprehension deficits from motor programming problems per se. Asking the patient to imitate gestures may help clarify these issues.

Nondominant cortical function is difficult to assess at the bedside and is an area in which the neuropsychologist can be of considerable assistance. The presence or absence of a cortical lesion can be determined with some reliability, but the more precise localization made possible in the left hemisphere by language assessment cannot be achieved in the right hemisphere. Construction, geographic orientation, time-telling, and neglect should be tested. Constructional abilities can be assessed by having the patient copy a drawing provided by the examiner. A Greek cross, a house, or a cube are examples of items simple enough for most normals but complex enough to elicit constructional deficits. Patients with nondominant cortical lesions typically copy details accurately but fail on the outline or general Gestalt, display neglect of the left side of the drawing, and "close in" by drawing part of their figure on part of the model (Benton, Hamsher, Varney, & Spreen, 1983). Geographic orientation can be tested by having the patient indicate positions of major cities on a map of his native state. Finally, time-telling can be assessed by having him draw clocks displaying various times and read times on clocks provided by the examiner.

Intention

Intention refers to executive functions subserved by frontal lobe systems. The frontal lobes are responsible for the selection, initiation, monitoring, and modification of responses on the basis of environmental demands and internal motivational states (Luria, 1980). The frontal lobes perform these functions in concert with subcortical structures and posterior association cortex via long subcortical white matter pathways. Intentional deficits may be found with lesions of the frontal lobes themselves; with subcortical lesions affecting the basal ganglia, thalamus, or white matter pathways; and with disorders of dopamine function.

Intentional function is difficult to evaluate at bedside, and abnormalities in intentional function are more frequently overlooked or misinterpreted than any other aspect of higher cortical function. It has been noted that in these patients the history may be more informative than the physical examination, but frontal lobe function is not unitary and several types of dysfunction may be noted. One characteristic constellation of complaints is apathy, loss of drive, a tendency to sit and do nothing all day, and change in voice. On examination, such patients often appear bradykinetic (slow moving), initiate little or no activity, do not speak unless spoken to, and respond with brief answers. This clinical picture is most characteristic of patients with subcortical disease. Alternatively, there may be a history of inappropriate behavior, loss of attention to social graces, low tolerance for frustration resulting in frequent explosive outbursts, and inappropriate or disorganized language. By examination, the most outstanding feature of such patients may be their apparent belligerence and lack of cooperation. Often language is normal in most respects but the patient has a great problem in organizing his language in such a way as to convey a concept effectively. This clinical picture is most characteristic of patients with cortical disease.

Commonly the entire clinical assessment of frontal lobe function consists of eliciting so-called frontal lobe release signs such as the grasp, root, suck, snout, and palmomental reflexes (see below). However, these signs are of very limited value because they are relatively insensitive, and they are often seen among normal elderly patients and therefore lack specificity as well with certain populations. The behavioral neurologist, therefore, often supplements the exam with tests of more complex frontal functions. Frontal lobe patients of any type, but particularly those with dominant hemisphere disease, often perform very poorly when asked to produce as many different words as possible beginning with a given letter in one minute. An equivalent nonverbal task failed predominantly by nondominant frontal patients consists of requesting the generation of as many unnameable shapes as possible in a minute (Jones-Gotman & Milner, 1977). Luria has also developed a number of bedside tests that are sensitive to frontal deficits in a wide variety of functional areas (see Malloy, Webster, & Russell, 1985; Luria, 1980).

Cranial Nerves

The cranial nerves and the pathways that control them span the entire intracranial neuraxis, and their examination is therefore of special importance. Neurologists refer to cranial nerves by their number, which corresponds roughly to the rostral to caudal sequence of their emergence from the brain (see Table 5.1). As will be discussed below, the effects of cranial nerve lesions depend on whether the lesion is infranuclear (below or peripheral to the nucleus), nuclear (in the nerve nucleus), or supranuclear (above or central to the nucleus).

The *olfactory nerve* (CN I) can be tested by presenting aromatic substances to each nostril. Since normal persons are often unable to identify specific smells, it is the ability to discriminate between smells that should be assessed. Complaints of loss of taste by patients might suggest dysfunction of CN VIII, IX, or X (see below), but are instead usually due to olfactory lesions because smell is such an important component of taste perception. The olfactory nerve is rarely tested anymore because olfactory loss commonly results from smoking and trauma, and structural lesions affecting olfaction, such as olfactory groove meningiomas, are generally detected by computed tomography (CT).

The *optic nerve* (CN II) is tested by examination of visual acuity, visual fields, pupillary responses, and the optic fundi. Visual acuity is measured by means of the familiar Snellen chart, which requires the patient to discriminate

TABLE 5.1 The Cranial Nerves and Their Functions

Number	Name	Function
I	Olfactory	Smell
II	Optic	Vision
III	Oculomotor	Horizontal and vertical eye movement
IV	Trochlear	Vertical eye movement
V	Trigeminal	Facial sensation and mastication
VI	Abducens	Horizontal eye movement
VII	Facial	Facial movement and taste
VIII	Auditory/ vestibular	Hearing and balance
IX	Glossopharyngeal	Pharyngeal sensation
X	Vagus	Visceral and autonomic function, swallowing, voice
XI	Accessory	Head turning, flexion, and extension
XII	Hypoglossal	Tongue movement

letters of various sizes, allowing objective comparison to normal 20/20 vision. Loss of visual acuity is usually related to ocular rather than brain disease. Optic nerve lesions manifest as progressively decreasing acuity in one eye, pallor of the optic disc, and an afferent pupillary defect (or Marcus-Gunn pupil) in which the degree of pupillary constriction from shining a light in the involved eye (the direct response) is less than that from shining the light in the opposite eye (the consensual response). Sudden visual loss, on the other hand, suggests a vascular lesion in either the opthalmic or posterior cerebral artery distributions.

Visual fields are tested by confrontation. The patient is instructed to fixate on the examiner's nose or forehead, and either one or two fingers are raised in each of the four visual quadrants. It is preferable to test each eye individually, and the test can be made more sensitive by simultaneously stimulating two horizontally adjacent quadrants to test for visual extinction. A field defect is an area of visual loss in both eyes, though the shape of the region of visual loss may not be the same in the two eyes. Central (or neurogenic) field defects can result from lesions anywhere in the visual pathways from the optic chiasm to the occipital lobes. Central field defects are always restricted to one quadrant or horizontal hemifield and do not cross the midline, unless, of course, there are bilateral lesions. Lesions of the chiasm produce loss of vision in the two temporal half fields (bitemporal hemianopia). Lesions of the optic tracts, lateral geniculate body, optic radiations, or occipital cortex produce quarter or half-field deficits that are on the same side in each eye (homonymous quandrantanopias or hemianopias). Cortical blindness is most commonly caused by bilateral posterior cerebral artery infarctions and may be characterized by spared vision in the center of the visual fields (macular sparing). Some patients with cortical blindness will also deny their visual loss and confabulate visual experiences (Anton's syndrome).

The optic discs (fundi) are examined with an opthalmoscope for evidence of swelling of the optic nerve head (papilledema), which can be produced by increased intracranial pressure and by inflammatory, vascular, or compressive lesions of the optic nerve itself.

The *oculomotor, trochlear,* and *abducens nerves* (CN III, IV, VI) control extraocular movement. Lesions of these cranial nerves or their respective nuclei in the brainstem produce dysconjugate gaze and double vision (diplopia). Third nerve lesions produce inability to elevate, depress, or adduct the ipsilateral eye with drooping of the eyelid (ptosis). Fourth nerve lesions produce defective depression of the ipsilateral eye and vertical diplopia. Sixth nerve lesions produce inability to abduct the ipsilateral eye. Supranuclear lesions produce conjugate gaze and pursuit defects, in general without double vision. Gaze refers to the ability to direct both eyes volitionally in a given direction. Pursuit refers to the ability to follow a moving object, usually the examiner's finger. Supranuclear lesions of the oculomotor nerves above the midbrain can be overcome by caloric testing (injecting cold water in one ear) or by the oculocephalic (doll's-head) maneuver, in which the examiner moves the head back and forth briskly while looking for lag in the return of the eyes to the primary position.

Pupillary abnormalities constitute a very important neurological sign. Third nerve lesions of a compressive nature produce ipsilateral pupillary dilation and loss of reactivity. Lesions involving the sympathetic pathways (which follow a very long and circuitous pathway through the brainstem, spinal cord, neck, and head) produce the combination of ipsilateral pupillary constriction (miosis) and ptosis known as Horner's syndrome.

The *trigeminal nerve* (CN V) innervates the ipsilateral muscles of mastication and subserves sensation over the ipsilateral face. The motor division is tested by palpating the muscles while the patient clenches his teeth. The sensory division is evaluated by testing sensation to all the major sensory modalities (see below) and by touching the cornea with a cotton wisp and observing the tendency to blink (corneal reflex). Unilateral diminution in this reflex signifies a fifth nerve (afferent arc) or a seventh nerve (efferent arc) lesion. Nuclear and infranuclear lesions of the fifth nerve produce ipsilateral loss of sensation within the distribution of one or more of the sensory divisions of the nerve. The ophthalmic division supplies the forehead, anterior scalp, and cornea; the maxillary division, the nose, upper lip, cheek, outer margin of the eye, and palate; the mandibular division, the lower lip, chin, anterior tongue, and jaw. Supranuclear lesions produce alteration of sensation over the entire contralateral face and diminution in the contralateral corneal reflex.

The *facial nerve* (CN VII) innervates the muscles of facial expression. Nuclear and infranuclear lesions (usually associated with so-called Bell's palsy) result in flaccid paralysis of the entire ipsilateral half of the face. Supranuclear lesions produce a contralateral paresis of the muscles of the lower half of the face, with relative sparing of the forehead.

The *auditory nerve* (CN VIII) has auditory and vestibular divisions. The auditory division may be tested adequately at the bedside by a combination of a simple test of hearing on each side (e.g., rubbing the fingers together softly or holding a ticking watch) and the Weber test. In the Weber test, a tuning fork is placed against the forehead, the vibration is conducted via bone, and lateralization of the perceived sound indicates: (1) a conductive loss on the side at which it is perceived, related to masking of environmental sound; or (2) a sensorineural loss on the opposite side. The Rinne test is a comparison of the relative loudness of a tuning fork held near the ear (air conduction) and held against the mastoid (bone conduction). Better bone than air conduction signifies middle-ear disease or a conductive hearing loss related to obstruction of the external ear. Vertigo usually signifies labyrinthine disease, but it also commonly occurs with acute lesions of the vestibular division or of the vestibular nuclei in the brainstem. Acutely, such lesions tend to produce tonic deviation of the eyes toward the side of the lesion, contralateral horizontal and rotary nystagmus, and a tendency to fall toward the side of the lesion.

The *glossopharyngeal nerve* (CN IX) subserves sensation and some movement of the pharynx and supplies the parotid salivary gland. Lesions result in loss of the gag reflex, with preservation of voluntary movement of the palate.

The *vagus nerve* (CN X) supplies motor innervation to the pharynx and larynx and autonomic innervation to all the viscera above the pelvis. The tenth nerve, particularly by virtue of its visceral autonomic role, is of major clinical import, but with respect to localization the only significant abnormality is contralateral palatal deviation, which signifies an infranuclear lesion. Infra- and supranuclear lesions are commonly associated with dysarthria (articulatory difficulty).

The *accessory nerve* (CN XI) supplies the sternocleidomastoid and trapezius muscles. Supranuclear lesions, the only type commonly observed, produce an inability to turn the head toward the contralateral side or shrug the contralateral shoulder.

The *hypoglossal nerve* (CN XII) supplies the tongue. The protruded tongue will deviate toward the side of a peripheral lesion and away from the side of a supranuclear lesion.

Sensory Examination

The sensory exam is the most difficult and unreliable part of the neurologic exam, due to its dependence on patient self-report, and it is particularly important for the examiner to formulate a hypothesis regarding localization before attempting the exam. A limited, carefully organized sensory exam may then be performed. Sensation is often divided into primary and secondary types. The primary sensory abilities involve detection of touch, pain, temperature, and vibration. The secondary sensory abilities involve discrimination of the parameters of sensation and include two-point discrimination, graphesthesia, stereognosis, baresthesia, and joint position sense. All sensations are mediated by the spinothalamic and dorsal column pathways of the spinal cord and by the thalamus, but secondary sensations require cortical processing.

Light touch is examined by lightly touching the skin with a wisp of cotton and having the patient report when he is touched, or by brushing the patient's skin with one's hand and inquiring about subjective sensory alteration. Pain is tested by touching the patient with a sharp object. Temperature is assessed by touching the patient with tubes of hot or cold water or, more commonly, with a cold tuning fork or reflex hammer. Vibration is tested by touching a vibrating tuning fork to bony prominences, such as the ankles, knees, or knuckles, and requiring the patient to report when the vibration ceases.

Secondary sensations are assessed by requiring the patient to discriminate single or double simultaneous touches with a pin on the fingertips or toes, identify numbers written on the hands or other parts of the body, identify objects placed in the hands, discriminate the heavier of two similar weights, reproduce passively induced positions of the fingers or limbs, and signal the first sensation of movement or the direction of movement in a passively manipulated phalanx or limb. Graphesthesia and position sense are the most commonly tested modalities and generally are sufficient.

Peripheral nerve lesions produce sensory loss in a peripheral neuronal distribution. Diseases affecting peripheral nerves diffusely produce a "stocking-glove" distribution sensory loss because the longest nerves are most severely affected. Diseases primarily affecting large fibers or myelin will produce disproportionate loss in vibratory and position sense, loss of deep tendon reflexes, and, in certain cases, wasting of distal musculature. Diseases primarily affecting small fibers will produce disproportionate loss of pain and temperature sensation, loss of sweating, and vasoregulatory abnormalities.

Other sensory deficits reflect more central localization of disease. Lesions of nerve roots produce sensory deficits in the dermatomes innervated via that root (radicular distribution). Lesions mainly affecting one-half of the spinal cord may produce ipsilateral loss of vibratory and position sense and contralateral loss of pain and temperature sense (Brown-Sequard pattern). Spinal cord lesions may also produce a well-defined loss of sensation in the dermatomes somewhere below the lesion (a sensory level). Infarction of the portion of the spinal cord supplied by the anterior spinal artery produces paraparesis, bilateral loss of pain and temperature sensation, and preservation of position and vibratory sensation. The lesion of syringomyelia (the formation of a cavity within the center of the spinal cord) selectively destroys spinothalamic fibers crossing in the anterior commissure of the cord and thus produces loss of pain and temperature sensation at all levels affected by the syrinx. Lesions above the sensory decussation (the pontomedullary junction) produce contralateral alteration in all sensory modalities. Lesions of the cerebral cortex produce differential loss of secondary sensations.

Motor Examination

The motor system is the "final common pathway" for all central nervous system output, making motor signs and symptoms the single most important source of information in the neurologic patient. The motor exam includes assessment of strength, bulk, fasciculations, abnormal movement, tone, fine motor movement, reflexes, and cerebellar and basal ganglia functions.

Strength is assessed by having the patient oppose movements by the examiner. For example, the patient is asked to spread his fingers against the inward squeeze of the examiner to test intrinsic hand muscles. Strength of various muscle groups is rated on a scale of 0-to-5, ranging from no movement to normal strength (see Table 5.2).

Muscle bulk and *abnormal movements* are evaluated through observation. The examiner takes note of atrophy (focal wasting of muscles) and fasciculations (small random twitches of muscles), both related to chronic denervation. Abnormal movements can take many forms, reflecting lesions in different motor systems. Descriptions of the common types of abnormal movement and the associated disease processes are displayed in Table 5.3.

Muscle tone is defined as resistance to passive stretch. It is particularly important in proximal muscles because it serves to maintain postures against the force of gravity and to stabilize the extremities so that fine motor movements may be executed with the hands and feet. Tone can be conveniently divided into static (or resting) and dynamic categories. Static tone is assessed by slowly moving an extremity back and forth. Dynamic tone is reflected in the briskness of deep tendon reflexes (see below) and in the presence or absence of spastic catches (clasped-knife response) during rapid passive extremity movement. Normally all muscles have some degree of resting tone, and all movement may be conceived of as the superimposition of a detailed motor program upon a programmed reduction in background tone. The maintenance of tone is

TABLE 5.2 Ratings of Motor Strength

5 = Normal strength
4 = Ability to overcome gravity plus additional resistance
3 = Ability to overcome gravity alone
2 = Movement without ability to oppose gravity
1 = Some muscular contraction but no joint movement
0 = No muscular contraction

TABLE 5.3 Abnormal Movements and Their Significance

Movement	Description	Localization	Common Etiologies
Tremor	Rhythmic oscillation of limbs or head: many different types	Basal ganglia Cerebellum Brainstem	Parkinsonism Cellebellar and brain-stem strokes and tumors Familial (essential) Physiologic
Chorea	Brief, irregular dance-like jerks of the limbs	Basal ganglia	Huntington's disease "Senile chorea" Sydenham's (rheumat-ic fever) Systemic lupus eryth-matosus
Athetosis	Fluid, often wormlike alternations of ex-tension and flexion, usually of hands and arms	Basal ganglia	Anoxic encephalop-athy Wilson's disease Other hereditary de-generative disease Severe proprioceptive sensory loss (pseudo-athetosis)
Dyskinesia	Includes chorea and athetosis, but may include various buccofacial move-ments	Basal ganglia	Neuroleptic use (tar-dive) Excessive levodopa Meige's syndrome
Ballism	Irregular, violent, flinging movements of the extremities	Subthalamus	Hypertensive micro-vascular disease
Clonus	Repetitive contraction produced by brisk, forceful extension of a muscle	Upper motor neuron	Any upper motor neuron lesion, usually spinal cord; associated with in-creased DTRs
Asterixis	Flapping movements of hands or fingers, especially when held in extension	Midbrain?	Hepatic encephalop-athy Midbrain lesion
Myoclonus	Quick, brief, usually random con-tractions of various muscles. May be rhythmic	Various rhythmic forms seen with le-sions of red nu-cleus, dentate, in-ferior olive.	Anoxic encephalop-athy Idiopathic (myoclonic dystonia) Hereditary degenera-tive disease Slow virus disease (e.g., Jakob-Creutzfeldt)

an exceedingly complex process, involving spinal cord flexion reflexes and descending influences from the vestibular nuclei, the brainstem reticular formation, and the cerebral cortex. The basal ganglia and the cerebellum participate indirectly. Fortunately, it is considerably easier to describe the localizing value of various tone abnormalities than it is to describe the underlying mechanisms (see below).

Fine motor movement refers to the ability to perform rapid discrete movements with the hands and feet and is dependent on the integrity of the pyramidal system. It is assessed by having the patient rapidly tap the thumb and index finger together in a pincer movement, alternately oppose the thumb to the tip of each succeeding finger, pick up a dime from a table top without sliding it off, or rapidly tap the foot.

Reflexes are involuntary motor responses to specific stimuli and can be divided into three classes: primitive, superficial, and deep tendon. Primitive reflexes are normally present at birth and disappear with maturation, but they may reappear in certain disease processes. They are sometimes termed "release" reflexes to indicate the release of lower, more primitive systems from descending inhibition as a result of damage to higher centers. Superficial reflexes are elicited by cutaneous stimulation, whereas deep tendon reflexes (DTRs) are elicited by sudden muscle stretch when the tendons are tapped with the reflex hammer. Descriptions of the types and significance of various reflexes are presented in Table 5.4.

Diseases of the muscles usually produce weakness, loss of tone (especially in the proximal musculature), and sometimes late loss of muscle bulk. Peripheral nerve or nerve root lesions (lower motor neuron lesions) produce weakness, wasting, fasciculations, and loss of tone, with reduced deep tendon reflexes, in the distribution of muscles innervated by the nerves or roots. Spinal cord lesions produce weakness that first becomes evident in hip flexors, progressing to weakness in both legs (paraparesis) or all four limbs (quadraparesis) and an increase in dynamic tone leading to hyperactive deep tendon reflexes and spastic catches. Lesions affecting mainly one-half of the cord produce ipsilateral paresis.

Brainstem lesions above the motor decussation produce weakness in the opposite side of the body (contralateral hemiparesis). Lesions above brainstem tone centers, which are located mainly in the pons and medulla, produce increases in both resting and dynamic tone. Large pontomedullary lesions produce extension of all extremities that may be so strong as to defy efforts by the examiner to overcome it (decerebrate posturing). Large lesions above the midbrain produce extension of the contralateral lower extremity, as well as flexion and pronation of the contralateral upper extremity (decorticate posturing). Lesions within the cerebral hemisphere may produce hemiparesis, but they can also cause selective degradation in fine motor movement with relative sparing of strength (the pyramidal syndrome). The locus of the lesion within the cortex will affect the pattern of deficit: middle and posterior cerebral artery

TABLE 5.4 Definition and Localizing Significance of Abnormal Reflexes

Reflex	Abnormal Response	Lesion Localization
Primitive "release"		
Myerson	Eye-closing in response to repeated tapping between the eyes that fails to habituate	Frontal lobe systems Basal ganglia
Snout	Brisk protrusion of lips when upper lip is tapped	Frontal lobe systems
Suck	Sucking movement of lips when object is placed between lips	Frontal lobe systems
Grasp	Hand closure when palm is stroked	Frontal lobe systems
Root	Oral movement as if to suck a nipple when corner of mouth is touched	Frontal lobe systems
Palmomental	Contraction of mentalis (chin) muscle when thenar eminence is briskly stroked	Frontal lobe systems
Jaw jerk	Jaw snaps shut when tapped, erroneously considered a release reflex, actually a DTR	Supranuclear CN V
Superficial		
Abdominal	Absent umbilical movement when abdomen is stroked	Upper motor neuron (UMN) lesion above T_7
Plantar	Dorsiflexion of great toe, called Babinski, Chaddock, Oppenheim, Gordon, etc., depending on mode of elicitation	Corticospinal tract
Cremasteric	Testis fails to rise when thigh is stroked	$T_{12}, L_{1,2}$
Anal wink	Sphincter fails to contract when perianal region is stroked.	S_{2-5}
Deep tendon		
Pectoral	Excessive or reduced contraction	UMN ($\uparrow$); $C_{5,6}$ ($\downarrow$)
Biceps	Excessive or reduced contraction	UMN ($\uparrow$); $C_{5,6}$ ($\downarrow$)
Brachioradialis	Excessive or reduced contraction	UMN ($\uparrow$); $C_{5,6}$ ($\downarrow$)
Triceps	Excessive or reduced contraction	UMN ($\uparrow$); C_{6-8} ($\downarrow$)
Finger jerk	Excessive or reduced contraction, also called Hoffman, Tromner	UMN ($\uparrow$); $C_{7,8}$ ($\downarrow$)
Patellar	Excessive or reduced contraction, also called knee jerk	UMN ($\uparrow$); L_{2-4} ($\downarrow$)
Achilles	Excessive or reduced contraction, also called ankle jerk	UMN ($\uparrow$); S_1 ($\downarrow$)

lesions produce paresis mainly of the arm, most marked distally and in extensors; anterior cerebral artery lesions produce paresis most marked in the leg; and watershed lesions (between anterior, middle, and posterior cerebral artery distributions) produce paresis most marked in the proximal extremities. Early hemispheric lesions may be associated with a subtle tendency to assume a decorticate posture manifested by slight flexion and pronation of the extended and supinated forearm (pronation drift). Diffuse cerebral disease commonly produces an irregularly alternating assistance and resistance to passive movement of an extremity (paratonia or Gegenhalten).

Cerebellar functions can be divided into those subserved by midline and by hemispheric regions. The midline cerebellum is involved in maintaining posture, balance, and gait, while the cerebellar hemispheres control the range, force, and direction of voluntary movements. The midline cerebellum is tested by observing the patient's posture and gait and by the heel-to-shin maneuver, in which the patient runs his heel lightly down his shin as smoothly as possible. The cerebellar hemispheres are tested by having the patient perform rapid alternating movements, such as rapidly pronating and supinating the hands, and by the finger-to-nose maneuver, in which the patient alternately touches his finger to his nose and to the examiner's finger.

Cerebellar disease is characterized by changes in posture and voluntary movement, which take a number of forms. Midline cerebellar disease affects mainly the axial musculature, resulting in difficulty in maintaining upright posture and a wide-based, unsteady gait (ataxic gait). Hemispheric cerebellar disease affects mainly the movement of the upper extremities. Dysmetria is indicated by inaccuracy of movements, classically with overshooting the target in the finger-to-nose maneuver. Ataxia on the finger-to-nose maneuver is characterized by a side-to-side oscillation that becomes progressively worse as the finger approaches the target. Dyssynergia refers to the absence of smooth coordination of multiple muscles, resulting in a jerky and disjointed movement. Dysdiadochokinesia is sloppiness in the execution of rapid alternating movements. Eye movements are also commonly affected by cerebellar lesions.

The basal ganglia are involved in regulating muscle tone and in the automatic execution of learned motor plans (Marsden, 1982). Basal ganglia disease produces a variety of abnormalities in tone (dystonia), movement (dyskinesia), and behavior, which to a certain extent are determined by the nature of the underlying disease. The most common disorder is Parkinson's disease, which produces bradykinesia, a fairly slow to-and-fro pill-rolling type of tremor most prominent in the distal upper extremities, and either plastic or cogwheel rigidity. Plastic rigidity (also known as lead pipe rigidity) is a constant resistence to slow passive movement, very much like the feeling of bending the old lead vent pipes. Cogwheel rigidity is a fine ratchety resistance to passive movement. Other types of movement disorders and common associated disease processes are described in Table 5.3.

CLINICAL EXAMPLES

Figures 5.1 through 5.3 are examples of neurologic examinations in three commonly encountered neurological disorders: cerebral infarct, tumor, and degenerative disease. The neurologist's findings are presented in the left column of each figure, using the symbols and shorthand with which results are recorded in the medical record; a translation of the findings is presented in the right column. There is no universally accepted standard for recording the neurological exam, but most of the abbreviations and figures presented here are in common usage. Familiarity with these conventions and with the rationale for the exam presented in previous sections should equip the reader to understand most neurologists' reports.

OTHER DIAGNOSTIC TECHNIQUES IN NEUROLOGY

A properly conducted neurological exam provides the clinician with the information needed to form one or more hypotheses concerning differential diagnosis. The neurologist can then order the tests that will provide the additional data necessary to reach a definitive diagnosis. In choosing such tests, the clinician considers the risks as well as potential benefits. For example, a history of episodic right-sided numbness and weakness, exam findings of a left carotid bruit (a systolic murmur heard at the root of the neck but not at the aortic area), and mild naming deficits might lead to the suspicion of left carotid artery disease. The physician may order an arteriogram to confirm and localize vascular disease, recognizing that while some mortality and morbidity is associated with the procedure, the patient may benefit from surgical treatment if the lesion can be better specified.

The remainder of this section will provide brief overviews of the methodology and utility of the more commonly used neurological diagnostic procedures.

Electroencephalography

The electroencephalogram (EEG) measures cerebral electrical activity by summating the electrical potentials from a relatively large population of neurons that lie beneath electrodes placed on the skull. The electrodes are usually placed in standard locations over the entire cranium, using skull landmarks in accordance with the international 10–20 system. In this system, the letter designates the lobe and the number the side over which the electrode is situated (odd for left, even for right). Thus, electrode F3 is located over the left frontal lobe.

In a normal resting adult EEG, the wave forms that appear in any of the electrode pair tracings (constituting one channel of the polygraph) are limited to alpha (8–13 Hz) and beta (> 13 Hz) frequencies. The slower theta (4–7 Hz) and delta (0–3 Hz) frequencies are usually indicative of pathology when present in the waking record, although they occur in large proportions of normal children and 10–15% of normal adults. Additional abnormalities include epileptic spikes, asymmetries between the hemispheres, focal slowing, and diffuse alterations in background rhythms. Sleep deprivation, flashing photic stimulation, and hyperventilation are commonly used to provoke seizure activity.

The EEG provides little information regarding etiology, and all such inferences are made indirectly. Today, the EEG is most useful in the evaluation of seizure disorders, providing data bearing on both the presence and type of epilepsy. Generalized disorders of attentional systems, whether of metabolic or structural origin, produce generalized slowing of background rhythms. With reference to brain structures, the EEG is of relatively little value in assessing the brainstem or cerebellum unless lesions in these areas impact on attentional systems. The EEG typically demonstrates focal slowing over cortical infarctions and tumors, with less dramatic changes with subcortical lesions. Subdural hematomas produce unilateral suppression of the background and loss of voltage. However, computed tomography (CT) has largely displaced the EEG in the evaluation of such lesions. Nevertheless the EEG may also be quite useful, in combination with a careful examination of higher cortical function, in discriminating cortical from subcortical disease in the stroke patient—a crucial therapeutic distinction that often cannot be made on the basis of the CT scan alone.

Recently an electrophysiological recording technique known as evoked potentials (EPs) has been developed. A computer repeatedly records a digitized, time-locked form of the cortical potential evoked by a sensory stimulus (e.g., a light flash, a click, or a small shock). In the process of summing hundreds or thousands of repetitions, the random EEG activity is averaged out and the tiny response evoked by the stimulus is amplified. The early components of EPs, occurring in the first 10 msec (auditory) to 130 msec (visual), are used by neurologists to detect clinically occult subcortical lesions (Dorfman, 1983). Unfortunately, EPs have been clearly useful in only one disease—multiple sclerosis. Certain late components (130–1000 msec) are associated with selective attention and other higher cortical processes and are therefore of special interest to neuropsychologists. Methods have recently been developed for mapping the topographical distribution of these EP components (Morihisa, Duffy, & Wyatt, 1983). These methods show promise for research on localization of these higher functions. However, the limited clinical usefulness and technical complexity of such measures make it highly unlikely that late component recording or mapping will ever become a standardized, widely available evaluative procedure (for reviews, see Hughes & Wilson, 1983; Chiappa & Ropper, 1982).

FIGURE 5.1. Sample neurological exam in a patient with a subacute embolic left posterior cerebral artery occlusion.

Notation	Interpretation
<u>SE</u>	Mental status examination.
Ⓡ -handed, HS educ WM.	Right-handed, high school educated white male.
Alert but mildly lethargic.	Responds readily but falls asleep if left alone.
OX3.	Oriented to person, place, & time.
Memory 6→, 4←, 3/3 @ 3',	Six digits forward and four backward on digit span.
remote ok.	Three out of three words recalled at three minutes.
Speech fluent but empty;	Mild comprehension & naming deficits.
↓ comprehension com-	
pound commands; ↓ naming	
low frequency items; repe-	
tition WNL.	
Clock-drawing, mapping ok;	Spatial functions normal, without neglect or
s̄ neglect, extinction.	extinction.
<u>CN</u>	Cranial nerves.
II VA 20/30 OU.	Visual acuity 20/30 both eyes.
◖ ◖	Right visual field defect, homonymous hemianopia.
Pupils 4→2	Right pupil normal size & reactive to light.
7 unreactive	Left pupil dilated & fixed.
Fundi benign.	Optic discs flat & sharp, without hemorrhage or
	exudate.
III, IV, VI Ⓛ 3rd palsy,	Inability to look to right voluntarily, abnormal
Ⓡ gaze paresis, ↓ pursuit	tracking of moving objects to left.
to Ⓛ	
V ↓ Ⓡ corneal, ↓ pp, st Ⓡ	Reduced right corneal reflex and ability to
face.	detect pinprick and simple touch on right face.
VII Ⓡ UMN paresis.	Facial weakness due to right upper motor
	neuron lesion.
VIII AA intact. Weber ML.	Auditory acuity normal. Weber test reported
	at midline, not lateralized.
IX, X ↓ shrug, ↓ head turn to	Reduced shrug and ability to turn head to right.
Ⓡ	
XII tongue → Ⓡ	Tongue deviates to right.

FIGURE 5.1. (*continued*)

Sensory

+ 1° modalities and graphes-   Decreased sensation in all primary modalities and
thesia (R).   in secondary modality of graphesthesia on right.

Motor

(R)HP, A>L, D>P, E>F.   Right hemiparesis, arm greater than leg, distal
                                    greater than proximal, extensors greater than
                                    flexors.

↓ FMM on (R), ↑ tone on (R).   Degraded fine motor movement and increased
                                    resting tone on right.

Cerebellar

FTN nl on (L).   Finger-to-nose maneuver normal on testable side.
Gait: falls to (R), circum-   Abnormal gait with falling to right & turning foot
ducts to R .   inward to right.

Reflexes

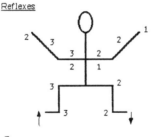 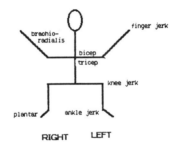

S̄ release   **RIGHT**   **LEFT**

                                    Hyperactive deep tendon reflexes and abnormal
                                    upgoing toes (extensor plantar response) on
                                    right. No frontal release signs.

Comment: The patient displayed mild arousal and concentration problems typical of impairment of function in the midbrain reticular formation. His language deficits (comprehension and naming poor, with intact repetition and fluent, empty spontaneous language) are characteristic of anomic aphasia and suggest a posterior left hemisphere lesion. Cranial nerve exam revealed gaze and pursuit deficits indicated supranuclear involvement of eye movement pathways; pupillary abnormalities and impairment of left-eye movement indicate a left 3rd nerve palsy; facial sensory and motor deficits, decreasing shrug and head turn, deviated tongue indicate supranuclear CN 5, 7, 11, 12 palsies. Right-field defect, decreased right-body sensation, right hemiparesis, gait disturbance, and abnormal right reflexes indicate left cerebral lesion. CT scan later revealed infarcted areas in the left occipital cortex, portions of the left inferior parietal lobule, the inferior left temporal lobe, the left cerebral peduncle, and the left third nerve. Deep tendon reflexes have become hyperactive as the lesion becomes chronic.

FIGURE 5.2. Sample neurological exam in a patient with a large left frontal lobe tumor.

Notation	Interpretation
Mental Status:	
Alert but easily distracted. Moderately uncooperative, requiring miltiple repetitions of commands before complying. Can perform only simple tasks, with mild tendency to perseverate and difficulty in maintaining set.	A deficit in control of attention, with indiscriminate shifts to other stimuli. Degradation in goal-oriented behavior leading to lack of cooperation and perseveration.
OXO. Poor FON.	Completely disoriented. Poor fund of knowledge indicated by failure to monitor ongoing activity (e.g. current events, television programs).
Language: Little spontaneous output, cannot provide coherent hx. No aphasic deficits in grammar, repetition, naming, no paraphasic errors.	Language itself is normal, but there is a reduced quantity and difficulty in organizing language to efficiently convey concepts, resulting in poor history.
Memory: 4→, 0/3 @ 3', poor remote.	Digit span four forward, no words recalled out of three at three minutes.
s̄ gross neglect. Other functions untestable.	Without apparent neglect.
C̲N̲ II VF FTC. VA NT. PERRLA. Ⓑ early papilledema.	Visual fields full to confrontation. Visual acuity not tested. Pupils equal, round, reactive to light and accomodation. Bilateral swelling of optic nerve head.
III, IV, VI EOM's full s̄ nystagmus.	Extraoccular movements normal, without nystagmus.
V Corneals =, Sensation intact.	Corneal reflexes symmetric, facial sensation normal.
VII Symmetric.	Normal facial movement.
VIII AA intact.	Auditory acuity normal.
IX, X Uvula ML, gag intact.	ML - midline.
XI shrug, head turn nl.	nl - normal limits.
XII ML, moves well.	

FIGURE 5.2. (*continued*)

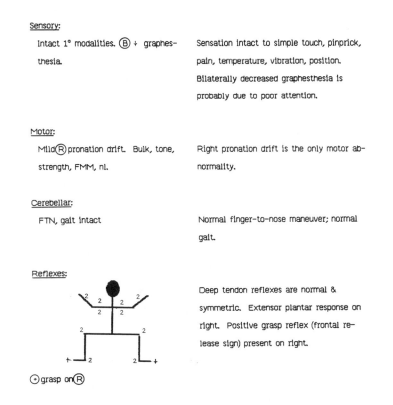

Sensory:

Intact 1° modalities. Ⓑ ↓ graphes-thesia.

Sensation intact to simple touch, pinprick, pain, temperature, vibration, position. Bilaterally decreased graphesthesia is probably due to poor attention.

Motor:

Mild Ⓡ pronation drift. Bulk, tone, strength, FMM, nl.

Right pronation drift is the only motor abnormality.

Cerebellar:

FTN, gait intact

Normal finger-to-nose maneuver; normal gait.

Reflexes:

Deep tendon reflexes are normal & symmetric. Extensor plantar response on right. Positive grasp reflex (frontal release sign) present on right.

⊕ grasp on Ⓡ

Comment: Hard neurologic signs (early papilledema, a right pronation drift, a right extensor plantar response) are relatively few but ominous. This patient has increased intracranial pressure and can be expected to deteriorate fairly rapidly as he begins to herniate. The easy distractibility, perseveration, lack of cooperation, disorganized language, and failure to monitor current events are typical of frontal impairment.

Computed Tomographic Scan

The computed tomographic (CT) scan is a relatively new imaging technique that allows the display of cross-sectional images of the brain. The technique involves directing an x-ray beam through the brain, beginning at a level that includes the orbit and brainstem. The radiation that emerges is absorbed by a detector on the opposite side of the brain. The emitter and detector are rotated around the brain section, a complex computer algorithm transforms the x-ray absorption data into density measurements, and these measurements are then displayed as a two dimensional image of the brain "slice." The CT scanner

FIGURE 5.3. Sample neurological exam in a patient with Alzheimer's disease of one-to-two years' duration.

Notation	Interpretation
Mental Status:	
Alert, Ⓡ handed, 2 yr college educ., pleasant, cooperative.	Normal level of arousal.
O x place & year.	Oriented as to place and year, but not to date.
Memory 0/3 at 3', 5→, remote fair. FON poor.	Remembered none of 3 objects at 3 minutes, digit span 5 forward, some deterioration in remote memory.
Language: good repetition; empty speech, very poorly organized; ↓ naming c̄ occ verbal para-phasias. ↓ comprehension compound commands. Calc: simple additions only. Praxis: persistent BPO errors. Thurstone:F:3. Cannot map, poor construction.	Anomic aphasia with occasional word-substitution errors. Calculations inappropriately poor for degree of education. Mild-to-moderate apraxia, with body-part-as-object errors. Word list generation: three words beginning with F in one minute. Severe spatial deficits.
C̱Ṉ 2 - 12 intact.	No cranial nerve abnormalities.
Sensory:	
Intact 1° modalities.	Sensation to primary modalities intact.
Ⓑ mildly ↓ graphesthesia.	Graphesthesia does not appear as good as it should in someone with this education.
Motor:	
Nl bulk, tone, strength, FMM s̄ drift.	Normal bulk, tone, strength, fine motor movement without drift.
Cerebellar:	
FTN, gait intact.	Finger-to-nose maneuver, gait normal.
Reflexes:	
2+, symmetric.	Normal deep tendon reflexes.
Ⓑ grasp, ⊕ snout, suck.	Frontal release signs present bilaterally.

then moves up to a higher level and repeats the process, producing a series of cross-sections encompassing the entire brain, from the base of the skull to the vertex. The patient is sometimes injected with contrast material that makes certain lesions (e.g., most tumors) more radiodense, producing a distinct image on the CT scan.

The CT scan has had a tremendous impact on neurological diagnosis because it is a relatively risk-free procedure capable of imaging most space-occupying lesions, infarcts, hemorrhages, and other structural changes in the brain with a simplicity and clarity unimaginable with previously available procedures such as the brain scan, cerebral angiogram, and pneumoencephalogram. Technological improvements in new scanners have greatly improved resolution, allowing imaging of subtle abnormalities. Some limitations remain, however, and the CT scan is relatively insensitive to small lesions near bone, recent infarcts, and disease processes that do not cause measureable changes in density.

There are a number of excellent atlases that can aid in correlating CT scan images with actual brain structures (e.g., Gado, Hanaway, & Frank, 1979; Matsui & Hirano, 1978), but precise localization of cortical lesions still remains a difficult task, even for the experienced neuroradiologist. Two systems have been developed to improve mapping of cortical lesions for purposes of neuropsychological research. One system, designed for lesion localization in aphasia, involves locating ventricular landmarks on the CT scan that are reliably related to language zones of the left hemisphere (Naeser, 1983). For example, in a CT scan done at about a 20 degree angle to the orbitomeatal line, Broca's area is directly lateral to the frontal horns of the lateral ventricles in the CT section, which also includes the Sylvian fissure, third ventricle, and quadrigeminal cistern. The involvement of other language-related structures, including Wernicke's area, the supramarginal gyrus, and the angular gyrus, can likewise be determined on other CT scan cuts by reference to the location of the lesion relative to ventricular landmarks. This system is of limited usefulness in more superior lesions that extend beyond the cuts in which the ventricles are displayed.

A second system that has more general utility has been developed by Mazzocchi and Vignolo (1978). This method involves determining the angle of the CT scan cuts by locating bony landmarks in the base of the skull. The anterior-to-posterior extent of the lesion is then measured on each cut, a proportional calculation is made, and the lesion is mapped on a standard

----

Comment: Although the formal neurological exam reveals little, the mental status examination is fairly typical of mid-stage Alzheimer's disease, demonstrating severe impairment of recent memory, moderate cognitive dysfunction, but minimal behavioral evidence of intentional dysfunction. In conjunction with a history of loss of skills, getting lost, mildly inappropriate behavior, poor memory for names and phone numbers, this exam is nearly diagnostic.

lateral diagram of the brain. This method can be modified by using a scout scan to determine the CT scan angle more precisely.

Nuclear Magnetic Resonance Scan

The nuclear magnetic resonance (NMR) scan (often called MRI for magnetic resonance imaging) is a new scanning technique based upon principles similar to the CT scan. However, the ultimate source of information in the NMR is not tissue density (and hence x-ray absorption), as in the CT, but rather the relative ease with which the direction of the axis of spin of hydrogen nuclei aligned in a large magnetic field can be reversed. Alternatively, fluorine, phosphorus, and any of several other elements may be used. The ease of reversal is determined by what compounds the average hydrogen ion is in within a given small cube of brain, which is related to the structural and physiological characteristics of the tissue. The NMR provides important advantages over CT scanning, including better image quality, especially near bone; sensitivity to largely physiological processes, such as demyelinated plaques in multiple sclerosis; and no requirement for radiation exposure or injection of contrast material. It is likely that hydrogen NMR scanners will largely supplant CT scanners over the next ten years. Phosphorus NMR scanners are less likely to become generally available because much greater power is required due to the scarcity of phosphorus relative to hydrogen. However, phosphorus scanners hold tremendous promise because their scans will be based upon local energy metabolism within the brain (for further discussion, see Buonanno, Kistler, DeWitt, Pykett, & Brady, 1983; Pykett, Newhouse, Buonanno, et al., 1982).

Arteriogram

The arteriogram (or angiogram) provides information on the location and integrity of cerebral blood vessels. In an ordinary x-ray or CT scan, cerebral vessels are not normally visible because they do not differ in radiodensity from surrounding tissue. In the arteriogram a radiodense contrast material is injected and a series of x-rays are taken as the contrast medium passes through vessels serving the brain, allowing them to be imaged on anterior and lateral views. Either the anterior circulation (anterior and middle cerebral arteries, filled via the carotids) or posterior circulation (basilar, posterior cerebral, and cerebellar arteries, filled via the vertebrals) can be imaged on a single series by injecting the contrast medium into the appropriate vascular system. Space-occupying lesions can be detected by observing their displacement of vessels from their normal position. Reduction in blood flow through vessels is revealed by narrowing (stenosis) of the vessels, and blockage is revealed by absence of vessels on the arteriogram. Today the cerebral arteriogram is most useful in evaluating diseases directly affecting blood vessels (such as atherosclerosis, vasculitis, arteriovenous malformations, and aneurysms) and in the detection or localization of lesions in regions where the CT scan is inherently inadequate, such as in the deep midline regions of the brain in the vicinity of the midbrain and in areas adjacent to bone.

A relatively new development in imaging cerebrovascular structures is digital subtraction angiography (DSA). In DSA the region of interest is x-rayed before the contrast material is injected, the flouroscopic images are converted to digital data, and this so-called masked image is stored for later analysis. The subsequent images taken while the contrast medium flows through the vessels are also digitized. The masked image is then digitally subtracted from the contrast images, resulting in clear, "unmasked" images of the blood vessels. DSA has some advantages over conventional angiography, including better contrast sensitivity allowing lower and safer doses. However, a number of problems, such as relatively poor spatial resolution and sensitivity to motion artifact, limit the clinical utility of DSA at present (Furlan, Weinstein, Little, & Modic, 1983).

Other Neurologic Procedures

Lumbar puncture is a procedure in which a needle is inserted into the spinal canal to withdraw cerebrospinal fluid (CSF) for laboratory examination. The CSF becomes abnormal in a wide variety of neurological diseases, but CSF evaluation is most useful in infectious diseases (meningitis, encephalitis, syphilis), multiple sclerosis, subarachnoid hemorrhage, and with meningeal involvement by cancer. In certain instances, radiographic contrast medium is injected into the spinal canal, which permits conventional x-ray imaging of the entire spinal canal and spinal cord to detect structural processes (myelography) or CT imaging of the spinal cord or posterior fossa (CT cisternography). A radioactive isotope may also be instilled into the lumbar subarachnoid space, followed by gamma-scanning to evaluate the pattern of CSF flow, as in suspected normal pressure hydrocephalus.

SUMMARY

The goal of this chapter has been to improve the reader's ability to understand and utilize the information contained in reports of the neurological exam and other neurodiagnostic procedures. Toward this end, we have emphasized the clinical importance of abnormal findings and the procedures of special interest to neuropsychologists, such as mental status assessment and lesion mapping. Neuropsychology is an interdisciplinary area, and quality research and clinical work can only come with thorough familiarity with the strengths and limitations of associated fields. Although space did not permit detailed discussion of many topics, it is hoped that the reader will be encouraged to pursue further knowledge of clinical neurology. Clinicians who make the effort to learn about behavioral neurology are likely to find these techniques particularly useful in bedside assessment, especially in cases where complex equipment and time-consuming procedures are impractical; in assessment of patients who are unable to cooperate with psychometric testing; and in delineating the specific deficits underlying failure on more complex tests.

REFERENCES

Benson, D. F., & Geschwind, N. (1971). Aphasia and related cortical disturbances. In A. B. Baker & L. H. Baker (Eds.), *Clinical neurology.* New York: Harper & Row.

Benton, A. L., Hamsher, K. D., Varney, N. R., & Spreen, O. (1983). *Contributions to neuropsychological assessment: A clinical manual.* New York: Oxford University Press.

Ben-Yishay, Y., Gerstman, L., Diller, L., & Haas, A. (1970). Prediction of rehabilitation outcomes from psychometric parameters in left hemiplegics. *Journal of Consulting and Clinical Psychology, 34,* 436–441.

Buonanno, F. S., Kistler, J. P., DeWitt, L. D., Pykett, I. L., & Brady, T. J. (1983). Proton (^{1}H) nuclear magnetic resonance (NMR) imaging in stroke syndromes. *Neurology Clinics, 1,* 243–262.

Chiappa, K. H., & Ropper, A. H. (1982). Evoked potentials in clinical medicine. *New England Journal of Medicine, 306,* 1205–1210.

Cummings, J. L., & Benson, D. F. (1983). *Dementia: A clinical approach.* Boston: Butterworths.

DeJong, R. N. (1979). *The neurologic examination* (4th ed.). Philadelphia: Lippincott.

Demeyer, W. (1980). *Technique of the neurologic examination: A programmed text.* New York: McGraw-Hill.

Diller, L., Ben-Yishay, Y., Gerstman, L. F., Goodkin, R., Gordon, W., & Weinberg, J. (1974). *Studies in cognition and rehabilitation in hemiplegia.* New York: New York University Medical Center, Institute of Rehabilitation Medicine.

Dorfman, L. J. (1983). Sensory evoked potentials: Clinical applications in medicine. *Annual Review of Medicine, 34,* 473–489.

Furlan, A. J., Weinstein, M. A., Little, J. R., & Modic, M. T. (1983). Digital subtraction angiography in the evaluation of cerebrovascular disease. *Neurology Clinics, 1,* 55–72.

Gado, M., Hanaway, J., & Frank, R. (1979). Functional anatomy of the cerebral cortex by computed tomography. *Journal of Computer Assisted Tomography, 3,* 1–19.

Geschwind, N. (1975). The apraxias: Neural mechanisms of disorders of learned movement. *American Scientist, 63,* 188–195.

Gilroy, J., & Meyer, J. S. (1979). *Medical neurology* (3rd ed.). New York: Macmillan.

Golden, C. J., Strider, F. D., Strider, M. A., Moore, G. G., & Gust, W. G. (1979). Neuropsychological effects of acute syphilitic involvement of the central nervous system: A case report. *Clinical Neuropsychology, 1,* 24–28.

Hecaen, H., & Albert, M. L. (1978). *Human neuropsychology.* New York: Wiley.

Heilman, K. M. (1979). Neglect and related disorders. In K. M. Heilman & E. Valenstein (Eds.), *Clinical neuropsychology* (pp. 268–307). New York: Oxford University Press.

Heilman, K. M., & Valenstein, E. (1979). Mechanisms underlying the unilateral neglect syndrome. *Annals of Neurology, 5,* 166–170.

Heilman, K. M., & Watson, R. T. (1977). The neglect syndrome—a unilateral defect of the orienting response. In S. Harnard (Ed.), *Lateralization in the nervous system.* New York: Academic Press.

Hughes, J. R., & Wilson, W. P. (1983). *EEG and evoked potentials in psychiatry and behavioral neurology.* Boston: Butterworths.

Jones-Gotman, M., & Milner, B. (1977). Design fluency: The invention of nonsense drawings after focal cortical lesions. *Neuropsychologia, 15,* 653–674.

Luria, A. R. (1980). *Higher cortical functions in man.* New York: Basic Books.

Malloy, P. F., & Webster, J. S. (1981). Detecting mild brain impairment using the Luria-Nebraska Neuropsychological Battery. *Journal of Consulting and Clinical Psychology, 49,* 768–770.

Malloy, P. F., Webster, J. S., & Russell, W. (1985). Tests of Luria's frontal lobe syndromes. *International Journal of Clinical Neuropsychology, 7,* 88–95.

Marsden, C. D. (1982). The mysterious motor function of the basal ganglia: The Robert Watenberg lecture. *Neurology, 32,* 514–539.

Matsui, R., & Hirano, A. (1978). *An atlas of the human brain for computerized tomography.* New York: Igaku-Shoin.

Mazzocchi, F., & Vignolo, L. A. (1978). Computer assisted tomography in neuro-psychological research: A simple procedure for lesion mapping. *Cortex, 14,* 136–144.

Milner, B. (1964). Some effects of frontal lobectomy in man. In J. M. Warren and K. Akert (Eds.), *The frontal granular cortex and behavior* (pp. 313–334). New York: McGraw-Hill.

Morihisa, J. M., Duffy, F. H., & Wyatt, R. J. (1983). Brain electrical activity mapping (BEAM) in schizophrenic patients. *Archives of General Psychiatry, 40,* 719–728.

Naeser, M. A. (1983). CT scan localization in cortical and subcortical aphasias. In A. Kertesz (Ed.), *Localization in neuropsychology* (pp. 63–120). New York: Academic Press.

Pykett, I. L., Newhouse, J. H., Buonanno, F. S., Brady, T. J., Goldman, M. R., Kistler, J. P., & Pohost, G. M. (1982). Principles of nuclear magnetic resonance imaging. *Radiology, 143,* 157–168.

Springer, S. P., & Deutsch, G. (1981). *Left brain, right brain.* San Francisco: W. H. Freeman.

Strub, R. L., & Black, F. W. (1977). *The mental status examination in neurology.* Philadelphia: F. A. Davis.

Van Allen, M. W., & Rodnitzsky, R. L. (1981). *Pictoral manual of neurologic tests* (2nd ed.). Chicago: Year Book Medical Publishers.

Watson, R. T., Valenstein, E., & Heilman, K. M. (1981). Thalamic neglect. *Archives of Neurology, 38,* 501–506.

6

The Halstead–Reitan Neuropsychological Test Battery

Ralph M. Reitan and
Deborah Wolfson

THEORY AND RATIONALE OF THE BATTERY

Any battery of tests that assesses human brain–behavior relationships must have three components: (1) content, or measurement of the types of psychological functions represented by the brain; (2) measurement strategies that permit application of the results to individual subjects; and (3) validation of the measurements through formal research procedures, with respect to clinical evaluations and applications.

Types of Brain-Related Functions

A neuropsychological test battery must be able to measure the full range of behavioral functions subserved by the brain. This aim is probably impossible to achieve completely, but we can measure many appropriate brain-related abilities. Historically the approach has been to evaluate persons with cerebral lesions, identify their deficits, and infer normal brain–behavior relationships by comparing persons with cerebral damage to persons who presumably have normal brains. The basic approach in neuropsychology, then, has been to relate consistent evidence of impairment to increasingly precise descriptions of underlying neuropathology.

In the early phases of such research the method generally used was to develop a "test" of brain damage. As more detailed investigations progressed, however, it became quite clear that the brain was a remarkably complex organ in terms of the behaviors that it subserved, and a series of tests would be necessary even to approximate the extensive range of strengths and weaknesses manifested by any single brain.

Another significant problem arose with the inferential procedure—comparisons of damaged and normal brains. First, there was undoubtedly a wide range of variation among normal brains in both level and structure of abilities. Imposed on this initial realization that normal brains vary considerably was the definite possibility that two brains sustaining similar damage might not demonstrate exactly the same behavioral deficits. Finally, using brain damage as the starting point for determining the characteristics of normal brains required that "brain damage" be assessed in terms of what it constituted. Studies of persons with various types of lesions, placed in different locations, occurring at different times and at different ages, made it quite clear that brain lesions showed a great deal of variability. Thus, researchers faced a very complicated situation and recognized that the difficulties implicit in validly describing the behavioral correlates of an individual brain were immense. It was apparent that procedures had to be standardized before any progress could be made. Since both normal and pathological brains were extremely variable, and since behavior was widely variable from one individual to another, scientists were unsure about just which behaviors should be measured. Some investigators, implicitly assuming that "brain damage is brain damage," elected to principally study only one type of lesion. This procedure allowed the researcher to vary the behavioral measurements and pursue initial findings in increasingly refined detail.

The alternative method was to develop a standardized neuropsychological test battery and administer that battery to patients with different types of brain lesions. In order to develop a valid and reliable neuropsychological test battery, certain procedures must be followed. Initially, many organizational problems must be solved, such as having patients with brain lesions available for testing; obtaining careful independent descriptions of the patients' brain lesions through the cooperation of neurologists, neurological surgeons, and neuropathologists; securing money and space to conduct examinations; and attending to the administrative details that are always present with large-scale research projects. It was necessary to study thousands of patients with brain lesions, correlate their test results with independent neurological data, and compare their performances to results obtained from control subjects. A standardized battery was developed and used so that the independent variables (brain lesions) could be varied while the dependent variables (neuropsychological test results) were held constant.

Another problem in developing a neuropsychological test battery concerned identifying *brain-related* variables as compared with behavioral manifestations that were principally dependent upon other types of influences. It is well recognized that a person's chronological age, education, socioeconomic status, medical history, personality, specific skills, and the host of variables that determine human individuality are all factors that contribute to an individual's psychological performance. It is not necessary to review the arguments of debate on the genetic-versus-environmental determinants of intelligence; we do, however, have to determine which aspects of psychological test results relate specifically to the biological condition of the brain. We have found that the best way to answer this question has been to examine carefully an individual's neuropsychological test data and, from that information, predict the neurological status. To implement this procedure data were collected on thousands of patients using a three-step process: (1) administering a comprehensive battery of neuropsychological tests to the patient without knowing any of the patient's neurological findings; (2) making a written prediction of the patient's neurological status based solely on his or her neuropsychological test results; and (3) comparing the neurological diagnosis with the neuropsychological test results.

Using this procedure, we have learned that certain variables contribute little to neurological conclusions (even though they may serve as comparison variables in certain respects), whereas other combinations of test results are of unequivocal significance. This procedure has permitted us to gradually refine clinical interpretation of results on individual subjects to a high degree of accuracy, as will be illustrated later.

Certain neuropsychological test data are particularly helpful in determining whether brain damage is present; other test results are especially useful for lateralizing and localizing cerebral damage; certain patterns of results relate to generalized or diffuse cerebral damage; other test results, particularly as they reflect the entire configuration of data, are used to differentiate the chronic, static lesion from the recent acutely destructive or rapidly progressive lesion; and still different findings aid the interpreter in deciding whether the cerebral damage was sustained during the developmental years or adulthood.

One can readily see that in addition to formal, controlled research studies (the type usually published in the literature) there are challenging tasks that involve development of valid clinical interpretation of results for individual subjects. Achieving this aim required the development of a test battery that represented at least a reasonable approximation of the behavioral correlates of brain function.

CONCEPTUAL MODEL OF THE BATTERY

The efforts to design a comprehensive set of neuropsychological measures led to a conceptual model of brain functions represented by the Halstead–Reitan Neuropsychological Test Battery. The battery consists of tests in five categories: (1) input measures; (2) tests of verbal abilities; (3) measures of spatial, sequential, and manipulatory abilities; (4) tests of abstraction, reasoning, logical analysis, and concept formation; and (5) output measures. The tests cover a broad range of difficulty: both very simple and quite complex tasks are included. Attention, concentration, and memory are distributed throughout the tests in the battery, just as they appear to occur in the tasks that people face in everyday living. Many of the tests require immediate problem-solving capabilities, others depend upon stored information, and some require simple perceptual skills that focus principally upon the sensory modalities of vision, hearing, and touch.

The tests in the Halstead–Reitan Battery that provide information regarding sensory integrity have also been designed or selected to give information regarding cerebral functioning. For example, rather than performing a test of tactile sensitivity that depends exclusively on receptor structures, we use tests (e.g., Tactile Finger Recognition) that also require a degree of cerebral cortical discrimination.

To aid in understanding the various complexities of central processing, the battery reflects a hierarchy of brain-related abilities. The first level of central processing represents attention, concentration, and memory (the ability to scan a range of prior experiences for comparison with immediate input) and can be identified as the "registration phase." The limiting point occurs at this level in some patients who have severe deficits.

After registering input material, the next step in central processing involves the specialized or differential functions of the cerebral hemispheres and depends upon the content of the test material. Some verbal tasks will stress the left cerebral hemisphere much less than others. Naming the capital of Italy, for example, is as much a verbal task as are responses to items on the Word-Finding test (Reitan, 1972). Nevertheless, many persons with significant left cerebral lesions who could name the capital of Italy have performed extremely poorly on the Word-Finding test. The difference concerns the extent to which the particular test item or procedure permeates the entire model. If the verbal task does not require involvement at the highest level of central processing (abstraction, reasoning, logical analysis, and concept formation), the damaged left cerebral hemisphere will be able to perform relatively well compared to normal expectations. However, if the verbal task requires a substantial element of concept formation and reasoning skills, the compromised left cerebral hemisphere will perform poorly. Of course, the damage may be so severe or in such a location that it will cause obvious impairment in specific language functions (aphasia), and such information would aid the interpreter in localizing the lesion.

The same types of considerations apply to right cerebral damage and impairment in the area of spatial, sequential, and manipulatory skills. Some patients with very serious or posteriorly located lesions in the right cerebral hemisphere will show evidence of constructional dyspraxia even when copying such simple figures as a square, cross, or triangle. Other patients may not show striking deficits on such simple tasks, but when abstraction and reasoning are involved in the constructional process (as in the Block Design subtest of the Wechsler Scale) a distinctly deficient performance may be obtained.

A neuropsychological test battery must also include items that evaluate the highest level of central processing, reasoning, and concept formation. These skills may be relatively independent of specific content requirements. The best example of this type of measure in the Halstead–Reitan Battery is the Category test, which requires complex abilities in the areas of attention, concentration, immediate memory, recognition and differentiation of spatial configurations, use of numerical symbols as a response mechanism, and formation of concepts on the basis of observation of recurring similarities and dissimilarities in the test items. Thus, limited ability at any of the levels of central processing may be responsible for a poor performance on the Category test. It is extremely important that a neuropsychological test battery evaluate this highest level of central processing to provide information relevant to the complexity of real-life situations.

Finally, output capabilities must be assessed. The effector organs of the body, the muscles and glands, are not evaluated in detail during neuropsychological assessment. However, motor functions on each side of the body are evaluated and compared and often provide valuable information about the status of a patient's cerebral functioning.

GENERAL VERSUS SPECIFIC MEASURES OF CEREBRAL STATUS

Goodglass and Kaplan (1979) have cited the importance of including both general and specific measures of brain functions in a neuropsychological test battery. Other approaches (Luria's, for example) have concentrated heavily on specific measures and do not include tests to evaluate the highest level of central processing. The Halstead–Reitan Battery was carefully designed to include both general and specific types of measures.

Measurement Strategies

Evaluation of brain-damaged subjects has shown that it is necessary to have a number of inferential strategies to be able to draw valid conclusions about brain–behavior relationships for the individual person (Reitan, 1966, 1967). These methods of inference had never been systematically included in neuropsychological assessment before development of the Halstead–Reitan Battery.

First, it is necessary to determine how well the subject performs on each of the measures included in the battery. This approach essentially refers to level of performance and, on most of the measures, is represented by a normal distribution for non-brain-damaged subjects. Since some persons perform quite well and others perform more poorly, it clearly would not be possible to accept a level-of-performance strategy alone as a basis for diagnosing cerebral damage. In other words, there are some persons who demonstrate above-average ability levels in spite of having sustained cerebral damage and some persons with below-average ability levels who do not have cerebral damage. A level-of-performance approach represents an interindividual inferential model. It is useful for comparing subjects, but offers relatively little direct information regarding the brain functions of the individual subject. (As the reader has probably noted, this is the model used in most research studies.)

A second approach, introduced by Babcock (1930), postulated that differences in levels of performance on various tests might denote impaired brain functions, or at least a loss of efficiency in psychological performances. This approach has also been used to compute the Deterioration Quotient, based on comparison of scores from different subtests of the Wechsler Scale (Wechsler, 1955). This method represents an intraindividual comparison procedure (a comparison of the subject's own performances on various tests) and helps identify the uniqueness of an individual's ability structure. Research with the tests included in the Halstead–Reitan Battery has produced a number of intraindividual patterns that are quite useful for assessing differential functions of the brain and identifying impaired areas within the brain.

A third approach incorporated into the Halstead–Reitan Battery is the identification of specific deficits on simple tasks of the type that occur almost exclusively among brain-damaged persons. Deficits on these simple tasks may not only identify the presence of cerebral damage but also indicate areas of maximal involvement (Wheeler & Reitan, 1962). The reader should be aware, however, that this inferential strategy fails to identify a significant proportion of brain-damaged persons who do not show the specific deficit in question (false negatives).

The fourth measurement strategy used in the Halstead–Reitan Battery to identify cerebral damage is one which compares motor and sensory-perceptual performances of the same type on the two sides of the body, thus permitting inferences regarding the functional status of homologous areas of the two cerebral hemispheres. This method is also based on intraindividual comparisons, using the subject as his or her own control. When positive findings occur they may have unequivocal significance for cerebral damage. A more detailed discussion of these inferential methods can be found in a previous publication (Reitan, 1967).

REVIEW OF RESEARCH FINDINGS

We will not attempt to present an exhaustive survey of published research concerned with validation of the Halstead–Reitan Battery, but a brief review may be helpful to the reader who wishes to have a general guide to this literature.

The Halstead–Reitan Battery has probably been researched in more detail than any other set of neuropsychological tests. Through the close cooperation between neuropsychologists, neurologists, neurological surgeons, and neuropathologists it has been possible to compose groups of subjects with definite, unequivocal evidence of cerebral damage and compare these persons with subjects who have no history or present evidence of cerebral damage or disease. This approach has a tremendous advantage over research oriented toward development of constructs such as intelligence, affective disorders, emotional maturity, and so forth. In attempting to validate psychological measures against such constructs, there has been the continual criterion problem of not having an unequivocal definition of the condition being evaluated. In neuropsychology, however, it has been possible not only to identify the presence or absence of cerebral damage but also to provide more detailed information regarding localization, type, duration, and acuteness or chronicity of lesion.

The initial approach in developing the Halstead–Reitan Battery was to compare control subjects to persons known to have diversified cerebral damage (heterogeneous types of lesions in various locations) and, based on these comparisons, to identify the tests that were sensitive to the general condition of the cerebral hemispheres. Numerous reports documenting the efficacy of the Halstead–Reitan Battery have appeared in the literature (including Boll, Heaton, & Reitan, 1974; Chapman & Wolff, 1959; Doehring & Reitan, 1961a; Doehring & Reitan, 1961b; Fitzhugh, Fitzhugh, & Reitan, 1960, 1961, 1962a, 1965; Heimburger, DeMyer, & Reitan, 1964; Heimburger & Reitan, 1961; Matthews, Shaw, & Kløve, 1966; Reed & Reitan, 1962, 1963a, 1963b, 1963c; Reitan, 1955a, 1955b, 1958, 1959a, 1959b, 1960, 1964, 1970a, 1970b; Reitan & Boll, 1971; Reitan & Fitzhugh, 1971; Reitan, Reed, & Dyken, 1971; Ross & Reitan, 1955; Shure & Halstead, 1958; Vega & Parsons, 1967; Wheeler, Burke, & Reitan, 1963; Wheeler & Reitan, 1962, 1963). The above references refer to studies of adult subjects and do not include the many investigations that have been performed using the Halstead–Reitan Neuropsychological Test Battery for Older Children or the Reitan–Indiana Neuropsychological Test Battery for Younger Children.

In order to evaluate the role of the Wechsler Scales concerning general intelligence in brain–behavior relationships, a similar range of investigations had to be completed. (Studies with adult subjects include Anderson, 1950; Doehring, Reitan, & Kløve, 1961; Fitzhugh, Fitzhugh, & Reitan, 1962b; Kløve, 1959; Matthews & Reitan, 1964; Reed & Reitan, 1963c; Reitan, 1955a, 1960, 1964, 1970b; Reitan & Fitzhugh, 1971; Wheeler, Burke, & Reitan, 1963; Wheeler & Reitan, 1963.) These studies demonstrated that the Wechsler Scales were generally not as sensitive as the tests devised by Halstead.

It has been shown, however, that persons with acutely destructive left cerebral lesions usually show significant impairment on the Verbal subtests and persons with acute right hemisphere damage will frequently have poor scores on the Performance subtests. Positive correlations between the specialized or lateralized psychological correlates of brain functions and the Wechsler Scales have been reported by Anderson (1950); Reitan (1955a); Doehring, Reitan, and Kløve (1961); Fitzhugh, Fitzhugh, and Reitan (1962b); Kløve and Reitan (1958); Matthews and Reitan (1964); and Meier and French (1966). These studies with the Wechsler Scale have been summarized by Matarazzo (1972) and Kløve (1974).

Other lateralization effects based on tests in the Halstead–Reitan Battery have been reported in a number of investigations (including Doehring & Reitan, 1961a, 1961b; Heimburger & Reitan, 1961; Heimburger, DeMyer, & Reitan, 1964; Kløve & Reitan, 1958; Reitan, 1959b, 1960, 1964; Wheeler, 1964; Wheeler & Reitan, 1963; Kløve, 1959). Reitan (1964) has also studied the effects of frontal versus posterior lesions in each cerebral hemisphere. In addition, several other variables have been investigated using data from the Halstead–Reitan Battery. Studies examining the differential effects of acute and chronic cerebral damage have shown that more severe and selective losses are usually present with acute damage, presumably because the brain has not had sufficient time to reorganize its functional status (Fitzhugh, Fitzhugh, & Reitan, 1961, 1962a, 1963).

Various types of cerebral deficits have also been studied in considerable detail. They include aphasia (Reitan, 1960; Doehring & Reitan, 1961b; Heimburger & Reitan, 1961); emotional problems and their influence on cognitive deficits (Fitzhugh, Fitzhugh, & Reitan, 1961; Dikmen & Reitan, 1974a; Dikmen & Reitan, 1974b; Dikmen & Reitan, 1977a; Dikmen & Reitan, 1977b; Reitan, 1970c, 1977); epilepsy (Reitan, 1976); and sensory-perceptual losses as related to intelligence (Fitzhugh, Fitzhugh, & Reitan, 1962c).

Other investigations have evaluated and compared various kinds of neurological disorders and types of lesions, including cerebral vascular disease (Reitan, 1970b; Reitan & Fitzhugh, 1971); brain tumors (Hom & Reitan, 1982, 1984); multiple sclerosis (Ross & Reitan, 1955; Forsyth, Gaddes, Reitan, & Tryk, 1971; Reitan, Reed, & Dyken, 1971); Huntington's chorea (Boll, Heaton, & Reitan, 1974); craniocerebral trauma (Reitan, 1973; Dikmen & Reitan, 1976, 1977a, 1977b, 1978; Dikmen, Reitan, & Temkin, 1983); alcoholism (Fitzhugh, Fitzhugh, & Reitan, 1960, 1965); drug abuse (Grant, Mohns, Miller, & Reitan, 1976); mental retardation (Matthews & Reitan, 1961, 1962, 1963; Davis & Reitan, 1966, 1967; Davis, Hamlett, & Reitan, 1966; Reitan, 1967); and aging effects (Reitan, 1955c, 1962, 1967, 1970a; Fitzhugh, Fitzhugh, & Reitan, 1963, 1964; Reed & Reitan, 1962, 1963a).

Although it is not possible to review these various studies in detail here, the reader may note that extensive research has been performed to establish the validity of neuropsychological measurements in a great number of clinical conditions. For the interested researcher, there is a considerable amount of data published in the recent literature to serve as a guide for developing clinical expertise. In addition, many publications (e.g., Reitan & Davison, 1974) include interpretations of clinical cases that illustrate the procedures used in applying research findings.

INTERPRETATION OF THE BATTERY

General aspects of the approach and procedure in interpreting results for individual subjects vary somewhat from one neuropsychologist to another, but there are commonalities that can be reviewed. We should note that interpretations of results for children differ from interpretations for adults (Reitan, 1984; Reitan, 1985); the present comments will be restricted to adult interpretations.

The general procedure is first to refer to results from the Wechsler Scale in an attempt to determine the subject's previous intellectual abilities. Wechsler subtests most useful in this respect are Information, Comprehension, Similarities, and Vocabulary. If these subtest scores are low, one cannot use them as a contrast for poor scores on neuropsychological (brain-sensitive) tests. If these scores are relatively good, one can presume that circumstances in the past have been adequate to permit development of these abilities; poorer scores on tests that are more specifically sensitive to the biological condition of the brain may be subject to interpretation as evidence of impairment. The Wechsler subtests may be used for more specific aspects of interpretation as well, but only after reviewing the results obtained with the remaining tests of the Halstead–Reitan Battery.

The next step in interpretation is to review the subject's scores on the four most sensitive measures of the battery: Halstead's Impairment Index, the Category test, Part B of the Trail-Making test, and the Localization component of the Tactual Performance test. If these tests were performed poorly and Wechsler scores suggest that the person had developed relatively normal abilities in the past, a presumption may be made that the person has suffered some neuropsychological deficit resulting from brain damage; inferences of severity may also be drawn. However, each of these four measures is a general indicator and does not have significance for localization of cerebral damage, even though focal lesions (regardless of localization) and generalized or diffuse damage may have pronounced effects on the general indicators.

The third step in interpretation is evaluating the measures that relate to lateralization and localization of cerebral damage. The inferential approaches of value in this regard concern patterns and relationships among test results, the occurrence of specific signs of cerebral damage, and comparisons of performances on the two sides of the body. The tests and findings most useful for this part of the interpretation include (1) the Wechsler Scale (Verbal versus Performance scores; selective deficits on individual subtests with relation to better scores on other subtests); (2) deviant performances on one hand as compared with the other on the Tactual Performance test; (3) disparities in finger-tapping speed of the two hands; (4) the presence of dysphasia; (5) evidence of constructional dyspraxia; (6) lateralized deficits on the Sensory-Perceptual examination (bilateral tactile, auditory, and visual stimulation; tactile finger recognition; and finger-tip number-writing perception); and (7) the presence of homonymous visual field losses.

These variables constitute arrays that can differ widely for individual subjects, making it impossible to offer a simple set of rules for evaluation of the indications of lateralization and localization. Competent interpretation must necessarily depend upon experience and expertise gained through studying results for a large number of individual subjects.

The next step in the interpretation is to discern the course of the lesion. Some brain lesions are progressive in nature, others are relatively static, and some are on a course of spontaneous recovery. Inferences regarding these possibilities can be drawn from the test results. The basic approach is to effect comparisons of certain tests with others, complemented by the extent to which the test results point toward a focal cerebral lesion. Most focal lesions tend to be progressive and cause serious generalized deficits as well as specific pathognomonic signs. It is possible, of course, for a lesion to be focal and relatively static, but such a lesion would be accompanied by specific focal signs and relatively better scores on at least some of the tests that are general indicators. In persons with static conditions, we have found that the Speech–Sounds Perception test and the Seashore Rhythm test are frequently done fairly well compared to some of the more brain-sensitive tests (e.g., the Category test). Part B of the Trail-Making test is also helpful in this respect: the results on this test are often comparatively good in persons who are in a recovery phase.

The final step in diagnostic neuropsychological interpretation involves compiling all of the data and drawing inferences about the type of lesion or neurological disorder that may be present. Skill in this area obviously requires knowledge of neurology and neuropathology, and the neuropsychologist should be familiar with the major categories of neurological disease and damage. Reviews of the specific neuropsychological characteristics of various types of lesions have been published (e.g., Hom & Reitan, 1982; Hom & Reitan, 1984), and in many instances it is clinically possible not only to differentiate between categories of lesions (such as intrinsic tumors, vascular lesions, and head injuries) but even to differentiate within categories (fast vs. slowly growing intrinsic tumors).

Although the above comments refer particularly to inferences regarding the neurological condition of the brain based upon neuropsychological measurements, inferences regarding the psychological significance of behavioral deficits are equally important. In fact, neuropsychological evaluation constitutes the only rigorous method of identifying impairment of *adaptive behavior* resulting from cerebral damage. The major areas of behavior related to impaired brain functions have already been reviewed above, and the Halstead–Reitan Battery has been developed and organized to reflect these major areas. The unique value of neuropsychological interpretation is the assessment and evaluation of intraindividual ability patterns as they relate to the condition of the brain. Although neurological diagnosis can be validly established using many other techniques and methods, the psychological consequences of cerebral damage are uniquely represented by neuropsychological evaluation.

In cases of static or improving brain lesions, the potential for brain retraining is an important issue. There is a great deal of interest in this concept, representing the spirit of the present times. Promising results have been obtained with individual subjects. In fact, during the past several years a formal training program called REHABIT has been developed by Reitan and, in many instances, results with individual subjects have far exceeded the degree of improvement seen in persons who were undergoing only spontaneous recovery (Reitan & Sena, 1983). The area of brain retraining is not only immensely complex but also a recent development in neuropsychology; detailed knowledge, beyond the fact that it is possible to facilitate recovery in certain individual persons, is relatively limited at this time.

ILLUSTRATIVE INTERPRETATION
OF INDIVIDUAL CASES

The cases to be presented will emphasize the significance and validity of the Halstead–Reitan Battery in inferring the neurological nature of cerebral damage. We must point out, however, that two cases are obviously inadequate to represent either the range of variability among subjects or the clinical applications of the evaluation.

It is well known that neurological diagnostic techniques have developed rapidly during the past 15 years and that definitive identification (diagnosis) of cerebral lesions can be achieved through the use of computed tomography (CT), positron emission tomography (PET), and nuclear magnetic resonance (NMR). There is little need for neuropsychological methods to diagnose the presence of an intrinsic brain tumor. On the other hand, there is a tremendous need for valid information regarding the behavioral deficits associated with brain lesions, including intrinsic tumors, and neuropsychological examination

PATIENT: __P.H.__ AGE: __67__ SEX: __M__ EDUCATION: __16__ HANDEDNESS: __R__

__X__ WECHSLER-BELLEVUE SCALE (FORM I) *Halstead's Neuropsychological Test Battery*
____ WECHSLER ADULT
      INTELLIGENCE SCALE __ R

VIQ	104	*Category Test*	*Discontinued*
PIQ	88		
FS IQ	90	*Tactual Performance Test*	
VWS	43	Dominant hand:	10.0 (1 block in)
PWS	9	Non-dominant hand:	10.0 (0 blocks in)
Total WS	52	Both hands:	8.0 (0 blocks in)
Information	13		Total Time _____
Comprehension	11		Memory _____
Digit Span	7		Localization _____
Arithmetic	4	*Seashore Rhythm Test*	
Similarities	8	Number Correct __15__	10
Vocabulary	13		
		Speech-sounds Perception Test	
Picture Arrangement	3	Number of Errors	34
Picture Completion	4		
Block Design	1	*Finger Oscillation Test*	
Object Assembly	0	Dominant hand	52	52
Digit Symbol	1	Non-dominant hand:	37

IMPAIRMENT INDEX: __0.9__

TRAIL MAKING TEST
Part A: _120_ seconds; _1_ errors
Part B: _227_ seconds; _1_ errors   Discontinued

Strength of Grip   Not done
Dominant hand: ____ kilograms
Non-dominant hand: ____ kilograms

Miles ABC Test of Ocular Dominance   Not done
Right eye: _____ Left eye: _____

Reitan-Klove Tactile Form Recognition Test   Not done
Dominant hand: _____ seconds; _____ errors
Non-dominant hand: _____ seconds; _____ errors

Reitan-Klove Sensory Perceptual Exam
RH ____ LH ____ Both H: RH ___ LH ___
RH ____ LF ____ Both H and F: RH ___ LF ___
LH ____ RF ____ Both H and F: LH ___ RF ___

RE ____ LE ____ Both E: RE ___ LE ___

RV ____ LV ____ Both: RV ___ LV ___
____ ____   ___ ___
____ ____   ___ ___

Tactile Finger Recognition
R 1 ___ 2 ___ 3 ___ 4 ___ 5 ___
L 1 ___ 2 ___ 3 ___ 4 ___ 5 ___

Finger-tip # Writing
R 1 ___ 2 ___ 3 ___ 4 ___ 5 ___
L 1 ___ 2 ___ 3 ___ 4 ___ 5 ___

MINNESOTA MULTIPHASIC   Not done
PERSONALITY INVENTORY

?	_____	Hy	_____
L	_____	Pd	_____
F	_____	Mf	_____
K	_____	Pa	_____
		Pt	_____
Hs	_____	Sc	_____
D	_____	Ma	_____
		Si	_____

Reitan-Klove Lateral Dominance Exam
                        Not done
Show me how you:
   throw a ball   _____
   hammer a nail   _____
   cut with a knife   _____
   turn a door knob _____
   use scissors   _____
   use an eraser   _____
   write your name _____

Record time used for spontaneous
name writing:
   Preferred hand   _____ seconds
Non-Preferred hand   _____ seconds

Show me how you:
   kick a football   _____
   step on a bug   _____

FIGURE 6.1 Results of neuropsychological examination: P.H.

Copy SQUARE See	Repeat TRIANGLE
Name SQUARE	Repeat MASSACHUSETTS
Spell SQUARE	Repeat METHODIST EPISCOPAL
Copy CROSS See	Write SQUARE
Name CROSS	Read SEVEN
Spell CROSS	Repeat SEVEN
Copy TRIANGLE See	Repeat/Explain HE SHOUTED THE WARNING
Name TRIANGLE	Write HE SHOUTED THE WARNING
Spell TRIANGLE	Compute 85 − 27 =
Name BABY	Compute 17 X 3 = "54" then corrected.
Write CLOCK	Name KEY
Name FORK	Demonstrate use of KEY
Read 7 SIX 2	Draw KEY See
Read MGW	Read PLACE LEFT HAND TO RIGHT EAR Place right hand to right ear.
Reading I	Place LEFT HAND TO RIGHT EAR RH to Left ear - self-corrected.
Reading II	Place LEFT HAND TO LEFT ELBOW LH to Right elbow - self-corrected.

REITEN-KLOVE SENSORY-PERCEPTUAL EXAMINATION

(Instance indicated where stimulus was not perceived or was incorrectly perceived.)

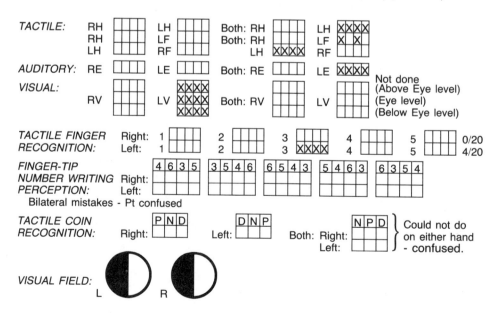

FIGURE 6.2 Reitan-Indiana Aphasia Screening Test: P.H.

is the best resource for filling this need. Identification of the behavioral correlates of such lesions is also a powerful manifestation of the validity of neuropsychological data. This is particularly true if the neuropsychological characterization of the lesion is sufficiently specific to provide unequivocal identification of the lesion in an individual case using *only* the test results.

Case #1: P.H.

Following the procedure outlined above, the first step in interpretation will be to inspect results obtained on the Wechsler Scale. At the time this man was examined the Wechsler–Bellevue Scale (Form I) was being administered. The patient earned a Verbal IQ (104) that was in the upper part of the average range and a Performance IQ (88) that was in the upper part of the low-average range (88). These values yielded a Full-Scale IQ (90) that was at the lower limit of the average range. (The reader may note that the Performance IQ seems to be quite high considering the limited credit that the patient was able to obtain on the individual Performance subtests. The inordinate age adjustment for older persons on the Wechsler–Bellevue Scale accounts for this apparent disparity).

Referring to the four Verbal subtests that generally provide the most valid information regarding the subject's prior intellectual development, we find that this man performed at the average level or above on three: Information, Comprehension, and Vocabulary. Considering the fact that the patient was a college graduate, it is likely that his score of 8 on Similarities, the fourth subtest in this group of indicators, reflects that he has suffered some degree of impairment on this test.

Of the Verbal subtests, Arithmetic is probably the most valid indicator of cerebral damage; however, compared with many of the other individual tests in the Halstead–Reitan Battery, it is not a particularly good index of brain dysfunction. In view of P.H.'s other scores, it is not surprising to see that he earned a poor score on Arithmetic as well.

The Digit Span subtest is often impaired in both brain-damaged and control subjects who are under the stress of illness and hospitalization. Therefore, this patient's score of 7 on Digit Span is not significant and does not contribute to the overall impression of his abilities that we have formulated so far.

Summarizing the results of the Verbal subtest scores, then, we can say that this man has had a relatively good intellectual level in the past, as demonstrated by his performances on measures that are most reflective of past intellectual acquisitions. P.H.'s scores on subtests requiring more immediate utilization of problem-solving skills suggest that he has experienced some diminution of these cognitive abilities.

Next, we will consider the Performance subtests of the Wechsler Scale. P.H. was able to make little progress on this section, although he did manage to

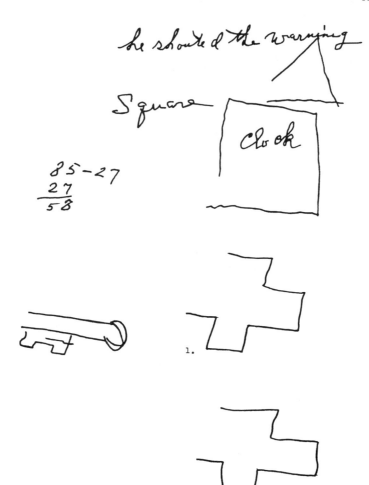

FIGURE 6.3 Drawing and writing attempts of P.H. on the Aphasia Screening Test.

score 3 points on the Picture Arrangement subtest and 4 points on the Picture Completion subtest.

On the Wechsler Scale, the Digit Symbol subtest is probably the most sensitive measure of the general effects of cerebral damage (regardless of lesion location). Picture Arrangement and Block Design are the subtests most sensitive to right cerebral damage. Not uncommonly, a person with a right cerebral lesion will have his highest Performance score on the Picture Completion subtest, demonstrating this test's low sensitivity to cerebral dysfunction.

Comparing P.H.'s pronounced deficits on the Performance subtests to the fairly good scores on the Verbal subtests, one could certainly raise a question of right cerebral damage in this man. Although not yet demonstrated in the literature, clinical experience suggests that involvement of the posterior part of the right cerebral hemisphere causes greater deficit on Performance than Verbal intelligence measures than do lesions of the right frontal lobe. In the case of this patient, results from the Wechsler Scale alone would be sufficient to question the integrity of the right cerebral hemisphere; as a general rule, though, scores on the Wechsler Scale considered by themselves are of equivocal significance.

The next step in the process of interpretation is evaluating the results on the four most sensitive measures in the Halstead–Reitan Battery. This man was severely impaired on all four of these indicators: Impairment Index—0.9; Category test—unable to do; Trails B—worked on for 227 seconds before the test was discontinued due to the patient's confusion; Tactual Performance test, Localization component—unable to do. It is apparent from these results that in spite of a well above-average Vocabulary score, this man was severely impaired in tasks that call for immediate adaptive abilities.

Considering this patient's results on these general indicators of cerebral status, it would not be surprising to find poor scores on measures that require close attention and concentration, indicating that even the first level of central processing was significantly impaired. In such a case it is likely that any lateralizing indicators will be derived from rather simple and discrete procedures and that the patient will have great difficulty with more complex tests that require continuing attention and organization of integral components and memory of one aspect of the test as compared with another (e.g., Category test and Tactual Performance test). In fact, the patient was scarcely able to make any progress at all on the Tactual Performance test. When a patient performs so poorly on all three trials of the test, no hypotheses regarding lateralization of damage can be made by comparing the performances of the two hands.

The lateralizing indicators of the battery are the next factors to be considered. P.H. demonstrated relatively few deficits related specifically to the status of the left cerebral hemisphere. He initially made an error when he responded to the arithmetic problem, 17×3. Research has documented that dyscalculia occurs about three times more frequently with left cerebral lesions than with right. Based on this mistake alone, though, it would be difficult to conclude that this patient had dyscalculia.

The patient became confused in reading "Place left hand to right ear," demonstrated this confusion when asked to perform the task, and responded incorrectly when asked to place his left hand to his left elbow. In this case one could question whether these mistakes actually constituted evidence of dyslexia and right-left confusion, or whether P.H.'s general state of confusion was sufficiently disabling to account for these errors. Although this question may not be answered unequivocally, it is clear that specific signs of left cerebral involvement were not very abundant. One might wonder whether the poor score on the Speech–Sounds Perception test represents a specific loss in the language area (particularly considering some of the good verbal subtest scores on the Wechsler Scale), but it is more likely that the requirement for close attention and continued concentration was the basis for the 34 errors on this measure. Thus, so far, the findings are not sufficient to support a hypothesis of a specific lesion of the left cerebral hemisphere.

However, a number of right cerebral deficits were identified. Besides the low Performance IQ as compared with the Verbal IQ, this patient showed distinct and definite evidence of constructional dyspraxia. He was not able to complete either the square or triangle correctly. He made fairly good progress with the cross, but when he reached the lower line of the left arm he became completely confused, did not know which way to turn, and refused to continue drawing the figure. He also had definite difficulty with the key, particularly on the left side.

Another significant sign of right cerebral damage was the finding of a left homonymous hemianopia, indicating involvement of the visual pathway on the right side at some point posterior to the optic chiasm. One can confidently infer that the geniculostriate tract was involved rather than the optic tract because of additional right cerebral indicators.

Among the findings most suggestive of right cerebral involvement were the results from the Sensory-Perceptual examination. Even though he made no mistakes in perceiving unilateral stimuli of either side, this man had great difficulty perceiving either a tactile or auditory stimulus to the left side when it was given in competition with a stimulus to the right side. Testing of perception of bilateral simultaneous visual stimuli was precluded by the left homonymous visual field loss. Although the patient did not have a great deal of difficulty on the left hand on tactile finger recognition, his only errors did occur on that side. Actually, it is quite surprising that P.H. could concentrate well enough to complete all 20 trials on his right hand without making a single error. On the more complex task of finger-tip number writing perception the patient was confused and could not respond correctly to stimuli given to either hand.

It is especially important to note that results of tests of bilateral simultaneous stimulation were positive only on the left side of the body and that not a single error, either with unilateral or bilateral simultaneous stimulation, occurred on the right side. In terms of cerebral damage, then, the lateralizing findings were quite convincing for right hemisphere dysfunction. The fact that the patient did not have difficulty in tactile finger localization on the left hand, except for one finger, should not be used to attenuate the significance of the pronounced lateralized deficit obtained with tests of bilateral simultaneous sensory stimulation. A general rule in neuropsychological interpretation is to depend upon distinct positive findings to infer brain damage and recognize that negative results, or the relative retention of premorbid abilities, may be due to many factors.

Finally, this man had normal finger-tapping speed in his right hand (52) but was comparatively slow with his left hand (37). He was still able to tap an average of 3.7 times per second with his left hand, but, expecting only about a

10% difference in favor of the preferred hand, we would have postulated that this man should have been able to tap about 4.7 times per second with his left hand.

It is important to note that when using a neuropsychological test battery all information is recorded and organized with relation to its predetermined significance. No aspect of the data is ignored. Every test must be considered, because the battery as a whole has been organized to represent cerebral functions generally and the entire cerebral cortex must be evaluated in order to gain a total picture of the individual's comparative strengths and weaknesses. The battery approach has a great advantage over other methods of evaluation because it provides a balanced evaluation of the functional status of the entire cerebral cortex for the individual subject.

Others (e.g., Christenson, 1975; Lezak, 1976) have argued that composing a battery appropriate for each individual subject, based upon the subject's complaints and the clinical judgment of the neuropsychologist, will provide an assessment for each patient that is pertinent and as economical as possible. However, if we had followed this method of evaluation and had examined the patient P.H. with only right hemisphere tests, we would never have known about the compelling nature of the right cerebral indicators as compared with the relative absence of left cerebral indicators. More importantly, perhaps, we would never have been aware of the severe generalized impairment this man was experiencing.

At this point we will summarize our findings on this patient. Considering the data from the entire battery, it was apparent that the right cerebral hemisphere was significantly involved and the lesion was of such a destructive nature that intellectual and cognitive functions were significantly deficient. It was also clear that the lesion principally involved the posterior part of the right cerebral hemisphere. Because of the slow finger-tapping speed with the left hand, we knew that the right posterior frontal area was also affected. The principal deficits on the Sensory-Perceptual examination involving tactile and auditory input suggested that the temporal and parietal lobes were areas of focal involvement. This inference was also supported by evidence of involvement of the right geniculostriate pathway, severe constructional dyspraxia, and pronounced deficits on the Performance subtests of the Wechsler Scale. Thus, there was evidence that P.H. had a large focal lesion involving the posterior part of the right cerebral hemisphere. The right cerebral deficits, as well as generalized confusion, could be produced by a lesion of this type. It did not appear that the left cerebral hemisphere was specifically involved; the overall general confusion may have been responsible for the small number of left cerebral indicators.

As a final step in interpretation, one must consider the types of lesions that could have been responsible for these findings. A critical item of information to keep in mind is that this man was not hemiplegic on his left side: he was still able to tap 3.7 times per second with his left hand. We had initially considered finger-tapping speed to be impaired on the left side; in light of the entire set of test results suggesting right cerebral damage, though, one might be amazed to find that P.H. had any finger-tapping speed at all on his left side. Persons who have suffered strokes causing severe lateralized deficits nearly always have severe motor impairments across from the damaged hemisphere (Hom & Reitan, 1982). Thus, if this man had experienced a stroke involving the right middle cerebral artery, he almost certainly would have had more severe motor impairment of the left upper extremity. Patients with intrinsic tumors sometimes have severe motor impairments corresponding with other indications of lateralized cerebral damage, but they often experience only a milder degree of deficit (Hom & Reitan, 1982; Hom & Reitan, 1984). Therefore, the relative retention of finger-tapping speed with the left hand, in spite of a degree of impairment, was a crucial finding in this case: it leaned the diagnostic conclusion toward a rapidly growing intrinsic tumor of the posterior part of the right cerebral hemisphere. On autopsy, it was confirmed that this man had a large astrocytoma, grade III, involving the right parietal–temporal occipital area.

Case #2: V.H.

This 59-year-old man was referred by an internist who had been asked to perform a complete physical examination of the patient. The internist had found no evidence of significant physical disease except for heavy drinking (and possible alcoholism) and an electrocardiogram that was reported as "borderline normal." The patient had been an outstanding salesman for a large firm for many years. V.H. felt that his difficulties had existed for about only three weeks and stated that he had tendencies toward forgetfulness, sometimes mumbled to himself, and often repeated himself. Although V.H. felt that these symptoms were of recent onset, he reported that others who worked with him had noticed these difficulties before he was aware of them himself. In fact, he brought with him a copy of a report of a physical examination that was essentially within normal limits, although the problems he complained of at the time of this examination were identified as having been of concern several months earlier. These complaints included difficulty with memory, poor taste in communication with his colleagues, and impaired business judgment. A review of these previous records indicated that the patient had been a heavy user of alcohol for many years, but, until the past six or eight months, had apparently been able to function relatively well. The internist who referred the patient for neuropsychological evaluation was concerned that the patient might have experienced some deterioration of cerebral functioning, even though objective evidence of brain disease or damage was not present in the physical or neurological examination.

This man earned a Verbal IQ that was in the upper part of the average range (106) and a Performance IQ that was in the upper part of the high-average range (119). These values yielded a Full-Scale IQ of 110, falling at the lower

PATIENT: __V.H.__ AGE: __59__ SEX: __M__ EDUCATION: __16__ HANDEDNESS: __R__

__X__ WECHSLER-BELLEVUE SCALE (FORM I)   *Halstead's Neuropsychological Test Battery*
____ WECHSLER ADULT
    INTELLIGENCE SCALE __ R

VIQ	106	*Category Test*		115
PIQ	119			
FS IQ	110	*Tactual Performance Test*		
VWS	47	Dominant hand:	11.7	
PWS	45	Non-dominant hand:	9.1	
Total WS	92	Both hands:	5.2	
Information	13			Total Time __25.9__
Comprehension	12			Memory __7__
Digit Span	7			Localization __5__
Arithmetic	9	*Seashore Rhythm Test*		
Similarities	6	Number Correct __24__		8
Vocabulary	14			
		Speech-sounds Perception Test		
Picture Arrangement	7	Number of Errors		5
Picture Completion	13			
Block Design	9	*Finger Oscillation Test*		
Object Assembly	9	Dominant hand	40	40
Digit Symbol	7	Non-dominant hand:	40	

IMPAIRMENT INDEX: __0.6__

TRAIL MAKING TEST
Part A: __37__ seconds; __0__ errors
Part B: __109__ seconds; __0__ errors   Discontinued

Strength of Grip   Not done
Dominant hand: __29.5__ kilograms
Non-dominant hand: __26.5__ kilograms

Miles ABC Test of Ocular Dominance   Not done
Right eye: __10__ Left eye: __0__

Reitan-Klove Tactile Form Recognition Test   Not done
Dominant hand: __18__ seconds; __0__ errors
Non-dominant hand: __12__ seconds; __0__ errors

Reitan-Klove Sensory Perceptual Exam
RH __0__ LH __0__ Both H: RH __0__ LH __0__
RH __0__ LF __0__ Both H and F: RH __0__ LF __0__
LH __0__ RF __0__ Both H and F: LH __0__ RF __0__

RE __0__ LE __0__ Both E: RE __0__ LE __0__

RV __0__ LV __0__ Both: RV __0__ LV __0__
   0   0   0   0
   0   0   0   0

Tactile Finger Recognition
R 1 __ 2 __ 3 __ 4 __ 5 __   0/20
L 1 __ 2 __ 3 __ 4 __ 5 __   0/20

Finger-tip # Writing
R 1 __ 2 __ 3 __ 4 __ 5 __   5/20
L 1 __ 2 __ 3 __ 4 __ 5 __   1/20

MINNESOTA MULTIPHASIC   Not done
PERSONALITY INVENTORY

?	60	Hy	60
L	66	Pd	60
F	50	Mf	61
K	57	Pa	50
		Pt	50
Hs	54	Sc	44
D	56	Ma	48
		Si	

Reitan-Klove Lateral Dominance Exam
                      Not done
Show me how you:
  throw a ball   R
  hammer a nail   R
  cut with a knife   R
  turn a door knob   R
  use scissors   R
  use an eraser   R
  write your name   R

Record time used for spontaneous
name writing:
  Preferred hand   __20__ seconds
  Non-Preferred hand __50__ seconds

Show me how you:
  kick a football   R
  step on a bug   R

No language difficulties on
Aphasia Exam.

FIGURE 6.4 Results of neuropsychological examination: V.H.

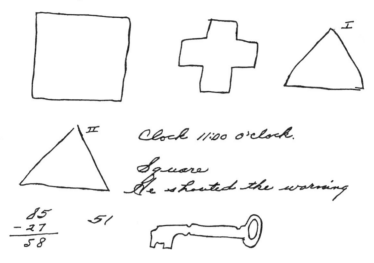

FIGURE 6.5 Drawing and writing of V.H. on the Aphasia Screening Test.

limit of the high average range. The Verbal subtests showed a considerable degree of variability: the Vocabulary score was well above average and the Similarities result was well below average. It would seem likely, on the basis of the low Similarities score, that the patient had experienced some reduction of Verbal IQ.

The distribution of scores on the Performance subtests was probably of more reliable significance with respect to impaired brain functions. The patient performed poorly on the Digit Symbol subtest, earning a score of 7. This variable is probably the most sensitive of all the Wechsler subtests to cerebral damage. In addition, the specifically poor score (7) on Picture Arrangement may well have been a reflection of cerebral dysfunction. Nevertheless, on the basis of the Wechsler Scale, it would have been difficult to draw any specific conclusion of cerebral damage. And if one had done so using the Wechsler Scale alone, the full consequences of cerebral impairment would have been missed.

We saw consistent evidence of cerebral impairment on the four most sensitive indicators of it in the Halstead–Reitan Battery. This man earned a Halstead Impairment Index of 0.6 (about 60% of the tests in the brain-damaged range), but it must be recognized that higher (poorer) Impairment Indexes are expected in older persons (Reitan & Wolfson, in press). Thus, in a 59-year-old man one could not confidently postulate cerebral damage on the basis of this Impairment Index score alone.

V.H. performed very poorly on the Category test (115 errors), especially when one considers his adequate IQ values. The patient's score (109 seconds) on Part B of the Trail-Making test was also in the brain-damaged range. On the Localization component of the Tactual Performance test his score (5) was just within normal limits. These results all suggest that the patient probably had some deterioration of brain functions.

In assessing the good versus the poor performances, it was apparent that in the past this man had had ability levels that were at least average or above. Some of these good scores were still reflected, especially in the Verbal subtests of the Wechsler Scale. For example, his Vocabulary score (14) was well above average. He also performed very well on the Speech–Sounds Perception test (5 errors). These values indicated that the patient had developed normally, had had good abilities in the past, and continued to have the ability to pay attention to specific stimulus material and maintain concentrated attention over time.

V.H. also showed normal results on tests of bilateral simultaneous stimulation and tactile finger recognition. These findings suggested that the patient did not have a focal destructive lesion of either cerebral hemisphere.

In spite of these good scores, the patient did show evidence of pronounced deficits. His principal deficiencies occurred on the Category test (115 errors) and the Tactual Performance test—total time 25.9 minutes. As with patients who show definite evidence of dementia, many patients with alcoholic deterioration (but without clinical dementia) also have difficulty with tasks that require them to define a problem as well as solve it. Prior research results (Fitzhugh, Fitzhugh, & Reitan, 1960; Fitzhugh, Fitzhugh, & Reitan, 1965) demonstrated that chronic alcoholics performed extremely poorly on the Category test in spite of having above-average IQ values and frequently had a general pattern of results that characterized diffuse cerebral dysfunction.

Proceeding with evaluation of V.H.'s test results, one would next refer to the lateralizing and localizing indicators. This man showed positive findings implicating each cerebral hemisphere. The fact that this right-handed man was able to tap no faster with his dominant hand than with his nondominant hand suggested left cerebral dysfunction. He also had tactile-perceptual difficulties on the right side. For example, he performed slowly on the Tactile Form Recognition test with his right hand and made significantly more errors in finger-tip number writing perception with his right than with his left hand.

Findings supporting right cerebral dysfunction included a somewhat slow performance with the left hand on the Tactual Performance test, a relatively low score on the Picture Arrangement subtest of the Wechsler Scale, and a clearly deficient performance in the attempt to copy the key. Deficits in copying the key were related particularly to a failure to represent corresponding notches on the stem near the handle and confusion about the spatial configuration of the "nose" of the key. Thus, in addition to results that pointed toward generalized involvement, the patient had positive findings to implicate each cerebral hemisphere.

The reader may wonder whether this patient might have had bilateral focal lesions, but this possibility was essentially ruled out by some of the better scores, even though they may have fallen in the brain-damaged range (Trails B, Speech–Sounds Perception test and some of the scores on the Wechsler subtests). In the context of the overall results it would definitely appear that neither the left nor right indicators were sufficient to implicate a specific, focal lesion of either the left or right cerebral hemisphere. Findings of this kind are suggestive of generalized cerebral involvement and, under these conditions, the extremely poor score on the Category test is characteristic of persons with chronic alcoholism.

The complaints of impaired memory and judgment were certainly related to basic impairment of reasoning processes and the ability to identify and organize relevant aspects of total situations. V.H.'s intact abilities, which largely represented skills acquired in the past, would have been important to consider when developing an overall plan for his rehabilitation; but the best advice, certainly, would have been for V.H. to discontinue use of alcohol. It is difficult to predict whether a person of this age, showing this degree of impairment, would demonstrate much spontaneous recovery, but on retesting even in 6 to 12 months a substantial degree of improvement sometimes occurs in persons who have totally discontinued use of alcohol.

CONCLUSIONS

This chapter has concentrated on clinical evaluation of the Halstead–Reitan Neuropsychological Test Battery. Several general conclusions are supported by these clinical evaluations and the research results cited. Experimental investigations and clinical practice with the Halstead–Reitan Battery over a period of about 30 years has led to (1) development of an understanding of the major behavioral and psychological categories of brain functions; (2) the development of measurement strategies, incorporated into the battery, that are basic for valid interpretation; and (3) an understanding of the data provided by the battery for clinical evaluation and application.

The Halstead–Reitan Battery has probably been researched more thoroughly than any other set of neuropsychological tests, although more investigation of the significance of deficits for everyday behavior is needed. Nevertheless, through evaluation of thousands of subjects, clinical interpretation has progressed to the point that neuropsychological examination of brain–behavior relationships is routinely of clinical value. In patients with known or suspected brain disease or damage, the test results relate directly to neurological findings, adding the important dimension of the behavioral consequences of brain disease or damage. Brain functions in persons who have sustained *no* brain damage are obviously no less important, and the future trend is in the direction of evaluation and application of the broad differences in brain functions among normal individuals.

REFERENCES

Anderson, A. L. (1950). The effect of laterality localization of brain damage on Wechsler–Bellevue indices of deterioration. *Journal of Clinical Psychology, 6,* 191–194.

Babcock, H. (1930). An experiment in the measurement of mental deterioration. *Archives of Psychology, 18,* 5–105.

Boll, T. J., Heaton, R. K., & Reitan, R. M. (1974). Neuropsychological and emotional correlates of Huntington's chorea. *Journal of Nervous and Mental Disease, 158,* 61–69.

Chapman, L. F., & Wolff, H. G. (1959). The cerebral hemispheres and the highest integrative functions in man. *Archives of Neurology, 1,* 357–424.

Christenson, A.-L. (1975). Luria's neuropsychological investigation: Text, manual, and test cards. New York: Spectrum.

Davis, L. J., Hamlett, I., & Reitan, R. M. (1966). Relationships of conceptual ability and academic achievement to problem-solving and experiential backgrounds of retardates. *Perceptual and Motor Skills, 22,* 499–505.

Davis, J., & Reitan, R. M. (1966). Methodological note on the relationships between ability to copy a simple configuration and Wechsler verbal and performance IQs. *Perceptual and Motor Skills, 22,* 281–332.

Davis, J., & Reitan, R. M. (1967). Dysphasia and constructional dyspraxia items and Wechsler verbal and performance IQ in retardates. *American Journal of Mental Deficiency, 71,* 606–608.

Dikmen, S., & Reitan, R. M. (1974a). Minnesota Multiphasic Personality Inventory correlates of dysphasic language disturbances. *Journal of Abnormal Psychology, 83,* 675–679.

Dikmen, S., & Reitan, R. M. (1974b). MMPI correlates of localized structural cerebral lesions. *Perceptual and Motor Skills, 39,* 831–840.

Dikmen, S., & Reitan, R. M. (1976). Psychological deficits and recovery of functions after head injury. *Transactions of the American Neurological Association, 101,* 72–77.

Dikmen, S., & Reitan, R. M. (1977a). Emotional sequelae of head injury. *Annals of Neurology, 2,* 492–494.

Dikmen, S., & Reitan, R. M. (1977b). MMPI correlates of adaptive ability deficits in patients with brain lesions. *Journal of Nervous and Mental Disease, 165,* 247–254.

Dikmen, S., & Reitan, R. M. (1978). Neuropsychological performance in post-traumatic epilepsy. *Epilepsia, 19,* 177–183.

Dikmen, S., Reitan, R. M., & Temkin, N. R. (1983). Neuropsychological recovery in head injury. *Archives of Neurology, 40,* 333–338.

Doehring, D. G., & Reitan, R. M. (1961a). Behavioral consequences of brain damage associated with homonymous field visual defects. *Journal of Comparative and Physiological Psychology, 54,* 489–492.

Doehring, D. G., & Reitan, R. M. (1961b). Certain language and non-language disorders in brain-damaged patients with homonymous visual field defects. *AMA Archives of Neurology and Psychiatry, 5,* 294–299.

Doehring, D. G., Reitan, R. M., & Kløve, H. (1961). Changes in patterns of intelligence test performances associated with homonymous visual field defects. *Journal of Nervous and Mental Disease, 132,* 227–233.

Fitzhugh, K. B., Fitzhugh, L. C., & Reitan, R. M. (1961). Psychological deficits in relation to acuteness of brain dysfunction. *Journal of Consulting Psychology, 25,* 61–66.

Fitzhugh, K. B., Fitzhugh, L. C., & Reitan, R. M. (1962a). The relationship of acuteness of organic brain dysfunction to Trail Making test performances. *Perceptual and Motor Skills, 15,* 399–403.

Fitzhugh, K. B., Fitzhugh, L. C., & Reitan, R. M. (1962b). Wechsler–Bellevue comparisons in groups with "chronic" and "current" lateralized diffuse brain lesions. *Journal of Consulting Psychology, 26,* 306–310.

Fitzhugh, K. B., Fitzhugh, L. C., & Reitan, R. M. (1963). Effects of "chronic" and "current" lateralized and non-lateralized cerebral lesions upon Trail Making tests performances. *Journal of Nervous and Mental Disease, 137,* 82–87.

Fitzhugh, K. B., Fitzhugh, L. C., & Reitan, R. M. (1964). Influence of age upon measures of problem solving and experiential background in subjects with long-standing cerebral dysfunction. *Journal of Gerontology, 19,* 132–134.

Fitzhugh, L. C., Fitzhugh, K. B., & Reitan, R. M. (1960). Adaptive abilities and intellectual functioning in hospitalized alcoholics. *Quarterly Journal of Studies on Alcohol, 21,* 414–423.

Fitzhugh, L. C., Fitzhugh, K. B., & Reitan, R. M. (1962). Sensorimotor deficits of brain-damaged subjects in relation to intellectual level. *Perceptual and Motor Skills, 15,* 603–608.

Fitzhugh, L. C., Fitzhugh, K. B., & Reitan, R. M. (1965). Adaptive abilities and intellectual functioning in hospitalized alcoholics: Further considerations. *Quarterly Journal of Studies on Alcohol, 26,* 402–411.

Forsyth, G. A., Gaddes, W. J., Reitan, R. M., & Tryk, H. E. (1971). Intellectual deficit in multiple sclerosis as indicated by psychological tests (Research Monograph No. 23). Victoria, B.C. (Canada): University of Victoria.

Goodglass, H., & Kaplan, E. (1979). Assessment of cognitive deficit in the brain-injured patient. In M. S. Gazzaniga (Ed.), *Handbook of Behavioral Neurobiology: Vol. 2.* (pp. 3–22). New York: Plenum Press.

Grant, I., Mohns, L., Miller, M., & Reitan, R. M. (1976). A neuropsychological study of polydrug users. *Archives of General Psychiatry, 33,* 973–978.

Heimburger, R. F., DeMyer, W., & Reitan, R. M. (1964). Implications of Gerstmann's syndrome. *Journal of Neurology, Neurosurgery and Psychiatry, 27,* 52–57.

Heimburger, R. F., & Reitan, R. M. (1961). Easily administered written test for lateralizing brain lesions. *Journal of Neurosurgery, 18,* 301–312.

Hom, J., & Reitan, R. M. (1982). Effect of lateralized cerebral damage upon con-tralateral and ipsilateral sensorimotor performances. *Journal of Clinical Neuropsychology, 4,* 249–268.

Hom, J., & Reitan, R. M. (1984). Neuropsychological correlates of rapidly vs. slowly growing intrinsic neoplasms. *Journal of Clinical Neuropsychology, 6,* 309–324.

Kløve, H. (1959). Relationship of differential electroencephalographic patterns of distribution of Wechsler–Bellevue scores. *Neurology, 9,* 871–876.

Kløve, H. (1974). Validation studies in adult clinical neuropsychology. In R. M. Reitan and L. A. Davison (Eds.), *Clinical neuropsychology: Current status and applications.* Washington, D.C.: V.H. Winston & Sons.

Kløve, H., & Reitan, R. M. (1958). The effect of dysphasia and spatial distortion of Wechsler–Bellevue results. *Archives of Neurology and Psychiatry, 80,* 708–713.

Lezak, M. (1976). *Neuropsychological assessment.* New York: Oxford University Press.

Matarazzo, J. D. (1972). *Wechsler's measurement and appraisal of adult intelligence.* Baltimore: Williams and Wilkins.

Matthews, C. G., & Reitan, R. M. (1961). Comparison of abstraction ability in retardates and in patients with cerebral lesions. *Perceptual and Motor Skills, 13,* 327–333.

Matthews, C. G., & Reitan, R. M. (1962). Psychomotor abilities of retardates and patients with cerebral lesions. *American Journal of Mental Deficiency, 66,* 607–612.

Matthews, C. G., & Reitan, R. M. (1963). Relationship of differential abstraction ability levels to psychological test performances in mentally retarded subjects. *American Journal of Mental Deficiency, 68,* 235–244.

Matthews, C. G., & Reitan, R. M. (1964). Correlations of Wechsler–Bellevue rank orders of subtest means in lateralized and non-lateralized brain-damaged groups. *Perceptual and Motor Skills, 19,* 391–399.

Matthews, C. G., Shaw, D., & Kløve, H. (1966). Psychological test performances in neurological and "pseudoneurologic" subjects. *Cortex, 2,* 244–253.

Meier, M. J., & French, L. A. (1966). Longitudinal assessment of intellectual functioning following unilateral temporal lobectomy. *Journal of Clinical Psychology, 22,* 22–27.

Reed, H. B. C., & Reitan, R. M. (1962). The significance of age in the performance of a complex psychomotor task by brain-damaged and non-brain-damaged subjects. *Journal of Gerontology, 17,* 193–196.

Reed, H. B. C., & Reitan, R. M. (1963a). Changes in psychological test performances associated with the normal aging process. *Journal of Gerontology, 18,* 271–274.

Reed, H. B. C., & Reitan, R. M. (1963b). A comparison of the effects of the normal aging process with the effects of organic brain damage on adaptive abilities. *Journal of Gerontology, 18,* 177–179.

Reed, H. B. C., & Reitan, R. M. (1963c). Intelligence test performances of brain-damaged subjects with lateralized motor deficits. *Journal of Consulting Psychology, 27,* 102–106.

Reitan, R. M. (1955a). Certain differential effects of left and right cerebral lesions in human adults. *Journal of Comparative and Physiological Psychology, 48,* 474–477.

Reitan, R. M. (1955b). Discussion: Symposium on the temporal lobe. *Archives of Neurology and Psychiatry, 74,* 569–570.

Reitan, R. M. (1955c). The distribution according to age of a psychologic measure dependent upon organic brain functions. *Journal of Gerontology, 10,* 338–340.

Reitan, R. M. (1958). The validity of the Trail Making test as an indicator of organic brain damage. *Perceptual and Motor Skills, 8,* 271–276.

Reitan, R. M. (1959a). The comparative effects of brain damage on the Halstead Impairment Index and the Wechsler–Bellevue Scale. *Journal of Clinical Psychology, 15,* 281–285.

Reitan, R. M. (1959b). *The effects of brain lesions on adaptive abilities in human beings.* Tucson, AZ: Reitan Neuropsychology Laboratories, Inc.

Reitan, R. M. (1960). The significance of dysphasia for intelligence and adaptive abilities. *Journal of Psychology, 50,* 355–376.

Reitan, R. M. (1962). The comparative psychological significance of aging in groups with and without organic brain damage. In C. Tibbitts & W. Donahue (Eds.), *Social and psychological aspects of aging* (pp. 880–887). New York: Columbia University Press.

Reitan, R. M. (1964). Psychological deficits resulting from cerebral lesions in man. In J. M. Warren & K. A. Akert (Eds.), *The frontal granular cortex and behavior.* New York: McGraw-Hill.

Reitan, R. M. (1966). Problems and prospects in studying the psychological effects of brain lesions in human beings. *Cortex, 2,* 127–154.

Reitan, R. M. (1967). Psychological assessment of deficits associated with brain lesions in subjects with normal and subnormal intelligence. In J. L. Khanna (Ed.), *Brain damage and mental retardation: A psychological evaluation.* Springfield, IL: Charles C. Thomas.

Reitan, R. M. (1970a). Measurement of psychological changes in aging. *Duke University Council on Aging and Human Development,* Proceedings of Seminars. Durham, NC: Duke University Press.

Reitan, R. M. (1970b). Objective behavioral assessment in diagnosis and prediction. In A. L. Benton (Ed.), *Behavioral change in cerebrovascular disease* (pp. 155–165). New York: Medical Department, Harper & Row.

Reitan, R. M. (1970c). Sensorimotor functions, intelligence and cognition, and emotional status in subjects with cerebral lesions. *Perceptual and Motor Skills, 33,* 275–284.

Reitan, R. M. (1972). Verbal problem solving as related to cerebral damage. *Perceptual and Motor Skills, 34,* 515–524.

Reitan, R. M. (1973). Psychological testing after craniocerebral injury. In J. R. Youmans (Ed.), *Neurological surgery* (Vol. II) (pp. 1040–1048). Philadelphia: W. B. Saunders.

Reitan, R. M. (1976). Psychological testing of epileptic patients. In P. J. Vinken & G. W. Bruyn (Eds.), *Handbook of clinical neurology: The epilepsies* (Vols. IX & X). New York: North Holland Publishing Company.

Reitan, R. M. (1977). Neuropsychological concepts and psychiatric diagnosis. In V. M. Rankoff, H. C. Stancer, & H. B. Kedward (Eds.), *Psychiatric diagnosis* (pp. 42–68). New York: Brunner/Mazel.

Reitan, R. M. (1984). *Aphasia and sensory-perceptual deficits in adults.* Tucson, AZ: Reitan Neuropsychology Laboratories, Inc.

Reitan, R. M. (1985). *Aphasia and sensory-perceptual deficits in children.* Tucson, AZ: Reitan Neuropsychology Laboratories, Inc.

Reitan, R. M., & Boll, T. J. (1971). Intellectual and cognitive functions in Parkinson's disease. *Journal of Consulting and Clinical Psychology, 37,* 364–369.

Reitan, R. M., & Davison, L. A. (Eds.). (1974). *Clinical neuropsychology: Current status and applications.* Washington, D.C.: V.H. Winston & Sons.

Reitan, R. M., & Fitzhugh, K. B. (1971). Behavioral deficits in groups with cerebral vascular lesions. *Journal of Consulting and Clinical Psychology, 37,* 215–223.

Reitan, R. M., Reed, J. C., & Dyken, M. L. (1971). Cognitive, psychomotor, and motor correlates of multiple sclerosis. *Journal of Nervous and Mental Disease, 153,* 218–224.

Reitan, R. M., & Sena, D. A. (1983, August). *The efficacy of the REHABIT technique in remediation of brain-injured people.* Paper presented at the meeting of the American Psychological Association, Anaheim, CA.

Reitan, R. M., & Wolfson, D. (1984). The emergence of clinical neuropsychology: Practical applications for psychologists. *Texas Psychologist, 36,* 5–13.

Reitan, R. M., & Wolfson, D. (in press). The Halstead–Reitan Neuropsychological Test Battery and aging. *The Clinical Gerontologist.*

Ross, A. T., & Reitan, R. M. (1955). Intellectual and affective functions in multiple sclerosis: A quantitative study. *AMA Archives of Neurology and Psychiatry, 73,* 663–677.

Shure, G. D., & Halstead, W. C. (1958). Cerebral localization of intellectual processes. *Psychological Monographs, 72* (12) (Whole No. 465).

Vega, A., & Parsons, O. A. (1967). Cross-validation of the Halstead–Reitan tests for brain damage. *Journal of Consulting Psychology, 31,* 619–625.

Wechsler, D. (1955). *Range of human capacities.* Baltimore: Williams & Wilkins.

Wheeler, L. (1964). Complex behavioral indices weighted by linear discriminant functions for the prediction of cerebral damage. *Perceptual and Motor Skills, 19,* 907–923.

Wheeler, L., Burke, C. J., & Reitan, R. M. (1963). An application of discriminant functions to the problem of predicting brain damage using behavioral variables. *Perceptual and Motor Skills, 16,* 417–440.

Wheeler, L., & Reitan, R. M. (1962). The presence and laterality of brain damage predicted from responses to a short Aphasia Screening test. *Perceptual and Motor Skills, 15,* 783–799.

Wheeler, L., & Reitan, R. M. (1963). Discriminant functions applied to the problem of predicting cerebral damage from behavior tests: A cross validation study. *Perceptual and Motor Skills, 16,* 681–701.

7

The Luria–Nebraska Neuropsychological Battery

Charles J. Golden and
Mark Maruish

Based on Luria's (1966, 1973) functional systems theory of brain organization, the Luria–Nebraska Neuropsychological Battery (LNNB) (Golden, Hammeke, Purisch, & Moses, 1984) has gained increasing acceptance as a reliable and valid battery for the assessment of brain functioning. The LNNB consists of 269 items representing approximately 700 test procedures. These comprise the battery's 11 ability scales, which are constructed to assess skills in 11 broad ability areas. In addition, two sensorimotor scales, a pathognomonic scale, and sets of localization and factor scales are also derived from the 269 items. Test results are interpreted by analysis of the patterns on all sets of scales, performance on individual items, and qualitative data.

Development of the LNNB represented an attempt by Golden and his associates to standardize and quantify methods used by the acclaimed Russian neuropsychologist, A. R. Luria, in the evaluation of brain-injured patients. Although it is reported that Luria was opposed to the standardization of his investigative techniques, it was believed that only through efforts in this direction would these valuable methods of assessment gain acceptance by colleagues in Western society. The items contained within the LNNB essentially represent the carrying of Christensen's (1975a,b) standardization of Luria's evaluation procedures a step further to include greater standardization in the administration and scoring of these procedures, as well as providing statistical norms against which performance can be judged. While providing a quantitative approach to assessment, the LNNB also allows for the integration of qualitative data (gleaned from behavioral observations and "testing-the-limits" strategies) in generating hypotheses regarding the nature of the patient's deficits.

The popularity the battery has gained among clinicians appears to be the result of several factors. These include a relatively short administration time (2–3 hr), the low price of the equipment necessary for the administration of the test items, and the portability of the test materials. Also, use of objective rules for interpretation (based on empirical data and clinical experience) allows the clinician to make reasonably accurate general statements about the neuro-psychological status of the patient, while the more sophisticated clinician has available extensive data for more complex interpretations.

THE LURIA–NEBRASKA SCALES

Clinical Scales

The 269 items presently contained on the LNNB are grouped into 11 ability scales, representing very broad skill areas outlined by Luria (1966). Items contained within each scale focus primarily on the ability suggested by the scale title. However, these items deliberately vary to test the interaction of the central skill with a variety of secondary input, output, or integrational abilities. Empirically derived scale scores for each item within a given scale are summed. The total score is subsequently converted to a T-score, based on normative data. Given the fact that no items in any of the scales are measures of a pure ability, a particularly high T-score (which would be indicative of impairment) could result from deficits other than those implied by the scale title.

The 11 basic ability scales are as follow:

Motor Items on this scale are designed to measure bilateral and bimanual motor coordination and speed, kinesthetic-based movement, oral-motor movement, and drawing ability and speed. The abilities to copy hand and arm movements from a model, to perform complex forms of praxis, and to use verbal commands to guide behavior are also measured.

Rhythm The patient's ability to attend to, discriminate among, and produce both verbal and nonverbal rhythmic stimuli is measured on this scale.

Tactile Tasks on this scale require the patient to identify the location and direction of tactile stimuli, discriminate among both hard and soft touches and painful stimuli, and identify numbers, letters, and shapes traced on the wrists. Position sense and the ability to identify objects placed in the hands are also assessed.

Visual The patient is asked to identify objects presented to him or her. Pictures of objects that are either clear, unfocused, or of high contrast quality, along with those of drawings of overlapping objects, must also be identified. Progressive matrix, clock-reading, clock-setting, and directional orientation tasks, as well as tasks measuring intellectual operations in space (e.g., counting the blocks in a pictured three-dimensional stack) are also included.

Receptive Speech The items here require the patient to discriminate between phonemes, and measure the ability to comprehend simple words, phrases, and sentences. Understanding of complex and inverted grammatical structures is also assessed.

Expressive Speech Items on this scale assess the patient's ability to articulate speech sound, words, and sentences presented either orally or visually. The ability to identify pictured or described objects, fluency and automatization of speech, and the ability to construct grammatically correct sentences are also measured.

Writing In addition to assessing motor writing abilities in general, phonetic analysis, the ability to copy and write from dictation letters, sounds, words, and phrases is assessed. A spontaneous writing task is also included.

Reading Items on this scale require the reading of letters, unfamiliar syllables, simple and complex words and sentences, and a simple paragraph. Two items requiring the synthesis of letters into sounds and words are also included.

Arithmetic Designed to measure basic arithmetic skills, this scale's items include tasks requiring the reading and writing of single- and multidigit numbers and Roman numerals, the performing of simple and complex computations, the comprehension of mathematical signs and number structure, and the performing of serial subtractions.

Memory Short-term memory for verbal and nonverbal stimuli under both interference and noninterference conditions is assessed here. Paired-associate learning and the ability to recall the gist of a paragraph are among the types of skills assessed here.

Intellectual Processes (Intelligence) This scale includes items that measure comprehension of thematic pictures and texts, concept formation (in the form of definitions, analogies, opposites, and elaboration of similarities, differences, and relationships between objects), and the ability to solve complex discursive mathematical problems.

Three other clinical scales are derived from the LNNB items:

Pathognomonic This scale consists of items drawn from ten of the ability scales. These items have been found to be highly sensitive to the presence of brain dysfunction. In addition to being the best indicator of brain integrity (among the clinical scales), it also provides an estimate of the degree to which the brain has compensated for sustained injuries.

Left Hemisphere Items measuring right-hand performance on the Motor and Tactile scales are included here. This scale provides specific information regarding the integrity of the left hemisphere sensorimotor strip (Broadman areas 1–4).

Right Hemisphere Included here are Motor and Tactile items measuring left-hand performance, thus rendering an indication of the intactness of the right hemisphere sensorimotor strip.

Localization Scales

Recognizing the potential effectiveness of utilizing specific items for the localization of lesions, McKay and Golden (1979a) selected sets of items that were more statistically sensitive to localized damage in one of eight areas of the brain (i.e., the frontal, sensorimotor, parietal-occipital, and temporal areas in the left and right hemispheres). Item selection was based on the performance of 53 brain-injured patients with lesions localized primarily to one of these eight areas. In Golden, Moses, Fishburne, and colleagues' (1981) cross-validation of these scales, accurate localization for 74% of their 87 patients with localized lesions occurred when either of the two highest scales was the criterion for classification. Also notable is the fact that the highest scale allowed for accurate lateralization in 92% of the cases.

Factor Scales

From studies that factor analyzed each of the ability scales (Golden, Sweet, et al., 1980; Golden, Osmon, et al., 1980; Golden, Hammeke, et al., 1981; Golden, Purisch, et al., 1980), a total of 34 factors was derived for these scales. A comparison of the performance of patients with localized lesions (from the Lewis, Golden, Moses, et al., 1979, and Golden, Moses, Fishburne, et al., 1981 studies) to that of a group of normal patients on scales designed to measure these factors was subsequently undertaken (McKay & Golden, 1981a). This resulted in the establishment of normative data for these scales. Also, four of the scales that were found not to discriminate between the normal and brain-damaged groups were deleted, leaving 30-factor scales. Although limitations in this set of scales (e.g., the number of items on each scale, findings of relatively low reliability for some differential ceilings) warrant caution in its use, the factor scales have been found to be beneficial in testing hypotheses drawn from examination of the clinical scales.

RESEARCH ON THE LURIA–NEBRASKA

Reliability

During the initial development of the LNNB, Golden, Hammeke, and Purisch (1980) sought to determine the degree to which the battery could be reliably scored. Using a different set of two raters for each of 5 patients who were administered the then 282 items, a 95% agreement rate (on the 1,410 pairs of scores) was obtained. Correlations between the two sets of raw scores for each patient ranged from .97 to .99. Although Bach, Harowski, Kirby, Peterson, and Schulein (1981) found somewhat lower interrater agreement when both normal and marginal responding were demonstrated by confederates, the results, on the whole, supported the initial finding of high interrater reliability.

In investigating the test–retest reliability with a small group of brain-impaired psychiatric patients, Golden, Berg, and Graber (1982) obtained an average correlation coefficient of .88 between the T-scores of the 11 ability scales and 2 sensorimotor scales from one testing to another (mean interval = 167 days). With a similar group tested during a longer mean interval of time (8.1 months), Plaisted and Golden (1982) obtained a mean correlation of .89 for the 11 ability scales, 2 sensorimotor scales, and the Pathognomonic scale. A mean correlation of .89 was also achieved for the localization scales. The reliability of the 30 factor scales was found to be much more variable, with the mean correlation equalling .75. Two of these scale correlations did not achieve significance at the .01 level.

Golden, Fross, and Graber (1981) sought to determine the split-half reliability of the 11 ability scales. For each scale, the total score of the even-numbered items was correlated with that of the odd-numbered items, using the results of 388 normal, neurologic, and psychiatric patients. The results of the three groups combined yielded correlations ranging from .89 to .93.

Alpha coefficients (which yield the mean reliability coefficients derived from all possible ways in which items can be grouped into halves) have been computed in several studies. Mikula (1981) obtained alphas ranging from .82 to .94 on the 14 clinical scales for his combined group of medical control and neurologic patients. From the LNNB results of 285 alcoholic, brain-damaged, and schizophrenic patients, Moses, Johnson, and Lewis (in press-a) obtained alphas ranging from .78 to .88 for the 14 summary scales; from .73 to .88 for the localization scales; and from .04 to .87 for the factor scales. Four of the 6 factor scales that were found not to meet the "minimum standards" for internal consistency (i.e., .5 or greater) were those derived from the Receptive Speech scale. This led the authors to question the stability of this scale's factor structure.

Moses, Johnson, and Lewis (in press-b,c) further investigated the LNNB's internal consistency by computing separate alphas for each set of scales for each of the three diagnostic groups that comprised their original sample. Comparison of each group's alphas for the summary and localization scales to those of the previous study led the authors to conclude that adequate reliability present to justify the clinical use of the 14 summary scales and 8 localization scales with brain-damaged patients. Sawicki, Maruish, and Golden (1983) also computed separate alphas for the 14 summary scales for large groups of brain-injured, schizophrenic, and mixed psychiatric patients, as well as for a group of normals. Those for the normal group ranged from .40 to .78, while the alphas for the other three groups ranged from the lower .80's to the lower .90's.

Recently, an alternate form of the LNNB (Form II) has been developed (Golden, Hammeke, Purisch, & Moses, 1984). The first 269 of the 279 items of this form are essentially the same as those on the original form. Only the specific content varies in the majority of these items. The last 10 items comprise the new Intermediate Memory scale. Ariel and Golden (1981) reported significant correlations from .79 to .87.

Validity

Golden, Hammeke, and Purisch (1978) selected 285 items from a pool of items constructed from Christensen's (1975a, 1975b) procedures. They were subsequently administered to 50 neurologic and 50 medical control patients and scored on a 0, 1, 2 system (with 0 indicating normal performance; 2, impaired performance; and 1, borderline performance). Two hundred eighty-five *t*-tests, comparing the performance of each group on all items, showed the controls to have performed significantly better on 253 of the items, and better on nearly all of the remaining items, far exceeding the 5% chance difference expected at the .05 level. Hammeke, Golden, and Purisch (1978) then administered the same items to 50 normals and 50 brain-impaired patients and summed the raw scores of all items in each of the clinical scales. The controls were found to have performed better on all summary measures. In addition, cutoff scores for each scale, derived to discriminate optimally between the groups, allowed for an accurate identification of at least 75% of the cases. Discriminant analysis using the 14 summary scores from both groups resulted in the accurate classification of 93% of the cases. Moses and Golden (1979), in cross-validation, administered the LNNB in its present form to a like group of subjects and achieved comparable results using Hammeke, Golden, and Purisch's cutoff scores and discriminant function. Duffala (1979/1981) found her group of 20 head trauma patients to perform significantly worse than 20 controls on the Pathognomonic and all ability scales except Visual.

Several studies have demonstrated the LNNB's ability to identify brain-impaired subjects. Bach (1983) found all but the Reading and Memory scores to discriminate between orthopedic, Parkinson's disease, and alcohol dementia patients. In light of the effects of age and education on LNNB performance found by Marvel, Golden, Hammeke, Purisch, and Osmon (1979) and seen again in their sample of normals, Golden, Moses, Graber, and Berg (1981) generated a regression equation to predict the average T-score of patients based on their age and educational level. When the 60 normals were combined with a group of 60 brain-damaged patients, and two or more scores (excluding Writing, Arithmetic, and the two sensorimotor scales) above the critical level (predicted average T-score plus 10) were used as the criterion for brain impairment, 84% of the total sample was accurately classified. Using this same criterion, similar total hit rates were achieved when normals were combined with groups of primary and secondary epileptics (85%, Berg & Golden, 1981), patients with relatively mild brain impairment (78%, Malloy & Webster, 1981), patients with various neurological disorders (77%, Sawicki & Golden, in press-a), patients with relatively discrete brain lesions (86%, Golden, Moses, Fishburne, et al., 1981), and elderly patients with either confirmed or suspected brain dysfunction (93%, Spitzform, 1982; 88%, MacInnes, Gillen, et al., 1983). Moses (in press-e) also found that this rule accurately classified 83% of his group of 165 brain-damaged patients.

The discriminant ability of the LNNB has undergone stringent testing in a number of studies designed to evaluate the degree to which schizophrenics can be differentiated from brain-damaged patients and the degree to which brain-damaged schizophrenics can be differentiated from those without brain impairment. Purisch, Golden, and Hammeke (1978) found accurate classification of 88% of 50 schizophrenic and 50 brain-damaged patients. The schizophrenics were also found to have significantly better performance on all scales but the Rhythm, Receptive Speech, Memory, and Intelligence scales. These findings (including the pattern of significant differences found between the two groups on the ability scales) were essentially the same as those obtained by Moses and Golden (1980) in a cross-validation study. Shelly and Goldstein (1983a) only partially replicated the Purisch, Golden, and Hammeke findings. The lack of complete replication was attributed to differences between their and the original brain-damaged groups.

Puente, Heidelberg-Sanders, and Lund (1982b) found schizophrenics to have performed significantly better than brain-damaged patients on all 14 LNNB summary scales. In another, similar study by the same authors (1982a), the schizophrenic group performed significantly better on all but the Expressive Speech and Pathognomonic scales and those four scales initially found by Purisch, Golden, and Hammeke to be nondiscriminating for these two populations. Moses, Cardellino, and Thompson (1983) combined two sets of samples of schizophrenic and neurologic patients and achieved a 74% hit rate for the total group using a discriminant function derived from the results of one of the sets of samples. This represented a drop from the previous hit rate (81%) obtained for the one sample from which the function was derived. Respective hit rates of 81% and 78% occurred when both the 14 individual scale T-scores and the sum of the 14 T-scores for each subject of the combined sets were submitted to discriminant analysis.

Noting that schizophrenics identified by the LNNB in previous studies as being brain damaged might actually have been brain impaired, Golden, Moses, et al. (1980) investigated the relationship between LNNB summary scores and ventricular size (a measure of cerebral atrophy). Eight of the 14 scales were found to correlate significantly with ventricular size. When submitted to multiple regression, a multiple correlation of .72 ($p < .001$) between ventricular size and the 8 LNNB scales was obtained. Four of the 6 scales that did not yield significant correlations were those found in previous studies not to discriminate between schizophrenics and brain-damaged patients. Rules for classifying schizophrenics as having enlarged ventricles were developed from these results and allowed for the accurate classification of 90% of the same subjects based on their LNNB performance.

Use of a revision of these rules by Golden, Graber, Moses, and Zatz (1980) lowered the hit rate to 81% for the identification of enlarged ventricles, but allowed for the accurate classification of 90% of schizophrenics in terms of whether or not they had enlarged sulci (another measure of cerebral atrophy). Using these same rules with a somewhat younger group of schizophrenics with nearly twice the number of hospitalizations as the previous sample, Golden, MacInnes, et al. (1982) achieved a 77% hit rate. A significant relationship ($p < .01$) between the 14 LNNB variables and ventricular size was again found, but the scales originally found to correlate individually with ventricular size were somewhat different than those found previously.

The ability of the LNNB to aid in the lateralization and localization of brain impairment was first investigated by Osmon, Golden, Purisch, Hammeke, and Blume (1979). Discriminant analysis allowed for accurate lateralization of dysfunction for 98% of the 60 subjects with either left or right hemisphere or diffuse damage. McKay and Golden (1979b), using the direction of the difference between the scores from empirically derived left and right hemisphere scales, were able to lateralize the site of dysfunction accurately for all of their initial subjects and for 83% of their cross-validation sample. Lewis, Golden, Moses, and colleagues (1979) found their eight groups of subjects with localized lesions (left and right frontal, temporal, sensorimotor, and parietal-occipital) to differ from each other in 20% of the comparisons of each group's scores on the 14 summary scales to those of each of the other groups.

Using patients determined to have localized lesions in one of eight areas (according to the criteria of Lewis, Golden, Moses, et al.), McKay and Golden (1979a) developed a set of 8 localization scales. The site of the dysfunction for these patients was subsequently identified with 89% accuracy when the highest localization scale T-score was used as the criterion. In cross-validation, Golden, Moses, Fishburne, et al. (1981) accurately identified the locus of the lesions in 74% of their 87 patients. The study also revealed the highest localization scale to achieve a better hit rate for lateralization than the direction of difference between the empirically derived lateralization scales (92% vs. 79%).

Further validation of the LNNB can be found in studies investigating its relationship to other neuropsychological, psychological, and physiological measures. The most important of these are those that have sought to determine its relationship to the Halstead–Reitan Neuropsychological Battery (HRNB). Vicente and colleagues (1980) and Golden, Kane, and colleagues (1981) found significant multiple R's between the LNNB scales and each of the HRNB measures investigated. They, along with Shelly and Goldstein (1982b), also noted significant correlations among many or all of the variables from both batteries. Comparability in the two batteries' discriminant ability was found in studies that utilized raters expert in the use of one or the other battery (Kane, Sweet, Golden, Parsons, & Moses, 1981) and objective rules (Johnson, Moses, Cardellino, & Bryant, 1983) as a means of classifying brain-impaired and nonimpaired subjects. Correlations of .60 or better were found between indices of global impairment for the two batteries (Johnson, Moses, Cardellino, & Bryant, 1983; Shelly & Goldstein, 1982b). After submitting the LNNB scales and HRNB measures together to factor analysis, Shelly and Goldstein (1982b, 1983b) concluded that both batteries assess similar abilities (i.e., language, nonverbal cognitive, perceptual–motor) and that laterality measures from the two batteries were tapping similar skills.

Investigations into the relationship between the LNNB and Wechsler Adult Intelligence Scale (WAIS) have revealed significant correlations between the LNNB ability scales and the WAIS subtests (McKay, Golden, Moses, Fishburne, & Wisniewski, 1981; Shelly & Goldstein, 1982a). Of particular note are the significant and high correlations that were found between the LNNB Intelligence scale and the three WAIS IQ's (McKay, Golden, Moses, Fishburne, & Wisniewski, 1981; Prifitera & Ryan, 1981; Picker & Schlottmann, 1982). Similar correlations were found between the Intelligence scale and WAIS-R IQ's (Dill & Golden, 1983). It should be noted that, to some extent, the relationship between the LNNB and the HRNB is due to the relationship of both to psychometric intelligence.

Research has also demonstrated relationships between LNNB scales and other psychological measures. Both Ryan and Prifitera (1982) and McKay and Ramsey (in press) found significant correlations ($p < .001$) between the LNNB Memory scale and the Memory Quotient derived from the Wechsler Memory Scale. Correlations between each of the LNNB summary and localization scales and the score of each of the five subtests of the Peabody Individual Achievement Test (PIAT) were significant (Gillen, Ginn, Strider, Kreuch, & Golden, in press). Also, the summary, factor, and localization scales that correlated the highest with the PIAT subtests were those that intuitively would be expected to do so. A similar pattern of correlations was obtained by Shelly and Goldstein (1982a) when the relationship between the 11 ability scales and the 3 subtests of the Wide Range Achievement Test was investigated.

Physiological measures of brain integrity have also been found to be related to LNNB scores. Zelazowski and colleagues' (1981) study of long-term alcoholics, as well as those studies previously mentioned, demonstrated significant relationships between the LNNB scales and both the ventricular brain and bicaudate ratios in a small group of demented elderly patients. However, they were unable to confirm Wolf's (1981) findings of significant relationships between the LNNB scales and brain density measures. MacInnes also failed to confirm Wolf's results (1981). He did find some significant relationships between regional cerebral blood flow and the localization scales (MacInnes, 1981; MacInnes, Golden, et al., 1982).

In studies of multiple sclerosis patients, Kaimann (1981) corroborated previous HRNB findings of sensory and motor impairment in this population. With essentially the same sample, Kaimann, Knippa, Schima, and Golden (1983) found a factor analysis-derived density factor to correlate significantly with ten of the LNNB ability scales, and sulcal width and cerebral distance factors to each correlate significantly with five of the ability scales. Performance on some of the scales was later reported to be related to demographic and illness variables as well (Kaimann, in press).

Support for the use of the LNNB has come from studies investigating populations that one would intuitively expect to have neurological and neuropsychological impairment. On the LNNB, 83% of Berg and Golden's (1981) epileptics were classified as impaired, and both of these groups differed from the normal controls in 11 of the summary scales. LNNB results indicated expected progressive cognitive deterioration over time in Huntington's disease patients in various stages of the illness (Moses, Golden, Berger, & Wisniewski, 1981). The effects of alcoholism and/or treatment of the same on LNNB performance were found to be as one might expect in studies by Chmielewski and Golden (1980), Gechter, Griffith, and Newell (1983), De Obaldia, Leber, and Parsons (1981), and Teem (1981). Normal controls were found to render better performances on the LNNB than groups of diabetics (Strider, 1982), dyslexics (Grey, 1982), and learning-disabled adolescents (Parolini, 1983), while greater neuropsychological dysfunction was indicated for violent or assaultive male schizophrenics or criminals than for their nonassaultive counterparts (Bryant, 1982; Scott, Martin, & Liggett, 1982; Bryant, Scott, Golden, & Tori, 1983; West, 1982; Scott, Cole, McKay, Leark, & Golden, 1982; McKay, 1981).

Other results have included the findings that substance-abusing schizophrenics performed better than nonabusing schizophrenics on all LNNB summary scales (Scott, Cole, McKay, Golden, & MacInnes, 1982) and that psychiatric patients experiencing visual hallucinations (often an indication of organic dysfunction) performed consistently better than counterparts experiencing auditory or no hallucinations on all ability scales after acute episodes were over (McKay, Golden, & Scott, 1981).

In that the LNNB is purported to be based on Luria's (1966, 1973) theory of the functional organization of the brain, its characteristics should reflect this theory. Also, results obtained from the battery should accurately reflect the status of abilities associated with the particular brain area predicted by the theory. Support for the functional systems theory being reflected in the LNNB comes from studies in which the majority of the 269 items were found to correlate highest with the score for the scale in which it is contained (Golden, Fross, & Graber, 1981), as well as from the Golden and Berg (1980a–d,

1981a–c, 1982a,b, 1983a–c) findings of significant ($p < .0001$) correlations between nearly all items and items from other scales. Several factor analytic investigations of the summary scales (Golden, Sweet, et al., 1980; Golden, Purisch, et al., 1980; Golden, Osmon, et al., 1980; Golden, Hammeke, et al., 1981; McKay & Golden, 1981b; Moses & Johnson, in press; Sawicki & Golden, 1986b; Moses, in press-a–d), as well as of the battery as a whole (McKay, Golden, Wolf, & Perrine, 1983), have generally resulted in the emergence of factors representing component abilities that would be predicted by Luria's theory. For the most part, deficit patterns of eight groups of patients with localized lesions have been found by Lewis, Golden, Moses, et al. (1979) and Golden, Moses, Fishburne, et al. (1981) to be consistent with those that one might expect, based on Luria's work. Also supportive of the LNNB's construct validity the robustness of the LNNB variables on a language factor derived from a factor analysis of LNNB and HRNB measures (Shelly & Goldstein, 1982a).

In general, the literature supports the contention that the LNNB is a reliable and valid instrument for the assessment of neuropsychological functioning. It has been shown to produce a relatively stable set of scores over time and to discriminate brain-damaged from normal patients at a level approximately equal to that found for the Halstead–Reitan battery. It has also been found to correlate highly with other neuropsychological, psychological, and physiological tests and measures and to display sensitivity to disorders that would be expected to cause disruption in cognitive processing. In addition, the construction of the LNNB is such that it adequately reflects Luria's theory of brain functioning.

Among current issues of importance are preliminary findings suggesting poor internal consistency for the factor and localization scales for some diagnostic groups (Moses, Johnson, & Lewis, in press-b,c), a relationship of clinical profile elevations to various demographic and treatment variables (e.g., Sawicki & Golden, 1986a), differences between different subtypes of schizophrenics (Purisch, Langell, & Golden, 1983; Langell, Purisch, Green, & Golden, 1983), and effects of depression on LNNB scores (Sweet, 1983).

INTERPRETATION OF THE LURIA–NEBRASKA

The empirical data gathered since the initial stages of development of the LNNB, as well as the experience gained from its clinical use with various diagnostic populations, have allowed for the formulation of general strategies of interpretation. These strategies are presented by both Moses, Golden, Ariel, and Gustavson (1983) and [Golden, Hammeke, and Purisch (1984),] and are summarized below. They permit the user to make some fairly accurate general statements regarding the patient's neuropsychological status. However, knowledge of these guidelines in no way makes one an expert in the use of the LNNB. Such expertise comes only with close familiarity with the anatomy and functioning of the nervous system, knowledge of the neuropsychological literature (including the works of Luria), and effective supervised clinical experience.

As with any neuropsychological instrument, even the most general interpretation of the results begins with the assumptions that the patient was sufficiently motivated to render his or her best performance and that the battery has been properly administered and scored. Inability to elicit maximum performance is not uncommon and subsequently must be taken into consideration when test data are analyzed. Proper administration and scoring of the LNNB can only come with detailed knowledge of the standardized test procedures, including the degree to which one can be flexible in these approaches. In addition, adequate background information obtained from interview data and medical records must be analyzed to determine whether variables that may influence test performance (e.g., medical, psychological, educational) are present.

The accuracy of the interpretation of the LNNB results at any level is dependent upon the user's ability to integrate all patient data. Demands for increased sophistication in interpretation will call not only for greater knowledge of brain functioning but also for more sophistication in integrating test and other data with such knowledge. For this reason, referral to those expert in the field should be made when what is called for is a description of how the patient's brain is functioning.

It is also important to note that use of the LNNB does not necessarily supplant or eliminate the need for the administration of other instruments. Occasionally, the examiner may want to investigate further the presence of deficits suggested by LNNB results or assess skills not measured by the LNNB (e.g., reading comprehension, remote memory). Administration of supplemental tests can only aid in increasing the knowledge that one has about the patient's strengths and deficits, and is recommended when time and financial factors are of no great consideration.

With these considerations in mind, methods of interpreting the results from the LNNB will be presented.

Identification of Brain Damage

Classification of a patient as having some form of brain damage using the LNNB is essentially determined by comparing his or her performance on the scales to that which would be predicted for a person of the same age and education. Education (an estimate of premorbid intellectual functioning) and age have been found to be significantly related to the average of the summary T-scores of 60 normal subjects (Golden, Moses, Graber, & Berg, 1981). From this data, a regression equation was developed to predict a mean T-score (or baseline) of the patient's performance. Adding 10 T-score points (one standard deviation) to this predicted mean establishes a "critical level," any T-scores above which are considered abnormal. The formula for determining the critical level is:

$$\text{Critical Level} = 68.8 = (.213 \times \text{Age}) - (1.47 \times \text{Education})$$

Age in the formula refers to actual age in years, except when the patient is 13 to 24 years of age, or older than 70. In the former instance, the age of 25 is used, while the age of 70 is used in the latter.

Education in the above formula refers to years of education, up to 20 years. Thus, a high school graduate is given credit for 12 years of education, and an individual who had dropped out of school after completing the eighth grade is given credit for 8 years of education. Regardless of the number of years needed to complete their degrees, those with bachelor's degrees are credited with 16 years of education, those with master's degrees are given 18 years, and those with doctoral degrees are credited with 20 years. At times, the examiner may need to adjust the number of years of education for which the patient is given credit, based on other considerations regarding his or her intellectual abilities. For example, an individual who was forced to discontinue his formal education after the eighth grade for financial reasons but is now the president of a prosperous business likely needs to be credited with a higher educational level. Likewise, a person who has graduated from high school as a result of social promotions likely should be credited with a much lower educational level. In these and similar cases, reading recognition–grade equivalent scores from academic achievement tests such as the WRAT or the PIAT may be useful in obtaining an estimate of the premorbid educational level. With individuals suffering from aphasic disorders, however, use of reading recognition or reading comprehension tests may be of little or no benefit.

Discrepancies between educational achievement and actual performance levels, as well as concerns over the quality of education received at a particular school, may be difficult to resolve. In such instances, another method of calculating the critical level may be used if a premorbid WAIS or WAIS-R IQ is known. In fact, use of the premorbid IQ may be preferable to the use of educational level in calculating the critical level, in that education, again, is essentially used to estimate premorbid intelligence. A regression formula to establish the critical level from premorbid WAIS IQ scores was derived by one of the authors, and is:

$$\text{Critical level} = 164.8 - (1.08 \times \text{WAIS FSIQ}) (.2 \times \text{Age})$$

Considerations in regard to the age variable here are the same as those described above. WAIS-R IQs may be used with this formula, but one needs to correct for the differences that have been found between the Wechsler measures in different populations. Other IQ estimates might also be substituted for the WAIS IQ, but this should be done with caution. It is important to realize that in cases with low premorbid IQs, use of this formula may be correcting for brain damage sustained early in life. For those with high premorbid IQs, the formula may overadjust the critical level. This is so because the LNNB has an upper limit of approximately 120 in estimating IQ. This necessitates raising critical levels derived from this formula that fall below 45 to a critical level of 45.

Unsuccessful attempts to obtain an accurate premorbid educational (intellectual) level by the methods described above necessitates the use of clinical judgment to arrive at an estimate. This should be based on all available information regarding the patient's premorbid functioning.

In most cases, the determination of an appropriate critical level will present no particular difficulty. Use of the prescribed formulas and guides will allow for a fairly accurate estimate of this cutoff value. However, there are summary scale profile patterns that should lead one to question whether the critical level is accurate and, subsequently, needs to be adjusted. Inaccurate critical levels may be due to poor estimates of educational achievement or to other factors that have not been considered and that may have a significant effect on premorbid functioning (e.g., geographical residence, socioeconomic status, occupation of parents).

Since all scores should fall within the range of the critical level or 20 points below this cutoff value, any score(s) falling more than 20 points below the critical level suggest(s) that the critical level is too high and needs to be adjusted. Adding 25 points to the lowest scale T-score will establish a new, more conservative critical level. This should then replace the original critical level if it is found to be lower. Given the statistical properties of the battery, adjustment of the critical level should also be considered in cases where two-thirds or more of the summary scales fall between the critical level and 10 points below it.

With the establishment of the critical level, determination of the probability of brain damage becomes relatively easy. In general, brain damage is indicated when three or more of the scores from the 11 ability scales and the Pathognomonic scale exceed the critical level, while only one or none of these scores above the critical level is indicative of normality. Given the correctness of the critical level, 85% to 90% of patients will be accurately classified. In cases where two scales are significantly elevated (above the critical level), the profile is likely to be abnormal if neither of the scales is the Arithmetic or Writing scale. If either (or both) of the two scales is the Arithmetic or Writing scale, one must determine the reason for the elevation(s). Elevations due solely to problems in spelling or calculation that are consistent with the patient's history can be ignored. Elevations due to motor writing problems (for the Writing scale), or to an inability to read or recognize numbers (for the

Arithmetic scale), should be considered significant and used in the application of the above rules.

Caution is warranted in the classification of profiles where elevations are due solely to educational deficits. This is usually indicated by elevations on only the Reading, Writing, and Arithmetic scales. Due solely to poor performance on those items requiring reading skills, the Expressive Speech scale is also elevated. This profile, or any one of the possible profiles resulting from the various scale elevation combinations, is commonly seen in individuals with poor school histories. In cases where the individual has had adequate exposure to this material but was unable to learn, the presence of brain damage is highly suggested. However, when no other deficits are noted on the LNNB and the individual appears not to have been exposed to the material for any number of reasons (including emotional disturbance unrelated to academic performance), the presence of brain damage is questionable.

Alertness to the presence of two other profile types may allow for the correct identification of some of the 10–15% of the brain-damaged patients misidentified by the use of the above rules. One of these has already been discussed in regard to considerations having to do with the determination of the critical level. This is the profile in which two-thirds or more of the scores fall between the baseline and the critical level. If, upon consideration, the critical level is deemed accurate, such a profile may indicate subtle yet real brain dysfunction. Further examination of the patient's performance (by a qualified neuropsychologist) is thus warranted. Also, a profile in which the difference between the highest and lowest scale T-scores exceeds 30 should be considered indicative of brain damage. However, when the highest scores(s) is (are) due solely to spelling and/or arithmetic calculation problems, it (they) should be ignored and the range recalculated using the next highest score.

Support for the initial hypothesis regarding the patient's brain status may come from examination of the localization scales. Here, two or more scales elevated above the critical level are associated with brain damage. The accuracy rate of this classification procedure is similar to that seen with the clinical scales. A difference of 30 or more points between the highest and the lowest scale T-scores is also highly suggestive of brain damage. If both the clinical and localization scale patterns indicate the presence of brain damage, the probability that the patient is actually brain damaged is increased. If the hypotheses suggested by the two sets of scales are not in concordance, consideration of subtle brain dysfunction or an interfering psychiatric disorder is warranted. In regard to using the localization scales to support initial hypotheses, it must be noted that performance on the left parietal-occipital scale (LPO) is highly related to academic achievement. A poor academic history may thus result in an elevation on this scale. Since this does not necessarily indicate brain dysfunction, one must exercise caution (given the above discussion on elevations on the academic scales) in using the performance on this scale to confirm or disconfirm previously generated hypotheses.

Scale and Pattern Analysis

The previously described methods of interpretation only permit the examiner to make very basic tentative statements regarding the status of the patient's brain. Frequently, this is all that is requested by referral sources. However, the results of the LNNB permit one trained in its use to go beyond making elementary statements to provide a description of the patient's neuropsychological functioning. This is accomplished by an overall analysis of the clinical, localization, and factor scales and individual items, combined with an analysis of qualitative data. It is beyond the scope of this chapter to go into any great depth in regard to the interpreting of LNNB results. To be discussed are ways of looking at the data that will allow the formulation of hypotheses regarding the integrity of the patient's brain.

Clinical Scale Elevations

In analyzing the results of the LNNB clinical scales, little emphasis is placed on interpreting scale elevations in and of themselves. This is so because all scales are composed of a set of heterogeneous items, such that an elevated scale score may reflect one or more of a number of deficits possibly caused by an injury in any part of the brain. However, when viewed in relationship to the other scales, elevations on individual scales allow one to begin generating hypotheses about the patient's neuropsychological status. The experienced clinician will, of course, arrive at these hypotheses only after other factors that affect scale elevations (e.g., peripheral or brainstem injuries, type and extensiveness of the neurological dysfunction, time since the injury, expressive or receptive language problems, premorbid functioning, psychiatric problems) have been taken into consideration.

While we will use language referring to specific brain areas, the reader must be cautioned about overinterpreting these statements in the rest of the chapter. A "left parietal" focus behaviorally refers to a certain pattern of deficits seen in such injuries, not to the injury itself. Physiologically, while the brain is somewhat localized, there is extensive intraindividual variation as well as a variety of disconnection syndromes and learning history problems that force one to regard the localization as reflecting not an actual brain but a behavioral model of the brain. With sufficient knowledge, localization to this model is both possible and useful in understanding a patient. However, the model does not predict to physiology on a one-to-one basis, nor would we expect it to, given current theories of brain function and development. Predictions to physiology require a much deeper understanding of the brain, the effects of demographic factors, and the complex interaction of these variables; such predictions also suffer from all the limitations, scientific and practical, of intuitive/clinical decision making. The reader should keep in mind these limitations and avoid localization statements that suggest a specific physiological (as opposed to behavioral) etiology for specific symptoms until they are well trained and experienced in the area.

Motor Interpretation of Motor scale elevations is best made by comparing this scale to Tactile and Left and Right Hemisphere scales. When these scales are not elevated, the Motor elevation suggests problems in performing complex motor tasks. Generalized impairment of the sensory and motor areas (often in the context of diffuse deficits) is suggested when all four scales are highly elevated. An anterior lesion is suggested when Motor is much higher than Tactile and one of the hemisphere scales is at least 10 points higher than the other (with the meaningfulness of this result increasing with the amount of difference between the two hemisphere scales).

Significant involvement of one sensorimotor area or related subcortical structures is indicated when Motor, Tactile, and one of the hemisphere scales are elevated, particularly if the difference between the two hemisphere scales is 20 points or more. This pattern is frequently seen in patients with unilateral middle cerebral artery strokes involving the sensorimotor area. Comparison of the raw scores of the first four items may be found useful in the absence of clear sensorimotor deficits. Here, left hand scores should be 90–110% of those of the right-hand scores, such that a left-hand score that is more than 110% of the right-hand score may be a sign of subtle left hemisphere loss. A left-hand score less than 90% of the right-hand score would suggest subtle right hemisphere dysfunction. This scale is neither sensitive to lower limb (leg) motor deficits nor particularly sensitive to subcortical disorders that do not affect voluntary motor movements.

Rhythm Right hemisphere injuries, which are usually in the more anterior areas (frontal and temporal lobes), or subcortical injuries in either hemisphere are most likely to be present when the Rhythm elevation is the highest. This is particularly the case when the highest elevations occur on Rhythm, Memory, Intelligence, and Arithmetic. This pattern can occur in left hemisphere disorders, but it is accompanied by at least subtle verbal deficits. When both Rhythm and Visual are elevated, either anterior or posterior lesions may be present. Here, the probability that the lesion is posterior increases with greater elevations on Visual. With the Right Hemisphere scale greatly elevated in relation to the Left Hemisphere scale, the possibility of a lesion crossing the sensorimotor area and involving posterior and anterior areas of the hemisphere must be strongly considered. Rhythm elevations are not uncommon in left hemisphere injuries; however, they are generally below those of the other scales. In general, very low elevations on Rhythm are inconsistent with right hemisphere lesions not involving the sensorimotor area.

Tactile When the Tactile elevation is the highest, it must be interpreted with equal regard to the Motor and two hemisphere scales. Generally, when the Tactile scale is equal to or much greater than the Motor scale, and one hemisphere scale is significantly elevated over the other, a posterior lesion in the hemisphere indicated is likely to be present. When both hemisphere scales are elevated, one must consider either a severe left hemisphere or bilateral injury. It is important to note that elevations on this scale may be due either to deficits in the patient's ability to integrate and identify all stimuli or to tactile/spatial deficits. The former will likely be revealed on other items requiring naming and identification and should lead one to consider the presence of a left parietal lesion. When Visual is also elevated, a right parietal-occipital involvement is likely to be present. Concentration problems will also cause errors on Tactile for many patients.

Visual A right hemisphere or left occipital lesion is suggested when the Visual scale is the highest. Although it can be elevated in other left hemisphere injuries, it likely will not be the highest scale. Right anterior or mild parietal disorders are suggested when deficits are noted on only the more complex tasks of the Visual scale. An elevation on Motor suggests a right hemisphere disorder is also present. Severe peripheral visual problems and subcortical lesions that impede visual processing may also result in patterns suggesting right hemisphere dysfunction. Problems due solely to naming should be interpreted as reflecting dominant hemisphere dysfunction.

Receptive Speech A left hemisphere injury is usually indicated when Receptive is the highest scale and is at least 15 points above the critical level. A less significant elevation (which remains the highest) resulting from problems with the more complex items of the scale may be seen with a lesion to the right anterior portion of the brain. This may particularly be the case when mild elevations on Receptive are combined with those on either Memory, Rhythm, Visual, and/or Intelligence and Arithmetic. However, when Receptive is more highly elevated, this will generally indicate a left hemisphere disorder.

Expressive Speech As with the Receptive scale, a left hemisphere disorder is indicated when Expressive is significantly elevated above the critical level. Mild elevations (resulting mostly from errors on the last, more complex items of the scale) may be associated with disorders of the right hemisphere.

Writing Elevations here may be the result of spelling, motor writing, and/or spatial deficits. Motor writing deficiencies suggest disorders in the hemisphere contralateral to the hand used for writing, while spatial deficits (when seen in other portions of the battery) should lead one to consider a right hemisphere lesion. Spelling deficits that had not been present premorbidly can result from injuries to either hemisphere.

Reading Left posterior disruption is almost always indicated with Reading scale deficits in individuals who had good reading skills premorbidly. However, left frontal lesions are suggested when highly educated individuals experience mild problems with complex words. Also, deficits due to spatial disruption (inability to follow a line of print) or neglect of the left side (for which the examiner should correct the patient) suggest right hemisphere disruption.

Arithmetic Performance on the Arithmetic scale may possibly be influenced by a lesion in any part of the brain or by preexisting deficits in some normals who are achieving at a level well below that which would be expected (based on years of education). Left hemisphere injury is suggested by an inability to read or write numbers. When difficulty is experienced only when dealing with the spatial aspects of numbers, a right hemisphere disorder is suggested. However, this might also be indicative of left hemisphere involvement.

Memory Very high elevations on Memory scale suggest left hemisphere dysfunction, while lower elevations may reflect dysfunction in either hemisphere. Along with Rhythm, the Memory scale is very sensitive to dysfunction of a subcortical nature. In fact, impaired performance on this scale often accompanies subtle subcortical dysfunction, particularly that of the temporal lobes.

Intelligence Although affected by injuries to either the anterior or posterior region, the Intelligence scale is generally more susceptible to posterior injuries. This scale may also reflect injuries to either hemisphere. A highly elevated Intelligence scale, combined with relatively elevated scores on Rhythm, Visual, Memory, and Arithmetic, indicates disturbance in the right hemisphere, while combinations with Expressive, Reading, and Writing suggest left hemisphere dysfunction.

Pathognomonic This scale not only discriminates best between normal and brain-damaged patients but also allows for a determination of the degree to which the patient has compensated for the brain injury. It is important to note here that the degree of compensation attained is generally affected by several factors, including the time since the injury, severity of permanent brain damage, premorbid functioning, and the nature of the disorder (progressive vs. static). When Pathognomonic is both quite high (i.e., usually 20 points above the critical level) and is the highest scale, an uncompensated injury is likely. Most frequently, this is seen with severe, acute injuries; however, it may also occur in patients with severe chronic dysfunction for which total compensation has not occurred. When quite high but approximately equal to the mean of the scales, compensation has probably occurred and some recovery of function has been demonstrated by the patient. A chronic injury that has generally recovered to the maximum expected level is suggested when Pathognomonic is high but is the lowest of the scales. With this same pattern but with Pathognomonic not as elevated, a less serious state of affairs is likely.

If Pathognomonic is not extremely elevated (less than 20 points above the critical level) but remains the most highly elevated scale, the injury may either be a recent one that is just starting to recover or a more long-standing one where general recovery has taken place but one or more areas of function have not been compensated for. This, then, would likely reflect a rather limited area of dysfunction. An elevated but not high score that is at the same level as the other scores suggests partial recovery with some (generally diffuse) dysfunction remaining.

When Pathognomonic is below the critical level, compensation has likely taken place. In this case and when it is the highest scale, the injury is likely to be compensated for but an area of dysfunction remains. It might also indicate a small, slow-growing lesion causing little disruption or the beginning of a very small, fast-growing lesion. When all scores fall below the critical level and Pathognomonic is either at or below the level of the other scales, a normal profile or a generally recovered injury is indicated.

Left and Right Hemisphere Scales These scales basically reflect sensorimotor functions and are interpreted with respect to the Motor and Tactile scales. The lateralization suggested by the difference between the two scales should be given serious consideration if it is 10 points or more. A difference of more than 20 points generally suggests sensorimotor strip involvement if no peripheral problems are present.

Pattern Analysis of the Clinical Scales

After initial hypotheses are generated from examination of the relationships of the clinical scales to each other, one may wish to proceed to a more global examination of the summary profile. From the work of Lewis, Golden, Moses, et al. (1979), and Golden, Moses, Fishburne, et al. (1981), LNNB summary profiles have been obtained for small groups of patients with localized lesions in either the left or right frontal, temporal, sensorimotor, or parietal-occipital areas. Comparison of the patient's profile to these average localized patterns may serve as a means of supporting initial localization hypotheses. The localized patterns are presented below.

Left Frontal For this group of patients, the highest scores are found on Expressive, Arithmetic, Receptive, and Pathognomonic. This combination of scales, as well as the next highest combination of scales (Writing, Reading, Motor, and Memory), point to left hemisphere difficulties. The equally mild elevations on the two hemisphere scales suggest an injury lying outside of the sensorimotor area. A lower score on Tactile (as compared to Motor), lack of visual deficits, and mild elevations on Reading and Writing (which are sensitive to posterior injuries) relative to the first combination of scales all point to an anterior locus of dysfunction. The elevation on Receptive and its relationship to Expressive are also consistent with a left anterior locus.

Further support for a conclusion of a left frontal focus can come from an examination of the types of errors made during the course of the testing. On

Expressive, the primary deficits are found on the items requiring spontaneous and complex speech, and possibly on the sequencing items. Clear expressive speech deficits, if present, will generally be found on the most complex items unless the lesion extends into the sensorimotor area. In this case, lateralized deficits will be noted on the Motor and Left Hemisphere scales. Conduction aphasia (generally representing a subcortical temporal lesion) should be considered if repetition errors are present and reading errors are not, or if such errors exist when Receptive is less than or equal to Expressive. Naming deficits on Expressive can be attributed to parietal injuries when these are the only errors noted.

Most frequently, Arithmetic errors are limited to the more complex calculation problems, particularly if these are performed mentally. Problems in complex number reading and writing errors, and errors due to impulsive responding, may also be seen. On the Receptive, Reading, and Writing scales, difficulty is encountered on the more complex items. Slow response rate, as well as deficits on the complex speech/motor items and those requiring bilateral motor movements or complex motor sequences, may be seen on the Motor scale. Indications of severe, lateralized motor impairment suggest involvement of the posterior frontal areas. Rhythm deficits are seen on the expressive and complex receptive items of this scale.

Right Frontal The highest elevations for the right frontal groups are found on Motor, Rhythm, Arithmetic, and Pathognomonic. This pattern may be seen in various right anterior injuries. However, the high elevation on Arithmetic and the elevations of Right Hemisphere over Left Hemisphere and Motor over Rhythm suggest a frontal rather than a temporal locus of dysfunction. In addition, the relatively low elevations on Receptive, Memory, and Intelligence (which are more sensitive to temporal lesions) are consistent with a frontal focus.

Examination of individual items reveals a particular pattern of deficits. On the Motor scale, these include slowness in performing left body side movement (not as pronounced as in sensorimotor lesions) and drawing speed, as well as problems on tasks requiring sequential processing. Rhythm errors tend to be worse on the Expressive items. When present, Tactile and Visual errors are found only on the complex spatial problems. The setting of time is generally harder than reading time on visual. Problems on Arithmetic are similar to those seen in left frontal injuries, with the possible added problem of working with sequencing numbers. Except in cases of mixed or reversed dominance, true dysgraphia or dyslexia will likely not be seen. If present, it is more like those seen in left frontal patients. Expressive deficits may be seen on items requiring sequencing (days of the week and counting). Spontaneous speech and the sequencing of sentences may be impaired due more to slowness than to impoverished speech production. Generally, Receptive errors are limited to items that are syntactically more complex and inverted.

Left Sensorimotor Elevations on Motor, Expressive, Left Hemisphere, Arithmetic, Intelligence, and Pathognomonic characterize these patients. Particularly characteristic is Left Hemisphere being greatly elevated over Right Hemisphere. Although this may be due solely to motor or tactile deficits of the right hand, it is generally due to both.

Deficits on Expressive are seen on both repetition and reading items, as well as on the more complex items. This is due to losses in basic motor speech. Although most characteristics of Broca's aphasia may be present, it is also possible that expressive speech skills will remain intact if the lesion is small and distant from the speech zone. Motor and Tactile errors generally reflect errors on items measuring right body side sensorimotor skills, bilateral coordination, and drawing skills. Due to either sensory or motor deficits, motor writing problems may occur. However, true construction dyspraxia is rare. Arithmetic deficits are similar to those found with the frontal patients, but the severity of the problems may increase if the lesion extends into the parietal area. Concrete thinking and problems with the discursive arithmetic problems (particularly noted on the most difficult problems) are seen with elevations on Intelligence.

Deficits on Reading, Visual, Rhythm, Receptive, and Memory are likely to be absent if care is taken to correct for any speech deficits that may be present. If such has not occurred, all scales may be elevated. If there is significant subcortical involvement, Memory deficits may be present. These will likely be seen on the verbal items of the scale. It is important to note that with stroke patients, it is not unusual to find a left sensorimotor pattern combined with patterns suggestive of involvement of one or more of the other areas.

Right Sensorimotor The pattern of elevations on Motor, Right Hemisphere, and Tactile seen with these patients is characteristic of right hemisphere disorders. Additional elevations on Rhythm, Visual, Memory, and/or Arithmetic might also be present if the lesion extends beyond the sensorimotor area. Motor deficits here are likely to represent mild constructional problems and left body side sensory and motor problems. Rhythm deficits are similar but less severe than those seen with right frontal injuries, while Tactile deficits are generally limited to the left body side. Bilateral dysgraphesthesia and astereognosis may also be noted. However, loss of spatial analysis, rather than bilateral perception problems, is primarily responsible for this.

Left Parietal-Occipital Elevations on Expressive, Reading, Writing, Arithmetic, Intelligence, and Receptive, as well as impairment of the verbal Memory items and the more complex spatial Visual items, attest to the severity of the disruption caused by lesions in this area. Visual deficits will increase and language deficits will decrease the more the occipital lobe is involved. If both areas are involved, deficits in both areas will be noted.

Patterns of deficits will allow for further localization. With occipital-parietal lesions, Arithmetic deficits will be noted. These may include loss of the ability to read and write numbers, to do simple calculations, or to comprehend the meaning of arithmetic signs (dyscalculia). Temporal-occipital lesions will result in Reading deficits, including an inability to associate letters and sounds in the presence of the ability to process auditory and visual information (dyslexia). Lesions more posterior to this area may result in an inability to recognize letters (visual dyslexia) and problems with other visual stimuli. Writing scale deficits, in the form of letter substitution and inability to write to dictation or spell phonemically, result from temporal-parietal lesions. Loss of all these skills, as well as naming problems (dysnomia) across all scales, may occur as a result of injury to the integrative temporal-parietal-occipital area.

Right Parietal-Occipital These patients show elevations on Motor, Tactile, Visual, and Right Hemisphere. The elevation on Left Hemisphere tends to be higher than that which is seen in other right-sided injuries. The difference between the two hemisphere scales is often much less than is seen with right sensorimotor lesions, and the mildness or absence of verbal scale elevations is quite different from that which is present in right temporal profiles. Left body side deficits are noted on both Motor and Tactile. Deficits on items requiring visual feedback bilaterally, other bilateral items, and constructional items may also be present on Motor, while bilateral dysgraphesthesia and astereognosis may be seen on Tactile. On the Visual scale, complex spatial items, spatial orientation items, and, in severe injuries, complex recognition items are performed poorly. Severe spatial disruption may also result in borrowing and carrying problems and difficulty in the alignment of numbers when performing arithmetic problems. Difficulty in comprehending visual material and solving discursive arithmetic problems may occur on the Intelligence scale.

Left Temporal An extreme elevation on Receptive, accompanied by lesser elevations on all of the verbal scales, is most characteristic of lesions in the posterior half of the temporal lobe. Deficits on Memory or a pattern similar to one found with frontal lesions (especially with extensive subcortical involvement) may characterize more anterior lesions. With the more posterior lesions, the profile begins to resemble the parietal-occipital profile. The extent of the disorder can be determined by examination of the Receptive scale. With an increase in basic errors will come an increase in the overall profile elevation. Deficits in comprehension of phonemes will be seen in the most severe cases, while less severe cases will result in difficulties in understanding all but the simplest language. Problems in phonemic analysis or association of phonemes to written letters will result in Reading deficits, while poor phonemic skills (except for overlearned material) will lead to Writing deficits. The patient's understanding of grammar and syntax will be impaired. Arithmetic problems presented auditorily will present more problems than those presented visually. Problems in comprehending questions and thinking abstractly may impair the Intelligence performance. Repetition will be more impaired than reading on Expressive, reflecting the comprehension problems. Deficits in both comprehension and repetition likely indicate a cortical (Wernicke's) aphasia. With repetition deficits in the presence of unimpaired comprehension and fluent speech, conduction aphasia (involving a subcortical temporal lesion) would be suspected. In either case, one will find spontaneous speech to be less impaired than what is seen in frontal or sensorimotor lesions.

Right Temporal Patients with lesions in this area show elevations on Motor, Rhythm, Visual, Receptive, Tactile, Intelligence, and Memory. Unlike the case with other right hemisphere lesions, Left Hemisphere is usually slightly elevated over Right Hemisphere (when peripheral or subcortical deficits are absent). This area's role in analyzing unfamiliar stimuli is seen in an improvement that occurs with repeat administration of graphesthesia items on Tactile and, similarly, on visually presented Motor items. Slowing is noted on constructional items, and the more complex visual discrimination and visual-spatial items are performed poorly. The ability to analyze nonverbal auditory stimuli is more impaired than in the right frontal patient. Problems in discriminating closely related phonemes and comprehending inverted and complex grammatical structures may be present on Receptive. Spontaneous speech, sequencing, and, occasionally, visual identification on Expressive may be impaired. Deficits on Memory usually reflect difficulties with the complex, interference, and visual items. Impaired interpretation of visual thematic and some verbal material, along with difficulty on the discursive arithmetic problems, usually appears on Intelligence.

Subcortical Very little data have been gathered on lesions that affect only the subcortical regions of the brain. Preliminary work suggests that subcortical involvement should be considered when a right hemisphere focus is suggested by the clinical scale profile pattern but not by an analysis of the cognitive symptoms, or when evidence of coexisting left and right hemisphere lesions is present. Discrepancies among patterns found on the clinical scales and those on the localization and factor scales (see below) should also alert one to the possibility of a subcortical disorder.

Mixed Lesions These will combine aspects of localized patterns and, in general, are much more common than the classical patterns. Unless one is experienced in localizing injuries and is specifically asked to do so, the examiner should focus on describing deficits, generating hypotheses about the patient's performance from hypotheses regarding localization, and determining the degree to which the three sets of scales are comparable.

Pattern Analysis of the Localization Scales

The empirically derived localization scales can provide the examiner with assistance in generating or confirming hypotheses regarding the nature of the cortical injury. The eight scales are most sensitive to injuries in different brain areas, but not exclusively so. (These scales will subsequently be referred to as

L1, L2, L3, L4, L5, L6, L7, L8.) As with the clinical scales, elevations on any of this set of scales are considered only within the context of their relationship to the other scales.

The scales have been found useful in formulating both general and specific hypotheses regarding the status of the patient's brain. The use of the scales for the determination of the presence of brain damage has already been discussed. If determined to be present, the scales can then assist in lateralizing the injury. In general, lateralization is most simply determined by looking at the highest scale. If the highest scale is a left hemisphere one (L1 to L4), then the injury is likely to be to the left hemisphere; if the highest scale is a right hemisphere one (L5 to L8), the injury is likely to be located in the right hemisphere. This method works best if the highest scale is at least 5 points above the next highest scale. If this is not the case, classification of the two highest scales (in order) may be helpful. In those cases where the two highest scales represent the same hemisphere (LL or RR), the hypothesis is clear. When the two highest scales are found to represent each of the hemispheres (LR or RL), lateralization is likely to be primarily in the hemisphere of the highest scale. Since the probability of error increases here, caution is advised in cases with these profiles.

Localization

Accuracy in localization is best attained when the two highest localization scales are used. When these two scales represent adjacent areas of the brain, an overlapping lesion is likely to be involved. If the three highest scales are within 5 points of each other, then this profile should be used. If the three scales are consistent with a single, large lesion (e.g., elevations on L5, L6, L8), then this becomes the most likely site of dysfunction. If the three scales are greatly disparate in their localization (e.g., L1, L3, L5), one must consider either a subcortical or diffuse disorder.

Initial hypotheses generated by the localization scales are, of course, investigated for accuracy through comparison with the other sets of scales, item patterns, and qualitative data. Consistency among all sources of information increases the likelihood of the initial localization hypothesis being valid. When only some of the deficits are accounted for by this method, the presence of a second area of dysfunction, suggested by secondary elevations, needs to be considered. When the initial hypothesis is generally not confirmed by comparison with the other data, a subcortical lesion must be considered. Here, subcortical interconnections between the areas represented by the two highest scales are first investigated. If this is not substantiated, the possibility of involvement of many areas (suggested by the lower elevations) needs to be considered. Since these scales were derived from items designed to measure cortical functioning, it is not surprising that they may not be adequate in localizing or describing a subcortical lesion. In these cases, other data obtained from history, observations, or neurological examination may be helpful in understanding the deficit.

Pattern Analysis of the Factor Scales

Further assistance in determining the nature of the deficits being investigated is provided by an analysis of the empirically derived factor scales. These scales include Kinesthetic-Based Movement and Oral-Motor Movements for the Motor scale; Rhythm and Pitch Perception for the Rhythm scale; Simple Tactile Sensation and Stereognosis for the Tactile scale; and Visual Acuity and Naming and Visual-Spatial Organization for the Visual scale. Receptive Speech scale factors include Phonemic Discrimination, Relational Concepts, Concept Recognition, Verbal-Spatial Relations, Word Comprehension, and Logical Grammatical Relations. Simple Phonetic Reading, Word Recognition, and Reading Polysyllabic Words comprise the Expressive Speech scale, while Reading Complex Material and Reading Simple Material comprise the Reading scale factors. Writing scale factors include Spelling and Motor Writing Skills. Factor scales for Arithmetic are Arithmetic Calculations and Number Reading. Memory scale factors include Verbal Memory and Visual and Complex Memory, while General Verbal Intelligence, Complex Verbal Arithmetic, and Simple Verbal Arithmetic comprise the scales derived from the Intelligence scale. The title of each of the factor scales may mislead those who are unfamiliar with these scales. Some titles provide a good description of the content of the items contained within the scales. Other scales are more general, making the titles somewhat misleading and thus requiring closer scrutiny of the items.

Factor scale profile patterns were examined by McKay and Golden (1981a) for patients with localized lesions. These provide the examiner with information regarding patterns of deficits that might be seen with localized areas of dysfunction. This additional information can be useful in attempting to confirm hypotheses formulated earlier.

Item Pattern and Qualitative Analysis

Analysis of all three sets of scales will lead one to arrive at a hypothesis that may represent the product of many revisions and modifications of the initial hypothesis. At this point, ideas regarding the nature of the disorder in question are tested against an analysis of individual items. Consistency of the item pattern (which items are missed, which items are performed adequately) strengthens one's confidence in one's hypothesis. Inconsistency, on the other hand, will necessitate further revision and, subsequently, checking again for consistency of the new hypothesis with the item pattern.

It is generally recommended that one initially entertain the likelihood of a single focus of dysfunction. Lack of substantiating evidence for the simple explanation would then necessitate considering more complex hypotheses, which, again, are checked against all available data. Of course, the ability to arrive at a hypothesis that adequately explains all of the results will depend upon the knowledge, experience, and skill of the interpreter.

An integrated hypothesis will also take into consideration qualitative information. These data have to do with the way in which the patient performed an item rather than whether his performance was adequate. It is obtained either through standard testing procedures or by initiating "testing-the-limits" procedures. At this time, a standardized system for scoring qualitative data is being developed. No data for groups of patients with localized lesions or normals are currently available. Even without such norms, however, the LNNB user who is knowledgeable about behavior associated with localized lesions can use qualitative data to verify or question his or her hypothesis. For example, observations of frequent impulsive or perseverative responding (both frequently seen in patients with frontal lobe disorders) would be consistent with a hypothesis of a left frontal lesion. If the hypothesis was that of a left parietal disorder, one would need to reconsider the hypothesis. It is also important to consider historical and other patient factors when doing any clinical case.

REFERENCES

Ariel, R., & Golden, C. J. (1981). *An alternate form of the Luria–Nebraska Neuropsychological Battery: Form II.* Paper presented at the meeting of the National Academy of Neuropsychologists, Orlando, FL.

Bach, P. J. (1983). *Empirical evidence mitigating against the diagnostic utility of the Luria–Nebraska Neuropsychological Battery.* Paper presented at the meeting of the International Neuropsychological Society, Mexico City.

Bach, P. J., Harowski, K., Kirby, K., Peterson, P., & Schulein, M. (1981). The interrater reliability of the Luria–Nebraska Neuropsychological Battery. *Clinical Neuropsychology, 3* (3), 19–21.

Berg, R. A., & Golden, C. J. (1981). Identification of neuropsychological deficits in epilepsy using the Luria–Nebraska Neuropsychological Battery. *Journal of Consulting and Clinical Psychology, 49,* 745–747.

Bryant, E. T. (1982). The relationship of learning disabilities, neuropsychological deficits, and violent criminal behavior in an inmate population (Doctoral dissertation, California School of Professional Psychology, Berkeley, 1982). *Dissertation Abstracts International, 43,* 3182B.

Bryant, E. T., Scott, M. L., Golden, C. J., & Tori, C. D. (1983). *Neuropsychological deficits, learning disability, and violent behavior.* Manuscript submitted for publication.

Chmielewski, C., & Golden, C. J. (1980). Alcoholism and brain damage: An investigation using the Luria–Nebraska Neuropsychological Battery. *International Journal of Neuroscience, 10,* 99–105.

Christensen, A. L. (1975a). *Luria's neuropsychological investigation.* New York: Spectrum.

Christensen, A. L. (1975b). *Luria's neuropsychological investigation: Manual.* New York: Spectrum.

De Obaldia, R., Leber, W. R., & Parsons, O. A. (1981). Assessment of neuropsychological functions in chronic alcoholic using a standardized version of Luria's neuropsychological technique. *International Journal of Neuroscience, 14,* 85–93.

Dill, R. A., & Golden, C. J. (1983). *WAIS-R and Luria–Nebraska intercorrelations.* Manuscript submitted for publication.

Duffala, D. (1979, 1981). Validity of the Luria–South Dakota Neuropsychological Battery for brain-injured persons (Doctoral dissertation, California School of Professional Psychology, Berkeley, 1978). *Dissertation Abstracts International, 39,* 4439B.

Gechter, G. A., Griffith, S. R., & Newell, T. G. (1983, August). *Changes in neuropsychological functions among detoxifying and recovering alcoholics as measured by the Luria–Nebraska Neuropsychological Battery.* Paper presented at the meeting of the American Psychological Association, Anaheim, CA.

Gillen, R. W., Ginn, C., Strider, M. A., Kreuch, T. J., & Golden, C. J. (in press). The relationship of the Luria–Nebraska Neuropsychological Battery to the Peabody Individual Achievement Test: A correlational analysis. *International Journal of Neuroscience.*

Golden, C. J., & Berg, R. A. (1980a). Interpretation of the Luria–Nebraska Neuropsychological Battery: The writing scale. *Clinical Neuropsychology, 2,* (1), 8–12.

Golden, C. J., & Berg, R. A. (1980b). Interpretation of the Luria–Nebraska Neuropsychological Battery by item intercorrelation: Items 1–24 for the Motor scale. *Clinical Neuropsychology, 2* (1), 8–12.

Golden, C. J., & Berg, R. A. (1980c). Interpretation of the Luria–Nebraska Neuropsychological Battery by item intercorrelation: I. Items 25–51 of the Motor scale. *Clinical Neuropsychology, 2* (3), 105–108.

Golden, C. J., & Berg, R. A. (1980d). Interpretation of the Luria–Nebraska Neuropsychological Battery by item intercorrelation: II. The Rhythm scale. *Clinical Neuropsychology, 2* (4), 153–156.

Golden, C. J., & Berg, R. A. (1981a). Interpretation of the Luria–Nebraska Neuropsychological Battery by item intercorrelation: III. The Tactile scale. *Clinical Neuropsychology, 3* (1), 25–29.

Golden, C. J., & Berg, R. A. (1981b). Interpretation of the Luria–Nebraska Neuropsychological Battery by item intercorrelation: VI. The Visual scale. *Clinical Neuropsychology, 3* (2), 22–26.

Golden, C. J., & Berg, R. A. (1981c). Interpretation of the Luria–Nebraska Neuropsychological Battery by item intercorrelation: VII. Receptive Language. *Clinical Neuropsychology, 3* (3), 21–27.

Golden, C. J., & Berg, R. A. (1982a). Interpretation of the Luria–Nebraska Neuropsychological Battery by item intercorrelation: VIII. The Expressive Speech scale. *Clinical Neuropsychology, 4* (1), 8–14.

Golden, C. J., & Berg, R. A. (1982b). Interpretation of the Luria–Nebraska Neuropsychological Battery by item intercorrelation: The Reading scale. *Clinical Neuropsychology, 4* (4), 176–179.

Golden, C. J., & Berg, R. A. (1983a). Interpretation of the Luria–Nebraska Neuropsychological Battery by item intercorrelation: Intellectual Processes. *Clinical Neuropsychology, 5* (1), 23–28.

Golden, C. J., & Berg, R. A. (1983b). Interpretation of the Luria–Nebraska Neuropsychological Battery by item intercorrelation: The Memory scale. *Clinical Neuropsychology, 5* (2), 55–59.

Golden, C. J., & Berg, R. A. (1983c). Interpretation of the Luria–Nebraska Neuropsychological Battery by item intercorrelation: The Arithmetic scale. *Clinical Neuropsychology, 5* (3), 122–127.

Golden, C. J., Berg, R. A., & Graber, B. (1982). Test–retest reliability of the Luria–Nebraska Neuropsychological Battery in stable, chronically impaired patients. *Journal of Consulting and Clinical Psychology, 50,* 452–454.

Golden, C. J., Fross, K. H., & Graber, B. (1981). Split-half reliability of the Luria–Nebraska Neuropsychological Battery. *Journal of Consulting and Clinical Psychology, 49*, 304–305.

Golden, C. J., Graber, B., Moses, J. A., & Zatz, L. M. (1980). Differentiation of chronic schizophrenics with and without ventricular enlargement by the Luria–Nebraska Neuropsychological Battery. *International Journal of Neuroscience, 11*, 131–138.

Golden, C. J., Hammeke, T., Osmon, D., Sweet, J., Purisch, A., & Graber, B. (1981). Factor analysis of the Luria–Nebraska Neuropsychological Battery: IV. Intelligence and Pathognomonic scales. *International Journal of Neuroscience, 13*, 87–92.

Golden, C. J., Hammeke, T. A., & Purisch, A. D. (1978). Diagnostic validity of a standardized neuropsychological battery derived from Luria's neuropsychological tests. *Journal of Consulting and Clinical Psychology, 46*, 1258–1265.

Golden, C. J., Hammeke, T. A., & Purisch, A. D. (1980). *A manual for the administration and interpretation of the Luria–Nebraska Neuropsychological Battery*. Los Angeles: Western Psychological Services.

Golden, C. J., Hammeke, T. A., Purisch, A. D., & Moses, J. A. (1984). *A manual for the administration and interpretation of the Luria–Nebraska Neuropsychological Battery*. Los Angeles: Western Psychological Services.

Golden, C. J., Kane, R., Sweet, J., Moses, J. A., Cardellino, J. P., Templeton, R., Vicente, P., & Graber, B. (1981). Relationship of the Halstead–Reitan Neuropsychological Battery to the Luria–Nebraska Neuropsychological Battery. *Journal of Consulting and Clinical Psychology, 49*, 410–417.

Golden, C. J., MacInnes, W. E., Ariel, R. N., Ruedrich, S. L., Chu, C., Coffman, J. A., Graber, B., & Bloch, S. (1982). Cross-validation of the Luria–Nebraska Neuropsychological Battery to differentiate chronic schizophrenics with and without ventricular enlargement. *Journal of Consulting and Clinical Psychology, 50*, 87–95.

Golden, C. J., Moses, J. A., Fishburne, F. J., Engum, E., Lewis, G. P., Wisniewski, A. M., Conley, F. K., Berg, R. A., & Graber, B. (1981). Cross-validation of the Luria–Nebraska Neuropsychological Battery for the presence, lateralization, and localization of brain damage. *Journal of Consulting and Clinical Psychology, 49*, 491–507.

Golden, C. J., Moses, J. A., Graber, B., & Berg, R. (1981). Objective clinical rules for interpreting the Luria–Nebraska Neuropsychological Battery: Derivation, effectiveness, and validation. *Journal of Consulting and Clinical Psychology, 49*, 616–618.

Golden, C. J., Moses, J. A., Zelazowski, R., Graber, B., Zatz, L. M., Gorvath, T. B., & Berger, P. A. (1980). Cerebral ventricular size and neuropsychological impairment in young chronic schizophrenics. *Archives of General Psychiatry, 37*, 619–623.

Golden, C. J., Osmon, D., Sweet, J., Graber, B., Purisch, A., & Hammeke, T. (1980). Factor analysis of the Luria–Nebraska Neuropsychological Battery: III. Writing, Arithmetic, Memory, Left, and Right. *International Journal of Neuroscience, 11*, 309–315.

Golden, C. J., Purisch, A., Sweet, J., Graber, B., Osmon, D., & Hammeke, T. (1980). Factor analysis of the Luria–Nebraska Neuropsychological Battery: II. Visual, Receptive, Expressive and Reading scales. *International Journal of Neuroscience, 11*, 227–236.

Golden, C. J., Sweet, J., Hammeke, T., Purisch, A., Graber, B., & Osmon, D. (1980). Factor analysis of the Luria–Nebraska Neuropsychological Battery: I. Motor, Rhythm, and Tactile scales. *International Journal of Neuroscience, 11*, 91–99.

Grey, P. T. (1982). A neuropsychological study of dyslexia using the Luria–Nebraska

Neuropsychological Battery. *Dissertation Abstracts International, 34,* 1236B. (University Microfilms No. 82–16, 284).

Hammeke, T. A., Golden, C. J., & Purisch, A. D. (1978). A standardized, short, and comprehensive neuropsychological test battery based on the Luria neuropsychological evaluation. *International Journal of Neuroscience, 8,* 135–141.

Johnson, G. L., Moses, J. A., Cardellino, J. P., & Bryant, E. (1983). *Development of an impairment index for the Luria–Nebraska Neuropsychological Battery.* Manuscript submitted for publication.

Kaimann, C. (1981, August). *A neuropsychological investigation of multiple sclerosis.* Paper presented at the meeting of the American Psychological Association, Los Angeles, CA.

Kaimann, C. R. (1986). A neuropsychological investigation of multiple sclerosis (Doctoral dissertation, University of Nebraska, Lincoln, 1983). *Dissertation Abstracts International.*

Kaimann, C., Knippa, J., Schima, E., & Golden, C. J. (1983). *Relationship of performance on the Luria–Nebraska Neuropsychological Battery to CT-scan findings in multiple sclerosis patients.* Manuscript submitted for publication.

Kane, R. L., Sweet, J. J., Golden, C. J., Parsons, O. A., & Moses, J. A. (1981). Comparative diagnostic accuracy of the Halstead–Reitan and standardized Luria–Nebraska Neuropsychological Batteries in a mixed psychiatric and brain-damaged population. *Journal of Consulting and Clinical Psychology, 49,* 484–485.

Langell, E. M., Purisch, A. D., Green, N., & Golden, C. J. (1983). *Left frontal lobe dysfunction in nonparanoid schizophrenics.* Manuscript submitted for publication.

Lewis, G. P., Golden, C. J., Moses, J. A., Osmon, D. C., Purisch, A. D., & Hammeke, T. A. (1979). Localization of cerebral dysfunction with a standardized version of Luria's neuropsychological battery. *Journal of Consulting and Clinical Psychology, 47,* 1003–1019.

Luria, A. R. (1966). *Higher cortical functions in man.* New York: Basic Books.

Luria, A. R. (1973). *The working brain.* New York: Basic Books.

MacInnes, W. D. (1981). *Aging and its relationship to neuropsychological and neurological measures.* Paper presented at the meeting of the National Academy of Neuropsychologists, Orland, FL.

McGill, J., & Uhl, H. S. (1983). *Aging, neuropsychological functioning, and brain density: Interrelationships.* Paper presented at the meeting of the American Psychological Association, Anaheim, CA.

MacInnes, W. D., Gillen, R. W., Golden, C. J., Graber, B., Cole, J. K., Uhl, H. S., & Greenhouse, A. H. (1983). Aging and performance on the Luria–Nebraska Neuropsychological Battery. *International Journal of Neuroscience, 19,* 179–190.

MacInnes, W. D., Golden, C. J., Sawicki, R. F., Gillen, R. W., Quaife, M., Graber, B., Uhl, H. S., & Greenhouse, A. J. (1982). *Aging, neuropsychological functioning, and regional cerebral blood flow: Interrelationships.* Manuscript submitted for publication.

Malloy, P. F., & Webster, J. S. (1981). Detecting mild brain impairment using the Luria–Nebraska Neuropsychological Battery. *Journal of Consulting and Clinical Psychology, 49,* 768–770.

Marvel, G. A., Golden, C. J., Hammeke, T., Purisch, A., & Osmon, D. (1979). Relationship of age and education to performance on a standardized version of Luria's neuropsychological tests in different patient populations. *International Journal of Neuroscience, 9,* 63–70.

McKay, S. (1981). The neuropsychological test performance of an assaultive psychiatric population (Doctoral dissertation, University of Nebraska, Lincoln, 1980). *Dissertation Abstracts International, 41,* 4269B.

McKay, S., & Golden, C. J. (1979a). Empirical derivation of experimental scales for localizing brain lesions using the Luria–Nebraska Neuropsychological Battery. *Clinical Neuropsychology, 1,* (2), 19–23.

McKay, S., & Golden, C. J. (1979b). Empirical derivation of neuropsychological scales for the lateralization of brain damage using the Luria–Nebraska Neuropsychological Test Battery. *Clinical Neuropsychology, 1,* (2), 1–5.

McKay, S. E., & Golden, C. J. (1981a). The assessment of specific neuropsychological skills using scales derived from factor analysis of the Luria–Nebraska Neuropsychological Battery. *International Journal of Neuroscience, 14,* 189–204.

McKay, S. E., & Golden, C. J. (1981b). Re-examination of the factor structure of the Receptive Language scale of the Luria–Nebraska Neuropsychological Battery. *International Journal of Neuroscience, 14,* 183–188.

McKay, S. E., Golden, C. J., Moses, J. A., Fishburne, F., & Wisniewski, A. (1981). Correlation of the Luria–Nebraska Neuropsychological Battery with the WAIS. *Journal of Consulting and Clinical Psychology, 49,* 940–946.

McKay, S. E., Golden, C. J., & Scott, M. (1981). Neuropsychological correlates of auditory and visual hallucinations. *International Journal of Neuroscience, 15,* 87–94.

McKay, S. E., Golden, C. J., Wolf, B. A., & Perrine, K. (1983). *Factor analysis of the Luria–Nebraska Neuropsychological Battery.* Manuscript submitted for publication.

McKay, S., & Ramsey, R. (in press). Correlation of the Wechsler Memory scale and the Luria–Nebraska Memory scale. *Clinical Neuropsychology,*

Mikula, J. A. (1981). The development of a short form of the standardized version of Luria's neuropsychological assessment (Doctoral dissertation, Southern Illinois University, Carbondale, 1979). *Dissertation Abstracts International, 41,* 3189B.

Moses, J. A. (in press-a). An orthogonal factor solution of the Luria–Nebraska Neuropsychological Battery items: I. Motor, Rhythm, Tactile, and Visual scales. *Clinical Neuropsychology,*

Moses, J. A. (in press-b). An orthogonal factor solution of the Luria–Nebraska Neuropsychological Battery items: II. Receptive Speech, Expressive Speech, Writing, and Reading scales. *Clinical Neuropsychology,*

Moses, J. A. (in press-c). An orthogonal factor solution of the Luria–Nebraska Neuropsychological Battery items: III. Arithmetic, Memory, and Intelligence scales. *Clinical Neuropsychology,*

Moses, J. A. (in press-d). An orthogonal factor solution of the Luria–Nebraska Neuropsychological Battery items: IV. Pathognomonic, Right Hemisphere, and Left Hemisphere scales. *Clinical Neuropsychology,*

Moses, J. A. (in press-e). The relative effects of cognitive and sensorimotor deficits on the Luria–Nebraska Neuropsychological Battery performance in a brain-damaged population. *Clinical Neuropsychology,*

Moses, J. A., Cardellino, J. P., & Thompson, L. L. (1983). Discrimination of brain damage from chronic psychosis by the Luria–Nebraska Neuropsychological Battery: A closer look. *Journal of Consulting and Clinical Psychology, 51,* 441–449.

Moses, J. A., & Golden, C. J. (1979). Cross validation of the discriminative effectiveness of the Standardized Luria Neuropsychological Battery. *International Journal of Neuroscience, 9,* 149–155.

Moses, J. A., & Golden, C. J. (1980). Discrimination between schizophrenic and brain-damaged patients with the Luria–Nebraska Neuropsychological Test Battery. *International Journal of Neuroscience, 14,* 95–100.

Moses, J. A., Golden, C. J., Ariel, R., & Gustavson, J. L. (1983). *Interpretation of the*

Luria–Nebraska Neuropsychological Battery (Vol. 1). New York: Grune & Stratton.

Moses, J. A., Golden, C. J., Berger, P. A., & Wisniewski, A. M. (1981). Neuropsychological deficits in early, middle, and late stages of Huntington's disease as measured by the Luria–Nebraska Neuropsychological Battery. *International Journal of Neuroscience, 14,* 95–100.

Moses, J. A., & Johnson, G. L. (in press). An orthogonal factor solution for the Receptive Speech scale of the Luria–Nebraska Neuropsychological Battery. *International Journal of Neuroscience.*

Moses, J. A., Johnson, G. L., & Lewis, G. P. (in press-a). Reliability analyses of the Luria–Nebraska Neuropsychological Battery summary, localization, and factor scales. *International Journal of Neuroscience.*

Moses, J. A., Johnson, G. L., & Lewis, G. P. (in press-b). Reliability analyses of the Luria–Nebraska Neuropsychological Battery summary, and localization scales by diagnostic group: A follow-up study. *International Journal of Neuroscience.*

Moses, J. A., Johnson, G. L., & Lewis, G. P. (in press-c). Reliability analyses of the Luria–Nebraska Neuropsychological Battery factor scales by diagnostic group: A follow-up study. *International Journal of Neuroscience.*

Osmon, D. C., Golden, C. J., Purisch, A. D., Hammeke, T. A., & Blume, H. G. (1979). The use of a standardized battery or Luria's tests in the diagnosis of lateralized cerebral dysfunction. *International Journal of Neuroscience, 9,* 1–9.

Parolini, R. (1983). Reading, spelling, and arithmetic disabilities: A neuropsychological investigation using Luria's methods (Doctoral dissertation, University of Nebraska, Lincoln, 1982). *Dissertation Abstracts International, 43,* 1996B.

Picker, W. T., & Schlottmann, R. S. (1982). An investigation of the Intellectual Processes scale of the Luria–Nebraska Neuropsychological Battery. *Clinical Neuropsychology, 4,* (3), 120–124.

Plaisted, J. R., & Golden, C. J. (1982). Test–retest reliability of the clinical, factor, and localization scales of the Luria–Nebraska Neuropsychological Battery. *International Journal of Neuroscience, 17,* 163–167.

Prifitera, A., & Ryan, J. J. (1981). Validity of the Luria–Nebraska Intellectual Processes scale as a measure of adult intelligence. *Journal of Consulting and Clinical Psychology, 49,* 755–756.

Puente, A. E., Heidelberg-Sanders, C., & Lund, N. (1982a). Detection of brain damage in schizophrenics measured by the Whitaker Index of Schizophrenic Thinking and the Luria–Nebraska Neuropsychological Battery. *Perceptual and Motor Skills, 54,* 495–499.

Puente, A. E., Heidelberg-Sanders, C., & Lund, N. L. (1982b). Discrimination of schizophrenics with and without nervous system damage using the Luria–Nebraska Neuropsychological Battery. *International Journal of Neuroscience, 16,* 59–62.

Purisch, A. D., Golden, C. J., & Hammeke, T. A. (1978). Discrimination of schizophrenic and brain-injured patients by a standardized version of Luria's neuropsychological tests. *Journal of Consulting and Clinical Psychology, 46,* 1266–1273.

Purisch, A. D., Langell, E. M., & Golden, C. J. (1983). *Performance of paranoid and nonparanoid schizophrenics on the Luria–Nebraska Neuropsychological Battery.* Manuscript submitted for publication.

Ryan, J. J., & Prifitera, A. (1982). Concurrent validity of the Luria–Nebraska Memory scale. *Journal of Clinical Psychology, 38,* 378–379.

Sawicki, R. F., & Golden, C. J. (in press-a). Examination of two decision rules for the global interpretation of the Luria–Nebraska Neuropsychological Battery summary profile. *International Journal of Neuroscience.*

Sawicki, R. F., & Golden, C. J. (in press, b). Multivariate statistical techniques in neuropsychology: I. Comparison of orthogonal rotation methods with the Receptive scale of the Luria–Nebraska Neuropsychological Battery. *Clinical Neuropsychology.*

Sawicki, R. F., Maruish, M. E., & Golden, C. J. (1983). *Comparison of alpha reliabilities of the Luria–Nebraska Neuropsychological Battery.* Manuscript submitted for publication.

Scott, M. L., Cole, J. K., McKay, S. E., Golden, C. J., & MacInnes, W. D. (1982). Neuropsychological performance in schizophrenics with histories of substance abuse. *International Journal of Neuroscience, 17,* 209–213.

Scott, M. L., Cole, J. K., McKay, S. E., Leark, R., & Golden, C. J. (1982). Neuropsychological performance of sexual assaulters and pedophiles. In J. Cole (Chair), *Psychological and neuropsychological concomitants of violent behavior.* Symposium conducted at the meeting of the American Psychological Association, Washington, DC.

Scott, M. L., Martin, R. L., & Liggett, K. R. (1982). Neuropsychological performance of persons with histories of assaultive behavior. In J. Cole (Chair), *Psychological and neuropsychological concomitants of violent behavior.* Symposium conducted at the meeting of the American Psychological Association, Washington DC.

Shelly, C., & Goldstein, G. (1982a). Intelligence, achievement, and the Luria–Nebraska Battery in a neuropsychiatric population: A factor analytic study. *Clinical Neuropsychology, 4* (4), 164–169.

Shelly, C., & Goldstein, G. (1982b). Psychometric relations between the Luria–Nebraska and Halstead–Reitan Neuropsychological Batteries in a neuropsychiatric setting. *Clinical Neuropsychology. 4* (3), 128–133.

Shelly, C., & Goldstein, G. (1983a). Discrimination of chronic schizophrenia and brain damage with the Luria–Nebraska Battery: A partially successful replication. *Clinical Neuropsychology, 5* (2), 82–85.

Shelly, C., & Goldstein, G. (1983b). *Relationships between language skills as assessed by the Halstead–Reitan Battery and the Luria–Nebraska language factor scales in a nonaphasic patient population.* Paper presented at the meeting of the American Psychological Association, Anaheim, CA.

Spitzform, M. (1982). Normative data in the elderly on the Luria–Nebraska Neuropsychological Battery. *Clinical Neuropsychology, 4* (3), 103–105.

Strider, M. A. (1982). Neuropsychological concomitants of diabetes mellitus (Doctoral dissertation, University of Nebraska, Lincoln, 1982). *Dissertation Abstracts International, 43,* 888B.

Sweet, J. J. (1983). Confounding effects of depression on neuropsychological testing: Five illustrative cases. *Clinical Neuropsychology, 5* (3), 103–109.

Teem, C. L. (1981). Neuropsychological functions in chronic alcoholism. *Dissertation Abstracts International, 42,* 791B. (University Microfilms No. 81–14, 380).

Vicente, P., Kennelly, M. A., Golden, C. J., Kane, R., Sweet., J., Moses, J. A., Cardellino, J. P., Templeton, R., & Graber, B. (1980). The relationship of the Halstead–Reitan Neuropsychological Battery to the Luria–Nebraska Neuropsychological Battery: Preliminary report. *Clinical Neuropsychology, 2* (3), 140–141.

Wolf, B. (1981). *Prediction of the Luria–Nebraska by changes in brain density.* Paper presented at the meeting of the American Psychological Association, Los Angeles, CA.

Zelazowski, R., Golden, C. J., Graber, B., Blose, I. L., Bloch, S., Moses, J. A., Zatz, L. M., Stahl, S. M., Osmon, D. C., & Pfefferbaum, A. (1981). Relationship of cerebral ventricular size to alcoholics' performance on the Luria–Nebraska Neuropsychological Battery. *Journal of Studies on Alcohol, 42,* 749–756.

8

The Kaufman Assessment Battery for Children: Development, Structure, and Application in Neuropsychology

Cecil R. Reynolds and
Randy W. Kamphaus

The Kaufman Assessment Battery for Children (K-ABC) (Kaufman & Kaufman, 1983a) is a recently published, individually administered clinical test of intelligence and achievement designed specifically for use with children from 2½ to 12½ years of age. The K-ABC was developed from a theoretical framework that to a large degree reflects a coalescence of the work of Luria and Vygotsky and American researchers with interests in cerebral specialization. As such, the K-ABC is of obvious interest to clinical neuropsychologists. This chapter will provide an overview of the K-ABC, its methods of development and standardization, and its technical properties; it will also point out *potential* applications in clinical neuropsychology. Definitive work on use of the K-ABC in this field lies in the future, but it has many characteristics that portend usefulness as part of neuropsychological assessment.

The impending release of the K-ABC was announced at the annual convention of the American Psychological Association, held in Washington, D.C., in August 1982. The K-ABC was eventually published on schedule in early April 1983. Since its release, the K-ABC has received considerable attention from both the lay (Starr, 1983; West, 1982) and professional (e.g., *Journal of*

Psychoeducational Assessment, Volume 1, 1983) presses, and a specialty newsletter devoted entirely to the K-ABC has started publication *(K-ABC Information/Edge)*. The Fall 1984 issue of the *Journal of Special Education* was devoted entirely to the K-ABC.

The previous work of the K-ABC authors, Alan S. and Nadeen L. Kaufman, is well known in the area of intellectual assessment. Alan Kaufman had had a major impact on the assessment of children's intelligence long prior to the K-ABC. As Research Associate at The Psychological Corporation, Kaufman was project director for development of the WISC-R and the McCarthy Scales, tasks to which he was well suited because of his studies at Columbia under the tutelage of Robert L. Thorndike. Subsequently, Kaufman's (1975) article on the factor analysis of the WISC-R standardization sample (still one of the most cited articles in WISC-R research) provided an important reminder to clinicians that, as was the case with the old WISC, the updated WISC-R produced three factors. Hence, it is not always possible to interpret the verbal and performance IQs as unitary dimensions. A possibly more legendary article by Kaufman (1976) cautioned psychologists against overinterpreting verbal and performance IQ discrepancies that were quite common in the general population.

Kaufman and Kaufman's first book, *Clinical Evaluation of Young Children with the McCarthy Scales* (1977), provided a logical framework for summary of major research findings for what was at the time a new, and somewhat unique, measure of intelligence. Prior to the K-ABC, however, Kaufman was probably best known for his text *Intelligent Testing with the WISC-R* (1979a). Anastasi (1982) says of Kaufman's book that

> [T]he most important feature of [Kaufman's] approach is that it calls for individualized interpretations of test performance, in contrast to the uniform application of any one type of pattern analysis . . .. The basic approach described by Kaufman undoubtedly represents a major contribution to the clinical use of intelligence tests. (p. 466)

Throughout his writings, however, one detects a sense of dissatisfaction with many aspects of existing intelligence tests.

In an article published in the *Journal of Research and Development in Education* (1979b), Kaufman set the stage for the development of the K-ABC. In that article, he maintained that "[I]ndividual intelligence testing has been remarkably resistant to change, despite advances in related fields such as psychology and neurology." Kaufman argued that substantive theoretical advances in intelligence research had gone unheeded in the conservative test-publishing industry and that the field lacked any true innovations since the work of Binet around the turn of the century. In developing his intelligent testing philosophy (an outgrowth of Wesman's 1968 intelligent testing approach), Kaufman gave great emphasis to the need for theory-driven assessment and interpretation of children's intelligence. Kaufman (1979b) then set the stage for the emphasis on theory in the development of the K-ABC. The Kaufmans' emphasis on assessing intelligence from a strong theoretical base is one characteristic of the K-ABC that, perhaps more than anything else, distinguishes it from its predecessors, and it is the derivation of that theory that creates much of interest to the neuropsychologist.

AN OVERVIEW OF THE SCALE

The Kaufmans' first test development goal for the K-ABC was to assess intelligence from a strong theoretical and research base (Kaufman & Kaufman, 1983a). The K-ABC intelligence scales are based on a model of sequential and simultaneous information processing. The theoretical underpinnings of the processing model were gleaned from a convergence of research and theory in a variety of areas but stemmed principally from Kaufman's evaluation and interpretation of research and theories in clinical neuropsychology (particularly Luria, 1966), cerebral specialization (Bogen, 1969; Sperry, 1968), and cognitive psychology (Neisser, 1967).

Simultaneous processing refers to the child's ability mentally to integrate input simultaneously in order to solve a problem correctly. Simultaneous processing frequently involves spatial, analogic, and organizational abilities (Kaufman & Kaufman, 1983a), as well as solving problems through the application of visual imagery. The Triangles subtest on the K-ABC (an analogue of Wechsler's Block Design task) is a prototypical measure of simultaneous processing. In order to solve these items correctly, one must mentally integrate the components of the design to "see" the whole. Similarly, the Spatial Memory subtest (a novel task) requires the child to memorize the spatial locations of stimuli and then identify the correct locations of the stimuli on a blank grid. Whether the tasks are spatial or analogic in nature, the unifying characteristic of simultaneous processing is the mental synthesis of the stimuli to solve the problem, independent of the sensory modality of the input.

Sequential processing, on the other hand, emphasizes the arrangement of stimuli in sequential or serial order for successful problem solving. In every instance, each stimulus is linearly or temporally related to the previous one (Kaufman & Kaufman, 1983a), creating a form of serial interdependence. An example from the K-ABC is the Word Order subtest, a task that requires the child to point to a series of silhouettes of common objects (e.g., tree, shoe, hand) in the sequence that the objects were named by the examiner—sometimes following a color-interference activity. In this task, and in other Sequential Processing subtests, the child has to place the stimuli in their proper order; it is not acceptable merely to reproduce the input without regard to the serial order. Other Sequential Processing tasks include Hand Movements, which involves visual input and a motor response, and Number Recall, which involves auditory input and a motor response. Therefore, the mode of presentation or response is not what determines the scale placement of a task; rather it is the mental processing demands of the task that are important (Kaufman & Kaufman, 1983a). Of course, no one with an intact brain uses only a single type of information processing to solve problems. These two methods of information processing are constantly interacting (even in the so-called split brain following commissurotomy, the two hemispheres of the brain often whisper to each other, even if they cannot talk), although one approach will usually take a lead role in processing. Which method of processing takes the lead role can change according to the demands of the problem or, as is the case with some individuals, persist across problem type (i.e., forming what Das, Kirby, & Jarman, 1979, refer to as habitual modes of processing). In fact, any problem can be solved through either method of processing. In most cases, one method is clearly superior to another. It is the latter case that makes the K-ABC a viable tool—the two scales are *primarily,* not exclusively, sequential and simultaneous processing measures. Pure scales do not exist, just as pure processing (all or none in one mode of processing) does not exist.

Of course, processing dichotomies are nothing new. What makes the processing dichotomy of the K-ABC so appealing is its breadth of support. Table 8.1 shows the definition of sequential and simultaneous processing adopted by the Kaufmans and quotes from other researchers in cerebral specialization and cognitive psychology who describe highly similar mental processes. Although neither the definitions nor the specific terms are identical, it is easy in this table to see far more overlap than difference between these concepts. Another appealing facet of this particular dichotomy is that it lends itself to designing interventions based on neuropsychological processing strengths (cf. Reynolds, 1981) and to evaluating the outcome of cognitive rehabilitation programs following brain trauma without the contaminating effects of academic achievement.

An equally important component of the K-ABC is the Achievement scale. This scale measures abilities that complement the intelligence scales. The Achievement scale contains measures of what have traditionally been identified as verbal intelligence (verbal concept formation and vocabulary), general information, and acquired school skills (arithmetic, letter and word reading, and word and sentence comprehension). Performance on the Achievement scales is viewed as an estimate of children's success in the application of their mental processing skills to the acquisition of knowledge from the environment (Kaufman, Kaufman, & Kamphaus, 1986). Knowing all the while that it is not possible to separate completely *what* you know (achievement) from *how well* you think (intelligence), the Kaufmans wanted to distinguish the two variables better than in the past. This requires a different conceptualization of intelligence that not all have been able to grasp, still clinging to measures of achievement such as Arithmetic and Expressive Vocabulary as the best measures of intelligence or *g* (e.g., Keith, 1986; Keith & Dunbar, 1984). Surely

TABLE 8.1 Definitions of the Two Types of Mental Processing That Underlie the K-ABC Intelligence Scales from the K-ABC Manual and from Several Theoretical Perspectives

Source	Labels for Process	Definitions
K-ABC Kaufman & Kaufman (1983a)	Sequential	"places a premium on the serial or temporal order of stimuli when solving problems" (p. 2)
	Simultaneous	"demands a gestalt-like, frequently spatial, integration of stimuli to solve problems with maximum efficiency" (p. 2)
Cerebral Specialization Nebes (1974) (summarizing model of Bogen, Levy-Agresti, and Sperry)	Analytic/propositional/ left hemisphere	"sequentially analyzes input, abstracting out the relevant details to which it associates verbal symbols in order to more efficiently manipulate and store the data" (p. 13)
	Synthetic/appositional/ right hemisphere	"organize(s) and treat(s) data in terms of complex wholes, being in effect a synthesizer with a predisposition for viewing the total rather than the parts" (p. 13)
Luria/Das Das, Kirby, & Jarman (1979)	Successive	"processing of information in a serial order. The important distinction between this type of information processing and simultaneous processing is that in successive processing the system is not totally surveyable at any point in time. Rather, a system of cues consecutively activates the components" (p. 89)
	Simultaneous	"the synthesis of separate elements into groups, these groups often taking on spatial overtones. The essential nature of this sort of processing is that any portion of the result is at once surveyable without dependence upon its position in the whole" (p. 89)
Cognitive Psychology Neisser (1967)	Sequential/serial	"viewed as a constructive process, it constructs only one thing at a time. The very definition of 'rational' and 'logical' also suggest that each idea, image, or action sensibly related to the preceding one, making an appearance only as it becomes necessary for the aim in view" (p. 297)

TABLE 8.1 *(continued)*

Source	Labels for Process	Definitions
		"A spatially serial activity is one which analyzes only a part of the input field at any given moment . . . On the other hand, *sequential* refers to the manner in which a process is organized; it is appropriate when the analysis consists of successive, interrelated steps" (p. 72)
	Parallel/Multiple	"carries out many activities simultaneously, or at least independently"

From Kaufman (1984). Reprinted with permission.

testing dyslexic youngsters' intelligence by evaluating their vocabulary or store of general information is inappropriate, if not quite as silly as using Arithmetic to assess the intelligence of a child with dyscalculia. This has long been a problem in certain aspects of neuropsychological assessment, where educational background and level of formal schooling can easily confound testing results. Outside of sensory measures and a relatively small number of other tests, it is seldom clear whether we are assessing processing problems or the result of the processing dysfunction or a specific educational deficit. The K-ABC, with its particular selection of co-normed tasks, seems to offer some real advantages in this regard.

The Intelligence scales consist of subtests that are combined to form scales of Sequential Processing, Simultaneous Processing, and the Mental Processing Composite, a summary score reflective of the sequential and simultaneous scales. On the separate Achievement scale, subtests are combined to form a global Achievement score. The K-ABC also includes a special short form of the Mental Processing Composite, known as the Nonverbal scale (comprised of tasks that can be administered in pantomime and that are responded to motorically), to assess the intelligence of children with speech or language handicaps, of hearing-impaired children, and of those who do not speak English. It is particularly useful as part of the assessment of children suspected of aphasia and certain of the apraxias. However, the Nonverbal scale is useful as an estimate of general intellectual level only and cannot be subdivided into Sequential or Simultaneous Processing scales.

All of the K-ABC global scales (Sequential Processing, Simultaneous Processing, Mental Processing Composite, Achievement, and Nonverbal) yield standard scores, with a mean of 100 and standard deviation of 15, to provide a commonly understood metric and to permit comparisons of mental processing with achievement for children suspected of learning disabilities. Furthermore, use of this metric allows for easy comparison of the K-ABC global scales to other major tests of intelligence and to popular individually administered tests of academic achievement, provided that the standardization samples are comparable (cf. Reynolds, 1984a). The availability of age-corrected deviation scaled scores for all intraindividual score comparisons offers another advantage to the neuropsychologist. The use of other equivalent-type score systems, such as age or grade equivalents, has long been a problem for interpretation of tests in child clinical neuropsychology (cf. Reynolds, 1982). Standard scores are clearly the most appropriate mechanism for score comparison and the analysis of fluctuations in individual performance, one of the hallmarks of current (and past) neuropsychological approaches to test interpretation.

The K-ABC is comprised of 16 subtests, not all of which are administered to any age group (see Table 8.2). Children aged 2½ are given 7 subtests, age 3 receives 9 subtests, ages 4 and 5 receive 11 subtests (but not precisely the same set of tasks, due to developmental and neuropsychological processing changes), age 6 receives 12 subtests, and the peak of 13 subtests is given to children aged 7 through 12½. Also, attempting to be sensitive to children's development, testing time ranges from about 30 minutes for 2½-year-olds to 1 hour 20 minutes (including the Achievement scale) for 7- to 12½-year-olds. The Mental Processing subtests yield standard scores with a mean of

TABLE 8.2 Subtests Administered to Each Age Group on the K-ABC

Scale	Subtest	2½	3	4	5	6	7 to 12½
Sequential	Hand Movements	X	X	X	X	X	X
	Number Recall	X	X	X	X	X	X
	Word Order			X	X	X	X
Simultaneous	Magic Window	X	X	X			
	Face Recognition	X	X	X			
	Gestalt Closure	X	X	X	X	X	X
	Triangles			X	X	X	X
	Matrix Analogies				X	X	X
	Spatial Memory				X	X	X
	Photo Series					X	X
Achievement	Expressive Vocabulary	X	X	X			
	Faces & Places	X	X	X	X	X	X
	Arithmetic		X	X	X	X	X
	Riddles		X	X	X	X	X
	Reading/Decoding				X	X	X
	Reading/Understanding						X
Total number of Subtests		7	9	11	11	12	13

10 and standard deviation of 3, modeled after the familiar Wechsler scaled score. Achievement subtests, on the other hand, yield standard scores with a mean of 100 and a standard deviation of 15, which permits direct comparisons of the mental processing global scales with individual achievement areas.

A brief description of the 16 K-ABC subtests, along with their age range, is given below. An asterisk identifies the subtests that are part of the K-ABC Nonverbal scale, a scale that is offered only for children aged 4 through 12½ years and that is described above.

K-ABC Subtests

Mental Processing Scale

Sequential Processing Scale
* *Hand Movements* (Ages 2½–12½ years)
Imitating a series of hand movements in the same sequence as the examiner performed them.
Number Recall (Ages 2½–12½ years)
Repeating a series of digits in the same sequence as the examiner said them.
Word Order (Ages 4–12½ years)
Touching a series of pictures in the same sequence as they were named by the examiner, with more difficult items employing a color-interference task.

Simultaneous Processing Scale
Magic Window (Ages 2½–4 years)
Identifying a picture that the examiner exposes by moving it past a narrow slit or "window," making the picture only partially visible at any one time.
* *Face Recognition* (Ages 2½–4 years)
Selecting from a group photograph the one or two faces that were exposed briefly in the preceding photograph.
Gestalt Closure (Ages 2½–12½ years)
Naming the object or scene pictured in a partially completed "inkblot" drawing.
* *Triangles* (Ages 4–12½ years)
Assembling several identical triangles into an abstract pattern that matches a model.
* *Matrix Analogies* (Ages 5–12½ years)
Selecting the picture or abstract design that best completes a visual analogy.
* *Spatial Memory* (Ages 5–12½ years)
Recalling the placement of pictures on a page that was exposed briefly.

* *Photo Series* (Ages 6–12½ years)
Placing photographs of an event in chronological order.

Achievement Subtests
  Expressive Vocabulary (Ages 2½–4 years)
  Naming the object pictured in a photograph.
  Faces & Places (Ages 2½–12½ years)
  Naming the well-known person, fictional character, or place pictured in a
  photograph or illustration.
  Arithmetic (Ages 3–12½ years)
  Answering a question that requires knowledge of math concepts or the
  manipulation of numbers.
  Riddles (Ages 3–12½ years)
  Naming the object or concept described by a list of three characteristics.
  Reading/Decoding (Ages 5–12½ years)
  Naming letters and reading words.
  Reading/Understanding (Ages 7–12½ years)
  Acting out commands given in written sentences.

Administration and Scoring

Administration and scoring procedures for the K-ABC are available in the
K-ABC Administration and Scoring Manual (Kaufman & Kaufman, 1983b).
One important aspect of the K-ABC administration that deserves special
mention, however, is the notion of teaching items. The first three items of each
mental processing subtest (the sample and the first two items appropriate for a
child's age group) are designated as teaching items. On these items the examiner is required to teach the task if the child fails on the first attempt at
solving the item. By "teaching the task" it is meant that the examiner is
allowed the flexibility to use alternate wording, gestures, physical guidance,
or even a language other than English to communicate the task *demands*
to the child. The examiner is not allowed to teach the child a specific strategy for solving the problem, however. This built-in flexibility is particularly
helpful to preschoolers, minority-group children, and exceptional children,
who sometimes perform poorly on a task in a traditional IQ test, not because
of a lack of ability, but because of an inability to understand the instructions
given. Kaufman (1983) discusses the concept of teaching items in greater
detail and he notes, as is evident from Table 8.4 (later in this chapter)
that this built-in flexibility has not adversely affected the reliability of the
K-ABC.
    The extensive use of sample practice items and teaching items on the K-ABC
helps to ensure that the various subtests actually measure what they were
intended to measure. Many intelligence tests contain basic language concepts,
such as "next," "same," "alike," "opposite," "backwards," and "after," that

less than half of children in kindergarten and a significant number of primary-grade children do not understand (Kaufman, 1978). Subsequently, a child may perform poorly on a test because of a very specific language deficit, when the test was intended to measure psychomotor speed, memory, spatial ability, or some other intellectual ability. Violations of standardized procedure to explain the directions to children make the obtained scores essentially unusable, since the amount and direction of error introduced through such procedures are unknown and are not constant across children (or across examiners). Since the K-ABC was standardized by using the sample and teaching items to ensure the child's understanding of the task, influences on performance are built into the normative data and the error introduced is included in the standard errors of measurement reported in the *K-ABC Interpretive Manual* (Kaufman & Kaufman, 1983a).

The K-ABC basal and ceiling rules, referred to as starting and stopping points in the *K-ABC Administration and Scoring Manual* (Kaufman & Kaufman, 1983b), are also somewhat different from those of many existing intelligence tests. The first rule for administering the K-ABC subtests is very straightforward: examiners are instructed to start and stop testing at the items designated as starting and stopping points for the child's age group. The set of items between the starting and stopping points are, therefore, designed, based on standardization data, to represent a full range of difficulty for the child's age group. This first basal and ceiling rule is very straightforward, but it is also rigid. Hence, several supplemental rules are given to allow examiners to find items of appropriate difficulty for children at the ends of the distribution of ability. The K-ABC also incorporates a very simple discontinue rule, one that is the same for *all* K-ABC subtests.

As noted earlier, the Nonverbal scale is intended for use with children for whom administration of the regular K-ABC (and virtually all other well-normed, standardized measures of intelligence) would be inappropriate: those who are hearing impaired, have speech or language disorders, other communication handicaps, or are limited English proficient. The Nonverbal scale yields a global estimate of intelligence; however, a method for profile interpretation of subtest scaled scores is offered in the *K-ABC Interpretive Manual* (Kaufman & Kaufman, 1983a). Most well-normed intelligence tests that are applicable to communications-handicapped children are very narrow and give a quite limited view of these children's intelligence (e.g., the Columbia Mental Maturity Scale). While the K-ABC Nonverbal scale has limitations in this regard, of those tests of mental ability with adequate technical/psychometric characteristics the K-ABC Nonverbal scale provides the broadest sampling of abilities. This breadth of assessment should enhance studies of these children and their development. The lack of adequately normed scales with any breadth of assessment has been a hindrance not only to clinical assessment of children with communications disorders but to research in the area (Reynolds & Clark, 1983). The Nonverbal scale of the K-ABC is the best-normed, psychometrically most sophisticated nonverbal scale presently available. Several features of the K-ABC also make it a very attractive scale for use in evaluating very low-functioning adolescents. Reynolds and Clark (1985) have described a useful approach to applying the K-ABC (and certain other tests) to this difficult population.

Standardization

The K-ABC was standardized on a sample of 2,000 children, using primarily 1980 U.S. Census figures. The sample was stratified by age, sex, geographic region, race/ethnic group, parental educational attainment (used as a measure of socioeconomic status), community size, and educational placement (regular class placement versus placement in one of a variety of programs for exceptional children). Educational placement is an infrequently used stratification variable. Typically, exceptional children are excluded from the standardization samples for individually administered tests. An attempt was made to include representative proportions of learning-disabled, mentally retarded, gifted and talented, and other special populations in the standardization sample according to data provided by the National Center for Education Statistics and the U.S. Office of Civil Rights. With all exceptional populations combined, the total percentage of exceptional children included in the K-ABC standardization sample was 6.9%, compared to 8.9% for the U.S. school-age population. An overview of the K-ABC standardization sample, indicating its match to the U.S. Census data for the variables of geographic region, race/ethnic group, parental education, and community size, is presented in Table 8.3. Overall, the match is quite good, although high socioeconomic status (SES) minorities (specifically blacks and Hispanics) were statistically significantly oversampled. The real effect was small, however, resulting in an overestimation of black and Hispanic populations' total scores by around two points on the Mental Processing Composite (overestimation here referring to the mean scores of these groups had their representation in the standardization sample been a perfect match to the 1980 U.S. Census Bureau statistics).

Reliability

Split-half reliability coefficients for the K-ABC global scales ranged from .86 to .93 (mean = .90) for preschool children, and from .89 to .97 (mean = .93) for children aged 5 to 12½ years. Mean internal consistency reliability coefficients for the global scales and the subtests are shown in Table 8.4. A test–retest reliability study was conducted with 246 children retested after a 2- to 4-week interval (mean interval = 17 days). The results of this study showed good estimates of stability that improved with increasing age. For the Mental Processing Composite, coefficients of .83, .88, and .93 were obtained for age groups 2½ through 4, 5 through 8, and 9 through 12½ respectively. Excellent

TABLE 8.3 Representation of the K-ABC Standardization Sample (Ages 2½ through 12½) by Geographic Region, Race/Ethnic Group, Parental Education, and Community Size

Region	K-ABC Sample (N)	(%)	U.S. Population (%)	Race or Ethnic Group	K-ABC Sample (N)	(%)	U.S. Population (%)
East	401	20.0	20.3	White	1,450	72.5	73.1
North Central	565	28.2	26.5	Total minorities	550	27.5	26.8
South	628	31.4	34.0	Black	311	15.6	14.5
West	406	20.3	19.2	Hispanic	157	7.8	9.1
				Native American, Asian, or Pacific Islander	82	4.1	3.2

Parental Education	K-ABC Sample (N)	(%)	U.S. Population (%)	Community Size	K-ABC Sample (N)	(%)	U.S. Population (%)
Less than high school education	384	19.2	21.1	Central city	579	28.9	27.9
High school education	813	40.6	41.1	Suburb or small town	876	43.8	43.8
Some college	413	20.6	19.8	Rural area	545	27.2	28.3
College degree	390	19.5	18.0				

test–retest coefficients in the .95 to .97 range were obtained for the Achievement scale at each age group. Further details of the test–retest study can be found on pages 81–84 of the *K-ABC Interpretive Manual* (Kaufman & Kaufman, 1983a).

The test–retest reliability coefficients for the global scales, and to a lesser extent the internal consistency (split-half) coefficients, show a clear developmental trend, with coefficients for the preschool ages being smaller than those for the school-age range. This trend is consistent with the known variability over time that characterizes preschool children's standardized test performance in general.

As is shown in Table 8.4, the reliability coefficients of the K-ABC subtests typically meet or exceed those for comparable intelligence tests (Kaufman & Kaufman, 1983a). Mean internal consistency reliability coefficients for the K-ABC subtests ranged from .72 to .89 for preschool children and from .71 to .92 for school age children. Test–retest coefficients for the subtests given in the *K-ABC Interpretive Manual* (Kaufman & Kaufman, 1983a) show the same predictable developmental trend identified for the global scales, and are consistent with the values for such traditional intelligence scales as the various Wechsler Scales and the McCarthy Scales.

TABLE 8.4 Average Reliability Coefficients for the K-ABC Scales and Subtests

Scale or Subtest	Preschool Children (Ages 2½ through 4) N=500 Mean r Across Age	School-Age Children (Ages 5 through 12½) N=1,500 Mean r Across Age
Global Scales[a]		
Sequential Processing	.90	.89
Simultaneous Processing	.86	.93
Mental Processing Composite	.91	.94
Achievement	.93	.97
Nonverbal	.87	.93
Mental Processing Subtests[b]		
1. Magic Window	.72	
2. Face Recognition	.77	
3. Hand Movements	.78	.76
4. Gestalt Closure	.72	.71
5. Number Recall	.88	.81
6. Triangles	.89	.84
7. Word Order	.84	.82
8. Matrix Analogies		.85
9. Spatial Memory		.80
10. Photo Series		.82
Achievement Subtests[b]		
11. Expressive Vocabulary	.85	
12. Faces & Places	.77	.84
13. Arithmetic	.87	.87
14. Riddles	.83	.86
15. Reading/Decoding		.92
16. Reading/Understanding		.91

Note: The values shown for preschool children are the mean coefficients for three age groups (2½, 3, and 4), and the values shown for school-age children are the mean coefficients for eight age groups.
[a]Composite score reliability coefficients were computed based on Guilford's (1954, p. 393) formula.
[b]All coefficients for the subtests were derived using the split-half method and corrected by the Spearman–Brown formula.

Validity

The *K-ABC Interpretive Manual* (Kaufman & Kaufman, 1983a) includes the results of 43 validity studies, an impressive amount of prepublication research that is all too uncommon in test manuals. Studies were conducted on aspects of construct, concurrent, and predictive validity. In addition, several of the studies were conducted with samples of exceptional children, including samples classified as hearing impaired, physically impaired, gifted, mentally retarded, and learning disabled.

Topics considered under construct validity include developmental changes, internal consistency, factor analysis, and convergent and divergent relationships to other measures. Of particular interest are the data on factor analysis and correlations with other tests. Since both of these areas of construct validity are discussed in detail in the K-ABC manuals and elsewhere (e.g., Reynolds, 1984b), only a synopsis of the findings in the *K-ABC Interpretive Manual* is given here.

Several prepublication factor analytic studies were conducted with early research editions of the K-ABC (Kaufman, Kaufman, Kamphaus, & Naglieri, 1982; Naglieri, Kaufman, Kaufman, & Kamphaus, 1981). In addition, Kamphaus, Kaufman, and Kaufman (1982) factor analyzed the published edition of the K-ABC using the 2,000 children from the standardization sample. All of these exploratory studies support the division of the intelligence scales into the Sequential and Simultaneous Processing scales. An overview of the findings from the Kamphaus, Kaufman, and Kaufman (1982) study is presented in Table 8.5.

Subsequent confirmatory factor analytic research provides strong support for the two-factor sequential and simultaneous processing model (Keith, 1986; Willson, Reynolds, Chatman, & Kaufman, in press) but is less enthusiastic in support of a distinct Achievement scale. Hence, it is possible to find a better mathematical fit to the subtests' structure when the Achievement scale subtests are included; however, the psychological meaning of such structures is highly suspect since they are being developed after the fact in a manner reminiscent of Monday morning quarterbacking and not from an *a priori* theoretical base, as did the Kaufmans. The subtests of the Achievement scale do show their largest loadings on a separate, clearly identifiable factor, as Kaufman and Kaufman (1983b) proposed, yet each shows large secondary and tertiary loadings on the two mental processing factors. Though some would interpret the Achievement scale as a good measure of verbal intelligence or perhaps even *g* (e.g., Keith, 1985), this seems ill advised since it involves so many assumptions regarding equal opportunity to acquire certain knowledge and is, in addition, extremely inferential, relying primarily upon acquired factual knowledge rather than the manipulation of information to solve a problem.

Of particular interest to various clinicians is the relationship of the K-ABC to the WISC-R. Numerous studies involving the K-ABC and WISC-R are reported in the *K-ABC Interpretive Manual* (Kaufman & Kaufman, 1983a). In a study of 182 children enrolled in regular classrooms, the Mental Processing Composite (MPC) correlated .70 with WISC-R Full-Scale IQ (FSIQ). Hence, the K-ABC Mental Processing scales and the WISC-R share a 49% overlap in variance. These findings indicate that the K-ABC does bear a substantial relationship to the widely used WISC-R; yet these data also indicate that the K-ABC is hardly a duplicate of the WISC-R, but possesses its own unique contribution to the field of intelligence measurement. Also of interest in this

**TABLE 8.5 Mean Sequential/Simultaneous Factor Loadings for
Preschool and School-Age Children**

Scale	Preschool (Ages 2½ through 4)		School-Age (Ages 5 through 12½)	
	Sequential	Simultaneous	Sequential	Simultaneous
Sequential Processing				
3. Hand Movements	*.60*	.19	*.37*	*.43*
5. Number Recall	*.64*	.28	*.77*	.15
7. Word Order	*.69*	.32	*.75*	.26
Simultaneous Processing				
1. Magic Window	.21	*.63*		
2. Face Recognition	.28	*.40*		
4. Gestalt Closure	.23	*.59*	.08	*.53*
6. Triangles	*.36*	*.47*	.20	*.72*
8. Matrix Analogies			.30	*.57*
9. Spatial Memory			.24	*.60*
10. Photo Series			.26	*.69*

Note: Factor loadings were obtained by principal factor analysis with varimax rotation. Factor loadings of .35 and above are italicized.

sample is the standard score difference between the MPC and FSIQ. The K-ABC, based on 1980 U.S. Census data, was shown to be about 3 points tougher (mean MPC = 113.6) than the WISC-R (mean FSIQ = 116.7), based on a sample of 182 children from regular classes (Kaufman & Kaufman, 1983a).

Relations With Neuropsychological Measures: Preliminary Data

Of particular importance to understanding how the K-ABC can contribute to neuropsychology will be learning how this new scale relates to existing measures commonly used in neuropsychological settings. To be useful in neuropsychological assessment, the K-ABC should be related to existing measures, but not so closely that its use with other preexisting scales is merely redundant. As yet, no data are available that relate the K-ABC to the myriad of Halstead–Reitan techniques; several comparisons with the Luria–Nebraska Children's Battery have been conducted. The first such report was by Snyder, Leark, Golden, Grove, and Allison (1983).

Snyder et al. (1983) evaluated 46 elementary school children (ages 8 to 12½) who had been referred for a variety of learning difficulties. All children were administered the K-ABC, WISC-R, and LNNB-CR as described in Golden (1981). Correlations between the K-ABC and LNNB-CR ranged from −.01 (LNNB-CR Writing Scale with K-ABC simultaneous) to −.64 (LNNB-CR Intelligence with K-ABC Sequential and MPC). The LNNB-CR Intelligence scale correlated highest of all LNNB-CR scales with the K-ABC global scales (SIM, −.54; SEQ, −.64; MPC, −.64; Nonverbal, −.51; ACH −.26). The K-ABC ACH scales correlated from −.50 to −.58 with the school-related scales of the LNNB-CR (e.g., Expressive Language, Reading). The K-ABC mental processing scales were also significantly related to each WISC-R IQ; correlations ranged from .35 between SEQ and PIQ to .72 between the MPC and FSIQ and the Nonverbal and FSIQ. The K-ABC ACH scale correlated .66 with FSIQ, .77 with VIQ, but only .28 with PIQ. After examining the overall pattern of correlations in the study, Snyder et al. concluded that the relationships revealed were "basically consistent" with the model of intelligence on which the K-ABC was based and the theoretical perspective of Luria in particular. Snyder et al. also concluded that the K-ABC provides additional information, beyond the WISC-R and LNNB-CR, that should be useful to the clinical neuropsychologist.

In a follow-up study with a larger sample of 65 children, Leark, Snyder, Grove, and Golden (1983) provide more detailed information. Table 8.6 displays the correlation matrix between the K-ABC global scales and the subscales of the LNNB-CR. Several interesting patterns emerge here. The LNNB-CR subscales that are known to be the most sensitive to brain impairment (Pathognomic and Intellectual) are clearly the most closely related to performance on all of the K-ABC global scales. Although there is very little overlap in item content from these scales to the K-ABC, the K-ABC seems sensitive to deficits in cortical functioning, at least at the level of the higher information processing functions of the brain. The SEQ-SIM distinction and the separate Achievement scale of the K-ABC receive support from the pattern of correlations in Table 8.6 as well. The school-related subscales of the LNNB-CR correlate considerably higher with the K-ABC ACH scale than with the mental processing scales. Clear differentiation occurs elsewhere as well. When evaluating correlations with the LNNB-CR Rhythm scale, one sees that the SEQ scale is significantly related to the Rhythm Scale ($r = −.40$) while the SIM scale is not ($r = −.13$). A similar pattern is observed for the LNNB-CR Receptive Speech scale. Additionally, the K-ABC Nonverbal scale is more highly correlated with the LNNB-CR Motor scale than is any other K-ABC scale. The Nonverbal and the SIM scales are more closely related to the LNNB-CR Visual scale than is the SEQ scale. Most of these relationships are intuitively obvious, but their actual occurrence, especially given the moderate magnitude of the relationships, is certainly encouraging with respect to potential contributions of the K-ABC to neuropsychological assessment and research. Two other recent studies address the use of the K-ABC in neuropsychologically related diagnosis and evaluation.

Telzrow, Redmond, and Zimmerman (1984) recently looked at the test score patterns of children classified into Boder's three subtypes of dyslexia— dysphonetics, dyseidetics, and mixed. These children could not be dif-

**TABLE 8.6 Correlations Between the K-ABC Global Scales and the
Luria–Nebraska Children's Battery Summary Scales ($n = 65$)**

Luria–Nebraska Scales	K-ABC Global Scales				
	Sequential	Simultaneous	MPC	Achievement	Nonverbal
Motor	−.382	−.424	−.456	−.242	−.481
Rhythm	−.405	−.132	−.282	−.370	−.199
Tactile	−.115	−.320	−.270	−.221	−.321
Visual	−.252	−.498	−.461	−.192	−.489
Receptive	−.515	−.355	−.482	−.600	−.427
Expressive	−.323	−.154	−.260	−.614	−.258
Writing	−.324	−.144	−.248	−.539	−.246
Reading	−.210	−.060	−.066	−.618	−.012
Arithmetic	−.307	−.152	−.258	−.607	−.202
Memory	−.471	−.300	−.427	−.629	−.356
Intelligence	−.567	−.570	−.645	−.439	−.599
Pathognomonic	−.598	−.469	−.606	−.649	−.656
Left SM	−.171	−.379	−.335	−.222	−.352
Right SM	−.075	−.319	−.244	−.091	−.301

From Leark et al. (1983). Reprinted with permission.

ferentiated on the basis of their Bannatyne patterns on the WISC-R. Boder's
subtypes were randomly distributed across Banatyne's suggested patterns. On
the K-ABC a significant relationship ($p < .01$) occurred between the Boder
classification and the pattern of Sequential-Simultaneous score differences on
the K-ABC. In particular, Boder's dysphonetic dyslexics were far more likely to
display a SIM greater than SEQ pattern than were the other diagnostic groups.
Although Telzrow et al. used a small sample ($N = 23$), the results are impressive with large effect sizes.

Morris and Bigler (1985) have investigated whether the K-ABC SEQ and
SIM scales can be related to left and right hemispheric functioning and whether
the K-ABC is better able to indicate neuropsychological deficits than the
WISC-R. In this study, 79 children aged 6 to 12 years were administered the
WISC-R, the K-ABC, and several neuropsychological measures of left and
right hemisphere functioning. Neuropsychological test scores were collapsed
into two composite scores for each subject, right hemisphere (RH) and left
hemisphere (LH). Twenty-five children who were right-handed and neurologically impaired were divided into three groups according to their K-ABC scores:
SIM < SEQ, SEQ > SIM, and SIM = SEQ. A one-way MANOVA revealed a
significant difference among these groups on the RH and LH scores ($p < .05$),
but not for WISC-R groups using VIQ=PIQ differences for classification ($p =
.41$). Further analyses revealed that the key to understanding these differences
was the inability of the WISC-R to detect RH dysfunction. While both scales
seemed to pick up left dysfunction, only the K-ABC could diagnose RH

problems at a statistically significant level. These results are also consistent with lateralization of sequential and simultaneous processing of the left and right hemispheres respectively, results also consistent with the findings of Leark et al. (1983).

The K-ABC seems to be related, both theoretically and empirically to neuropsychological functioning, even at this early stage in its career. The moderate but consistent relationships with other neuropsychological batteries bodes well for its use, indicating that it does provide additional information. It also seems more closely related than the Wechsler series to recent neuropsychological models of higher cognitive processes. The Wechsler series is much more researched at this point, however, and we should proceed cautiously with the K-ABC; existing data are very promising and dictate that research should continue full speed ahead.

Implications for Educational Rehabilitation

Another test development goal for the K-ABC was to develop a children's intelligence test that yields scores capable of providing guidance to educational interventions (Kaufman & Kaufman, 1983a). Chapter 7 of the *K-ABC Interpretive Manual* (Kaufman & Kaufman, 1983a) provides a framework for educational intervention. In this chapter various approaches to remediating academic problems in children are reviewed (e.g., modality training and processing training) and their advantages and disadvantages discussed. Based on this review of other approaches to remediation, the Kaufmans propose that interventions based on K-ABC results should focus on the design of instructional programs that teach the relevant academic skill using curriculum materials that capitalize on a child's mental processing strengths and that de-emphasize the child's weaknesses. Some pilot studies using the model, which produced positive results, are also described and more extensive projects are underway.

The K-ABC thus adopts a strength model of remediation, as opposed to deficit-centered ability-training models, such as the ITPA, that permeate much of current (and past) special education practice. The K-ABC approach to remediation is not an ability-training model at all—it does not attempt to train or remediate any underlying cognitive deficits. Rather, the K-ABC philosophy is reflected in the attitude that the best remedial program for a child who cannot read is to teach the child to read, but to do so using methods and materials optimally related to the child's best information-processing skills. The focus is clearly on direct instruction in the child's area of academic deficit, allowing children to exploit their preference for processing in a particular way. The structure of the K-ABC provides theoretical guidance to this admittedly nebulous area of educational research and practice, sorely needed guidance (cf. Reynolds, 1981) that is focused on instruction, not peripheral activities.

The K-ABC provides a clear model for using neuropsychological data and theories to make inferences regarding important aptitudes for the individual learner. A model for matching neuropsychological aptitudes to treatment approaches that is nicely complemented by the K-ABC has been presented by Hartlage and Telzrow (1983). Their model teaches "circumvention" of dysfunctional areas of the brain to develop compensatory (not remedial) skills and then to capitalize on the child's strengths. Hartlage and Telzrow's approach is very much in line with the K-ABC philosophy and may be particularly useful to the neuropsychologist in designing rehabilitation approaches from K-ABC results, thus expanding the potential utility of the K-ABC in clinical application in neuropsychology.

EARLY POSTPUBLICATION RESEARCH

It appears that the K-ABC is going to spur a considerable amount of research, as is evidenced by the interest generated in the scholarly as well as lay presses. Research on the K-ABC already began to appear in journals and on the programs of professional meetings even before the formal publication of the scale. Articles and paper presentations are beginning to appear on factor analyses of the K-ABC (Kaufman & Kamphaus, 1984; Willson, Reynolds, Chatman, & Kaufman, 1986), age progression of the K-ABC subtests (Reynolds, Willson, & Chatman, 1983), correlations of the K-ABC with other tests (Bing & Bing, 1984; Harrison & Kamphaus, 1984; McLoughlin & Ellison, 1984; Naglieri & Haddad, 1984; Snyder, Leark, Golden, Grove, & Allison, 1983; Zins & Barnett, in press), profile interpretation of the K-ABC with normal (Naglieri & Kamphaus, 1986) and special populations (Reynolds & Clark, 1984, 1986), and the use of the K-ABC with Appalacian children (Clark, 1984), trainable mentally retarded children (Kaplan & Klanderman, 1984), learning-disabled children (Klanderman, Perney, & Kroeschell, 1984), and gifted children (McCallum & Karnes, 1984). Certainly, the plethora of postpublication research and special journal issues devoted to the K-ABC will make the K-ABC a well-researched and therefore better understood test instrument.

A disappointing aspect of the postpublication research available to date is that no research has appeared regarding the K-ABC model of educational translation. One hopes that this is due to the youth of the K-ABC. One of our fears is that, faced with a lack of research in this area, clinicians will have only intuition and theory to guide their practice.

EARLY REVIEWS OF THE K-ABC

As of this writing the K-ABC has been reviewed for *The Reading Teacher* (Narrett, in press), the 9th edition of the *Mental Measurements Yearbook* (Anastasi, 1985), and the *Journal of Psychoeducational Assessment* (Das,

1984), although other reviews are undoubtedly being prepared. The most thorough reviews are those by Anastasi and Das.

Anastasi expresses concern that some statements in the manuals may buttress common misconceptions about the nature of performance on intelligence tests. Specifically, statements about separating the assessment of acquired knowledge (achievement) from problem-solving ability (mental processing) masks the fact that even information-processing skills are impacted by a child's experiential background. Space does not permit discussion of the full review, but the following statement seems eloquently to sum up Anastasi's review:

> The K-ABC is an innovative cognitive assessment battery, whose development meets high standards of technical quality. When used by a qualified professional, it is a promising instrument for dealing with important practical testing needs. It should, however, be presented to the testing community with suitable cautions against probable misuses.

Das's review, on the other hand, focuses more on the theoretical basis for the K-ABC. Although he describes the subtests as reliable, interesting to children, and accompanied by clear administration procedures, he faults the *K-ABC Interpretive Manual* in several areas. He cites the *K-ABC Interpretive Manual* as lacking evidence of the degree to which the K-ABC assesses *g*. More importantly, he states that the K-ABC does not measure the whole brain, but that using Luria's (1966) formulation, the K-ABC measures only one of the "three major divisions of cortical functions." Given that the K-ABC is only for use with children from the ages of 2½ to 12½ and given that any cognitive device is to some degree a measure of Luria's block-one functions, this seems a particularly curious criticism. Many, if not most, of the crucial intellective aspects of the frontal lobe–block-three functions are not functional to a large extent until the age of about 12 years or so. Attempts to provide any kind of thorough assessment of the cognitive self-regulatory decision-making and planning functions of the third Lurian block are currently considered futile for the most part (e.g., Golden, 1981). Even the several versions of the Americanized standardized version of the Children's Luria–Nebraska Neuropsychological Battery do not attempt to assess such functions at these younger ages.

CONCLUSIONS

In this chapter we have attempted to provide the reader with an overview of the K-ABC, including its genesis in the Kaufmans' work in intellectual assessment, a brief description of the major properties of the instrument, and a summary of some of the early reviews of the K-ABC. The K-ABC is a controversial test instrument that is generating unprecedented research and discussion of issues in intellectual assessment. Despite its controversial nature, it has obtained a degree of acceptance in the assessment of handicapped children unrivaled since the introduction of the WISC in 1949. The K-ABC has promoted interest in theoretical issues in intelligence testing by clinicians and spurred academicians to become more keenly involved in practical issues in intellectual assessment. Perhaps an enduring legacy of the K-ABC will be that it, as much as any other intelligence test, has promoted discussion that may lead to innovation in the practice of intellectual assessment. Whatever the final outcome of the evaluation of its own specific usefulness in the assessment of children, few can argue that the latter is not a major contribution to psychology and to education.

REFERENCES

Anastasi, A. (1982). *Psychological testing* (5th ed.). New York: Macmillan.

Anastasi, A. (1984). The K-ABC in historical and contemporary perspective. *Journal of Special Education, 18,* 357–366.

Anastasi, A. (1985). In J. V. Mitchell (Ed). *Ninth Mental Measurement Yearbook.* Lincoln, NE: University of Nebraska Press.

Bing, S., & Bing, J. (1984, April). *Relationship between the K-ABC and PPVT-R for preschoolers.* Paper presented at the meeting of the National Association of School Psychologists, Philadelphia, PA.

Bogen, J. E. (1969). The other side of the brain: Parts, I, II, and III. *Bulletin of the Los Angeles Neurological Society, 34,* 73–105, 135–162, 191–203.

Clark, R. (1984, April). *Research with the K-ABC and an Appalachian sample.* Paper presented at the meeting of the National Association of School Psychologists, Philadelphia, PA.

Das, J. P. (1984). Review of the Kaufman Assessment Battery for children [K-ABC]. *Journal of Psychoeducational Assessment, 2,* 83–88.

Das, J. P., Kirby, J., & Jarman, R. F. (1979). *Sequential and simultaneous cognitive processes.* New York: Academic Press.

Guilford, J. P. (1954). *Psychometric methods.* 2nd Ed. New York: McGraw Hill.

Golden, C. J. (1981). The Luria–Nebraska Children's Battery: Theory and initial formulation. In G. Hynd & S. Obrzut (Eds.), *Neuropsychological assessment and the school age child: Issues and Procedures,* New York: Grune & Stratton.

Harrison, P. L., & Kamphaus, R. W. (1984, April). *Comparison between the K-ABC and Vineland Adaptive Behavior Scales.* Paper presented at the meeting of the National Association of School Psychologists, Philadelphia, PA.

Hartlage, L. C., & Telzrow, C. F. (1983). The neuropsychological basis of educational intervention. *Journal of Learning Disabilities, 16,* 521–528.

Kamphaus, R. W. (1983, August). *The relationship of the Kaufman Assessment Battery for Children (K-ABC) to diagnostic measures of academic achievement.* Paper presented at the meeting of the American Psychological Association, Anaheim, CA.

Kamphaus, R. W., Kaufman, A. S., & Kaufman, N. L. (1982, August). *A cross-validation study of sequential-simultaneous processing at ages 2-1/2–12-1/2 using the Kaufman Assessment Battery for Children (K-ABC).* Paper presented at the meeting of the American Psychological Association, Washington, D.C.

Kaplan, R. J., & Klanderman, J. W. (1984, April). *Neuropsychological profile of T.M.H. youngsters assessed with the K-ABC.* Paper presented at the meeting of the National Association of School Psychologists, Philadelphia, PA.

Kaufman, A. S. (1975). Factor analysis of the WISC-R at eleven age levels between 6½ and 16½ years. *Journal of Consulting and Clinical Psychology, 43,* 145–147.

Kaufman, A. S. (1976). Verbal-performance IQ discrepancies on the WISC-R. *Journal of Consulting and Clinical Psychology, 44,* 739–744.

Kaufman, A. S. (1978). The importance of basic concepts in the individual assessment of preschool children. *Journal of School Psychology, 16,* 207–211.

Kaufman, A. S. (1979a). *Intelligent testing with the WISC-R.* New York: Wiley-Interscience.

Kaufman, A. S., (1979b). Cerebral specialization and intelligence testing. *Journal of Research and Development in Education, 12,* 96–107.

Kaufman, A. S. (1983). Some questions and answers about the Kaufman Assessment Battery for Children (K-ABC). *Journal of Psychoeducational Assessment, 1,* 205–218.

Kaufman, A. S. (1984). K-ABC and controversy. *Journal of Special Education, 18,* 409–444.

Kaufman, A. S., & Kamphaus, R. W. (1984). Factor analysis of the Kaufman Assessment Battery for Children (K-ABC) for ages 2½ through 12½ years. *Journal of Educational Psychology, 76,* 623–637.

Kaufman, A. S., & Kaufman, N. L. (1977). *Clinical evaluation of young children with the McCarthy scales.* New York: Grune & Stratton.

Kaufman, A. S., & Kaufman, N. L. (1983a). *K-ABC interpretive manual.* Circle Pines, MN: American Guidance Service.

Kaufman, A. S., & Kaufman, N. L. (1983b). *Kaufman Assessment Battery for Children (K-ABC) administration and scoring manual.* Circle Pines, MN: American Guidance Service.

Kaufman, A. S., Kaufman, N. L., & Kamphaus, R. W. (1986). The Kaufman Assessment Battery for Children (K-ABC). In C. S. Newmark (Ed.), *Major psychological assessment instruments.* Newton, MA: Allyn and Bacon.

Kaufman, A. S., Kaufman, N. L., Kamphaus, R. W., & Naglieri, J. A. (1982). Sequential and simultaneous factors at ages 3–12-1/2: Developmental changes in neuropsychological dimensions. *Clinical Neuropsychology, 4,* 74–81.

Keith, T. K. (1985). Questioning the K-ABC: What does it measure? *School Psychology Review, 14,* 2–21.

Keith, T. K., & Dunbar S. B. (1984). Hierarchical factor analysis of the K-ABC: Testing alternative models. *Journal of Special Education, 18,* 367–376.

Klanderman, J. W., Perney, J., & Kroeschell, Z. B. (1984, April). *Comparisons of the K-ABC and WISC-R for LD children.* Paper presented at the meeting of the National Association of School Psychologists, Philadelphia, PA.

Leark, R. A., Snyder, T., Grove, T., & Golden, C. J. (1983, August) *Comparison of the K-ABC standardized neuropsychological batteries: Preliminary results.* Paper presented to the annual meeting of the American Psychological Association, Anaheim, CA.

Luria, A. R. (1966). *Human brain and psychological processes.* New York: Harper & Row.

McCallum, R. S., & Karnes, F. (1984). The test of choice for assessment of gifted children: A comparison of the K-ABC, WISC-R, and Stanford Binet. *Journal of Psychoeducational Assessment, 2,* 57–63.

McLoughlin, C. S., & Ellison, C. L. (1984, April). *Comparison of scores for normal preschool children on the Peabody Picture Vocabulary Test–Revised and the Achievement Scale of the Kaufman Assessment Battery for Children.* Paper presented at the meeting of the National Association of School Psychologists, Philadelphia, PA.

Morris, J. M., & Bigler, E. (1985, January) *An investigation of the Kaufman Assessment Battery for Children (K-ABC) with neurologically impaired children.* Paper presented to the annual meeting of the International Neuropsychological Society, San Diego.

Naglieri, J. A., & Haddad, F. (1984). Learning disabled children's performance on the Kaufman Assessment Battery for Children: A concurrent validity study. *Journal of Psychoeducational Assessment, 2,* 49–56.

Naglieri, J. A., & Kamphaus, R. W. (in press). Interpreting the subtest profile on the Kaufman Assessment Battery for Children. *Clinical Neuropsychology.*

Naglieri, J. A., Kaufman, A. S., Kaufman, N. L., & Kamphaus, R. W. (1981). Cross-validation of Das' simultaneous and successive processes with novel tasks. *Alberta Journal of Educational Research, 27,* 264–271.

Narrett, C. M. (in press). Review of the Kaufman Assessment Battery for Children (K-ABC). *The Reading Teacher.*

Nebes, R. D. (1974). Hemispheric specialization in commissuorotomized man. *Psychological Bulletin, 81,* 1–14.

Neisser, U. (1967). *Cognitive Psychology.* New York: Appleton-Century-Crofts.

Reynolds, C. R. (1981). Neuropsychological assessment and the habilitation of learning: Considerations of the search for the aptitude X treatment interaction. *School Psychology Review, 10,* 343–349.

Reynolds, C. R. (1982). The importance of norms and other psychometric concepts to assessment in clinical neuropsychology. In R. N. Malatesha & L. C. Hartlage (Eds.), *Neuropsychology and cognition* (Vol. II). The Hague: Martinus Nijhoff, pp. 55–76.

Reynolds, C. R. (1984a). Critical measurement issues in learning disabilities. *Journal of Special Education,*

Reynolds, C. R. (1984b) K-ABC. Special issue of *Journal of Special Education, 18*(3).

Reynolds, C. R., & Clark, J. H. (Eds.) (1983). *Assessment and programming for children with low incidence handicaps.* New York: Plenum Publishing.

Reynolds, C. R., & Clark, J. H. (1984, November) *Profile analysis of standardized intelligence test performance of very high IQ children.* Paper presented to the annual meeting of the National Association for Gifted Children, St. Louis.

Reynolds, C. R., & Clark, J. H. (1985). Profile analysis of standardized intelligence test performance of very low functioning individuals. *Journal of School Psychology.*

Reynolds, C. R., Willson, V. L., & Chatman, W. (1983, March). *Relationships between age and raw score increases on the Kaufman Assessment Battery for Children.* Paper presented at the meeting of the National Association of School Psychologists, Detroit, MI.

Snyder, T. J., Leark, R. A., Golden, C. J., Grove, T., & Allison, R. (1983, March). *Correlations of the K-ABC, WISC-R, and Luria–Nebraska Children's Battery for exceptional children.* Paper presented at the meeting of the National Association of School Psychologists, Detroit, MI.

Sperry, R. W. (1968). Hemisphere deconnection and unity in conscious awareness. *American Psychologist, 23,* 723–733.

Starr, D. (1983). Split-brain I.Q. test. *Omni, 5*(10), 35.

Telzrow, C., Redmond, C., & Zimmerman, B. (1984, October). *Dyslexic subtypes: A comparison of the Bannatyne, Boder, and Kaufman models.* Paper presented at the annual meeting of the National Academy of Neuropsychologists, San Diego.

Wesman, J. (1968). Intelligent testing. *American Psychologist, 23,* 267–274.

West, S. (1982). A smarter test for intelligence? *Science, 82,* 3(9), 14.

Willson, V. L., Reynolds, C. R., Chatman, S., & Kaufman, A. S. (in press). Confirmatory analysis of sequential and simultaneous processing factors for children ages 2-1/2 to 12-1/2 years. *Journal of School Psychology.*

Zins, J. E., & Barnett, D. W. (in press). A validity study of the K-ABC, WISC-R, and Standford Binet with non-referred children. *Journal of School Psychology.*

PART III
Treatment

9

Single Case Design for Neuropsychology

Jeffrey S. Webster,
Robert McCaffrey, and
Reda R. Scott

Case studies have had considerable impact on both neuropsychology and behavioral psychology. Consider, for example, the degree to which present neuropsychological conceptualizations of language mechanisms have been influenced by Paul Broca's study of the aphasic patient Leborgne in 1861 (Restak, 1984). Likewise, examine how current behavioral approaches to treating anxiety-based disorders have been influenced by Mary Cover Jones's (1924) treatment of a single patient, Peter. Since these early, relatively simple studies, single case methodology has been improved to allow the use of more sophisticated and powerful strategies with the individual subject.

Advances made by basic experimental neuropsychologists in the area of single case design have improved the ability to identify and describe deficits resulting from focal brain injuries and unusual information processing syndromes. In contrast, advances made by behavior therapists in the area of single case design have improved the ability to demonstrate the efficacy of a given therapeutic or training technique. With reference to neuropsychology, behavioral single case designs are most directly relevant to the retraining of patients with brain injury. However, behavioral strategies can also contribute to the description of brain–behavioral relationships essential to sound experimental neuropsychological investigation. The goal of this chapter is to demonstrate the considerable overlap between single case strategies of both basic experimental neuropsychology and behavior therapy.

BASIC EXPERIMENTAL NEUROPSYCHOLOGISTS' METHODS FOR IMPROVING STUDY OF THE UNIQUE SINGLE CASE

When using behavior of brain-injured patients as a neuropsychological index, various levels of interpretation can be made. At the most direct level, the measured behavior is a sample of a behavioral problem, as in the case of a poor Wechsler Memory Scale (WMS) Logical Memory score interpreted as indicating the subject has trouble repeating information that is orally presented. At this level no inferences are made regarding the presentation of this behavioral deficit at other levels of interpretation (e.g., implications for information processing, neurostructural integrity, etc.). As will be discussed later, such a direct level of interpretation is encouraged in behavior analysis.

Failure on a neuropsychological test can also be viewed as a sign that a support subsystem is malfunctioning. The hypothesized subsystem can have either information processing or biological referents. In the case of information processing, the inability to recall paragraphs from the WMS represents a breakdown in subsystems essential to encoding, storage, and/or retrieval of verbal information. When the focus of research is determining the value of a biological subsystem, performance on the WMS might be used to understand what the thalamus or other brain structures contribute to memory. Subject selection criteria and experimental design differ according to whether research focuses on biological or information processing questions.

Subject Selection

Neurobiological Research

When single case design is used in neurobiological model building, considerable neurodiagnostic data must be available on the subject to document the presence of the injury of interest and the absence of other injuries or abnormalities that could obscure the results. Measures of both brain structure and activity should be available, making CT scans and electroencephalography essential.

The etiology of the injury is also important, because the type of insult is predictive of the diffuseness of neurological damage. Disorders known to be focal in nature and of abrupt onset are most desirable for this type of research. Thus, patients with small strokes would be preferable to those with acceleration/deceleration traumatic injury in which diffuse axonal shearing is likely.

With reference to rate of onset, patients who have undergone successful surgical treatment for rapidly growing tumors are better subjects than those with successful treatment of slower growing tumors, because in the latter case "spontaneous" recovery and compensation may have altered the typical function of the structure (Gouvier, Webster, & Blanton, Chapter 11, this volume).

It is difficult to determine the most opportune time for testing patients following injury. Testing too soon may confound the influence of primary lesion effects with generalized influences of the injury process on the brain (e.g., edema, diaschesis), while waiting too long can result in contamination of the primary influences with the recovery process.

Subjects selected for study should have few concurrent problems that will potentially obscure results. Psychiatric disorders, severe cardiovascular limitations, chronic pain, and diabetes are examples of conditions that may affect neuropsychological performance independently of any recent damage. Also, longstanding neurological disease weakens the conclusions one can draw. For example, many conclusions regarding language in the right hemisphere were based upon commissurectomized epileptics who had suffered seizure disorders since early childhood. Springer and Deutsch (1981) have questioned the generalizability of conclusions based on this sample because of the possibility that the underlying disease producing the long-term seizure disorder had altered the functional neuroanatomy of these subjects.

Information Processing Research

Criteria for subject selection are somewhat different in information processing research, wherein brain-injured patients serve to test components of models that cannot be tested any other way because they are too interwoven and occur too quickly in the intact brain. The only means of validating a given component is to show that focal brain damage affects a cognitive activity in a way predicted by the model. Figure 9.1 shows an early model of memory, which proposes that orally presented material directly enters both short- and long-term memory stores (Shallice & Warrington, 1970). Because this model posits that short- and long-term memory operate in parallel, it predicts that some brain-injured patients will show very poor short-term memory but normal long-term memory. In a now classic case study, Warrington and Shallice (1969) demonstrated this pattern of strengths and weaknesses in a patient.

Information processing researchers' emphasis on finding pure forms of neuropsychological deficits has lessened the importance of etiology and/or location of lesions. Instead, subjects are chosen by the presence of specific deficits in the absence of evidence supporting alternative hypotheses, such as low intellectual ability and deprived learning history (Shallice, 1979). In addition, as with neurobiological research, the ideal subject for information processing research should have no history of serious psychiatric problems and other nonneurological deficits potentially contributing to the performance.

Background Assessment of the Subject

Both neurobiological and information processing research require a general description of the subject's strengths and weaknesses, including tests of cognition, language, memory, perception, and motor functions. In this phase of

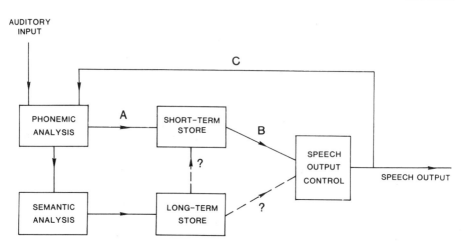

FIGURE 9.1. Suggested model for processing in auditory verbal memory experiments. *Source:* From "Independent Functioning of Verbal Stores: A Neuropsychological Study," by T. Shallice and E. K. Warrington, 1970, *Quarterly Journal of Experimental Psychology, 22,* 261– 273. Copyright © 1970 by the *Quarterly Journal of Experimental Psychology.* Reprinted by permission of the Experimental Psychology Society.

experimentation, it is best to use tests with substantial normative data. Such tests will allow the conversion of test results to standard scores, thus providing direct comparison of performance across the various tasks as long as all tests were standardized on very similar samples (Lezak, 1983; Anastasi, 1976).

Standard scores are typically generated by transforming the raw score to a Z score (score-mean/standard deviation), except when tests have significantly skewed distributions. In this case, it is preferable to normalize the distribution by converting scores to a frequency distribution and transforming them to percentiles. Anastasi (1976) provides a detailed description of this procedure. The resultant normalized standard scores and Z scores can be transformed to more convenient scales, such as stainines, deviation IQs, and the more commonly used T scores.

The use of standard scores facilitates the establishment of individual standards of comparison, which refer to the performance level expected if the subject had not received the injury. These standards serve as a reference point for the interpretation of performance levels across tasks. A WAIS Full-Scale IQ estimate of 100, for example, would have a different meaning if the individual standard of comparison indicated the patient should be functioning in the top 5% of the population.

The best standard, obviously, is preinjury test performance, but these data are rarely available. The most common method of idiographic estimation has been to use test data for predicting preinjury performance levels. Various tests from the Wechsler Adult Intelligence Scale have been recommended for this purpose. Based on the assumption that Verbal test scores reflect crystallized intelligence (i.e., abilities less likely to be influenced by aging, injury, or other types of change), the Vocabulary test (Yates, 1954) and the combination of the Information and Comprehension tests (Gouvier, Bolter, Veneklasen, Hutcherson, & Long, 1983) were suggested as the best index of premorbid abilities. However, when injuries affect the ability to comprehend questions, produce language, organize answers, and evaluate output, such complex language tests are sensitive to the injury and are, therefore, poor measures of premorbid ability. McFie (1975) suggested that the most stable test from the Performance subtests of the WAIS, Picture Completion, be used in conjunction with the Vocabulary test to estimate preinjury abilities, with the stipulation that when either test score is very depressed, the other should be used alone.

An alternative approach for generating individual comparison standards is to weight demographic factors and generate an expectancy score. Wilson and colleagues (1978) subjected several demographic characteristics (age, sex, education, occupation, and race) of normals to regression analysis and found they could predict WAIS summary scores. The formulae were developed on the WAIS standardization sample, which had an average educational attainment of 10.1 years. Recent statistics indicate the median educational attainment was 12.3 years in 1975 (U.S. Bureau of Census). To adjust for these changes the authors suggested the resultant educational product be multiplied by .82. Empirical investigations of Wilson et al.'s (1978) formulae have shown that the resultant estimations have been highly correlated with the actual WAIS scores. Unfortunately, the formula has consistently misclassified 30 to 50% of the individual cases (Klesges, Sanches, & Stanton, 1981; Bolter, Gouvier, Veneklasen, & Long, 1982). Typically, the formula overestimates the actual IQ score (Klesges et al., 1981). Adjusting the education estimate, however, has improved the results substantially (Klesges et al., 1981; Bolter et al., 1982). A similar formula was recently developed for predicting summary scores of the WAIS-R based on the subject's age, education, race, sex, occupation, and region (Barona, Reynolds, & Chastain, 1984). Although the formula has yet to be cross-validated, this method of estimating occupation and other demographic variables appears to be much improved over Wilson et al.'s (1978) formula.

To date, no empirical basis for selecting one summary formula over another has emerged. As a guideline, if VIQ and PIQ are significantly different and no history of learning disability is evident, the authors would use the higher of the two tests. If VIQ and PIQ are not significantly different, the FSIQ estimate would be used.

Demographic factors are not always an accurate estimate of premorbid abilities, as witnessed in the bright student who left school in the 10th grade to help with family finances. Such cases have led researchers to develop individual comparison standards incorporating both demographic information and data from the subject's present test performance. Gouvier et al. (1983) improved prediction, based on Wilson et al.'s (1978) formula, by including age-corrected Information and Comprehension scores into the formula. Estimates for normal subjects were accurate nearly 90% of the time. Unfortunately, the formula faired less well than Wilson et al.'s original with head-injured patients suffering injuries affecting WAIS subtests. Thus, Gouvier et al. recommended its use only with patients whose performance on the Verbal scales appeared to be within normal limits.

Lezak (1983) advocated the use of the best performance method for generating individual comparison standards. Her method utilizes test scores as well as observations and historical data in an effort to estimate the highest level of performance the individual has produced. Fundamental to this method is the assumption that in intact, well-adjusted adults, there is little scatter among the tests. Any marked discrepancy among performance levels across tasks reflects ". . . evidence of disease, developmental anomalies, cultural deprivation, emotional disturbance, or some other condition that has interfered with the full expression of the person's intellectual potential" (pp. 94–95). However, this approach would not be appropriate in the case of the overachiever who has excelled beyond his or her natural ability by persistent study and who may perform better on tests of vocabulary and arithmetic than on other tests because of rote learning. Lezak also contended that a single high score on a memory test should not be used as an individual comparison standard, as memory tests do not correlate well with measures of cognition.

While the merits of Lezak's suggestion may be limited because of the dispute over the power of the G-factor in the breadth of higher cortical functions (Gould, 1981), her insistence on surveying the subject's historical accomplishments, present activities, and residual abilities is very important. Her system's subjectivity is not a limitation at present, since no system for estimating individual comparison standards has produced substantial empirical support.

Recommendations for Generating an Individual Comparison Standard

It is evident that there is no completely satisfactory system for generating an individual comparison standard. Instead, there are several methods from which the researcher or clinician can choose. The following are the authors' recommendations for selecting a particular method. First, it is important to collect as much background data as possible. School, military service, and occupational records should be investigated, and requests for these records should specify exactly what is needed. The authors have found that specifically requesting psychological testing data often results in getting such records from educational systems when a general request for information may not result in any indication that psychological testing had been completed.

Next, test scores on neuropsychological instruments with adequate normative information should be converted to normalized standard scores and plotted in some fashion (see Long & Wagner, Chapter 20, this volume). Given the available background data and the pattern of neuropsychological test scores, a method for generating an individual comparison standard should emerge. If all scores are low and the subject's medical history suggests diffuse injury while his or her personal history suggests above-average performance prior to the injury, the best basis for estimation is demographic data. In contrast, if neuropsychological data show substantial scatter and the specific subtests used in generating the individual comparison standard are among the highest scores, then methods incorporating performance scales as well as demographic data should be considered. This is especially true when a demographic variable is problematic, as in the case of a high school graduate with a D+ average who apparently obtained his or her degree on the basis of a series of social promotions rather than performance.

The chosen method should then be calculated and plotted. The authors propose that the expected score should be exceeded by some of the subject's actual test scores unless he or she has generalized structural/physiological impairment. If the subject's pattern of deficits shows variability, and his or her higher scores are in the normal range of the general population, the expected average should not exceed these scores. When this happens, alternative means of calculating individual comparison standards should be considered. However, when making such a decision, sensory, motor, and memory tests should be excluded because of their weak relationship with tests of cognition. Along with data from neuropsychological tests, this analysis must include tests of psychopathology and self-appraisal of deficits as suggested by Chelune and Moehle (Chapter 18, this volume).

Specific Hypothesis Testing

Dissociation and Double Dissociation

Once the initial testing has clearly indicated the subject's areas of strengths and weaknesses, the experimenter must demonstrate the specific deficits that make the patient an unusual or interesting subject. The first step in this process is to show that neuropsychological test scores reflecting activity in the subsystem of interest are not only low but also significantly lower than both the individual standard of comparison and the other test scores. When such a pattern is evident, the functions of interest are said to be *dissociated* from other cognitive functions. It has been suggested that a difference of one standard deviation between the target task and comparison tasks *suggests* dissociation, while a difference of two standard deviations actually *demonstrates* dissociation (Lezak, 1983; Shallice, 1979).

A more powerful demonstration of the presence of an isolated deficit is *double dissociation*, which was initially suggested by Teuber (1955) for group designs but which is also applicable to single case methodology (Shallice,

1979). In this design, two demographically comparable subjects who have lesions in differing brain areas are tested on two tasks, one of which is of theoretical interest (Task A) and the other of which (Task B) is significantly correlated with the first task in normals but may not be of interest in the present study. When the design works as planned, the performance of the subject of interest (Subject 1) will show dissociation with poor performance on Task A and much better performance on Task B. In contrast, the second subject (Subject 2) ideally will show the opposite pattern. The second subject's reversal of the other's pattern demonstrates that the first subject's dissociation cannot be a result of complexity differences across tasks, or greater sensitivity of Task A to the nonspecific effects of brain injury. Hence, the double dissociation technique provides greater support that Subject 1's brain injury produced the poor performance on Task A than does dissociation alone. Kinsbourne (1971) contends that Subject 2 need not have a focal brain injury if only Subject 1 is of interest. Nonetheless, the control subject should not have a lesion compromising the same brain area or information processing subsystem because the results would be ambiguous. If the control subject showed the same dissociation as the experimental subject, this might be the result of both subjects' having damage to the same structures. On the other hand, if the control subject did not show dissociation, this could be interpreted as a failure to replicate Subject 1's findings and, therefore, as evidence that the initial experiment had poor external validity. Consequently, it is best to know as much as possible about the status of the control subject's brain (both lesion and lesion-free areas) so that any ambiguity can be addressed directly.

Generation of New Tasks for Testing Hypotheses

At this point in assessment, a patient's deficits need to be assessed more carefully to determine whether they add new information for biological and/or information processing model building. Typically, this requires the generation of new tasks designed to test the hypotheses of interest. The source of hypotheses can include not only the literature from human neuropsychology but also that of cognitive psychology, psycholinguistics, comparative psychology, and cybernetics. The resultant tasks must include positive investigations to establish the presence of the deficits of interest and negative investigations to demonstrate that other factors potentially responsible for the observed behavior do not play a significant role (Shallice, 1979).

In developing these tasks it should be realized that any results must be replicated with other subjects in order to have a significant impact on the field. Consequently, it is unwise to make these tests too specific to the ability level of the individual patient. Instead, each test should contain items likely to be passed by all neurologically normal subjects, regardless of educational level, as well as items likely to be failed by some normals and by most well-compensated brain-injured individuals showing residual problems in the functions of interest.

Ideally, the resultant tests should be of comparable difficulty for normals since tasks that dissociate because of complexity differences make positive and negative investigations meaningless in brain-injured patients. Item difficulty in psychometric research is often determined by administering the test to a normal sample and analyzing how many subjects fail each item. As an alternative, experimental psychologists have established difficulty ratings for many types of stimulus items. Thorndike and Lorge (1944) rated 30,000 words by their frequency of occurrence in the English language. Others have used subjective ratings by college students to determine the characteristics and complexity of stimulus items. Toglia and Battig (1978), for example, established ratings of the categorizability, meaningfulness, familiarity, and pleasantness of 2,854 words. Similar ratings for nonsense syllables were provided by Hilgard (1951), who also included lists for the level of similarity of various paired associates. Paivio, Yuille, and Madigan (1968) presented level-of-concreteness ratings for 925 nouns. Handel and Garner (1966) had subjects rate the level of pleasantness for meaningless visual patterns, and Snodgrass and Vanderwart (1980) have presented ratings for the meaningfulness, complexity, and familiarity of a set of pictures. Ratings of the quality and intensity of emotional expression in photographs of faces are also available for test construction (Ekman & Friesen, 1975). These various lists have been used sparingly but with great success in neuropsychology (Goodglass & Kaplan, 1983).

For dissociation to be of interest in basic experimental neuropsychological research, it needs to occur not only between tests of comparable difficulty but also between tests that are highly correlated in normals. Fortunately, at this point in assessment, hypotheses of interest typically concern highly related cognitive functions, since these are the only interesting comparisons in contemporary neurobiological and information processing research. Consequently, well conceived hypotheses and well designed tasks are likely to share considerable variance in normals. If experimentation reveals a dissociation, it is still preferable to confirm the typical interrelationships of the tests with a group of normals ($n > 10$) to assure they are highly correlated. If the first two phases of experimentation support the uniqueness of the subject and his or her theoretical importance to experimental neuropsychology, testing may continue over months and sometimes years. For example, Milner's subject, H. M., who suffered bilateral hippocampal damage, has been studied for over three decades (Milner, Corkin, & Teuber, 1968). Hence, some of the recommended validation procedures in this chapter can be postponed until after the initial assessment is completed and after the investigator has collected data suggesting the psychometric properties of the tasks are worth pursuing.

Nonspecific Error in Single Case Designs for Basic Experimental Neuropsychology

Sources of Error

In single case design, nonspecific error cannot be averaged out; it must be directly addressed. One source of error stems from the subject's expectations about personal performance. These expectations may be established prior to the injury, as in the patient who claims to have always had a poor memory and who fails to put forth adequate effort to learn a complicated list of items. Other expectations may be established during the initial recovery process when the general brain response to injury (e.g., brain edema, diaschesis) produces temporary deficits that rapidly clear. If the patient has had a traumatic experience soon after the injury while trying to perform a previously mastered skill, he or she may not have tried it again prior to the neuropsychological evaluation. Consequently, early deficits reported by the patient should be reexamined to determine if they are still relevant.

Another strategy in isolating legitimate postinjury deficits is to analyze the reliability of a deficit by administering several tests of varying complexity that should be failed if the subsystem of interest is malfunctioning. A failure on a single test without support from very similar tests suggests psychological factors may play an important role in the failure.

Temporary nonspecific effects can also influence test performance. General health issues such as pain, cardiac efficiency, seizures, metabolic disturbances, and sleep disturbance are among the problems that can directly as well as indirectly influence attention, concentration, and memory, thereby diminishing cognitive abilities depending on these support functions. Similarly, the subject's emotional status can result in poorer performance than would be expected under normal circumstances. Sometimes emotional distraction may be induced by the testing itself, as in the case of the subject given a verbal memory test which he or she cannot perform because of skill deficits. This failure can evoke a catastrophic reaction that, in turn, may disrupt performance on all subsequent memory tests. Low motivation, either of psychological or neuropsychological origin, will also influence performance.

Strategies for Reducing Nonspecific Error

Most temporary factors influencing performance can be minimized by repeating testing on different days in different orders. While there may be concern over practice effects, repeated exposure to tests that the subject cannot perform because of true neuropsychological deficits should produce minimal improvements unless the subject learns a compensatory technique minimizing the impact of the deficit subsystem. Yet, even if compensation occurs, it simply supplies more interesting information about how the brain functions without the subsystem of interest and, as such, adds to the single case analysis. In cases where practice effects may be detrimental, however, alternate forms can be easily designed. Additionally, the impaired subsystem should be important to a variety of tasks; hence, it can be tested across sessions with different, but related, tasks. For example, a subject showing left hemispatial neglect on a test of letter cancellation should also show the same pattern on a vigilance task in which stimulus items are presented to the temporal fields. Consequently, the vigilance task can be used to assess the reliability of the neglect if the experimenter fears the subject has had too much exposure to the letter cancellation task.

To analyze further the suspected mediating factor (e.g., pain, fatigue), some form of rating scale should be used concurrently with neuropsychological evaluation. Biomedical measures, such as blood glucose levels in diabetics, should also be followed when relevant and available, since changes in such measures signal metabolic changes that produce generalized effects on neuropsychological performance. In some instances, the mediating factor may be under the direct control of the experimental situation, as in the case of anticipatory test anxiety producing headaches or a lengthy car trip to the testing center producing fatigue or back pain. In such cases, modification of typical testing procedures may be necessary, such as going to the patient's home for testing or conducting relaxation exercises to reduce tension prior to testing.

Motivational limitations can be overcome by allowing time for developing an empathic, supportive relationship with the subject, as well as informing him or her about the importance of the experiment. Emphasizing the partnership between the experimenter and the subject in helping other patients is essential, because the subject is often much more willing to cooperate if he or she knows that the testing may benefit others as well. Further analysis of the role of motivation can be examined through the use of performance feedback and tangible rewards, when appropriate.

Progress In Basic Experimental Case Study Design

When it has been adequately shown that the subject has an unusual set of strengths and deficits, his or her problems are attributable to brain injury, and the deficits are important to model building in basic experimental neuropsychology, what are the next steps with this patient? Typically, a series of experiments is conducted that involves months, and more commonly years, of testing aimed at either further challenges to the conceptualization of the patient's deficits or additional elaboration of the effects of the deficits on other neuropsychological functions. In some cases, additional neuropsychologists may conduct experimentation with the patient; in others, the patient may serve as the control in a double dissociative investigation of a second patient's unique pattern of deficits. Also, other patients with similar deficits can be studied, because replication is the strongest support for external validity, even in single case design. Probably the most thoroughly studied and celebrated subject in single case experimentation was H.M., a patient with profound memory loss following bilateral injury to his hippocampal and medial temporal lobe areas. The following section presents a summary of Milner and her colleagues' excellent series of studies of this fascinating patient. It is presented as an example of single case design at its best.

The Study of H.M.

Background History H.M. was a young white male who had suffered severe grand mal and petit mal seizures since the age of 16. Initial radiological and neurological examinations were unremarkable, but his EEG showed diffuse slowing. His seizures were assumed to have resulted from a bicycle accident occurring when he was 9 years old. After continued worsening of his condition, he was treated surgically at the age of 29 by the bilateral excision of mid-temporal tissue, including the prepyreform gyrus, uncus, amygdala, hippocampus, and hippocampal gyrus. The lesion was limited superiorly and laterally by the temporal horns and extended approximately three centimeters posteriorly to the medial portion of the petrios ridge. The surgery resulted in a decrease of both grand mal and petit mal seizures and a reduction of anticonvulsant medications. H.M. was only one of 10 cases in the initial paper concerning the effects of bilateral hippocampal injury on human memory (Scoville & Milner, 1957). He became the focus of subsequent study because he was the only subject having no history of psychiatric problems.

Assessment of Strengths and Weaknesses Following surgery H.M. showed improvement on the Wechsler–Bellevue from a presurgical FSIQ of 104 to a postsurgical FSIQ of 121. An extensive battery of tests revealed normal abilities in perception, abstract thinking, and problem solving. In contrast, H.M. evinced profound deficits on tests of memory, indicating poor recall of events following his injury and a three-year retrograde amnesia manifest in failure on orientation questions. (He thought the date was March, 1953, when testing actually took place in April, 1955). Furthermore, his MQ from the Wechsler Memory Scale (WMS) was 64, almost four standard deviations below his FSIQ on the Wechsler–Bellevue. His long-term memory deficits were so profound that if one task was interrupted with another, he denied ever having taken the original test when it was presented again. Despite these deficits, he did quite well on card games and sorting tasks, which seem to depend heavily on some form of immediate/short-term memory. For example, on the Wisconsin Card Sorting Test (WCST) (Grant & Berg, 1948) he completed six categories in 84 cards. Despite this performance, however, he was unaware that the categories were changed and reported that he had been using the same principle of categorization throughout the task (Milner, Corkin, & Teuber, 1968). Because of the devastating effects of this surgery on H.M.'s memory, Scoville (1968) appropriately urged that the procedure never be performed again. Consequently, single case methodology provided the only means of studying this fascinating and unusual subject.

Specific Hypothesis Testing The initial analysis of H.M. revealed that his immediate memory functions may have been intact while his long-term functions were dysfunctional. Several researchers investigated this apparent dissociation more closely. Drachman and Arbit (1966) studied immediate span versus supraspan in H.M., first by determining the longest digit span he could recall and then by investigating whether the length of this string could be increased with performance feedback and repeated exposure to a longer string of digits. H.M. recalled a maximum of six digits, which was only slightly lower than normals who can typically recall eight digits. In contrast, his supraspan performance was also six digits as he failed to improve at all over 25 additional trials. These data supported the hypothesis that his immediate recall was near normal while his ability to learn presumably through the facilitation of long-term memory was nonexistent.

Wickelgren (1968), a major proponent of the strength theory of short-term memory, stated, "H.M.'s apparently normal short-term memory traces provide a remarkable opportunity to test theories of short-term memory under conditions where one can be quite sure that little or no long-term memory is contaminating the results" (p. 235). Taking advantage of this opportunity of working with H.M., he replicated several of his experiments previously conducted with college students. In Experiments 1 and 2, H.M. heard lists of numbers followed by either a single number (Experiment 1) or three numbers (Experiment 2). He was then asked if the number had occurred in the previous list. The percentage accuracy of detection per serial position of the target number(s) (first, second, third . . . last position) was calculated as an index of the rate of short-term trace decay. The results indicated that H.M. did best if the target stimulus occurred toward the end and progressively worse if it occurred toward the beginning of the list. Overall, H.M.'s performance on these tasks was consistent with that of Wickelgren's college students, with the exception that H.M. showed only a slight primacy effect, suggesting long-term memory was contributing little to overall performance. In Experiment 3, H.M. heard two tones varying in pitch that were separated by a constant tone varying in duration (0.25 to 8 sec). H.M. was to indicate if the two stimulus tones were the same or different. The results indicated that his rate of short-term decay appeared to be reasonably well fit by a single exponentially decaying trace that did not differ from those decay rates established for normals. This set of experiments illustrates H.M.'s importance not only to neurobiological model building but also to information processing model building.

Corkin (1968) noted that, despite H.M.'s poorer performance on verbal learning tasks, he demonstrated learning and retention of fairly complex motor tasks such as mirror drawing (Milner, 1966). These data suggested that motor learning may rely on brain structures other than the hippocampal temporal regions and that H.M. may have had adequate brain function to perform selective motor learning. This hypothesis was not unprecedented, since it had long been noted that motor learning in normals seemed qualitatively different from other kinds of learning. For example, quite complex motor skills (e.g., skating and swimming) are acquired most efficiently in childhood, do not show much loss through lack of practice, and do not correlate highly with IQ.

To test her hypothesis, Corkin (1968) had H.M. perform on a Rotary Pursuit, a bimanual tracking and tapping task, for several days. He performed within the range of Corkin's normal controls ($n = 6$) and showed retention of performance levels across seven days. Anecdotal evidence suggested that "testing habits" also had been maintained. He could grossly describe what needed to be done on the Rotary Pursuit task, for example, and could spontaneously recall specific rules, such as, no touching of the spring mechanism with the stylus.

Similar results were observed on the Gollin figures, a complex, nonmotoric perceptual task, in which H.M. had to identify pictures varying in completeness. H.M., who was 40 years of age at the time, was compared with 10 normal male subjects ranging in age from 39 to 46 years. His performance was indistinguishable from the normal controls over the initial learning trials. When the test was readministered one hour later, however, he denied having taken the test previously, even though he scored 48% better than he did on the initial trials.

While H.M. performed quite well on the previously mentioned perceptual and motor learning tasks, Milner and her colleagues recognized that mastery of only a few skills was needed to perform optimally on these tasks. In addition, acquisition of these skills did not depend upon memory of previous steps or reinforcement history.

To investigate H.M.'s skill on perceptual motor tasks requiring more discrete skills as well as greater dependence on memory, these researchers had H.M. complete both visually and tactually guided mazes. His skill on maze tasks was compared with various small homogeneous groups of patients with focal cortical injuries, and his performance was shown to be worse than groups of right and left temporal as well as frontal patients on both tactually (Corkin, 1965) and visually (Milner, 1965) guided maze learning when the maze contained many steps beyond memory span. In contrast, when these mazes were greatly simplified to include as few as three turns, his learning improved as did his retention across days. Nevertheless, his learning rate and retention across days were far lower than the other patient groups and normals. Further testing showed no transfer of training from the master maze to a slightly more complex visual maze (Milner, 1965). These authors concluded that H.M. mastered mazes only when their choice-points were well within his immediate memory span, again illustrating the importance of long-term memory to learning lengthy serial tasks and the contribution of the hippocampus to this learning process (Milner et al., 1968). In addition to their conclusions, it is important to note that the dissociation between simple motor and verbal learning was reliable and has since been shown to occur with Korsakoff's patients as well (cf. Butters, 1984).

Once H.M.'s specific deficit in long-term memory was accepted, he was used as a control subject in other case studies and group designs. Milner et al. (1968), for example, contrasted H.M.'s performance on the WCST and a delayed face recognition task with the performance of K.M., a patient who had sustained bilateral removal of the anterior portion of both frontal lobes. Double dissociation was clearly demonstrated, since H.M. scored normally on the WCST and very poorly on the recognition task, while K.M. showed the opposite pattern.

Jones (1974) contended that the memory disorder for verbal information experienced by patients with left hemisphere lesions sparing the hippocampus were less general and more material-specific than those of patients with hippocampal lesions. More specifically, she proposed that when the hippocampus was spared, the principal memory deficit involved the processing of verbal information as opposed to its storage. Consequently, if an alternative, intact way of processing verbal information is used, these patients should show improvement in verbal memory. For example, Jones (1974) investigated the application of imagery to facilitate paired-associate learning. Using this alternative processing procedure, the association between the words *cigarette* and *typewriter,* for example, was the visualization of a typewriter smoking. Via group methodology, this researcher demonstrated that imagery facilitated paired-associate learning in left temporal lobe lesion patients and also in right temporal lobe lesion patients (an unexpected finding). In contrast, H.M. and a patient with unilateral left hippocampal damage, H.B., showed no improvement in paired-associate recall, suggesting that their memory deficits and that of the cortically lesioned patients were qualitatively different.

Through research with H.M., a tremendous amount of information was gleaned about memory function and the importance of the hippocampus. Milner and her colleagues' carefully controlled and programmatic research uncovered the dissociation of short-term and long-term memory in humans and provided empirical support for formerly established theories on the differences between motor and other forms of learning. Other subjects showing striking and important patterns of deficits have been similarly studied (cf. Shallice, 1979).

BEHAVIORAL SINGLE CASE DESIGN FOR APPLIED NEUROPSYCHOLOGY

The previous sections have described the use of case study procedures developed by basic experimental neuropsychologists to test brain–behavior models. From this perspective, behavior has been viewed as a sign of either information processing or neurobiological interactions. This section will discuss methods developed by behavior therapists, who use a less theoretical and more intervention-oriented approach to single case methodology. To distinguish this methodology from that used in experimental neuropsychology, these methods will be collectively referred to as behavioral single case designs (BSCD). The most direct application of BSCD to neuropsychology is in the planning and evaluation of treatment for the cognitive and interpersonal problems of the brain-injured patient.

Single case design has typically been used to provide a finely grained analysis of problem behavior, which clarifies the maintaining variables so that procedures for modifying behavior can be applied efficiently. More specifically, the assessor uses these procedures to (1) describe the clinical target behavior(s) with reference to their maintaining conditions, (2) select the best treatment available to achieve therapeutic goals, and (3) evaluate and revise treatment as the therapy is being applied.

BSCDs share several common characteristics with within-subject group designs. Both test hypotheses of interest by measuring a dependent variable under various levels of an independent variable, and both use repeated measurement to evaluate the effectiveness of the experimental manipulation. In addition, the strength of both designs is based on how effectively alternative hypotheses are refuted by the results. Hence, in planning a BSCD, clinicians address many of the same challenges as they would in planning a group design. Specifically, clinicians must directly address those events independent of the manipulation of the independent variable that may account for changes in the dependent variable, as well as threats to internal validity, such as the influence of history, maturation, repeated testing, and instrumentation changes during experimentation (Campbell & Stanley, 1963).

It is more difficult to address challenges to external validity (generalizability to other subjects, populations, settings, treatment variables, and measurement variables) with single case methodology (Barlow & Hersen, 1984; Kazdin, 1982). Nonetheless, replications of the procedures across several subjects can directly evaluate these concerns (Sidman, 1960). Despite the inherent external validity problems of all forms of single case design, it is notable that the results from such methods generally have been consistent with those from subsequently conducted group designs (Kazdin, 1982; Shallice, 1979).

Selecting Target Behaviors

BSCDs are used most frequently to demonstrate that the technique of interest has a positive clinical impact on the patient. Thus, the experimenter must provide justification that a change in the target behavior will produce an ecologically relevant change in the patient's life. Teaching the subject better ways of learning and recalling lists of words is, in and of itself, of small consequence. Showing that this skill generalizes to remembering telephone numbers, buying groceries, and other daily tasks would indeed demonstrate ecological validity. Consequently, when the training tasks are more laboratory-like than practical, positive demonstrations must include measurement of real-life behaviors to which the training should generalize. These measures do not necessarily have to be unobtrusively recorded samples of spontaneous behavior, but they should be as close as possible to naturally occurring everyday behavior. As an example, Webster et al. (1984) developed an obstacle course to assess the transfer of stationary scanning training to scanning during complicated movement in patients with hemispatial neglect. The runways in this obstacle course were designed to the specifications of the average home's hallways and door widths. This course was actually preferable to unobtrusive monitoring in the hallways of the rehabilitation center where this study was conducted, since the hallways had been widened for the handicapped, making them much too broad to serve as a test of safe movement in the home or, for that matter, other institutional settings. Furthermore, the obstacle course allowed for the design of hazardous conditions with special relevance for spatial-neglecting patients, such as the placement of obstacles on the right and left to investigate the influence of simultaneous stimulation on safe ambulation. Consequently, most BSCD investigations will require the inclusion of measures with direct ecological relevance although these measures may still be contrived.

Methods of Recording a Target Behavior

Once a general target behavior has been selected, its definition must be operationalized to make it observable, discrete, easily recorded, and readily quantifiable in terms of its presence, frequency of occurrence, intensity, and/or duration. The operational refinement of the observed activity allows for sufficient clarity to assure that the dependent measure is being recorded reliably.

The recording of target behaviors can be accomplished in many ways. Frequency measures require the recording of each occurrence of a target behavior over a specified time period. For example, Zlutnick, Mayville, and Moffat (1975) recorded the number of daytime seizures experienced by epileptics. When intervals differ across recording sessions, frequency data can be transformed to rate measures (frequency/time).

One weakness in the use of raw frequency is that behavioral events occurring at extremely high rates can be difficult for human observers to record. For example, recording the frequency of Wernicke's aphasics' paraphasic errors would be extremely problematic because of the difficulty both in discriminating subtle errors from normal speech and in keeping up with the high rate of occurrence. For such high-rate behaviors, interval scoring techniques have been developed in which blocks of time rather than raw frequency of the behaviors are the focus of measurement. Raters score whether the target behavior has or has not occurred at least once over a predetermined interval (typically 10 sec or more). Generally, recording intervals are alternated with observation intervals to allow the recording of the response before the resumption of monitoring. Often tape recorders are used to signal the beginning and end of recording intervals, thereby assuring that raters are observing the behavior and recording at the same time. Because one monitors the presence or absence of behavior in interval recording, it is possible to monitor more than one behavior at a time. Hence, time sampling allows for monitoring patterns of behaviors, and this can be optimal when the target behavior of the assessment is a complex response requiring many discrete actions. Time sampling may also be the observational method of choice when the assessor is examining the specific impact of the intervention and wishes to monitor other behaviors that should not change if, indeed, the manipulation alone is accounting for the specific behavioral changes.

Another means of recording activity is to use the duration of behavior. Such measurement is especially useful for monitoring behavioral events that are continuous rather than discrete. Examples include the duration of a tonic-clonic seizure or the persistence of a patient with severe frontal lobe deficits on an unsupervised task.

Behavioral checklists have also been used for discrete classification of presence or absence, as well as appropriateness or inappropriateness, of a behavior. Many discrete categories are used in general behavioral checklists such as the Vineland Social Maturity Scale. The present authors have used a presence/absence checklist format for appropriate dressing to evaluate patients with right middle cerebral artery strokes and dressing apraxia. Recently, behaviorists have also used more complex Likert-scales to record global ratings of a given performance over an extended behavioral sample. Global ratings have been used principally in the social skills literature and have provided data on aspects of performance, including overall social competence and overall physical attractiveness (McFall, 1977). Webster, Gouvier, and Doerfler (1983) used a similar method to rate the spontaneous verbalizations of a closed head–injured patient with "confused" language by using tape recorded samples of each of five presented statements and having raters judge on a three-point scale the appropriateness of his speech (1 = completely on task; 2 = generally on task, but somewhat tangential; 3 = off task). Surprisingly, there was high agreement across all three categories, indicating that a more precise definition was not necessary for this level of discrimination.

One problem with global ratings is that they supply little specific information about either the process by which judgments are made or the characteristics of the actual behavior. To add precision to global scales, attempts have been made to anchor points of the scale to specific criteria (McFall, 1977). Instead of rating the effectiveness of assertive behavior on a 1 (not effective) to 5 (effective) scale, researchers have anchored scales by more objective endpoints, as in the case of a rating of assertiveness from 1 (the patient complies with the request without qualification) to 5 (the patient refused to do the task under any circumstances).

Measurement Agreement

Regardless of the methods used to collect data on target behaviors, there must be substantial agreement among the raters in order to assure that (1) the data are being scored consistently across experimental phases, (2) the data are not affected by a bias of an individual rater, and (3) the target behavior is sufficiently well defined to allow subsequent replication by others (Kazdin, 1982). Generally, interrater agreements are determined by comparing the data records of two raters who have independently rated the same sample of behaviors. These data are then subjected to various methods for estimating the degree of interrater agreement.

The frequency ratio interrater agreement method involves the comparison of the two observers' totals for the occurrence of a given behavior and is calculated by dividing the smaller by the larger total and multiplying by 100. Although this method appears frequently in the literature, most researchers contend it has serious problems. The most critical problem is that the total scores do not necessarily indicate that the two raters frequently agreed on the occurrence of individual events. As long as the different events being counted by the two raters occur at roughly the same frequency, agreement will appear quite high.

Another interrater agreement measure, the point-by-point agreement ratio, improves upon the frequency ratio by requiring trial-by-trial comparisons of rater reliability. Thus, the number of times the two raters agreed on each of the trials is divided by the number of the trials. This method is best suited for observational studies in which there are more discrete opportunities, such as trials, during which the behavior can occur. Often a behavior may occur so infrequently that the inclusion of agreements during trials when nothing happened inflates the point-by-point ratio. In such cases it is recommended that only the occurrence trials be counted.

Pearson product moment correlations have also been used as a means of investigating interobserver agreement across several days (Kazdin, 1982). The one problem with this index is that a high correlation coefficient does not necessarily indicate a high degree of point-by-point agreement. If Rater A reliably scores fewer events than Rater B, interrater reliability via Pearson's technique could be quite high, even though it would be quite low using the previously mentioned techniques.

For all methods of calculating interobserver agreement, ratios above .79 are generally considered evidence that the data were reliably collected. Nevertheless, these estimates do not always indicate what they seem to, because they are influenced by the rate of the target behavior. Moreover, if a behavior occurs very frequently the agreement estimates are likely to be inflated by chance agreements.

Most applied research papers still report point-by-point agreement despite the problem of base-rate bias. Kazdin (1982) has suggested that at present studies should report estimates of both occurrence and nonoccurrence rater agreement, as well as a reliability estimate based on chance alone. Another contemporary guideline is that agreement checks should occur in no fewer than 20% of the observations and should be drawn equally from all portions of the assessment (Hersen & Barlow, 1976). With reference to the latter, successful intervention changes the base rate of the target behavior, thus alternating the chance agreement factor. In addition, as the behavior begins to change in the targeted direction there may be greater likelihood of bias in recording, thereby necessitating more checks by a second observer who is ideally blind to the experimental condition and, if possible, to the purpose of the study.

High interrater reliabilities do not assure that the two raters are consistently following the operationally defined scoring system across time. Kent and Foster (1977) refer to this tendency for observers to change the definitions over the course of treatment as *observer drift*. When observers frequently work together and discuss the outcomes of session assessments, they may stray from the original definitions, perhaps in order to improve interrater reliabilities (Hawkins & Dobes, 1977). One way to control observer drift is to retrain observers continually over the course of the investigation. A set of criterion video tapes that were rated at the onset of an investigation can be rerated by the observers and feedback provided on consistency with the original criteria (Johnson & Bolstad, 1973). Feedback for applying definitions has been shown to reduce drift from the initial behavioral criteria (DeMaster, Reid, & Twentyman, 1977).

Interrater agreement is also influenced by the observers' expectations regarding checks on their reliability. Generally, observers show higher interrater agreement when checks are obtrusive, or at least predicted, than when they are unobtrusive (Kent, Kanowitz, O'Leary, & Cheiken, 1977; Kent, O'Leary, Diament, & Dietz, 1974; Taplin & Reid, 1973). Unfortunately, obtrusive checks may also alter the reported rate of the target behavior. For example, Romanczyk, Kent, Diament, and O'Leary (1973) found that the rate of recording disruptive behavior increased when observers knew that a reliability check was in effect. Kazdin (1982) recommends that these reactive effects can be kept to a minimum if the observers believe they are always being checked. Thus, when a rater does not expect that accuracy will be checked, interrater reliability should be done unobtrusively. However, since unobtrusive checks are so difficult to conduct, one might alternatively create the expectation that all observations are being checked, perhaps using audio- or videotape equipment, to at least reinforce the possibility of constant monitoring. Analogue studies have shown that when observers suspect that their recording may be monitored at any given time, they are not only more reliable but also more accurate in using the operational definitions and monitoring system (Reid, 1970; Taplin & Reid, 1973).

As with any form of experimentation, observational data may also be affected by the expectations of the observers regarding the experimental hypotheses and the feedback given observers about the results of their observations (Kent & Foster, 1977). Of the two sources of bias, the feedback the experimenter provides appears to have the greater influence (O'Leary, Kent, & Kanowitz, 1975). Although research suggests that observers need not be blind to the experimental hypotheses, feedback on their observations should be restricted to concerns over interrater reliability and consistency of data recording (Kent et al., 1974; Kent & Foster, 1977).

Different Types of Behavioral Single Case Designs

The A–B Design

The most basic improvement over the uncontrolled case study is the A–B design, which consists of a baseline (A) phase and a treatment (B) phase. During the baseline phase, the investigator records the occurrences of the target behavior(s) until it is stable or a stable pattern emerges. Most authors recommend that the A phase contain a minimum of three data points that show little change across samples or indicate changes inconsistent with the direction expected if the experimental manipulation has the predicted effect. During the treatment (B) phase, the therapeutic or experimental variable is introduced and remains in effect until the stability of the change in the target behavior has been established. Similar to the recommendations for the baseline phase, the B phase should continue until the data are stable across trials (at least three) or the magnitude of the target behavior consistently changes in a direction inconsistent with the trends observed during baseline. The baseline phase should serve as a guide to the length of time the B phase must be in effect. When baseline data show considerable variability, the treatment phase should be extended to refute the hypothesis that the observed changes are spontaneous fluctuations in performance independent of treatment or the result of transient nonspecific influences associated with treatment's initiation, such as novelty. Barlow and Hersen (1984) recommend that the B phase should contain as many data points as the A phase.

The A–B design represents a considerable improvement over the use of the uncontrolled case study, since it quantifies a specific target behavior and allows the direct comparison of this behavior during baseline with that during treatment, when the therapeutic variable(s) is introduced. Nonetheless, the A–B design provides a relatively weak demonstration because it does not control for abrupt changes in an uncontrolled variable that could influence the target behavior. For example, the authors recently worked with a head-injured client whose anger-control problems were most apparent in the presence of his co-workers. Concurrent with the onset of treatment, this client lost his job and the number of his anger outbursts were greatly reduced. In this example, an abrupt environmental change (his firing) confounded the manipulation of the independent variable (anger control program), a problem the A–B design cannot partial out.

The A–B design can be modestly improved by simultaneously monitoring other behaviors or by testing alternative hypotheses for changes in the target behavior. This is similar to conducting the negative investigations described in the sections on single case design for experimental neuropsychology. For example, it could be argued that if "spontaneous recovery" of function following brain insult accounted for changes during the treatment phase, then such improvements should also be apparent on monitored behaviors that were unlikely to be influenced by training. To isolate generalization of training from the effects of spontaneous recovery likely to affect many neuropsychological subsystems equally, the other behaviors should be relatively independent of the targeted behavior but of comparable complexity. When only the target behavior changes, the results support with greater confidence the hypothesis that changes in the target behavior could not be attributable to spontaneous recovery. However, it would be impractical and, perhaps, impossible to assess all alternative hypotheses in this manner. The following is an example of the use of the A–B design with brain-injured patients.

Case Example The subject was a 46-year-old black female who had suffered generalized psychomotor seizures since age 13. Despite documented compliance with medication the subject still experienced an average of four seizures per week. During the baseline phase, she was asked to record each occurrence of a seizure-like episode over a 9-week period. In addition, serum anticonvulsant levels (Dilantin and phenobarbital) were assessed on three occasions during baseline. At the end of baseline, the experimenters initiated a 7-week program of stress management training consisting of training in relaxation, assertion, and problem-solving skills. The total package is described in greater detail in Raczynski, Webster, Jordan, Cliett, and Thompson (1984). The results are shown in Figure 9.2. The top portion of the figure shows changes in subjective seizure frequency following training. While the data indicate a fairly substantial reduction in self-reported seizures, the limitations of the design make it difficult to determine the variables leading to this change. The bottom portion of Figure 9.2 presents serum levels of the anticonvulsants Dilantin and phenobarbital. While serum levels show some variability across measurements, they remain in the therapeutic range for both medications and do not support the hypothesis that changes in the dependent measure were a function of changes in anticonvulsant dosage or medication compliance. These data strengthen the A–B design by demonstrating that medication could not account for improvements occurring during the B phase. However, many other alternative hypotheses would need to be dismissed before a strong case could be made that stress management training alone accounted for the observed changes in seizure frequency.

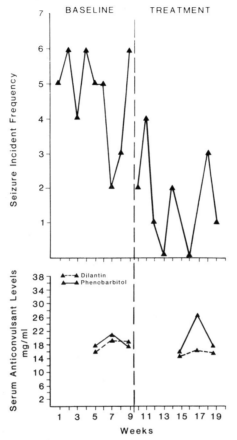

FIGURE 9.2 The effects of stress management treatment on self-reported seizure frequency: An A–B design.

The phases of the A–B design can also be reversed in order (B–A) and involve changes in treatments (B1–B2) rather than adhering to a strict baseline and treatment format. The B1–B2 design, for example, may be the only appropriate design when a manipulation is imposed upon a general treatment program, such as ongoing occupational and physical therapy within a rehabilitation center. More importantly, all single case designs should help evaluate the systematic manipulations of variables and, to that end, they should be flexible enough to accommodate most problem behaviors and settings.

A–B–A Design

The A–B–A design extends the A–B design by adding a phase in which the treatment condition is withdrawn. If the target behavior changes in the predicted direction with treatment and then returns to baseline levels during the subsequent A phase, then a stronger statement can be made about the controlling effects of the treatment variable. Clearly, it is much more unlikely that the observed changes in the target behavior are due to an uncontrolled variable if changes are present only when treatment is in effect. As with an A–B design, the strong support for the effectiveness of the manipulation is dependent upon the magnitude and stability of the changes. The guidelines for the A–B design also apply to the A–B–A design.

While the A–B–A design represents an improvement over the A–B designs, there are problems in its application to neuropsychological research. First, the changes in the target behaviors occurring during the B phase may be difficult to withdraw, because they may be readily reinforced by the natural environment. For example, training the head-injured patient to use more adaptive and appropriate social skills may result in a noticeable, if not dramatic, change in social reinforcement from his or her family and acquaintances. Withdrawing the rewards for such behavior in the laboratory may have little impact because the skills are maintained by the patient's improved relationships with others. Such problems can often occur when training an individual with acquired injuries, because most targeted changes were within the patient's repertoire prior to his injury. In this case, training primarily facilitates accessibility or control of the targeted responses rather than trains a completely novel set of skills. Consequently, in the authors' experience, reacquisition and maintenance can sometimes occur quickly in brain-injured patients, especially when their deficits are mild. When the change is likely to be maintained, the withdrawal of treatment should occur as soon as treatment stability is established so as to increase the likelihood of a return to baseline later.

To insure the desired return to baseline, some researchers have used a reversal approach in which the pretreatment level of the target behavior is reinforced (Leitenberg, 1973). For example, if training involved reinforcing a patient for shorter response times on a reaction time device, the follow-up (reversal) condition would involve reinforcing slower response times. If the change in contingencies produced a lengthening in response time, it would be clear that the contingencies were also responsible for the shorter reaction time in the B phase.

Unfortunately, in many cases returning the target behavior to pretreatment levels via either withdrawal or reversal of contingencies could have serious ethical implications, especially considering that the A–B–A design ends with a nontreatment phase. Clearly, when the goal of intervention is to effect clinically meaningful changes in behavior, the investigator must go beyond the A–B–A design. As an adjunctive procedure to assessment, however, the A–B–A design has considerable utility to the clinical neuropsychologist who wishes either to test the limits in an assessment or to pilot a retraining technique before mobilizing resources for treatment.

Case Example The patient was a 58-year-old female who had suffered a closed head injury in a bicycle accident in which she had been thrown to the pavement. She was in a coma for two and one-half weeks. A CT scan on the day of her accident revealed lowered density in the left frontal area. The first author assessed her four months later and found that she had profound intellectual, memory, and attentional deficits based on a fairly comprehensive neuropsychological assessment, including the WAIS-R, Wechsler Memory Scale, Benton Visual Retention Test, Trails A and B, and a variety of Lurian tasks. A critical question at this time was whether she could benefit from some form of retraining.

Among her many deficits, the most basic problem seemed to be inability to sustain attention, which prevented prolonged concentration essential to the effectiveness of subsequent complex retraining. Thus, a reaction time assessment procedure was initiated to assess the effectiveness of performance feedback on sustained attention. The training device consisted of a programmable calculator and printer. The stimulus was presented via the printer, and reaction time was recorded by the calculator. During feedback conditions the patient's reaction time and the number of successive trials in which she had performed faster than a criterion speed (in the present example, 600 ms) were printed. To facilitate the effectiveness of the feedback, the subject was required to read aloud the printout. In addition, performance-related feedback was provided by the experimenter.

The results of training are seen in Figure 9.3. Two target variables were investigated: reaction time and the range of reaction times for each five-trial interval. During the A phase, fairly slow reaction times were observed, with considerable intertrial variability. The introduction of feedback resulted in a marked decrease in both reaction time and intertrial variability. A return to baseline resulted in increases in both response parameters. By limiting training to a few trials (30) and a short period of time (15 minutes), the chances were increased that a withdrawal of treatment would also result in a return to pretreatment performance levels. The results were interpreted as indicating that this patient's consistency and concentration could be influenced by the level of performance feedback and that she was functionally ready to benefit from extensive training to improve self-regulation of attention.

As with the A–B design, the phases of the A–B–A design can be modified to accommodate the question and experimental setting. In addition, concurrent monitoring of other variables is helpful in further demonstrating the specific effects of training and the refutation of alternative hypotheses.

A–B–A–B Design

The A–B–A–B design ends on a treatment phase that is obviously an advantage over the A–B–A design when the intervention is designed to facilitate relatively permanent behavior change. This design is simply an extension of the A–B–A

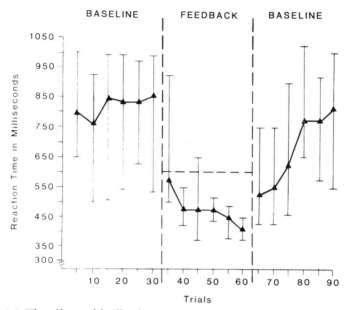

FIGURE 9.3 The effects of feedback on reaction time (RT) and reaction time variability. (Each point is an average RT for a 5-trial sample, and each vertical line represents the range of the RTs during that sample.)

design and necessitates the data stability and magnitude of the simpler design in order to demonstrate powerful and unequivocal experimental relationships. While the A–B–A–B design eschews some of the ethical liabilities of the A–B–A design, it still necessitates the withdrawal of treatment. Fortunately, the temporary withdrawal of most treatments will not result in harming the patient or his family, thereby making this design a very valuable means of establishing the effectiveness of a therapeutic approach. Because this design requires a replication of both the baseline and treatment conditions, the A–B–A–B design provides one of the strongest single case demonstrations of a treatment's effect. It is also a demanding test that is often failed because of a carry-over effect during the replication phase. The authors have found this approach especially helpful when probing the effectiveness of a compensatory strategy that is intended for subsequent extensive training.

Case Example This subject was a 50-year-old male who had suffered a stroke involving the right middle cerebral artery and right thalamus following an attempted surgical repair of an intracerebral aneurysm 2½ years prior to the evaluation. At the time of assessment, he had a left homonymous hemianopsia, mild left-sided hemiparesis, and moderate problems with left hemi-inattention. Performance on items requiring considerable scanning suggested that this subject preferred to begin such tasks on the far right side and then move to the left. In addition, he frequently neglected to move his eyes to the far left and/or moved them too slowly to detect objects on the left when the task was paced by the experimenter. A probe was used to investigate the potential effectiveness of a compensatory strategy requiring that he search from the far left to the right and utilize a verbal mnemonic ("look left"). Two two-digit numbers were simultaneously presented over a CRT with one number placed in the left visual hemispace and the other in the right hemispace. Each set of numbers was displayed for $1\frac{1}{2}$ sec, with a 5 sec interresponse time. The subject was instructed to respond by pressing a button if either number on the screen contained a "5." Following a baseline consisting of 45 trials, a training phase was initiated in which each trial was preceded by the visual prompt, "Look left," which was presented for 2 sec before the trial. After 45 trials under this condition (B phase) more baseline data were collected, followed by a return to the "Look left" condition. Figure 9.4 shows these results. As can be seen, the verbal/visual prompt was effective.

The previous example also reveals a major limitation of extended A–B–A–B designs. Carry-over effects that tend to obscure the experimental effect will usually be present. In the present example, the second baseline performance is better than the first, as is the second treatment performance. However, it is not necessary to have an exact replication of the previous phase to show distinct differences in the dependent variable under the influence of the levels of the independent variable.

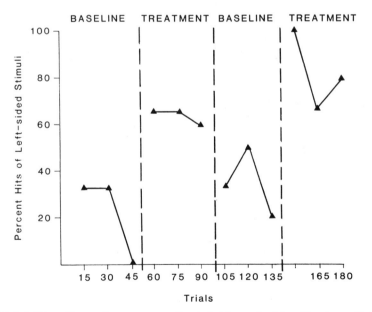

FIGURE 9.4 The effects of prompts to "look left" on the identification of left-sided stimuli during a vigilance task performed by a subject suffering left neglect.

Other Replication Designs

Single case methodology is meant to be as flexible as necessary to accommodate the questions of interest and to handle any surprises occurring during the course of the experiment. Consequently, many other replication BSCDs have been described and are reviewed in Barlow and Hersen (1984) and Kazdin (1982).

Multiple Baseline Designs

Multiple baseline designs require no withdrawal or reversal of contingencies to demonstrate the effects of a training procedure. Instead, a number of behaviors measured over time serve as baselines against which changes can be evaluated. The experimenter then applies a training procedure to one of the behaviors and continues to monitor the others to see if they change as well. When changes occur only in the targeted response, there is support that the specific quality of the treatment produced the observed change. If all the measures change, however, considerable ambiguity exists. One must question whether or not some other variable produced the change (e.g., spontaneous recovery or some other uncontrolled variable). Alternatively, one must consider whether the treatment affected all the behaviors equally (e.g., nonspecific treatment effects, poorly chosen baseline measures).

The monitored measures can come from various sources. They can be the same behavior measured in different settings (multiple baseline across settings), different behaviors in the same individual (multiple baseline across behaviors), or, more commonly, the same behavior across different subjects (multiple baseline across subjects). Each component of a multiple baseline design can be conceptualized as a logical extension of the A–B design. In this respect, it is a fairly weak demonstration of a treatment effect. Accordingly, as a general rule multiple baseline designs should contain at least three behaviors, settings, or patients because the greater the number of replications, the more powerful is the demonstration yielded by the design (Barlow & Hersen, 1973).

Case Example Gianutsos and Gianutsos (1986) used a multiple baseline across behaviors design to study the effects of EMG biofeedback on movement of the hemiplegic arms of stroke patients. The measures used for this design were EMG output from the protagonist and antagonist muscle pairs for shoulder flexion, elbow extension, and finger extension. Visual feedback of EMG activity was used as the independent variable and was systematically applied first to the muscles regulating shoulder flexion, then to elbow extension, and finally to finger extension. As seen in Figure 9.5, baseline EMG activity for muscles used in shoulder flexion was variable but did not show a trend in the targeted direction (increasing activity). When feedback-assisted training was initiated (signified by the broken line), immediate increases in activity were observed in these muscles whereas no changes were observed in finger extension and only slight changes were noted in the muscles of elbow extension. Five sessions later, feedback-assisted training was initiated with the muscles of elbow extension producing more gradual changes in the targeted direction in this muscle group without influencing finger extension. Finally, five sessions later the muscles of finger extension received feedback-assisted training. These results clearly show that the greatest gains were accomplished in specific muscle groups when feedback was directly applied to facilitate the protagonist and inhibit the antagonist. Nonetheless, some carry-over was observed across measures, at least with regard to elbow extension.

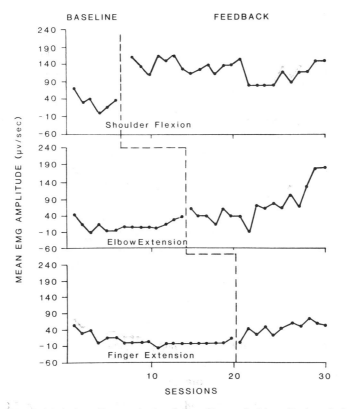

FIGURE 9.5 Multiple baseline analysis of the effects of video displayed electromyographic feedback on mean electromyographic amplitude recorded from progatonist/antagonist muscle pairs of the hemiparetic upper extremity. (Each section of the graph represents the combined score of the protagonist/antagonist pair obtained by subtracting the m.v. second value of the antagonist muscle from that of the protagonist muscle. This is an abbreviated and simplified adaptation from the original figure).

Source: From "Single Case Experimental Approaches to the Assessment of Interventions in Rehabilitation Psychology," by R. Gianutsos and J. Gianutsos, 1986, in *Handbook of Contemporary Rehabilitation Psychology,* by B. Caplan (Ed.), Springfield, IL.: Charles Thomas. Copyright © 1986 by Charles Thomas. Adapted by permission.

Because it is very difficult to avoid impinging on other behaviors or settings in a single individual when multiple baseline designs are used, experimenters have more commonly employed the multiple baseline across subjects design. In this case, the subjects have similar strengths and deficits and are matched on important demographic characteristics. Baseline measurement should begin on the same day for all subjects, as a way to control the effects of changes in setting or instrumentation. Additionally, care should be taken to discourage subjects from comparing treatments. This is especially a concern when the subjects come from a single institution or rehabilitation setting.

Case Example A multiple baseline design across subjects was used to demonstrate the efficacy of a visual scanning training procedure to minimize neglect in three subjects with right hemispheric strokes. Webster et al. (1984) monitored error rates of the subjects on a task requiring the subjects to identify the position of lights presented on a light board 6 ft-wide. Training consisted of teaching the subjects to verbally guide their gaze into the left visual space by saying "anchor left" and providing feedback concerning omitted lights. As shown in Figure 9.6, Subjects 1, 2, and 3 received two, three, and four baseline assessment sessions respectively. Training was initiated with Subject 1, one week later with Subject 2, and one week later with Subject 3. As can be seen in Figure 9.6, striking reductions in errors in the left visual space followed the initiation of training in all three subjects. These authors also measured the subjects' performance on an obstacle course with barriers on the right and left. They did not use this as an independent measure for training within the context of a multiple baseline design because they anticipated that scanning training would generalize to this obstacle course. They believed performance on the light board and the obstacle course were poor in these subjects principally because they did not look to the left sufficiently often. Thus, training them to look left should have impact on both behaviors, which, indeed, it did. This illustrates the necessity of choosing sufficiently dissimilar behaviors for multiple baseline designs across behaviors if some of the behaviors are to be used for assessing specificity as opposed to generalization of training.

Simultaneous Treatment Designs

As with most repeated measures designs, the previously mentioned single case strategies make it difficult to compare the effectiveness of two treatment techniques with the same subject because of carry-over effects. Recently, Kazdin and Hartmann (1978) introduced the simultaneous treatment design, which attempts to make treatment comparisons possible. This strategy begins by observing a target behavior under at least two different circumstances or times of day. Once stable baseline parameters are established, two interventions are implemented concurrently but during different observational times or settings. The interventions are varied across observational periods so that their effects can be separated from the influence of settings and time. If

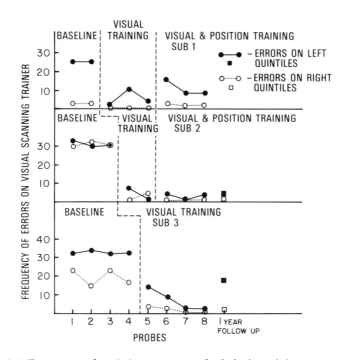

FIGURE 9.6 Frequency of omission errors on the light board during visual scanning probes.

Source: From "Visual Scanning Training with Stroke Patients," by J. S. Webster, S. Jones, P. Blanton, R. Gross, G. F. Beissel, and J. D. Wofford, 1984, *Behavior Therapy, 15,* p. 137. Copyright © 1984 by the Association for the Advancement of Behavior Therapy. Reprinted by permission.

one of the interventions emerges as better than the other, it is then applied to all observational circumstances in an attempt to replicate this effect.

Case Example This subject was a 42-year-old male who reported severe memory loss since suffering viral encephalitis 10 years prior to his evaluation by the first author. A neuropsychological evaluation revealed good short-term recall for verbal material, moderately poor recall of designs, and very limited delayed recall of information regardless of its stimulus properties. Aside from very mild visual perceptual problems, other neuropsychological functions appeared intact.

Further discussion with this patient and his wife revealed that his most devastating problems involved his inability to recall reliably the names of his customers. In an attempt to replicate this problem in the laboratory, the authors presented frontal photographs of individuals and gave them names that the patient was to learn. He was instructed to repeat each name aloud one time and to try to remember it in his typical way. On immediate recall he did

quite well, recalling 100% of the names. However, his recall declined substantially when he was shown the pictures 15 minutes later. (See Figure 9.7.)
To assess this deficit further, two compensatory strategies were introduced.
Strategy 1 was an adaptation of a common memory technique used by professional mnemonists, requiring that the patient find an unusual facial
characteristic of the person to be remembered and pair it with his name so as to
create a paired-associate relationship to facilitate name recall. For example, a
person named Thompson who had a large nose might be remembered by
imagining his nose to be a giant thumb and relating it to his surname via the

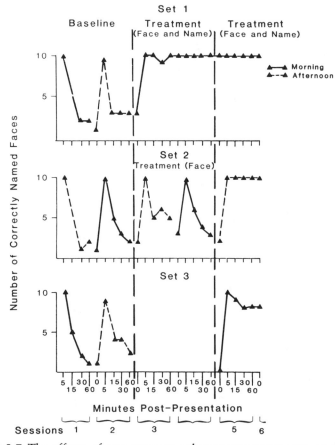

FIGURE 9.7 The effects of two memory enhancement treatments on the recall of
names from faces. [Treatment (face) consisted of associating a name with a prominent
facial characteristic. Treatment (face and name) added the visualization of the name in
the facial characteristics. The subject received Treatment (face and name) with Set 1
faces during the morning of the first treatment week and the afternoon of the second.
He received Treatment (face) with Set 2 faces during the afternoon of the first week and
morning of the second. Treatment (face and name) was used with all sets of faces during
the final session].

association "Tom Thumb." Strategy 2 elaborated on the first strategy by requiring that the patient not only find a facial characteristic but also associate more correctly the name and the landmark by visualizing the name within the facial area. Using this strategy, the patient was required not only to see the thumb on the man's face but also to see "Thompson" spelled out by the folds of his nose. This elaboration was included because of the patient's generally poor performance on difficult paired-associate items during baseline, which suggested he was not able to generate the name if its relationship with the facial feature was too abstract or indirect.

This patient was seen only one day per week, during the morning and afternoon, because of the distance he had to travel to attend the sessions. Three sets of pictures, each containing ten faces, were presented during baseline. As seen in Figure 9.7, the three sets of faces were introduced to the subject without any compensatory technique, with Sets 1 and 3 being introduced in the morning and Set 2 being introduced in the afternoon. The subject was then shown the faces at 5-, 15-, 30- and 60-min intervals and asked to name them. As can be seen, he did progressively worse over time. On the second baseline day the sets were again shown to the subject, but in this instance Sets 1 and 3 were shown in the afternoon, while Set 2 was shown in the morning. Before introducing the faces to the subject, his recall was probed (0-min trial), revealing minimal retention from the previous week. He was reintroduced to the faces, and trials once again occurred at 15-, 30-, and 60-min intervals. All subsequent sessions followed this format. Following the demonstration that each group consisted of comparably difficult stimulus items, the interventions began. One set of pictures was used with each strategy, while the third set of faces was used later for replication. During the first week of training, Strategy 2 (face + name) was used during the morning session and Strategy 1 (face only) during the afternoon. The order was reversed during the second week.

As can be seen in Figure 9.7, Strategy 2 produced the best results, especially across weeks. Strategy 2 was introduced to Set-2 and to Set-3 faces after it had been shown that Strategy 2 had facilitated memory regardless of whether it was utilized in the morning or afternoon. The results supported the effectiveness of this memory procedure, since recall of both Set-2 and Set-3 pictures improved with the introduction of the second strategy. The replication of effects with Set 3 was done to demonstrate that improvement observed with Set-2 faces was not simply a result of the extensive exposure prior to the introduction of Strategy 2.

Changing Criterion Design

The changing criterion design is another recent innovation to single case methodology. When it is successful, it allows a convincing demonstration of the effectiveness of a treatment without the withdrawal of the procedure. Specifically, the level of the independent variable is adjusted over time and changes in the dependent variable are observed (Hartmann & Hall, 1976). The procedure is effective if the level of the dependent variable changes with variations of the independent variable.

Case Example Six months prior to seeing the first author, this 38-year-old male suffered a closed head injury that produced pronounced concentration deficits. A reaction time training program identical to that described in the example of the A–B–A design was employed and required the subject to respond by pressing a button each time the number 5 was presented on the LED display. Performance feedback was immediately provided for accuracy and speed of response. Initially, the criterion time limit was any time faster than 750 ms, but it was reduced by increments of 50 to 100 ms as his performance improved. Such gradual performance change could also be a natural result of skill mastery, as opposed to a result of the systematic variation of the feedback criterion. To demonstrate more convincingly the power of feedback, the fourth adjustment of the criterion was an increase in the acceptable reaction time (see Figure 9.8). This change actually resulted in an increase

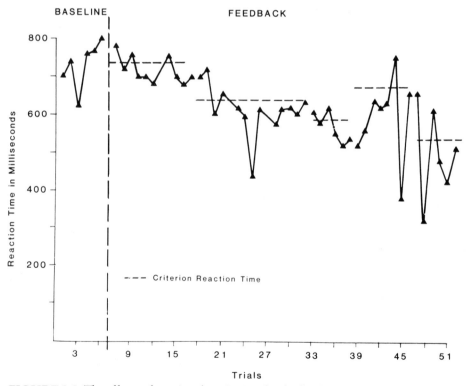

FIGURE 9.8 The effects of varying the criterion for feedback on the reaction time of a brain-injured patient.

in the subject's reaction time, thus demonstrating that the changes in reaction time were under the control of feedback and not simply reflective of a gradual mastery of the task.

Steps Following the Demonstration of Efficacy of Training

When the BSCD results are clear and unambiguous from graphs alone, there is no need for statistical analysis following the demonstration of training efficacy. However, in cases where the results are less clear (e.g., unstable baseline, an initial study in an area, and/or limited control of the subject's behavior), specific statistical procedures should be used (Kazdin, 1982). For a review and discussion of statistical procedures to be used with BSCDs the reader should refer to Barlow and Hersen (1984), Kazdin, (1982), and Kratochwill (1978).

Regardless of whether or not statistical analyses have been performed, the experimenter must demonstrate that positive changes in the target behavior following the onset of treatment have some impact on the subject's life beyond the laboratory. The initial step in this process is to show that training transfers to other related tasks. Sometimes these tasks can be analogues, such as paired associates, digit span, story recall, and other verbal learning tasks used to assess transfer of training following successful treatment for recall of word lists. Typically, it is preferable to use tasks with more ecological validity, such as recalling telephone numbers, grocery lists, and work instructions because they provide a direct link to real-life activities and encourage the subject to apply his or her new skills to problems of daily living.

It is also important to investigate generalization of training to other settings, since the skills learned in therapy must be used in settings of daily living if they are to have clinical utility. Webster and Scott (1983), for example, telephoned their head-injured patient at his home to test the generalization of self-instructional training aimed at improving concentration during conversations. Significant others can also replicate testing in more relevant settings. In addition, indirect evidence of improvement in skill can be collected using data such as work reports and job promotions. These measures, however, should be used only as supplements to more direct assessment of generalization across settings.

Failures to generalize may result in very interesting and unexpected findings. In some cases it may not signal the failure of the training task per se but rather the failure of the patient to use the technique without prompting, indicating that a different set of skills aimed at increasing the spontaneous use of the compensatory skill must be added to the training package. In other cases, the real-life setting may be influenced by variables not incorporated in training, such as the impact of competing irrelevant noise or the effect of an unfair and demanding supervisor. When these variables are identified, they can easily be added to training.

Maintenance of Training

Applied research also requires evidence that the effects of training are relatively permanent. Editorial boards of behavioral journals often recommend from 6 to 12 months of follow-up assessments. Applied neuropsychological research necessitates more frequent follow-ups to separate out the effects of training from spontaneous recovery typically occurring after acquired injury. Follow-up assessments should be scheduled for at least four-week intervals during the initial few months. Assessment should include replications of both positive and negative investigations, with the latter to measure directly generalized improvements typical of spontaneous recovery. Maintenance failures should be fully investigated, and either booster training sessions or supplemental training should be undertaken.

Replications

Replicating results with other subjects is obviously the strongest support for the external validity of the results from a BSCD. Replications need not be restricted to identical treatment of another subject (direct replications), but can include systematically applied additions to the treatment package that not only replicate but also extend findings (systematic replication) (Sidman, 1960). For example, Webster et al. (1984) showed that stationary scanning training improved obstacle course performance in three stroke patients suffering from visual neglect. Gouvier et al. (1984) replicated these results with two subjects and also demonstrated that adding a verbal compensatory strategy, designed to correct distance estimation errors in the left visual space, further enhanced obstacle course performance.

Single case designs can also be used in conjunction with group designs, especially in the early stages of a research area. The flexibility of single case designs allows for relatively inexpensive experimentation aimed at developing powerful clinical techniques. Once these procedures appear to be established, group designs can be used to better examine the external validity of the results and the cost-effectiveness of the treatment package. One should be cautioned, however, that the training requirements of group designs (fixed session length and number) may be too restrictive to replicate single case results unless a very powerful clinical procedure has been developed beforehand. Following group experimentation, the experimenter may return to single case design to investigate any unusual finding.

CONCLUSIONS

In this chapter the use of single case designs in neuropsychology has been divided into a set of techniques for basic experimentation and a set of techniques for applied research. Such a division has been made simply for convenience. With reference to basic experimentation, behavioral single case designs (BCSDs) can be essential to an elegant description of a specific deficit by demonstrating that a compensatory strategy that restores the functions believed to be impaired in the subject does indeed improve performance. Luria (1980) was a major advocate of such an addition to experimental analysis. Among his many applications was the use of an A–B–A design to demonstrate that motor regulation was facilitated by loud vocal speech in frontal lobe patients. This demonstration was used to support his contention that the frontal lobes' contribution to self-regulation was in the form of private speech. Another example of the use of BSCD in basic neuropsychology is the previously mentioned use of an A–B design by Jones (1974) to show that imagery that helped patients with left temporal lobe lesions recall words did not improve the recall of H.M. or other patients with hippocampal lesions.

Applied researchers can also improve their work through the adoption of basic neuropsychological guidelines for single case design. Although their subjects rarely have pure deficits, the subject's strengths and weaknesses must be adequately described to develop both an appropriate training procedure and an accurate means of assessing treatment progress. Procedures from basic research can help in this endeavor. In addition to increasing precision in describing the subject, guidelines from basic research encourage the clinician to utilize existing brain–behavioral models in case conceptualization. This may, in turn, refine their skill at hypothesis generation, encourage the maximum use of existing information from basic neuropsychological research and facilitate communication with basic researchers.

In sum, neuropsychological research with brain-injured patients is difficult under the best of circumstances. Single case designs provide an inexpensive, efficient means for systematic study of the interesting patient.

REFERENCES

Anastasi, A. (1976). *Psychological testing* (4th ed.). New York: Macmillan.

Barlow, D. H., & Hersen, M. (1973). Single-case designs: Uses in applied clinical research. *Archives of General Psychiatry, 29,* 319–325.

Barlow, D. H., & Hersen, M. (1984). *Single case experimental design: Strategies for studying behavioral change* (2nd ed.). New York: Pergamon.

Barona, A., Reynolds, C. R., & Chastain, R. (1984). A demographically based index of premorbid intelligence for the WAIS-R. *Journal of Consulting and Clinical Psychology, 52,* 885–887.

Bolter, J. F., Gouvier, W. D., Veneklasen, J. A., & Long, C. J. (1982). Using demographic information to predict premorbid I.Q.: A test of clinical validity with head trauma patients. *Clinical Neuropsychology, 4,* 171–174.

Butters, N. (1984). The clinical aspects of memory disorders: Contributions from experimental studies of amnesia and dementia. *Journal of Clinical Neuropsychology, 6,* 17–36.

Campbell, D. T., & Stanley, J. C. (1963). *Experimental and quasi-experimental designs for research.* Chicago: Rand McNally.

Chelune, G. J., & Moehle, K. A. (1986). Neuropsychological assessment and everyday functioning. In D. Wedding, A. M. Horton, & J. S. Webster (Eds.), *The neuropsychology handbook: Clinical and behavioral perspectives.* New York: Springer Publishing Co.

Corkin, S. (1965). Tactually-guided maze learning in man: Effects of unilateral cortical excision and bilateral hippocampal lesions. *Neuropsychologia, 3,* 339–351.

Corkin, S. (1968). Acquisition of motor skill after bilateral medial temporal lobe excision. *Neuropsychologia, 6,* 255–265.

DeMaster, B., Reid, J., & Twentyman, C. (1977). The effects of different amounts of feedback on observers' reliability. *Behavior Therapy, 8,* 317–329.

Drachman, D. A., & Arbit, J. (1966). Memory and the hippocampal complex: II. Is memory a multiple process? *Archives of Neurology, 15,* 52–61.

Ekman, P., & Friesen, W. V. (1975). *Unmasking the face: A guide to recognizing emotions for facial expressions.* Englewood Cliffs, NJ: Prentice-Hall.

Gianutsos, R., & Gianutsos, J. (in press). Single case experimental approaches to the assessment of interventions in rehabilitation psychology. In B. Caplan (Ed.), *Handbook of contemporary rehabilitation psychology.* Springfield, IL: Charles C. Thomas.

Goodglass, H., & Kaplan, E. (1983). *The assessment of aphasia and related disorders* (2nd ed.). Philadelphia: Lea & Febiger.

Gould, S. J. (1981). *The mismeasure of man.* New York: Norton.

Gouvier, W. D., Bolter, J. F., Veneklasen, J. A., Hutcherson, W. L., & Long, C. S. (1983). Development and cross validation of an improved index of premorbid intelligence. *Clinical Neuropsychology, 5,* 42.

Gouvier, W. D., Cottam, G., Webster, J. S., Beissel, G. F., & Wofford, J. D. (1984). Behavioral interventions with stroke patients for improving wheelchair navigation. *International Journal of Clinical Neuropsychology, 6,* 186–190.

Gouvier, W. D., Webster, J. S., & Blanton, P. D. (1986). Cognitive retraining with brain-damaged patients. In D. Wedding, A. M. Horton, & J. S. Webster (Eds.), *The neuropsychology handbook: Clinical and behavioral perspectives.* New York: Springer Publishing Co.

Grant, D. A., & Berg, E. (1948). A behavioral analysis of degree of reinforcement and ease of shifting to new responses in a Weigl-type card sorting problem. *Journal of Experimental Psychology, 38,* 404–411.

Handel, S., & Garner, W. R. (1966). The structure of visual pattern associates and pattern goodness. *Perception and Psychophysics, 1,* 33–38.

Hartmann, D. P. (1977). Consideration in the choice of interobserver reliability estimates. *Journal of Applied Behavioral Analysis, 10,* 103–116.

Hartmann, D. P., & Hall, R. V. (1976). The changing criterion design. *Journal of Applied Behavioral Analysis, 9,* 527–532.

Hawkins, R. P., & Dobes, R. W. (1977). Behavioral definitions in applied behavior analysis: Explicit or implicit? In B. C. Etzel, J. M. LeBlanc, & D. M. Baer (Eds.), *New directions in behavioral research: Theory, methods, and applications. In honor of Sidney W. Bijou* (pp. 167–188). Hillsdale, NJ: Erlbaum.

Hersen, M., & Barlow, D. H. (1976). *Single-case experimental designs: Strategies for studying behavior change.* New York: Pergamon.

Hilgard, E. R. (1951). Methods and procedures in the study of learning. In S. S. Stevens (Ed.), *Handbook of experimental psychology* (pp. 517–567). New York: Wiley.

Johnson, S. M., & Bolstad, O. D. (1973). Methodological issues in naturalistic observation: Some problems and solutions for field research. In L. A. Homerlynck, L. C. Hardy, & E. J. Mash (Eds.), *Behavior change: Methodology, concepts, and practice* (pp. 7–67). Champaign, IL: Research Press.

Jones, M. C. (1924). A laboratory study of fear: The case of Peter. *Journal of Genetic Psychology, 31,* 308–315.

Jones, M. K. (1974). Imagery as a mnemonic aid after left temporal lobectomy: Contrast between material-specific and generalized memory disorders. *Neuropsychologia, 12,* 21–30.

Kazdin, A. E. (1982). *Single-case research designs: Methods for clinical and applied settings.* New York: Oxford University Press.

Kazdin, A. E., & Hartmann, D. P. (1978). The simultaneous treatment design. *Behavior Therapy, 5,* 912–923.

Kent, R. N., & Foster, S. L. (1977). Direct observational procedures: Methodological issues in naturalistic settings. In A. R. Ciminero, K. S. Calhour, & H. E. Adams (Eds.), *Handbook of behavioral assessment* (pp. 279–328). New York: Wiley.

Kent, R. N., Kanowitz, J., O'Leary, K. D., & Cheiken, M. (1977). Observer reliability as a function of circumstances of assessment. *Journal of Applied Behavioral Analysis, 10,* 317–324.

Kent, R. N., O'Leary, K. D., Diament, C., & Dietz, A. (1974). Expectation bias in observational evaluation of therapeutic change. *Journal of Consulting and Clinical Psychology, 42,* 774–780.

Kinsbourne, M. (1971). Cognitive deficits: Experimental analysis. In J. L. McGaugh (Ed.), *Psychobiology* (pp. 285–349). New York: Academic Press.

Klesges, R. C., Sanches, V. C., & Stanton, A. L. (1981). Cross validation of an adult premorbid functioning index. *Clinical Neuropsychology, 3,* 13–15.

Leitenberg, H. (1973). The use of single-case methodology in psychotherapy research. *Journal of Abnormal Psychology, 82,* 87–101.

Lezak, M. D. (1983). *Neuropsychological assessment* (2nd ed.). New York: Oxford University Press.

Long, C. J., & Wagner, M. S. (1986). Computer applications in neuropsychology. In D. Wedding, A. M. Horton, & J. S. Webster (Eds.), *The neuropsychology handbook: Clinical and behavioral perspectives.* New York: Springer Publishing Co.

Luria, A. R. (1980). *Higher cortical functions in man* (2nd ed.). New York: Basic Books.

McFall, R. M. (1977). Analogue methods in behavioral assessment: Issues and prospects. In J. D. Cone & R. P. Hawkins (Eds.), *Behavioral assessment: New directions in clinical psychology* (pp. 152–177). New York: Brunner/Mazel.

McFie, J. (1975). *Assessment of organic intellectual impairment.* London: Academic Press.

Milner, B. (1965). Visually-guided maze learning in man: Effects of bilateral hippocampal, bilateral frontal, and unilateral cerebral lesions. *Neuropsychologia, 3,* 317–338.

Milner, B. (1966). Amnesia following operation on the temporal lobes. In C. W. M. Whitty & O. L. Zargwill (Eds.), *Amnesia* (pp. 109–133). London: Butterworth.

Milner, B., Corkin, S., & Teuber, H. L. (1968). Further analysis of the hippocampal amnesic syndrome: 14-year follow-up study of H. M. *Neuropsychologia, 6,* 215–234.

O'Leary, K. D., Kent, R. N., & Kanowitz, J. (1975). Shaping data collection congruent with experimental hypotheses. *Journal of Applied Behavioral Analysis, 8,* 43–51.

Paivio, A., Yuille, J. C., & Madigan, S. A. (1968). Concreteness, imagery, and meaningfulness values for 925 nouns. *Journal of Experimental Psychology: Monograph Supplement, 76,* 1–9.

Raczynski, J. M., Webster, J. S., Jordan, J. E., Cliett, J., & Thompson, J. K. (1984). Stress management training in epilepsy. *Assert, 3,* 1–2.

Reid, J. B. (1970). Reliability assessment of observational data: A possible methodological problem. *Child Development, 41,* 1143–1150.

Reitan, R. M. (1974). Methodological problems in clinical neuropsychology. In R. M. Reitan & L. A. Davison (Eds.), *Clinical neuropsychology: Current status and applications* (pp. 19–46). New York: Wiley.

Restak, R. (1984). *The brain*. New York: Bantam Books.

Romanczyk, R. G., Kent, R. N., Diament, C., & O'Leary, K. D. (1973). Measuring the reliability of observational data: A reactive process. *Journal of Applied Behavior Analysis, 6,* 175–184.

Scoville, W. B. (1968). Amnesia after bilateral mesial temporal lobe excision: Introduction of case H. M. *Neuropsychologia, 6,* 211–213.

Scoville, W. B., & Milner, B. (1957). Loss of recent memory after bilateral hippocampal lesions. *Journal of Neurology, Neurosurgery, and Psychiatry, 20,* 11–21.

Shallice, T. (1979). Case study approach in neuropsychological research. *Journal of Clinical Neuropsychology, 1,* 183–211.

Shallice, T., & Warrington, E. K. (1970). Independent functioning of verbal stores: A neuropsychological study. *Quarterly Journal of Experimental Psychology, 22,* 261–273.

Sidman, M. (1960). *Tactics of scientific research*. New York: Basic Books.

Sidman, M., Stoddard, L. T., & Mohr, J. P. (1968). Some additional observations of immediate memory in a patient with bilateral hippocampal lesions. *Neuropsychologia, 6,* 245–254.

Smith, R. S. (1983). A comparison study of the Wechsler Adult Intelligence Scale with the Wechsler Adult Intelligence Scale-Revised in a college population. *Journal of Consulting and Clinical Psychology, 51,* 414–419.

Snodgrass, J. G., & Vanderwart, M. (1980). A standardized set of 260 pictures: Norms for name agreement, image agreement, familiarity, and visual complexity. *Journal of Experimental Psychology: Human Learning and Memory, 6,* 174–215.

Springer, S. P., & Deutsch, G. (1981). *Left brain, right brain*. San Francisco: Freeman.

Taplin, P. S., & Reid, J. B. (1973). Effects of instructional set and experimenter influence on observer reliability. *Child Development, 43,* 547–554.

Teuber, H. L. (1955). Physiological psychology. *Annual Review of Psychology, 9,* 267–296.

Thorndike, E. L., & Lorge, I. (1944). *The teachers word book of 30,000 words*. New York: Teachers College Press.

Toglia, M. P., & Battig, W. F. (1978). *Handbook of semantic word norms*. Hillsdale, NJ: Erlbaum.

Warrington, E. K., & Shallice, T. (1969). The selective impairment of auditory verbal short-term memory. *Brain, 92,* 885–896.

Webster, J. S., Gouvier, W. D., & Doerfler, L. (1983, March). *Computer applications in cognitive rehabilitation*. Paper presented at the meeting of the Southeastern Psychological Association, Atlanta, GA.

Webster, J. S., Jones, S., Blanton, P., Gross, R., Beissel, G. F., & Wofford, J. D. (1984). Visual scanning training with stroke patients. *Behavior Therapy, 15,* 129–143.

Webster, J. S., & Scott, R. R. (1983). The effects of self-instructional training on attentional defects following head injury. *Clinical Neuropsychology, 5,* 69–74.

Wickelgren, W. A. (1968). Sparing of short-term memory in an amnesic patient: Implications for the strength theory of memory. *Neuropsychologia, 6,* 235–244.

Wilson, R. S., Rosenbaum, G., Brown, G., Rourke, D., Witman, D., & Grisell, J. (1978). An index of premorbid intelligence. *Journal of Consulting and Clinical Psychology, 46,* 1554–1555.

Yates, A. J. (1954). The validity of some psychological tests of brain damage. *Psychological Bulletin, 51,* 359–379.

Zlutnick, S. I., Mayville, W. T., & Moffat, S. (1975). Modification of seizure disorders: The interruption of behavior chains. *Journal of Applied Behavior Analysis, 8,* 1–12.

10
Behavioral Neuropsychology: Behavioral Treatment for the Brain-Injured*

Arthur MacNeill Horton, Jr. and Scott W. Sautter

Concurrent with the recent medical and technological advances in facilitating the survival of those with brain damage have been dramatic increases in the number of brain-impaired individuals. The problems of management and rehabilitation of brain-impaired individuals demand thoughtful consideration and attention by health care professionals. This chapter will provide a perspective on the interface between neuropsychology and behavior therapy. Certain conceptual models for behavioral intervention with brain-damaged persons will be overviewed in order to generate a workable treatment paradigm. Empirical data from the available literature has been selectively reviewed and will be offered to demonstrate the current state of research-based knowledge. Clinical challenges, promising techniques for research, and tentative conclusions regarding the interface between neuropsychology and behavior therapy will be highlighted.

Behavioral neuropsychology may be defined as the application of behavior therapy techniques to problems of organically impaired individuals while applying a neuropsychologically based assessment and treatment perspective. That is, the

*The authors' contributions to this chapter were made in their capacities as private citizens and were without support or endorsement by either the Veterans Administration or the U.S. Department of Education and the National Institute of Handicapped Research.

careful delineation of data from neuropsychological assessment strategies would enhance the generation of tentative hypotheses in relation to the antecedent variables (either external or internal) for observed conditions of psychopathology. This neuropsychological perspective will significantly aid the behavior therapist's ability to make accurate discriminations as to the origin of the client's maladaptive behavior. Further, the development of a thoughtful treatment plan and its skillful application could be facilitated by a specific task analysis of behavior deficits implicating impairment of higher cortical functioning. (Horton, 1979, p. 20)

The rationale for incorporating a behavioral neuropsychological perspective derives from changes in the field of clinical neuropsychology—from emphasis on neurodiagnostics to a focus on treatment planning and outcome evaluation. Moreover, demographic and epidemiological data, theoretical issues, empirically based research to date, and increases in the population of brain-damaged individuals lead to a straightforward conclusion that the time has come to provide a working behavioral neuropsychology treatment paradigm.

THEORETICAL ISSUES

A number of theoretical issues concern the relationship of neuropsychology and contemporary behavior therapy models, and a discussion may provide clarity in developing the interface of the two fields. This discussion is limited by space and is inadequate to give it full justice; however, comments relative to the inclusion of a neuropsychological perspective within a behavioral model are appropriate.

The relationship of neuropsychology and behavior therapy will be approached from two separate perspectives. The first perspective is related to researchers and clinicians who do not identify themselves as behavior therapists. These individuals may well promote a model of behavior therapy lacking in all of its conceptual richness. The second perspective attempts to model the views of researchers and clinicians who do identify themselves as behavior therapists. It is self-evident that there are inherent difficulties in developing a consensual definition of behavior therapy that all behavior therapists would readily embrace. Therefore, the second perspective is offered as the favored approach of the authors rather than the monolithic agreement of behavior therapists as a whole. With a clear understanding of these limitations the following discussion is offered.

Horton and Miller (1984) related that the radical behavioral model, in its most extreme sense, has rejected unobservable variables as inadequate in the functional analysis and study of human behavior. That is, thoughts, unexpressed and expressed feelings are unnecessary to explain stimulus-response actions. Many would agree that there is considerable wisdom in carefully objectifying the variables in question when empirically evaluating human behavior, because of the complexity of its dynamics. However, it may be fallacious to assume that the radical behaviorist model can combine all inferred variables in the same conceptual category.

It is a truism that radical behavior therapists would agree that unobservable factors in studying human behavior are not appropriate factors for study in behavior therapy (Skinner, 1938). These behavior therapists would insist on utilizing a strict stimulus-response model of behavior that is observable. However, the fact remains that persons outside of the behavior therapy establishment continue to view radical behaviorism as synonymous with and tantamount to behavior therapy. The question of the place of inferred variables that are not observable stimulus-response actions of an organism should be raised (Mahoney, 1974), particularly those variables that might serve the development of interfacing neuropsychology and behavior therapy. A tentative solution is offered to substantiate the claim that an enlarged behavioral neuropsychology paradigm is appropriate and warranted at this time (Horton, 1979).

A solution to this dilemma involves the identification and discussion of two separate and distinct classes of inferred variables. Craighead, Kazdin, and Mahoney (1976) referred to these as *intervening variables* and *hypothetical constructs*. On a theoretical level, intervening variables are not amenable, being limited by our present state of technology to direct observation by conventional behavioral techniques. Examples of intervening variables would be thoughts or feelings (Horton, 1979). Conversely, hypothetical constructs have a more empirical or physiological function, which can be assessed with our present techniques, than do intervening variables (Craighead, Kazdin, & Mahoney, 1976). The crux of the matter is that hypothetical constructs are derived from observable physiological referents. The importance of this distinction cannot be emphasized enough. As Horton (1979) stated, the major advantage is that at some point, by some method, the existence or nonexistence of hypothetical constructs can be observed, verified, and documented. As an example of direct observation, neuropsychological test data suggesting that a patient has a right hemisphere brain tumor could be readily verified by means of neuroradiological procedures. The fact of observability and documentation of the maladaptive behavior from a physiological referent is important. This distinction promotes the validity of utilizing hypothetical constructs for use in delineating etiology for behavior therapy. At the present time, methods for direct objective verification of thoughts or feelings have not yet been adequately developed; therefore, intervening variables are not as appropriate for the determination of antecedent conditions of maladaptive behavior in behavior therapy.

Neuropsychological variables are best viewed as hypothetical constructs, and their inclusion in the interface between neuropsychology and a behavior therapy treatment paradigm has quite different implications than inclusion of intervening variables. An impressive knowledge base of brain–behavior relationships has been published (Golden, 1978; Heilman & Valenstein, 1979; Luria, 1966; Reitan & Davison, 1974), and because of the particular nature of neuropsychological variables the time for their inclusion in an enlarged behavioral treatment paradigm is justified.

The viewpoint of the authors follows that of self-identified behavior therapists, and the second perspective regarding the interface of neuropsychology and behavior therapy originates with that conceptual issue. Horton (1981) related that a salient trend in contemporary behavior therapy, concerning clinical sophistication of behavioral assessment and therapy, has evolved. One of the most important directions of this evolving trend for neuropsychology and behavior therapy is the rationale for and development of an empirical test for what can best be considered behavioral techniques. Hayes and Zettle (1980) have presented a cogent argument and issues for conceptual discussion in judging whether a particular technique is appropriate for use as a behavioral technique in behavior therapy. They first clarified the differences between the technical aspects (the means of application) and conceptual dimensions (the means of discussing that application) of behavior therapy. They presented arguments for the selection of conceptual dimensions rather than the technical aspects in discriminating among techniques that can be considered behavioral.

A technique or method for observing and documenting behavior should be considered behavioral if it can be empirically tested and discussed in terms of behavioral principles. Consequently, the topographical details or etiology of the particular techniques or methods are not the decisive factors in including or discounting it as being behavioral. In other words, the antecedents and consequences of the behavior are observed to generate tentative hypotheses as to its *purpose* instead of simply observing and documenting environmental details. The overriding point is that methods that can be discussed in terms of behavioral principles and that provide objectively assessed outcomes, leading to empirical verification, are behavioral techniques. An example of this sort of reasoning would be that empirically based assessment techniques, such as the Minnesota Multiphasic Personality Inventory, should be considered as having the same degree of behavioral respectability as more traditional behavior therapy assessment procedures, such as fear surveys or self-monitoring protocols. The implication of this discussion is that if behavioral therapy is defined in a conceptual sense, then clinical neuropsychological instruments can and should be discussed in terms of behavioral principles. Therefore, the Halstead–Reitan Neuropsychological Battery, the Luria–Nebraska Neuropsychological Battery, and the McCarron–Dial assessment systems should be considered as behavioral techniques. Hayes and Zettle (1980) characterized behavior therapy as a clinical science that is based upon clinical realities; and, in keeping with this salient trend, behavior therapy may best be served from the incorporation of the conceptual view as the preferred perspective in the selection of assessment methods. Hence, there exist solid theoretical grounds for developing the interface between neuropsychology and behavior therapy. In the best tradition of behaviorism the bottom line will be the empirical verification of how much this blend of neuropsychology and behavioral therapy contributes to facilitation of patient care.

Horton and Miller (1984) have provided clarification regarding the understanding of the neuropsychological perspective in this developing interface because of the advent and probability of increasing technological changes in the field of clinical neuropsychology. It would be detrimental to the burgeoning field of behavioral neuropsychology to identify any single set of neuropsychological assessment techniques, due to the inherent problems that would follow such a narrow scope. Rather, a more sagacious attitude toward the development of behavioral neuropsychology would be to identify major guidelines for procedures, based upon the unique characteristics of the human brain and interfaced with traditional, contemporary, and evolving behavior therapy techniques. The introduction of parameters and conceptual schemes regarding a proposed treatment paradigm would more likely be relatively independent of foreseeable changes and outgrowths in neurodiagnostic methods and procedures.

The future viability of the Halstead–Reitan Neuropsychological Battery and the Luria–Nebraska Neuropsychological Battery in neurological, neurosurgical, psychiatric, and rehabilitative medicine, as well as educational and vocational settings can be seen as functioning independently of behavioral neuropsychology. To provide support for the perspective of the behavioral neuropsychology treatment paradigm it is necessary to discuss the ways and means of integrating data from the two fields. Thus, a need exists for a workable and empirically viable treatment methodology derived from a sound theoretical base.

CONCEPTUAL MODELS

Diller and Gordon (1981a), from an excellent chapter in the *Handbook of Clinical Neuropsychology,* posited three conceptual approaches as models of mental life and called their approaches those of the chemist, the biologist, and the behavioral engineer. They compared and contrasted the three perspectives with respect to each method's purpose, major concepts, and critical neuropsychological issues. The result was the incorporation of conceptual problem selection, task analysis, and treatment perspectives (Diller & Gordon, 1981a). These three models of mental life will be renamed for the purposes of this chapter as those of the clinical psychologist (for chemist), the neurologist (for biologist), and the behavior therapist (for behavioral engineer) (Horton & Wedding, 1984).

Horton and Wedding (1984) described these perspectives, stating that the clinical psychologist utilizes psychometric tests to study mental life and test profiles to delineate strengths and weaknesses in functioning. In contrast, the neurologist employs knowledge of neurodevelopmental procedures and responses to altered conditions of performance to describe functioning. The behavior therapist views mental life by observing behavior and abstracting its purpose through the application of stimulus-response contingencies to describe the patient's functioning. In other words, the psychologist looks at test scores, the neurologist looks at neuroanatomy, and the behavior therapist looks at behavior (Horton & Wedding, 1984). Further clarification of these models may be offered by reference to their implications and applications for intervention and treatment strategies (Diller & Gordon, 1981a).

In support of an assessment and treatment paradigm based on behavioral neuropsychology, Diller and Gordon (1981a) concluded that the three approaches should be integrated in a complementary rather than competitive manner. It is self-evident that a sophisticated understanding of each perspective is necessary to facilitate appropriate intervention with the patient and the presenting problems. Without a firm grasp of each perspective's content and theory one would be hard pressed to integrate them in a meaningful and practical way. That is, a rote or mechanical application of any of the three in isolation would be neither appropriate nor justified. In a discussion of the amalgamation of the clinical psychologist's, neurologist's, and behavior therapist's perspectives and applications, Horton and Wedding (1984) stated that this integration could produce publicly verifiable, objectively stated outcomes, and provide behavioral treatment procedures for the application of behavioral neuropsychology in a meaningful way. With careful and thoughtful persistence, therapeutic changes may take place and generalize to new skills, tasks, and settings.

Thus, there appears to be a degree of consensus regarding the need for a blending of the clinical psychologist's, neurologist's, and behavior therapist's approaches to viewing a patient's mental life. Just as a clinician would not wish to base a diagnostic decision about the presence or absence of brain impairment on a single assessment measure, neither would the clinician view therapy for brain-damaged clients as being effective from a single approach or perspective. The ultimate test of integrating neuropsychology and behavior therapy into an assessment and treatment paradigm will, of course, be how much empirical support can be gathered to support this hypothesis. In the next section, a brief review of previously employed assessment and treatment paradigms will be offered to demonstrate efficacious means of utilizing their best qualities.

Contributions to clinical neuropsychology from Luria (1966) and Diller and his associates (1974) have been expertly dealt with elsewhere in this text. For a more comprehensive and detailed analysis of these approaches the reader is referred to Chapters 7 and 11 of this book. Quite simply, Luria has provided a view of the brain as consisting of a complex functional organization for production of behavior. Assessment stems from describing intact functional systems from which compensatory strategies for rehabilitation are derived. Conversely, Diller and his associates have concentrated their efforts on describing areas of functional deficits in a hierarchical fashion in order to progress systematically through remedial rehabilitation of those deficits. A third contribution to the field of clinical neuropsychology has been put forth by Lewinsohn, which appears to provide a unique assessment-treatment paradigm.

Lewinsohn's Model

As is well known, Peter Lewinsohn has received worldwide recognition for his work on the behavioral theory of depression. As is less well known, he has also made important contributions to clinical and behavioral neuropsychology. Of particular relevance to this chapter is his research on the remediation of memory deficits in brain damaged individuals (Lewinsohn, Danaher, & Kikel, 1977).

Lewinsohn and his colleagues at the University of Oregon Human Neuropsychology Laboratory devoted major efforts to the evaluation of clinical memory remediation methods for brain-injured adults. A byproduct of his research program was the development of a clinical paradigm for working with brain-damaged individuals (Glasgow, Zeiss, Barrera, & Lewinsohn, 1977). These are as follows:

Step 1: General assessment of neuropsychological functioning

Step 2: Specific assessment of neuropsychological functioning

Step 3: Laboratory evaluation of intervention strategy

Step 4: *In vivo* application of intervention strategy

General Assessment

The goal of the first step is to understand the patient's neuropsychological functioning in terms of normative data. Put another way, how does the patient compare to patients with similar demographic characteristics and the same diagnosis? This viewpoint, of course, compares the patient to other patients of similar type.

In order to answer these sets of questions, standardized neuropsychological test batteries have significant advantages. Instruments like the Halstead–Reitan Neuropsychological Test Battery (including, of course, the age-appropriate Wechsler scales and, if appropriate, the Minnesota Multiphasic Personality Inventory) and the Luria–Nebraska Neuropsychological Test Battery have been subjected to empirical validation and reliability studies. Related data have been gathered regarding normal performance for particular types of patients. Moreover, coverage of a wide number of areas of neuropsychological functioning is assured through the use of a standardized battery. By providing data on areas of strength as well as weakness, treatment planning is facilitated.

Specific Assessment

The goal of the second step is to understand the patient's problem in terms of his or her unique individual functioning, that is to say, the specific parameters of the patient's problem. If the hallmark of the first step of the Lewinsohn Model, as seen by the authors, is the use of a psychometrically validated neuropsychological test battery, then the hallmark of the second step is a behavioral assessment that includes, in addition to examination of the topographical details of the patient's behavior, exploring the purpose and personal meaning of the patient's behavior. By way of illustration is the case of Ms. J.

Glasgow, Zeiss, Barrera, and Lewinsohn (1977), in the first step of the model, administered the Wechsler Adult Intelligence Scale (WAIS) and the Halstead–Reitan Neuropsychological Test Battery (HRNTB) to Ms. J., who obtained a WAIS Full-Scale IQ of 114 and a Halstead Impairment Index of .25. By contrast, in the second step, selections from a reading-skills training program of informational presentations and narrative prose were chosen to evaluate the actual dimensions of her self-reported semantic memory functions (which were causing school-related difficulties); in short, a direct qualitative assessment of the behavior in question. [For a more detailed example of behavioral assessment in neuropsychology, see Horton and Wedding (1984)].

Laboratory Evaluation

The goal of the third step is to test the value of specific intervention for the patient's problem in a controlled environment. In a setting where the various parameters of a treatment method can be either held constant or precisely varied, it is possible to make precise statements regarding cause-and-effect relationships. Therefore, questions of treatment validity can be meaningfully addressed.

In vivo Application

The goal of the fourth step is to translate the successful laboratory intervention into the real world. It is perhaps trite to say that this is the stage where many techniques that were successful in the laboratory setting prove to be inadequate to the rigors of the real world. Quite often, additional efforts are needed to engineer a successful *in vivo* performance of a treatment technique. For example, two issues of concern are incentive systems and fidelity of treatment. First, attention may need to be devoted to generating occasions of reinforcement for engaging in the preferred intervention. In the case of memory aids, for instance, patients often fail to use them because it is easier, at the moment, not to. Second, the strength of treatment needs to be considered. Just as various drugs have therapeutic windows, behavioral treatment methods have specific levels at which they must be maintained in order to be efficacious. It may be that additional strategies must be added or that specific intervention must be adjusted to fit more appropriately the particular circumstances of the patient's unique environment and life style, or both.

A related consideration is the question of how the treatment conditions can be maintained in the real world. While the induction of behavior change in the *in vivo* situation is praiseworthy in and of itself, many conditions are chronic and some attention should be devoted to arranging environmental cues and contingencies in such a manner that the therapeutic intervention is maintained over an extended period of time and over the variety of different situations that the person is likely to encounter.

In summary, it can be averred that Lewinsohn's model provides a valuable paradigm for conceptualizing the steps necessary for clinical intervention with brain-injured patients. One final point, however, should be kept firmly in mind. While the theme of this chapter is the use of neuropsychological test batteries, it would be a misreading to assume that other neurodiagnostic methods are excluded. Rather, the clear intent is to include whatever standardized, valid, and reliable methods neuroscience can develop. More specifically, the use of techniques such as the CT scan, PET scan, and BEAM in the context raises no conceptual difficulties (Horton & Wedding, 1984). Given the current state of contemporary neuroscience and the varieties of neurodiagnostic advances in the last two decades, it would be unwise to expect anything other than rapid technological progress in science's quest to view, describe, and understand the brain and, by extension, the human mind.

GUIDELINES FOR BEHAVIORAL NEUROPSYCHOLOGY

At this point, some consideration as to how treatment recommendations for behavior change procedures are generated from neuropsychological data would appear warranted. It is important to state that the current basis for empirical research in this area consists of remarkably few studies. Thus, a lesser degree of scientific certainty is all that is available. Perhaps related to the paucity of research data on treatment options for the brain injured is the rather complex nature of the problem. It would seem almost trite to evoke once again images of how complex the human brain is, how much information is stored in the mind, and how creative humans are with mental capacities. Given the complexity of human information processing there are even more ways it can go wrong in the case of brain injury; thus, the problem of dealing with a subject matter of almost infinite variety. Still, some overall generalizations are possible. The following comments will suggest some guidelines that appear to have at least face validity and the weight of some clinical lore. It is, of course, freely admitted that in some cases empirical evidence is wanting.

In order to facilitate clarity of expression, some simplifying assumptions will be made. For example, it is proposed that the three dimensions described by Manfred Meier (1974) will be crucial. They are from left to right, from front to back, and from top to bottom; simply, the three dimensions of objects. In talking about the brain, Horton and Wedding (1984) refer to these three dimensions as *laterality, caudality,* and *dorsality* respectively. As stated by Horton and Wedding (1984):

> These terms are selected for the sake of convenience and are not intended to be of exact neuroanatomical significance or precision. These suggestions presuppose rather focal cortical lesions. (p. 216)

Laterality

As is well known, the two cerebral hemispheres have different modes of cognitive processing (Horton & Wedding, 1984). As has been noted many times before in a variety of contexts, the left cerebral hemisphere, assuming right-handedness, is more specialized for language arts and analytical thought. By contrast, assuming right-handedness, the right cerebral hemisphere is more specialized for processing the spacial aspects of data and the mode of thought is more intuitive (Sperry, 1961). In short, choice of modes of communication, therapy tasks, and the process of therapeutic management are dependent upon laterality considerations (Horton & Wedding, 1984).

In order to illustrate this point it may be helpful to consider the following case example of a man who sustained a traumatic injury to the right cerebral hemisphere (Horton, 1979b). The patient, an aircraft mechanic, had fallen off the wing of an airplane (while the airplane was on the ground). The man had been referred for "behavior modification" because he exhibited inappropriate social behavior in a sheltered workshop situation. Neuropsychological and behavioral analysis of the patient and his difficulties revealed an interesting chain of events. Apparently, the patient began his socially inappropriate behavior only after he had been assigned some perceptual-motor tasks. It is noteworthy that these tasks involved his impaired visuo-spacial and manual manipulation skills which are, of course, subserved by the right cerebral hemisphere. When seen in the controlled setting of a neurology ward, the patient's inappropriate behavior was easily extinguished by verbal reprimands. The point worth remembering is that an earlier analysis of the patient's pattern of neuropsychological strengths and weaknesses could have produced a more realistic rehabilitation plan; it is quite likely that if he had been assigned tasks within his level of adaptive ability, then no socially inappropriate behavior would have been elicited from him. More detailed discussion of this issue can be obtained in Horton and Wedding (1984), Golden (1978), or Luria (1963).

Caudality

Caudality, in the sense it is used here, refers to the anterior-posterior dimension of the cerebral cortex. The implications of caudality of brain injury for the planning of behavior change strategies are quite straightforward. As hypothesized by Luria (1966), the frontal lobes are critically important in the planning, executing, and verifying of human behavior. Luria (1966) also postulated that the temporal, parietal, and occipital lobes were vitally important in the reception, integration, and analysis of auditory, somatosensory, and visual data, respectively, from the internal and external environment. Clearly, the implications of injury to the prefrontal (or "far-frontal," as Karl Pribam has suggested it be called) cortex are of clinical importance. A patient with compromised frontal lobe functioning can be expected to exhibit a lessened ability to solve problems in novel situations. Often, this translates into poor self-management skills. Luria (1966), referring to his work with brain-injured Russian soldiers after World War II, noted the difficulties of rehabilitating patients with frontal lobe lesions. He commented that in most cases the patients with impairment of the prefrontal region were unable to work unsupervised and thus had to be kept in a sheltered workshop situation. In a nutshell, the prognosis for self-direction and independent action was poor. As observed by Horton and Wedding (1984), often a patient with intact frontal lobe functioning would adapt better to independent living than a patient with a frontal lobe lesion, despite the fact that on either standardized neuropsychological batteries, such as the Halstead–Reitan, or neurodiagnostic devices, such as the CT scan, the frontal lobe patient demonstrated objective evidence of a lesser degree of overall brain damage.

A related issue is the value of cognitive-behavioral treatment methods for this population. Meichenbaum (1977) has been a leader in promoting the use of self-instructional therapy to develop self-control skills. A likely outgrowth of his work would be to adapt self-instructional therapy for the patient with frontal lobe lesions, as has already been done with impulsive children.

Dorsality

As previously asserted, the term *dorsality* will be used within the context of this chapter to refer to the top–bottom dimension of human brain functioning. An important aspect of dorsality is the observation that there are personality alternatives secondary to certain types of brain injury. Sometimes, previously controlled negative personality traits may be accentuated after the onset of a cortical lesion, according to the triune brain theory of Paul MacLean (1973). Briefly, MacLean postulates that the evolution of the human brain can be seen as the development in sequence of three separate neurocognitive systems. Each layer shares some functions with each other layer, but the newer layers add more sophisticated levels of mental functioning. Still, the older layers remain active and play a role in producing behavior. The closer the layer to the bottom, the more primitive and emotional the actions; the closer to the top, the more complex and civilized the actions.

As observed by Horton and Wedding (1984): "The overall effect is a multifaced and at times contradictory picture of base motivation, warm emotion and logical abstraction" (p. 49). With respect to clinical implications, it is fair to say that a great deal of additional work must be completed before it is possible to generate meaningful recommendations. In short, the current knowledge base concerning dorsality issues is inadequate.

EMPIRICAL RESEARCH

At this point, attention will be directed to the existing research evidence for the use of behavior modification/therapy with the brain-injured population. The intent of this section is to examine critically the contemporary scientific status of this new area of clinical research. The focus will be on behavioral treatment methods. Because the topic of cognitive retraining is covered thoroughly in Chapter 11 of this volume, it will not be addressed here. It is, of course, acknowledged that these categorizations are arbitrary and other conceptualizations might have equal or superior logical warrant. Moreover, despite the best efforts of the editors some overlap in content is unavoidable. Thus, with a full realization of the limitations of the enterprise, the following comments are offered.

Horton and Miller (1984) have averred:

> Rather dramatically, it can be seen that the majority of research evidence concerning behavior therapy or behavior modification has dealt with a single conceptualization of learning. Indeed it would appear difficult to find more than a few studies using an approach other than operant conditioning in the literature on behavior therapy and brain damage as long as seizure disorders are excluded.

In perhaps the earliest review of the use of behavior modification with the brain injured, Ince (1976) reviewed 24 studies, of which 23 used operant methods (e.g., positive reinforcer, time-out, feedback). As might be expected, given the initial nature of these efforts, essentially all were one- or two-patient case reports (20 or 83% to be exact). Later reviews by Horton (1979; 1982) reflected an increasing sophistication in this literature but clearly indicated that much additional research was necessary. A particularly noteworthy paper was a general review of cognitive intervention with brain-injured adults by Diller and Gordon (1981b) that included the earlier work of Ince. The present selective review of research is an attempt to complement the contribution of Diller and Gordon (1981b) and, by extension, Ince (1976). Essentially, this review attempts to identify studies not included in the Ince (1976) review and to include studies published from 1976 through 1983. There are over 30 studies that can be cited in addition to those already identified by Ince (1976) and cited by Diller and Gordon (1981b). They include: Blyth, 1969; Brannigan and Young, 1978; Campbell and Stremel-Campbell, 1982; Carlin and Armstrong, 1968; Carter et al., 1980; Cinciripini et al., 1980; Deaton and Citron, 1983; Foxx and Azrin, 1972; Gerber et al., 1981; Gerber and Spevack, 1981; Hall and Broden, 1967; Hartlage and Horton, 1981; Horton, 1979b; Horton and Howe, 1981; Horton and Howe, 1982; Kumchy and Koris, 1981; Montgomery and Cleeland, 1980; Muir and Milan, 1982; Murphy, 1976; Reidy, 1979; Ribes-inesta and Guzman, 1974; Rinke et al., 1978; Rothschild et al., 1975; Rusch et al., 1980; Salvatore, 1976; Salzinger et al., 1970; Sellick and Peck, 1981; Stanton et al., 1979; Sufrin, 1975; Turner et al., 1978; Waye, 1980; Webster and Scott, 1985; Wilson and McCulley, 1970. These papers include a number of control group studies, among them: Denton and Citron, 1983; Dolan and Norton, 1977; Hartlage and Horton, 1981; and Sufrin, 1975. As each study has been abstracted elsewhere (Horton & Miller, 1985), they will not be reviewed here. Readers wishing additional information, such as specific details regarding patient characteristics and behavioral techniques utilized, should see Horton and Miller, 1985.

To a large measure, these research studies speak for themselves. Along with the previously cited reviews (Diller & Gordon, 1981b; Horton, 1979; Horton, 1982; Ince, 1976), they provide a convincing basis for the use of behavior modification/therapy methods with the brain injured.

In closing this section, perhaps it would be best to recall the earlier observation of Horton (1982) in reviewing much of the same research:

A limitation of this literature is the generally neurologically simplistic adaptation of behavioral treatment methodology. Only recently have more sophisticated applications been attempted. . . . Still, the uniformly positive results suggest great promise in this area for future application. (p. 101)

FUTURE PERSPECTIVES

In a somewhat cursory fashion, four areas that hold promise will be briefly discussed in regard to neglected populations, various treatment methods, different views on conceptualizations, and assessment techniques. It is important that some brain-damaged groups have not received adequate attention. Horton and Decker (1981) have stated that the learning-disabled child does grow up but does not completely grow out of maladaptive functioning. This population was officially recognized in 1981 by the U.S. Department of Education's Rehabilitation Services Agency, which mandated that learning-disabled adults must be served within each state's vocational rehabilitation agency. Further, despite a massive amount of data implicating brain impairment among alcoholics (Butters & Cermack, 1980) and aged individuals (Horton, 1979), relatively few efforts have been made to rehabilitate and provide remediation of the consequences of brain damage.

New technological treatment approaches with brain-impaired individuals is a rich area for study. Seron, Delocke, Mouland, and Rousselle (1980) have adapted computer technology to create computer-based therapy programs for remediating writing problems in aphasic populations. William Lynch (1983), in a similar vein, has adapted video games for cognitive retraining at the Palo Alto Veterans Hospital. The integration of behavioral and pharmacological medication has provided yet another interesting treatment intervention (Pirozzolo, Campanella, Christensen, & Lawson-Kerr, 1981). The research on physostigmine and lecithin, and their effects on verbal memory in posttraumatic amnesia, appears to be a worthwhile area of study (Goldberg, Gerstman, Mattis, Hughes, Sirio & Binder, 1982; Walton, 1982).

A third promising area of new research, which may transform current theoretical models, involves new conceptualizations of appropriate variables. The concepts of sensory reinforcement (Rincover, Newsom, Lovas, & Koegel, 1977) and cognitive modifiability (Feurstein, 1980) hold tremendous promise for enriching current thoughts on the learning abilities of brain-damaged individuals. Similarly, new assessment techniques are evolving. Computer technology may play an important role with respect to assessment methods. (For a closer look at present and potential computer applications in neuropsychology, see Chapter 20, this volume.) A computerized behavioral approach to cognitive assessment has been developed by Perez, Brown, Cooke, Pickett, Rivera, and Grabois (1980). Also, John's (1977) computer-based applications of neurometric assessment holds great promise for future investigations. The Luria–Nebraska Neuropsychological Battery has proven to be an exciting assessment instrument (Golden, Hammeke, & Purisch, 1978).

CONCLUSION

The preceding remarks were intended to describe the current status of behavioral neuropsychology. To that end, a definition was proposed and defended. In addition relevant theoretical issues were examined and conceptual models explored. In the interest of providing practical guidance some rational-clinical suggestions for designing behavioral neuropsychology interventions were presented. Next, a selective review of research studies utilizing behavior modification/therapy with the brain injured was presented and some future perspectives were shared.

As would appear self-evident, the ultimate value of an area of scientific inquiry lies in its potential to solve human problems. Thus, the value of behavioral neuropsychology will rest upon the contributions it makes toward the solution of the cognitive, affective, and behavioral problems encountered by brain-damaged individuals. The expectation and hope is that this chapter will help meet the challenge to alleviate emotional distress and to promote the social adaptation of individuals who have suffered cerebral injury.

While it would be premature to suggest that many problems have been solved, it is also true that nothing is obtained without risk. At this point one might reflect and take comfort in the words of Neal Miller, the father of biofeedback: "We need to be cautious in what we claim but bold in what we try."

REFERENCES

Blyth, Z. (1969, July–August). Group treatment for handicapped children. *Journal of Psychiatric Nursing and Mental Health Services,* 172–173.

Bollinger, R. L., & Stout, C. E. (1976). Response-contingent small-step treatment. Performance-based communication intervention. *Journal of Speech and Hearing Disorders, 41,* 40–49.

Brannigan, C., & Young, R. (1978). Social skills training with the MDB adolescent: A case study. *Academic Therapy, 13* (4), 401–404.

Butters, N., & Cermak, L. (1980). *Alcoholic Korsakoff syndrome: An information-processing approach to amnesia.* New York: Academic Press.

Campbell, C., & Stremel-Campbell, K. (1982). Programming "loose training" as a strategy to facilitate language generalization. *Journal of Applied Behavior Analysis, 15,* 295–301.

Carlin, A. S., & Armstrong, H. E. (1968). Rewarding social responsibility in disturbed children: A group play technique. *Psychotherapy: Theory, research and practice, 5,* 169–174.

Carter, L. T., Caruso, J. L., Languirand, M. A., & Bernard, M. A. (1980). Cognitive skill remediation in stroke and non-stroke elderly. *Clinical Neuropsychology, 2,* 109–113.

Cinciripini, P., Epstein, L., & Kotanchik, N. (1980). Behavioral intervention for self-stimulatory, attending and seizure behavior in a cerebral palsied child. *Journal of Behavior Therapy and Experimental Psychiatry, 11,* 313–316.

Craighead, W. E., Kazdin, A. E., & Mahoney, M. J. (1976). *Behavior modification: Principles, issues, and applications.* Boston: Houghton Mifflin.

Deaton, A., & Citron, C. (1983, August). *The development of group intervention strategies for impulsive adolescents with cognitive and language deficits.* Paper presented at the annual convention of the American Psychological Association, Anaheim, CA.

Diller, L. (1976). A model for cognitive retraining in rehabilitation. *Clinical Psychologist, 29,* 13–19.

Diller, L., Ben-Yishay, Y., Gerstman, L. I., Goodkin, R., Gordon, W., & Weinberg, J. (1974). Studies in cognition and rehabilitation in hemiplegia (Rehabilitation Monograph No. 50). New York University Medical Center, Institute of Rehabilitation Medicine.

Diller, L., & Gordon, W. A. (1981a). Rehabilitation and clinical neuropsychology. In S. B. Filskov & T. J. Boll (Eds.), *Handbook of clinical neuropsychology* (pp. 461–682). New York: Wiley.

Diller, L., & Gordon, W. A. (1981b). Intervention for cognitive deficits in brain-injured adults. *Journal of Consulting and Clinical Psychology, 49,* 882–834.

Dolan, M. P., & Norton, J. C. (1977). A programmed training technique that uses reinforcement to facilitate acquisition and retention in brain damaged patients. *Journal of Clinical Psychology, 33,* 496–501.

Feurenstein, R. (1980). *Instrument enrichment: An intervention program for cognitive modifiability.* Baltimore, MD: University Park Press.

Forsland, C., & Errickson, E. (1978, May). A behavioral approach to physical rehabilitation: A case study. *Journal of Psychiatric Nursing and Mental Health Services,* 48–51.

Foxx, R. M., & Azrin, N. H. (1972). Restitution: A method of eliminating aggressive-disruptive behavior of retarded and brain damaged patients. *Behavior Research and Therapy, 10,* 15–27.

Fredericksen, L., & Rosenbaum, M. (1979). The behavioral control of tardive dyskinesia: Evaluation of three types of feedback. *Journal of Behavior Therapy and Experimental Psychiatry, 10,* 299–302.

Gerber, G., Major, M., Adams, J., & Spevack, M. (1981, November). *Stimulation of cognitive functioning in a young severely-impaired closed head injury patient: The role of behavior modification strategies.* Paper presented at the meeting of the Association for Advancement of Behavior Therapy, Toronto.

Gerber, G., Rivard, C., & Spevack, M. (1980, December). *Increasing compliance and attention in a severely brain damaged patient using behavioral intervention.* Paper presented at the meeting of the Association for Advancement of Behavior Therapy, New York.

Gerber, G., & Spevack, M. (1981, November). *Increasing cognitive functioning in a severely brain-damaged patient using behavioral interventions.* Paper presented at the meeting of the Association for Advancement of Behavior Therapy, Toronto.

Gianutsos, R., & Gianutsos, J. (1979, February). *Rehabilitating the verbal information processing of brain-injured patients: An experimental demonstration using the single-case methodology.* Paper presented at the seventh annual meeting of the International Neuropsychological Society, New York.

Glasgow, R. E., Zeiss, R. A., Barrera, M., Jr., & Lewinsohn, P. M. (1977). Case studies on remediating memory deficits in brain damaged individuals. *Journal of Clinical Psychology, 33,* 1049–1054.

Goldberg, E., Gerstman, L., Mattis, S., Hughes, J., Sirio, C., & Binder, R. (1982). Selective efforts of cholinergic treatment of verbal memory in post-traumatic amnesia. *Journal of Clinical Neuropsychology, 4* (3), 219–234.

Golden, C. J. (1978). *Diagnosis and rehabilitation in clinical neuropsychology.* Springfield, IL: C. C. Thomas.

Golden, C. J., Hammeke, T. A., & Purish, A. D. (1978). Diagnostic validity of a standardized neuropsychology battery derived from Luria's neuropsychological tests. *Journal of Consulting and Clinical Psychology, 46,* 1258–1265.

Hall, R. V., & Broden, M. (1967). Behavior changes in brain-injured children through social reinforcement. *Journal of Experimental Child Psychology, 5,* 463–479.

Hartlage, L., & Horton, A. M., Jr. (1982, August.) Behavioral neuropsychology and rehabilitation: A group comparison study. In J. Lutzer (Chair), *Behavioral approaches to rehabilitation and health psychology.* Symposium conducted at the annual convention of the American Psychological Association, Los Angeles.

Hayes, S. C., & Zettle, R. D. (1980). On being "behavioral." The technical and conceptual dimensions of behavioral assessment and therapy. *The Behavior Therapist, 3* (3), 4–6.

Heilman, K. M., & Valenstein, E. (1979). *Clinical neuropsychology.* New York: Oxford University Press.

Horton, A. M., Jr. (1979). Behavioral neuropsychology: Rationale and research. *Clinical Neuropsychology, 1* (2), 20–23.

Horton, A. M., Jr. (1979b). Behavioral neuropsychology: A clinical case study. *Clinical Neuropsychology, 1* (3), 44–47.

Horton, A. M., Jr. (1981). Behavioral neuropsychology in the schools. *School Psychology Review, 10,* 367–372.

Horton, A. M., Jr. (1982). Behavioral neuropsychology: A brief rationale. *The Behavior Therapist, 5,* 100–102.

Horton, A. M., Jr., & Decker, E. B. (1981). Neuropsychological assessment of an adult's minimal brain dysfunction: A case study. *Perceptual and Motor Skills, 51,* 676–678.

Horton, A. M., Jr., & Howe, N. R. (1981). Behavioral neuropsychology and the traumatic brain injured adult: A case study. *Proceedings of the 5th annual postgraduate course on the rehabilitation of the brain-injured adult* (pp. 18–19). Richmond, VA: Virginia Commonwealth University.

Horton, A. M., Jr. & Howe, N. (1982). Behavior therapy with an aged alcoholic: A case study. *International Journal of Behavioral Geriatrics, 1* (3), 17–18.

Horton, A. M., Jr., & Miller, W. G. (1984). Brain damage and rehabilitation. In C. J. Golden (Ed.), *Current topics in rehabilitation psychology.* (pp. 77–105). New York: Grune & Stratton.

Horton, A. M., Jr., & Miller, W. G. (1985). Neuropsychology and behavior theory. In M. Hersen, R. M. Eisler, & P. M. Miller (Eds.), *Progress in behavior modification,* Vol. 19 (pp. 1–55). New York: Academic Press.

Horton, A. M., Jr., & Wedding, D. (1984). *Clinical and behavioral neuropsychology: An introduction.* New York: Praeger.

Ince, L. P. (1976). *Behavior modification in rehabilitation medicine.* Springfield, IL: C. C. Thomas.

John, E. R. (1977). Neurometrics: Clinical applications of electrophysiology. In E. R. John & R. W. Thatcher (Eds.), *Functional neuroscience* (Vol. 2). Hillsdale, NJ: Lawrence Erlbaum Associates.

Kumchy, C., & Kores, P. (1981). Behavioral management of a neurologically impaired pediatric inpatient. *Archives of Physical Medicine and Rehabilitation, 62,* 289–291.

Kusher, H., & Know, A. W. (1973). Application of the utilization technique to the behavior of a brain-injured patient. *Journal of Communication Disorders, 6,* 151–154.

Leftoff, S. (1979). Perceptual retraining in an adult cerebral palsied patient: A case of deficit in cross-modal equivalence. *Journal of Clinical Neuropsychology, 1,* 227–241.

Lewinsohn, P. M., Danaher, B. G., & Kikel, S. (1977). Visual imagery as a mnemonic aid for brain-injured persons. *Journal of Consulting and Clinical Psychology, 45,* 717–727.

Luria, A. R. (1963). *Restoration of function after brain injury.* New York: Macmillan.

Luria, A. R. (1966). *Higher cortical functions in man* (B. Haigh, Trans.) New York: Basic Books.

Lynch, W. J. (1983). *A guide to Atari video computer programs for rehabilitation settings.* Unpublished manuscript.

MacLean, P. D. (1973). *On the evolution of three mentalities.* Toronto: University of Toronto Press.

Mahoney, M. J. (1974). *Cognition and behavior modification.* Cambridge, MA: Ballinger.

McMordie, W. R. (1976). Reduction of perseveration in appropriate speech in a young male with persistent anterograde amnesia. *Journal of Behavior Therapy and Experimental Psychiatry, 7,* 67–69.

Meichenbaum, D. H. (1977). *Cognitive behavior modification.* New York: Plenum Press.

Meier, M. (1974). Some challenges for clinical neuropsychology. In R. M. Reitan and L. A. Davison (Eds.), *Clinical neuropsychology: Current status and applications* (pp. 289–324). Washington, DC: V. A. Winston & Sons.

Montgomery, G., & Cleeland, C. (1980, August). *Behavioral treatment in the management of Parkinsonian symptoms.* Paper presented at the annual convention of the American Psychological Association, Montreal.

Muir, K., & Milan, M. (1982). Parent reinforcement for child achievement: The use of a lottery to maximize parent training effects. *Journal of Applied Behavioral Analysis, 15* (3), 455–460.

Murphy, M. E. (1976). Modified time-out procedures for controlling tantrum behavior in public places. *Behavioral Therapy, 7,* 412–413.

Palmer, K., & Marshall, P. (1980, December). *A behavioral approach to tardive dyskinesia.* Paper presented at the meeting of the Association for Advancement of Behavior Therapy, New York.

Perez, F., Brown, G., Cooke, N., Pickett, A., Rivera, V., & Grabois, M. (1980). Stroke patients: A computerized behavioral approach to cognitive assessment and retraining. *Archives of Physical Medicine and Rehabilitation, 61,* 500 (abstract).

Pirozzolo, F. J., Campanella, D. J., Christensen, K., & Lawson-Kerr, K. (1981). Effects of cerebral dysfunction on neurolinguistic performance in children. *Journal of Consulting and Clinical Psychology, 49,* 791–806.

Reidy, T. (1979). Training appropriate eating behavior in a pediatric rehabilitation setting: Case study. *Archives of Physical Medicine and Rehabilitation, 60* (5), 226–230.

Reitan, R. M., & Davison, L. A. (1974). *Clinical neuropsychology: Current status and application.* Washington, DC: V. H. Winston and Sons.

Ribes-inesta, E., & Guzman, E. (1974). Effectiveness of several suppression procedures in eliminating a high-probability response in a severely brain-damaged child. *Interamerican Journal of Psychology, 8,* 29–39.

Rincover, A., Newsom, D. C., Lovas, I. I., & Koegel, R. L. (1977). Some motivational properties of sensory reinforcement in psychotic children. *Journal of Experimental Child Psychology, 24,* 312–323.

Rinke, C., Williams, J., Floyd, K., & Smith-Scott, W. (1978). The effects of prompting and reinforcement on self-bathing by elderly residents of a nursing home. *Behavior Therapy, 9,* 873–881.

Rothschild, A., Guilford, A. M., & McConnell, J. V. (1975). An investigation of the use of operant conditioning techniques in the treatment of a 64-year-old aphasic. *Journal of Biological Psychiatry, 17,* 33–36.

Rusch, M., Grunert, B., Erdmann, B., & Lynch, M. (1980). Cognitive retraining of brain-injured outpatient rehabilitation. *Archives of Physical Medicine and Rehabilitation, 61,* 472 (abstract).

Salvatore, A. P. (1976). Training an aphasic adult to respond appropriately to spoken commands by feeling pause duration within commands. *Clinical Aphasiology Conference Proceedings,* 172–191.

Salzinger, K., Feldman, R. S., & Portnoy, S. (1970). Training parents of brain-injured children in the use of operant conditioning procedures. *Behavior Therapy, 1,* 4–32.

Sellick, K., & Peck, C. (1981). Behavioral treatment of fear in a child with cerebral palsy using a flooding procedure. *Archives of Physical Medicine and Rehabilitation, 62* (8), 398–400.

Seron, X., Delocke, G., Moulard, G., & Rousselle, M. (1980). A computer-based theory for treatment of aphasic subjects with writing disorders. *Journal of Speech and Hearing Disorders, 45* (1), 45–58.

Shelley, K. B., Potter, R. E., & McDermon, J. R. (1975). Using reinforcement therapy and precision teaching techniques with adult aphasics. *Journal of Behavior Therapy and Experimental Psychiatry, 6,* 301–305.

Skinner, B. F. (1938). *The behavior of organisms.* New York: Appleton-Century-Crofts.

Sperry, R. W. (1961). Cerebral organization and behavior. *Science, 133,* 149.

Stanton, K., Flowers, C., Kuhl, P., Miller, R., & Smith, C. (1979). Language oriented training program to teach compensation of left side neglect. *Archives of Physical Medicine and Rehabilitation, 60,* 540 (abstract).

Sufrin, E. M. (1975). *The effects of a behavior modification treatment program on a neurologically handicapped population.* Unpublished doctoral dissertation, University of Southern California, Los Angeles.

Tucker, D. M., Shearer, S. L., & Murray, J. D. (1977). Hemispheric specialization and cognitive behavior therapy. *Cognitive Therapy and Research, 1,* 263–273.

Turner, S. M., Hersen, M., & Bellack, A. S. (1978). Social skills training to teach prosocial behavior in an organically impaired and retarded patient. *Journal of Behavior Therapy and Experimental Psychiatry, 9,* 253–258.

Walton, R. (1982). Lecithin and physostigmine for post-traumatic memory and cognitive deficits. *Psychosomatics, 23* (4), 435–436.

Waye, M. (1980). Treatment of an adolescent behavior disorder with a diagnosis of Huntington's chorea. *Journal of Behavior Therapy and Experimental Psychiatry, 11,* 239–242.

Webster, J., Jones, S., Blanton, P., Gross, R., Beissel, G., & Wofford, J. (1984). Rehabilitation of patients with visual field cuts. *Behavior Therapy, 15,* 129–143.

Webster, J., & Scott, R. (1983). The effects of self-instructional training on attentional deficits following head injury. *Clinical Neuropsychology, 5* (2), 69–74.

Weinberg, J., Diller, L., Gordon, W., Gerstman, L., Leiberman, N., Lakin, P., Hodges, G., & Ezrachi, O. (1977). Visual scanning training effect on reading-related tasks in acquired right brain damage. *Archives of Physical Medicine and Rehabilitation, 58,* 479–486.

Weinberg, J., Diller, L., Gordon, W., Gerstman, L., Lieberman, A., Lakin, P., Hodges, G., & Ezrachi, O. (1979). Training sensory awareness and spatial organization in people with right brain damage. *Archives of Physical Medicine and Rehabilitation, 60,* 491–496.

Wilson, E. D., & McCulley, C. (1970). The use of patient-teachers in a maximum-security psychiatric unit. *Hospital and Community Psychiatry,* February 37–38.

11

Cognitive Retraining with Brain-Damaged Patients

William Drew Gouvier, Jeffrey S. Webster, and
Paul D. Blanton

INTRODUCTION

Patients are far more impaired immediately after a brain injury than they will be weeks later, and functional recovery typically continues for some time. Nevertheless, many patients never regain sufficient adaptive skills to resume employment or recover enough functional independence to allow their spouses to return to work. The degree of residual functional loss is staggering in both human and monetary terms. In 1977, for example, more than 122,000 Americans were institutionalized because of stroke (NCHS, 1977) and another 793,000 victims were disabled (Mills & Thompson, 1978). Figures based on 1976 data indicate that stroke resulted in over $3 billion worth of direct care costs and from $3 to $5 billion in indirect costs such as loss of income due to the spouses' inability to resume work (Weinfeld, 1981).

Similar statistics exist for head injury. A recent national survey, for example, estimated that 422,000 Americans suffered head injuries in 1974, producing a rehabilitation cost estimate of almost $4 billion annually (Anderson & McLaurin, 1980). Traumatic head injuries are also the major cause of disability in young adults (Anderson & McLaurin, 1980), producing severe occupational limitations during the most financially productive years and at a time when reserve capital has not been established. Furthermore, survivors can expect a normal lifespan (Levin, Benton, & Grossman, 1982), thereby compounding the financial burden.

Given the increasing number of patients surviving cerebral injury, programs are needed to improve the brain-injured patients' and their families' quality of life and potential economic independence. Medical rehabilitation programs for the brain injured have traditionally focused on the early stages of recovery in which motor, arousal, and elementary speech deficits are prominent. Data on the effectiveness of these rehabilitation programs suggest that treatment is most successful if it is initiated soon after the insult (Stern, McDowell, Miller, & Robinson, 1970) and that moderately impaired patients are more likely to improve than very severely injured patients (Harasymiw & Albrecht, 1979; Johnston & Keith, 1983; Lind, 1982). Gains of early treatment do not assure later success in employment and other complex human activities, however (Cope & Hall, 1982). Deficits in memory, perceptual abilities, problem solving, and social appropriateness appear to limit occupational and interpersonal success far more than simple motor and speech deficits (Lewinsohn & Graf, 1973; Lezak, 1978b). These results clearly indicate that rehabilitation specialists must treat the cognitive and emotional sequelae of brain injury in order to rehabilitate these patients successfully.

The focus of this chapter will be on training activities developed to remediate cognitive and interpersonal deficits of the brain-injured patient. Collectively, these techniques will be referred to as cognitive retraining. Cognitive retraining is intended to benefit patients and families by changing the patients' employment status, or at least their functional independence, thereby allowing others greater freedom.

Although we chose to define cognitive retraining by its end point, much is to be gained by systematically studying the process of retraining. Careful observation using quasi-experimental and experimental designs is necessary both to create a retraining technology of scientific merit and to contribute to our understanding of brain–behavior relationships.

All too often, therapists working with the brain impaired have resorted to simple applications of procedures used for similar purposes with other populations instead of developing techniques based on experimental models of brain function, neuropathology, and recovery of function. For example, mnenomic devices developed to facilitate normal memory processes are frequently applied to the very different memory deficits of various groups of amnestic patients. When such techniques work it is gratifying, but when they fail or provide only limited benefit, which is more often the case, the results rarely suggest an alternative approach or directions for subsequent experimentation. This point is best supported by the general lack of programmatic research in cognitive retraining of memory deficits. Ideally, investigators will borrow far more from cognitive psychology, experimental neuropathology, and neuropsychology during the assessment of a given patient's deficits, far more from behavioral biology and neuropsychology during the development of therapeutic approaches, and far more from behavioral psychology in the development of the technology to facilitate acquisition of a skill and measurement of its effectiveness (see Webster, McCaffrey, & Scott, Chapter 9, this volume).

The following sections will present not only a review of recent cognitive retraining studies but also a survey of issues that pertain to case conceptualization and to the development of viable retraining plans for the individual client. When planning retraining the following questions should be considered: (1) How are normal higher cortical functions organized, and how have they been altered by the injury? (2) Which of the patient's deficits are likely to recover spontaneously, and which are likely to need compensatory training? (3) What natural physiological and structural changes may be occurring during the recovery of function process, and how can they be capitalized upon? (4) What techniques have been empirically demonstrated to produce improvement given the type of deficit and the patient's specific neuropathology?

Higher Cortical Functions

Luria's proposed system of higher cortical function has great utility for our subsequent discussion of both the effects of brain injury on functional activity and its subsequent amelioration through retraining. Our bias is partially based on the fact that Luria is one of the few applied neuroscientists to view cognitive retraining as a means of furthering the study of brain–behavioral organization and not just as a noble service to those afflicted. We concur with Luria's (1980) statement:

> By suggesting to the patient that he use various aids in order to solve the problem presented to him, we can discover which components of the process studied are disturbed and which remain intact. A careful examination of the dynamics of the disturbed function in the course of retraining thus provides an approach to the true qualification of the defect and enables primary disturbances of function to be distinguished from various types of disturbances of functional systems. (p. 396)

Luria did not view a complex higher cortical function as a product of a particular tissue or organ, but rather as the coordinated effect of several brain areas. Hence, he rejected a strict localizationist approach, with its reliance on one cortical center for one brain function. He also rejected the equipotentiality approach to higher cortical function, instead positing that particular brain regions were specialized for specific aspects of a functional activity (regions of specificity). Wernicke's area and surrounding cortical zones, for example, were best suited for auditory to verbal transformations; however, execution of a more complex activity, such as the repetition of the spoken word, would involve a far more extensive functional system coordinating lexical and basic motor program units with the accurate reception of auditory verbal signals.

Luria (1963) and other Russian theorists (Mecacci, 1979) also contended that regions of specificity were organized in a hierarchical order and that this order changed with experience and development. Thus, a disturbance in higher cortical activity varies as a function of ontogenetic stage. Damage to auditory analyzers specified for phonemic analysis of words, for example, would have greater functional consequences in children, who are forming a working vocabulary and therefore depend more on "sounding out" new words, than adults, who have an extensive working vocabulary at the time of the injury. Golden and Maruish (1986) present a more comprehensive discussion of the developmental aspects of Luria's theory in Chapter 7 of this volume.

Luria also proposed that normal functional activity was dependent on three global functional units that guide mental functions. The first of these regulates the level of activation and state of vigilance and consists of the reticular formation, limbic system, and mesial basal frontal lobes. This system provides the appropriate background arousal and emotional "drive" to maximally regulate the higher cortical functional systems. Injuries to these areas can cause lethargy and emotional flatness, which in turn impair higher functional systems when in fact these latter areas may not be directly injured at all.

The second unit has as its function the registration, analysis, and storage of information, and depends on the integrity of the occipital, parietal, and temporal lobes. The third functional unit programs and regulates mental activity producing the adjustments necessary for complex, flexible human activity. Luria contended that this unit was regulated by the frontal lobe areas anterior to the precentral gyrus.

Luria's theory highlights the need for a revision of the concept of behavioral syndrome following brain injury. For Luria, a syndrome is an index of a disturbance of a functional system, but does not reveal which of the cerebral structures employed in the functional system has been damaged. For example, the patient may not be attending (functional unit 1), he may not be able to analyze the relevant signals (functional unit 2), or he may not be actively trying to retain the information (functional unit 3). To determine which functional activities may be responsible for the deficits, Luria suggested testing a series of hypotheses that assess the various functional units on tasks, dissociating them from the impaired functional system. This approach is much like that employed by a good car mechanic who traces an engine failure by sequentially testing each segment of the malfunctioning system to see which part(s) may be responsible for the breakdown.

The principal lesson Luria teaches is that the neuropsychologist involved in rehabilitation must be prepared not only to identify areas of weakness but also to generate hypotheses about why a complex psychological task was failed. The generation of these hypotheses require both an understanding of functional organization of the nervous system and knowledge of what the insult has done to the brain's structure and physiological activity.

Neuropathology of Acquired Injuries

Sudden injury to brain tissue through either stroke or head trauma produces both primary and secondary effects. Primary injuries are those that involve the death of neurons, while secondary effects involve a loss of neuronal efficiency resulting from one of several of the brain's general responses to the injury.

Primary Injury

When the brain is suddenly injured, neurons die. The pattern of neuronal death, however, varies with the type of brain injury. Cerebrovascular accidents typically produce neuronal death in circumscribed areas, as do nonmetastatic brain tumors (see Wedding, Chapter 3 of this volume). In contrast, neuronal death from traumatic brain injury can be quite widespread and diffuse, although none of these primary injury sites may be as extensive as those produced by stroke or tumor (Levin et al., 1982). Since neuronal tissue does not spontaneously regenerate, areas of primary injury are lost permanently, making the etiology of the brain injury helpful in predicting which functions will be affected permanently and which are likely to recover (Knopman, Selnes, Niccum, Rubens, Yock, Larson, 1983; Luria, 1963).

The extent of neuronal loss can increase after the injury because of spreading degeneration from dead tissue. *Retrograde degeneration* refers to the eventual death of a cell following injury to its axon. Because axons can be of considerable length, cell death can be very remote from the site of initial injury. *Anterograde degeneration* occurs when the distal portion of a severed axon becomes necrotic, producing synaptic terminal degeneration. There is also evidence for *transneuronal degeneration,* in which the spread of the necrosis destroys cells across the synaptic junction (Woolsey, 1978). It is unclear, however, whether transneuronal degeneration results from an extension of the degenerative process or simply from a loss of afferents to that neuron (see Cowan, 1970, for a review).

Secondary Injuries

General Response to Injury Like other tissue, the brain swells when damaged. This edema may contribute to primary brain injury because of squeezing and herniation of other brain areas, as well as the occlusion of blood supply to remote brain structures (Levin et al., 1982). Brain edema can also raise cerebrospinal fluid (CSF) pressure by obstructing the ventricular system, thereby squeezing periventricular neuronal structures (Powell, 1981).

Brain function is also affected by the relative difference in circulatory pressure between the hemispheres when the vascular system of one side is compromised by injury. Dyken and Nelson (1964) studied arteriograms of patients with congenital hemiplegia and found that part of the blood supply to the injured hemisphere was siphoned off by the intact hemisphere, thus diverting nourishment necessary for the affected hemisphere. These effects typically allow cell survival but do not support optimal functional activity in the affected cells. Other studies using cerebral blood flow and PET scan measures have supported these findings (Kuhl et al., 1980; Overgaard, Mosdale, & Tweed, 1981; Tolonen, 1981). Much of the brain's general response to injury is time-limited, as edema and its side effects tend to subside within a few weeks, except when brain swelling has caused structural damage.

Site-Specific Secondary Effects While the extent of the generalized effects is often determined by the severity of the injury, the secondary deficits described in this section are more related to the specific injury site. Monakow (1969) called these effects *Diaschisis* from the Greek word meaning to "split apart" and described the temporary inactivation of a functional system through the raising of excitability thresholds with the subsequent normalization of these thresholds over time. Decreased afferent input to the system can also produce neuronal depression and perhaps even cell death (Guillery, 1972; Valverde, 1971), and transneuronal degeneration findings suggest that disease processes can "jump the synapse."

Behavioral evidence suggests that lesions to one part of a functional system may also result in neuronal depression across the system and that this depression is reversible. For example, injections of amphetamines, which presumably reduce neuronal inhibition, have reversed apparently permanent behavioral losses following lesions in animals (for a review, see Braun, 1978), as have the anticholinesterase drugs neostigmine and eserine (Luria, 1963; Luria et al., 1969). Luria (1963) emphasized that only functions outside the areas of primary tissue destruction were enhanced with this technique for overcoming what he called "protective inhibition" (Pavlov, 1966).

Specific secondary effects can also be produced if the area of neuronal injury is instrumental in a support function of general brain activity. Included under this heading would be processes such as production of neurotransmitters, the regulation of arousal, and/or support of other complex activities like sleep (Guilleminault, Faull, Miles, & Van der Hoed, 1983; Vecht, Woerkom, Tellhen, & Minderhoud, 1975, 1976). Woerkom, Minderhoud, Gottschal, and Nicolai (1982) found that the injection of L-dopa and/or physostigmine (which enhances cholinergic neurotransmission) produced clinical improvement in 64% of their chronic comatose patients. These improvements were not dramatic; nevertheless, the authors believed that the drugs may have facilitated recovery from coma. Subjects who failed to improve with the drugs showed clinical signs that brain stem mechanisms were permanently damaged.

Another secondary effect of a brain injury may be the loss of inhibitory control on behaviors that compete with the primary behavior. For example, injury to frontal areas may produce motor perseveration, which interferes with writing, drawing, and so forth (Luria, 1980). Similarly, injury to the speech zones can "release" production of paraphasic language which competes with normal word selection (Kolb & Whishaw, 1980).

Nonbrain Injuries and Their Influences on the Clinical Picture

Other factors can also play an indirect role in the manifestation of behavioral deficits following brain injury. In the case of traumatic injury, the brain is not necessarily the only injured body part. Spinal and muscular skeletal injury may produce considerable pain which undoubtedly distracts and fatigues the patient, thereby exacerbating his or her "real" neuropsychological problems. Pituitary injury following closed head injury can also disrupt memory and higher cortical function and may produce systemic complications such as diabetes (Levin et al., 1982). Stroke can also produce central pain as well as pain secondary to muscular spasticity. In addition, it should be remembered that stroke typically represents the presence of widespread cardiovascular disease, which directly affects other organ systems, and thus leads to further impairments in brain functioning.

Psychosocial Background and Its Impact on the Clinical Picture

Brain injury is imposed upon the patient's premorbid psychological and physical state. Factors that have been identified as influencing recovery of function include cerebral dominance, premorbid intellectual abilities, age, social support, motivation to improve, and premorbid mental stability (Golden, 1978; Heilman & Valenstein, 1979).

All things being equal, greater recovery is expected in patients with higher economic and intellectual accomplishment prior to the injury (Keenan & Brassell, 1974). Age and handedness can also influence outcome of brain injury. Comparable injuries can be expected to affect the aged more than young adults (Golden, 1978). With reference to handedness, sinistrals tend to show greater recovery from unilateral injuries than do dextrals. Injury to the brain rarely makes the individual more adaptive; thus, poor premorbid emotional stability is a good predictor of postinjury adjustment problems (Golden, 1978). Further complicating the picture is the fact that lesions to various brain sites can produce significant emotional changes even in patients who were premorbidly normal (see Heilman & Satz, 1983, for a review). Brain injury can also influence the adjustment of the family unit (Lezak, 1978b). Recent evidence suggests that the family's ability to cope with the patient's changes may be the key factor in how emotionally disabling the patient's physical and intellectual deficits will be (McKinlay & Brooks, 1984).

The preceding limited review indicates that many factors other than neuropsychological test performance should be considered in generating hypotheses about impairment of various functional systems. First is the contribution of primary neuronal destruction, based on the nature of the insult and neurodiagnostic test results. Second are the generalized secondary effects, which are likely to be time limited. Third are the effects of primary cell destruction on supportive brain activity, such as production of neurotransmitters, the generating of tonic and phasic arousal, and facilitation of sleep, all of which are essential to optimal higher cortical function and information processing. Fourth, a functional system can also be indirectly impaired as other systems are no longer inhibited and actively compete with its activity. In addition, pain, cardiovascular problems, and other factors affecting both the patient's psychological and physiological health can influence his or her presenting picture. Finally, background factors such as IQ, age, and social support must be considered in accounting for the level of deficits presented by the patient.

Recovery of Function

Three mechanisms of recovery of function have been suggested: spontaneous recovery, reorganization of functional systems, and compensation for a functional deficit. Much of this literature is based on animal models of brain function; however, researchers have attempted to draw parallels between these models and applied problems in human neuropathology.

Spontaneous Recovery

Most of the research on spontaneous recovery involves training an animal to perform a specific response, lesioning the animal's brain so that the response no longer appears in its repertoire, and then observing to see if the response recovers. While recovery of a lost function (e.g., response) is impressive, it is no guarantee that the animal is using the same functional system to accomplish the task as it did prior to the injury. Therefore, it is important to measure how recovered tasks are performed (Gentile, Green, Nieburgs, Schmelzer, & Stein, 1978; Laurence & Stein, 1978; LeVere & LeVere, 1982). What is taken to be spontaneous recovery may often be the development of different functional systems. Given these results, the degree of true spontaneous recovery may be far less than predicted by the early animal work on recovery of function.

Considerable recovery can occur if the monitored behavior is regulated by brain tissue that is only temporarily compromised. Severe aphasic deficits often resolve over time when they are secondary to cerebral edema (Luria et al., 1969). Also, visual hemi-inattention (neglect and extinction) becomes much less severe over time when the right frontal and/or the posterior parietal lobe sustains no permanent damage (Hier, Mondlock, & Caplan, 1983). Such behavioral recovery usually parallels pathophysiological improvement.

LeVere and LeVere (1982) argue that lesioned subjects are "optimizers," attempting to compensate for a loss in efficiency of a given functional system by using a compensatory functional system. These authors contend that compensation occurs even if the injured functional system is relatively intact and recovers to near premorbid levels of efficiency in accomplishing the task once the initial stages of brain recovery are completed. Behavioral recovery finally occurs when the patient encounters situations in which the compensatory system is inadequate and he must resort to trying the old system again. Their theory would predict that preventing the development of compensatory strategies would reduce the degree of disability and increase the speed of the recovery process. The theory receives considerable support from experimental work with both rodents and monkeys (see LeVere, 1975, 1980, for reviews). For example, after unilateral spinal deafferentation, monkeys rarely use their ipsilateral limbs in any useful fashion unless the unaffected impaired limb is physically restrained (see reviews by Guth, 1974; LeVere, 1980). Lashley (1935) reported similar results in monkeys with lesions at the neocortical level. His subjects would only use their contralateral limbs when the other limb was physically restrained or made more hemiparetic by a subsequent cortical lesion. Neither LeVere nor Luria proposes that the resultant functional system is an exact replica of its preinjury representation; rather, they contend that part of the system is replaced, perhaps less efficiently, by the same function under control of spared tissue surrounding the lesion (LeVere, 1975) or another functional unit (Luria, 1980).

Reorganization

Under reorganization we will consider both structural and physiological means of maximizing the use of the remaining functional system. Reorganization differs from simple compensation in that it implies the use of the intact portions of the functional system in the subsequent postinjury, recovered behavior. Compensation, in contrast, means that a wholly alternative system is used to accomplish the task.

Structural Changes Two forms of neuronal sprouting have been described: axon regeneration and collateral sprouting. In axonal regeneration the destroyed axons regrow and connect to a viable synaptic terminal. This form of regeneration takes place quite efficiently in the mammalian peripheral nervous system but not within the CNS (Burgess & Horch, 1973). Although some growth is observed, rarely do the new axons reach their original target or make functional connections (Cotman & McGaugh, 1980). Interestingly, mammals are unique among the vertebrates in their inability to show spontaneous axonal regeneration (Cotman & McGaugh, 1980).

Collateral sprouting differs from axonal regeneration in that undamaged fibers grow and form new connections in place of those lost. Sprouting can originate from both adjacent and contralateral fibers (Cotman, Gentry, & Steward, 1977; Steward, Cotman, & Lynch, 1976; Zimmer & Hjorth-Simonsen, 1975). Interestingly, these newly sprouted fibers can form electrophysiologically functional synapses (Wilson, Levey, & Steward, 1979), and the new growth causes only quantitative increases and rearrangements of previously existing connections. Few qualitatively new pathways are formed (Cotman & Nieto-Sampedro, 1982).

Artificial techniques have been developed to facilitate mammalian axonal regeneration and collateral sprouting. For example, severed axons will grow into and make synaptic connections with extraneural tissue placed near the injury (Bjorklund & Stenevi, 1971). Recently it has been shown that fetal tissue can be transplanted into the brains of injured animals, resulting in viable and functional synaptic connections (Cotman & Nieto-Sampedro, 1983; Lewis & Cotman, 1983). Transplanting neural tissue into the brain has the advantage over other types of transplantation in that immune cells cannot cross the blood–brain barrier; hence, such tissue is unlikely to be rejected by the host general immune system (Kolata, 1983), but is still somewhat suscept-ible to rejection via specific secondary systems (Cotman & McGaugh, 1980; Manthorpe et al., 1983; Sabel, Slavin, & Stein, 1984).

In a recent review, Kolata (1983) describes several exciting preliminary studies. Tissue from the adrenal glands (which produce dopamine) was trans-planted to cerebral tissue of two patients suffering severe Parkinson's disease. Both patients reportedly needed less exogenous dopamine (L-dopa) following surgery. Another promising finding was that rats receiving brain implants showed not only neuronal recovery but some functional recovery of memory skills as well. It should be remembered that this neural sprouting research has been accomplished by placing exogenous tissue or neurotrophic substances in the brain. Without these steps, axonal regeneration and other forms of sprout-ing in the CNS are minimal.

Physiological Processes Wall and his colleagues (Wall, 1980; Wall & Egger, 1971) have demonstrated that when CNS areas are disconnected from the peripheral sites they innervate, they show a spreading of electrophysiological excitability. Wall suggested such changes involve the release, or in his words, the "unmasking," of relatively inefficient synapses that are anatomically es-tablished within the functional system but that have been under inhibitory control prior to the brain injury. Hughlings Jackson (1932) and Luria (1963) have also suggested unmasking as a potential explanation for recovery of function. Unmasking may be undermined by surviving neuronal tissue that is still producing inhibitory control over redundant areas but is not functioning well enough to regulate the functional system. For example, the contralateral motor function of infantile epileptics receiving hemispherectomy in adulthood improves considerably, as do their cognitive and memory functions (Smith, 1974). Glees (1980) has presented rather convincing evidence that release of ipsilateral hemispheric control accounted for his patients' improvement in motor function. Posthemispherectomy motor improvements involved all but the return of fine motor activity, a finding that matches the known ipsilateral input to the upper extremity. In further support of the release of a redundant mechanism, Krynauw (reported by Smith, 1974) noted that EEG activity, in the hemisphere ipsilateral to his infantile hemiplegics' affected limbs, fell within normal limits following removal of the pathological hemisphere. It should be remembered that all patients studied in these experiments have had aberrant systems since early childhood. Given that functional localization is an ontogenetic as well as phylogenetic phenomenon, the less impaired hemisphere of infantile epileptics and hemiplegics probably regulated many more functions than that of the unimpaired individual. Normal adults suffering abrupt injury of a comparable magnitude may not fare as well. In fact, adult tumor victims receiving hemispheric resection have shown devastating neuropsychological deficits following surgery (Smith, 1974).

The next physiological mechanism proposed to support recovery of function is denervation supersensitivity. When cortical zones receive decreased input, the postsynaptic terminals increase their sensitivity to the relevant neurotransmitter (Laurence & Stein, 1978). If such a process involves an increase in the number of postsynaptic receptors, as is suggested by chemotherapy treatment of patients with affective disorders, then such changes may make it easier for sprouting axons to reconnect with the original sites (Powell, 1981). However, denervation supersensitivity has limits in that it can facilitate recovery only when the synapse is left partially intact. Most severe acquired brain injuries produce fairly massive primary insults in which denervation supersensitivity may only play a minor role in the recovery process. Nevertheless, it may be an important factor in the recovery following mild cerebral injury.

Despite this promise centering upon the potential for structural and physiological recovery of function, limits remain. When massive injury occurs to structures essential to the functional activity, most researchers and clinicians would agree that natural recovery mechanisms are inadequate. In such instances, functional recovery may be facilitated by compensatory training—that is, teaching the subject a different, yet effective, way of performing the functional activity. The rest of this chapter will review the considerable literature that involves teaching brain-impaired humans to use alternative strategies to perform functional tasks.

COMPENSATORY TRAINING

Interventions Targeting Attention and Vigilance

Many cognitive deficits result from reduced arousal and attentional abilities that provide the background tone upon which higher cortical functions are based. Hence, reduced ability to behave effectively may represent impairment in levels of arousal and alertness, rather than impaired higher cortical functions per se. Even in the presence of deficits in higher cortical functions, impairments in arousal are often present. Consequently, many comprehensive programs for the brain injured first assess and treat these basic arousal and attentional deficits before addressing specific deficits in perceptual integration, memory, planning, and so forth. Miller (1980) has demonstrated that brain-damaged patients can learn to improve their simple reaction time to a level comparable with nonimpaired individuals, given sufficient training. Since this ability to attend and react appears so essential for other learning to take place, it is not surprising that training in simple reaction time is the first step in the Orientation Remedial Module of New York University (NYU 1978, 1979, 1980a, 1981, 1982, 1983), the Cognitive Rehabilitation programs of Gianutsos and Klitzner (1981), The Foundations Skills programs (Bracy, 1982), and the computerized training programs used at Braintree Hospital (Mikula, 1983). Once simple reaction time tasks are mastered, patients are prepared to advance to more complex tasks.

Reaction time training is not the only technique for improving attention and vigilance. Gross, Ben-Nahum, and Munk (1982) describe a procedure that can be used in the training of attention and memory span. This procedure involves presenting a linear array of numbers, letters, or symbols. The therapist masks one or two consecutive symbols and moves the mask along the array, instructing the patient to name the next symbol to be uncovered. This task places demands on attention, concentration, and memory; it can be made more stringent by masking successively longer strings of symbols or by moving the mask along the array more quickly. Such a training procedure could be readily adapted for automatic administration, feedback, and response recording on a minicomputer.

Orientation Remedial Module

A number of computer programs have been designed to ameliorate basic deficits in attention and concentration. One of the earliest of these program packages was the Orientation Remedial Module (ORM) (NYU, 1978, 1979, 1980a), originally developed using electromechanical programming equipment and only recently (NYU, 1983) transformed into a completely computerized system.

The ORM consists of five tasks to be mastered successfully as a prerequisite to participating in higher-level cognitive retraining or resocialization activities (Ben Yishay & Diller, 1981). All tasks are presented with a testing probe specific to the task, followed by training practice on that task. These tasks range in their complexity and response demands so that each successive task builds upon the skills acquired in the preceding one. Thus, on the first task the patient is instructed to respond by pressing a key whenever a small white signal light is presented. Latency feedback is given to the patient in an analog visual format. When patients' progress plateaus or reaches the ceiling level, they advance to training on the "Zeroing Accuracy Conditioner" (ZAC), which forces patients to time their responses *in relation* to changing environment cues.

The ZAC presents a patient with a clocklike face with a single hand that can rotate at different speeds as controlled by the trainer. The patient is required to stop the hand at a particular marking (e.g., 12:00 or 9:00) on the face within a given number of rotations. At low speeds of rotation, the hand stops almost simultaneously with the patient's response, but at higher speeds it coasts to a stop. Training advances to the next task when a criterion level of performance is reached.

The third task involves training patients to be actively vigilant in scanning their environment and seeking out signals. This is done with a program called the "Visual Discrimination Conditioner," which requires the patient to monitor display panels simultaneously. Training can involve gradually increasing the distance between the display panels, gradually fading the number of preparatory cues provided, or gradually reducing the duration of stimulus "on-time" and interstimulus intervals. Patients are provided with performance feedback, praise, and encouragement to become even more vigilant, and training is discontinued when performance reaches criterion levels.

The next task trains patients to respond on the basis of self-generated internal cues rather than externally provided cues. This "Time Estimation" task proceeds through a series of steps involving (1) synchronized finger tapping or upper body rocking with the ticking second hand of a stopwatch, (2) synchronized tapping or body rocking with an imagined stopwatch hand, (3) synchronized head nodding with the imagined stopwatch, and (4) "keeping time" with the imagined stopwatch hand without any body movements.

The last task in the ORM involves the integration of previously trained skills and trains the patient to synchronize bodily responses with complex environmental signals. Practice on the "Rhythm Synchrony Conditioner" requires that the patient tap on a response key in synchrony with a prerecorded series of Morse-code-like tones that are presented both auditorily and visually. Success on this task requires that patients attend to the rhythm sequence, internalize it, anticipate the next "beat" in the sequence, and precisely time and synchronize their responses. Patients have to start their responses at the same time as the target tones and maintain them for the duration of the target tones.

Foundation Skills Programs

A similar group of computer programs for training improved attention, reaction, and discrimination skills among brain-injured patients is the Foundation Skills programs (Bracy, 1982). These are ten different programs designed to begin training using basic visual and auditory reaction time tasks. Training proceeds to multimodality reaction tasks which require the patient to alternate between initiating and inhibiting responses signaled by visual and auditory stimuli. Once initial Foundation Skills programs are mastered, more complex computerized activities are gradually introduced.

For example, a training session might involve practice on a sequence of four tasks: (1) visual reaction time, (2) auditory reaction time with visual prestimulus, (3) auditory reaction time, and (4) visual reaction time with auditory prestimulus. This sequence challenges the patient to be flexible in shifting from task to task, to learn to initiate responses to the (regularly changing) appropriate stimulus, and to inhibit responses to inappropriate prestimuli. With mastery of each of the tasks in this alternating series, patients are thought to be ready to advance to even more complex and demanding tasks (Bracy, 1983).

Computer Programs for Cognitive Rehabilitation

A third group of computer programs for cognitive rehabilitation was developed by Gianutsos & Klitzner (1981). These include three perceptual programs and four memory programs, all of which involve a substantial component of attention and concentration. Among the three perceptual programs, the Speeded Reading of Word Lists (SRWL) can be used to identify and treat problems in four areas of visual information processing, namely, anchoring at the left margin, horizontal scanning, word identification, and monitoring the periphery (Gianutsos, Glosser, Elbaum, & Vroman, 1983). A second perceptual program is the Reaction Time Measure of Visual Fields (REACT). In this program stimuli appear unpredictably to left or right of center in the upper, middle, and lower regions of the visual fields.

The Searching for Shapes (SEARCH) program is designed to identify hemifield differences in attention and responsiveness. It involves quickly matching an abstract shape to one hidden in an 8 × 8 array of comparable shapes. It is useful for patients who need to overcome unilateral inattention, as well as for those who need to improve their careful visual searching habits and avoid making hasty judgments.

Although not computerized, the Search-a-Word task is also included in the Gianutsos programs. This task is analogous to the SEARCH program in that the patient is required to find a three-letter target word from a 13 × 13 array of letters. This allows further measurement of left- and right-sided search times, and can be helpful in differentiating inattention from sensory-based imperceptions.

The first of the memory programs is a Free Recall task that presents six lists of 12 words for immediate recall, and six lists of 12 words that have interpolated reading between list presentation and recall. Scoring guides are presented that permit the differentiation of short-term from long-term recall.

The Memory Span program is presented as an exercise in short-term storage; for persons with problems in transient memory, work on this task can be a prerequisite to work on long-term retention. The program presents 30 lists of unpredictable length in six rounds of five lists each. In the first round, patients are instructed to remember the last two words in the list, and in each successive round they are asked to remember one additional word at the end of the list.

The Triplet Recall task is patterned after the Peterson and Peterson (1959) interference memory task, which requires that patients remember three-word triplets under conditions of no delay or with interpolated reading intervals of three, six, or nine words in length. Within the limits imposed by ceiling performance, this task allows the differentiation of short-term from long-term recall.

The Sequence Recall program presents 21 trials in which lists of words, nonsense words, pictures, or shapes are presented. Patients are asked to identify the listed stimuli in order from a "menu" containing the listings and distracting stimuli. Parameters of list length, stimulus type, and error discontinuation can be adjusted to offer a broad range of difficulty, and the programs may be useful for those who are aphasic or nonfluent in English.

Gianutsos and associates have recently offered a second set of programs designed to offer a greater variety of training tasks and intended to be used after more basic deficits in memory and perception have been addressed. We had not had the opportunity to review these at the time of writing.

Other Programs

Specialized programs for cognitive rehabilitation are not essential for patients to be able to benefit from the practice in memory, visual perception, and eye–hand coordination that computer-controlled activities offer. Lynch (1981) has compiled a guide listing a variety of Atari video games suitable for cognitive rehabilitation, with a description of the games, equipment required, and suggestions of the kinds of problems that could be treated with each. Further description of the use of electronic games in cognitive rehabilitation, along with representative case examples, can be found in Lynch (1982, 1983).

Bridging the gap between deficits of attention and memory impairment, Webster and Scott (1983) describe the treatment of a 24-year-old closed head injury patient who presented for treatment with a complaint of memory deficits. Careful analysis of the neuropsychological assessment data suggested that this patient's memory weakness arose secondary to difficulties in sustaining prolonged attention and concentration. Targeting these attention and concentration deficits, Webster and Scott adapted Meichenbaum's (1973) self-instructional training strategy to teach their patient to monitor covertly exactly what he was listening to by subvocally repeating whatever he heard. Impressive improvements in memory functioning were observed, and these gains were maintained at follow-up. Rusch, Grunert, Erdmann, and Lynch (1980) describe other applications of self-instructional training in cognitive rehabilitation.

Memory

External Memory Aids

Impairment of memory functions is a common outcome of head injury (Levin, Benton, & Grossman, 1982), and recovery of memory functions often lags behind recovery of other abilities (Lezak, 1979). Some researchers have investigated the efficacy of using external memory aids to enhance memory.

These strategies have ranged from the use of notebooks and schedules to home computers (Parente & Anderson, 1983). Although some success with external aids has been reported, Newcombe (1982) has identified one disadvantage to the use of external memory aids: the subject frequently needs to be trained to use these aids; if the subject does not use the device effectively, little hope exists that memory deficits may be remediated.

Gouvier (1982) has suggested that patients wear a wristwatch equipped with an hourly chime so as to remind themselves to check their schedule books. This memory intervention works only when the client uses the watch as a signal to check the schedule; if this is not done, the intervention will be of little benefit. However, Fowler, Hart, and Sheehan (1972) have reported that a similar intervention, coupled with verbal praise for compliance, was effective in enhancing the promptness and employability of a 28-year-old closed head injury patient.

At present, little data have been reported on the efficacy of home computers in improving memory following cerebral insult. Parente and Anderson (1983) report two single-subject design cases (AB design) in which home-based computer training in organizing material into categories, chunking of number strings, and mnemonic mediation of to-be-learned material was effective in improving Wechsler Memory Scale scores and improving recall for passages, attention and concentration, and cued learning. Likewise, Gianutsos (1981) reports that her Memory Span and Triplet Recall computer tasks (Gianutsos & Klitzner, 1981) were helpful in remediating short- and long-term memory deficits in a postencephalitic amnesic.

Memory: Visual Imagery

The success of visual imagery in enhancing the recall of information in normal subjects (Crovitz & Harvey, 1979) has led investigators to consider its effects in improving the memory abilities of brain-injured persons. Early clinical reports were encouraging in that persons with acquired verbal memory deficits were able to improve verbal memory greatly through the use of a peg-word vivid visual imagery mnemonic (Patten, 1972). Peg-word systems involve learning a list of peg-words and associated visual images, such as one-bun, two-shoe, three-tree, and so forth. Once this list is memorized, new information to be remembered (e.g., items from a shopping list) is paired with each peg-word to form an interactive visual image. To recall items, the user of this mnemonic device proceeds down the list, attempting to recreate the visual image of each item associated with the memorized peg-words. Thus, the early implications were that brain-injured subjects could profit from the same memory-enhancing strategies as normals. Cermak (1975), in a study of the effects of visual imagery cuing upon recall in Korsakoff patients, hypothesized that the memory-enhancing effects of imagery were due to the provision of cues at both encoding and retrieval levels. Another method, such as verbal mediation, was not as effective for this group of patients because such a strategy provided cuing only at either the time of encoding or retrieval, but not both.

The benefits of imagery training have, however, been questioned. Lewinsohn, Danaher, and Kikel (1977) studied the effects of imagery formation upon the recall of paired-associates and face–name associations. It was found that although imagery-trained subjects (both normals and brain damaged) showed increased acquisition and 30-min recall of material, these gains were not maintained at 1-week follow-up. Obviously, some provision for maintenance of the effect is needed before these laboratory interventions can be generalized to real-life applications.

Glasgow, Zeiss, Barrera, and Lewinsohn (1977) presented a case in which they attempted to use visual imagery to improve a 23-year-old male student's poor learning of peoples' names. Preliminary studies in the laboratory with the patient indicated that visual-imagery-mediated retention of five name–face pairs was greater than memory without imagery. The intervention strategy was composed of four steps: (1) repeat the to-be-remembered name several times, (2) transform name into a high-imagery noun, (3) select the most outstanding feature of the person's face, and (4) form an image linking the modified name with the outstanding feature. Unfortunately, however, this strategy did not enhance face–name learning in real-life settings because the subject was given to forming complex images that required lengthy visualization durations. A simplified imagery technique (having the subject write down names forgotten and then visualize them three times per day) was sufficient to reduce daily name forgetting to one-fourth the pretreatment amount.

Gasparrini and Satz (1979) compared rote verbal memorization and visual imagery strategies in paired-associates learning for 30 left-brain-damaged patients, all of whom had sustained cerebrovascular accidents. As expected, visual imagery fostered better recall. In a second study using this same population, these two groups were combined, and the effects of visual imagery were then compared against verbal mnemonic encoding in an AB-BA order. The results of this second study suggested that visual mnemonics were superior to semantic elaboration mnemonics, but this conclusion remains questionable, since half of the subjects had already had extensive training in forming visual mediators for paired-associates, while none of the subjects had prior practice in forming verbal mediators for paired-associate learning.

Although for normals bizarre interacting images are not required in enhancing recall (Hauck, Walsh, & Kroll, 1976), some evidence exists that brain-damaged subjects are unable to generate, or have great difficulty in generating, their own imagery mnemonics and actually recall experimenter-provided visual images much better (Crovitz, Harvey, & Horn, 1979). These authors indicate that the source of difficulty may lie in the fact that brain-injured subjects are restricted to concrete modes of thought and have problems in generating images due to impaired ability in processing information foreign to their immediate situation. Unfortunately, little information exists on how to overcome patient deficits in acquiring imagery mnemonics to help in reducing memory deficits. One possible strategy may be to elaborate visual images from pictures of to-be-remembered stimuli. As Bevan and Feuer (1977) have indicated, showing pictures of the objects to be visualized presents this information in a more concrete manner than does creating a visual image from verbal descriptors. Thus, combining verbal guidance in forming visual images with concrete pictures may bypass the problems with concreteness of thought in the brain-damaged patient and may be of help in facilitating encoding and recall. This strategy might also be used with narrative stories designed to facilitate encoding and recall, such as those described by Bower and Clark (1969) and Crovitz (1979).

Jones (1974) has indicated that visual imagery is an efficacious treatment strategy only for certain groups of brain-damaged individuals, and only under certain conditions. She studied paired-associate learning in groups of patients who had experienced surgical resection of right or left temporal lobe tissue and compared these groups with patients with bilateral temporal lobe damage and normal controls. Prior to training, right temporal lobe patients performed at a level comparable to controls, while left temporal lobe patients and the bilateral patients were impaired. Training in visually associating the word pairs led to improvement of the deficiencies of the left temporal group for concrete (easily imaged) words, but not abstract words. The bilateral group failed to show significant improvement on either sort of word, suggesting limitations in their ability to use either verbal or visual mnemonics. Similar problems and limitations in memory training have been reported by Wilson (1982).

The use of visual imagery as a memory-enhancing strategy for brain-injured individuals is far from unequivocal. As Glasgow and colleagues (1977) have indicated, although these procedures have produced some positive results, more controlled research is needed to help identify which procedures are most appropriate for given disorders.

Memory: Semantic Elaboration

Another memory-enhancing strategy that has been used with brain-injured individuals is semantic elaboration. Under these conditions the subject is required to form some sort of meaningful relationship (typically verbal) between to-be-remembered stimuli. As research has indicated (e.g., Bellezza & Reddy, 1978; Newcombe, 1982), subject-generated memory-enhancing cues are more likely to improve recall than are imposed strategies if the self-generated strategies have a high likelihood of being recalled. Therefore, semantic elaboration strategies may prove useful in those situations in which the subject is unable to generate highly memorable images. Such elaborative encoding has been identified as facilitating recall for nonverbal stimuli (Siegel & Siegel, 1976). For example, a semantic elaboration strategy for paired-associate learning might involve forming a sentence out of the word pairs (e.g., *crush* the *dark* stone).

An early study that compared the effects of visual imagery and semantic elaboration strategies in 31 right temporal lobectomy patients (Jones-Gotman & Milner, 1978) revealed that the use of semantic elaboration strategies was beneficial for the right temporal lobe patients in improving recall. This study is important in that it emphasizes the use of a strategy best suited for a particular type of brain damage. Similarly, mnemonic strategies should match the patient's preference. For example, Webster, Hammer, and Moss (1980) attempted to train a postencephaletic patient to recall peoples' names by using verbal associations such as "Webster, like the dictionary." This patient reported that he preferred using personally meaningful associations such as (hypothetically) "Webster, like Ben Webster, my old friend from Louisiana." For this patient, his use of personally meaningful associations led to more consistent improvements in recall than the use of the associations that were provided to him. Other reports of the usefulness of elaboration mnemonics can be found in Bower and Clark (1969), Gianutsos (1980, 1981), Gianutsos and Gianutsos (1979), and Malec and Questad (1983).

Glasgow and colleagues (1977) used Robinson's (1970) PQRST technique to improve a brain-injured woman's recall of written information. The PQRST strategy is a structured technique for reading and studying information to be remembered. Their patient was trained to (1) *Preview* the information to be read, (2) form *Questions* about that information, (3) carefully *Read* the information with a goal of answering the questions, (4) *State* the answers to the questions, and (5) *Test* for retention by asking and answering the questions again after the material had been read and the preceding steps completed. Glasgow and colleagues (1977) also suggest adding a final step, (6) *Verify* the answers by checking back into the material that has been read. This strategy was then applied to the acquisition of real-world information (e.g., newspaper stories). When the PQRST strategy was applied to this information, the subject rated her memory as improved (negative self-statements decreased), and retention of newly learned information was improved at ½-week and 1-week intervals relative to rote rehearsal.

Memory: Providing Encoding and Retrieval Cues

Another strategy that has been reported as successful in improving recall in brain-injured patients has been the providing of encoding and retrieval cues for to-be-remembered information (Crovitz, 1979; Jaffe & Katz, 1975). This strategy has typically been used in those cases in which the subject has a disorder such as Korsakoff's psychosis, which greatly interferes with the ability to both encode and retrieve information, in which previously mentioned strategies (i.e., imagery and semantic elaboration) would not improve recall.

Jaffe and Katz (1975) report the memory-enhancing effects of providing encoding and retrieval cues for a 52-year-old Korsakoff's patient using a multiple baseline design. Although the patient was able to recognize about 14 out of 25 words correctly throughout training recall, recall performance improved only under conditions in which storage and retrieval cues were provided. Seeing that such a strategy was effective, the authors taught their patient two full names, as well as his locker location and its contents, with cuing and fading. This comprised the first learning he had shown in his five years of hospitalization. This memory training was effective in facilitating recall of information necessary to more independent functioning.

Crovitz (1979) has suggested the use of mnemonic encoding principles (Higbee, 1977) in the "Airplane List" to improve recall for lists of unrelated words. This strategy involves presenting stimuli in a fashion that encourages deep and elaborate encoding by forming a connected story of bizarre visual images, with graded retrieval cuing presented to maximize information retrieval. Thus, to remember a list beginning with the words, *airplane, giraffe, bologna,* and *moon,* the patient has the following passage read to him:

> The first word is *airplane.* Remember that however you like. The next word is *giraffe,* because the airplane is filled with giraffes sitting in the seats. The next word is *bologna,* because each giraffe is holding a bologna and taking bites out of it. The next word is *moon,* because the moon is really made out of bologna, not green cheese. . . . (p. 131)

The therapist might use the following cues to facilitate recall: What was on the airplane? It is animals. . . . It starts with the letter "G". . . . They have long necks. . . . What is the next word? It is something they are eating. . . . It starts with the letter "B." Is it bacon or bologna? . . . Even in the presence of severe memory impairment, such techniques to foster deep encoding of new information can get information stored in memory and can also provide additional cues for prompting recall of that information.

Language: Aphasia

The treatment of aphasic disorders has chiefly fallen within the realm of speech pathology and aphasiology. This literature is extensive and beyond the scope of this chapter (see Sullivan & Kommers, 1977, for a review), which will be limited to supplemental techniques used as an adjunct to traditional speech therapy. While some research has shown that treated aphasics make better recovery than do nontreated aphasics (Basso, Capitani, & Vignolo, 1979; Sarno & Levita, 1979), cognitive rehabilitation intervention strategies can complement the effects of traditional speech therapy.

Gardner, Zurif, Berry, and Baker (1976) demonstrated that eight globally aphasic patients were able to master a visual communications system even though they did not improve in their verbal communicative abilities. This finding supports the idea that intersystemic reorganization is possible. However, the impact of this intervention upon quality of life is likely to be quite limited, since these patients could not communicate with others outside the laboratory who did not know the system. A similar project that taught a nonverbal communication system to patients and their families has been reported by Glass, Gazzaniga, and Premack (1973). This is an important step in bridging the gap between laboratory-based interventions and those with the potential for real impact on patients' quality of life. Functional reorganization of speech through the inclusion of right hemispheric abilities also has been demonstrated. Melodic Intonation Therapy (MIT) has been shown to facilitate verbal communication in nine aphasic patients who had reached a plateau with traditional speech therapy (Sparks, Helm, & Albert, 1974). All subjects participated in a two-leveled training program that stressed the melodic and rhythmic aspects of speech under differing conditions of therapist assistance.

Diller and colleagues (NYU, 1974) have found that training spouses of aphasics in behavior modification techniques produced modest, yet significant, increases in aphasics' functional speech. The training for the spouses consisted of two different procedures: (1) sessions with spouses alone, in which the spouse was given a brief overview of behavior modification techniques and their use to change speech patterns, and (2) sessions with the couple in which feedback was given to the spouse as to how she or he responded to the aphasic partner. The authors noted that although this successful instruction strategy could be taught within a 3- to 6-week period by trained speech therapists, difficulties in treatment implementation arose in cases of poor patient–spouse relationships. Thus, attention needs to be directed at interpersonal factors that may impede program success. Thomsen (1981) suggests that recovery can be facilitated by early intervention, continuity of care, and consideration of familial and interpersonal factors.

Language: Alexic and Reading Disorders

Another problem that follows brain injury is disruption of an individual's reading abilities. A variety of these disorders exists (see Heilman & Valenstein, 1979, for a review), yet because of their association with more devastating disruptions in communicative abilities, reading disorders are not commonly seen in isolation. Although the research in this particular area is sparse, the findings are encouraging and further remediation studies are warranted.

Carmon, Gordon, Bental, and Harness (1977) reported a case of alexia with agraphia secondary to progressive left cerebral atrophy. This patient, who was a librarian before being forced to leave her job, retained good pattern recognition, visual perception, and memory skills. In each training session she was trained to associate from 10 to 20 written words with their spoken (auditory) representation by rote paired-associate learning. Each word presented to her in training was printed in different typefaces on individual cards, in order to maximize the likelihood that her word recognition skills would generalize. In this manner the patient had acquired a reading vocabulary of approximately 800 words at the time of publication. The subject was, however, unable to generalize her reading ability to plurals and variants of learned words, thus suggesting that a more primitive functional system, which did not involve complex grammatical/lexical functions, was utilized in training.

Contrasted with this is the methodology used in a case of alexia without agraphia (Moyer, 1979). In this case the remediation was directed at increasing the patient's reading speed, not at increasing reading vocabulary. In this study the subject was given a weekly 600-word passage to read and reread as quickly as possible for approximately ½ hour per day. The patient's reading speed was measured each week, feedback about performance changes was provided, and over the 12-week training period he showed a significant (50%) increase in reading rate. The patient reported being satisfied with his improved abilities. In this case the remediation strategy may have been effective because the subject's component skills for processing written language were intact, and the treatment focused on "painfully slow word-by-word reading," thus stressing the importance of thorough evaluation of the disability and interventions that targeted the problem itself rather than presumed underlying skills.

A vertical reading strategy used by Gheorghita (1981) was also effective in significantly improving the reading abilities of 60 aphasics of various typologies. She suggests that by not using an overlearned scanning style in looking at letters or words, the patients had the opportunity to concentrate on one lexical element at a time. This additional time for concentrating on each element is believed to have helped patients become more aware of their mistakes. Three variants of the intervention strategy were used, with vertical letters in words, horizontal syllables for vertical words, and vertical passages with each word presented horizontally. Assessment on dependent measures (50 single words and 120 word passages, presented both horizontally and vertically) revealed that vertically presented material was read better than horizontal material. Although some subjects reached near-normal reading fluency in the vertical mode, the findings of this research are clinically limited because the author did not attempt progressively to shape and fade the subjects from vertical fluency to regular horizontal reading. Despite this drawback, the findings are significant because they suggest that remediation of reading disability secondary to brain trauma is possible.

At present there is little research on the rehabilitation of reading disorders. Basic research (Bakker, Moerland, & Goekoop-Hoetkens, 1981; Gheorghita, 1981) suggests that these deficits can be remediated somewhat, but the clinical utility of these methods is somewhat limited. At present the case study methodology suggests (Carmon et al., 1977; Moyer, 1979) that reading deficits may be improved through specifically targeted interventions that are dependent upon adequate assessment. As Carmon and colleagues (1977) have noted, "The real problem is not *how to teach* an alexic patient to read, but rather to *teach him how* to read" (p. 49, italics added).

Retraining Perceptual/Cognitive Deficits

There are approximately two million hemiplegics in the United States (Diller et al., NYU, 1974), 50% of whom are estimated to be of working age. Unfortunately, less than 10% of those patients who receive rehabilitation actually return to work. Two reasons are given for this poor outcome: (1) deficient functional language abilities in right hemiplegics, and (2) decreased perceptual skills in left hemiplegics. Perceptual/cognitive deficits have great impact upon visual-spatial memory (DeRenzi, 1968) and driving abilities (Sivak, Olson, Kewman, Won, & Henson, 1981).

In an attempt to address and to remediate the perceptual-cognitive deficits that are commonly found after right brain damage, several investigators have attempted to use visual-scanning training (Diller & Weinberg, 1977). In essence, scanning training attempts to train the subject to attend to and survey the entire stimulus field before or while making responses. Scanning training has been conducted through the use of lightboards (Diller et al., NYU, 1974; Diller & Gordon, 1981b; Webster et al., 1984), letter cancellation tasks (Diller et al., NYU, 1974), and computer-generated stimulus arrays (Gianutsos et al., 1983; Gianutsos & Grynbaum, 1982).

Diller and colleagues (NYU, 1974) used a lightboard to facilitate the remediation of scanning behavior in right-brain-damaged patients. This lightboard contained 20 colored lights and a small target that was moved around the perimeter of the board at various speeds. Using a training procedure that incorporated two different tasks, visual tracking (of the target into impaired visual fields) and visual search, the authors found that lightboard training, when coupled with additional higher-level perceptual training (body awareness and size estimation), was effective in improving patients' awareness of space and remediating visual-spatial neglect.

Webster and colleagues (1984) have examined the generalization of lightboard scanning to wheelchair navigation. Using a multiple baseline, single-subject research design, the authors also considered such questions as the ability of subjects to use speech mediation to help in increasing scanning behavior. The experimental results indicate that lightboard scanning improved dramatically for all subjects.

Letter cancellation also showed improvement, but there was still a greater preponderence of left-sided omission errors. Navigation abilities showed variable improvement across subjects; however, it was noted that error severity decreased with scanning training (e.g., fewer direct collisions). These results were maintained at one-year follow-up. This study indicates that lightboard scanning training did generalize to a wheelchair ambulation task and that these results were maintained for a period of one year. Gouvier, Cottam, Webster, Beissel, and Wofford (1984) extended this research by specifically targeting wheelchair navigation. By conducting scanning training under various conditions of movement and incorporating additional training exercises as the need emerged (e.g., distance estimation training), clinically significant improvements in wheelchair navigation were obtained in both subjects.

Weinberg and colleagues (1977) gave 25 experimental right-brain-damaged subjects one month of scanning training and compared them to 32 right-brain-damaged patients who received only a standard rehabilitation program. The two groups were matched on a variety of neurological and demographic variables. The authors hypothesized that visual neglect underlies the perceptual problems in right brain damage. Subjects were compared before and after training on a variety of tasks: primary training tasks [Wide Range Achievement Test (WRAT) reading, writing, and arithmetic], secondary related tasks (e.g., letter cancellation), and tertiary general cognitive tasks [face counting, facial recognition, Wechsler Adult Intelligence Scale (WAIS) Digit Span, WAIS Object Assembly, picture completion, double simultaneous stimulation, confrontation, and motor impersistence]. Results indicate that the severely neglecting experimental subjects showed improvement on all tasks except facial matching, Object Assembly, and impersistence, while severely neglecting controls showed no improvement. In fact, the greatest amount of improvement was noted among the most severely impaired patients, who improved to a level equivalent to that of the untreated mildly neglecting patients. Mildly impaired patients who received the experimental treatment showed less improvement than the severe patients. An informal follow-up report suggests that these improvements for the experimental groups were well maintained while controls frequently became worse. Diller and associates (NYU, 1974) have studied generalization effects and have found that block design training (based on the WAIS Block Design subtest) improved left hemiplegic subjects' performances on other psychometric measures. In addition, the authors determined that the amount of cuing subjects required in order to learn a particular design was a direct function of initial competence levels. However, by using a method of "saturation cuing" (in which cues are hierarchically arranged in a descending order by the amount of information provided), the authors were able to demonstrate improvement for left hemiplegics on WAIS Object Assembly, Bender–Gestalt rotation, Purdue Pegboard, and motor impersistence (Ben-Yishay, Diller, Gerstman, & Gordon, 1970). A recent study (Gordon et al., 1985) indicates that training in visual scanning, body awareness, and perceptual organization facilitates more rapid recovery of function than no treatment, and that treated subjects reported higher self-satisfaction ratings with lower ratings of anxiety and hostility.

Young, Collins, and Hren (1983) compared the effects of block design training with other scanning tasks in improving perceptual/cognitive deficits incurred in right hemispheric damage. Three groups were studied: one received

1 hr of occupational therapy (OT) per day (for 20 days); another received 20 min of OT, 20 min of cancellation training, and 20 min of scanning training per day; while the third received 20 min of block design training, 20 min of cancellation training, and 20 min of lightboard scanning training per day. Dependent variables were WAIS Performance subtests, letter cancellation, WRAT, copying addresses, and counting faces. Results indicate that overall, the two experimental groups surpassed the OT controls on scanning, reading, and writing, and the third group showed superior performance to the second. After discharge, the two experimental groups continued to improve while the control group's performance on dependent measures declined. Again, these experimental results support the position that cognitive rehabilitation directed at perceptual deficits adds an additional effect to other traditional therapies; however, the authors did not report on changes in activities of daily living (ADL). Thus the impact of this training may have been limited only to a narrow range of behaviors, and the OT controls may have surpassed the experimental patients in some regards.

Diller and colleagues (Gordon et al., 1985; NYU, 1980b; Weinberg et al., 1979) have devised a comprehensive package aimed at assessing and remediating the perceptual deficits that frequently accompany right hemisphere brain damage. Both the evaluation and remediation procedures are divided into three Visual Information Processing (VIP) subsections. Each of these visual information processing subsections contains specific tasks and each is believed to be associated with different forms of cognitive-perceptual behavior. In both assessment and training, the patient is taken through the VIP modules in a hierarchical fashion. The VIP I module represents assessment and training for those behaviors related to visual exploration, systematic visual scanning, and academic skills. The second visual information processing module (VIP II) involves behaviors associated with body schema, somatosensory awareness, and size estimation. The final module (VIP III) assesses and remediates deficits in pattern organization and sequential analysis. Several principles are central to the visual information training program: (1) establishing the patient's understanding of the problem, (2) providing an external anchoring point for the patient, (3) pacing of task performance, (4) providing immediate performance-based feedback, and (5) the training of habitual environmental scanning in a left-to-right direction. Further information on these modules and treatment results can be found in Gordon et al. (1985) and Horton and Miller (1984).

The goal of these assessment/remediation programs is to document and rehabilitate perceptual/cognitive deficits, which are present in many patients who sustain right-sided brain damage. Such training programs are of great importance because perceptual-cognitive deficits are implicated as a major factor in the failure of brain-injured persons to return to work and assume an autonomous life style (NYU, 1983). The effectiveness of the NYU perceptual/ cognitive retraining programs in remediating deficits associated with right brain damage is described in several published reports (Gordon et al., 1985; Weinberg et al., 1977, 1979, 1982). Other studies analyzing and treating perceptual and sensory deficits associated with brain damage include Castro-Caldas and Salgado (1984), Gianutsos et al. (1983), Weinberg et al. (1982), and Zihl (1980).

ADL Training

The loss of one's ability to function autonomously is one of the greatest consequences of cerebral injury. This autonomous function decline may be due to the physical limitations caused by injury (e.g., hemiparesis) or due to perceptual/cognitive deficits that severely limit the brain-injured individual's ability to deal with his environment efficiently. Historically, restoration of individual autonomy has been the goal of all therapeutic domains (e.g., speech therapy, physical therapy, occupational therapy). Yet, despite their efforts many patients never return to autonomous living. Thus the role of the behavioral neuropsychologist in enhancing the effect of ADL training through systematic task analysis, program development, and cue fading becomes evident.

Stanton et al. (1983) presented the case of a 44-year-old female who had sustained a cerebrovascular accident and who, after 9 weeks in the rehabilitation setting, had failed to master safe transfers. Careful task analysis revealed that there were 26 separate steps involved in making safe transfers. The patient was given step-by-step instructions in each step and was provided with a verbal check for each. She was then given a self-monitoring sheet listing the 26 steps, to allow her to evaluate her transfer behavior. Once this was mastered, the training trials were faded and the 26 steps were reduced to 13 larger steps. The patient's performance was scored for both performance and judgment errors, with advancement criteria being less than one error per trial for three days. Results indicate that the patient was able to master the desired behavior before discharge.

Several studies (Golper, Rau, & Marshall, 1980; Sivak, Olson, Kewman, Won, & Henson, 1981) have identified impaired perceptual/cognitive abilities as major factors impeding an effective return to driving following brain injury. Sivak and colleagues (1981) assessed three groups of subjects on three sets of tests: (1) 12 tests of perceptual and cognitive skills, (2) a set of five driving tasks performed in a closed course, and (3) performance in in-traffic driving. The subject groups included an experimental group, all of whom had sustained brain injury, a spinal-cord-injury group (included to rule out the effects of nonbrain CNS injury), and a non-CNS–injured control group. Results of assessment reveal that the experimental group performed significantly poorer than either control group on the perceptual/cognitive tests. Persons with brain damage also performed less well than able-bodied controls on several measures of closed- and open-road driving. Two cognitive/perceptual tests correlated significantly with on-road driving: rod-and-frame and symbol digit modalities (both written and oral forms). The brain-injured subjects also showed poorer driving performance (as measured by a Composite Driving Index) than either spinal-cord-injured or normal controls. Although subjects both with and without brain damage who scored well on certain perceptual/cognitive tasks also tended to show good driving abilities, different tests predicted good driving ability for the two groups. This suggests that although perceptual deficits do greatly interfere with driving abilities, the driving task itself may be dependent on different skills for brain-damaged and normal individuals.

Given this demonstration that perceptual deficits do correlate with impaired driving performance, Sivak and colleagues (1985) attempted to demonstrate that remediation of perceptual/cognitive deficits would correlate with improved driving ability. Prior to treatment, subjects were assessed on a variety of perceptual skills (picture completion, picture arrangement, block design, symbol digit, trail making test, and cancellation). Subjects were also given a driving evaluation on an in-traffic course with five reliable categories of driving performance. The subjects received between 8 and 10 hours of perceptual training over five to nine sessions on tasks of cancellation, pathfinding, pattern visualization/identification, visual line-tracing, pattern matching, and design construction and analysis. Results of this study indicate that subjects showed varying degrees of perceptual skill change (post–pre) and that driving ability (as measured by the Composite Driving Index) improved for most. There was a significant correlation ($r = .73$, $p < .025$) between the change in the driving index and the changes in perceptual skills.

The above studies suggest that the retraining of perceptual/cognitive deficits can have a direct effect upon the driving ability of brain-injured individuals. Thus, the ability of the psychologist to break behaviors down into their components may be quite helpful in formulating a remediation program— either for improving transfers or for improving driving ability.

Social Factors in Brain Trauma: Implications for Rehabilitation

Concomitant with the perceptual, cognitive, and intellectual changes that occur with cerebral insult, there are also likely to be changes in the personality of the brain-injured individual. These may include a wide range of personality changes: a decrease in the ability to appreciate humorous material (Gardner, Ling, Flamm, & Silverman, 1975), marked changes in functional abilities (Lezak, 1978a, 1978b), decreases in the ability to cope with daily stressful situations (Bloch & Bloch, 1972), and the development of postmorbid behavior patterns that are socially inappropriate (Craine, 1982; Horton, 1979b). Unfortunately, without sufficient attention given to the reduction of the impact of these changes on personality, affective lability, and social functioning, rehabilitation techniques directed at increasing independence may be in vain (Horton, 1978, 1979a, 1982). As Tucker (1981) has mentioned, disordered affective states may need to be addressed before the disordered cognitive status can be treated.

Weddell, Oddy, and Jenkins (1980) noted that a number of marked changes in social functioning occur in closed head injury patients. These include dramatic decreases in work, leisure activities, and interpersonal contacts; and all activity changes were related to the degree of personality change. As Lezak (1978a) notes, perplexity, distractibility, and fatigue accompany all brain injuries and can easily lead to confusion, anxiety, and depression. These symptoms are often missed in consultation cases; this is tragic, as they can be treated through education and the use of coping strategies (Bloch & Bloch, 1972; Lezak, 1978a). Although functional overlay of the organic behavior changes occurs, to attribute a majority of deviations from premorbid behavior patterns to such constructs as conversion hysteria, affective overreactions, or secondary gain (Carter, 1967) is overly simplistic. With an accurate case conceptualization, intervention will be more effective and efficient (Horton, 1978).

A number of intervention strategies are available to the clinical neuropsychologist, ranging from behavioral modification techniques (Horton, 1979b; Ince, 1976) to dealing with specific interpersonal issues that arise as a result of the brain trauma (Kaplan De-Nour & Bauman, 1980) to the use of videotape recorded feedback (Axley, Foster, & Baker, 1983; Helffenstein & Wechsler, 1982). The intervention strategy that one eventually utilizes depends on several factors, including extent of the trauma, location of the neuropsychologist within the health care system, premorbid intelligence of the patient, the patient's ability to benefit from feedback and insight into deficits, presenting complaints, and extent of disruptive behavior. Regardless of the intervention strategy chosen, a working knowledge of psychopathology and brain–behavior relationships is of utmost importance for the clinical neuropsychologist (Brinkman, 1979; Incagnoli, 1982).

The clinical neuropsychologist's intervention need not be confined to the patient; the family of the brain-damaged individual is likely to be stressed and may require therapeutic intervention. Although Oddy, Humphrey, and Uttley (1978) have indicated that family and marital relationships appear to withstand changes in the brain-injured person's life style, considerable stress is present in the situation and must be acknowledged. In fact, the wives of head-injury patients who present with the greatest degree of personality changes tend to have higher scores on Eysenck's neuroticism scale, although the direction of any causal relationship here remains to be determined (McKinlay & Brooks, 1984). The closed head injury not only creates adjustment problems for the patient, but also for the family (Lezak, 1978b). In particular, the social and psychological ties to the patient and the unrealistic expectations for recovery are likely to place a great deal of pressure upon spouses and dependent children. Depression is not uncommon among family members. The spouses of brain-damaged men appear to go through a crisis period at one year postinjury (Rosenbaum & Najenson, 1976). Their hopes for a complete recovery diminish, and they are required to give much to a person who, because of deficits in interpersonal skills, gives little in response (LaBaw, 1968). Supportive psychotherapy and educational counseling are appropriate for family members. As Lezak (1978b) indicates, this may improve the family's adjustment and their subsequent care of the patient. Counseling is needed to readjust family expectations, to provide management advice, and to allow and encourage family members to acknowledge their own needs.

Other Applications: Older Adults

Cognitive retraining interventions have been applied to populations other than the brain damaged, and considerable research has focused on applying these procedures to problems that are common among the aged and children.

One of the most common complaints among the aged is memory impairment. Since cognitive retraining interventions have been shown to affect memory disturbances among the brain damaged, there is no reason why they might not be useful with nonbrain-damaged elderly people. Poon, Fozard, and Treat (1978) reviewed the etiology of memory disorders among the aged and identified problems in the evaluation of memory dysfunction among members of this population. The most significant problem in assessment is the differentiation between complaints about memory as opposed to measurable psychometric deficits. Treat, Poon, Fozard, and Popkin (1978) suggest that close attention to three facets of memory intervention programs will help ensure their success. First, the program's content should include specific techniques to increase attention paid to the to-be-remembered information, thus leading to improved encoding and organization of the material during acquisition and retrieval, especially when used in conjunction with mnemonic elaboration strategies. Second, participants should be trained (if necessary) in the underlying skills necessary to use the strategies (cf., Lahey & Drabman, 1974). The use of group treatment allows formation of a peer support system that provides reinforcement to boost motivation to put the trained skills to use. Finally, within any group, the presence of individual differences among the participants, and the individual tailoring of the program goals to take these differences into account, will help ensure success of the overall program.

Many of these suggestions were incorporated into a series of studies by Zarit and colleagues. Zarit, Gallagher, and Kramer (1981) studied 47 older patients and reported that memory complaints correlated more strongly with measured affective status than with memory performance per se. These participants then received seven sessions of either specific memory skills training groups or interpersonal growth experience therapy groups. Both conditions led to improved memory performance and reduced subjective complaints, the only difference being that the memory training group showed improved memory performance earlier in the seven weeks. Not surprisingly, posttreatment analysis of complaints revealed that complaint reductions were more strongly associated with affective improvement than memory improvement.

In a similar vein, Zarit, Cole, and Guider (1981) studied 44 nonbrain-damaged elderly persons who were enrolled in either four sessions of memory training or four sessions of current events groups. In this study, both groups reduced their subjective complaints, but groups receiving the memory training program, which included practice in categorization, face–name associations, imagery elaboration, and forming personally relevant associations to help remember the information showed greater improvements in memory performance than the current events groups. A second study compared the memory training program with untreated waiting-list participants. Again, no relationship between memory complaints and actual performance was noted, but the training program led to significant improvements in recall for related materials, unrelated materials, and face–name learning.

Other aspects of cognitive performance among the elderly have also been targeted. For example, Meichenbaum (1974) reports that elderly participants were able to benefit from problem-solving training that was presented to them in a self-instructional format. Older adults can also be trained in conservation skills (Hornblum & Overton, 1976) and in problem-solving skills that do not require the use of self-instructional training (Sanders & Sanders, 1978; Sanders, Stern, Smith, & Sanders, 1975). In conducting such training, however, Sanders and Sanders (1978) caution against the use of extrinsic reinforcement in tasks that may be intrinsically rewarding because the extrinsic rewards may take away the personal satisfaction from learning and thus reduce retention of the learning. A similar point is raised by Bandura (1969).

Other Applications: Children

Cognitive training interventions have been applied to problems of learning-disabled children with mixed results. For example, Miller, Sabatino, and Miller (1977) evaluated commercially available perceptual discrimination training programs versus no treatment with 112 learning-disabled and normal children and found that none of the programs had any significant effect on their drawing task dependent variable. Myers and Hammill (1976) reviewed 81 studies that attempted to train skills correcting the "underlying" perceptual-motor, visual discrimination, and/or auditory sequential deficits proposed to cause learning disabilities. They conclude their review in agreement with Koppitz (1971), stating that the overwhelming majority of these programs are ineffective in influencing academic performance and maintaining that the focus of treatment should be on more task-oriented remedial methods (Lee, Koenigsknecht, & Mulhern, 1975). This emphasis is further amplified by Treiber and Lahey (1983), whose review concludes that there is no good evidence supporting the remediation of "underlying deficits." Nor is there appreciable evidence that such training generalizes to other nontrained domains. They suggest that focus is never necessary on processing deficits or incompatible behaviors, but rather on the specific academic deficiency at the most molar possible level, shifting to a more molecular level only when needed to permit molar intervention (cf., Lahey & Drabman, 1974).

These strong statements might best be tempered in light of the reports of Braggio and colleagues (1980), who describe a procedure for operationally determining the optimal mode(s) of information processing in learning-disabled children. Results indicate that material presented to the children in their optimal modes is learned and retained better than material presented in a nonoptimal mode. Their findings suggest that learning and social adjustment can be maximized by tailoring information presentations to match the learners' best mode. This suggestion is supported by other research (Bakker et al., 1981; Doyle, 1983). Given that academic deficits can be targeted directly, what sorts of techniques are most useful? Self-instructional training (Meichenbaum & Goodman, 1971) has been shown to promote improved problem-solving and pattern-matching performance among impulsive children, and training strategic response strategies (e.g., "respond so as to rule out the greatest number of alternatives") has been shown to be superior to simple rule-governed strategies (e.g., "don't select uninformative choices, respond only to stimuli that can tell you something") (McKinney & Haskins, 1980). Self-instructional procedures are also effective in remediating deficits in social behavior and impulse control exhibited by children (Finch & Spirito, 1980; Kneedler, 1980).

Program Structure for Vocationally Oriented Cognitive Retraining

Ever since Ferguson (1950) demonstrated that severely disabled individuals can do productive (and competitive) work, day treatment programs for the disabled have been gaining popularity. Green and De La Cruz (1981) point out that day treatment programs offer an alternative to full-time institutionalization, and also help bridge the gap between acute hospitalization and return to community living. Day treatment programs offer a number of advantages, including cost savings over institutionalization, the fact that they can help alleviate the burden of day-to-day supervision for the family, and their potential for promoting improved social adjustment and eventual return to work.

Katz, Galatzer, and Kravetz (1978) evaluated changes in brain-injured veterans and their families' perceptions of functioning in relation to their participation in a sheltered workshop. Veterans were accepted into the program from 4 to 24 years posttrauma, and they worked all jobs, supervised all labor, and were responsible for managing the workshop for two years. Relative to untreated controls, the veterans saw significant improvements in family relationships, social relationships, vocational abilities, and independence, with no perceived changes in economic or medical conditions. By contrast, families reported significant improvements in all areas except family relationships. Control patients and their families tended to report deterioration of functioning in most of these areas over the two years of the study.

Rosenbaum, Lipsitz, Abraham, and Najenson (1978) describe another sheltered workshop approach to the rehabilitation of traumatically brain-injured war veterans. Their comprehensive program, involving the team services of psychologists, social workers, speech pathologist, and others, had three general goals: (1) to modify problems in the patients' behavior via psychotherapy, cognitive retraining, prostheses, and vocational training, (2) to create a supportive environment within the project to promote improved behavior via the therapeutic milieu, group therapy, and work groups and, (3) to generalize the therapeutic effects to the community at large via family therapy and groups, employer contacts, and defense department and welfare liaisons. These authors concluded that behavioral problems and socio-environmental factors were the biggest obstacles to successful reintegration into the community.

Evaluation of Cognitive Retraining Results

It is not sufficient to deliver cognitive retraining interventions to brain-impaired patients; the results of such interventions must be systematically evaluated in order to ascertain the relative effectiveness of different procedures or approaches. Ideally, such evaluations would be conducted using research designs that allow one to infer that the observed changes are related to the intervention, and not to extraneous factors. Both group and single subject designs can serve this purpose, provided that the designs are sufficiently adequate to permit interpretation of the results (Mahoney, 1978).

It is equally important, however, that evaluators attach clinical significance to their reports of statistically significant findings (Meyerson & Kerr, 1979). Thus it would not be sufficient to report that when collapsed across subjects, average levels of behavior change were statistically significant. Further data regarding the proportion of patients who improve versus those who do not are needed to appraise accurately the significance of such findings.

It is becoming a growing social imperative to demonstrate not only that rehabilitation programs produce changes in patients' level of functioning, but also that those changes are effected with the lowest possible cost. Cope and Hall (1982) suggest that this end can be best served by early rehabilitation intervention with head injury patients because the treatment can focus on the primary injury effects and time and effort are not required to reverse the preventable secondary complications. Similarly, Rusk, Block, and Lowman (1969) demonstrated that a disproportionate amount of time is spent treating secondary preventable complications when rehabilitation is postponed, and Cogstad and Kjellman (1976) showed that there is better functional outcome in patients whose rehabilitation program is continuous with their acute care. But not all disabled patients return to work or taxpaying status, so it is problematic to use these factors in attempting to define the cost-effectiveness of rehabilitation programs. Recognizing this, Albrecht and Harasymiw (1979) offer a technique for evaluating life function change per dollar cost that can be used to evaluate rehabilitation effectiveness in all patients, whether they return to work or not. An advantage of this indicator is that it permits comparisons between the outcomes and cost-effectiveness of different programs along a single standard scale.

After Rehabilitation: Return to Work

The best possible outcome following a disabling injury to the brain is for the patient to return successfully to his or her premorbid occupation. Hook (1976) emphasizes the need for early intervention to maximize the likelihood of successful return to premorbid or downgraded employment, and the importance of a team approach to patient management. Hook identifies nine factors that are associated with poor recovery, warning rehabilitation workers to take such factors into consideration when setting goals and planning treatment. Dresser and colleagues (1973) confirm the observation of Symonds (1937) that it is not just the nature of the injury that matters, but also the characteristics of the brain that receives the damage. The best outcomes come from good premorbid brains that receive less severe injuries. Prognosis worsens with poorer premorbid levels of functioning and increasing injury severity.

Successful return to work can be enhanced by including work samples in the assessment and treatment of patients with brain dysfunction in order to make the assessment findings more pertinent to the patient's premorbid life style, and to make treatment more relevant to the patient (Anchor, Sieveking, Peacock, & Pressley, 1979). Three recent studies that have done this have reported a much better rate of successful return to work than the 55% figure reported by Dresser and colleagues (1973). In these studies (Jellinek & Harvey, 1982; Musante, 1983; Wechsler, 1983) the vocational specialists worked hand-in-hand with neuropsychologists and cognitive therapists to evaluate present levels of functioning in comparison to premorbid occupational requirements. These factors became integral parts of the treatment plan, and actual job samples were incorporated into treatment in order to enhance patients' motivation, the face validity of retraining activities, and the likelihood that treatment gains would generalize outside the rehabilitation environment to the workplace. This is a direction in which cognitive retraining efforts can be expected to expand and flourish.

CASE CONCEPTUALIZATION

Our overall assumptions are: (1) cognitive training is an emerging field with few hard and fast principles to serve as guidelines at this time, and (2) the field can only advance through recognition that it is a multidisciplinary field requiring the integration of diverse data bases. Together these assumptions emphasize the need to be well prepared to enter this field through training in such areas as cognitive psychology, neuropathology, experimental neuropsychology, rehabilitation psychology, and behavioral psychology. At the same time, neuropsychologists must be open to advances in other fields. Conceptual flexibility and a willingness to embrace new information, even if it contradicts old assumptions, are essential.

This integration will consist of general guidelines we use in case conceptualization for the retraining of brain-injured patients. Our stages of retraining include the following: (1) the initial assessment, (2) the individualized assessment, and (3) the initiation of training and its progressive evaluation.

The Initial Assessment

In the initial assessment, data from diverse areas are collected in order to understand on a molar level the patient's neuropsychological status, interpersonal history, occupation–educational history, medical history, and current life stressors. Testing at this level includes screening of such diverse abilities as memory, intellect, sensorimotor skill, perception, language, and complex praxic function. In addition, self-report questionnaires are included to assess psychopathology and complaints of cognitive deficits.

Our laboratories secure the privilege of contacting significant others in order to verify or expand upon the patient's complaints. This is necessary because (1) the patient is often unaware of the quality and extent of his problems and (2) the spouse's ability to cope with the situation is predictive of the patient's emotional adjustment, especially later in the recovery process (McKinlay & Brooks, 1984). We will also secure school records as a means of estimating pre-accident abilities and characteristics, since these factors have been shown to affect recovery of function. In addition, employers may be contacted to validate estimates of the patient's premorbid functioning and to provide information about jobs the patient has held. Of course, when litigation is an issue such contact with the employer is often impossible.

Medical records are also secured, including CT and EEG reports when available. Whenever possible, we try to obtain the CT scan and a sample of the EEG and have our staff neurologists review them because there is considerable variability across readers. In addition, we have found that the natural history of recovery can give clues to subtle functional deficits that may linger; hence, all the physician's notes are requested, rather than a general summary. For example, when the patient's initial aphasia rapidly clears, he is sometimes left with a subtle anomia only detectable on tests with high ceilings, such as the Boston Naming Test (Kaplan, Goodglass, & Weintraub, 1983). Summary reports often fail to mention such short-lived deficits, and without knowing that the patient had been transiently aphasic, interpretation of subtle language deficits would become more difficult.

The final phase of this initial assessment is interviewing the patient. Of principal importance are the patient's presenting complaints and his prior medical and psychological history.

Individualized Assessment

In this phase, data from the various sources of information in the initial assessment are integrated to generate hypotheses about cognitive deficits that may account for the patient's problems with independence. The goal is to uncover the impaired functional units that account for the presenting syndrome. With reference to structural/physiological aspects, facts about the type of injury, initial sequelae (e.g., length of coma, first symptoms), time since injury, structural/physiological damage, and the patient's general health are integrated to generate hypotheses about which functional deficits revealed by the patient's complaints and neuropsychological performance might result from primary injuries. If the patient, for example, shows profound aphasia following a car accident but has a normal CT and only mildly abnormal EEG with left-sided slowing, we might predict that significant recovery of language functions may be possible with retraining. Also, establishing the presence of psychological factors such as elective mutism or reluctant speech should be investigated more closely in this case. Depending upon the circumstances we may also suggest a second neurological examination to assure that no worsening of the patient's condition has taken place.

The neuropsychological results are evaluated with respect to data on present stress, psychopathology, and premorbid ability (e.g., occupation and educational performance). These data are then compared with the patient's and significant other's complaints of problems in daily functioning to help identify the neuropsychological syndromes.

Following this, hypotheses are generated to tease out those factors contributing to the deficit. When the deficit appears to result from brain injury we must then ask what aspects of the functional system are impaired. When the resultant hypotheses cannot be addressed by the data collected during initial assessment, subsequent testing and data gathering are performed. For example, if results from the initial assessment suggest various problems may relate to arousal/attentional deficits, the following hypotheses could be proposed and evaluated:

1. The patient is not motivated to do well.
2. He is experiencing previously undetected petit mal seizures.
3. He is suffering a sleep disturbance resulting in concentration problems during the day.
4. He is unable to inhibit irrelevant activity rather than simply unable to remain alert.

5. He is suffering a modality/material-specific attentional problem as opposed to a general arousal deficiency per se.
6. He is using a faulty compensatory strategy that does not promote improved attention.

The role of the individualized assessment phase is to test the hypotheses of importance that will further the understanding of the patient's problems and the generation of appropriate training strategies. To be realistic, some hypotheses may not be assessed immediately because of cost-benefit issues, as in the case of sleep disturbance problems that may only be detectable with considerable expense by a sleep laboratory. Nonetheless, these hypotheses should remain viable in case the lack of progress in treatment points to the probability that they may be accounting for the patient's problem.

The Initiation of Training and Its Progressive Modification

After case conceptualization, a training strategy is designed. Such a strategy needs to address the chosen hypotheses pertaining to which functions are impaired, while also taking into account the patient's idiosyncrasies and preferences. Additionally, a means of accountability should be provided to assess progress. Preferably, the assessment results should be graphically charted, along with normative and estimated premorbid levels, thus serving as a motivator for the patient who does not appreciate his progress. Comprehensive assessment also keeps the therapist in touch with subtle changes, some of which may be unexpected. For example, improvement in one function can reveal other deficits inaccessible before training (Diller & Gordon, 1981a), as in our experience with patients suffering left spatial hemiakinesia who, once taught to look to left space, showed left visual hemifield perceptual disturbances (Gouvier et al., 1984). Consequently, assessment and treatment are a continuing, serial process lasting throughout therapy.

The nature of the progressive recovery from brain damage requires that therapists be able to change and adjust their models of case conceptualization as the recovery process proceeds. This evolution of case conceptualization follows the simple to complex procession that patients demonstrate in recovery. Thus, for the profoundly impaired patient early in recovery who has difficulty practicing even a simple reaction time task, a rather simple-minded conceptualization of his problem as limited to the domains of attending and responding will probably suffice. Through the use of verbal praise and encouragement, tangible rewards, and therapist charting of his progress, the patient can often be engaged in the training task and his performance can improve. As the patient progresses, however, the therapist will need to modify and refine the case conceptualization to identify more precisely the pattern of deficits that the patient continues to display.

As patients continue to recover and target goals become more complex, their deficits may become more subtle and are likely to be multidetermined. In addition, there is an increasing level of uncertainty in the therapist's case conceptualization. Thus, it becomes easier for a therapist to regard a high-functioning patient's persisting problems as representing manifestations of premorbid personality and adjustment disorders. While such hypotheses may be accurate, they should be introduced only when other hypotheses generated from the patient's history and assessment data have been evaluated and ruled out.

One final word of caution concerns the potential overenthusiasm of some professionals involved in rehabilitating brain-injured individuals. Cognitive retraining is a fledgling therapy technique. Professionals engaged in this activity should exercise the utmost restraint in extolling the virtues of cognitive retraining or computerized practice exercises for brain-injured patients. Popular magazines and newspapers that publish exaggerated claims about cognitive retraining are raising unrealistic hopes among thousands of distressed patients and families. The inevitable disillusionment that will result from this may prevent professionals from doing the tedious research that is necessary to prove what good, if any, can be achieved through the development and application of the technology of cognitive retraining.

REFERENCES

Albrecht, G., & Harasymiw, S. (1979). Evaluating rehabilitation outcome by cost function indicators. *Journal of Chronic Diseases, 32,* 525–533.

Anchor, K., Sieveking, N., Peacock, C., & Pressley, B. (1979). Work behavior sampling in vocational assessment: Applications for neuropsychological methodology. *Clinical Neuropsychology, 1*(3), 51–53.

Anderson, D., & McLaurin, R. (1980). Report on the National Head and Spinal Cord Injury Survey. *Journal of Neurosurgery, 53* (Suppl.), 1–43.

Axley, W., Foster , & Baker, A. (1983). Audiovisual feedback: An exercise in self-awareness for the head injured patient. *Cognitive Rehabilitation, 1*(6), 8–10.

Bakker, D., Moerland, R., & Goekoop-Hoetkens, M. (1981). Effects of hemisphere-specific stimulation on the reading performance of dyslexic boys: A pilot study. *Journal of Clinical Neuropsychology, 3,* 155–159.

Bandura, A. (1969). *Principles of behavior modification.* New York: Holt, Rinehart and Winston.

Basso, A., Capitani, E., & Vignolo, L. (1979). Influence of rehabilitation on language skills in aphasic patients. *Archives of Neurology, 36,* 190–196.

Bellezza, F., & Reddy, B. (1978). Mnemonic devices and natural memory. *Bulletin of the Psychonomic Society, 11,* 277–280.

Ben-Yishay, Y., & Diller, L. (1981). Rehabilitation of cognitive and perceptual deficits in people with traumatic brain damage. *International Journal of Rehabilitation Research, 4,* 208–210.

Ben-Yishay, Y., Diller, L., Gerstman, L., & Gordon, W. (1970). Relationship between initial competence and ability to profit from cues in brain-damaged individuals. *Journal of Abnormal Psychology, 75,* 248–259.

Bevan, W., & Feuer, J. (1977). The facilitative role of imagery in episodic memory: Multiple cues or active construction? *Bulletin of the Psychonomic Society, 10,* 172–174.

Bjorklund, A., & Stenevi, U. (1971). Growth of central catecholamine neurons into smooth muscle grafts in the rat mesencephalon. *Brain Research, 31,* 1–20.

Bloch, G., & Bloch, N. (1972). Traumatic and post-traumatic neuroses. *Industrial Medicine, 41*(10), 5–8.

Bower, G., & Clark, M. (1969). Narrative stories as mediators for serial learning. *Psychonomic Science, 14,* 181–182.

Bowers, D., & Heilman, K. (1980). Material-specific hemispheric activation. *Neuropsychologia, 18,* 309–319.

Bracy, O. (1982). *Cognitive rehabilitation programs for brain injured and stroke patients.* Indianapolis: Psychological Software Service.

Bracy, O. (1983). Computer based cognitive rehabilitation. *Cognitive Rehabilitation, 1*(1), 7–8, 18.

Braggio, J., Braggio, S., Hall, A., Allman, T., Peyton, L., & Karan, D. (1980). Validating optimal response modes in learning disabled children. *Perceptual and Motor Skills, 51,* 1335–1345.

Braun, J. (1978). Time and recovery from brain damage. In S. Finger (Ed.), *Recovery from brain damage: Research and theory* (pp. 165–197). New York: Plenum Press.

Brinkman, S. (1979). Rehabilitation of the neurologically impaired patient: The contribution of the neuropsychologist. *Clinical Neuropsychology, 2*(2), 39–43.

Burgess, P., & Horch, K. (1973). Specific regeneration of cutaneous fibers in the cat. *Journal of Neurophysiology, 36,* 101–114.

Carmon, A., Gordon, H., Bental, E., & Harness, B. (1977). Retraining in literal alexia: Substitution of a right hemisphere perceptual strategy for impaired left hemisphere processing. *Bulletin of the Los Angeles Neurological Societies, 47,* 41–50.

Carter, A. (1967). The functional overlay. *Lancet, ii,* 1196–1200.

Castro-Caldas, A., & Salgado, V. (1984). Right hemifield alexia without hemianopia. *Archives of Neurology, 41,* 84–87.

Cermak, L. (1975). Imagery as an aid to retrieval for Korsakoff patients. *Cortex, 11,* 163–169.

Cogstad, A., & Kjellman, A. (1976). Rehabilitation prognosis related to clinical and social factors in brain injured of different etiology. *Social Science and Medicine, 10,* 283–288.

Cope, D., & Hall, K. (1982). Head injury rehabilitation: Benefit of early intervention. *Archives of Physical Medicine and Rehabilitation, 63,* 433–437.

Cotman, C., Gentry, C., & Steward, O. (1977). Synaptic replacement in the dentate gyrus after unilateral entorhinal lesion: Electron microscopic analysis of the extent of replacement of synapses by the remaining entorhinal cortex. *Journal of Neurocytology, 6,* 455–464.

Cotman, C., & McGaugh, J. (1980). *Behavioral Neuroscience.* New York: Academic Press.

Cotman, C., & Nieto-Sampedro, M. (1982). Brain function, synapse renewal, and plasticity. *Annual Review of Psychology, 33,* 371–401.

Cotman, C., & Nieto-Sampedro, M. (1983). Trophic influences on the in vivo survival of transplanted cholinergic neurons: A model system for the study of neuronal loss in Alzheimer's disease. In *Banbury report 15: Biological aspects of Alzheimer's disease* (pp. 275–283). Cold Springs Harbor, NY: Cold Spring Laboratory.

Cowan, W. (1970). Anterograde and retrograde transneuronal degeneration in the central and peripheral nervous system. In W. Nauta & S. Ebbesson (Eds.), *Contemporary research methods in neuroanatomy* (pp. 217–251). New York: Springer-Verlag.

Craine, J. (1982). Principles of cognitive rehabilitation. In L. Trexler (Ed.), *Cognitive rehabilitation: Conceptualization and intervention.* (pp. 83–98). New York: Plenum Press.

Crovitz, H. (1979). Memory retraining in brain-damaged patients: The airplane list. *Cortex, 15,* 131–134.

Crovitz, H., & Harvey, M. (1979). Visual imagery vs. semantic category as encoding conditions. *Bulletin of the Psychonomic Society, 13,* 291–292.

Crovitz, H., Harvey, M., & Horn, R. (1979). Problems in the acquisition of imagery mnemonics: Three brain damaged cases. *Cortex, 15,* 225–234.

Dean, R. (1986). Lateralization of cerebral functions. In D. Wedding, A. Horton, & J. Webster (Eds.), *The neuropsychology handbook: Behavioral and clinical perspectives.* New York: Springer Publishing Co.

DeRenzi, E. (1968). Nonverbal memory and hemispheric side of lesion. *Neuropsychologia, 6,* 181–189.

Diller, L., & Gordon, W. (1981a). Rehabilitation and clinical neuropsychology. In S. Filskov & T. Boll (Eds.). *Handbook of clinical neuropsychology* (pp. 702–733). New York: Wiley.

Diller, L., & Gordon, W. (1981b). Interventions for cognitive deficits in brain-injured adults. *Journal of Consulting and Clinical Psychology, 49,* 822–834.

Diller, L., & Weinberg, J. (1977). Hemi-inattention in rehabilitation: The evolution of a rational remediation program. In E. Weinstein & R. Friedland (Eds.), *Advances in neurology* (Vol. 18) (pp. 63–82). New York: Raven Press.

Doyle, W. (1983). The effectiveness of color-coded cues in remediating reversals. *Journal of Learning Disabilities, 15,* 227–230.

Dresser, A., Meirowsky, A., Weiss, G., McNeel, M., Simon, G., & Caveness, W. (1973). Gainful employment following head injury. *Archives of Neurology, 29,* 111–116.

Dyken, M., & Nelson, G. (1964). Changes in local blood flow characteristics in chronic unilateral brain damage. *Acta Neurologica Scandinavia, 40,* 361–368.

Ferguson, T. (1950). The idea of a sheltered workshop. In S. Licht & V. Greenwood (Eds.), *Occupational therapy and rehabilitation* (pp. 73–82). Baltimore: Williams & Wilkins.

Finch, A., & Spirito, A. (1980). Use of cognitive training to change cognitive processes. *Exceptional Education Quarterly, 1,* 31–41.

Fowler, R., Hart, J., & Sheehan, M. (1972). A prosthetic memory: An application of the prosthetic memory concept. *Rehabilitation Counseling Bulletin, 16,* 80–85.

Gardner, H., Ling, P., Flamm, L., & Silverman, J. (1975). Comprehension and appreciation of humorous material following brain damage. *Brain, 98,* 399–412.

Gardner, H., Zurif, E., Berry, T., & Baker, E. (1976). Visual communication in aphasia. *Neuropsychologia, 14,* 275–292.

Gasparrini, B., & Satz, P. (1979). A treatment for memory problems in left hemisphere CVA patients. *Journal of Clinical Neuropsychology, 1,* 137–150.

Gentile, A., Green, S., Nieburgs, A., Schmelzer, W., & Stein, D. (1978). Disruption and recovery of locomotor and manipulatory behavior following cortical lesions in rats. *Behavioral Biology, 22,* 417–455.

Gheorghita, N. (1981). Vertical reading: A new method of therapy for reading disturbances in aphasics. *Journal of Clinical Neuropsychology, 3,* 161–164.

Gianutsos, R. (1980). What is cognitive rehabilitation? *Journal of Rehabilitation, 46* (July–August), 36–40.

Gianutsos, R. (1981). Training the short and long term recall of a postencephalitic amnesic. *Journal of Clinical Neuropsychology, 3,* 143–153.

Gianutsos, R., & Gianutsos, J. (1979). Rehabilitating the verbal recall of brain-injured patients by mnemonic training: An experimental demonstration using single case methodology. *Journal of Clinical Neuropsychology, 1,* 117–135.

Gianutsos, R., Glosser, D., Elbaum, J., & Vroman, G. (1983). Visual imperception in brain injured adults: Multifaceted measures. *Archives of Physical Medicine and Rehabilitation, 64,* 456–461.

Gianutsos, R., & Grynbaum, B. (1982). Helping brain injured people to contend with hidden cognitive deficits. *International Rehabilitation Medicine, 5,* 37–40.

Gianutsos, R., & Klitzner, C. (1981). *Handbook: Computer programs for cognitive rehabilitation.* Bayport, NY: Life Science Associates.

Glasgow, R., Zeiss, R., Barrera, M., & Lewinsohn, P. (1977). Case studies on remediating memory deficits in brain-damaged individuals. *Journal of Clinical Psychology, 33,* 1049–1054.

Glass, A., Gazzaniga, M., & Premack, D. (1973). Artificial language training in global aphasics. *Neuropsychologia, 11,* 95–104.

Glees, P. (1980). Functional reorganization following hemispherectomy in man and small experimental lesions in primates. In P. Bach-y-Rita (Ed.), *Recovery of function: Theoretical considerations for brain injury rehabilitation* (pp. 106–126). Baltimore: Park Press.

Golden, C. (1978). *Diagnosis and rehabilitation in clinical neuropsychology.* Springfield, IL: Charles C Thomas.

Golden, C., & Maruish, M. (1986). The Luria–Nebraska Neuropsychological Battery. In D. Wedding, A. Horton, & J. Webster (Eds.), *The neuropsychology handbook: Behavioral and clinical perspectives.* New York: Springer Publishing Co.

Golper, L., Rau, M., & Marshall, R. (1980). Aphasic adults and their decisions on driving: An evaluation. *Archives of Physical Medicine and Rehabilitation, 61,* 34–40.

Gordon, W., Hibbard, M., Egelko, S., Diller, L., Shaver, M., Lieberman, A., & Ragnarsson, K. (1985). Perceptual remediation in patients with right brain damage: A comprehensive program. *Archives of Physical Medicine and Rehabilitation, 66,* 353–359.

Gouvier, W. (1982). Using the digital alarm chronograph in memory retraining. *Behavioral Engineering, 7,* 134.

Gouvier, W., Cottam, G., Webster, J., Beissel, G., & Wofford, J. (1984). Behavioral interventions with stroke patients for improving wheelchair navigation. *International Journal of Clinical Neuropsychology, 6,* 186–190.

Green, L., & De La Cruz, A. (1981). Psychiatric day treatment as alternative to and transition from full-time hospitalization. *Community Mental Health Journal, 17,* 191–202.

Gross, Y., Ben-Nahum, Z., & Munk, G. (1982). Techniques and application of simultaneous information processing. In L. Trexler (Ed.), *Cognitive rehabilitation: Conceptualization and intervention* (pp. 223–238). New York: Plenum Press.

Guilleminault, C., Faull, K., Miles, L., & Van der Hoed, J. (1983). Post-traumatic excessive daytime sleepiness: A review of 20 patients. *Neurology, 33,* 1584–1589.

Guillery, R. (1972). Binocular competition in the control of geniculate cell growth. *Journal of Comparative Neurology, 144,* 117–127.

Guth, L. (1974). Axonal regeneration and functional plasticity in the central nervous system. *Experimental Neurology, 45,* 606–654.

Harasymiw, S., & Albrecht, G. (1979). Admission and discharge indicators as aids in optimizing comprehensive rehabilitation services. *Scandinavian Journal of Rehabilitation Medicine, 11,* 123–128.

Hauck, P., Walsh, C., & Kroll, N. (1976). Visual imagery mnemonics: Common vs. bizarre mental images. *Bulletin of the Psychonomic Society, 7,* 160–162.

Heilman, K., & Satz, P. (1983). *Neuropsychology of human emotion.* New York: Guilford Press.

Heilman, K., & Valenstein, E. (1979). *Clinical neuropsychology.* New York: Oxford University Press.

Helffenstein, D., & Wechsler, F. (1982). The use of Interpersonal Process Recall (IPR) in the remediation of interpersonal and communication skill deficits in the newly brain injured. *Clinical Neuropsychology, 4,* 139–143.

Hier, D., Mondlock, J., & Caplan, L. (1983). Recovery of behavioral abnormalities after right hemisphere stroke. *Neurology, 33,* 345–350.

Higbee, K. (1977). *Your memory: How it works and how to improve it.* Englewood Cliffs, NJ: Prentice-Hall.

Hook, O. (1976). Neuropsychological aspects of motivation. *Scandinavian Journal of Rehabilitation Medicine, 8,* 97–106.

Hornblum, J., & Overton, W. (1976). Area and volume conservation among the elderly: Assessment and training. *Developmental Psychology, 12,* 68–74.

Horton, A. (1978). Behavioral neuropsychology: A tentative definition. *Behavioral Neuropsychology Newsletter, 1,* 1–2.

Horton, A. (1979a). Behavioral neuropsychology: Rationale and research. *Clinical Neuropsychology. 2*(2), 20–23.

Horton, A. (1979b). Behavioral neuropsychology: A clinical case study. *Clinical Neuropsychology, 2*(3), 44–46.

Horton, A. (1982). Behavioral neuropsychology and the rehabilitation of neurologically impaired patients. *Bulletin of the National Academy of Neuropsychologists, 2*(4), 10.

Horton, A., & Miller, W. (1984). Brain damage and rehabilitation. In C. Goldon (Ed.), *Current topics in rehabilitation psychology.* Orlando, FL: Grune & Stratton.

Hughlings-Jackson, J. (1932). In J. Taylor (Ed.), *Selected writings of John Hughlings Jackson* (Vol. 2). London: Hodder & Stoughton.

Incagnoli, T. (1982). The role of the clinical neuropsychologist in rehabilitation. *Bulletin of the National Academy of Neuropsychologists, 2*(4), 11–12.

Ince, L. (1976). *Behavior modification in rehabilitation medicine.* Springfield, IL: Charles C. Thomas.

Jaffe, P., & Katz, A. (1975). Attenuating anteriorgrade amnesia in Korsakoff's psychosis. *Journal of Abnormal Psychology, 84,* 559–562.

Jellinek, H., & Harvey, R. (1982). Vocational/educational services in a medical rehabilitation facility: Outcomes in spinal cord and brain injured patients. *Archives of Physical Medicine and Rehabilitation, 63,* 87–88.

Johnston, M., & Keith, R. (1983). Cost-benefits of medical rehabilitation. *Archives of Physical Medicine and Rehabilitation, 64,* 147.

Jones, M. (1974). Imagery as a mnemonic aid after left temporal lobectomy: Contrast between material-specific and generalized memory disorders. *Neuropsychologia, 12,* 21–30.

Jones-Gotman, M., & Milner, B. (1978). Right temporal-lobe contribution to image-mediated verbal learning. *Neuropsychologia, 16,* 61–71.

Kaplan, E., Goodglass, H., & Weintraub, S. (1983). *The Boston Naming Test.* Philadelphia: Lea & Febiger.

Kaplan De-Nour, A., & Bauman, A. (1980). Psychiatric treatment in severe brain injury: A case report. *General Hospital Psychiatry, 2,* 23–34.

Katz, S., Galatzer, A., & Kravetz, S. (1978). The physical, psycho-social, and vocational effectiveness of a sheltered workshop for brain-damaged war veterans. *Scandinavian Journal of Rehabilitation Medicine, 10,* 51–57.

Keenan, J., & Brassell, E. (1974). A study of factors related to prognosis for individual aphasic patients. *Journal of Speech and Hearing Disorders, 39,* 257.

Kneedler, R. (1980). The use of cognitive training to change social behaviors. *Exceptional Education Quarterly, 1,* 65–74.

Knopman, D., Selnes, O., Niccum, N., Rubens, A., Yock, D., & Larson, D. (1983). A longitudinal study of speech fluency in aphasia: CT correlates of recovery and persistent nonfluency. *Neurology, 33,* 1170–1178.

Kolata, G. (1983). Brain-grafting work shows promise. *Science, 221,* 1277.

Kolb, B., & Whishaw, I. (1980). *Fundamentals of human neuropsychology.* San Francisco: W. H. Freeman.

Koppitz, E. (1971). *Children with learning disabilities—A five year follow-up study.* New York: Grune & Stratton.

Kuhl, D., Phelps, M., Kowell, A., Metter, E., Selin, C., & Winter, J. (1980). Effects of stroke on local cerebral metabolism and perfusion: Mapping by emission computed tomography of ^{18}FDG and ^{13}NH$_3$. *Annals of Neurology, 8,* 47–60.

LaBaw, W. (1968). Closed brain injury. *Medical Times, 96,* 821–829.

Lahey, B., & Drabman, R. (1974). Facilitation of the acquisition and retention of sight-word vocabulary through token reinforcement. *Journal of Applied Behavioral Analysis, 7,* 307–312.

Lashley, K. (1935). The mechanism of vision: XII Nervous structures concerned in habits based on reactions to light. *Comparative Psychology Monographs, 11,* 43–79.

Laurence, S., & Stein, D. (1978). Recovery after brain damage and the concept of localization of function. In S. Finger (Ed.), *Recovery from brain damage: Research and theory* (pp. 402–407). New York: Plenum Press.

Lee, L., Koenigsknecht, R., & Mulhern, S. (1975). *Interactive language development teaching.* Evanstown, IL: Northwestern University Press.

LeVere, N., & LeVere, T. (1982). Recovery of function after brain damage: Support for the compensation theory of the behavioral deficit. *Physiological Psychology, 10,* 165–174.

LeVere, T. (1975). Neural stability, sparing and behavioral recovery following brain damage. *Psychological Review, 82,* 344–358.

LeVere, T. (1980). Recovery of function after brain damage: A theory of the behavioral deficit. *Physiological Psychology, 8,* 297–308.

Levin, H., Benton, A., & Grossman, R. (1982). *Neurobehavioral consequences of closed head injury.* New York: Oxford University Press.

Lewinsohn, P., Danaher, B., & Kikel, S. (1977). Visual imagery as a mnemonic aid for brain-injured persons. *Journal of Consulting and Clinical Psychology, 45,* 717–723.

Lewinsohn, P., & Graf, M. (1973). A follow-up study of persons referred for vocational rehabilitation who have suffered brain injury. *Journal of Community Psychology, 1,* 57–62.

Lewis, E., & Cotman, C. (1983). Neurotransmitter characteristics of brain grafts: Stratial and septal tissues from the same laminated input to hippocampus. *Neuroscience, 8,* 67.

Lezak, M. (1978a). Subtle sequelae of brain damage: Perplexity, distractibility, and fatigue. *American Journal of Physical Medicine, 57,* 9–15.

Lezak, M. (1978b). Living with the characterologically altered brain injured patient. *Journal of Clinical Psychiatry, 39,* 592–598.

Lezak, M. (1979). Recovery of memory and learning functions following traumatic brain injury. *Cortex, 15,* 63–72.

Lind, K. (1982). Synthesis of studies on stroke rehabilitation. *Journal of Chronic Disease, 35,* 133–149.

Luria, A. (1963). *Restoration of function after brain injury.* New York: Macmillan.

Luria, A. (1980). *Higher cortical functions in man* (2nd ed.). New York: Basic Books.

Luria, A., Naydin, V., Tsvetkova, L., & Vinarskaye, E. (1969). Restoration of higher cortical function following local brain damage. In P. Vinken & G. Brugh (Eds.), *Handbook of clinical neurology* (pp. 368–433). New York: Wiley.

Lynch, W. (1981). *A guide to Atari videocomputer programs for rehabilitation settings* (rev. ed.). Palo Alto, CA: Veterans Administration.

Lynch, W. (1982). The use of electronic games in cognitive rehabilitation. In L. Trexler (Ed.), *Cognitive rehabilitation: Conceptualization and intervention* (pp. 263–274). New York: Plenum Press.

Lynch, W. (1983). Cognitive retraining using microcomputer games and commercially available software. *Cognitive Rehabilitation, 1*(1), 19–22.

Mahoney, M. (1978). Experimental methods and outcome evaluation. *Journal of Consulting and Clinical Psychology, 46,* 660–672.

Malec, J., & Questad, K. (1983). Rehabilitation of memory after craniocerebral trauma: Case report. *Archives of Physical Medicine and Rehabilitation, 64,* 436–438.

Manthorpe, M., Nieto-Sampedro, M., Skaper, S., Lewis, E., Barbin, B., Longo, F., Cotman, C., & Varon, S. (1983). Neurotrophic activity in brain wounds of the developing rat: Correlation with implant survival in the wound cavity. *Brain Research, 267,* 47–56.

McKinlay, W., & Brooks, D. (1984). Methodological problems in assessing psychosocial recovery following head injury. *Journal of Clinical Neuropsychology, 6,* 87–99.

McKinney, J., & Haskins, R. (1980). Cognitive training and the development of problem solving strategies. *Exceptional Education Quarterly, 1,* 41–52.

Mecacci, L. (1979). *Brain and history: The relationship between neurophysiology and psychology in Soviet research.* New York: Brunner/Mazel.

Meichenbaum, D. (1973). Cognitive factors in behavior modification: Modifying what clients say to themselves. In C. Franks & G. Wilson (Eds.), *Annual review of behavior therapy: Theory and practice.* New York: Brunner/Mazel.

Meichenbaum, D. (1974). Self-instructional strategy training: A cognitive prosthesis for the aged. *Human Development, 17,* 259–272.

Meichenbaum, D., & Goodman, J. (1971). Training impulsive children to talk to themselves: A means of developing self-control. *Journal of Abnormal Psychology, 77,* 115–126.

Meyerson, L., & Kerr, N. (1979). Research strategies for meaningful rehabilitation research. *Rehabilitation Psychology, 26,* 228–238.

Mikula, J. (1983, February). *A computerized approach to training visual attention and visual imagery in closed head injury.* Paper presented at the 11th annual meeting of the International Neuropsychological Society, Mexico City.

Miller, E. (1980). The training characteristics of severely head injured patients: A preliminary study. *Journal of Neurology, Neurosurgery, and Psychiatry, 43,* 525–528.

Miller, S., Sabatino, D., & Miller, T. (1977). Influence of training in visual perceptual discrimination on drawings by children. *Perceptual and Motor Skills, 44,* 479–487.

Mills, E., & Thompson, M. (1978). Economic costs of stroke in Massachusetts. *New England Journal of Medicine, 299,* 415–418.

Monakow, C. von. (1969). *Diaschisis.* In K. Pribram (Ed.), *Brain and behavior 1. Mood, states and mind* (pp. 27–37). Baltimore: Penguin.

Moyer, S. (1979). Rehabilitation of alexia: A case study. *Cortex, 15,* 139–144.

Musante, S. (1983). Issues relevant to the vocational evaluation of the traumatically head injured client. *Vocational Evaluation and Work Adjustment Bulletin, 16*(2), 45–49.

Myers, P., & Hammill, D. (1976). *Methods for learning disorders.* New York: Wiley.

National Center for Health Statistics. (1977). *Profile of chronic illness in nursing homes U.S.* August 1968–April, 1974. Vital and Health Statistics, Series 13, No. 29, Hyattsville, MD. USDHEW, December.

New York University, Institute of Rehabilitation Medicine. (1974). *Studies in cognition and rehabilitation in hemiplegia* (Rehabilitation Monograph No. 50). New York: NYUIRM.

New York University, Institute of Rehabilitation Medicine. (1978). *Working approaches to remediation of cognitive deficits in brain damaged persons* (Supplement to the 6th Annual Workshop for Rehabilitation Professionals). New York: NYUIRM.

New York University, Institute of Rehabilitation Medicine. (1979). *Working approaches to remediation of cognitive deficits in brain damaged persons* (Supplement to the 7th Annual Workshop for Rehabilitation Professionals). New York: NYUIRM.

New York University, Institute of Rehabilitation Medicine. (1980a). *Working approaches to remediation of cognitive deficits in brain damaged persons* (Supplement to the 8th Annual Workshop for Rehabilitation Professionals). New York: NYUIRM.

New York University, Institute of Rehabilitation Medicine. (1980b). *Methods for the evaluation and treatment of visual perceptual difficulties in right brain damaged individuals* (Supplement to the 8th Annual Workshop for Rehabilitation Professionals). New York: NYUIRM.

New York University, Institute of Rehabilitation Medicine. (1981). *Working approaches to remediation of cognitive deficits in brain damaged persons* (Supplement to the 9th Annual Workshop for Rehabilitation Professionals). New York: NYUIRM.

New York University, Institute of Rehabilitation Medicine. (1982). *Working approaches to remediation of cognitive deficits in brain damaged persons* (Supplement to the 10th Annual Workshop for Rehabilitation Professionals). New York: NYUIRM.

New York University, Institute of Rehabilitation Medicine. (1983). *Working approaches to remediation of cognitive deficits in brain damaged persons* (Supplement to the 11th Annual Workshop for Rehabilitation Professionals). New York: NYUIRM.

Newcombe, F. (1982). The psychological consequences of closed head injury: Assessment and rehabilitation. *Injury: The British Journal of Accident Surgery, 14,* 111–136.

Oddy, M., Humphrey, M., & Uttley, D. (1978). Subjective impairment and social recovery after closed head injury. *Journal of Neurology, Neurosurgery, and Psychiatry, 41,* 611–616.

Overgaard, J., Mosdal, C., & Tweed, W. (1981). Cerebral circulation after head injury, part 3: Does reduced regional cerebral blood flow determine recovery of brain function after blunt head injury? *Journal of Neurosurgery, 55,* 63–74.

Parente, F., & Anderson, J. (1983). Techniques for improving cognitive rehabilitation: Teaching organization and encoding skills. *Cognitive Rehabilitation, 1*(4), 20–22.

Patten, B. (1972). The ancient art of memory. *Archives of Neurology, 26,* 25–31.

Pavlov, I. (1966). An attempt of a physiologist to digress into the domain of psychiatry. In M. Kaplan (Ed.), *Essential works of Pavlov* (pp. 360–366). New York: Bantam Books.

Peterson, L., & Peterson, M. (1959). Short term retention of individual verbal items. *Journal of Experimental Psychology, 58,* 193–198.

Piasetsky, E. (1982). The relevance of brain–behavior relationships for rehabilitation. In L. Trexler (Ed.), *Cognitive rehabilitation: Conceptualization and intervention.* New York: Plenum Press.

Poon, L., Fozard, J., & Treat, N. (1978). From clinical and research findings on memory to intervention programs. *Experimental Aging Research, 4,* 235–253.

Powell, G. (1981). *Brain function therapy.* London: Gower.

Robinson, E. (1970). *Effective study.* New York: Harper & Row.

Rosenbaum, M., Lipsitz, N., Abraham, J., & Najenson, T. (1978). A description of an intensive treatment project for the rehabilitation of severely brain injured soldiers. *Scandinavian Journal of Rehabilitation Medicine, 10,* 1–6.

Rosenbaum, M., & Najenson, T. (1976). Changes in life patterns and symptoms of low mood as reported by wives of severely brain injured soldiers. *Journal of Consulting and Clinical Psychology, 44,* 881–888.

Rusch, M., Grunert, B., Erdmann, B., & Lynch, N. (1980). Cognitive retraining of brain injured adults in outpatient rehabilitation. *Archives of Physical Medicine and Rehabilitation, 61,* 472.

Rusk, H., Block, J., & Lowman, E. (1969). Rehabilitation following traumatic brain damage: Immediate and long term follow-up results in 127 cases. *Medical Clinics of North America, 53,* 677–684.

Sabel, B., Slavin, M., & Stein, D. (1984). G_{M1} ganglioside treatment facilitates behavioral recovery from bilateral brain damage. *Science, 225,* 340–341.

Sanders, J., Stern, H., Smith, M., & Sanders, R. (1975). Modification of concept identification performance in older adults. *Developmental Psychology, 11,* 824–829.

Sanders, R., & Sanders, J. (1978). Long-term durability and transfer of enhanced conceptual performance in the elderly. *Journal of Gerontology, 33,* 408–412.

Sarno, M., & Levita, E. (1979). Recovery of treated aphasia in the first year post-stroke. *Stroke, 10,* 663–670.

Siegel, M., & Siegel, D. (1976). Improving memory for color. *Bulletin of the Psychonomic Society, 7,* 461–464.

Sivak, M., Hill, C., Henson, D., Butler, B., Silber, S., & Olson, P. (1985). Improved driving performance following perceptual training of persons with brain damage. *Archives of Physical Medicine and Rehabilitation, 65,* 163–167.

Sivak, M., Olson, P., Kewman, D., Won, H., & Henson, D. (1981). Driving and perceptual/cognitive skills: Behavioral consequences of brain damage. *Archives of Physical Medicine and Rehabilitation, 62,* 476–483.

Smith, A. (1974). Dominant and nondominant hemispherectomy. In M. Kinsbourne & W. Smith (Eds.), *Hemispheric disconnection and cerebral function* (pp. 5–33). Springfield, IL: Charles C Thomas.

Sparks, R., Helm, N., & Albert, M. (1974). Aphasia rehabilitation resulting from Melodic Intonation Therapy. *Cortex, 10,* 303–316.

Stanton, K., Pepping, M., Brockway, J., Bliss, L., Frankel, D., & Waggener, S. (1983). Wheelchair transfer training for right cerebral dysfunctions: An interdisciplinary approach. *Archives of Physical Medicine and Rehabilitation, 64,* 276–280.

Stern, P., McDowell, F., Miller, J., & Robinson, M. (1970). Effects of facilitation exercise techniques in stroke rehabilitation. *Archives of Physical Medicine and Rehabilitation, 51,* 526–531.

Steward, O., Cotman, C., & Lynch, G. (1976). A quantitative autoradiographic and electrophysiological study of the reinervation of the dentate gyrus by the contralateral entorhinal cortex following ipsilateral entorhinal lesions. *Brain Research, 114,* 181–200.

Sullivan, M., & Kommers, M. (1977). *Rationale for adult aphasia therapy.* Omaha: University of Nebraska Press.

Symonds, C. (1937). Mental disorders following head injuries. *Proceedings of the Royal Society of Medicine, 30,* 1081–1094.

Thomsen, I. (1981). Neuropsychological treatment and longtime follow-up in an aphasic patient with very severe head trauma. *Journal of Clinical Neuropsychology, 3,* 43–51.

Tolonen, U. (1981). Quantitive ^{99m}Technetium cerebral circulation time in brain infarction. *Acta Neurologica Scandinavia, 64,* 337–352.

Treat, N., Poon, L., Fozard, J., & Popkin, S. (1978). Toward applying cognitive skill training to memory problems. *Experimental Aging Research, 4,* 305–319.

Treiber, F., & Lahey, B. (1983). Toward a behavioral model of academic remediation with learning disabled children. *Journal of Learning Disabilities, 16,* 111–116.

Tucker, D. (1981). Lateral brain function, emotion, and conceptualization. *Psychological Bulletin, 89,* 19–46.

Valverde, F. (1971). Rate and extent of recovery from dark rearing in the visual cortex of the mouse. *Brain Research, 33,* 1–11.

Vecht, C., Woerkom, I., Tellhen, A., & Minderhoud, J. (1975). Homovanillic acid and 5-hydroxyindole-acetic acid cerebrospinal fluid levels. *Archives of Neurology, 32,* 792–797.

Vecht, C., Woerkom, I., Tellhen, A., & Minderhoud, J. (1976). On the nature of brain stem disorders in severe head injured patients: I. Changes in cerebral neurotransmitter metabolism. *Acta Neurochirurgica, 32,* 23–35.

Wall, P. (1980). Mechanisms of plasticity of connection following damage in adult mammalian nervous systems. In P. Bach-y-Rita (Ed.), *Recovery of function: Theoretical considerations for brain injury rehabilitation* (pp. 91–105). Baltimore: Park Press.

Wall, P., & Egger, M. (1971). Formation of new connections in adult rat brains after partial deafferentation. *Nature, 232,* 542–545.

Webster, J., Hammer, D., & Moss, R. (1980, August). Functional analysis of brain disorder: A model for assessment and rehabilitation. Symposium presentation at the 14th annual convention of the Association for the Advancement of Behavior Therapy, New York.

Webster, J., Jones, S., Blanton, P., Gross, R., Beissel, G., & Wofford, J. (1984). Visual scanning training with stroke patients. *Behavior Therapy, 15,* 129–143.

Webster, J., McCaffrey, R., & Scott, R. (1986). Single case design for neuropsychology. In D. Wedding, A. Horton, & J. Webster (Eds.), *The neuropsychology handbook: Behavioral and clinical perspectives.* New York: Springer Publishing Co.

Webster, J., & Scott, R. (1983). The effects of self-instructional training on attentional deficits following head injury. *Clinical Neuropsychology, 5,* 69–74.

Wechsler, F. (1983, October). The work environment as a cognitive retraining laboratory. Paper presented at the meeting of the National Academy of Neuropsychologists, Houston, TX.

Weddell, R., Oddy, M., & Jenkins, D. (1980). Social adjustment after rehabilitation: A two year follow-up of patients with severe head injury. *Psychological Medicine, 10,* 257–263.

Wedding, D. (1986). Neurological disorders. In D. Wedding, A. Horton, & J. Webster (Eds.), *The neuropsychology handbook: Behavioral and clinical perspectives.* New York: Springer Publishing Co.

Weinberg, J., Diller, L., Gordon, W., Gerstman, L., Lieberman, A., Lakin, P., Hodges, G., & Ezrachi, O. (1977). Visual scanning training effect on reading-related tasks in acquired right brain damage. *Archives of Physical Medicine and Rehabilitation, 58,* 479–486.

Weinberg, J., Diller, L., Gordon, W., Gerstman, L., Lieberman, A., Lakin, P., Hodges, G., & Ezrachi, O. (1979). Training sensory awareness and spatial organization in people with right brain damage. *Archives of Physical Medicine and Rehabilitation, 60,* 491–496.

Weinberg, J., Piasetsky, E., Diller, L., & Gordon, W. (1982). Treating perceptual organization deficits in nonneglecting RBD stroke patients. *Journal of Clinical Neuropsychology, 4,* 59–75.

Weinfeld, F. D. (ed.) (1981). National survey of stroke. *Stroke, 12,* (Suppl. #1), *i*-1-91.

Wilson, B. (1982). Success and failure in memory training following cerebral vascular accident. *Cortex, 18,* 581–594.

Wilson, R., Levey, W., & Steward, O. (1979). Functional effects of lesion-induced plasticity: Long-term potentiation in normal and lesion-induced temporo dentate connections. *Brain Research, 176,* 65–78.

Woerkom, T. van, Minderhoud, J., Gottschal, T., & Nicolai, G. (1982). Neurotransmitters in the treatment of patients with severe head injuries. *European Neurology, 21,* 227–234.

Woerkom, T. van, Teelken, A. van, & Minderhoud, J. (1977). Difference in neurotransmitter metabolism in frontotemporal-lobe contusion and diffuse cerebral contusion. *Lancet, i,* 812–813.

Woolsey, T. (1978). Lesion experiments: Some anatomical considerations. In S. Finger (Ed.), *Recovery from brain damage: Research and theory* (pp. 71–89). New York: Plenum Press.

Young, G., Collins, D., & Hren, M. (1983). Effects of pairing scanning training with block design training in the remediation of perceptual problems in left hemiplegics. *Journal of Clinical Neuropsychology, 5,* 201–212.

Zarit, S., Cole, K., & Guider, R. (1981). Memory training strategies and subjective complaints of memory in the aged. *The Gerontologist, 21,* 158–164.

Zarit, S., Gallagher, D., & Kramer, N. (1981). Memory training in the community aged: Effects on depression, memory complaint, and memory performance. *Educational Gerontology, 6,* 11–27.

Zihl, J. (1980). "Blindsight": Improvement of visually guided eye movements by systematic practice in patients with cerebral blindness. *Neuropsychologia, 18,* 71–77.

Zimmer, J., & Hjorth-Simonsen, A. (1975). Crossed pathways from the entorhinal area to the fascia dientata II. Provokable in rats. *Journal of Comparative Neurology, 161,* 71–102.

12
Family Therapy Issues in Neuropsychology*

Mitchell Rosenthal
and
Cheri Geckler

The neurobehavioral consequences of brain damage frequently result in major changes in life style for both the patient and the entire family unit. Cognitive and behavioral changes necessarily place pressures on the family to accommodate, in effect creating a crisis situation and the need for reorganization. A family refusing to acknowledge the presence of any real or permanent change in one of its members, through denial, only exacerbates the stresses created by the realities of living with a brain-damaged family member (Romano, 1974; Lezak, 1978; Bond, 1983). Historically, clinicians tended to focus on physical aspects of disability, thereby relegating psychosocial and family aspects to a status of lower priority. In the past decade, however, the latter have been recognized for their importance in facilitating progress in rehabilitation, thereby promoting attempts to understand the multidimensional character of family support networks.

Research supporting the beneficial effects of family involvement has evolved from both psychiatric and a variety of medical subspecialties. Investigating renal disease, Ebra (1975) reported that the structure and synchrony of family relationships may determine the outcome of rehabilitation. Similarly, Litman (1966) found that family support, defined as encouragement, acceptance, and active interest, was significantly related to a patient's progress during

*Portions of this chapter were included in an earlier work by the senior author, "Strategies for Intervention with Families of Brain Injured Patients." In B. Edelstein & E. Couture, *Behavioral Assessment and Rehabilitation of the Traumatically Brain-Damaged*. New York: Plenum Press. Reprinted with permission of the Publisher.

orthopedic rehabilitation. Additional reports from other diagnostic groups, such as progressive dementia (Mace & Rabins, 1982), schizophrenia (Falloon, Boyd, McGill, Razani, Moss, & Gilderman, 1982) and aphasic disorders (Turnblom & Myers, 1952) attest to the positive influence that family members may have on the rehabilitation process.

To understand how best to mobilize family support, it is important to understand both the impact of brain injury on a family member and the framework that makes a family a functional unit. With that knowledge base, the need for therapeutic intervention can be assessed and the type of intervention strategy can be determined.

IMPACT OF BRAIN INJURY

The disruptive effect of brain injury on family functioning has been widely documented. As noted by Blayzk (1983), the crisis associated with head injury begins almost immediately posttrauma. Confronted with the shocking disparity of a family member who was healthy one minute and is seemingly lifeless the next, numerous emotions are necessarily generated; denial is most frequently pivotal, especially in the early stages (Romano, 1974). Combined in varying degrees with feelings of shock, incomprehension, anger, guilt, and grief, both individual and family equilibrium fall vulnerable to disruption (Bruhn, 1977; Shontz, 1978). In a study of 13 families having a brain-injured member, Romano (1974) reported denial, manifested in various forms, as the most enduring response; it was found that families who failed to progress as expected through the stages frequently associated with loss (denial, anger, bargaining, depression, and, finally, acceptance) (Kübler-Ross, 1969) persisted with denial. Whether seen in terms of a "sleeping beauty" fantasy (i.e., the belief that one day the patient will awaken and be his former self) or in terms of refusals to acknowledge prominent physical, mental, and behavioral changes, such coping strategies eventuate in family difficulties. Needs of the injured remain unmet as members strive toward homeostasis, rejecting demands to accommodate to reality.

A family faced with significant and often confusing changes in one of its members must somehow accommodate if the family is to survive as a cohesive structure. Retaining expectations of premorbid functional levels creates one form of stress that may have serious repercussions on family dynamics (Lezak, 1978). Several studies have focused specifically on identifying the various other sources of family stress. Panting and Merry (1972) found a lack of information concerning prognosis, insufficient support, and uncertainty about what to prepare for as key contributors to family stress. Furthermore, Bond (1972) reports from a study of 52 patients with severe brain injury that mental rather than physical deficits were more closely associated with adverse effects upon family cohesion. Adding to the list, Malone (1977) found role changes particularly problematic for families. Secondary difficulties stemmed from guilt, financial pressures, and both health and disciplinary problems. The last issue is particularly relevant because of its frequent association with reports of personality and behavioral changes resulting from brain injury (Bond, 1983; Lezak, 1978). Health and disciplinary problems have repeatedly been indicated as precipitating the greatest burden on family members (McKinlay, Brooks, Bond, Martinage, & Marshall, 1981; Oddy, Humphrey, & Uttley, 1978). An additional psychosocial factor which is affected by brain injury is social involvement. Rosenbaum and Najensen (1976) studied the reactions of wives of brain-injured Israeli soldiers and found that they had more restricted social lives than either the wives of males with spinal cord injuries or of control subjects.

In a similar vein, rapid advances in the acute neurosurgical management of head-injured adults during the past decade have given rise to an ever-increasing number of survivors of severe brain injury. However, unlike other severely disabled adults (e.g., those with spinal cord injuries), the brain-injured adult usually displays a variety of cognitive and behavioral deficits that adversely affect the patient's ability to function effectively within the community and family systems. Such deficits are often of indefinite duration and can result in prolonged dependence on family members. This state of dependence is frequently linked to the inability of the head-injured adult to achieve an adequate measure of social and vocational rehabilitation.

Predominant in research directed toward the nature and effects of traumatic brain injury have been findings that describe the specific medical, functional, and vocational outcomes that follow brain damage (Evans, Bull, Devenport, Hall, Jones, Middleton, Russell, Stichburg, & Whitehead, 1976; Jennett & Teasdale, 1976; Levine & Grossman, 1978; Najensen, Mendelson, Schechter, David, Mintz, & Grosswasser, 1974). However, little attention has been directed to the impact of the disability upon the family system and toward identifying potential strategies for minimizing family stress and maximizing family adaptation. As a result, even the most heroic of early neurosurgical efforts and subsequent physical rehabilitation may be of little consequence if the patient cannot be successfully integrated into the family unit and regain a useful function within society.

The uncertain hope for recovery, combined with the burdensome reality of caring for a head-injured person, results in an almost continual state of stress and disequilibrium. Feelings of burden, isolation, and anger are at times universal among family members. Over a period of time, unless the family system restructures itself to accommodate to these demands, some degree of disintegration will result.

This brief review suggests that head injury can result in significant problems for the families of head-injured adults and that methods for managing these problems need to be developed to optimize the rehabilitation of these patients.

THEORETICAL FRAMEWORK

Family, by definition, is more than a "simple static collection of people with different roles" (Wiley, 1983, p. 271). A family is a multidimensional system in which members develop patterns for relating to one another and learn to assume roles to maintain the whole as a functional unit. The essential purposes of a family are twofold: to guide and protect members through the process of growth and selectively to transmit cultural values and orientations. Its organization, which acts to influence and qualify both the experiences of members and resultant interpretation of self as an individual member of society, is crucial. Organization is dependent upon some degree of coordination among those participating in the unit. Jackson (1965) describes the family as a rule-governed system. Members thus interact in an organized, repetitive manner that becomes a pattern or governing principle of family life. In this way, an individual learns to communicate, interact with, and relate to others both within and outside the family. As noted by Minuchin (1974), mutual expectations develop among family members, thus further regulating and validating particular behaviors or communications.

By conceptualizing the family in these terms, general systems theory, as described by Bertalanaffy (1969), is readily applicable: "every organism is a system, a dynamic ordering of parts and processes that interact reciprocally." The family, too, is a system comprised of units, organized by rules, and made dynamic by transactional patterns between members and exchanges beyond. According to Satir (1971), an open system will enhance growth. Flexibility of rules or norms is one defining characteristic, operationalized by accommodations to individual needs.

A closer look at family structure reveals that within the broad system exist subsystems made distinct by boundaries and unique by separate goals, role functions, and responsibilities. Each member of the family is assigned a particular set of roles or task functions necessary to maintain the unit. For example, the father may be recognized as the principal wage earner, arbiter of conflicts, and decision maker. He is also a member of several distinct subsystems, including the marital dyad and father–son and father–daughter units. Each of these subsystems has a unique, dynamic character. For example, the marital dyad may involve the goals of mutual support and the responsibility for faithfulness and continued financial security. The father–child system may include the goal of guidance, the role of nurturance, and the responsibility for security. Each family member belongs to a number of subsystems in which unique roles are assigned, alliances formed, and relative status within the system established. Boundaries are crucial dividers that protect the integrity of the subsystem network. Minuchin (1974) observes that unless boundaries are sufficiently well defined and balanced through flexibility, a family will not function properly. In an enmeshed system, behavior or stress in one area immediately reverberates across boundaries, interfering with other subsystems. Equally dysfunctional is the disengaged system where boundaries are excessively rigid, thereby limiting communication among members. Thus boundaries must be firm yet sufficiently flexible to permit realignment with changing circumstances. A family must maintain continuity yet at the same time accommodate to change. To control this process adequately, a broad range of transactional patterns must be available, as well as the flexibility to mobilize them when necessary (Minuchin, 1974).

A family lacking the means to contend with change will become dysfunctional. In this sense, rules may be excessively rigid, role positions fixed, and the ability to shift into alternative patterns of interacting limited (Satir, 1971). Rather than accommodating to altered demands, either within or outside the system, attention is focused on maintaining the status quo. Under these circumstances the family as a dynamic system will fail in its purpose to promote individual growth and may begin to disintegrate or foster a series of dysfunctional, symptomatic behaviors.

Brain injury of a family member necessarily demands some realignment. As mentioned above, sudden onset and the frequently dramatic changes that occur in cognitive and personality functioning elicit a range of responses from the family. Denial may superficially predominate, yet an undercurrent of stress is likely to build. Significant stress among family members has been repeatedly observed as professional medical involvement declines, the recovery rate plateaus, and the family is confronted daily with the needs and demands of the injured person. It is at this point that flexible transactional patterns and an open family system are critical. Importantly, this event has an equally strong potential to elicit family growth as family dissolution. Roles assumed by various members may change, as well as status and responsibility levels. The responsible, supportive, and financially resourceful father–husband may no longer be able to assume his prior status, thereby necessitating accommodations within several family subsystems. The type of counseling or therapeutic intervention must be assessed according to the system's precrisis functional abilities. For some the goal will be simply to provide as much descriptive and prognostic information as is available. For other families, already dysfunctional, the goal of therapy necessarily involves opening a closed system by either strengthening or loosening subsystem boundaries or facilitating role change by restructuring the way family members perceive one another's capabilities. By altering transactional patterns to conform more closely with a change in context and an uncertain future, the reorganized system will have achieved a greater level of complexity and adaptive capacity. This is particularly crucial for maximizing the injured person's functional recovery.

SIGNIFICANT COGNITIVE AND BEHAVIORAL DEFICITS AFFECTING FAMILY FUNCTIONING

To intervene successfully with the families of the brain injured, it is critical initially to identify the nature and variety of cognitive and behavioral deficits that can create stress and disrupt the family system. The following listing is not all-inclusive; rather, it is a brief description of selected deficits and issues that can create maladaptive interactions within the family system.

Presence of Cognitive Deficits

Following neurologic insult, cognitive deficits tend to persist for an indefinite time. Although significant recovery of formal intellectual function may be observed, residual problems in maintaining attention, processing complex information, storing and retrieving information, and problem solving are often present and present significant obstacles to the patient and family. In some cases, there is a generalized deficit in intellectual functioning. In the case of Alzheimer's disease, one may find a disorientation to surroundings and familiar faces, which can be devastating to family members. After the patient's discharge from the hospital, as in the case of a person with severe cognitive deficits following a stroke, families must often face the reality of providing 24-hour supervision because of the patient's inability to be left alone.

Disorders of Communication

In the case of brain injury, communication disorders, including various forms of aphasia, dysarthria, and apraxia, can impair the patient's ability to cope and communicate. Impaired communication skills can adversely affect a person's ability to function independently in activities of daily living or in vocational pursuits and thus create a greater burden for significant others.

Emotional Regression

As Symonds (1937) noted in his discussion of brain-injured adults, the patient is often observed to be "less of a man and more of a child." It is frequently the case that the newly brain-injured adult demonstrates behavior patterns reminiscent of childhood and adolescence. The patient may display childlike dependency, crave constant attention, display inappropriate affect, or engage in violent temper tantrums. The parent or spouse of the patient may be dismayed and confused by this behavior and express confusion as to the appropriate methods of managing it. Often, significant others may unwittingly contribute to the maintenance of these behaviors by providing attention and positive reinforcement when they occur.

Frontal Lobe Behavior

Often a patient with brain injury displays a constellation of behavior identified as a "frontal lobe syndrome." As described by Freedman, Kaplan, and Sadock (1975, pp. 218–219), damage to the frontal lobes may result in a variety of behaviors including aspontaneity, lethargy, flat or dulled affect, irritability, loss of initiative, and lack of goal-directedness. In addition, there may be a loosening of inhibitions, lack of regard for social graces and moral standards, impaired ability to abstract, and inappropriate sexual behavior.

Withdrawal from Social Contacts

The patient with severe brain injury suffers a severe blow to his or her self-esteem on account of apparent physical or mental deficits, as well as a perceived loss of self-worth and identity as a productive, well-functioning, competent individual. Usually, feelings of decreased self-esteem are reinforced by the loss of peer contact and social relationships (which often occurs within 3 to 6 months after return to the community). Brain-injured adults perceive themselves as different, handicapped, brain damaged, and unattractive and tend to isolate themselves or be isolated from their peer groups in the community.

Inappropriate Social Behavior

As mentioned earlier, the behavior of the brain-injured adult often resembles that of a young child or adolescent. In observing the behavioral patterns of brain-injured adults, one notes that such patients are unaware of the consequences and implications of their behavior. Often the patient engages in verbal or motor perseveration, pathological laughter, or inappropriate sexual behavior. The presence of this constellation of behaviors is a source of embarrassment and frustration for the family. Inappropriate sexual behavior is especially troublesome for families who are confused as to its etiology (functional or organic) and uncertain as to the best method of managing it.

Depression

Often the recovery of the brain-injured adult is accompanied by a gradually progressive awareness of the multifaceted loss in physical and mental functioning imposed by the injury. Despite the restoration of mobility skills, the patient may be less able to participate in strenuous physical exercise (e.g., athletic activities) or routine activities (e.g., walking to the bathroom). Although the person may perform most self-care activities independently, residual perceptual-motor problems can preclude the resumption of driving an automobile. Often the injury results in changes in appearance, such as scars and cranial defects, that can greatly alter body image and self-concept. Due to the persistence of cognitive deficits such as memory impairment and a slower rate of information processing, the patient may have an acquired learning disability that will interfere with the successful resumption of vocational activities or academic pursuits.

The result of this recognition of loss in psychosocial function and rewarding activities is frequently an onset of depression. Depression may be observed in the form of decreased activity level, self-derogation, negative affect, feelings of worthlessness, and occasionally suicidal ideation. The brain-injured person may say "I wish I were still in a coma" or "Why did they save my life if there's nothing for me." In a patient with a cerebrovascular accident, the presence of organically based emotional lability may further complicate the clinical picture. The presence of depression may have a major impact upon the family, who feel impotent and frustrated. The brain-injured person who experiences depression is likely to be more passive, dependent, and less productive, thus imposing a greater burder on family members, who feel a sense of responsibility for maintaining the emotional well-being of their loved ones.

Inability to Resume Premorbid Role Within the Family

Because of such deficits, the brain-injured adult is usually prevented from resuming premorbid roles within the family. In the marital relationship, it is often observed that the brain-injured husband who was formerly the assertive partner is now the passive one. Whereas the brain-injured patient may have been a "breadwinner," the family may now be dependent on federal and state agencies for financial support.

Frequently, siblings experience guilt feelings about their brain-injured relative and will report dismay at the changes in role relationships that occur. The likelihood of alterations in role relationships is greatly enhanced when the patient sustains significant cognitive and behavioral deficits. The observed changes in the patient can be a stimulus for marital discord. Whereas, in the initial six to twelve months postinjury the spouse may be quite willing and able to accept these changes, with the realization that the partner "may never be the same" comes an overwhelming stress on the spouse's coping mechanisms. The recognition that known mental changes may be permanent is extremely difficult for parents to recognize and accept.

The cognitive and behavioral deficits described represent a sampling rather than an exhaustive listing of the potential problems of the brain-injured adult that can impair the functioning of the family unit. It is noteworthy that the impact of these deficits is rarely experienced by the patient or family unit until discharge from the rehabilitation hospital into the community. At that point, however, contact with the home health care team has probably diminished, and the family feels alone when dealing with these overwhelming problems. Families may be reluctant to seek out appropriate professional help. It is therefore imperative that health care professionals anticipate family distress and establish the appropriate mechanisms for providing family support prior to the patient's discharge from the hospital.

ASSESSING THE NEED FOR FAMILY INTERVENTION

Just as early neurological diagnosis and surgical intervention is often necessary to save the life of the brain-injured patient, so is early assessment of the need for intervention and direction of the appropriate intervention technique often necessary to preserve a healthy family unit. The diagnostic process may be viewed as consisting of at least three major components: (1) analyzing the premorbid history of patient and family, (2) identifying the severity and potential duration of mental and physical deficits, and (3) understanding "signals" from the family that would appear to reflect the need for intervention.

Analyzing Premorbid History

The complexity of the process of rehabilitation of the brain-injured adult is partly attributable to the uniqueness of each patient and family. In the case of traumatic brain injury, it has often been observed that the head-injured population seems to consist of a significant percentage of young people with a history of antisocial behavior or impulse-control problems. It is not surprising that excessive alcohol intake is correlated with the occurrence of brain injury. In other cases, drug intake may be a contributing factor to the events surrounding a traumatic brain injury. By interviewing family members or significant others, it is often possible to obtain a detailed (although not completely objective) picture of both patient and family prior to the injury. Important components of this history might include a description of intellectual and academic function; peer, marital, and family relationships; vocational history; avocational activities; and antisocial or unusual behavioral problems. Though less sophisticated and accurate than an x-ray or CT scan, the resulting profile provides a necessary baseline for the assessment of the patient and family.

It is often the case that a strong correlation exists between a newly disabled person's premorbid history and level of postmorbid adjustment. Therefore, the 19-year-old head-injured victim who had a poor work history, impaired peer relationships, and had shown frequent antisocial or rebellious behavior may be prone to significant postinjury adjustment problems. Conversely, the 19-year-old who was successfully employed, had an active and rewarding social life, and had good peer and family relationships may achieve a satisfactory adjustment to the injury. Although this is an oversimplification, it is often observed in clinical practice that there is an important relationship between premorbid history and postmorbid adjustment.

In this regard, it would also be useful to understand the patient and family's ability to handle stress. Did the presence of stress stimulate an expression of aggression, avoidance, or denial? Could the patient tolerate certain stresses better than others (e.g., work vs. family)? The presence of chronic disability secondary to brain injury poses a continuous series of stresses that would greatly tax the resources of an intact (i.e., non-brain-injured) individual.

Identifying the Severity and Duration of Deficits

The ability to predict recovery of mental and physical function is still a very problematic area in brain-injury research. Although Jennett and Bond (1975) and others have developed tools, such as the Glasgow Coma and Outcome Scales, that help predict outcome, it is still difficult to specify the extent, nature, and duration of specific mental and physical deficits for any single patient. This issue is of central importance for the patient and family who are struggling to accept the permanence of the injury and plan effectively for the future.

Although physical deficits are often greatly reduced at six months postinjury, residual deficits in vision, hearing, mobility, self-care, strength, coordination, and balance may exist. The patient whose vision may be compromised as a result of the injury and prove to be insensitive to remedial measures may be greatly limited in activities of daily living (ADL) or vocational productivity, thus requiring a greater dependence on family for supervision of daily activities. Helping the patient and family acknowledge and accept these limitations can be a formidable yet critical task for the helping professional.

The prediction of residual mental sequelae is even more difficult due to a variety of factors, including a generally slower and less consistent pattern of recovery, environmental factors that may aid or adversely affect the recovery process, and problems in objectively measuring the course of recovery in such areas as memory, social skills, and personality. The family is often informed that some mental sequelae of head injury are likely to exist indefinitely. Such information is frequently by physicians and is difficult for family members to accept.

The clinical neuropsychologist or rehabilitation psychologist is often the best member of the team to address this issue. On the basis of extensive neuropsychological examination and clinical observations, the psychologist should be able to provide a detailed explanation of the nature of specific neurobehavioral deficits. The more difficult task is to provide the family with an answer as to the potential duration of these deficits and the likelihood of improvement. Given the uncertainties inherent in neurologic recovery and the lack of precision in our diagnostic instruments, it is incumbent on the psychologist to provide an educated guess as to the recovery of a selected mental function without making absolute statements. An assessment of the family's willingness to accept and utilize this information is crucial to the determination of the appropriate intervention strategy.

Understanding "Signals" from the Family

Within a rehabilitation setting, it is a rare event when the family of a patient approaches the staff to request assistance in coping with the catastrophic effects of the brain injury. Yet, if the family is to play a central role in the rehabilitation process, it is necessary that rehabilitation specialists recognize certain expressed concerns that may signal a need for family intervention. These concerns may be verbalized to any member of the rehabilitation team (i.e., physician, physical therapist, nurse), as opposed to the identified psychosocial team member (i.e., psychologist, social worker).

A frequent signal may be the expression of anxiety or fear about prognosis. Statements such as "I don't know if I can manage if he can't recover" or "Will my son ever be the same?" are indications that the family is having difficulty. Another need for family intervention may be observed when the family expresses confusion and helplessness concerning observed behavioral problems. As mentioned earlier, behavioral deficits are often upsetting and alarming to families who do not understand why the behavior is occurring. Assistance may be required to explain the nature of these deficits—their etiology and relationship to premorbid behavior—and to help the family manage their problems. Another concern expressed by families involves the change in role relationships. This is especially the case in marital relationships, where one partner may have been the dominant, assertive individual and now becomes the passive-dependent one. This is also the case where the brain-injured victim was an important figure in the life of a sibling and can now no longer be relied on for emotional support and assistance. These alterations in role relationships are likely to create disruptions in family functioning. Often, as discharge from the inpatient rehabilitation setting approaches, there is a sudden realization by family members as to the level of emotional/physical dependency demanded by the injured relative. Although families are often quite willing and able to assume a great burden of responsibility and care, the recognition of the scope of the problem is often overwhelming. A family member frequently has to relinquish a job, hire home health aides, or adopt a much more restricted life style than in the past. A parent may become consumed with the burden of care and thus lose perspective on his or her own needs. Such a situation can create tension and stress within the family system.

High-Risk Families

Certain patients and families may be considered in greatest need for family intervention due to high-risk factors. The term *high-risk* reflects the greater probability that such families would become disrupted by the advent of the brain injury and therefore be less equipped to facilitate the recovery process.

The first category of high-risk families would be those with a premorbid history of dysfunction or with evidence of maladaptive interaction patterns. Families with a history of alcoholism, marital discord, or antisocial behavior would be apt to be overwhelmed by the burden of adjusting to the presence of a brain-injured relative. Also included within this category would be patients whose premorbid behavior tended to be impulsive, reckless, and reflective of poor social judgment. The presence of brain injury has often been observed to intensify these maladaptive behaviors due to the disinhibition caused by many brain injuries.

Another group of high-risk families are those in which the patient demonstrates severe, chronic cognitive and/or behavioral deficits. For example, a patient with a frontal lobe injury is likely to be perceived as an entirely different individual, lacking in drive, affect, and initiative. The presence of such behaviors is likely to disrupt the day-to-day functioning of the family unit greatly. A patient with severe cognitive deficits, such as memory loss, is likely to require intensive assistance and supervision in everyday activities. A point may be reached where the constant care and emotional support required cannot be provided consistently or effectively. Such a family is clearly in need of intervention.

Finally, those families in which denial is utilized for a prolonged period have great difficulty in realistically planning for the future. In such cases, the inability to accept the permanence of the deficit may cause family members to develop unrealistic expectations of their relative, unwittingly creating additional frustration and unrewarding experiences. This problem is illustrated by families who insist that their brain-injured relative is capable of returning to work or school when in fact the reverse is often the case. Feelings of failure and pessimism are felt by the patient when such return to work or school is premature and inappropriate.

TYPE OF FAMILY INTERVENTION TECHNIQUES

Four categories of family intervention strategies may be proposed. These include (1) patient-family education, (2) family counseling, (3) family therapy, and (4) family support groups.

Patient-Family Education

Recently, many rehabilitation centers have developed group programs for patient-family education. These sessions are designed to provide basic information about the nature of brain injury and its consequences and to help families gain a greater understanding and acceptance of the disability. These are usually held at the rehabilitation facility during the evening hours (to allow for maximal attendance by family members). The sessions usually comprise a series of 1- to 2-hour meetings covering a wide range of topics. A model for patient-family education was developed by Diehl (1978) and her colleagues at the Medical College of Virginia. In this program, patients with brain injury (e.g., stroke and head injury) and their families attend 10 sessions over a period of 5 weeks. The format is a combined lecture-discussion approach, with actual demonstrations of techniques and procedures, as well as audiovisual aids and handout materials. During these sessions, a wide variety of topics is presented and discussed, including the nature of brain injury, the rehabilitation process, the recovery process, psychosocial deficits, mobility skills, perceptual-motor deficits, and community resources. Because the material is presented in a structured educational format, patients and families react positively to the program and feel comfortable in sharing their own frustrations and experiences. Although the group is primarily educational in design and focus, peer support is a natural byproduct. This method of intervention has been well-received and is likely to benefit most families with the early stages of recovery from brain injury.

Family Counseling

Another level of intervention often practiced by rehabilitation professionals is family counseling. This type of intervention is often directed toward the family of the brain-injured patient. The purpose of family counseling is to assist the family in dealing with their overwhelming feelings of loss and helplessness and to help the family in understanding and accepting the disability and its potential consequences. (e.g., increased dependence, impaired cognitive and behavioral functioning, decreased physical abilities). Often, this intervention is initiated by the psychosocial member of the rehabilitation team. It is useful to commence family counseling sessions within the inpatient rehabilitation program, although precise timing will vary according to the needs and desires of the individual family.

In these sessions, family members (often the parents or spouses of victims) are given the opportunity to express their feelings of guilt, anguish, anger, sadness, and loss. The family is given the opportunity to ask questions about the nature of the disability, prognosis, and level of care that may be required. An additional goal of family counseling is to provide much-needed emotional support. Families of individuals who experience head injury and subsequent prolonged periods of hospitalization are often taxed to the limit of their adaptive resources. Seemingly endless visits to the hospital may necessitate changes in family work schedules, impose strain on marital and parent-child relationships, and create physical stresses that may lead to psychosomatic illnesses. Often, perceived progress is painstakingly slow and the ultimate goal of restoration of premorbid function appears to be an impossible dream. As discharge approaches, families become apprehensive since they have been given an implicit or explicit message that a plateau has been reached. During the transition from hospital to community, the counselor can play a key role in helping the family anticipate future problems and be more psychologically and physically prepared to assume the burden of care. Frequently, the patient and family may maintain unrealistic expectations that restoration of function will magically occur once the patient can return home. To prevent an experience of overwhelming disappointment and frustration, the counselor can gently prepare the family for the realities of life with a brain-injured relative and maintain close communication to provide the additional support so often needed but rarely requested.

Case History

The case of J. G. exemplifies typical issues that arise in family counseling. J. G., a 23-year-old unmarried male, was injured in a collision in a car driven by his roommate on the way home from a party. J. G. sustained a severe brain injury resulting in 4 weeks of coma and diffuse brain damage; his roommate also sustained a severe brain injury. After 3 months of hospitalization, the patient was independent in ADL and mobility skills but continued to experience mild residual deficits in cognitive functioning, dysarthria, impaired coordination, decreased motor speed, periodic violent outbursts, and inappropriate sexual behavior. During the hospitalization, the family met weekly with a psychologist in family counseling sessions. The family vented its anger about the circumstances surrounding the injury, particularly toward the roomate, who was driving the car while intoxicated. Fears about the patient's ultimate mental recovery were expressed, as well as concerns about his future ability to work and live independently. Upon J. G.'s discharge, sessions were continued for several months. Many concerns were discussed, including questions about the patient's ability to drive an automobile and/or to resume drinking; effects of seizure medication on arousal, sexual functioning, and ability to be left alone; and so on. Methods of managing inappropriate behavior were suggested.

This case illustrates the variety of needs for ongoing family counseling and emotional support during hospitalization and after discharge into the community. In many cases, families are resistant to participating in a counseling relationship during the hospitalization, perhaps due to the presence of denial. After discharge, however, the family is often confronted with the reality of living with a brain-injured relative and family members are more likely to acknowledge the presence of problems and experience feelings of helplessness. Uncertainty regarding appropriate management techniques can often lead to inconsistency and feelings of guilt and inadequacy. Maintenance of ongoing contact in periodic family counseling sessions can help minimize the deleterious effects of these problems and their disruptive impact upon the family.

Family Therapy

Another technique that may be utilized to assist the families of brain-injured patients is family therapy. Glick and Kessler (1974, p. 4) define family therapy as "a professionally organized attempt to produce behavioral changes in a disturbed marital or family unit by essentially counteractive, non-physical methods." The chief objective of family therapy is to alter maladaptive communication and interaction patterns within the family system. The focus in family therapy is directed toward developing an increased understanding of the family's current mode of interaction and providing active intervention to resolve the dysfunctional communication and produce more satisfying and rewarding family relationships. In contrast to family counseling, the focus in family therapy is on the family system as a whole rather than the brain-injured patient .

In cases involving traumatic brain injury, family therapy may be limited to a select number of families where there is high risk (as described earlier) and where the brain-injured patient is cognitively intact to the degree that he or she can meaningfully participate in the sessions. The goals of family therapy include but are not limited to the following:

1. To provide a supportive environment where all family members can freely verbalize feelings about the trauma and its effect upon the family.
2. To educate the family about the nature of the deficit in communication and interaction and develop methods for resolving conflicts within the relationship patterns of the family system.
3. To examine and clarify role relationships and restructure roles and responsibilities within the family system.

Ideally, family therapy is initiated prior to discharge, since the need for this type of intervention should have been clearly defined. However, in reality, it is difficult for the family to express readiness to participate in this process until the patient has returned home and specific problems become manifest. Some specific techniques that can be employed in family therapy include the following:

1. Emphasizing the mutuality of responsibility for the maladaptive communication and interaction within the family, shifting the burden of guilt and blame from the identified patient to the family system.
2. Analyzing and emphasizing the positive aspects of the family system, reinforcing evidence of appropriate and healthy interaction that occurs within the sessions.
3. Exploring dysfunctional patterns of interaction by reenacting family conflicts and assisting family member in problem solving to alleviate conflicts.
4. Prescribing homework assignments for the family to practice outside the sessions so as to foster generalization of behavior change. Homework assignments may be defined as specific tasks that family members are asked to perform between sessions to create desirable behavior change.

These tasks may include altered methods of communication between parent and child, specific problem-solving techniques to employ when conflicts arise, or perhaps alternative and more adaptive ways of expressing feelings and frustrations.

Case History

The following case example is presented to illustrate some of the above concepts. M. G., a 17-year-old high-school senior, was admitted to the hospital for surgical repair of an arteriovenous (A-V) malformation. As a consequence of the procedure, the patient had a right-sided hemiparesis and residual deficits in language, memory, and personality function. His capacity to recall recently learned information was decreased. He experienced a great deal of emotional lability and depression. His family unit consisted of his parents and a 13-year-old sister. Through the course of his hospitalization (approximately 4 months), he made great strides in recovery of cognitive abilities but continued to experience great difficulty in coping with the behavioral changes imposed by his injury. The family was also experiencing a great deal of stress in attempting to understand and accept the changes in him. Premorbidly, the patient had been a high achiever academically in a private school and had been quite athletic. Family therapy sessions were initiated with a focus on assisting family members to understand and accommodate to the manifest changes. During the course of the family therapy sessions, the patient was able to express many of his feelings of grief and loss and found great support from his parents. In fact, his frequent crying spells and emotional lability greatly diminished. The patient's sister voiced her feelings about being ignored and feeling guilty during the period of her brother's illness. She revealed that her grades had suffered due to her inability to concentrate in school. The sessions helped the sister to verbalize these feelings and enable her parents to consider ways of meeting her needs as well as those of the patient.

Family therapy helped to establish a more open communication system within the family and allowed the burden of responsibility for the care of the patient to be shifted to the entire family system. The therapy sessions provided a nonthreatening atmosphere in which the patient could communicate his feelings and achieve greater self-esteem. In addition, members of the family were able to clarify their roles and responsibilities and become more comfortable in relating to each other.

Family Support Groups and Organizations

The preceding intervention strategies are described as helpful methods that rehabilitation professionals might consider for incorporation into their overall treatment programs. However, for a variety of reasons, health care professionals are not always the ideal resource for families. In recent years, the notion of peer counseling and support has gained prominence within the field of rehabilitation.

Within the past few years, parents and spouses of brain-injured patients have joined together to form support groups and grass-roots organizations to address the unmet needs of this population. The Easter Seal Society has developed the "stroke club" model of peer support, in which survivors of stroke gather together on a regular basis to listen to lectures, have informal discussions, or socialize. In 1980, families of several head-injured victims in Massachusetts coalesced to form an organization known as the National Head Injury Foundation. This organization now has more than 25 state chapters nationwide and is engaged in a wide variety of activities to assist the victims of traumatic brain injury. An important activity of the organizaion has been the stimulation of family support groups throughout the country. Families of patients with other neurologic disorders, such as Alzheimer's disease, Huntington's chorea, and Parkinson's disease, have also organized to increase public awareness of these disorders and provide needed assistance for families.

Support groups and self-help organizations run by consumers provide an important alternative source of counseling and support that may be more effective than services provided by health care professionals. The perspective provided by families is unique, since they have experienced the anger, frustration, despair, and uncertainty associated with the process of recovering from brain injury. The opportunity to attend regular support groups or meetings with those experiencing similar problems reduces feelings of social isolation and helplessness.

CONCLUSION

An individual with a neurologic disability presents both a great challenge and potential burden for relatives. Initially, family members have to accommodate to the shock of a traumatic injury or cerebral disease of recent onset. After a period of time, it becomes necessary for the family members to attempt to comprehend the multitude of neurobehavioral deficits that may now characterize the behavior of their loved one. It is often the case that the altered status of the patient has a tremendous impact upon the functioning of the entire family unit. Part of the problem is due to the diminished capacity of the brain-injured person to live independently and return to a meaningful, satisfying, and productive life style.

The presence of these deficits often compels the family of the brain-injured victim to assume a central role in the care and management of their loved ones's life. Thus the needs of family members must be addressed so that the newly rehabilitated brain-injured patient will not be placed in a chaotic, inconsistent, unstructured environment. The usually persistent presence of cognitive and behavioral deficits long after the injury places many demands and stresses upon the family; these are likely to lead to disruption of the family system unless the necessary psychosocial intervention is provided.

The preceding discussion has presented a theoretical framework and a model for family intervention that can be applied to the rehabilitation of the patient with acquired brain damage. In dealing with the families of the brain injured, it is necessary to view the family as an entire unit. Physical limitations, cognitive deficits, and behavioral abnormalities change interaction patterns within the family. Preexisting patterns of communication are greatly altered, and stress and disequilibrium become almost constant.

Within the early phases of recovery from brain injury within the hospital setting, patient-family education would be the treatment of choice. At this point, most families are interested in learning about the nature of brain injury and the recovery process but not yet ready to confront the rather frightening problems that lie ahead. The brief, focused, educational group format allows families to gain an understanding of the injury and ask questions about the future.

As the patient approaches the end of inpatient rehabilitation, many families can benefit from periodic family counseling sessions. These sessions are useful in identifying problems that may be encountered when the patient returns home. The counselor can aid the family in developing a realistic assessment of the patient's abilities and limitations. In addition, the counselor can help family members work through their grief and the feelings of loss accompanying a growing recognition of the significant and perhaps permanent changes in cognitive and behavioral functioning manifested by their loved one.

A selected number of families are in need of family therapy, which involves a psychotherapeutic process whereby communication and interaction patterns within the family are explored and, one hopes, altered. This type of intervention is usually effective only when the entire family unit, including the patient, can participate in the sessions. It is recommended for high-risk families, in which there is a significant premorbid history of family dysfunction or a persistent tendency to deny the disability and its consequences. The goal of family therapy is to shift the focus from the brain-injured patient to the family system and to develop specific techniques to alter maladaptive patterns of interaction within the family.

A newer form of family intervention has been developed by the consumer community. Organizations have been developed by parents and spouses of the brain injured to provide education, referral information, and peer support. Family support groups have been developed where emotional support is provided within an environment that may be less threatening and provide greater reassurance than is available in the traditional health care setting.

The inclusion of family intervention in the broad scope of treatment provided for the brain injured is a relatively new concept. To date, studies have not been conducted demonstrating that family intervention significantly alters the ultimate prognosis, outcome, and quality of life for the brain-injured victim. However, there is an increasing body of clinical evidence suggesting that family intervention should be considered as a primary rather than secondary or optimal mode of treatment in the comprehensive rehabilitation management of the brain-injured patient.

REFERENCES

Bertalanaffy, L. (1969). *General systems theory.* New York: George Braziller.

Blazyk, S. (1983). Developmental crisis in adolescents following severe head injury. *Social Work in Health Care, 80,* 55–59.

Bond, M. (1976). Assessment of psychosocial outcome of severe head injury. *Acta Neurochirugica, 34,* 57–70.

Bond, M. (1983). Effects on the family system. In M. Rosenthal, E. Griffith, M. Bond, & J. Miller (Eds.), *Rehabilitation of the head injured adult.* Philadelphia: F. A. Davis.

Bruhn, J. (1977). Effects of chronic illness on the family. *Journal of Family Practice,* 4(6), 1057–1060.

Diehl, L. (1978, June). *Patient-family education.* Paper presented at the 2nd annual conference on the Rehabilitation of the Traumatic Brain Injured Adult, Williamsburg, VA.

Ebra, G. (1975). Rehabilitation considerations in end stage renal disease. *Journal of Applied Rehabilitation Counseling,* 6,(2), 96.

Evans, C. D., Bull, C. F., Devenport, M. J., Hall, P. M., Jones, J., Middleton, F. R., Russell, G., Stichbury, J. C., & Whitehead, B. (1976). Rehabilitation of the brain damaged survivor. *Injury, 8,* 80–97.

Falloon, I., Boyd, J., McGill, C., Razani, J., Moss, H., & Gilderman, A. (1982). Family management in the prevention of exacerbations of schizophrenia: A controlled study. *New England Journal of Medicine, 306,* 1437–1440.

Freedman, A. M., Kaplan, H. I., & Sadock, B. J. (Eds.). (1975). *Comprehensive textbook of psychiatry* (Vol. 1), Baltimore: Williams & Wilkins.

Glick, I. D., & Kessler, D. R. (1974). *Marital and family therapy.* New York: Grune & Stratton.

Jackson, D. (1965). The study of the family. *Family Process,* 4(1), 1–20.

Jennett, B., & Bond, M. R. (1975). Assessment of outcome after severe brain damage. *Lancet, 1,* 480–484.

Jennett, B., & Teasdale, G. (1976). Predicting outcome in individual patients after severe closed head injury. *Lancet, 1,* 1081–1084.

Kübler-Ross, E. (1969). *On death and dying.* New York: Macmillan.

Levin, H., & Grossman, R. G. (1978). Behavioral sequelae of closed head injury. *Archives of Neurology, 35,* 720–727.

Lezak, M. (1978). Living with the characterologically altered brain injured patient. *Journal of Clinical Psychiatry, 39,* 592–698.

Litman, T. (1966). The family and physical rehabilitation. *Journal of Chronic Disease,* 19, 211–217.

Mace, N., & Rabins, P. (1982). *The 36 hour day: a family guide to caring for a person with Alzheimer's disease, relating dementing illnesses and memory loss in later life.* Baltimore: Johns Hopkins Press.

Malone, R. (1977). Expressed attitudes of families of aphasics. In J. Stubbins (Ed.), *Social psychology and aspects of disability.* Baltimore: University Park Press.

McKinlay, W. W., Brooks, D. N., Bond, M. R., Martinage, D. P., & Marshall, M. M.

(1981). The short-term outcome of severe blunt head injury as reported by relatives of the injured person. *Journal of Neurology, Neurosurgery and Psychiatry, 44,* 527–533.

Minuchin, S. (1974). *Families and family therapy.* Cambridge, MA: Harvard University Press.

Najenson, T., Mendelson, L., Schechter, I., David, C., Mintz, N, & Grosswasser, Z. (1974). Rehabilitation after severe head injury. *Scandinavian Journal of Rehabilitation Medicine, 6,* 5–14.

Oddy, M., Humphrey, M., and Uttley, D. (1978). Stresses upon relatives of head injured patients. *British Journal of Psychiatry, 133,* 507–513.

Panting, A., & Merry, P. (1972). The long term rehabilitation of severe head injuries with particular reference to the need for social and medical support for the patient's family. *Rehabilitation, 38,* 33–37.

Rhodes, S. (1977). A developmental approach to the life cycle of the family. *Social Casework. 22,* 301–311.

Romano, M. (1974). Family response to traumatic head injury. *Scandinavian Journal of Rehabilitation Medicine, 6*(1), 257–263.

Rosenbaum, M., & Najenson, T. (1976). Changes in life patterns and symptoms of low mood as reported by wives of severely brain-injured soldiers. *Journal of Consulting and Clinical Psychology, 44,* 881–888.

Satir, V. (1971). The family as a treatment unit. In J. Haley (Ed.), *Changing families.* New York: Grune & Stratton.

Shontz, F. (1978). Psychological adjustment to physical disability: Trends in theories. *Archives of Physical Medicine and Rehabilitation, 59,* 251–254.

Symonds, C. P. (1937). Mental disorders following head injury. *Proceedings of the Royal Society of Medicine, 30,* 1081–1092.

Turnblom, M. & Myers, J. (1952). A group discussion program with families of aphasic patients. *Journal of Speech and Hearing Disorders, 17,* 393–396.

Wiley, S. (1983). Structural treatment approach for families in crisis. *American Journal of Physical Medicine, 62*(6), 271–286.

Wright, G. (1980). *Total rehabilitation.* Boston: Little, Brown.

PART IV
Special Populations

13

The Neuropsychology of
Head Injuries

William Gene Miller

Traumatic head injury is responsible for more deaths and disabilities than any other neurological cause in patients under 50 years of age (Berkow & Talbott, 1977). An estimated 7 million head injuries occur each year in the United States (Caveness, 1977), with over 100,000 deaths and 500,000 admissions to hospitals. Fifty thousand persons, most under the age of 30, are left with disabilities that preclude resumption of normal lives (National Head Injury Foundation, 1982). As a result of the life-saving neurosurgical management in modern trauma centers (Bakay & Glasauer, 1980; Jennett & Teasdale, 1981), the number of persons surviving head injuries from motor vehicle accidents, assaults, and athletic mishaps increases steadily. The direct and indirect costs of this "silent epidemic" have been estimated at $3.9 billion per year (Kalsbeek, McLaurin, Harris, & Miller, 1980), but no one can place a price tag on the shattered lives of the victims of severe head injury, who often inherit a humpty-dumpty world (Warrington, 1983).

Accurate ascertainment of the number of head injuries is difficult because of problems in patient identification, definitions of severity of injury, exclusion of patients with mild injury who are not admitted to hospitals, and omission from reports of persons who died prior to reaching a hospital (Field, 1976). Therefore, there is a wide range of incidence rates reported in the literature (Annegers, Grabow, Kurland, & Laws, 1980; Jennett & MacMillan, 1981; Kalsbeek et al., 1980).

Regardless of the incidence rates, the consequences of head injury can hardly be overestimated. The features of the posttraumatic symptom-complex are varied and seldom fully recognized by professionals, patients, or family members. Levin, Benton, and Grossman (1982), however, have offered an excellent and comprehensive analysis of the neurobehavioral consequences of closed head injury that is must reading for professionals in this field. A selective review of the voluminous literature on the neurobehavioral sequelae of head injury will be presented in this chapter in order to define the current state of knowledge. Emphasis will be placed on the effects of closed head injury in adults.

PATIENT CHARACTERISTICS AND ASSOCIATED VARIABLES

The consequences of traumatic head injury are dependent on a number of variables, including type of injury (penetrating or closed), cause of injury (vehicle accident or fall), severity of injury (mild or severe), age and sex, locus of lesion, preexisting risk factors, and socioeconomic status. The results of any study in the area of head injury must be interpreted in the context of these variables. Further, the reader should be cognizant of the measures used and the time frame within which observations were made.

Type of Injury

Penetrating (open) head injuries, typically produced by gunshot wounds or by fragments from exploding shells, involve perforation of the skull and laceration of the brain tissue in the path of the intruding object (Levin et al., 1982; Lezak, 1983). Some authors (Jennett & Teasdale, 1981) include compound depressed fractures of the skull vault and fractures of the skull base caused by nonmissile accidents under the category of open head injuries.

An adequate description of penetrating (open, missile) injury is complicated by at least two important factors. First, the injury may not be quite as circumscribed or focal as was depicted in the early literature on the topic (Newcombe, 1969). The intruding object (missile) may cause damage throughout the brain as a result of shock waves and cavitation or pressure effects (Grubb & Coxe, 1978; Gurdjian & Gurdjian, 1976; Kirkpatrick & DiMaio, 1978), and there may be secondary effects such as edema (Kirkpatrick & DiMaio, 1978), hematoma (West, 1981), infection (Adams, 1982), and posttraumatic epilepsy (Meirowsky, 1982). The resulting impairments in mental slowing, attention, concentration, and memory (Lezak, 1983) tend to look like those associated with diffuse brain damage from closed head injury. Secondly, case selection, that is, military or civilian, may confound the depiction of penetrating injuries. Studies of military cases reveal a predominance of fragment wounds over bullet wounds and a greater mortality among the latter (Hammon, 1971; Newcombe, 1969; Semmes, Weinstein, Ghent, & Teuber,

1960; Teuber, Battersby, & Bender, 1960). However, studies of civilian cases include mostly gunshot wounds (Rich, 1980), and many of these wounds are self-inflicted (Freytag, 1963; Kirkpatrick & DiMaio, 1978; Lillard, 1978). The differences between military and civilian cases limit some of the generalizations about global outcome (Dresser, Meirowsky, Weiss, McNeel, Simon, & Caveness, 1973; Teuber, 1975) and about the specific neuropsychological sequelae of penetrating injuries (Newcombe, 1969; Semmes et al., 1960; Teuber et al., 1960).

Closed (nonmissile, blunt, diffuse) head injury typically results from blunt trauma associated with acceleration/deceleration forces to the head (Gurdjian, 1971). Linear and rotational acceleration of the brain within the skull puts stresses on nerve fibers and blood vessels that can stretch them to the point of shearing (Strich, 1956, 1970). Mounting evidence suggests that this mechanical shearing and tearing of nerve fibers upon impact causing widespread lesions in the brain is the "primary" mechanism of closed head injury (Adams, Mitchell, Graham, & Doyle, 1977; Lezak, 1983). Coup and contrecoup macroscopic lesions also contribute to impact brain injury (Grubb & Coxe, 1978; Gurdjian, 1971; Lezak, 1983), but their role in closed head injuries may have been exaggerated (Levin et al., 1982). Midbrain lesions, in the presence of widespread injury, are frequently found in patients dying from the direct effects of closed head trauma (Rosenblum, Greenberg, Seelig, & Becker, 1981). In addition, systemic or secondary mechanisms such as brain swelling, increased intracranial pressure, and hemorrhage may exacerbate the immediate effects of impact (Jennett & Teasdale, 1981; Levin et al., 1982). Tertiary or delayed effects, that is, ventricular enlargement and posttraumatic epilepsy, also contribute to the complications of closed head injury (Jennett & Teasdale, 1981; Levin, Meyers, Grossman, & Sarwar, 1981). Although arbitrary distinctions can be made between "impact" and the "systemic" mechanisms, secondary events occur rapidly (within an hour of injury) and require early monitoring and management (Jennett & Teasdale, 1981). Full discussions of the structural and physiological alterations resulting from head injury are given by Bakay and Glasauer (1980), Jennett and Teasdale (1981), and Levin et al. (1982).

Closed head injury, particularly in motor vehicle accidents, does not occur in isolation. Many victims endure multiple traumas. Rimel and Jane (1983), in a study of 1,248 patients, found that 82% of the patients admitted to the hospital had one or more extracranial injuries, that is, lacerations, orthopedic fractures, abdominal injuries, and chest injuries.

The diffuse brain damage that accompanies most severe head injuries tends to compromise mental speed, attention and concentration, cognitive efficiency, high-level concept formation, and complex reasoning abilities (Gronwall & Sampson, 1974; Levin et al., 1982; Lezak, 1983; Roberts, 1979; Van Zomeren, 1981).

Cause of Injury

There is no uniformity in the literature in the use of terms for classifying the cause of injury, but there is evidence to suggest that motor vehicle accidents account for the majority of all closed head injuries, with falls being the second major causative factor (Kalsbeek et al., 1980). Annegers and colleagues (1980) suggested that 37% of injuries are caused by automobile and motorcycle accidents and that 27% are due to falls and domestic mishaps. Assaults, industrial accidents, and sports mishaps account for 17% of head trauma. Age is related to causation in that falls contribute disproportionately to head injuries in young children and in older adults (Levin et al., 1982).

Severity of Lesion

The degree of severity of injury has been lumped into overlapping categories of mild, moderate, and severe. Estimates of severity based on loss of consciousness vary from no alteration in level of consciousness to 1 hour of unconsciousness for "mild" injury, and from 6 hours to more than 7 days of unconsciousness for "severe" injury (Bond, 1983a; Jennett & Teasdale, 1981; Van Zomeren, 1981). "Moderate" injury is usually defined by exclusion from mild or severe categories. No category, such as "profound" severity, exists for patients who are unconscious for months. Thus, there is no absolute measure of what constitutes a severe injury.

The major criteria for estimating the severity of closed head injury have been the duration and depth of coma, and the duration of posttraumatic amnesia (PTA), that is, the period of gross confusion and amnesia for ongoing events after the patient emerges from coma (Levin et al., 1982). Although coma—that is, a state in which there is no eye opening, an inability to follow commands, and no utterance of recognizable words (Teasdale and Jennett, 1974)—is widely viewed as a characteristic feature of closed head injury, prolonged loss of consciousness is relatively uncommon (less than one-third of cases) in consecutive head injury admissions to major trauma hospitals (Clifton et al., 1980).

In an attempt to produce a reliable and practical procedure for the assessment of altered consciousness, Teasdale and Jennett (1974) developed the Glasgow Coma Scale, which evaluates three components of wakefulness (eye opening, motor response, and verbal response) independently of each other. Coma is defined as the absence of eye opening, inability to obey commands, and failure to utter recognizable words. This definition corresponds to a total Glasgow Coma Scale score of 8 or less (out of a possible 15 points) and is an important watershed because patients with such scores are regarded as having had a "severe" injury (Bond, 1983a). However, the score of 8 or less, as noted earlier, may exclude the majority of head-injured patients who may nonetheless manifest significant neurobehavioral sequelae (Levin et al., 1982).

Although the Glasgow Coma Scale has gained wide acceptance and use, there are problems in the interpretation of "purposeful" motor responses and in respect to global distinctions between "consciousness" and "unconsciousness." Some of the problems can be resolved if successive ratings are made at regular intervals (Levin et al., 1982). The measurement of change over the first 72 hours provides a more valid index of severity than the scores at the time of admission to the hospital (Jennett et al., 1979). A relationship between depth of coma and quality of outcome has been demonstrated by Overgaard et al. (1973). Only 7% of patients showing the most severe degree of coma made a "good recovery," as compared to 82% of those patients who had been merely somnolent.

The severity of injury also has been defined by the period of posttraumatic amnesia (PTA), that is, the time between injury and recovery of continuous memory (Russell, 1971; Russell & Smith, 1961). It is important to note that Russell included both the length of coma and the period of anterograde amnesia (loss of memory for events after trauma) in the estimation of posttraumatic amnesia (Levin et al., 1982). Russell and Smith (1961) related the duration of PTA to the severity of injury in the following manner: PTA of less than 1 hour = mild injury; PTA of 1–24 hours = moderate injury; PTA of 1–7 days = severe injury; and PTA of more than 7 days = very severe injury. Jennett (1983) expanded the categories to include very mild (PTA of less than 5 minutes), very severe (PTA of 1 to 4 weeks), and extremely severe (PTA of more than 4 weeks) injuries. The retrospective nature of the assessment of posttraumatic amnesia, however, is open to criticism (Levin et al., 1982). Patients may not be able to differentiate between information derived from other persons after termination of posttraumatic amnesia and information obtained at some earlier point in the recovery process. Some patients with mild injury have "islands of memory," that is, memory of a postinjury event followed by a period of amnesia (Gronwall & Wrightson, 1980). In this context, it is important to establish when full memory for day-to-day events is recovered.

Levin, O'Donnell, and Grossman (1979) developed an instrument, the Galveston Orientation and Amnesia Test (GOAT), to focus on prospective rather than retrospective assessment of amnesia after head injury. Serial scores on the GOAT yield a recovery curve that is useful in characterizing the early phase of recovery in the noncomatose patient (Levin et al., 1982).

When considered in combination, duration/depth of coma and duration of posttraumatic amnesia can provide a moderate early estimate of the severity of injury. By adding neurological indicants, especially intracranial hematoma and neuroopthalmalogical signs, the predictive power of severity of injury with its implications for neurobehavioral outcome is increased (Levin, Grossman, Rose, & Teasdale, 1979). Longer coma and protracted posttraumatic amnesia yield an increasingly poor prognosis for the patient.

It is worth noting that the subtle neurobehavioral consequences of seemingly "mild" head injury may have been grossly underestimated. Many patients experience persisting symptoms (headaches, memory problems, and emotional stress) that interfere with personal, social, and vocational adjustment. Deservedly, increasing attention has been given to mild head injuries in recent years (Dikmen, Reitan, & Temkin, 1983; Gronwall, 1977; Gronwall & Wrightson, 1974, 1980, 1981; McLean, Temkin, Dikmen, & Wyler, 1983; Rimel, Giordani, Barth, Boll, & Jane, 1981; Wrightson & Gronwall, 1980).

Age and Sex

A high incidence of closed head injury in adolescents and young adults (ages 15 to 30) has been consistently reported in the literature (Field, 1976; Kraus, 1980a; Rimel & Jane, 1983). The study of head injury in Olmstead County, Minnesota (Annegers et al., 1980), indicated a steep rise in incidence rates at ages 15 to 24 and a secondary peak after age 70. Head injury admissions in children reach a peak at ages 4 to 8 (Craft, 1972). Jennett and Teasdale (1981) reviewed the effects of age on outcome and found that within a series of closed head injury patients, in which the Glasgow Coma Scale score was below 8 for 6 or more hours, the probability of death increased exponentially as a function of age at the time of injury.

Head injury is about three times more common in males than in females. The ratio of male to female hospital admissions is about 4 to 1, but declines to about 2 to 1 in patients over 70 years old (Field, 1976; Kerr, Kay, & Lassman, 1971; Kraus, 1980b). The male incidence rate rises to a peak in the 15-20-24 age range (Levin et al., 1982; Rimel and Jane, 1983).

Locus of Lesion

Although severe closed head injury usually results in diffuse damage, there is evidence to suggest disproportionate damage to certain areas of the brain. Ommaya and Gennarelli (1974) reported that diffuse injury produced by shear strain was greater in areas of bony protrusion and in rough surfaces of the skull. Thus, the frontal and temporal lobes of the brain are more likely to absorb the brunt of damage. In contrast, shear strain was found to be slight in areas of smooth surfaces of the skull such as the occipital lobes.

In addition, focal mass lesions such as contusions (bruises) and intracranial hematomas (space-occupying blood clots) may be produced by closed head injury. Both contusions and hematomas are common in the orbital surfaces of the frontal and temporal lobes (Levin et al., 1982).

These focal lesions, superimposed on diffuse injury, may result in problems in the regulation and control of activity, in conceptual and problem-solving behavior, and in various aspects of memory and learning (Lezak, 1979, 1983). The more severe the injury, the more likely the patient will display deficits associated with frontal and temporal lobe injuries (Brooks, 1972; Levin, Grossman, & Kelly, 1976b; Lezak, 1979).

Preexisting Risk Factors

With respect to predisposing causes for injury, alcohol consumption has been implicated in 29% of head injuries in males who are 15 or older and in 10% of head injuries in females (Field, 1976). Rimel and Jane (1983), in their study of head injury, found that 25% of the patients interviewed had received some type of professional treatment for alcohol abuse. Depending on the study, chronic alcoholics may constitute as many as one-half the head injuries reported as being severe (Field, 1976).

Another issue is whether persons who sustained a head injury are at greater risk of incurring a subsequent head injury. Annegers et al. (1980) found that after a head injury the incidence rate in adults was three times that of a first head injury in a general population and that after a second head injury the rate jumps to eight times that of the general population. Rimel and Jane (1983), in their series, found that 31% of all patients studied were previously hospitalized for a head injury. Based on these data, adult patients who sustain a head injury are at high risk of a subsequent head injury.

A somewhat controversial risk factor suggested in the literature is that head-injured patients are not a random sample of the population, but may be more representative of people who are maladjusted risk takers (Bond & Brooks, 1976; Fahy, Irving, & Millac, 1967; Jamieson & Kelly, 1973; Jennett, 1972). However, as noted by McLean et al. (1983), previous studies have either used no control groups or have used types of controls (hospital workers and university students) that could inflate the differences between head-injured patients and control subjects. The relationship between preinjury "maladjustment" and posttraumatic outcome has not been established.

Socioeconomic Status

British, Australian, American, and Canadian studies have suggested a relationship between socioeconomic level and head injury. Kerr et al. (1971), in their study of admissions to Newcastle General Hospital, implicated an association between low socioeconomic level and a high frequency of head injury. Data from admissions for head injury in Oxford disclosed an overrepresentation of the lower socioeconomic groups in patients 20 to 64 years of age (Field, 1976). Selecki, Hoy, and Ness (1967, 1968), in an Australian study, found that laborers and craftsmen were disproportionately represented and that the lower socioeconomic classes had considerably more head injuries caused by assaults and household mishaps. Motor vehicle accidents, however, were not related to socioeconomic level. In the University of Virginia series, reported by Rimel and

Jane (1983), head-injured patients were predominantly from a lower socioeconomic class.

Finally, although socioeconomic levels may be less strongly related to head injury at either extreme in age, Klonoff (1971), in a study of children brought to the emergency room of Vancouver General Hospital, found a disproportionate number of children who had fathers of lower occupational status and who lived in congested residential areas.

Bond and Brooks (1976) have postulated that members of the upper socioeconomic levels may have greater mental capacity and range of skills than persons from the lower socioeconomic groups. Consequently, socioeconomic status may be positively correlated with outcome in terms of employment, leisure activities, and social functioning. However, this conclusion awaits adequate documentation.

GLOBAL OUTCOME

Traumatic head injury, as noted earlier, predominantly affects adolescents and young adults and produces tremendous financial, personal, and social problems for the patients and their families. Consequently, several authors have directed efforts to predict outcome after head injury (Najenson et al., 1974; Roberts, 1979; Stover & Zeiger, 1976). "Outcome" generally refers to the adequacy with which a patient's life style is resumed, including the efficiency of performance of the routine activities of daily life (Levin et al., 1982). Langfitt (1978) maintains that outcome measures may assist clinicians in providing useful prognostic information to patients and their families and in assessing the effectiveness of different treatment modalities in promoting the recovery process after head injury.

However, there is considerable diversity of opinion about outcome after head injury. Specialists who are primarily concerned with the management of the acute phase of head injury, that is, with the survival of the patient and with the prevention of devastating physical and mental impairment, often view outcome in a different light than do rehabilitation specialists and vocational counselors who deal with the adjustment problems of patients in the later posttraumatic period (Benton, 1979; Jennett, 1975). Neurosurgeons who focus on immediate outcome may give a rating of "excellent" outcome to patients who are hemiplegic and dysphasic (Jennett, 1972). Similarly, physicians and family members often overlook subtle cognitive changes in head-injured patients (Fuld & Fisher, 1977).

Further, although somewhat peripheral in the present context, there is continuing controversy about the mechanisms of recovery from brain damage, for example, diaschisis, regrowth of axons, collateral sprouting, supersensitivity, plasticity, equipotentiality, radical reorganization, and behavioral compensation (Bach-y-Rita, 1980; Finger, 1978; Finger & Stein, 1982; Fletcher &

Satz, 1983; Luria, 1973; Porter & Fitzsimons, 1975; Smith, 1983; Stein, Rosen, & Butters, 1974). Regardless of the mechanisms involved, many professionals suggest that the greater part of natural recovery, that is, recovery of those functions directly attributable to activity of the brain, takes place within 6 months after injury, and that 80% to 95% of recovery is expected within 12 to 18 months following trauma (Bond & Brooks, 1976; Porter & Fitzsimons, 1975). Later improvements may occur but are diminished in comparison. Contrary to these data, however, Dikmen and colleagues (1983) argue that conclusions regarding the slowing of recovery after the first year may be premature.

Finally, large-scale group studies of outcome do not account for individual variation in either the rate or the direction of change over time, and the extent of such variation appears to be quite substantial (Benton, 1979). Some patients may exhibit a decline in cognitive efficiency after an initial gain. Lezak (1979) has reported a "secondary regression" in cognitive function in several patients 18 months after trauma.

Mortality

Jennett and associates (1977), in a study of 700 patients with severe head injuries from centers in Scotland, the Netherlands, and Los Angeles, reported a relatively uniform mortality of approximately 50% at each center. Subsequent investigations, perhaps reflecting some heterogeneity in head injuries and variations in the interval between injury and admission to a neurosurgical trauma center, have reported a lower mortality rate of about 30% (Becker et al., 1977; Clifton et al., 1980; Marshall, Smith, & Shapiro, 1979a,b; Miller et al., 1981). Levati, Farina, Vecchi, Rossanda, and Marrubini (1982), in a study of 215 patients, reported a mortality rate of 39.5%.

Thus, a patient who sustains a head injury of sufficient severity to be rated below 8 on the Glasgow Coma Scale has a 50% to 70% chance of survival, even with the best current medical care (Levin et al., 1982), and the probability of death appears to increase exponentially as a function of age at the time of injury (Jennett & Teasdale, 1981).

Morbidity

Outcome studies at different centers have included a variety of terms, for example, "serious," "partial," and "slight," for classification of the disability status of the head-injured patient. Jennett and Bond (1975), in an attempt to introduce some standardization into the assessment of global outcome, developed the Glasgow Outcome Scale to categorize brain-damaged patients (head-injured and nontrauma coma) on the basis of a predetermined characteristic, level of overall capability or dependency. The original scale included five categories: death, persistent vegetative state, severe disability, moderate disability, and good recovery. Each of the four categories of survival is a composite of physical, cognitive, and social functioning. Jennett and Teasdale (1981) reported a high level of interrater reliability for this widely used instrument.

Persistent vegetative state, a term proposed by Jennett and Plum (1972), describes patients who remain speechless and devoid of meaningful contact with other persons for weeks or months. However, such patients manifest sleep-waking cycles and periodically open their eyes (Plum & Posner, 1980). Widespread cerebral white matter damage and brainstem lesions have been implicated in these patients (Jennett & Teasdale, 1981; Strich, 1970).

Jennett and Teasdale (1981) suggested that in many cases the vegetative state can be recognized with confidence one month after trauma and that, in those patients still vegetative at three months postinjury, the possibility of regaining an independent existence can be virtually excluded. Sixty percent of those patients declared vegetative at three months were dead at one year postinjury. Jennett and Teasdale view the vegetative state as death postponed. Higashi et al. (1977), in a review of 38 closed head injury patients in the vegetative state, found that 45% of these patients were still alive at the end of a 3-year follow-up interval. Some patients, with excellent medical and nursing care, may live for as long as 18 to 20 years.

It is important to note in this context that patients frequently pass through a vegetative state phase during the course of recovery from severe head injury (Levin et al., 1982). Further, there are reports of patients who regain consciousness and benefit from rehabilitation efforts after remaining comatose for as long as 6 years (Tanhecho & Kaplan, 1982). Some centers offer sensory stimulation programs for comatose patients during the early stages of postinjury (McGonagle, Carper, & Balicki, 1983). Such procedures, at the very least, have the potential of preventing the "persistent vegetative state" from becoming a self-fulfilling prophecy.

Severely disabled patients were described by Jennett and Bond (1975) as conscious but dependent on others for daily support by reason of mental and/or physical disability. Although many of these patients are institutionalized, some patients, with exceptional family support, reside at home. The severely disabled patient is capable of some degree of self-care but may have limited communication and locomotion abilities. The frequency of severe disability varies considerably in the different series of patients at various centers. The category of severely disabled was three times as common among patients treated in Los Angeles as among those treated in San Diego (Levin et al., 1982).

Moderate disability, as a category of outcome, is used to designate patients who are independent in daily activities but are disabled. These patients can use public transportation and can work in a sheltered environment, but have varying degrees of motor and neuropsychological deficits, as well as personality changes (Jennett and Teasdale, 1981). Levin et al. (1979), however, found that the designation of outcome within the middle range of recovery is difficult, and that the "moderate disability" category encompasses a wide range of neuropsychological functioning and social adjustment.

Good recovery implies the resumption of a preinjury life style. The patients may have some mild impairments and may or may not return to work. Jennett and Bond (1975) did not use resumption of work as a criterion, however, because employment is contingent on a number of factors, including local economic conditions and disability benefits. Estimates of the frequency of "good recovery" vary markedly across studies, but Levin et al. (1982) suggest that one-third to one-half of the survivors of severe head injury, with optimal treatment, can achieve such status.

Jennett and Teasdale (1981) reported outcome data on more than 500 survivors of severe head injury at postinjury intervals of 3 months, 6 months, and 12 months. At 12 months, 3% of the patients were vegetative, 16% were severely disabled, 31% were moderately disabled, and 50% were rated as having made a good recovery. Of those who had made a good or moderate recovery, two-thirds had reached this level within 3 months after injury, and 90% had done so by 6 months. Only 10% of those patients who were severely or moderately disabled at 6 months were in a better category 1 year after injury.

Bond and Brooks (1976), in an attempt to determine the outcome of severe head injury on daily living, assessed the relationship between the physical, mental, and social aspects of recovery in patients over a period of 24 months. The difference between physical disability ratings at 6 months and at 24 months was not significant. The greater part of physical recovery was within the first 6 months. A similar pattern of recovery was found for mental abilities, that is, intellectual and mnemonic functions. Verbal skills seemed to reach their final level earlier than performance or nonverbal skills. Psychosocial variables had a major influence upon recovery, particularly in the later stages when the physical and mental deficits were fixed.

On the basis of these data and research with the Glasgow Outcome Scale over the past few years, Bond (1979) developed a three-stage conceptual description of recovery for severely head-injured patients. Stage one lasts a matter of days, and the patient is unconscious. Management priorities are intensive physical care and family intervention. The features of stage two are the end of posttraumatic amnesia and the period of maximum recovery of basic physical and mental functions. Stage two extends up to 6 months postinjury. Management priorities in this stage are continued physical care, including physical therapy and occupational therapy, psychological and social rehabilitation, and group and family therapy. During this second stage, relatives often entertain false hopes about the eventual level of recovery in the patient, and this becomes apparent to those responsible for management. Stage three begins when recovery of basic physical and mental deficits slows, usually between 3 and 6 months postinjury. In the third stage final levels of disability are revealed, and patients and relatives are faced with adapting to the presence of fixed disabilities. In more than half of these patients, mental deficits overshadow physical deficits. Management priorities are psychological and social rehabilitation.

Thus, studies using the Glasgow Outcome Scale support the view that almost all patients who make a "good recovery" do so by 6 months postinjury. This recovery curve also has been proposed in reports other than those using the Glasgow outcome categories (Roberts, 1976, 1979). Later improvements in functioning do occur, but are viewed as diminished in comparison to recovery in the first 6 months posttrauma (Bond, 1979; Jennett & Teasdale, 1981).

However, as noted earlier, global outcome measures do not provide sufficient detail about subtle, long-term recovery in individual patients. The Glasgow Outcome Scale is too coarse for an accurate assessment of patients who vary widely in educational background, premorbid neuropsychological status, severity of injury, and motivational levels. This instrument does not measure subtle cognitive changes over time. Different functions improve at varying rates (Kertesz, 1979; Lezak, 1979, 1983). The rate and nature of improvement are almost always uneven, and are not easily subsumed under a composite heading of physical, mental, and social functioning.

Additional Indices of Outcome

If resumption of work is added as a criterion of outcome, additional issues must be addressed, including the percentage of students in the population sample, the definition of work (sheltered workshop or competitive employment), and the level of employment (preinjury or lowered status). Unfortunately, there are few answers to these questions. Existing studies suggest that few victims of motor vehicle accidents who have sustained severe head injuries ever resume their studies or return to gainful employment; if they do return to work, it is likely to be at a lower level than before the injury (Lezak, 1983).

Oddy and associates (Oddy, Humphrey, & Uttley, 1978a,b; Oddy & Humphrey, 1980) followed a series of 50 young adult head-injured patients for a period of 2 years and found that most (38) eventually were able to return to work. However, in a study of 50 closed head injury patients who had been deeply unconscious for at least 24 hours, Thomsen (1974) found that only 8% had resumed their preinjury work 30 months after trauma. Levin et al. (1979) found that 44% of 27 young adult patients with severe injury were employed at follow-up 1 year postinjury. Gilchrist and Wilkinson (1979) reported that 39% of 70 closed head injury patients under 40 years of age at time of injury were working at the time of follow-up (9 months to 15 years after injury).

Najenson, Groswasser, Mendelson, and Hackett (1980), in a study of 147 patients followed up on at least once 6 months or more after discharge, found that 39% were unemployed and/or unemployable, 18% were in sheltered work, 25% were in unskilled work, and 18% were in skilled work. Final employment results were affected mainly by cognitive deficits and by behavioral disturbances as judged by social consequences. Ben-Yishay (1982), reporting preliminary findings on the outcome of the first 20 trainees in the head injury project at the New York University Institute of Rehabilitation Medicine, found 50% were engaged in part-time or full-time competitive work, 40% were in noncompetitive or subsidized work, and 10% were not working. None of these trainees, who had a mean age at injury of 26 years, a mean education of 14.3 years, a mean duration of coma of 45 days, a mean Full-Scale IQ of 110 on the Wechsler Adult Intelligence Scale, and a mean time since injury of 36 months upon admittance to the project, returned to work at a preinjury level of work competence.

Thus, outcome data based on resumption of work manifest tremendous variation, and contain inherent limitations due to a number of factors, including disability benefits. Although litigation and compensation are often discussed in this context as having adverse effects on the return to work, there is little evidence for such statements (Irving, 1972; Oddy et al., 1978b; Rimel et al., 1981).

Finally, the long-term psychosocial consequences of head injury and the resulting impact on family and friends are often neglected or inadequately characterized in the outcome data (Walker, Caveness, & Critchley, 1969). Brooks and associates (Brooks & Aughton, 1979a,b; Brooks, McKinlay, & Bond, 1979) devised a structured interview to assess the subjective (perceived stress) and objective (observable changes in family routine, health, or housing) burdens that the trauma imposes on the patient's family. The greatest family burden was in dealing with the patient's personality and emotional changes. This finding has been supported in several studies (Oddy et al., 1978a,b; Panting & Merry, 1972; Rosenbaum & Najenson, 1976). Many head-injured patients with severe injuries display impaired initiative and apathy, defective social judgment, childishness and selfishness, lack of concern, impulsiveness, irritability, and low frustration tolerance (Gronwall, 1976; Levin & Grossman, 1978; Panting & Merry, 1972; Rosenbaum & Najenson, 1976). The wives of the victims of severe head injury are often depressed, and eventual divorce is relatively common (Panting & Merry, 1972).

Lezak (1978) has offered some constructive advice for counseling the family members of head-injured patients. Discussions of the effects of head injury on the family system and methods of education/intervention are presented by Bond (1983b), Diehl (1983), and Rosenthal and Muir (1983) in a recent publication, and by Rosenthal and Geckler in Chapter 12 of this volume.

SPECIFIC SEQUELAE AND RECOVERY

It has been established with some degree of certainty that the long-term mental sequelae of closed head injury are more disabling than the physical sequelae (Bond & Brooks, 1976; Jennett & Teasdale, 1981; Oddy & Humphrey, 1980; Porter & Fitzsimons, 1975; Weddell, Oddy, & Jenkins, 1980). However, there is no agreement in the literature on which of the patient's behaviors belong under the rubric of "mental" and which belong under the rubric of "physical." Ben-Yishay and Diller (1983) abandoned the traditional classifications and suggested that the assessment of functional disorders should encompass scrutiny of content variables (intelligence, perceptual-motor skills), process variables (attention, memory, problem solving), and modifying variables (initiative, endurance, emotional components).

The following presentation is based on traditional, overlapping categories of physical and neuropsychological sequelae, and emphasis will be placed on memory and cognitive-intellectual functions, with some mention of the perceptual-motor, linguistic, and behavioral consequences of head injury.

Measurement Issues

There are only a few serial assessments of adult patients with closed head injuries (Bond, 1975; Dikmen & Reitan, 1976; Dikmen et al., 1983; Lezak, 1979; Mandleberg, 1975, 1976; Mandleberg & Brooks, 1975; Parker & Serrats, 1976). Consequently, the state of knowledge in the area of long-term recovery is quite fragmentary. However, there is some evidence that a differential potential for recovery probably exists in accordance with the severity of injury. Persons surviving severe head injuries may have limited potential for improvement, as noted in an earlier section, and may reach that potential fairly rapidly, that is, within 6 months (Bond & Brooks, 1976; Jennett & Teasdale, 1981). Patients with moderate or mild head injury may continue to improve over a prolonged period (Dikmen et al., 1983). Levin and colleagues (1982) leave no doubt that patients with normal premorbid intelligence, moderate coma duration (1–3 days), preserved oculovestibular response, reactive pupils, and absence of intracranial hematoma/hemiparesis/aphasia have the best prognosis for recovery.

Attempts to assess the sequelae of head injury have been flawed by a number of variables, including those enumerated in the first section of the chapter, such as severity and premorbid characteristics, and also by the failure to use uniform intervals between injury and measurement, the use of disparate measures, and the absence of appropriate controls (Levin et al., 1982). Thus, caution is justified in generalizing about recovery after head injury.

Physical Deficits

The frequency of various kinds of physical deficits after head injuries of varying severity is not known. However, there is evidence that physical deficits are common after severe injury. Roberts (1979), in a study of more than 300 patients, found that 40% of the patients were hemiparetic. In a report on 150 survivors after severe injury, Jennett and Teasdale (1981) found that 49% were hemiparetic, 29% were dysphasic, 21% were both hemiparetic and dysphasic, and 5% were hemianopic. Cranial nerve palsies were evident in 32% of the patients. A full discussion of the impact of cranial nerve deficits on the quality of outcome is presented in Levin et al. (1982).

Physical sequelae, particularly locomotion and communication disorders, often have a significant impact on work capacity (Tobis, Puri, & Sheridan, 1982; Weddell et al., 1980). In addition, rehabilitative efforts and social recovery may be adversely affected by physical sequelae (Grosswasser, Mendelson, Stern, Schechter, & Najenson, 1977; Lundholm, Jepsen, & Thornval, 1975; Najenson et al., 1975), but mounting evidence suggests that the neuropsychological sequelae present the more serious obstacle to recovery.

Memory Function

Disturbance in memory is the most frequently voiced complaint of the posttraumatic patient (Benton, 1979). Memory, however, is a very broad concept that encompasses a number of different functions, including, but not limited to, short-term memory, long-term (semantic and episodic) memory, and visual memory (Lachman, Lachman, & Butterfield, 1979; Wingfield & Byrnes, 1981). Short-term or immediate memory is a limited capacity system that holds approximately seven chunks of information over periods of less than one minute (Atkinson & Shiffrin, 1968; Miller, 1956). Long-term or remote memory is a system of unlimited capacity, involving rehearsal, repetition, organization, and storage of information over a period of years. In addition, visual memory, that is, recognition of abstract figures, location of objects in space, or pictures, is often distinguished from auditory memory (Nickerson, 1965; Standing, Conezio, & Haber, 1970). Visual memory may be short term or long term (Cooper & Shepard, 1973; Shepard & Metzler, 1971). Schacter and Crovitz (1977) have provided a helpful review of the quantitative research in memory function after closed head injury.

Attempts to document deficits in short-term (immediate) memory in head-injured patients have yielded varied results. Mandleberg and Brooks (1975) found that Digit Span was the only subtest on the Wechsler Adult Intelligence Scale that differentiated posttraumatic cases from controls when the former were tested 3 years after injury. Brooks (1975), however, found that neither forward repetition nor reversal of digits discriminated between head-injured patients and closely matched controls. Smith (1974), examining patients 10 years or more postinjury, found forward repetition of digits to be significantly impaired in those whose site of impact was on the right side of the head. Thomsen (1977) found that auditory digit span was still reduced more than 2 years after severe head injury in patients with residual aphasia. However, Digit Span may be a relatively insensitive test, and it is questionable that the forward repetition of digits is a measure of short-term memory (Levin et al., 1982). Mildly injured patients may display no evidence of reduced forward span, and persistent deficits in digit span of severely injured patients seem primarily confined to backward span.

Levin et al. (1976b), in testing recognition of irregularly shaped designs, found that patients with closed head injury complicated by protracted coma or oculovestibular deficit presented evidence of impaired short-term visual memory when tested at long intervals after injury.

Only a few studies have explored long-term (remote) memory in posttraumatic patients. Levin, Grossman, and Kelly (1977a) adopted the technique of Squire and Slater (1975), in which the recognition of names of television programs of earlier years is assessed to investigate memory functions in patients with brain disease (including some cases with closed head injury). They found a significant deficit in remote memory among the brain-disordered patients, as reflected in their poor identification of television programs broadcast 3 to 10 years prior to the assessment. In a recent application of Buschke's selective reminding procedure (Buschke, 1973; Buschke & Fuld, 1974), Levin and Eisenberg (1979) studied patients with closed head injury of varying severity and found significant deficits in long-term storage and retrieval of verbal material in those patients with a mass lesion or diffuse injury. The severity of injury was associated with persisting memory deficits. McLean et al. (1983), in a study of 20 patients with mild injury, also used a selective reminding test as a measure of memory. Results indicated that these patients had significant deficit at 3 days, but not at 1 month postinjury.

Visual (visuospatial) memory, in studies of patients with cerebral lesions other than head injury, has been associated with damage to the right hemisphere (Milner, 1974, 1978). Only a few studies of visual memory in head-injured patients have been reported. Brooks (1972) studied visual memory in 27 patients by testing reproduction of geometric designs and the complex Rey design and performance on the continuous recognition memory task of Kimura (1963). The closed head injury group performed below the level of the control group on all tasks with the exception of reproduction of geometric designs. Recognition memory after closed head injury was further studied by Brooks (1974), who administered Kimura's task to 34 patients after resolution of posttraumatic amnesia (ranging from 2 to 300 days). The closed head injury group had excessive false negative errors and a lower corrected score. Hannay, Levin, and Grossman (1979) investigated continuous recognition memory using a series of 110 line drawings with 47 patients recovering from closed head injuries of varying severity. Patients with severe injury had an excessive number of false alarms (misindentifying a new stimulus as one previously seen). More than two-thirds of the patients with severe injury achieved a total score that fell below the range of scores in the control group. Controls and mildly injured patients did not differ in their performance.

Cognitive-Intellectual Functions

The judgment of whether a head-injured patient is intellectually impaired often depends on the assessment measure used, that is, a brief mental status exam versus an omnibus test battery (Benton, 1979). Although the frequent use of the Wechsler Adult Intelligence Scale (WAIS) has enhanced comparison across studies of cognitive-intellectual functioning in head-injured patients, the WAIS is not a comprehensive measure of cognitive functions and is not sensitive to many subtle sequelae of closed head injury (Levin et al., 1982). The IQ scores on the WAIS may indicate little impairment in overall level of intellectual function, but more focused tests may reveal specific deficits in linguistic, perceptual, or mnemonic functions.

Studies of intellectual functioning during the early stages of recovery after closed head injury were reported in the 1940s by Ruesch and co-workers (Ruesch & Moore, 1943; Ruesch & Bowman, 1945; Ruesch, 1946). They found that patients with brief periods of coma and/or confusion and no hematoma recovered markedly on measures of cognitive speed, visuomotor speed, and Wechsler-Bellevue Scale items within 1 to 3 months of injury. Gronwall and Wrightson (1974) found that nearly all patients admitted to the hospital for mild head injury (posttraumatic amnesia less than 24 hours) had retained a normal rate of information processing on a cognitive stress test, the Paced Auditory Serial Addition Test (PASAT), by 35 days postinjury.

Although data are more available for long-term intellectual recovery than for the early phases of recovery, there is substantial disagreement in the literature concerning the potential for restitution of intellectual functioning (Levin et al., 1982). Mandleberg and Brooks (1975) studied 40 severely injured patients serially with the WAIS over a 3-year period. They found progressive improvement in function from 6 weeks to 3 years, with significant differences in the IQ scores between the earlier assessments and the final examination. The results indicated no significant differences between a control group and the final performances of the posttraumatic patients. Abilities assessed by the Verbal Scale of the WAIS recovered rapidly (within 5 months). At the 10-month interval postinjury, mean Full-Scale and Performance-Scale IQs were significantly lower than those of the controls, but at the 36-month interval these differences had disappeared.

Levin and colleagues (1979) gave the WAIS to 27 patients with severe closed head injury. The median duration of follow-up exceeded a year. In contrast to previous studies suggesting that intellectual ability after severe injury eventually recovers to a normal level, this study indicated that residual intellectual level corresponded to global outcome as measured by the Glasgow Outcome Scale. All severely disabled patients and several moderately disabled patients exhibited marked cognitive impairment.

Employing the Halstead–Reitan Neuropsychological Test Battery and the Trail-Making test, Dikmen and colleagues (1983) examined 27 adult patients with mild to severe head injuries over an 18-month period. The results indicated improvement over time for both relatively simple and more complex tasks, that is, simple and complex motor and manipulatory skills, alertness, attention, memory, quickness and flexibility of thought processes, concept formation, reasoning, and logical analysis. These findings gave little evidence that improvement in neuropsychological deficit areas slows appreciably after the first year. The authors argued that those patients with substantial losses show a greater amount of improvement but also a greater amount of residual deficit, which represents the remaining nonrecovered portion of the initial loss. Patients with less initial impairment show a smaller amount of improvement and a smaller remaining residual deficit.

Language Functions

The findings of Heilman, Safran, and Geschwind (1971) suggested that a frank aphasic disorder occurs only rarely (13 cases among 750 hospital admissions) after closed head injury. Levin et al. (1976a), in a study of 50 young adults with closed head injuries of varying severity, noted that minimal aphasia was a common sequel of closed head trauma. In the latter study, the authors administered the Multilingual Aphasia Examination (Benton and Hamsher, 1978), and found that 40% of the patients had deficits in picture naming. Circumlocution and paraphasic errors were often disclosed by the testing. On the other hand, only a few patients had difficulty with sentence repetition. Most of the patients, however, were seen shortly after recovery from confusion and disorientation.

Recovery from aphasia after an interval of at least six months after closed head injury was investigated by Levin, Grossman, Sarwar, and Meyers (1981) in 21 patients. The Multilingual Aphasia Examination and portions of other aphasia batteries were administered at the time of follow-up. Nine patients had fully recovered from acute aphasia, but 12 patients had residual language deficits. Decreased word-finding and naming difficulties were the most common deficits. Further, generalized language deficit was associated with global cognitive impairment as measured by the WAIS.

Although aphasia is evident in a small proportion of closed head-injured patients, it is more likely to occur in patients with mass lesions of the dominant hemisphere or in patients with diffuse injury (Levin et al., 1982). However, minimal aphasia may be present in patients without obvious aphasia, and dysarthria may occur with aphasia or in isolation. Symptoms of hemispheric disconnection (writing disorders, ideomotor praxis, and tactile naming) may be present more often than previously thought, particularly in severe injuries (Levin et al., 1982). A detailed discussion of language disorders after closed head injury has been presented by Levin (1981).

Perceptual-Motor Skills

The effects of closed head injury on perceptual-motor skills have been relatively unexplored. However, studies published to date suggest that retardation of response speed persists after severe injury and that performance on complex reaction time and perceptual-motor tasks is frequently impaired (Levin et al., 1982).

Miller (1970), in a study of simple and complex visual reaction times of 5 young adults who were tested between 3 and 12 months after closed head injuries, reported that complex reaction time, but not simple reaction time, was slowed in these patients. Van Zomeren and Deelman (1978) reported on a longitudinal study of 57 head-injured patients who were divided into mild, moderate, and severe injury groups according to duration of coma. On a choice reaction procedure, the reaction time in patients 2 years after severe injury was still slower than the reaction time of 90% of the subjects in a control group. Choice reaction time, however, had recovered to normal values in the mild and moderately injured subgroups. Van Zomeren (1981) has interpreted these findings in the context of deficits in attention and speed of information processing as sequelae of severe head injury.

Levin, Grossman, and Kelly (1977b) assessed the recognition of unfamiliar faces in 46 patients with closed head injury, including 6 cases with intracranial hematoma. Defective performance was found in more than one-quarter of the closed head injury patients who had been comatose for periods of more than a few minutes. Focal hematoma involving the right hemisphere contributed to visuoperceptive deficits in two of the six cases with focal lesions. However, this study was undertaken soon after patients had reached a normal level of orientation and does not shed light on long-term recovery of perceptual abilities.

Behavioral-Psychiatric Consequences

Personality changes and emotional disorders of head-injured patients are frequently reported by relatives and by rehabilitation staff as the greatest obstacles to full restoration within the family and the community. Unfortunately, most studies of behavioral disturbances after head injury are descriptive in nature and use the terminology of traditional psychiatric nosological categories, that is, psychoses, neurotic reactions, and personality disorders (Lishman, 1973, 1978). The third edition of the *Diagnostic and Statistical Manual for Mental Disorder* (DSM-III) of the American Psychiatric Association includes head trauma under the "Organic Personality Syndrome."

Stern (1978) has described three chronological phases of psychiatric symptoms after head injury. Phase one begins with the recovery of consciousness and is characterized by posttraumatic amnesia, disorientation, agitation, and aggression. Transient episodes of schizophrenic-like behavior may occur. The second, or subacute phase, begins when the acute symptoms remit and is characterized by introversion, egocentricity, defects of memory and judgment, and catastrophic anxiety reactions to changes. Phase three corresponds to relatively permanent changes in personality, such as judgment disorders, emotional shallowness, and absence of anticipation.

One of the few quantitative studies of long-term behavioral disturbance was conducted by Levin et al. (1979). Twenty-seven patients with severe closed head injuries were followed for at least 6 months postinjury. Behavioral outcome was assessed by the completion of the Glasgow Outcome Scale and the Brief Psychiatric Rating Scale (Overall & Gorham, 1962). Chronic socioeconomic dependence was found in moderately or severely disabled patients (as rated on the Glasgow Outcome Scale) who exhibited prolonged thinking disturbance and withdrawal-retardation. These patients had little comprehension of their cognitive deficits and would either focus on minor residual symptoms or deny any sequelae. Motor slowing and aspontaneity contributed to the ratings of withdrawal-retardation. Complaints of residual cognitive deficit were evident in 59% of the patients. Depressed mood, marital/family problems, and increased anxiety were also common in the series. Four of the patients (14%) had severe psychiatric disturbance, with two being diagnosed as psychotic.

Levin et al. (1982), after a review of the evidence on behavioral and psychiatric disturbances, concluded that the so-called postconcussional symptoms (headache, dizziness, fatigue, memory deficit, anxiety, irritability, hypersensitivity to noise, diminished concentration, hypochondriacal concern, and insomnia) and psychoses that emerge during the second (subacute) phase of head injury and later subside are a function of the degree of severity of injury.

SOME FINAL WORDS

National telethons promote the visibility of cerebral palsy and muscular dystrophy, yet traumatic head injury, with many more new cases each year than both of these neurological disorders, remains a silent epidemic. Nonetheless, a voluminous literature from several centers is accumulating. There is, however, great need for more refined classifications of outcome, for uniform measures of long-term cognitive/behavioral sequelae, for well-designed single-case studies of recovery, and for investigation of pharmacological intervention.

In addition, clinical neuropsychologists need to access the contributions of both the information-processing paradigm and the behavioral paradigm, the latter so eloquently presented by Horton and Sautter in Chapter 10 of this volume, in addressing the characterization and remediation of the cognitive/ behavioral sequelae of head injury. Finally, the professionals who witness the aftermath of vehicular accidents need to interact with advocacy groups in designing and promoting *preventive* measures regarding alcohol consumption and the use of safety devices.

REFERENCES

Adams, D. B. (1982). Wound ballistics: A review. *Military Medicine, 147,* 831–835.

Adams, J. H., Mitchell, E. E., Graham, D. I., & Doyle, D. (1977). Diffuse brain damage of immediate impact type. *Brain, 100,* 489–502.

American Psychiatric Association. (1980). *Diagnostic and statistical manual of mental disorders* (3rd ed.). Washington, DC.

Annegers, J. F., Grabow, J. D., Kurland, L. T., & Laws, E. R. (1980). The incidence, causes, and secular trends of head trauma in Olmsted County, Minnesota, 1935–1974. *Neurology, 30,* 912–919.

Atkinson, R. C., & Shiffrin, R. M. (1968). Human memory: A proposed system and its control processes. In K. W. Spence and J. T. Spence (Eds.), *The psychology of learning and motivation* (Vol. 22) (pp. 89–195). New York: Academic Press.

Bach-y-Rita, P. (Ed.). (1980). *Recovery of function: Theoretical considerations for brain injury rehabilitation.* Baltimore: University Park Press.

Bakay, L., & Glasauer, F. E. (1980). *Head injury.* Boston: Little, Brown.

Becker, D. P., Miller, J. D., Ward, J. D., Greenberg, R. P., Young, H. F., & Sakalas, R. (1977). The outcome from severe head injury with early diagnosis and intensive management. *Journal of Neurosurgery, 47,* 491–502.

Benton, A. L. (1979). Behavioral consequences of closed head injury. In G. L. Odom (Ed.), *Central nervous system trauma research status report* (pp. 220–231). Bethesda, MD: NINCDS, National Institutes of Health.

Benton, A. L., & Hamsher, K. deS. (1978). *Multilingual Aphasia Examination.* (Manual, revised). Iowa City: University of Iowa Press.

Ben-Yishay, Y. (Ed.). (1982). *Working approaches to remediation of cognitive deficits in brain damaged persons* (Rehabilitation Monograph No. 64). New York: New York University Medical Center, Institute of Rehabilitation Medicine.

Ben-Yishay, Y., & Diller, L. (1983). Cognitive deficits. In M. Rosenthal, E. R. Griffith, M. R. Bond, & J. D. Miller (Eds.), *Rehabilitation of the head injured adult* (pp. 167–183). Philadelphia: F. A. Davis.

Berkow, R., & Talbott, J. H. (Eds.). (1977). *The Merck manual of diagnosis and therapy* (13th ed.). Rahway, NJ: Merck.

Bond, M. R. (1975). Assessment of the psychosocial outcome after severe head injury. In R. Porter & D. W. Fitzsimons (Eds.), *Outcome of severe damage to the central nervous system* (Ciba Foundation Symposium 34) (pp. 141–157). New York: Elsevier.

Bond, M. R. (1979). The stages of recovery from severe head injury with special reference to late outcome. *International Rehabilitation Medicine, 1,* 155–159.

Bond, M. R. (1983a). Standardized methods of assessing and predicting outcome. In M. Rosenthal, E. R. Griffith, M. R. Bond, & J. D. Miller (Eds.), *Rehabilitation of the head injured adult* (pp. 97–113). Philadelphia: F. A. Davis.

Bond, M. R. (1983b). Effects on the family system. In M. Rosenthal, E. R. Griffith, M. R. Bond, & J. D. Miller (Eds.), *Rehabilitation of the head injured adult* (pp. 209–217). Philadelphia: F. A. Davis.

Bond, M. R., & Brooks, D. N. (1976). Understanding the process of recovery as a basis for the investigation of rehabilitation for the brain injured. *Scandinavian Journal of Rehabilitation Medicine, 8,* 127–133.

Brooks, D. N. (1972). Memory and head injury. *Journal of Nervous and Mental Diseases, 155,* 350–355.

Brooks, D. N. (1974). Recognition, memory, and head injury. *Journal of Neurology, Neurosurgery, and Psychiatry, 37,* 794–801.

Brooks, D. N. (1975). Long and short term memory in head injured patients. *Cortex, 11,* 329–340.

Brooks, D. N., & Aughton, M. E. (1979a). Psychological consequences of blunt head injury. *International Rehabilitation Medicine, 1,* 160–165.

Brooks, D. N., & Aughton, M. E. (1979). Cognitive recovery during the first year after severe blunt head injury. *International Rehabilitation Medicine, 1,* 166–172.

Brooks, D. N., McKinlay, W., & Bond, M. R. (1979, June). *The burden on the relatives of head injured adults.* Paper presented to the second European conference of the International Neuropsychological Society, Noordvijkerhout, The Netherlands.

Buschke, H. (1973). Selective reminding for analysis of memory and learning. *Journal of Verbal Learning and Verbal Behavior, 12,* 543–550.

Buschke, H., & Fuld, P. A. (1974). Evaluating storage, retention, and retrieval in disordered memory and learning. *Neurology, 24,* 1019–1025.

Caveness, W. F. (1977). Incidence of craniocerebral trauma in the United States, 1970–1975. *Annals of Neurology, 1,* 507.

Clifton, G. L., Grossman, R. G., Makela, M. E., Miner, M. E., Handel, S., & Sadhu, V. (1980). Neurological course and correlated computerized tomography findings after severe closed head injury. *Journal of Neurosurgery, 52,* 611–624.

Cooper, L. A., & Shepard, R. N. (1973). Chronometric studies of the rotation of mental images. In W. G. Chase (Ed.), *Visual information processing* (pp. 75–176). New York: Academic Press.

Craft, A. W. (1972). Head injury in children. In P. J. Vinken & G. W. Bruyn (Eds.), *Handbook of clinical neurology* (Vol. 23) (pp. 445–458). New York: Elsevier.

Diehl, L. N. (1983). Patient-family education. In M. Rosenthal, E. R. Griffith, M. R. Bond, & J. D. Miller (Eds.), *Rehabilitation of the head injured adult* (pp. 395–406). Philadelphia: F. A. Davis.

Dikmen, S., & Reitan, R. M. (1976). Psychological deficits and recovery of functions after head injury. *Transactions of the American Neurological Association, 101,* 72–77.

Dikmen, S., Reitan, R. M., & Temkin, N. R. (1983). Neuropsychological recovery in head injury. *Archives of Neurology, 40,* 333–338.

Dresser, A. C., Meirowsky, A. M., Weiss, G. H., McNeel, M. L., Simon, G. A., & Caveness, W. F. (1973). Gainful employment following head injury. Prognostic factors. *Archives of Neurology, 29,* 111–116.

Fahy, T. J., Irving, M. H., & Millac, P. (1967). Severe head injuries. *Lancet, 2,* 475–479.

Field, J. H. (1976). *Epidemiology of head injury in England and Wales: With particular application to rehabilitation.* Leicester, England: Printed for H. M. Stationery Office by Willsons.

Finger, S. (Ed.). (1978) *Recovery from brain damage: Research and theory.* New York: Plenum Press.

Finger, S., & Stein, D. G. (1982). *Brain damage and recovery: Research and clinical perspectives.* New York: Academic Press.

Fletcher, J. M., & Satz, P. (1983). Age, plasticity, and equipotentiality: A reply to Smith. *Journal of Consulting and Clinical Psychology, 51,* 763–767.

Freytag, E. (1963). Autopsy findings in head injuries from firearms. *Archives of Neurology, 76,* 215–225.

Fuld, P. A., & Fisher, P. (1977). Recovery of intellectual ability after closed head-injury. *Developmental Medicine and Child Neurology, 19,* 495–502.

Gilchrist, E., & Wilkinson, M. (1979). Some factors determining prognosis in young people with severe head injuries. *Archives of Neurology, 36,* 355–358.

Gronwall, D. (1976). Performance changes during recovery from closed head injury. *Proceedings of the Australian Association of Neurology, 13,* 143–147.

Gronwall, D. (1977). Paced auditory serial-addition task: A measure of recovery from concussion. *Perceptual and Motor Skills, 44,* 367–373.

Gronwall, D., & Sampson, H. (1974). *The psychological effects of concussion.* Auckland, New Zealand: Auckland University Press.

Gronwall, D., & Wrightson, P. (1974). Delayed recovery of intellectual function after minor head injury. *Lancet, 2,* 605–609.

Gronwall, D., & Wrightson, P. (1980). Duration of post-traumatic amnesia after mild head injury. *Journal of Clinical Neuropsychology, 2,* 51–60.

Gronwall, D., & Wrightson, P. (1981). Memory and information processing capacity after closed head injury. *Journal of Neurology, Neurosurgery, and Psychiatry, 44,* 889–895.

Groswasser, Z., Mendelson, L., Stern, M. J., Schechter, I., & Najenson, T. (1977). Reevaluation of prognostic factors in rehabilitation after severe head injury. Assessment thirty months after trauma. *Scandinavian Journal of Rehabilitation Medicine, 9,* 147–149.

Grubb, R. L., & Coxe, W. S. (1978). Trauma to the central nervous system. In S. G. Eliasson, A. L. Prensky, & W. B. Hardin, Jr. (Eds.), *Neurological pathophysiology* (2nd ed.). New York: Oxford University Press.

Gurdjian, E. S. (1971). Mechanisms of impact injury of the head. In *Head injuries: Proceedings of an international symposium held in Edinburgh and Madrid* (pp. 17–22). Edinburgh, Scotland: Churchill Livingstone.

Gurdjian, E. S., & Gurdjian, E. S. (1976). Cerebral contusions: Reevaluation of the mechanism of their development. *Journal of Trauma, 16,* 35–51.

Hammon, W. M. (1971). Analysis of 2187 consecutive penetrating wounds of the brain from Vietnam. *Journal of Neurosurgery, 34,* 127–131.

Hannay, H. J., Levin, H. S., & Grossman, R. G. (1979). Impaired recognition memory after head injury. *Cortex, 15,* 269–283.

Heilman, K. M., Safran, A., & Geschwind, N. (1971). Closed head trauma and aphasia. *Journal of Neurology, Neurosurgery, and Psychiatry, 34,* 265–269.

Higashi, J., Sakata, Y., Hatans, M., Abiko, S., Ihara, K., Katayama, S., Wakuta, Y., Okamura, T., Veda, H., Zenke, M., & Aoki, H. (1977). Epidemiological studies on patients with a persistent vegetative state. *Journal of Neurology, Neurosurgery, and Psychiatry, 40,* 876–885.

Irving, J. G. (1972). Impact of insurance coverage on convalescence and rehabilitation of head-injured patients. *Connecticut Medicine, 36,* 385–391.

Jamieson, I. G., & Kelly, D. (1973). Crash helmets reduce head injuries. *Medical Journal of Australia, 2,* 806.

Jennett, B. (1972). Prognosis after severe head injury. *Clinical Neurosurgery, 19,* 200–207.

Jennett, B. (1975). Scale, scope and philosophy of the clinical problem. In R. Porter & D. W. Fitzsimons (Eds.), *Outcome of severe damage to the central nervous system* (Ciba Foundation Symposium 34) (pp. 3–21). New York: Elsevier.

Jennett, B. (1983). Scale and scope of the problem. In M. Rosenthal, E. R. Griffith, M. R. Bond, & J. D. Miller (Eds.), *Rehabilitation of the head injured adult* (pp. 3–8). Philadelphia: F. A. Davis.

Jennett, B., & Bond, M. (1975). Assessment of outcome after severe brain damage. *Lancet, 1,* 480–487.

Jennett, B., & MacMillan, R. (1981). Epidemiology of head injury. *British Medical Journal, 282,* 101.

Jennett, B., & Plum, F. (1972). Persistent vegetative state after brain damage. *Lancet, 1,* 734–737.

Jennett, B., & Teasdale, G. (1981). *Management of head injuries.* Philadelphia: F. A. Davis.

Jennett, B., Teasdale, G., Braakman, R., Minderhoud, J., Heiden, J., & Kurze, T. (1979). Prognosis of patients with severe head injury. *Neurosurgery, 4,* 283–289.

Jennett, B., Teasdale, G., Galbraith, S., Pickard, J., Grant, H., Braakman, R., Avezaat, C., Maas, A., Minderhoud, J., Vecht, C. J., Heiden, J., Small, R., Caton, W., & Kurze, T. (1977). Severe head injuries in three countries. *Journal of Neurology, Neurosurgery, and Psychiatry, 40,* 291–298.

Kalsbeek, W. D., McLaurin, R. L., Harris, B. S. H., III, & Miller, J. D. (1980). The National Head and Spinal Cord Injury Survey: Major findings. *Journal of Neurosurgery, 53* (Suppl.), 19–31.

Kerr, T. A., Kay, D. W. K., & Lassman, L. P. (1971). Characteristics of patients, type of accident, and mortality in a consecutive series of head injuries admitted to a neurosurgical unit. *British Journal of Preventive and Social Medicine, 25,* 179–185.

Kertesz, A. (1979). *Aphasia and associated disorders:* Taxonomy, localization and recovery. New York: Grune & Stratton.

Kimura, D. (1963). Right temporal lobe damage. *Archives of Neurology, 8,* 264–271.

Kirkpatrick, J. B., & DiMaio, V. (1978). Civilian gunshot wounds of the brain. *Journal of Neurosurgery, 49,* 185–198.

Klonoff, H. (1971). Head injuries in children: Predisposing factors, accident conditions, accident proneness and sequelae. *American Journal of Public Health, 61,* 2405–2417.

Kovner, R., Mattis, S., & Goldmeier, E. (1983). A technique for promoting robust free recall in chronic organic amnesia. *Journal of Clinical Neuropsychology, 5,* 65–71.

Kraus, J. F. (1980a). A comparison of recent studies on the extent of the head and spinal cord injury problem in the United States. *Journal of Neurosurgery, 53* (Suppl.), 35–43.

Kraus, J. F. (1980b). Injury to the head and spinal cord: The epidemiological relevance of the medical literature published from 1960 to 1978. *Journal of Neurosurgery, 53* (Suppl.), 3–10.

Lachman, R., Lachman, J. L., & Butterfield, E. C. (1979). *Cognitive psychology and information processing: An introduction.* Hillsdale, NJ: Lawrence Erlbaum.

Langfitt, T. W. (1978). Measuring the outcome from head injuries. *Journal of Neurosurgery, 48,* 673–678.

Levati, A., Farina, M. L., Vecchi, G., Rossanda, M., & Marrubini, M. (1982). Prognosis of severe head injuries. *Journal of Neurosurgery, 57,* 779–783.

Levin, H. S. (1981). Aphasia in closed head injury. In M. T. Sarno (Ed.), *Acquired aphasia* (pp. 427–463). New York: Academic Press.

Levin, H. S., Benton, A. L., & Grossman, R. G. (1982). *Neurobehavioral consequences of closed head injury.* New York: Oxford University Press.

Levin, H. S., & Eisenberg, H. M. (1979, October). *Verbal learning and memory in relation to focal and diffuse effects of closed head injury.* Paper presented at Academy of Aphasia meeting, San Diego, CA.

Levin, H. S., & Grossman, R. G. (1978). Behavioral sequelae of closed head injury: A quantitative study. *Archives of Neurology, 35,* 720–727.

Levin, H. S., Grossman, R. G., & Kelly, P. J. (1976a). Aphasic disorder in patients with closed head injury. *Journal of Neurology, Neurosurgery, and Psychiatry, 39,* 1062–1070.

Levin, H. S., Grossman, R. G., & Kelly, P. J. (1976b). Short-term recognition memory in relation to severity of head injury. *Cortex, 12,* 175–182.

Levin, H. S., Grossman, R. G., & Kelly, P. J. (1977a). Assessment of long-term memory in brain damaged patients. *Journal of Consulting and Clinical Psychology, 45,* 684–688.

Levin, H. S., Grossman, R. G., & Kelly, P. J. (1977b). Impairment of facial recognition after closed head injuries of varying severity. *Cortex, 13,* 119–130.

Levin, H. S., Grossman, R. G., Rose, J. E., & Teasdale, B. (1979). Long-term neuropsychological outcome of closed head injury. *Journal of Neurosurgery, 50,* 412–422.

Levin, H. S., Grossman, R. G., Sarwar, M., & Meyers, C. A. (1981). Linguistic recovery after closed head injury. *Brain and Language, 12,* 360–374.

Levin, H. S., Meyers, C. A., Grossman, R. G., & Sarwar, M. (1981). Ventricular enlargement after closed head injury. *Archives of Neurology, 38,* 623–629.

Levin, H. S., O'Donnell, V. M., & Grossman, R. G. (1979). The Galveston orientation and amnesia test: A practical scale to assess cognition after head injury. *Journal of Nervous and Mental Diseases, 167,* 675–684.

Lezak, M. D. (1978). Living with the characterologically altered brain injured patient. *Journal of Clinical Psychiatry, 39,* 592–598.

Lezak, M. D. (1979). Recovery of memory and learning functions following traumatic brain injury. *Cortex, 15,* 63–70.

Lezak, M. D. (1983). *Neuropsychological assessment* (2nd ed.). New York: Oxford University Press.

Lillard, P. L. (1978). Five years experience with penetrating crainiocerebral gunshot wounds. *Surgical Neurology, 9,* 79–83.

Lishman, W. A. (1973). The psychiatric sequelae of head injury, A review. *Psychological Medicine, 3,* 304–318.

Lishman, W. A. (1978). *Organic psychiatry: The psychological consequences of cerebral disorder.* Boston: Blackwell.

Lundholm, J., Jepsen, B. N., & Thornval, G. (1975). The late neurological, psychological, and social aspects of severe traumatic coma. *Scandinavian Journal of Rehabilitation Medicine, 7,* 97–100.

Luria, A. R. (1973). *The working brain.* New York: Basic Books.

Mandleberg, I. A. (1975). Cognitive recovery after severe head injury. 2. Wechsler Adult Intelligence Scale during post-traumatic amnesia. *Journal of Neurology, Neurosurgery, and Psychiatry, 38,* 1127–1132.

Mandleberg, I. A. (1976). Cognitive recovery after severe head injury. 3. WAIS verbal and performance IQ's as a function of post-traumatic amnesia duration and time from injury. *Journal of Neurology, Neurosurgery, and Psychiatry, 39,* 1001–1007.

Mandleberg, I. A., & Brooks, D. N. (1975). Cognitive recovery after severe head injury. 1. Serial testing on the Wechsler Adult Intelligence Scale. *Journal of Neurology, Neurosurgery, and Psychiatry, 38,* 1121–1126.

Marshall, L. F., Smith, R. N., & Shapiro, H. M. (1979a). The outcome with aggressive treatment in severe head injuries. Part I: The significance of intracranial pressure monitoring. *Journal of Neurosurgery, 50,* 20–25.

Marshall, L. F., Smith, R. W., & Shapiro, H. M. (1979b). The outcome with aggressive treatment in severe head injuries. Part II: Acute and chronic barbiturate administration in the management of head injury. *Journal of Neurosurgery, 50,* 26–30.

McGonagle, E., Carper, M., & Balicki, M. (1983). Greenery: An integrated approach to cognitive rehabilitation of the head injured patient. *Cognitive Rehabilitation, 1,* 8–12.

McLean, A., Jr., Temkin, N. R., Dikmen, S., & Wyler, A. R. (1983). The behavioral sequelae of head injury. *Journal of Clinical Neuropsychology, 5,* 361–376.

Meirowsky, A. M. (1982). Notes of posttraumatic epilepsy in missile wounds of the brain. *Military Medicine, 147,* 632–634.

Miller, N. E. (1970). Simple and choice reaction time following severe head injury. *Cortex, 6,* 121–127.

Miller, G. A. (1956). The magical number seven plus or minus two: Some limits on our capacity for processing information. *Psychological Review, 63,* 81–97.

Miller, J. D., Butterworth, J. F., Gudeman, S. K., Faulker, J. E., Choi, S. C., Selhorst, J. B., Harbison, J. W., Lutz, H. A., Young, H. F., & Becker, D. P. (1981). Further experience in the management of severe head injury. *Journal of Neurosurgery, 54,* 289–298.

Milner, B. (1974). Sparing of language functions after early unilateral brain damage. *Neurosciences Research Progress Bulletin, 12,* 213–217.

Milner, B. (1978). Clues to the cerebral organization of memory. In P. A. Buser & A. Rougeul-Buser (Eds.), *Cerebral correlates of conscious experience* (INSERM Symposium No. 6) (pp. 139–153). New York: Elsevier North-Holland Biomedical Press.

Najenson, T., Grosswasser, Z., Mendelson, L., & Hackett, P. (1980). Rehabilitation outcome of brain damaged patients after severe head injury. *International Rehabilitation Medicine, 2,* 17–22.

Najenson, T., Grosswasser, Z., Stern, M., Schechter, I., David, C., Berghaus, N., & Mendelson, L. (1975). Prognostic factors in rehabilitation after severe head injury. *Scandinavian Journal of Rehabilitation Medicine, 7,* 101–105.

Najenson, T., Mendelson, L., Schechter, I., David, C., Mintz, N., & Grosswasser, Z. (1974). Rehabilitation after severe head injury. *Scandinavian Journal of Rehabilitation Medicine, 6,* 5–14.

National Head Injury Foundation (1982). *The silent epidemic.* (Available from National Head Injury Foundation Inc., 18A Vernon Street, Framingham, MA).

Newcombe, F. (1969). *Missile wounds of the brain: A study of psychological deficits.* New York: Oxford University Press.

Nickerson, R. S. (1965). Short-term memory for complex meaningful visual configurations: A demonstration of capacity. *Canadian Journal of Psychology, 19,* 155–160.

Oddy, M., & Humphrey, M. (1980). Social recovery during the year following severe head injury. *Journal of Neurology, Neurosurgery, and Psychiatry, 43,* 798–802.

Oddy, M., Humphrey, M., & Uttley, D. (1978a). Stresses upon the relatives of head-injured patients. *British Journal of Psychiatry, 133,* 507–513.

Oddy, M., Humphrey, M., & Uttley, D. (1978b). Subjective impairment and social recovery after closed head injury. *Journal of Neurology, Neurosurgery, and Psychiatry, 41,* 611–616.

Ommaya, A. K., & Gennarelli, T. A. (1974). Cerebral concussion and traumatic unconsciousness: Correlation of experimental and clinical observations on blunt head injuries. *Brain, 97,* 633–654.

Overall, J. E., & Gorham, D. R. (1962). The brief psychiatric rating scale. *Psychological Reports, 10,* 799–812.

Overgaard, J., Hvid-Hansen, O., Land, M., Pedersen, K., Christensen, S., Haase, J., Hein, O., & Tweed, W. (1973). Prognosis after head injury based on early clinical examination. *Lancet, 2,* 631–635.

Panting, A., & Merry, P. H. (1972). The long term rehabilitation of severe head injuries with particular reference to the need for social and medical support for the patient's family. *Rehabilitation, 38,* 33–37.

Parker, S. A., & Serrats, A. F. (1976). Memory recovery after traumatic coma. *Acta Neurochirurgery, 34,* 71–77.

Plum, F., & Posner, J. (1980). *The diagnosis of stupor and coma.* Philadelphia: F. A. Davis.

Porter, R., & Fitzsimons, D. W. (Eds.) (1975). *Outcome of severe damage to the central nervous system* (Ciba Foundation Symposium 34). New York: Elsevier.

Rich, N. M. (1980). Missile injuries. *American Journal of Surgery, 139,* 414–420.

Rimel, R., Giordani, M., Barth, J., Boll, T., & Jane, J. (1981). Disability caused by minor head injury. *Neurosurgery, 9,* 221–228.

Rimel, R. W., & Jane, J. A. (1983). Characteristics of the head-injured patient. In M. Rosenthal, E. R., Griffith, M. R. Bond, & J. D. Miller (Eds.). *Rehabilitation of the head injured adult* (pp. 9–21). Philadelphia: F. A. Davis.

Roberts, A. H. (1976). Long term prognosis of severe accidental head injury. *Proceedings in the Royal Society of Medicine, 59,* 137–140.

Roberts, A. H. (1979). *Severe accidental head injury: An assessment of long-term prognosis.* New York: Macmillan.

Rosenbaum, M., & Najenson, T. (1976). Changes in life patterns and symptoms of low mood as reported by wives of severely brain-injured soldiers. *Journal of Consulting and Clinical Psychology, 44,* 881–888.

Rosenblum, W. I., Greenberg, R. P., Seelig, J. M., & Becker, D. P. (1981). Midbrain lesions: Frequent and significant prognostic feature in closed head injury. *Neurosurgery, 9,* 613–620.

Rosenthal, M., Griffith, E. R., Bond, M. R., & Miller, J. D. (Eds.). (1983). *Rehabilitation of the head injured adult.* Philadelphia: F. A. Davis.

Rosenthal, M., & Muir, C. A. (1983). Methods of family intervention. In M. Rosenthal, E. R. Griffith, M. R. Bond, & J. D. Miller (Eds.), *Rehabilitation of the head injured adult* (pp. 407–419). Philadelphia: F. A. Davis.

Ruesch, J. (1946). Intellectual impairment in head injuries. *American Journal of Psychiatry, 100,* 480–496.

Ruesch, J., & Bowman, K. M. (1945). Prolonged post-tramatic syndromes following head injury. *American Journal of Psychiatry, 102,* 145–163.

Ruesch, J., & Moore, B. E. (1943). Measurement of intellectual functions in the acute stage of head injury. *Archives of Neurology, 50,* 165–170.

Russell, W. R. (1971). *The traumatic amnesias.* New York: Oxford University Press.

Russell, W. R., & Smith, A. (1961). Post-traumatic amnesia in closed head injury. *Archives of Neurology, 5,* 19–29.

Schacter, D. L., & Crovitz, H. F. (1977). Memory function after closed head injury: A review of the quantitative research. *Cortex, 13,* 150–176.

Selecki, B. R., Hoy, R. J., & Ness, P. (1967). A retrospective survey of neuro-traumatic admissions to a teaching hospital: Part 1. General aspects. *Medical Journal of Australia, 2,* 113–117.

Selecki, B. R., Hoy, R. J., & Ness, P. (1968). Neurotraumatic admissions to a teaching hospital: A retrospective survey. Part 2. Head injuries. *Medical Journal of Australia, 1,* 851–855.

Semmes, J., Weinstein, S., Ghent L., & Teuber, H.-L. (1960). *Somatosensory changes after penetrating brain wounds in man.* Cambridge, MA: Harvard University Press.

Shepard, R. N., & Metzler, J. (1971). Mental rotation of three-dimension objects. *Science, 171,* 701–703.

Smith, A. (1983). Overview or "underview"? Comment on Satz and Fletcher's "emergent trends in neuropsychology: An overview." *Journal of Consulting and Clinical Psychology, 51,* 768–775.

Smith, E. (1974). Influence of site of impact on cognitive impairment persisting long after severe closed head injury. *Journal of Neurology, Neurosurgery, and Psychiatry, 37,* 719–726.

Squire, L. R., & Slater, P. C. (1975). Forgetting in very long-term memory as assessed by an improved questionnaire technique. *Journal of Experimental Psychology: Human Learning and Memory, 1,* 50–54.

Standing, L., Conezio, J., & Haber, R. N. (1970). Perception and memory for pictures: Single-trial learning of 2560 visual stimuli. *Psychonomic Science, 19,* 73–74.

Stein, D. G., Rosen, J. J., & Butters, N. (Eds.). (1974). *Plasticity and recovery of function in the central nervous system.* New York: Academic Press.

Stern, J. M. (1978). Cranio-cerebral injured patients. *Scandinavian Journal of Rehabilitation Medicine, 10,* 7–10.

Stover, S. L., & Zeiger, H. E., Jr. (1976). Head injury in children and teenagers: Functional recovery correlated with duration of coma. *Archives of Physical Medicine and Rehabilitation, 57,* 201–205.

Strich, S. J. (1956). Diffuse degeneration of the cerebral white matter in severe dementia following head injury. *Journal of Neurology, Neurosurgery, and Psychiatry, 19,* 163–185.

Strich, S. J. (1970). Lesions in the cerebral hemispheres after blunt head injury. In S. Sevitt & H. B. Stoner (Eds.), *The pathology of trauma* (pp. 166–171). London: BMA House.

Tanhecho, J., & Kaplan, P. E. (1982). Physical and surgical rehabilitation of patient after 6-year coma. *Archives of Physical Medicine and Rehabilitation, 63,* 36–38.

Teasdale, G., & Jennett, B. (1974). Assessment of coma and impaired consciousness: A practical scale. *Lancet, 2,* 81–84.

Teuber, H.-L. (1975). Recovery of function after brain injury in man. In R. Porter & D. W. Fitzsimons (Eds.), *Outcome of severe damage to the central nervous system* (Ciba Foundation Symposium 34) (pp. 159–190). New York: Elsevier.

Teuber, H.-L., Battersby, W. S., & Bender, M. B. (1960). *Visual field defects after penetrating missile wounds of the brain.* Cambridge, MA: Harvard University Press.

Teuber, H.-L., Battersby, W. S., & Bender, M. B. (1960). *Visual field defects after penetrating missile wounds of the brain.* Cambridge, MA: Harvard University Press.

Thomsen, I. V. (1974). The patient with severe head injury and his family. *Scandinavian Journal of Rehabilitation Medicine, 6,* 180–183.

Thomsen, I. V. (1977). Verbal learning in aphasic and non-aphasic patients with severe head injuries. *Scandinavian Journal of Rehabilitation Medicine, 9,* 73–77.

Tobis, J. S., Puri, K. B., & Sheridan, J. (1982). Rehabilitation of the severely brain-injured patient. *Scandinavian Journal of Rehabilitation Medicine, 14,* 83–88.

Van Zomeren, A. H. (1981). *Reaction time and attention after closed head injury.* Lisse, The Netherlands: Swets & Zeitlinger B. V.

Van Zomeren, A. H., & Deelman, B. G. (1978). Long-term recovery of visual reaction time after closed head injury, *Journal of Neurology, Neurosurgery, and Psychiatry, 41,* 452–457.

Walker, A. E., Caveness, W. F., & Critchley, M. (Eds.). (1969). *The late effects of head injury.* Springfield, IL: C. C Thomas.

Warrington, J. M. (1983). *Humpty dumpty syndrome.* Winona Lake, IN: Light & Life Press.

Weddell, R., Oddy, M., & Jenkins, D. (1980). Social adjustment after rehabilitation: A two year follow-up of patients with severe head injury. *Psychological Medicine, 10,* 257–263.

Weinberg, J., Piasetsky, E., Diller, L., & Gordon, W. (1982). Treating perceptual organization deficits in nonneglecting RBD stroke patients. *Journal of Clinical Neuropsychology, 4,* 59–65.

West, C. C. H. (1981). A short history of the management of penetrating missile injuries of the head. *Surgical Neurology, 10,* 145–149.

Wingfield, A., & Byrnes, D. L. (1981). *The psychology of human memory.* New York: Academic Press.

Wrightson, P., & Gronwall, D. (1980). Time off work and symptoms after minor head injury. *Injury, 12,* 445–454.

14

The Neuropsychology of Alcoholism

Christopher Ryan and
Nelson Butters

Until quite recently, most researchers interested in the neuropsychology of alcohol studied either the transient changes in information-processing ability that are associated with acute intoxication, or the permanently disabling neuropsychiatric disorders that are found in the small proportion of alcoholics who develop Korsakoff's syndrome or alcoholic dementia. Both approaches have provided, and continue to provide, important data about certain brain mechanisms, particularly those subserving memory, and the sensitivity of these processes to the toxic effects of ethanol. With the growth of clinical neuropsychology during the past 15 years, however, there has been a dramatic increase in interest in the more pragmatic issues of assessment and treatment planning. As a consequence, investigators have begun to focus their attention on "neurologically intact" alcoholics, that very large population of individuals who have been drinking heavily for several years yet show no clinically obvious evidence of brain damage on mental status examination. When neuropsychological testing is conducted several weeks after the beginning of detoxification, these alcoholics often manifest subtle cognitive deficits, particularly on tests assessing problem-solving, visuoperceptual and visuomotor skills, and learning and memory ability. With continued sobriety, the severity of those subclinical deficits may decline spontaneously, although the rate and pattern of improvement appear to be unpredictable.

In this chapter, we review the recent experimental literature on neuropsychological deficits associated with chronic alcohol abuse, discuss several theories that have been advanced to explain these findings, and examine how different alcoholismic factors (e.g., liver disease, family history of alcoholism, duration of sobriety) may moderate or amplify the nature and extent of cognitive impairment. We have approached this task from the perspective of the practicing clinician who must not merely determine whether a particular alcoholic patient is "organic," but must comprehensively assess the patient's neuropsychological strengths and weaknesses so that cognitive remediation plans can be formulated, if necessary, and reasonable recommendations made about long-term prognosis. Although most clinicians continue to rely on standardized test batteries such as the Halstead–Reitan Battery (see Parsons & Farr, 1981, for review; see also Chapter 6, this volume), we shall emphasize how various tests, initially used in research on groups of alcoholic subjects, can be profitably applied in a clinical setting to evaluate the individual with a history of chronic alcohol consumption.

ASSESSMENT OF THE ALCOHOLIC PATIENT

Alcoholic Korsakoff's Syndrome

While our primary concern in this chapter is with the alcoholic who has relatively subtle, subclinical impairments, there are two important reasons to begin with a brief discussion of the alcoholic Korsakoff patient. First, those patients have been studied extensively in the experimental laboratory, and a large number of tasks and paradigms have been developed to examine their cognitive status (e.g., Butters & Cermak, 1980; Talland, 1965). Second, clinicians are often asked to evaluate an alcoholic patient because of a suspicion that the person may be "a Korsakoff." Conducting such an examination requires assessment techniques that may be very different from those used with more intact patients.

Alcoholic Korsakoff's syndrome is characterized by a remarkably circumscribed memory disorder. These patients continue to perform within normal limits on standardized tests of intelligence, but show a profound anterograde amnesia, as well as a retrograde amnesia. Deficits are also evident on measures of problem solving and hypothesis testing (Oscar-Berman, 1973) and on a variety of visuospatial tasks (Bertera & Parsons, 1978; Kapur & Butters, 1977; Glosser, Butters, & Kaplan, 1977), but these appear trivial when compared with the learning and memory impairments. Surprisingly, Korsakoff patients have an intact immediate memory capacity, as indexed by their normal digit span, and have no difficulty accessing and using information from semantic memory, as demonstrated by their normal scores on the WAIS Information and Vocabulary subtests (Butters & Cermak, 1976; Cutting, 1978a; Victor, Herman, & White, 1959). Their ability to learn motor skills and retain general rules and procedures also appears to be intact, for they readily master pursuit rotor (Cermak, Lewis, Butters, & Goodglass, 1973) and mirror reading tasks (Martone, Butters, Payne, Becker, & Sax, 1984).

Anterograde amnesia is an inability to hold new information in memory for more than a few seconds. Because of this impairment, the Korsakoff patient remains disoriented in time and place, is unable to learn the names of doctors and nurses, cannot remember three words 10 seconds after hearing them, and has no recollection of major events that were experienced minutes earlier (Cermak & Butters, 1973). Neither rote rehearsal nor the use of verbal or visual mnemonics is very effective in facilitating recall (Cermak, 1980), although certain types of cuing techniques may temporarily improve performance (Huppert & Piercy, 1978; Warrington & Weiskrantz, 1974). In addition to their dense anterograde amnesia, alcoholic Korsakoff patients are unable to recall accurately events that had occurred in the remote past. This retrograde memory disturbance appears to follow a temporal gradient, such that events experienced in the 10 to 20 years prior to the onset of illness are less likely to be remembered than those experienced during childhood and early adulthood (Albert, Butters, & Levin, 1979; Marslen-Wilson & Teuber, 1975; Seltzer & Benson, 1974).

Accompanying this memory disorder is a dramatic change in personality. Most alcoholic Korsakoff patients show an apathy or flattened affect reminiscent of that seen in mental patients who have undergone frontal lobotomies. That is, they have become passively compliant individuals who make few demands and offer few complaints and who have apparently lost all interest in alcohol (Butters, 1981; Cutting, 1978b). These patients typically lack any insight into their memory disorder, and usually deny having any cognitive problems whatsoever. In addition, they will occasionally confabulate, or produce responses that are false, and even bizarre, when asked about events that have occurred in the recent past. At one time confabulation was thought to be a cardinal symptom of Korsakoff's syndrome, but most clinicians now regard it to be an infrequent event that is *not* related to the severity of the patient's memory disorder or to his suggestibility (Mercer, Wapner, Gardner, & Benson, 1977). In our experience, confabulatory behavior is most likely to occur early in the course of the disorder; chronic patients who have had the disease five or more years rarely confabulate (Butters, 1984).

Extensive neuropsychological testing is usually not necessary to make a diagnosis of Korsakoff's syndrome. In most instances the Wechsler Adult Intelligence Scale (WAIS) and the Wechsler Memory Scale (WMS) will provide enough information to differentiate the Korsakoff patient from both the demented alcoholic and the neurologically intact alcoholic. The Wechsler Memory Scale has been designed so that healthy persons of average or bright average intelligence will earn a "Memory Quotient," or MQ, that is approximately equal to their IQ (Wechsler, 1945). Thus, any deviation reflects some kind of memory disorder, and the greater the deviation, the more profound the disorder. A number of investigators have used a 15-point difference between IQ and MQ as diagnostic of an amnestic disturbance (Cutting, 1982; Wilkinson & Carlen, 1980). In our research, we have considered persons to have Korsakoff's syndrome if their WAIS Verbal IQ score is 90 or more (i.e., in the "normal" range) *and* their MQ is at least 20 points lower. We rely on Verbal IQ, rather than Full-Scale IQ, because the verbal subtests provide a better estimate of premorbid intelligence in alcoholics. Most people who have consumed alcohol excessively earn quite low Performance IQs (and hence, lower Full-Scale IQs) because of impaired visuomotor functioning. This is particularly evident on the Digit Symbol, Object Assembly, and Block Design subtests, tasks on which both neurologically intact alcoholics (Goldstein & Shelly, 1982; Long & McLachlan, 1974; Fitzhugh, Fitzhugh, & Reitan, 1965) and alcoholic Korsakoff patients (Butters & Cermak, 1980; Victor et al., 1959) tend to have most difficulty. In contrast, Korsakoff patients perform as well as nonalcoholics on the WAIS Information, Vocabulary, Arithmetic, Digit Span, Similarities, and Picture Completion subtests (Butters, 1981).

The mnestic deficit of the alcoholic Korsakoff patient is so pervasive that performance is impaired on virtually all WMS subtests. This is illustrated in Table 14.1, which compares the performance of a group of 10 middle-aged alcoholic Korsakoff patients with demographically similar groups of neurologically intact alcoholics and nonalcoholic controls (Ryan & Butters, 1980a). Unlike the two other groups of subjects, Korsakoff patients are clearly impaired on the Information and Orientation subtests—two tasks that measure orientation in time and place, and memory for events occurring in the recent past. Their immediate memory for visual information (Visual Reproductions) is also impaired, as is their capacity to recall connected discourse (Logical Memory). In addition, verbal learning ability (Associate Learning) is disrupted, although not completely. Indeed, after three study trials, Korsakoff patients are often able to master all 6 of the "easy" associates (e.g., baby/cries), but rarely learn more than 1 of the 4 "hard" associates (e.g., crush/dark). On the other hand, they are able to concentrate and follow instructions (Mental

TABLE 14.1 Mean Scores (± SD) of Alcoholic Korsakoff Patients, Neurologically Intact Alcoholics, and Nonalcoholic Control Subjects on Wechsler Memory Scale Subtests

	Alcoholic Korsakoffs	Alcoholics	Nonalcoholic Controls
Mean age	55	54	55
Years of education	12.2 ± 2.1	11.3 ± 2.3	12.1 ± 1.4
WAIS Verbal IQ	106.1 ± 12.2	115.2 ± 6.7	116.7 ± 9.4
WMS Memory Quotient	76.2 ± 10.9	108.7 ± 19.9	116.9 ± 15.1
WMS raw scores			
Information	2.7 ± 1.3	5.6 ± 0.9	5.9 ± 0.3
Orientation	2.2 ± 1.3	4.9 ± 0.3	4.9 ± 0.3
Mental Control	6.4 ± 2.7	7.2 ± 1.7	7.5 ± 1.8
Memory Passages	4.8 ± 3.2	8.7 ± 2.3	9.4 ± 2.1
Digits Total	11.6 ± 2.1	11.5 ± 1.5	11.7 ± 2.2
Visual Reproductions	3.5 ± 1.9	7.7 ± 3.4	8.1 ± 2.4
Associate Learning	6.1 ± 1.3	13.1 ± 2.8	13.8 ± 3.5

Control) and to hold information in immediate memory (Digit Span), as well as other subjects.

Alcoholic Dementia

The existence of alcoholic dementia as a unique clinical syndrome remains controversial. Some writers have maintained that those alcoholics showing evidence of *global* intellectual impairment are actually suffering from an Alzheimer-type degenerative dementia or a multiinfarct dementia that is completely unrelated to their history of alcoholism. Others have suggested that the severe intellectual deterioration occasionally seen in alcoholics is invariably caused by a nutritional deficiency or a liver disorder, and that alcohol plays only a secondary role in the etiology of the dementia (for reviews, see Victor, 1975; Victor & Banker, 1978). With the rising popularity of both viewpoints during the past 40 years, there has been a corresponding decline in the frequency with which the diagnosis of alcoholic dementia is made and an increase in the diagnosis of other disorders, particularly Korsakoff's syndrome (Lishman, 1981; Cutting, 1978b; Horvath, 1975). As a consequence, less is known about the neuropsychology of alcoholic dementia than about most other dementiform disorders.

In a recent review of this literature, Cutting (1982, p. 151) has argued that the syndrome of alcoholic dementia has been "unjustifiably neglected" by clinicians and that it is, in reality, a not uncommon complication of chronic alcohol abuse. He asserts that individuals with this disorder can be readily differentiated from both alcoholic Korsakoff patients and from neurologically intact alcoholics. Data from a retrospective chart review study of patients classified as having alcoholic dementia or Korsakoff's syndrome demonstrate several important differences between these two groups (Cutting, 1978b). Compared to Korsakoff's syndrome, alcoholic dementia had a gradual rather than an acute onset, was more likely to occur in women, and was associated with a longer drinking history. Despite their much higher incidence of electroencephalographic abnormalities, patients with an alcoholic dementia were less likely to show evidence of ocular abnormalities, particularly nystagmus. A follow-up study of these patients demonstrated that those with alcoholic dementia were more likely to show improvement (though not complete recovery) over time, so long as they remained abstinent.

On formal neuropsychological testing, these demented alcoholics performed poorly on all WAIS subtests and hence earned lower than average Verbal, Performance, and Full-Scale IQ scores. Table 14.2 indicates that, unlike Korsakoffs, the demented alcoholics had marked difficulty on the Vocabulary, Comprehension, Digit Span, and Picture Completion subtests and were far more likely to earn scaled scores below 9 on those tests. Although Wechsler Memory Scale scores were not reported, both types of patients were found to be disoriented in time and place and impaired on all mnestic measures. This

**TABLE 14.2 Mean WAIS Scores for Patients with
Korsakoff's Syndrome or Alcoholic Dementia**

	Korsakoff's Syndrome	Alcoholic Dementia
Number of cases	21	24
Verbal IQ	104	89
Performance IQ	98	85
Vocabulary	12.2	8.4
Comprehension	11.0	8.1
Digit Span	11.0	7.4
Picture Completion	9.2	6.4
Arithmetic	7.8	7.3
Similarities	8.2	5.7
Object Assembly	7.7	5.2
Block Design	7.1	5.9
Picture Arrangement	5.8	5.3
Digit Symbol	4.9	3.6

overall pattern of results is very different from that seen in the neurologically intact alcoholic, who earns scores on both the WAIS and WMS that are well within the normal range. Because language functions were not evaluated in a systematic fashion, it is not known whether confrontation naming and verbal fluency deficits are as common in demented alcoholics as they are in patients with an Alzheimer-type degenerative dementia (e.g., Rosen, 1980). On the basis of their clinical observations, however, Seltzer and Sherwin (1978) have suggested that language abnormalities are *not* characteristic of alcoholic dementia.

The assessment of patients suspected of having an alcoholic dementia is clearly hampered by the lack of detailed neuropsychological and neuropathological research into that disorder. At the present time, the most reasonable diagnostic criteria appear to be those established by the American Psychiatric Association (1980) for "dementia associated with alcoholism." Three features are essential for that diagnosis:

1. Widespread, clinically obvious intellectual impairment appears in the alcoholic and is so serious that it interferes with the person's ability to function socially and occupationally.
2. This impairment persists despite 3 or more weeks of abstinence.
3. All other causes of dementia, other than chronic, heavy consumption of alcohol, are excluded by history, physical examination, and laboratory tests.

According to these criteria, the truly demented alcoholic should show deficits on virtually *all* neuropsychological measures. Not only are learning and memory processes disrupted, but problem-solving, visuomotor coordination, and constructional skills are also significantly impaired. While there are many specialized tests available that can be used to assess these functions, we find that the WAIS and WMS usually provide sufficient information about the individual's overall level of functioning for differential diagnosis. In attempting to discriminate the demented alcoholic from the individual with an Alzheimer-type degenerative disorder, periodic reassessment should prove to be of particular value. Patients with alcoholic dementia should show no change in functioning—or some improvement—over time if they remain sober, whereas the patient with Alzheimer's disease will show a worsening level of performance.

Estimating premorbid intelligence is critical in determining whether an individual is currently performing at a significantly lower level (i.e., at least 15 points), and is thus demented. One approach to this problem has been taken by Wilson and his associates (1979), who have used a series of demographic variables (age, race, sex, occupation, and education) to derive a formula that appears to predict premorbid IQ with a remarkably high level of accuracy. We have operated under the assumption that when Verbal IQ is lower than 90, and the MQ is 10 or more points lower still, the person is demented if there is evidence from their educational and occupational background that they had functioned at a higher level some time in the past. As Cutting (1978b) has demonstrated, all WAIS subtest scores are usually depressed, including Vocabulary and Digit Span. This "rule" must be modified when one is evaluating a patient who once functioned at a very high level (e.g., college professor, physician). In that case, a Verbal IQ score of 100 or 105 could still be considered indicative of significant deterioration, since a score of at least 120 or 125 would normally have been expected. Because no Wechsler Memory Scale data have been reported for demented alcoholics, we can rely only on our clinical findings, which suggest that these individuals show deficits on all subtests, including Mental Control. Because of their difficulty concentrating, they often have difficulty learning even the "easy" word pairs on the Associate Learning subtest.

Alcohol-Related Subclinical Impairments

Although they are relatively rare disorders (Lishman, 1981; Victor & Banker, 1978; Horvath, 1975), both Korsakoff's syndrome and alcoholic dementia are quite easy to identify because they are characterized by such profound cognitive deficits. Far more problematic for the clinician is the identification of neuropsychological impairments in that much larger group of alcoholics and problem drinkers who show no obvious behavioral evidence of brain dysfunction. Indeed, recent research carried out with this population of neurologically intact alcoholics has produced such inconsistent findings from one study to another that conclusions about the consequences of chronic alcohol use have ranged from ". . . cautious optimism that even very heavy alcohol use is not related to neuropsychological impairment in the alcoholic who is in his or her late 30s" (Grant, Adams, & Reed, 1979, p. 1268), to "disabling intellectual impairment may be the earliest complication of chronic alcoholism and may arise early in the alcoholic career" (Lee, Møller, Hardt, Haubek, & Jensen, 1979, p. 759).

This general lack of agreement in the literature on the relationship between drinking and neuropsychological functioning reflects not only the tremendous difficulty one faces in studying *subtle* changes in central nervous system (CNS) processes, but the problems associated with searching for those deficits in an unusually heterogeneous subject population. For example, if one were to survey several large outpatient alcohol treatment facilities one would probably find that clients come from very different educational and occupational backgrounds, range in age from 16 to 70 or older, have been drinking heavily for anywhere between 1 and 50 or more years, and suffer from a variety of alcohol-related medical and/or psychiatric disturbances. Unfortunately, all of those variables are known to influence cognition. In fact, a number of recent studies have clearly demonstrated that both neuropsychological test scores and neuroradiological measures of cerebral atrophy are correlated with the subject's age (Craik, 1977; Carlen, Wilkinson, Wortzman, Holgate, Cordingley, Lee, Huszer, Moddel, Singh, Kiraly, & Rankin, 1981), the duration (Tarter, 1973; Cala & Mastaglia, 1981) and pattern (Eckardt, Parker, Noble, Feldman, & Gottschalk, 1978; Bergman, Axelsson, Idestrom, Borg, Hindmarsh, Makower, & Mutzell, 1983) of alcohol consumption, the duration of sobriety prior to testing (Brandt, Butters, Ryan, & Bayog, 1983; Ron, Acker, Shaw, & Lishman, 1982), the use of drugs other than alcohol (Hill & Mikhael, 1979; Grant, Reed, Adams, & Carlin, 1979), and the incidence of alcohol-related medical complications such as nutritional deficiency (Guthrie, 1980; Albert, Butters, Rogers, Pressman, & Geller, 1982) and liver dysfunction (Rehnstrom, Simert, Hansson, Johnson, & Vang, 1977; Smith & Smith, 1977). Performance on many neuropsychological tests is also affected by subjects' educational and occupational background (Finlayson, 1977; West, Hill, & Robins, 1977), their premorbid level of intellectual competence (Lezak, 1976), and their affective state (Weingartner, Cohen, Murphy, Martello, & Gerdt, 1981). Thus, anyone interested in studying the neuropsychology of alcoholism must control for, or otherwise take into account, the myriad demographic and alcoholism-related factors that interact to produce the pattern of cognitive impairment found in the alcoholic individual. In addition, one must have available a set of measures that are sensitive to relatively small changes in information-processing ability.

It should be obvious that virtually any pattern of neuropsychological deficit can be seen in alcoholics, depending on what sorts of subjects are selected, how soon after the beginning of detoxification they are tested, and the particular assessment measures used (cf. Klisz & Parsons, 1979). In the remainder of this section we examine these interrelationships in more detail.

General Measures of Intelligence

One of the earliest attempts to assess cognitive changes in the neurologically intact alcoholic was made by David Wechsler (1941). When he administered the Wechsler–Bellevue (W–B) Intelligence Scale to male alcoholics who had been drinking heavily for at least 10 years, he found no evidence of generalized intellectual deterioration, for IQ scores fell well within the normal range (mean = 98.3). However, when he compared the individual subtest scores of the alcoholics with those from his normative sample, he found a distinctive pattern of deficit. Alcoholics performed as well as normals on all subtests except Similarities, Digit Span, Digit-Symbol, and Object Assembly—tasks that were thought to depend on abstract reasoning, perceptual organization, and new learning.

This basic observation has subsequently been replicated by numerous investigators (for a review, see Kleinknecht & Goldstein, 1972). When detoxified, neurologically intact alcoholics are evaluated with the Wechsler–Bellevue or Wechsler Adult Intelligence Scales, they invariably earn IQ scores that are in the average or bright average range, but perform significantly more poorly than nonalcoholics on one or more subtests, with Block Design, Object Assembly, and Digit-Symbol being most frequently affected (Fitzhugh et al., 1965; Goldstein & Shelly, 1971; Long & McLachlan, 1974; Parsons & Farr, 1981). While many writers have interpreted this pattern of results as indicative of a visuoperceptual deficit, which, in turn, reflects an alcohol-induced right hemisphere dysfunction (e.g., Jones, 1971; Jones & Parsons, 1972), a very different explanation has been offered by Kaldegg (1956). Studying a group of bright (median IQ = 120), middle-aged alcoholics whose poorest performances appeared on Object Assembly, Kaldegg examined the approach taken by his subjects to rapidly assembling the jigsaw-type puzzles comprising that subtest. Despite their high level of intelligence, most of the subjects failed to use any sort of systematic problem-solving strategy, but behaved in a trial-and-error fashion: "They should have thought in advance, but they were planless . . ." (1956, p. 617).

The failure of many alcoholics to approach challenging, relatively unfamiliar tasks in a planned, systematic way may be responsible for their impaired performance on certain neuropsychological tasks. Indeed, of the various Wechsler subtests, both Block Design and Object Assembly seem to be particularly dependent on the use of efficient information-processing strategies (Schorr, Bower, & Kiernan, 1982; Das, 1980; Luria & Tsvetkova, 1964). On the other hand, sophisticated strategies are unnecessary for optimal performance on subtests like Information, Comprehension, Vocabulary, or Picture Completion, where the subject merely retrieves highly overlearned information from remote memory. The Digit Symbol subtest appears to be unusually sensitive to virtually *any* type of subtle brain dysfunction, perhaps because optimal performance depends upon the effective integration of several different processes, including attention, visual scanning, psychomotor speed, and associative learning (Glosser, Butters, & Kaplan, 1977; Kapur & Butters, 1977).

The tendency of alcoholic patients to have particular difficulty on tasks that are functionally complex is also seen on the Luria–Nebraska Neuropsychological Battery. When Chmielewski and Golden (1980) administered this collection of 269 items to a group of detoxified, neurologically intact male alcoholics and to a comparable group of nonalcoholic medical patients, they found significant between-group differences on only the Visual-Spatial, Receptive Speech, Arithmetic, Memory, Intellectual, and Pathognomonic scales. A detailed item-by-item analysis demonstrated that alcoholic patients had the most difficulty on those tasks requiring the greatest amount of "cortical integration" (Chmielewski & Golden, 1980, p. 9). For example, alcoholics performed as well as controls when asked to recall the gist of a brief story, repeat meaningful sentences, or recall a short list of related words, but their level of performance deteriorated significantly when they were asked to form associations between words and a series of unrelated pictures or recall a longer list of unrelated words—two tasks that require the organization, association, and storage of a relatively large amount of information. Comparing the performance of alcoholics and nonalcoholics on an extensive, somewhat different, collection of neuropsychological measures, Gudeman and his colleagues (1977, p. 39) reached a similar conclusion: ". . . unless well integrated through years of overlearning, the chronic alcoholic patient has difficulty in tasks and situations that require an ongoing integration and modification of behavioral responses on the basis of immediate perceptual feedback."

Abstract Reasoning

Given the difficulty alcoholics have on tasks requiring "cortical integration" and "mental flexibility," one would expect them to show severe impairments on tests specifically designed to assess abstract-reasoning ability. Investigators using a number of different types of abstraction tests have demonstrated that this generalization is accurate, but only under certain circumstances.

Perhaps the most commonly used measure of deductive reasoning is the Halstead Category test. On this test the subject sees a series of slides (e.g., three circles) and is told to guess the principle underlying the series (e.g., number) by pressing one of four levers. Each response is followed by immediate feedback about its accuracy. Six increasingly difficult subtests are presented, along with a seventh "memory" subtest. In an extensive review of this literature, Parsons and Farr (1981) report that alcoholics performed more poorly than nonalcoholic controls in 93% of the studies. The one study in their survey that showed no evidence of impairment (Grant et al., 1979) had been restricted to younger alcoholics who had been drinking for a relatively short period of time (mean = 6 years).

Other investigators have also demonstrated that both age and duration of drinking have a significant effect on the number of Category test errors. When Jones and Parsons (1971) administered this test to younger and older groups of alcoholics, only the older alcoholics were found to be impaired; younger alcoholics performed as well as nonalcoholic controls. When they assessed the effects of duration of drinking on performance by assigning alcoholics to either a short- or long-duration group, they found that those who had been drinking for a long period of time tended to make more errors than age- and education-matched alcoholics who had been drinking for a significantly shorter period of time.

A very similar pattern of results has been reported on the Wisconsin Card Sorting test, a deductive reasoning task considered to be particularly sensitive to damage in the frontal regions of the brain. In this test, the subject is presented with a deck of cards on which are printed one of four symbols in one of four colors, and is told to place each card into one of four bins (marked with one red triangle, two green stars, three yellow crosses, and four blue circles) according to some principle that must be deduced on the basis of feedback provided by the examiner. After the subject has made 10 consecutive correct responses, the examiner shifts to another sorting principle. Tarter and Parsons (1971) found that middle-aged alcoholics had no difficulty acquiring the first concept ("color") as rapidly as controls, but required significantly more trials to master successive concepts. Not only did the alcoholics make more errors than controls, but they made qualitatively different errors. Unlike normal subjects or patients with frontal lobe damage who tend to make perseverative errors, the alcoholics studied by Tarter and Parsons had difficulty maintaining the correct cognitive set and tended to shift *prematurely* to a different (and incorrect) sorting principle.

When Tarter (1973) later compared the Wisconsin performance of long-term alcoholics (more than 10 years of heavy drinking) with a demographically similar group of short-term alcoholics, he found that the two groups differed in their responsiveness to examiner-provided feedback. Both groups made more premature-shift errors than controls, but when the short-term alcoholics were told they had made an error, they used that information and tried a different sorting principle on the next trial. The long-term alcoholics, in contrast, failed to modify their behavior following feedback, and continued to perseverate with the same incorrect strategy.

Using a somewhat different type of task, Klisz and Parsons (1977) have demonstrated that the inability to test hypotheses in a systematic fashion is the cardinal deficit underlying the poor performance of alcoholics on measures of deductive reasoning. In their investigation, they administered a task, initially developed by Levine (1966), to study the problem-solving strategies of groups of alcoholics differing in age and duration of drinking. For each problem, subjects were shown a set of cards on which there were two stimuli that differed from each other on the basis of background color, letter of the alphabet, size, and location. They were told to guess which of the two stimuli was correct by pointing to the appropriate side of the card and were given feedback about the accuracy of their guess after the first, sixth, eleventh, and sixteenth trials. By analyzing responses on each of the *non*reinforced trials, it is possible to determine which "hypothesis" subjects have adopted and then examine how they modify it following feedback.

Compared to nonalcoholic controls, the alcoholics studied by Klisz and Parsons approached this hypothesis-testing task less systematically and required more time to complete each problem. During the nonreinforced trial sequences they failed to use a particular hypothesis consistently, and after a feedback trial they were less likely to adopt a win-stay/lose-shift strategy. Their inconsistent behavior cannot be attributed to any sort of memory deficit, since a similar pattern of results was obtained in a second, "memory aid" condition, in which markers indicating the correct stimulus were left in view on each of the four feedback trial cards. Unlike participants in previous studies (e.g., Tarter, 1973), long-term alcoholics were not more impaired than short-term drinkers. There was, however, a significant interaction between age and group: older alcoholics performed far worse than either age-matched controls or younger alcoholics, whereas younger alcoholics performed much more like age-matched nonalcoholics.

Taken together, these studies suggest that alcoholics, particularly those who are older and have been drinking heavily for a longer period of time, manifest significant problem-solving deficits. Deficits are most apparent on nonverbal, relatively unfamiliar tasks and seem to result from an inability to generate appropriate hypothesis-testing strategies (Laine & Butters, 1982) and to use feedback to modify behavior in a consistent fashion (Tarter, 1973). As we have suggested elsewhere (Ryan & Butters, 1983), this failure to use hypothesis-testing strategies in a planned, systematic way may underlie most, if not all, of the information-processing impairments found in chronic alcoholics. Although the Shipley–Hartford Institute of Living Scale and Raven's Progressive Matrices have also been used to examine abstract reasoning ability in alcoholics (Jones & Parsons, 1972) and heavy social drinkers (Parsons & Fabian, 1982; Parker & Noble, 1980; Parker, Birnbaum, Boyd, & Noble, 1980), these tasks appear to be relatively less sensitive to alcohol-related impairments and tend to provide less information about the neuropsychological mechanism underlying the deficit, compared with measures like the Category test, the Wisconsin Card Sorting test, and Levine's hypothesis-testing paradigm.

Visuospatial and Visuomotor Ability

The failure of alcoholics to perform normally on nonverbal problem-solving tasks is not limited to measures of abstract reasoning. Significant deficits have also been found on a wide range of visuoperceptual and visuomotor tasks that require visual scanning, contour analysis, and rapid responding.

Two of the most sensitive, and most commonly used, clinical measures of visual information-processing efficiency are the Trail-Making test and the WAIS Digit-Symbol Substitution test (DSST). The DSST is a coding task in which the subject scans an array of numbers, substituting numbers for letters according to a code presented at the top of the page. In the standard administration procedure (Wechsler, 1955), the raw score is merely the number of correct substitutions made in 90 seconds. The Trail-Making test (Reitan, 1958) can be thought of primarily as a visual search task made up of two different subtests. On Part A, the subject connects, in order, 25 numbers randomly distributed across a page. On Part B, numbers and letters are presented, and the subject must alternate between the two, rapidly connecting the stimuli in consecutive order (e.g., 1-A-2-B). Detoxified alcoholics are far slower than controls on both of these tasks (e.g., Fitzhugh et al., 1965; O'Leary, Radford, Chaney, & Schau, 1977; Butters, Cermak, Montgomery, & Adinolfi, 1977; Goldstein & Shelly, 1971), although it should be kept in mind that most other patients having psychiatric disorders or mild brain dysfunction also perform quite slowly on these tasks.

While there have been few experimental analyses of the neuropsychological deficit(s) responsible for the typical alcoholic's slow performance on the Trail-Making test, several investigations have determined that the low scores earned by alcoholics on the DSST are *not* merely secondary to motor retardation, but reflect a higher-order perceptual impairment (Glosser et al., 1977; Kapur & Butters, 1977). For example, when Kapur and Butters administered the DSST, an associative learning test (Symbol-Digit Learning test), and an embedded figures test (Boston Embedded Figures test) to middle-aged alcoholics, they found impairments on all three tests, as well as significant correlations between DSST scores and performance on the other two tests. These results suggest that two somewhat different mechanisms are responsible for the DSST impairment in alcoholics. First, because they learn the 9 digit-symbol associations more slowly than nonalcoholics, they must refer more frequently to the code presented at the top of the page. Second, because they have more difficulty analyzing and integrating visual contour information (as indicated by their poor embedded figures performance), they are unable to identify visual stimuli as efficiently as controls. Both of these rather subtle deficits act synergistically to slow the recoding process. This process may be slowed further by a third type of deficit—a reduction in visual scanning efficiency, which has also been found in detoxified chronic alcoholics (Bertera & Parsons, 1978).

Several other tests have been employed with varying degrees of success to assess the visuospatial abilities of alcoholics. The Boston Embedded Figures test (Kapur & Butters, 1977) has been found to be very useful in measuring alcoholics' capacity to analyze the figural-spatial properties of visual stimuli. On each test trial, subjects are presented with a card containing a relatively simple line drawing in the upper portion and four complex patterns below. Their task is to identify rapidly the pattern containing the target stimulus.

Brandt and his associates (1983) have reported that both younger and older alcoholics are impaired on this test, relative to age- and education-matched controls. Moreover, this impairment does not appear to improve spontaneously with continued abstinence, since alcoholics who had been continuously sober for nearly 7 years performed as poorly as those who had been sober for 1 to 2 months. Alcoholics have also been found to have significant difficulty on the Group Embedded Figures test (Oltman, Raskin, & Witkin, 1971), a test having a short-term memory component as well as visual scanning and contour analysis components (Donovan, Queisser, & O'Leary, 1976).

An unfortunate problem with the assessment of visuospatial and visuomotor problems in the individual alcoholic is that the results often have only limited clinical utility. Knowing that an alcoholic has difficulty scanning visual arrays, for example, provides important, albeit nonspecific, evidence that this particular individual is not functioning at a normal level, yet that information typically plays no role in formulating treatment plans or rehabilitation strategies. In many ways, these are "silent" deficits, since alcoholics rarely note that they are having significant visual information-processing deficits, whereas they frequently express a great deal of concern about the fact that they are having difficulty thinking clearly or remembering things. On the other hand, the presence of these deficits has led to the development of theories localizing the effects of chronic alcohol abuse to the frontal region of the brain, or to the right hemisphere (for review, see Tarter, 1976, 1980), and has provided researchers with evidence that in the abstinent alcoholic, different cognitive functions recover at very different rates (e.g., Brandt et al., 1983; Ryan, DiDario, Butters, & Adinolfi, 1980).

Learning and Memory

Those of us in clinical practice constantly hear alcoholics report that "my memory isn't as good as it used to be." In spite of those complaints, however, it has been notoriously difficult to demonstrate the presence of clinically significant learning and memory deficits in the typical detoxified, neurologically intact alcoholic. With few exceptions (e.g., Ryan & Butters, 1980b; Brown, Gopinathan, & Slobogin, 1984), most alcoholics who have been detoxified for 3 or more weeks perform well within normal limits on standard clinical memory assessment instruments.

It is only within the past 5 years that investigators have begun to develop more challenging measures of learning and memory ability and have, as a consequence, frequently (Ryan, 1980; Ryan & Butters, 1980b; Riege, Holloway, & Kaplan, 1981; Brandt et al., 1983; Cutting, 1978c; Miglioli, Buchtel, Campanini, & DeRisio, 1979), but not always (e.g., Parsons & Prigatano, 1977; Yohman & Parsons, in press), succeeded in demonstrating the presence of subtle mnestic deficits. In general, the tests most sensitive to both the transient effects of acute alcohol intoxication and the relatively permanent effects of chronic alcohol abuse are those that require subjects to process a great deal of unfamiliar information, particularly nonverbal information, in a short period of time (for a review, see Ryan & Butters, 1983). On the other hand, tests requesting recall of information learned in the remote past (e.g., knowledge of famous people or events) are performed quite well (Albert, Butters, & Brandt, 1980), although there is some rather controversial evidence suggesting that recall of certain types of remote information (e.g., vocabulary knowledge) may be disrupted in detoxified alcoholic patients (Draper & Manning, 1982).

In our experience, the Symbol-Digit Learning test (SDLT) (Kapur & Butters, 1977) has proven to be an unusually powerful measure of the ability to encode new information efficiently. A large number of studies have demonstrated that this easily administered, multitrial, paired-associate learning task is successful in detecting significant deficits in both younger and older chronic alcoholics (e.g., Ryan & Butters, 1980a,b; Albert et al., 1982) who have been continuously abstinent for several months (Ryan, DiDario, Butters, & Adinolfi, 1980) or years (Brandt et al., 1983). Briefly, the subject is presented with 7 unfamiliar symbols, each paired with a single digit. During the study phase, each symbol-digit pair is presented visually for 3 seconds. Following presentation of the entire list, the subject is tested by showing the symbol alone as a retrieval cue and asking for the appropriate number. Immediately after each response, the correct symbol-digit pair is presented for an additional 3 seconds. Four such test trials are administered.

We suspect that alcoholics have so much difficulty with this task because of their tendency to use relatively simple encoding strategies. Rather than transforming each symbol into some sort of meaningful representation ("that looks like a carpenter's T-square"), long-term alcoholics are more likely to focus on the structural characteristics of the symbols ("that has two lines that are perpendicular"), relying on a strategy that does not allow subjects readily to differentiate one stimulus cue from another. Because of the resulting increase in proactive interference, they will learn the list at a slower rate than controls (Ryan, Butters, Montgomery, Adinolfi, & DiDario, 1980).

Evidence of a significant associative learning deficit has recently been obtained using a more "ecologically valid" test—a face/name paired-associate learning test. Becker and his colleagues (1983a) presented groups of alcoholics and nonalcoholic control subjects with 12 pictures of men's faces, each paired with a highly associative surname (e.g., Carpenter, Plant, Spear). The paradigm was very similar to that used with the SDLT. On the study trial, each face was exposed for 10 seconds and the subject was told "this is Mr . . ." The subject was then tested by presenting each face to him and asking for the name. Whenever he made an error, he was told the correct name and given an additional 4 seconds to study the face. This process continued for 9 test trials, or until the subject correctly named all 12 faces. An analysis of the acquisition phase data demonstrated that performance declined as a function of age for both alcoholics and nonalcoholics, although alcoholics, as a group, made significantly fewer correct responses than nonalcoholics and learned at a slower rate.

Although verbal paired-associate learning tasks have also been used to assess mnestic processes in alcoholics (e.g., Ryan, 1980), it now appears that those tasks may not be as consistently sensitive as the nonverbal SDLT or the Face/Name Learning test. In our experience, and that of other investigators (e.g., Yohman & Parsons, in press), performance on verbal associative learning tests is quite variable from one study to another, perhaps because various task parameters (e.g., list length, study time, associative similarity) and subject characteristics (e.g., age, occupational and educational background) exert an unusually powerful influence. For example, Ryan (1980) demonstrated clinically significant verbal learning deficits in a group of older detoxified alcoholics, using a very long list of 24 pairs of unrelated words presented at the rather slow rate of 10 seconds per pair. Ryan and Butters (1980b) were also successful in finding statistically significant differences between younger and older alcoholics and comparable age-matched nonalcoholic control subjects, using a shorter list of 10 pairs presented at a more rapid rate (2 sec/pair). On the other hand, Yohman and Parsons (in press) found no differences when they tested somewhat younger groups of alcoholics and nonalcoholics with an even shorter list of 7 word pairs, presented at an intermediate rate (6 sec). There are probably important differences in the educational and occupational backgrounds of the subjects in those three studies, as well as in their drinking histories. Nevertheless, it seems clear that the demand characteristics of the learning task will have a critical effect on outcome. If alcoholics have more difficulty than nonalcoholics in using associative mnemonics, those tasks that require processing unfamiliar information in a brief period of time will be performed more poorly than will those that provide more time to process less information.

Because certain types of short-term memory tasks require subjects to process a great deal of information at a rapid rate, they have been found to be quite useful in detecting alcohol-related mnestic impairments. For example, a number of studies from our laboratory have demonstrated that groups of older and younger detoxified long-term alcoholics are significantly impaired, relative to age-matched controls, on the Four Word Short-Term Memory test (Ryan & Butters, 1980b; Brandt et al., 1983). On each trial, four unrelated words are read to the subject at the rate of one word per second. Immediately thereafter, the subject hears a three-digit number from which he begins counting backward by threes until the examiner asks for the words, 15 or 30 seconds later. This task provides an excellent estimate of how efficiently verbal information can be encoded and held in memory for several seconds, because the mental arithmetic task prevents the subject from rehearsing the words during the retention interval.

Two recent studies have demonstrated that this task may be particularly useful in monitoring both the *recovery* of information-processing ability following prolonged abstinence and the *development* of very subtle information-processing deficits associated with nonalcoholic social drinking. Brandt and his associates (1983) administered this test to groups of chronic alcoholics who had been continuously abstinent for 1 to 2 months, 1 to 3 years, or more than 5 years, and found that those alcoholics who had been abstinent for more than 5 years showed a significant degree of recovery of short-term memory functioning, since they performed as well as nonalcoholic controls, and significantly better than alcoholics who had been abstinent for less than 5 years. In contrast, both the 1- to 3-month-abstinent and 1- to 3-year-abstinent groups were significantly impaired, relative to the group of nonalcoholic control subjects. Taking a very different approach, MacVane and her co-workers (1982) increased the difficulty of the test by presenting 5 words on each trial, rather than 4, and administering this to groups of nonalcoholic social drinkers. When they correlated performance with various drinking parameters, they found small, but statistically reliable relationships between test scores and both the current amount consumed per drinking occasion and the amount consumed during their heaviest drinking period.

Many subjects find this test to be extraordinarily frustrating and complain vociferously about having to count backward by threes rapidly and accurately. Nevertheless, it is becoming increasingly clear that of all the neuropsychological tests currently available, the Four (or Five) Word Short-Term Memory test may be one of the most sensitive measures of alcohol-related changes in overall mental efficiency.

Recovery of Function Following Detoxification

Virtually any traumatic or neurotoxic insult to the central nervous system produces neuropsychological deficits that tend to reduce in severity over time (Stein, Rosen, & Butters, 1974). For alcoholic individuals, recovery occurs most rapidly in the first few weeks following the beginning of detoxification, although it may continue, albeit at a much slower pace, over the next several years.

Many studies have demonstrated that when alcoholics or heavy drinkers are evaluated within their first week of sobriety, significant cognitive impairments appear on most neuropsychological tests (e.g., Jonsson, Cronholm, & Izikowitz, 1962; Burdick, Johnson, & Smith, 1970), including measures of language function (Rada, Porch, Dillingham, Kellner, & Porec, 1977) and very simple verbal learning ability (Sharp, Rosenbaum, Goldman, & Whitman, 1977). Within the next 1 to 2 weeks, however, this clinically obvious "organic brain syndrome" will normally remit spontaneously (Acker, 1982), although a recent psychopharmacological study has indicated that the rate of recovery may be accelerated somewhat by administering therapeutic doses of certain antihypoxidotic/nootropic drugs (e.g., Piridoxilate) (Saletu, Saletu, Grünberger, & Mader, 1983). After 3 to 6 weeks of sobriety, the recovery process appears to level off, leaving most alcoholics with the relatively subtle, "subclinical" deficits described above (cf. Grünberger et al., 1976; Clarke & Haughton, 1975; Page & Linden, 1974; Claiborn & Greene, 1981; Goldman, Williams, & Klisz, 1983; Grant, Adams, & Reed, 1984). Because neuropsychological status is so unstable in the recently detoxified alcoholic, little information about long-term clinical prognosis is gained by evaluating patients who have been abstinent for less than 3 or 4 weeks.

Whether alcoholics will ultimately show complete recovery of cognitive functions following long-term sobriety is an issue that is still being debated. It now appears that the process of recovery may continue for at least 5 years, with different cognitive processes recovering at very different rates. In general, simple language skills seem to recover completely within a matter of weeks (Sharp et al., 1977; Rada et al., 1977), whereas performance on tests of visuomotor, visuospatial, and abstract-reasoning ability may continue to improve—yet not reach completely normal levels—over the course of a year or more (Long & McLachlan, 1974; Berglund, Leijonquist, & Horlen, 1977; Schau, O'Leary & Chaney, 1980). The slowest rate of spontaneous change appears on measures of learning and memory. Three groups of investigators, using very different mnestic tests, reported essentially no improvement whatsoever following one year of sobriety (Yohman, Parsons, & Leber, 1985; Ryan, DiDario, Butters, & Adinolfi, 1980; Günberger, Krypsin-Exner, Masarik, & Wessely, 1975). Indeed, despite 7 years of sobriety, the alcoholic subjects studied by Brandt and his colleagues (1983) continued to perform as poorly as recently detoxified alcoholics on a paired-associate learning test, though they did show a significant improvement in performance on a test of short-term memory.

Rehabilitation specialists have recently demonstrated that various types of cognitive remediation techniques are remarkably effective in improving the linguistic, mnestic, and problem-solving skills of seriously brain-damaged patients (for review, see Goldstein & Ruthven, 1983), and it is possible that such techniques may similarly facilitate recovery in alcoholics. Unfortunately, there have been few systematic studies of the long-term efficacy of cognitive remediation programs with these individuals. In most of the work published to date, memory retraining procedures have been applied to relatively small numbers of severely amnestic alcoholic Korsakoff patients, with little or no success (Goldstein, Ryan, Turner, Kanagy, Barry, & Kelly, 1985; Cermak, 1980; Jaffe & Katz, 1975). However, because there is evidence that neurologically intact alcoholics derive a great deal of benefit when they are provided with associative mnemonics (Binder & Schreiber, 1980; Ryan, 1980) or are repeatedly readministered the same learning and memory tests (Guthrie, 1980) or concept-formation tests (Jenkins & Parsons, 1980; Fabian & Parsons,

1983), we are optimistic that formal cognitive retraining programs will hasten the course of recovery of function in this less seriously impaired group of alcoholics.

THEORIES OF IMPAIRMENT

In an effort to explain the interrelationships between alcohol use, brain dysfunction, and behavioral change, three somewhat different neurobehavioral theories have been advanced (for detailed reviews, see Tarter, 1980; Bolter & Hannon, 1980; Ryan & Butters, 1983). Although none of these offer a completely satisfactory explanation, all have been instrumental in stimulating some very intriguing research.

Right Hemisphere Hypothesis

Because the performance of alcoholic patients is quite similar to that of neurological patients who have had traumatic or vascular damage to the right side of the brain, it has been hypothesized that alcohol selectively damages structures within the right cerebral hemisphere. Like right hemisphere patients, most detoxified alcoholics show relatively well preserved verbal information-processing skills, but have difficulty on visuoperceptual (Kapur & Butters, 1977) and visuomotor tests (Glosser et al., 1977), as well as on virtually any learning (Ryan & Butters, 1980b), memory (Miglioli et al., 1979), or problem-solving test (Jones & Parsons, 1972) having a visual component.

This hypothesis predicts that chronic alcoholics will show signs of lateralized brain damage when evaluated with various neuroradiological techniques. While it is known that certain disease processes (e.g., herpes simplex encephalitis) or toxic exposures (e.g., carbon monoxide poisoning) may selectively damage circumscribed regions within the brain (e.g., hippocampus), there is currently little evidence that the brain damage seen in alcoholic patients is restricted to the right cerebral hemisphere. Neither computerized tomography (Carlen et al., 1981; Ron, 1983) nor pneumoencephalography (Hudolin, 1980; Brewer & Perrett, 1971) has succeeded in demonstrating that the mild to moderate degree of cortical atrophy often seen in alcoholics is more prominent in the right hemisphere. Furthermore, when Goldstein and Shelly (1980) reexamined the neuropsychological status of alcoholics using a comprehensive test battery and a series of neuropsychological "keys" or decision rules to predict the locus of damage, they too found little evidence of a characteristic right hemisphere disturbance: 37.5% of their subjects were classified as having diffuse brain damage, while 19% were classified as having primarily left hemisphere damage and 21.5% were considered to show primarily right hemisphere damage.

We suspect that alcoholics perform so poorly on so-called right hemisphere tasks not because they have incurred lateralized brain damage, but because they have suffered diffusely distributed brain damage that produces an overall reduction in mental efficiency. This type of generalized dysfunction will cause an individual to *appear* to have relatively more difficulty with right hemisphere tasks, because those tasks are likely to rely on skills that are less well practiced (e.g., rapidly reproducing an unfamiliar design with a series of colored blocks), and hence are more intellectually demanding, than most verbal tasks (e.g., answering vocabulary questions that draw on previously acquired information).

Frontal System Hypothesis

On the basis of results demonstrating that alcoholic subjects have particular difficulty on a variety of abstract-reasoning tasks (Tarter, 1973; Jones & Parsons, 1972), Tarter (1976, 1980) has postulated that chronic alcohol abuse selectively disrupts the "frontal system"—a series of interconnected nuclei located in the frontal, limbic, and diencephalic regions of the brain that mediates the initiation and regulation of complex behaviors (Luria, 1973). Alcoholics, like neurological patients with damage in these areas, frequently have a great deal of difficulty formulating efficient information-processing strategies (Klisz & Parsons, 1977; Luria & Tsvetkova, 1964), using feedback about errors to modify behavior (Konow & Pribram, 1970; Tarter, 1973), learning new information (Benton, 1968; Ryan, 1980), and scanning visual arrays in search of a designated target (Teuber, Battersby, & Bender, 1951; Bertera & Parsons, 1978). Neuroanatomical studies of chronic alcoholics have also indicated that while they often show widespread brain damage, the greatest degree of pathology tends to be seen in the frontal and diencephalic regions of the brain (Cala, Jones, Mastaglia, & Wiley, 1978; Feuerlein & Heyse, 1970; Courville, 1955).

This hypothesis not only appears to integrate a great deal of neuropsychological and neuroanatomical data, but is consonant with many clinicians' impression that alcoholics tend to be impulsive individuals who have serious problems organizing and regulating their behavior. Unfortunately, there is increasing evidence that the learning, visual-scanning, and problem-solving deficits so frequently seen in patients with frontal damage may not be *unique* to those patients, but may be found in individuals who have experienced a sufficiently large lesion *anywhere* in the brain (Chapman & Wolff, 1959; Willanger, 1970). In many ways, this is not at all surprising, given the rich structural and biochemical interconnections between the frontal regions of the brain and essentially all other cortical and subcortical regions. As a consequence, it is currently impossible to determine whether the "frontal signs" seen in alcoholics are truly indicative of damage localized to a single region, or whether they more likely reflect the presence of diffuse brain damage.

Premature Aging Hypothesis

The many superficial similarities between middle-aged alcoholics and elderly nonalcoholics have led several writers to speculate that chronic alcohol abuse causes premature aging. As we have discussed elsewhere (Ryan & Butters, 1984), there are actually two somewhat different versions of this hypothesis. The "accelerated aging" view maintains that alcohol (and alcoholism-related medical disorders) serves as an agent that somehow speeds up the biological process of aging. Thus, the neurobehavioral changes that would normally appear at, say, the age of 50, would appear 10 or 15 years earlier in the heavy drinker. This position predicts that alcoholics, regardless of age, should manifest a certain degree of impairment, but only on those tests that are sensitive to age-related changes in performance. The alternative "increased vulnerability" interpretation maintains that age is merely a risk factor that increases the likelihood that alcoholics will develop neurobehavioral deficits. According to this position, the functional and structural changes that normally occur in the aging brain render older individuals more sensitive to the harmful effects of *any* toxic substance. Thus, neurobehavioral deficits should be found primarily in older alcoholics and should not necessarily resemble those seen in normal elderly individuals.

Earlier observations provided some empirical support for each version of this hypothesis. Cognitive deficits have been found in both younger and older alcoholics, and many parallels have been noted between the performances of alcoholic subjects and older nonalcoholics (Ryan & Butters, 1980b). Moreover, a number of neuropathological and neuroradiological studies have noted that the brain of the typical middle-aged alcoholic seems to resemble that of the elderly nonalcoholic (Courville, 1955; Cala & Mastaglia, 1981; Carlen et al., 1981). In contrast, other investigators have reported that when they compared the performances of younger and older alcoholics with appropriate groups of age-matched controls, only the older alcoholics showed significant cognitive deficits (Jones & Parsons, 1971; Klisz & Parsons, 1977; Bertera & Parsons, 1978).

These different versions of the premature aging hypothesis have recently stimulated a great deal of research. While all the results are not yet in, it now appears that there is only a partial overlap between the neurobehavioral changes associated with the process of normal aging and those associated with chronic alcohol consumption. When alcoholics are compared with elderly nonalcoholics on measures of divided attention (Becker, Butters, Hermann, & D'Angelo, 1983b), learning and memory (Riege, Tomaszewski, Lanto, & Metter, 1984), or tactual perception (Oscar-Berman, Weinstein, & Wysocki, 1983), one finds a highly variable picture, with alcoholics sometimes resembling nonalcoholics, sometimes not, depending on the nature of the task, the age of the subjects, and the duration of drinking. As Becker and his colleagues (1983b, p. 217) have noted ". . . it would appear that alcohol and aging may both result in diffuse brain damage, and subsequently in some overlap of cognitive impairments, but that the particular constellation of brain structures and psychological mechanisms compromised may be different in the two cases."

THE ETIOLOGY OF NEUROPSYCHOLOGICAL DEFICITS IN ALCOHOLICS

Most laymen, and many health professionals, continue to believe that the cognitive changes seen in chronic alcoholics are due solely to the ethanol neurotoxicity of ethanol. While animal studies have demonstrated that alcohol and its metabolites can readily produce structural and functional changes in the brain (Melgaard, 1983), there is growing evidence that cognitive processes may also be adversely affected by the subclinical vitamin deficiencies and liver disorders that are often associated with alcoholismic behavior (Lee et al., 1979). In addition, several investigators have recently speculated that many of the neuropsychological deficits seen in alcoholics may not be a *consequence* of drinking behavior, but may *predate* it (Tarter & Alterman, 1983). According to this viewpoint, both the predisposition to become alcoholic and the development of neurobehavioral impairments reflect the same genetically transmitted disturbance in neurological organization.

Neurotoxic Effects of Ethanol

Research conducted by Freund and his colleagues has provided some of the most compelling evidence that ethanol is a potent neurotoxin (Freund, 1973). In one series of studies, rats and mice were maintained for 3 to 9 months on a nutritionally adequate liquid diet containing 35% ethanol and were then allowed to detoxify for approximately 2 weeks before being tested in an avoidance learning shuttle-box paradigm (Freund, 1970; Freund & Walker, 1971; Walker & Freund, 1971). Not only did the ethanol-fed animals learn more slowly than pair-fed control animals maintained on an isocaloric sucrose diet, but they showed a "dose-response" relationship, such that rate of learning was inversely correlated with duration of ethanol feeding. Moreover, there was little recovery of function following prolonged sobriety: ethanol-fed animals continued to perform more poorly than age-matched control animals after 4½ months of detoxification (Freund & Walker, 1971). Neurohistological studies of mice have demonstrated that the morphological changes associated with chronic ethanol ingestion occur primarily in the dendrites, with both a reduction in the number of dendritic spines and a decrease in the degree of dendritic arborization. These changes have been found in a number of different brain regions, although they are most prominent in the hippocampus and dendate gyrus (Riley & Walker, 1978).

Alcoholism–Related Vitamin Deficiencies

The well-studied neurobehavioral changes associated with the Wernicke-Korsakoff syndrome are generally regarded to be a consequence of a chronic deficiency of certain vitamins, particularly thiamine (Victor, Adams, & Collins, 1971; Dreyfus & Victor, 1961). Because significant cognitive deficits are often seen in nonalcoholics who are seriously malnourished, and in animals fed diets deficient in certain nutrients (Campbell & Biggart, 1939; De Wardener & Lennox, 1947; Botez, Fontaine, Botez, & Bachevalier, 1977; Witt & Goldman-Rakic, 1983), some writers have suggested that essentially *all* of the neurobehavioral deficits found in alcoholics are secondary to malnutrition (e.g., Victor & Adams, 1961). Although it is extremely difficult to obtain reliable information about alcoholics' nutritional status, there is evidence to suggest that many of them do experience at least a subclinical degree of malnutrition. Not only do they tend to rely on alcohol, rather than nutritionally adequate diets, to supply calories (Hillman, 1973), but they often manifest an inability to absorb nutrients efficiently from the food they do consume (Baker, Frank, Zetterman, Rajan, tenHove, & Leevy, 1975; Tomasulo, Kater, & Iber, 1968). As a result, when examined shortly after the beginning of detoxification, alcoholics frequently show significantly reduced levels of most vitamins, including thiamine (Hell, Six, & Salkeld, 1976; Devgun, Fiabane, Paterson, Zarembski, & Guthrie, 1981). To date, there have been few systematic studies delineating the relationship between nutritional levels and neuropsychological functioning in the alcoholic who has been detoxified for several weeks. It does appear, however, that the degree of cognitive impairment seen in alcoholics immediately after the beginning of detoxification may be related to certain nutritional variables, particularly folic acid levels (Albert, Butters, Rogers, Pressman, & Geller, 1982; Guthrie & Elliott, 1980).

Liver Dysfunction

Although it is well known that patients with cirrhosis may sometimes develop a dementia or "hepatic encephalopathy," this very serious neurological complication of liver disease affects a relatively small proportion of cirrhotic patients (Hoyumpa, Desmond, Avant, Roberts, & Schenker, 1979). Within the past 10 years, however, investigators have demonstrated that many individuals with either alcoholic or nonalcoholic liver disease manifest neuropsychological deficits as well as evidence of cortical atrophy that may be more serious than that found in alcoholics without liver disease (Rikkers, Jenko, Rudman, & Freides, 1978; Acker, Aps, Majumdar, Shaw, & Thomson, 1982; Tarter, Hegedus, Van Thiel, Schade, Iwatsuki, & Starzl, 1984). For example, when Gilberstadt and his associates (1980) administered a comprehensive battery of neuropsychological tests to groups of demographically similar alcoholics with and without Laennec's cirrhosis, they found that the cirrhotic alcoholics earned significantly lower WAIS Performance IQ scores and performed more poorly than the noncirrhotic alcoholics on those tests requiring rapid responding and psychomotor integration. Moreover, these test scores were unrelated to drinking history but were significantly correlated with certain indicators of liver dysfunction, including serum albumin level and fasting venous ammonia level. Other researchers have reported that these deficits are not necessarily permanent, but will reduce following a surgically induced improvement in liver function (Rehnstrom, Simert, Hansson, Johnson, & Vang, 1977; Rikkers et al., 1978).

Given the high incidence of both clinical and subclinical liver disease in chronic alcoholics, as well as the behavioral similarities between impairments seen in alcoholics and those seen in cirrhotics, one is tempted to speculate that it is the toxic effects of liver disease, rather than alcohol intake per se, that are primarily responsible for the cognitive deficits found in the neurologically intact alcoholic. Because virtually all chronic alcoholics may incur long periods of subclinical liver disturbances and nutritional abnormalities while consuming large amounts of ethanol (Mendelson, 1970), it is impossible to determine which single factor has caused the neurobehavioral deficits seen in these individuals. Indeed, it is likely that all of these factors, interacting with one another, contribute to the development of the brain disturbances found in alcoholics (Mendelson, 1971; Elton, 1983).

Antecedent Neurobehavioral Deficits in Alcoholics

There is increasing support for the hypothesis that the development of alcoholism, like many other psychiatric disorders, is influenced by genetic factors. Family studies have clearly demonstrated that children born of alcoholics but raised in nonalcoholic households are later more likely to develop alcoholism than those without a family history of alcoholism (e.g., Schuckit, Goodwin, & Winokur, 1972; Cloninger, Bohman, & Sigvardsson, 1981). Postulating that the genetic characteristics that underlie the development of alcoholism may also induce a significant degree of neurological disorganization, several researchers have carried out a series of neurobehavioral studies in a search for possible biologic markers of this inherited predisposition.

Static ataxia, or body sway at rest, has been identified by Lipscomb and his colleagues (1979) as one such marker. When they measured body sway in a group of *nonalcoholic* male young adults, they found that those with a family history of alcoholism tended to sway significantly more while standing for 1 minute with eyes closed than those who had no alcoholic first-degree relatives. While most of these subjects were social drinkers, the degree of static ataxia was not related to the subject's past drinking history or to his current drinking practices. These results suggest that nonalcoholics with a family history of alcoholism manifest a motor impairment that is remarkably similar to that frequently seen in chronic alcoholics (Goldstein, Chotlos, McCarthy, & Neuringer, 1968). At the present time, however, we have no way of knowing whether those subjects who swayed the most will go on, 5 or 10 years in the future, to develop alcoholism.

Taking a somewhat different approach, Pollock and her associates (1983) recorded electroencephalograms (EEGs) from young men at risk for developing alcoholism before and after consumption of a small amount of ethanol. They found that men who had alcoholic fathers, and hence had a high risk of developing alcoholism, were more likely than a group of demographically similar low-risk men to show greater decrease in the mean alpha frequency following administration of a single dose of alcohol. Changes were most evident in the posterior scalp regions and were lateralized to the right hemisphere. As in the study by Lipscomb and associates, no subject in either group met criteria for alcoholism, nor were there any statistically significant between-group differences in blood alcohol concentrations at the time of testing or in subjects' estimates of amount of alcohol consumed in the previous week. These data suggest that men who are at risk for developing serious drinking problems may have nervous systems that are unusually sensitive to the effects of ethanol.

The neuropsychological status of subjects with and without a family history of alcoholism has recently been investigated by Schaeffer, Parsons, and Yohman (1984). They administered a battery of tests to groups of alcoholic and nonalcoholic males, 24 to 60 years of age, who had a positive or negative family history (parents or siblings) of alcoholism. Comparing nonalcoholics with and without a positive family history of alcoholism, Schaeffer and her associates found that those with a positive family history performed significantly more poorly on a series of perceptual-motor tests and on several measures of abstract reasoning. While the differences between the two *alcoholic* subgroups failed to reach statistical significance, the resultant trends were in the predicted direction: alcoholics with a positive family history tended to perform more poorly than those with a negative family history. These findings support the hypothesis that a subtype of alcoholics—specifically, those alcoholics with a family history of alcoholism—may have a series of cognitive deficits that predate their alcoholismic behavior.

Our discussion of etiology indicates that the various neurobehavioral changes seen in heavy drinkers are produced not by a single toxic agent, but by the complex interaction of a number of alcoholismic (e.g., liver status, drinking history), organismic (e.g., age), and genetic (e.g., family history of alcoholism) factors. It remains to be seen whether researchers will be successful in disentangling these factors so that they can go on to predict which drinkers are most likely to develop serious neuropsychological deficits and which are not.

REFERENCES

Acker, W. (1982). Objective psychological changes in alcoholics after the withdrawal of alcohol. *British Medical Bulletin, 38,* 95–98.

Acker, W., Aps, E. J., Majumdar, S. K., Shaw, G. K., & Thomson, A. D. (1982). The relationship between brain and liver damage in chronic alcoholic patients. *Journal of Neurology, Neurosurgery, and Psychiatry, 45,* 984–987.

Albert, M. S., Butters, N., & Brandt, J. (1980). Memory for remote events in alcoholics. *Journal of Studies on Alcohol, 41,* 1071–1081.

Albert, M. S., Butters, N., & Levin, J. (1979). Temporal gradients in the retrograde amnesia of patients with alcoholic Korsakoff's disease. *Archives of Neurology, 36,* 211–216.

Albert, M. S., Butters, N., Rogers, S., Pressman, J., & Geller, A. (1982). A preliminary report: Nutritional levels and cognitive performance in chronic alcohol abusers. *Drug and Alcohol Dependence, 9,* 131–142.

American Psychiatric Association. (1980). *Diagnostic and statistical manual of mental disorders* (3rd ed.). Washington, DC: APA.

Baker, H., Frank, O., Zetterman, R. K., Rajan, K. S., tenHove, W., & Leevy, C. M. (1975). Inability of chronic alcoholics with liver disease to use food as a source of folates, thiamine and vitamin B6. *American Journal of Clinical Nutrition, 28,* 1377–1380.

Becker, J. T., Butters, N., Hermann, A., & D'Angelo, N. (1983a). Learning to associate names and faces. *Journal of Nervous and Mental Disease, 171,* 617–623.

Becker, J. T., Butters, N., Hermann, A., & D'Angelo, N. (1983b). A comparison of the effects of long-term alcohol abuse and aging on the performance of verbal and nonverbal divided attention tasks. *Alcoholism, 7,* 213–219.

Benton, A. L. (1968). Differential behavioral effects in frontal lobe disease. *Neuropsychologia, 6,* 53–60.

Berglund, M., Leijonquist, H., & Horlen, M. (1977). Prognostic significance and reversibility of cerebral dysfunction in alcoholics. *Journal of Studies on Alcohol, 38,* 1761–1770.

Bergman, H., Axelsson, G., Idestrom, C.-M., Borg, S., Hindmarsh, T., Makower, J., & Mutzell, S. (1983). Alcohol consumption, neuropsychological status, and computer-tomographic findings in a random sample of men and women from the general population. *Pharmacology, Biochemistry and Behavior, 18* (Suppl. 1), 501–505.

Bertera, J. H., & Parsons, O. A. (1978). Impaired visual search in alcoholics. *Alcoholism, 2,* 9–14.

Binder, L. M., & Schreiber, V. (1980). Visual imagery and verbal mediation as memory aids in recovering alcoholics. *Journal of Clinical Neuropsychology, 2,* 71–73.

Bolter, J. F., & Hannon, R. (1980). Cerebral damage associated with alcoholism: A reexamination. *Psychological Record, 30,* 165–179.

Botez, M. I., Fontaine, F., Botez, T., & Bachevalier, J. (1977). Folate-responsive neurological and mental disorders. *European Neurology, 16,* 230–246.

Brandt, J., Butters, N., Ryan, C., & Bayog, R. (1983). Cognitive loss and recovery in long-term alcohol abusers. *Archives of General Psychiatry, 40,* 435–442.

Brewer, C., & Perrett, L. (1971). Brain damage due to alcohol consumption: An air-encephalographic, psychometric, and electroencephalographic study. *British Journal of Addiction, 66,* 170–182.

Brown, E. R., Gopinathan, G., & Slobogin, P. (1984, February). *Assessment of memory in chronic alcoholics with unreported memory deficits.* Paper presented at the twelfth annual meeting of the International Neuropsychological Society, Houston, TX.

Burdick, J. A., Johnson, L. C., & Smith, J. W. (1970). Measurements of change during alcohol withdrawal in chronic alcoholics. *British Journal of Addiction, 65,* 273–280.

Butters, N. (1981). The Wernicke-Korsakoff syndrome: A review of psychological, neuropathological and etiological factors. In M. Galanter (Ed.), *Currents in Alcoholism* (Vol. 8) (pp. 205–232). New York: Grune & Stratton.

Butters, N. (1984). Alcoholic Korsakoff's syndrome: An update. *Seminars in Neurology, 4,* 226–244.

Butters, N., & Cermak, L. S. (1976). Neuropsychological studies of alcoholic Korsakoff patients. In G. Goldstein & C. Neuringer (Eds.), *Empirical studies of alcoholism,* (pp. 153–193). Cambridge, MA: Ballinger.

Butters, N., & Cermak, L. S. (1980). *Alcoholic Korsakoff's syndrome: An information-processing approach to amnesia.* New York: Academic Press.

Butters, N., Cermak, L. S., Montgomery, K., & Adinolfi, A. (1977). Some comparisons of the memory and visuoperceptive deficits of chronic alcoholics and patients with Korsakoff's disease. *Alcoholism, 1,* 73–80.

Cala, L. A., Jones, B., Mastaglia, F. L., & Wiley, B. (1978). Brain atrophy and intellectual impairment in heavy drinkers: A clinical, psychometric, and computerized tomography study. *Australian and New Zealand Journal of Medicine, 8,* 147–153.

Cala, L. A., & Mastaglia, F. L. (1981). Computerized tomography in chronic alcoholics. *Alcoholism, 5,* 283–294.

Campbell, A. C. P., & Biggart, J. H. (1939). Wernicke's encephalopathy: Its alcoholic and nonalcoholic incidence. *Journal of Pathology and Bacteriology, 48,* 245–262.

Carlen, P. L., Wilkinson, A., Wortzman, G., Holgate, R., Cordingley, J., Lee, M. A., Huszar, L., Moddel, G., Singh, R., Kiraly, L., & Rankin, J. G. (1981). Cerebral atrophy and functional deficits in alcoholics without clinically apparent liver disease. *Neurology, 31,* 377–385.

Cermak, L. S. (1980). Improving retention in alcoholic Korsakoff patients. *Journal of Studies on Alcohol, 41,* 159–169.

Cermak, L. S., & Butters, N. (1973). Information processing deficits of alcoholic Korsakoff patients. *Quarterly Journal of Studies on Alcohol, 34,* 1110–1132.

Cermak, L. S., Lewis, R., Butters, N., & Goodglass, H. (1973). Role of verbal mediation in performance of motor tasks by Korsakoff patients. *Perceptual and Motor Skills, 37,* 259–262.

Chapman, L. F., & Wolff, H. G. (1959). The cerebral hemispheres and the highest integrative functions in man. *Archives of Neurology, 1,* 357–423.

Chmielewski, C., & Golden, C. J. (1980). Alcoholism and brain damage: An investigation using the Luria–Nebraska Neuropsychological Battery. *International Journal of Neuroscience, 10,* 99–105.

Claiborn, J. M., & Greene, R. L. (1981). Neuropsychological changes in recovering men alcoholics. *Journal of Studies on Alcohol, 42,* 757–765.

Clarke, J., & Haughton, H. (1975). A study of intellectual impairment and recovery rates in heavy drinkers in Ireland. *British Journal of Psychiatry, 126,* 178–184.

Cloninger, C. R., Bohman, M., & Sigvardsson, S. (1981). Inheritance of alcohol abuse: Cross-fostering analysis of adopted men. *Archives of General Psychiatry, 38,* 861–868.

Courville, C. B. (1955). *Effects of alcohol on the nervous system of man.* Los Angeles: San Lucas Press.

Craik, F. I. M. (1977). Age differences in human memory. In J. E. Birren & K. W. Schaie (Eds.), *Handbook of the psychology of aging* (pp. 580–605). New York: Van Nostrand Reinhold.

Cutting, J. (1978a). A reappraisal of alcoholic psychoses. *Psychological Medicine, 8,* 285–295.

Cutting, J. (1978b). The relationship between Korsakov's syndrome and 'alcoholic dementia.' *British Journal of Psychiatry, 132,* 240–251.

Cutting, J. (1978c). Specific psychological deficits in alcoholism. *British Journal of Psychiatry, 133,* 119–122.

Cutting, J. (1982). Alcoholic dementia. In D. F. Benson & D. Blumer (Eds.), *Psychiatric aspects of neurologic disease* (Vol. 2) (pp. 149–165). New York: Grune & Stratton.

Das, J. P. (1980). Planning: Theoretical considerations and empirical evidence. *Psychological Research, 41,* 141–151.

Devgun, M. S., Fiabane, A., Paterson, C. R., Zarembski, P., & Guthrie, A. (1981). Vitamin and mineral nutrition in chronic alcoholics including patients with Korsakoff's psychosis. *British Journal of Nutrition, 45,* 469–473.

De Wardener, H. E., & Lennox, B. (1947). Cerebral beriberi. *Lancet, 1,* 11–17.

Donovan, D. M., Queisser, H. R., & O'Leary, M. R. (1976). Group Embedded Figures test performance as a predictor of cognitive impairment among alcoholics. *International Journal of the Addictions, 11,* 725–739.

Draper, R. J., & Manning, A. (1982). Vocabulary deficit and abstraction impairment in hospitalized alcoholics. *Psychological Medicine, 12,* 341–347.

Dreyfus, P. M., & Victor, M. (1961). Effects of thiamine deficiency on the central nervous system. *American Journal of Clinical Nutrition, 9,* 414–425.

Eckardt, M. J., Parker, E. S., Noble, E. P., Feldman, D. J., & Gottschalk, L. A. (1978). The relationship between neuropsychological performance and alcohol consumption in alcoholics. *Biological Psychiatry, 13,* 551–565.

Elsass, P., Lund, Y., & Ranek, L. (1978). Encephalopathy in patients with cirrhosis of the liver: A neuropsychological study. *Scandinavian Journal of Gasteroenterology, 13,* 241–247.

Elton, M. (1983). Do brain damage and liver disease interrelate in advanced abusers of alcohol? *Acta Psychiatrica Scandinavica, 68,* 437–444.

Fabian, M. S., & Parsons, O. A. (1983). Differential improvement of cognitive functions in recovering alcoholic women. *Journal of Abnormal Psychology, 92,* 87–95.

Feuerlein, W., & Heyse, H. (1970). Die weite der 3. hirnkammer bei alkoholikern. *Archiv für Psychiatrie und Nervenkrankheit, 213,* 78–85.

Finlayson, M. A. (1977). Test complexity and brain damage at different educational levels. *Journal of Clinical Psychology, 33,* 221–223.

Fitzhugh, L. C., Fitzhugh, K. B., & Reitan, R. M. (1965). Adaptive abilities and intellectual functioning of hospitalized alcoholics: Further considerations. *Quarterly Journal of Studies on Alcohol, 26,* 402–411.

Freund, G. (1970). Impairment of shock avoidance learning after long-term alcohol ingestion in mice. *Science, 168,* 1599–1601.

Freund, G. (1973). Chronic central nervous system toxicity of alcohol. *Annual Review of Pharmacology, 13,* 217–227.

Freund, G., & Walker, D. W. (1971). Impairment of avoidance learning by prolonged ethanol consumption in mice. *Journal of Pharmacology and Experimental Therapeutics, 179,* 284–292.

Gilberstadt, S., Gilberstadt, H., Zieve, L., Buegel, B., Collier, R. O., & McClain, C. J. (1980). Psychomotor performance defects in cirrhotic patients without overt encephalopathy. *Archives of Internal Medicine, 140,* 519–521.

Glosser, G., Butters, N., & Kaplan, E. (1977). Visuoperceptual processes in brain-damaged patients on the Digit-Symbol Substitution test. *International Journal of Neuroscience, 7,* 59–66.

Goldman, M. S., Williams, D. L., & Klisz, D. K. (1983). Recoverability of psychological functioning following alcohol abuse: Prolonged visual-spatial dysfunction in older alcoholics. *Journal of Consulting and Clinical Psychology, 51,* 370–378.

Goldstein, G., & Ruthven, L. (1983). *Rehabilitation of the brain-damaged adult.* New York: Plenum Press.

Goldstein, G., Chotlos, J., McCarthy, R., & Neuringer, C. (1968). Recovery from gait instability in alcoholics. *Quarterly Journal of Studies on Alcohol, 29,* 38–43.

Goldstein, G., Ryan, C., Turner, S., Kanagy, M., Barry, K., & Kelly, L. (1985). Three methods of memory training for severely amnesic patients. *Behavior Modification, 9,* 357–374.

Goldstein, G., & Shelly, C. (1971). Field dependence and cognitive, perceptual and motor skills in alcoholics: A factor analytic study. *Quarterly Journal of Studies on Alcohol, 32,* 29–40.

Goldstein, G., & Shelly, C. (1980). Neuropsychological investigation of brain lesion localization in alcoholism. In H. Begleiter (Ed.), *Biological effects of alcohol* (pp. 731–743). New York: Plenum Press.

Goldstein, G., & Shelly, C. (1982). A multivariate neuropsychological approach to brain lesion localization in alcoholism. *Addictive Behaviors, 7,* 165–175.

Grant, I., Adams, K., & Reed, R. (1979). Normal neuropsychological abilities of alcoholic men in their late thirties. *American Journal of Psychiatry, 136,* 1263–1269.

Grant, I., Adams, K., & Reed, R. (1984). Aging, abstinence, and medical risk factors in the prediction of neuropsychologic deficit among long-term alcoholics. *Archives of General Psychiatry, 41,* 710–718.

Grant, I., Reed, R., Adams, K., & Carlin, A. (1979). Neuropsychological function in young alcoholics and polydrug abusers. *Journal of Clinical Neuropsychology, 1,* 39–47.

Grünberger, J., Krypsin-Exner, K., Masarik, J., & Wessely, P. (1975). Psychoorganische ausfälle bei alkoholkranken nach einjähriger abstinenz. *Nervenarzt, 46,* 384–390.

Grünberger, J., Krypsin-Exner, K., Masarik, J., & Wessely, P. (1976). Das "residualsyndrom" bei alkoholkranken nach 5-jähriger abstinenz. *Schweizer Archiv für Neurologie, Neurochirgerie, und Psychiatrie, 118,* 295–305.

Gudeman, H. E., Craine, J. F., Golden, C. J., & McLaughlin, D. (1977). Higher cortical dysfunction associated with long term alcoholism. *International Journal of Neuroscience, 8,* 33–40.

Guthrie, A. (1980). The first year after treatment: Factors affecting time course of reversibility of memory and learning deficits in alcoholism. In H. Begleiter (Ed.), *Biological effects of alcohol* (pp. 757–770). New York: Plenum Press.

Guthrie, A., & Elliott, W. A. (1980). The nature and reversibility of cerebral impairment in alcoholism: Treatment implications. *Journal of Studies on Alcohol, 41,* 147–155.

Hell, D., Six, P., & Salkeld, R. (1976). Vitamin-B1-mangel bei chronischen athylikern und sein klinisches korrelat. *Schweizer Medizinischer Wochenschrift, 106,* 1466–1470.

Hill, S. Y., & Mikhael, M. A. (1979). Computerized transaxial tomographic and neuropsychological evaluations in chronic alcoholics and heroin abusers. *American Journal of Psychiatry, 136,* 598–602.

Hillman, R. W. (1973). Alcoholism and malnutrition. In B. Kissin & H. Begleiter (Eds.), *The biology of alcoholism* (Vol. 3) (pp. 513–581). New York: Plenum Press.

Horvath, T. B. (1975). Clinical spectrum and epidemiological features of alcoholic dementia. In J. G. Rankin (Ed.), *Alcohol, drugs, and brain damage* (pp. 1–16). Ontario: Addiction Research Foundation.

Hoyumpa, A. M., Desmond, P. V., Avant, G. R., Roberts, R. K., & Schenker, S. (1979). Hepatic encephalopathy. *Gasteroenterology, 76,* 184–195.

Hudolin, V. (1980). Impairments of the nervous system in alcoholics. In D. Richter (Ed.), *Addiction and brain damage,* (pp. 168–200). Baltimore: University Park Press.

Huppert, F. A., & Piercy, M. (1978). The role of trace strength in recency and frequency judgments by amnesic and control subjects. *Quarterly Journal of Experimental Psychology, 30,* 347–353.

Jaffe, P. G., & Katz, A. N. (1975). Attenuating anterograde amnesia in Korsakoff's psychosis. *Journal of Abnormal Psychology, 84,* 559–562.

Jenkins, R. L., & Parsons, O. A. (1980). Recovery of cognitive abilities in male alcoholics. In M. Galanter (Ed.), *Currents in alcoholism* (Vol. 5) (pp. 285–296). New York: Grune & Stratton.

Jones, B. M. (1971) Verbal and spatial intelligence in short- and long-term alcoholics. *Journal of Nervous and Mental Disease, 153,* 292–297.

Jones, B. M., & Parsons, O. A. (1971). Impaired abstracting ability in chronic alcoholics. *Archives of General Psychiatry, 24,* 71–75.

Jones, B. M., & Parsons, O. A. (1972). Specific vs generalized deficits of abstracting ability in chronic alcoholics. *Archives of General Psychiatry, 26,* 380–384.

Jonsson, C.-O., Cronholm, B., & Izikowitz, S. (1962). Intellectual changes in alcoholics: Psychometric studies on mental sequels of prolonged intensive abuse of alcohol. *Quarterly Journal of Studies on Alcohol, 23,* 221–242.

Kaldegg, A. (1956). Psychological observations in a group of alcoholic patients. *Quarterly Journal of Studies on Alcohol, 17,* 608–682.

Kapur, N., & Butters, N. (1977). An analysis of visuoperceptive deficits in alcoholic Korsakoffs and long-term alcoholics. *Journal of Studies on Alcohol, 38,* 2025–2035.

Kleinknecht, R. A., & Goldstein, S. G. (1972). Neuropsychological deficits associated with alcoholism. *Quarterly Journal of Studies on Alcohol, 33,* 999–1019.

Klisz, D., & Parsons, O. A. (1977). Hypothesis-testing in younger and older alcoholics. *Journal of Studies on Alcohol, 38,* 1718–1729.

Klisz, D., & Parsons, O. A. (1979). Cognitive functioning in alcoholics: The role of subject attrition. *Journal of Abnormal Psychology, 88,* 268–276.

Konow, A., & Pribram, K. H. (1970). Error recognition and utilization produced by injury to the frontal cortex in man. *Neuropsychologia, 8,* 489–491.

Laine, M., & Butters, N. (1982). A preliminary study of the problem-solving strategies of detoxified long-term alcoholics. *Drug and Alcohol Dependence, 10,* 235–242.

Lee, K., Møller, L., Hardt, F., Haubek, A., & Jensen, E. (1979). Alcohol-induced brain damage and liver damage in young males. *Lancet, 2,* 759–761.

Levine, M. (1966). Hypothesis behavior by humans during discrimination learning. *Journal of Experimental Psychology, 71,* 331–338.

Lezak, M. (1976). *Neuropsychological assessment.* New York: Oxford University Press.

Lipscomb, T. R., Carpenter, J. A., & Nathan, P. E. (1979). Static ataxia: A predictor of alcoholism? *British Journal of Addiction, 74,* 289–294.

Lishman, W. A. (1981). Cerebral disorder in alcoholism: Syndromes of impairment. *Brain, 104,* 1–20.

Long, J. A., & McLachlan, F. C. (1974). Abstract reasoning and perceptual-motor efficiency in alcoholics. *Quarterly Journal of Studies on Alcohol, 35,* 1220–1229.

Luria, A. R. (1973). *The working brain: An introduction to neuropsychology.* London: Penguin.

Luria, A. R., & Tsvetkova, L. A. (1964). The programming of constructive activity in local brain injuries. *Neuropsychologia, 4,* 95–107.

MacVane, J., Butters, N., Montgomery, K., & Farber, J. (1982). Cognitive functioning in men social drinkers: A replication study. *Journal of Studies on Alcohol, 43,* 81–95.

Marslen-Wilson, W. D., & Teuber, H.-L. (1975). Memory for remote events in anterograde amnesia: Recognition of public figures from news photographs. *Neuropsychologia, 13,* 347–352.

Martone, M., Butters, N., Payne, M., Becker, J. T., & Sax, D. S. (1984). Dissociations between skill learning and verbal recognition in amnesia and dementia. *Archives of Neurology, 41,* 965–970.

Melgaard, B. (1983). The neurotoxicity of ethanol. *Acta Neurologica Scandinavica, 67,* 131–142.

Mendelson, J. H. (1970). Biologic concomitants of alcoholism. *New England Journal of Medicine, 283,* 24–32, 71–81.

Mendelson, J. H. (1971). Effects of alcohol on the central nervous system. *New England Journal of Medicine, 284,* 104–105.

Mercer, B., Wapner, W., Gardner, H., & Benson, D. F. (1977). A study of confabulation. *Archives of Neurology, 34,* 429–433.

Miglioli, M., Buchtel, H. A., Campanini, T., & DeRisio, C. (1979). Cerebral hemispheric lateralization of cognitive deficits due to alcoholism. *Journal of Nervous and Mental Disease, 167,* 212–217.

O'Leary, M. R., Radford, L. M., Chaney, E. F., & Schau, E. J. (1977). Assessment of cognitive recovery in alcoholics by use of the Trail Making Test. *Journal of Clinical Psychology, 33,* 579–582.

Oltman, P. K., Raskin, E., & Witkin, H. A. (1971). *Group embedded figures test.* Palo Alto, CA: Consulting Psychologists Press.

Oscar-Berman, M., (1973). Hypothesis testing and focusing behavior during concept formation by amnesic Korsakoff patients. *Neuropsychologia, 11,* 191–198.

Oscar-Berman, M., Weinstein, A., & Wysocki, D. (1983). Bimanual tactual discrimination in aging alcoholics. *Alcoholism, 7,* 398–403.

Page, R. D., & Linden, J. D. (1974). "Reversible" organic brain syndrome in alcoholics. *Quarterly Journal of Studies on Alcohol, 35,* 98–107.

Parker, E. S., & Noble, E. P. (1980). Alcohol and the aging process in social drinkers. *Journal of Studies on Alcohol, 41,* 170–178.

Parker, E. S., Birnbaum. I, M., Boyd, R. A., & Noble, E. P. (1980). Neuropsychologic decrements as a function of alcohol intake in male students. *Alcoholism, 4,* 330–334.

Parsons, O. A., & Fabian, M. S. (1982). Comments on cognitive functioning in men social drinkers: A replication study. *Journal of Studies on Alcohol, 43,* 178–182.

Parsons, O. A., & Farr, S. D. (1981). The neuropsychology of alcohol and drug use. In S. B. Filskov & T. J. Boll (Eds.), *Handbook of clinical neuropsychology* (pp. 320–365). New York: Wiley.

Parsons, O. A., & Prigatano, G. P. (1977). Memory functioning in alcoholics. In I. M. Birnbaum & E. S. Parker (Eds.), *Alcohol and human memory* (pp. 185–194). Hillsdale, NJ: Lawrence Erlbaum.

Pollock, V. E., Volavka, J., Goodwin, D. W., Mednick, S. A., Gabrielli, W. F., Knop, J., & Schulsinger, F. (1983). The EEG after alcohol administration in men at risk for alcoholism. *Archives of General Psychiatry, 40,* 857–861.

Rada, R. T., Porch, B. E., Dillingham, C., Kellner, R., & Porec, J. B. (1977). Alcoholism and language function. *Alcoholism, 1,* 199–205.

Rehnstrom, S., Simert, G., Hansson, J. A., Johnson, G., & Vang, J. (1977). Chronic hepatic encephalopathy: A psychometrical study. *Scandinavian Journal of Gastroenterology, 12,* 305–311.

Reitan, R. M. (1958). Validity of the Trail Making test as an indicator of organic brain damage. *Perceptual and Motor Skills, 8,* 271–276.

Riege, W. H., Holloway, J. A., & Kaplan, D. W. (1981). Specific memory deficits associated with prolonged alcohol abuse. *Alcoholism, 5,* 378–385.

Riege, W. H., Tomaszewski, R., Lanto, A., & Metter, E. J. (1984). Age and alcoholism: Independent memory decrements. *Alcoholism, 8,* 42–47.

Rikkers, L., Jenko, P., Rudman, D., & Freides, D. (1978). Subclinical hepatic encephalopathy: Detection, prevalence, and relationship to nitrogen metabolism. *Gastroenterology, 75,* 462–469.

Riley, J. N., & Walker, D. W. (1978). Morphological alterations in hippocampus after long-term alcohol consumption in mice. *Science, 201,* 646–648.

Ron, M. A. (1983). The alcoholic brain: CT scan and psychological findings. *Psychological Medicine* (Suppl. 3), 1–33.

Ron, M. A., Acker, W., Shaw, G. K., & Lishman, W. A. (1982). Computerized tomography of the brain in chronic alcoholism: A survey and follow-up study. *Brain, 105,* 497–514.

Rosen, W. G. (1980). Verbal fluency in aging and dementia. *Journal of Clinical Neuropsychology, 2,* 135–146.

Ryan, C. (1980). Learning and memory deficits in alcoholics. *Journal of Studies on Alcohol, 41,* 437–447.

Ryan, C., & Butters, N. (1980a). Further evidence for a continuum of impairment encompassing male alcoholic Korsakoff patients and chronic alcoholics. *Alcoholism, 4,* 190–198.

Ryan, C., & Butters, N. (1980b). Learning and memory impairments in young and old alcoholics: Evidence for the premature-aging hypothesis. *Alcoholism, 4,* 288–293.

Ryan, C., & Butters, N. (1983). Cognitive deficits in alcoholics. In B. Kissin & H. Begleiter (Eds.), *The pathogenesis of alcoholism* (Vol. 7) (pp. 485–538). New York: Plenum Press.

Ryan, C., & Butters, N. (1984). Alcohol consumption and premature aging: A critical review. In M. Galanter (Ed.), *Recent Developments in Alcoholism* (Vol. 2) (pp. 223–259). New York: Plenum Press.

Ryan, C., Butters, N., Montgomery, K., Adinolfi, A., & DiDario, B. (1980). Memory deficits in chronic alcoholics: Continuities between the "intact" alcoholic and the alcoholic Korsakoff patient. In H. Begleiter (Ed.), *Biological effects of alcohol* (pp. 701–718). New York: Plenum Press.

Ryan, C., DiDario, B., Butters, N., & Adinolfi, A. (1980). The relationship between abstinence and recovery of function in male alcoholics. *Journal of Clinical Neuropsychology, 2,* 125–134.

Saletu, B., Saletu, M., Grunberger, J., & Mader, R. (1983). Spontaneous and drug-induced remission of alcoholic organic brain syndrome: Clinical, psychometric, and neurophysiological studies. *Psychiatry Research, 10,* 59–75.

Schaeffer, K. W., Parsons, O. A., & Yohman, J. R. (1984). Neuropsychological differences between male familial and nonfamilial alcoholics and nonalcoholics. *Alcoholism, 8,* 347–351.

Schau, E. J., O'Leary, M. R., & Chaney, E. F. (1980). Reversibility of cognitive deficit in alcoholics. *Journal of Studies on Alcohol, 41,* 733–740.

Schorr, D., Bower, G. H., & Kiernan, R. (1982). Stimulus variables in the Block Design task. *Journal of Consulting and Clinical Psychology, 50,* 479–487.

Schuckit, M. A., Goodwin, D. A., & Winokur, G. (1972). A study of alcoholism in half siblings. *American Journal of Psychiatry, 128,* 1132–1136.

Seltzer, B., & Benson, D. F. (1974). The temporal pattern of retrograde amnesia in Korsakoff's disease. *Neurology, 24,* 527–530.

Seltzer, B., & Sherwin, I. (1978). "Organic brain syndromes": An empirical study and critical review. *American Journal of Psychiatry, 135,* 13–21.

Sharp, J. R., Rosenbaum, G., Goldman, M. S., & Whitman, R. D. (1977). Recoverability of psychological functioning following alcohol abuse: Acquisition of meaningful synonyms. *Journal of Consulting and Clinical Psychology, 45,* 1023–1028.

Smith, H. H., & Smith, L. S. (1977). WAIS functioning of cirrhotic and noncirrhotic alcoholics. *Journal of Clinical Psychology, 33,* 309–313.

Stein, D., Rosen, J., & Butters, N. (1974). *Plasticity and recovery of function in the central nervous system.* New York: Academic Press.

Talland, G. A. (1965). *Deranged memory.* New York: Academic Press.

Tarter, R. E. (1973). An analysis of cognitive deficits in chronic alcoholics. *Journal of Nervous and Mental Disease, 157,* 138–147.

Tarter, R. E. (1976). Empirical investigations of psychological deficit. In R. E. Tarter & A. A. Sugerman (Eds.), *Alcoholism: Interdisciplinary approaches to an enduring problem* (pp. 359–394). Reading, MA: Addison-Wesley.

Tarter, R. E. (1980). Brain damage in chronic alcoholics: A review of the psychological evidence. In D. Richter (Ed.), *Addiction and brain damage* (pp. 267–297). Baltimore: University Park Press.

Tarter, R. E., & Alterman, A. I. (1983). The transmission of psychological vulnerability: Implications for alcoholism etiology. *Journal of Nervous and Mental Disease, 171,* 147–154.

Tarter, R. E., Hegedus, A. M., Van Thiel, D. H., Schade, R. R., Iwatsuki, S., & Starzl, T. E. (1984). Nonalcoholic cirrhosis associated with neuropsychiatric dysfunction in the absence of overt evidence of hepatic encephalopathy. *Gastroenterology, 86,* 1421–1427.

Tarter, R. E., & Parsons, O. A. (1971). Conceptual shifting in chronic alcoholics. *Journal of Abnormal Psychology, 77,* 71–75.

Tarter, R. E., & Ryan, C. M. (1983). Neuropsychology of alcoholism: Etiology, phenomenology, process, and outcome. In M. Galanter (Ed.), *Recent developments in alcoholism* (Vol. 1) (pp. 449–469). New York: Plenum Press.

Teuber, H. L., Battersby, W. S., & Bender, M. S. (1951). Performance of complex visual tasks after cerebral lesions. *Journal of Nervous and Mental Disease, 114,* 413–429.

Tomasulo, P. A., Kater, R. M. H., & Iber, F. L. (1968). Impairment of thiamine absorption in alcoholism. *American Journal of Clinical Nutrition, 21,* 1340–1344.

Victor, M. (1975). Neurologic disorders due to alcoholism and malnutrition. In A. B. Baker & L. H. Baker (Eds.), *Clinical neurology* (Vol. 2) (pp. 1–83). Philadelphia: Harper & Row.

Victor, M., & Adams, R. D. (1961). On the etiology of the alcoholic neurologic diseases with special reference to the role of nutrition. *American Journal of Clinical Nutrition, 9,* 379–397.

Victor, M., Adams, R. D., & Collins, G. H. (1971). *The Wernicke-Korsakoff syndrome.* Philadelphia: F. A. Davis.

Victor, M., & Banker, B. Q. (1978). Alcohol and dementia. In R. Katzman, R. D. Terry, & K. L. Bick (Eds.), *Alzheimer's disease: Senile dementia and related disorders* (*Aging,* Vol. 7) (pp. 149–170). New York: Raven Press.

Victor, M., Herman, K., & White, E. E. (1959). A psychological study of the Wernicke-Korsakoff syndrome. *Quarterly Journal of Studies on Alcohol, 20,* 467–479.

Walker, D. W., & Freund, G. (1971). Impairment of shuttle box avoidance learning following prolonged alcohol consumption in rats. *Physiology and Behavior, 7,* 773–778.

Warrington, E. K., & Weiskrantz, L. (1974). The effect of prior learning on subsequent retention in amnesic patients. *Neuropsychologia, 12,* 419–428.

Wechsler, D. (1941). The effect of alcohol on mental activity. *Quarterly Journal of Studies on Alcohol, 2,* 279–285.

Wechsler, D. (1945). A standardized memory scale for clinical use. *Journal of Psychology, 19,* 87–95.

Wechsler, D. (1955). *Wechsler Adult Intelligence Scale manual.* New York: Psychological Corporation.

Weingartner, H., Cohen, R. M., Murphy, D. L., Martello, J., & Gerdt, C. (1981). Cognitive processes in depression. *Archives of General Psychiatry, 38,* 42–47.

Weingartner, H., Faillice, L. A., & Markley, H. G. (1971). Verbal information retention in alcoholics. *Quarterly Journal of Studies on Alcohol, 32,* 293–303.

West, P. A., Hill, S. A., & Robins, L. N. (1977). The Canter Background Interference Procedure (BIP): Effects of demographic variables on diagnosis. *Journal of Clinical Psychology, 33,* 765–771.

Wilkinson, D. A., & Carlen, P. L. (1980). Relationship of neuropsychological test performance to brain morphology in amnesic and nonamnesic chronic alcoholics. *Acta Psychiatrica Scandinavica* (Suppl.), *286,* 89–101.

Willanger, R. (1970). *Intellectual impairment in diffuse cerebral lesions.* Copenhagen: Munksgaard.

Wilson, R. S., Rosenbaum, G., & Brown, G. (1979). The problem of premorbid intelligence in neuropsychological assessment. *Journal of Clinical Neuropsychology, 1,* 49–54.

Witt, E. D., & Goldman-Rakic, P. S. (1983). Intermittent thiamine deficiency in the rhesus monkey. II. Evidence for memory loss. *Annals of Neurology, 13,* 396–401.

Yohman, J. R., Parsons, O. A., & Leber, W. R. (1985). Lack of recovery in male alcoholics' neuropsychological performance one year after treatment. *Alcoholism, 9,* 114–117.

Yohman, J. R., & Parsons, O. A. (in press). Verbal abilities in alcoholics. *Journal of Clinical Psychology.*

15

The Neuropsychology of Normal Aging and Dementia: An Introduction

Barbara H. Nolan, Andrew A. Swihart,
and
Francis J. Pirozzolo

As the proportion of the population living beyond the age of 65 has increased, the absolute number of individuals afflicted with dementia has also increased. Although precise estimates of the prevalence of dementia are lacking, there is undisputed agreement that dementia constitutes a major public health problem. Various studies have estimated the prevalence of severe dementia to be 1.3 to 6.2% in persons over the age of 65, with milder impairment in 2.6 to 15.4% of persons in this age group (Mortimer, Schuman, & French, 1981). Alzheimer's disease, the most prevalent of the dementias, is the most frequent cause of institutionalization of the elderly. According to the National Institute on Aging, over $27 billion were spent in the United States toward the care of these patients in 1983. Public awareness has recently increased concerning this disabling condition, and, perhaps not coincidentally, significant progress has been made in the basic and clinical sciences in understanding the disease.

Although by far the most well known of the dementias, Alzheimer's disease is only one of numerous dementing disorders. Other disorders producing dementia include multiinfarct dementia, Parkinson's disease, Huntington's disease, Pick's disease, normal pressure hydrocephalus, progressive supranuclear palsy, Creutzfeldt-Jacob disease, and pseudodementia. In most cases, the symptomatology of the dementing illness is superimposed on changes characteristic of normal aging. Such normal, age-related changes are numerous and occur at both the neurobiological and neuropsychological levels. Hence, before the neuropsychologist can fully understand the dementias, a working knowledge of the changes produced by the normal aging process must be obtained.

This chapter, then, will present a brief review of the changes occurring with normal aging, followed by a more detailed review of the various dementing disorders, with particular emphasis upon Alzheimer's disease.

NORMAL AGING

Numerous changes occur with normal aging. Significant changes are frequently noted in sensory functions, in motor functions, and in cognitive functions, including intelligence, memory, language, and visuospatial abilities. In addition, characteristic age-related neuromorphological and neurochemical changes occur. "Normal aging" is often conceptualized as being composed of two components: the primary, nonpathological aging process and the secondary, pathological processes that often occur comcomitantly with aging (e.g., hypertension, atherosclerotic processes, etc.). This distinction acknowledged, it must be noted that the elderly person free of secondary processes is more the exception than the rule. This review will concentrate, however, on the primary, nonpathological changes.

Sensory and Motor Functions

Normal aging is associated with numerous alterations in sensory functioning. Age-related declines have been noted within each sensory modality (Botwinick, 1984; Corso, 1981; Ordy, Brizzee, & Beavers, 1980). Although sensory declines in the various modalities differ in age of onset and rate of decline, significant decrements generally do not begin prior to late middle age. That is, change is typically slight up through age 40 or 50, but after this time marked declines frequently occur (Botwinick, 1984).

Age-related changes in the visual system documented to date include decreased acuity, reduced color and brightness discrimination, decreased sensitivity to low levels of illumination, increased sensitivity to glare, constriction of visual field size, decreased depth perception, and reduced efficiency in ocular motility, including accommodation, convergence, upgaze, and pursuit and saccadic movements (Cohen & Lessell, 1984; Fozard, Wolf, Bell, McFarland, & Podolsky, 1977). The most common manifestation in the auditory system is progressive binaural loss of hearing, especially for high-frequency sounds (an age-related process known as presbycusis) (Corso, 1977; Hayes & Jerger, 1984). In addition to changes in the visual and auditory systems, age-related changes occur in somatosensory, vestibular, and kinesthetic systems (see Baloh, 1984; Kenshalo, 1977), as well as chemical sense systems involving smell and taste (see Engen, 1977).

Numerous changes in the motor system are associated with aging (Mortimer, Pirozzolo, & Maletta, 1982). Changes include decreased muscle strength, slowing of movements, impaired fine motor coordination, disturbances in balance control mediated by the postural reflex system, and loss of agility (Mortimer et al., 1982; Welford, 1977; Woollacott, Shumway-Cook, & Nashner, 1982). Murray, Kory, and Clarkson (1969) describe a characteristic walking pattern of the elderly consisting of decreased speed and stride length, broader-based gait, and increased toeing-out.

Cognitive Functions

Intelligence

The question of whether or not intelligence declines with age has historically been a matter of some controversy, but in recent years research has begun to produce a consensus concerning this issue. It is no longer considered helpful or meaningful to frame the question in the broad terms used above (i.e., "Does intelligence decline with age?"). The key issue is not a decline in intellectual ability *in general,* but rather, the compromise of certain *specific* intellectual functions (Botwinick, 1977, 1984; Hochanadel & Kaplan, 1984; Horn, 1982; Horn & Cattell, 1967). Research findings suggest that there is little or no decrement in any specific area of intellectual performance up to age 50 or 60 (Botwinick, 1977). When specific cognitive skills do begin to decline, a "classic aging pattern" is described in which scores on Verbal subtests of the Wechsler Adult Intelligence Scale (WAIS) remain relatively stable with increasing age, while scores on Performance subtests decline (Botwinick, 1977, 1984; Hochanadel & Kaplan, 1984).

One theoretical conceptualization of intellectual abilities postulates a distinction between "fluid" and "crystallized" intelligence (Horn, 1982; Horn & Cattell, 1967). Crystallized intellectual abilities are those based on learning and experience assimilated throughout the life span, and they have been demonstrated to remain stable, or even improve slightly, with advancing age. Fluid intellectual abilities, on the other hand, are those involving problemsolving with novel, unfamiliar material in tasks requiring the apprehension of more complex relations and, frequently, perceptual-integrative and manipulative skills (Baltes & Willis, 1982). Such abilities have been demonstrated to decline selectively with advancing age. This dichotomy of intellectual abilities is compatible with the classic aging pattern. That is, relatively preserved Verbal subtests rely on the use of previously stored information that is manipulated in familiar ways (and thus reflect crystallized intelligence), whereas Performance subtests require the manipulation of novel material in unfamiliar ways (and thus reflect fluid intelligence).

Memory

Age-related decrements in memory functioning are well documented. However, these decrements are more apparent in some tasks than in others (for detailed reviews, see Botwinick & Storandt, 1974; Craik, 1977; Craik & Rabinowitz, 1984; Craik & Trehub, 1982; and Poon, Fozard, Cermak, Arenberg, & Thompson, 1980). The pattern of normal loss of mnestic efficiency that accompanies aging can be qualitatively distinguished from various disorders of memory (Morley, Haxby, & Lundgren, 1980). Although it is generally accepted that performance dealing with old memories either is not impaired or is impaired to a much lesser extent than performance dealing with new memories, conclusive evidence awaits more controlled study (Botwinick, 1984).

Age-related changes in the learning of new memories has been described as characterized by a dissociation between primary and secondary memory functions (Craik, 1977; Wright, 1982). Changes in primary memory (the process by which retained material is maintained in conscious attention) are reported as minimal, unless conditions require divided attention or reorganization of the material. In contrast, significant age decrements are noted in performance requiring retrieval from secondary memory (information acquired in the past, but which is not part of current conscious awareness). Thus in tests of new learning with immediate recall, the primary memory component is relatively unaffected, whereas the secondary memory component is affected (Craik, 1977).

This age-related decrement in secondary memory has been attributed to deficiencies in both acquisition and retrieval procedures (Craik, 1977, 1984). Less effective acquisition procedures are associated not with a failure to perceive, but rather with decreased efficiency in mental operations, which results in less elaborate encoding (Sanders, Murphy, Schmitt, & Walsh, 1980). Less efficient retrieval procedures are associated with an attenuated ability to elaborate minimal retrieval cues to reconstruct the original experience (Craik, 1977, 1984). Performance can be altered as a function of task conditions; effective processing can be induced by highly structured task conditions or hindered by task conditions that provide little guidance or that require a high degree of active, novel manipulation (Craik, 1984; Craik & Rabinowitz, 1984).

Language

Although language capabilities generally have been considered unaffected by the aging process, available evidence now suggests that certain age-related language changes do occur (for more detailed reviews, see Albert, 1981; Brookshire & Manthie, 1980; Obler & Albert, 1984). While some components of language appear somewhat vulnerable to the effects of aging (beginning at around age 60), other components appear relatively resilient, or may even be enhanced (Albert, 1980, 1981; Obler, 1980). Discourse (i.e., spontaneous and responsive speech) becomes more elaborate, as opposed to the more abbreviated style characteristic of middle-aged adults (Albert, 1981; Obler, 1980). That is, the elderly tend to use more total words, more words per theme (yet fewer themes), more complicated syntax (e.g., more frequent and more complex embedded clauses), more detail, and more modifiers (e.g., adjectives and adverbs). On the other hand, when language generation is timed, as in verbal fluency tasks (the generation of a list of words within a particular semantic category, or beginning with a certain letter, in a fixed time period), performance declines with age (Albert, 1981).

Under certain conditions, naming performance also declines with age (Goodglass, 1980; Obler & Albert, 1984). Active naming (e.g., object naming to confrontation) declines with age, while passive naming (e.g., word recognition) remains preserved, or may even increase, with age. To compensate for naming difficulties, elderly persons frequently employ the strategies of circumlocution or synonym substitution (Goodglass, 1980).

Finally, subtle decrements in sentence comprehension frequently do occur with advancing age (Feier & Gerstman, 1980). Consequently, the elderly become more dependent on language context and nonverbal cues (Albert, 1981). It should be noted that decrements in sentence comprehension may reflect not only a decline in language comprehension per se, but also declines in auditory acuity, attention, memory, and speed of processing (Albert, 1981; Feier & Gerstman, 1980). Brookshire and Manthie (1980) observe that even though changes in language capabilities in the elderly may be detected by formal testing, these changes are more than likely not sufficient to interfere significantly with communication in daily life.

Visuoperceptual Abilities

Declines in certain spatial and nonspatial visuoperceptual abilities occur with advancing age (see Benton, Hamsher, Varney, & Spreen, 1983; Botwinick, 1984; Fozard et al., 1977). No consistent changes are observed in visual form discrimination (Benton et al., 1983). On the other hand, age-related declines occur in tasks requiring perceptual flexibility (e.g., reporting reversals in perspective of a two-dimensional cube or reporting two alternate percepts that may be seen in a single figure), spatial integration, figure/ground discrimination, visual closure, facial recognition, line orientation judgment, and three-dimensional block construction (Benton et al., 1983; Botwinick, 1984; Cerella, Poon, & Fozard, 1981; Eslinger & Benton, 1983; Fozard et al., 1977). Botwinick (1984) proposes two factors to account for many of the above-mentioned declines: an increased requirement in processing time to perceive complex stimuli and a greater persistence of the stimulus trace in the nervous system, which interferes with processing of subsequent stimuli. Besides decrements in visuoperceptual abilities, other age-related factors can play a role in lowered performance, including decreased visual acuity, decreased perceptual spans and ocular scanning rates, and increased cautiousness (Fozard et al., 1977). Botwinick (1984) emphasizes that timing effects are significant for older people and that the lack of time constraints often lessens the degree of performance decrement.

Behavioral Slowing

One of the most consistent changes noted in aging is behavioral slowing. Slowing can be seen in both the peripheral and central processing of sensory information, as well as in motor activities (Birren, Woods, & Williams, 1980; Cerella, Poon, & Williams, 1980; Welford, 1977, 1982). Learning processes are affected by this slowness and are thus less efficient. Slowing of central processes has been attributed to a lowering of signal-to-noise ratios (Welford, 1982). This decrease can be due to both an attenuation of the signal and to an increase in the level of noise. The elderly are thought to compensate for lower signal-to-noise ratios by taking extra time so that signal strength can be accumulated and noise can be averaged out. This phenomenon of slowing has been studied extensively through the use of reaction time paradigms (Cerella et al., 1980; Welford, 1977).

Neuromorphology

Normal aging produces numerous neuromorphological changes at both gross and microscopic levels in the brain (for detailed reviews, see Brizzee, Ordy, Knox, & Jirge, 1980; Kemper, 1984; Petit, 1982). At the gross level, computerized tomography (CT) scans of the elderly often reveal mild enlargement of the ventricular system and widening of cortical sulci (Freedman, Knoefel, Naeser, & Levine, 1984). In addition, brain weight decreases by approximately 11% between age 19 (the age at which maximum brain weight is attained) and age 86, with the most significant weight decrease beginning at approximately age 60 (Brizzee et al., 1980; Dekaban & Sadowsky, 1978).

Numerous studies have revealed age-related changes at the microscopic level, including neuronal loss, atrophy of dendritic processes, amyloid deposition, lipofuscin accumulation, granulovacuolar degeneration, and the appearance of senile (neuritic) plaques, neurofibrillary tangles, and Hirano bodies (Brizzee et al., 1980; Kemper, 1984; Petit, 1982; Scheibel, 1981). These age-related changes differ in age of onset, along with rate and extent of progression (Kemper, 1984).

Cell counts have revealed significant cortical neuronal loss with aging (Brody, 1955; Henderson, Tomlinson, & Gibson, 1980; Shefer, 1972). Although neuronal loss appears to be widespread in cortical and hippocampal areas, some areas (i.e., temporal and frontal regions) are more vulnerable than other areas (Brizzee et al., 1980; Brody, 1955; Kemper, 1984). The magnitude of cell loss with age has also been shown to vary with cell type and size. Cortical cell counts have revealed greater loss of large neurons as compared to small neurons and glial cells (Henderson et al., 1980). Further, the pyramidal Betz cells of the precentral gyrus appear especially vulnerable to aging (Scheibel, 1981; Scheibel, Tomiyasu, & Scheibel, 1977).

Although significant neuromorphological changes are known to be a part of normal aging, the functional consequences of such changes are not clear. The observation that considerable age-related cell loss can exist without obvious clinical impairment suggests the possibility of a neuronal "reserve" and compensatory neuronal and chemical changes (Henderson et al., 1980; Mortimer et al., 1982).

Neurochemistry

Normal aging is associated with selective changes in neurotransmitter systems (for detailed reviews, see Cote & Kremzner, 1983; Selkoe & Kosik, 1984). Most investigations have assessed the activities of synthetic and degradative enzymes associated with specific neurotransmitter systems rather than the neurotransmitters themselves. The most striking age-related changes occur in the catecholamine systems; declines in synthetic enzyme activity, increases in degradative enzyme activity, and decreases in absolute number of receptor sites have all been documented (Cote & Kremzner, 1983; Selkoe & Kosik, 1984; Wong et al., 1984). Reports of changes in the cholinergic system have been inconsistent (Bartus, Dean, Beer, & Lippa, 1982; Cote & Kremzner, 1983; Selkoe & Kosik, 1984). Age-related changes in the gamma-aminobutyric acid (GABA) system have been reported for selected brain regions (Selkoe & Kosik, 1984). Interpretation of the functional significance of these neurotransmitter system changes is extremely complex and remains unclear. Finally, little is known about specific changes in neuropeptide metabolism during aging (Selkoe & Kosik, 1984).

Neurophysiological Measures

Multiple neurophysiological systems demonstrate change with advancing age. Cerebral blood flow studies demonstrate age-related reduction in gray matter blood flow, particularly in prefrontal regions (Meyer & Shaw, 1984; Tachibana et al., 1984). Findings from positron emission tomography studies assessing the effects of aging on local cerebral glucose utilization have, however, been inconsistent. Some investigators have found age-related decreases in cerebral glucose utilization (e.g., Kuhl, Metter, Riege, & Phelps, 1982), while other investigators have found no age-related decreases (e.g., de Leon et al., 1983).

Electrophysiological measures have also been applied to the analysis of aging effects. Electroencephalogram (EEG) studies of normal aged individuals indicate mild slowing of alpha frequency (but no lower than 8 cycles per second) and intermittent slow wave activity over temporal regions (but with delta activity no greater that 5% of the time recorded) (Hansch et al., 1980; Katz & Harner, 1984; Pedley & Miller, 1983). Aging is also associated with consistent slowing in auditory, visual, and somatosensory evoked potentials and with less consistent changes in responsivity to cognitive event–related potentials (i.e., P300 and contingent negative variation) (Pedley & Miller, 1983; Polich & Starr, 1984).

In conclusion, normal aging is associated with numerous characteristic sensory, motor, cognitive, neuromorphological, and neurochemical changes. The clinician is faced with the complex task of discriminating between changes consistent with normal aging and changes indicative of dementia. Of course, this task will be more difficult early in the course of a dementing illness, when clinical signs are more subtle, as compared to the more obvious signs in advanced stages of deterioration. Despite such difficulties, accurate differential diagnosis is, of course, of crucial importance for subsequent appropriate patient care.

THE DEMENTIAS

Definition

Unfortunately there is no succinct, unambiguous definition of dementia. However, dementia can generally be defined as acquired, persistent, diffuse deterioration of cognitive ability produced by brain dysfunction. The term *dementia* often implies an insidious onset and a progressive, irreversible course. However, the definition is sometimes stretched to include processes with somewhat more acute onset or a static or reversible course. Deterioration is described as diffuse to distinguish dementia from relatively isolated disturbances that occur with focal brain lesions (e.g., aphasia or amnesia syndromes). The term *dementia* does not represent a single disease entity, but rather encompasses many forms of dementing processes. Each of the individual dementias has its own characteristic clinical course, predominant neuropsychological pattern, neuropathology, known (or presumed) etiology, and treatment approach.

Neuropsychologically, dementia is manifested by disturbances in intelligence, memory, language, visuoperception, and a variety of other higher cortical functions, along with changes in orientation, mood, personality, and behavior. However, few (if any) dementias are truly diffuse in earlier stages. Relative sparing of some cognitive functions, combined with deterioration of others, produces identifiable neuropsychological patterns among the various dementing processes. These unique neuropsychological patterns are reviewed below.

Alzheimer's Disease

Alzheimer's disease (AD) accounts for more cases of dementia than any other single etiological category. In a review of hospital-based studies conducted from 1972 to 1982, Cummings and Benson (1983) report that AD was diagnosed in 22 to 57% of the cases presenting with dementia. AD typically begins after age 50; however, cases of onset prior to this age have been reported (Heston, 1983). AD is characterized by insidious onset and a gradual, progressive course. Although uncommon, plateau periods of arrested progression of up to three years' duration have been observed in individual patients (Katzman, 1983).

The length of survival after onset is variable. Heston (1983) reports survival rates ranging from 2 to 14 years. An early age at onset tends to be associated with greater severity, shortened survival period, and greater risk to relatives (Heston, 1983). Although a predominance of females has been observed in some studies (e.g., Roth, 1978), this sex differential has not been substantiated in other studies (e.g., Heston, Mastri, Anderson, & White, 1981). Traditional nosology has divided patients into presenile (onset before age 65) and senile (onset after age 65) groups. However, empirical support for this distinction, based solely on age at onset, is currently quite sparse, and in this review the term AD will refer to patients of both presenile and senile onset.

Clinical Course

The clinical manifestations of AD are often divided into three stages. It should be kept in mind that not all patients will manifest all symptoms of each stage, nor will they necessarily manifest the individual symptoms in the order described. Further, manifestations of more than one stage may be present concurrently. Nevertheless, conceptualizing the clinical symptomatology in stages of progressive deterioration is useful for both clinical and research purposes. The interested reader is referred to Cohen, Kennedy, and Eisdorfer (1984), Cummings and Benson (1983), DSM-III (1980), Reisberg, Ferris, and Crook (1982), and Schneck, Reisberg, and Ferris (1982) for more detailed clinical descriptions.

The onset of the mild stage, or the "forgetfulness phase," is marked by memory impairment for recently learned information or recent events, as opposed to relatively intact recall of information pertaining to life events from the distant past. The individual tends to forget where things are placed, has difficulty remembering names, and often needs statements repeated to facilitate memory. The individual may have difficulty remembering appointments and may have to write things down more frequently in order to remember them. The memory deficit at this stage is generally subtle, but can usually be demonstrated through formal psychometric testing. Other cognitive deficits at this stage may include the onset of anomia, mild declines in judgment and problem solving, and deficiencies in visuospatial and visuoconstructional skills.

Although at this mild stage the degree of cognitive loss usually does not significantly interfere with daily life (including employment), it more than likely will bring about affective changes. Long before professional help is sought and a diagnosis established, the individual may recognize that something is wrong and experience concern or anxiety. Changes in personality and behavior can also involve withdrawal from social situations and depressive reactions. At this mild stage, neurological findings are usually negative.

While the differentiation between normal aging and AD is very difficult in the mild stage, progressive deterioration into the moderate stage of impairment allows a more definitive diagnosis. In this moderate stage, or the "confusional phase," deficits become readily apparent to the observer. Deficits apparent during the previous stage worsen, and new areas of cognitive impairment become evident. These areas may include confusion, disorientation, concentration difficulties, and the onset of agnosia, apraxia, alexia, agraphia, and acalculia. Memory for recent events becomes particularly impaired, while memory for the past remains relatively intact. The individual tends to get lost in traveling to unfamiliar locations. Word- and name-finding deficits become readily apparent to others; however, recognition vocabulary remains largely spared.

The degree of cognitive impairment at this moderate stage significantly interferes with daily life (including employment). The ability to handle such routine activities as shopping or managing personal and household finances is usually significantly impaired. Personality and behavioral changes may also occur, often involving the replacement of earlier anxiety with lack of insight and/or denial. The individual may exhibit restlessness secondary to cognitive abulia (i.e., the individual may not be able to carry a thought long enough to determine a purposeful course of action). In addition, irritability, suspiciousness, emotional lability, flattening of affect, and further withdrawal from challenging situations often occur. Neurological findings may include slight hypertonicity and regressive reflexes (e.g., glabellar, snout, palmomental, etc.).

The severe stage, or the "dementia phase," of impairment again involves continuing deterioration of the above-mentioned abilities and new, additional signs of degeneration. In addition to impairment of recent memory, recall of past as well as personal information becomes deficient. At times, the individual may forget major life facts or be unable to recognize significant others (e.g., spouse, children). Disorientation to both time and place and severe confusional episodes occur. Language usually deteriorates to severe receptive and expressive aphasia.

In this third stage, the individual can no longer survive without assistance. In the middle of this stage, the individual will begin to require assistance with basic activities of daily living, such as dressing, bathing, and toileting. Changes in personality and behavior, which can be quite variable, may involve aspontaneity, decreased alertness, continued denial, anxiety, severe agitation, delusions, paranoid ideation, obsessiveness, hallucinations, and depression. Transient episodes of crying or previously nonexistent violent behavior may occur. Psychopharmacological intervention may be necessary at this stage to treat agitation.

Neurological signs, which become progressively more pronounced in this severe stage, usually include hypertonia, postural and gait disturbances, abnormal reflexes, and dyskinesia. Eventually, all basic psychomotor skills, including the ability to walk, are lost. At the end of the final stage, stupor and coma occur, if death has not already resulted from aspiration, infection, or other illness.

Neuropsychological Pattern

Obviously, the pattern of neuropsychological performance characterizing AD is dependent upon the stage of severity of this progressive disease process. Declines are first seen in fluid intellectual abilities, while crystallized intellectual abilities tend to remain unaffected until later in the disease course (Pirozzolo, 1982). AD patients characteristically show deficiencies in memory, spatial orientation, visual-spatial reasoning, mental tracking, naming ability, and word-list generation, while performance on tasks tapping long-term language abilities (e.g., WAIS Information and Vocabulary subtests) and basic motor functioning remain relatively unaffected until late stages (Obler & Albert, 1984; Pirozzolo, 1982). Since research has focused most intensively upon memory and language dysfunction in AD, the changes in these cognitive abilities will be more fully enumerated below. It should be kept in mind that declines in dementia are described in reference to performance expected of a "normal" person of equivalent age.

Memory failures are the most prominent and often the first symptom noted in AD (for greater detail, see Miller, 1971; Morley et al., 1980; Weingartner et al., 1981). In the initial stages, primary memory (e.g., digit span forward) and remote memory for past life events are relatively unaffected, but undergo increasing decline with the progression of the disease (Weingartner et al., 1981). In contrast, secondary memory (e.g., free recall and paired-associate learning) is severely affected (Miller, 1971; Weingartner et al., 1981). This impairment has been attributed to ineffective encoding of incoming material, which in turn may be secondary to any of a number of more fundamental defects: impaired access to semantic structures in memory, markedly reduced capacity of short-term memory store, and difficulty in transfer between short-term and long-term storage (Miller, 1971; Weingartner et al., 1981).

Deterioration of language abilities frequently follows a unique pattern in AD (see Obler & Albert, 1984, for more detail). Impaired naming and word-list generation usually occur early in the disease course, in contrast to relatively spared abilities in discourse, comprehension, and repetition (Kirshner, Webb, Kelly, & Wells, 1984; Obler & Albert, 1984; Rosen, 1980). In the middle stages of AD, discourse becomes increasingly devoid of meaning and incoherent, secondary to increased word-finding difficulties and circumlocutions and a decreased ability to follow a line of thought (Obler & Albert, 1984). In general, syntactic and phonological aspects, repetition of short high-frequency items, and mechanical aspects of speech are relatively preserved, in contrast to impoverished semantic content and progressively deteriorating comprehension (Cummings, Benson, Hill, & Read, 1985; Kirshner et al., 1984; Obler & Albert, 1984). In late stages of AD, patients often appear not to comprehend what is said to them and are thus no longer amenable to structured testing. Verbalizations may consist of only a few short emotional outbursts, stereotypies, echolalia (repetition of words and phrases addressed to the patient), palilalia (repetition of patient's own words and phrases), and logoclonia (repetition of the final syllable of a word) (Cummings et al., 1985). The progression of language deterioration frequently results in terminal mutism (Obler & Albert, 1984).

Neuromorphological Changes

Neuromorphological signs of AD are found at both the gross and microscopic levels. At the gross level, changes may not be apparent early in the disease, but frequently become quite significant in the disease's later stages. At that time, CT study frequently reveals ventricular dilation and cortical atrophy characterized by sulcal enlargement (de Leon & George, 1983; Freedman et al., 1984). In addition, loss in brain weight may be accentuated (Kemper, 1984).

At the microscopic level, AD is characterized by the classic triad of neuritic (senile) plaques, neurofibrillary tangles, and granulovacuolar degeneration, as well as neuronal loss. Although these histological features are sometimes observed in the brains of nondemented elderly (Tomlinson, Blessed, & Roth, 1968), the severity and localization of these abnormalities in AD differentiate the two processes.

Neuronal loss of approximately 30% beyond that found in nondemented controls has been documented in a variety of cortical areas (Shefer, 1972; Tomlinson, 1982). The pathological process appears to affect larger neurons more often than smaller neurons (Terry, Peck, DeTeresa, Schechter, & Horoupian, 1981). Areas of most pronounced neuronal loss involve temporal lobe (particularly hippocampus and amygdala) and temporoparietal and frontal association cortex, while primary motor and sensory areas are relatively spared (Brun & Gustafson, 1976; Shefer, 1972; Terry et al., 1981). In addition, more recent findings reveal significant neuronal loss in specific basal forebrain and brainstem nuclei (i.e., nucleus basalis of Meynert, medial septal nucleus, locus ceruleus, and dorsal tegmental nucleus) (Mann, Yates, & Marcyniuk, 1984b; Nakano & Hirano, 1982; Whitehouse et al., 1982). Discussion of degeneration in these nuclei, and the significance of such, is taken up below in the section on the neurochemistry of AD.

Neuritic plaques are a characteristic histologic feature found in AD. These plaques are central masses of amyloid fibrils surrounded by clusters of abnormal, enlarged nerve processes and terminals. Plaques are found primarily in cortical regions (particularly temporal lobe), hippocampus, and amygdala (Kemper, 1984; Tomlinson, 1982; Wisniewski, 1983), but may also occur in other brain regions, including thalamus and hypothalamus (McDuff & Sumi, 1985). The role of plaques in the symptomatology of AD is unknown.

Neurofibrillary tangles, another characteristic histologic feature of AD, are bundles of paired helical filaments that accumulate within cell bodies of neurons and that displace and intermingle with apparently otherwise normal cytoplasmic elements. These filaments are composed of a highly insoluble protein that accumulates to take over a large portion of cell space (Iqbal & Wisniewski, 1983). Tangles show a predilection for the hippocampal formation and amygdala but also occur in other brain areas, including temporal and frontal cortex (with relative sparing of primary motor and sensory areas), thalamus, hypothalamus, nucleus basalis of Meynert, and locus ceruleus (Ball, 1977; Kemper, 1984; McDuff & Sumi, 1985; Tomlinson, 1982; Wilcock, 1983). Investigators have concluded that tangles provide a more consistent indicator of the severity of AD than plaques (Tomlinson, 1982; Wilcock, 1983).

Granulovacuolar degeneration, the final histologic feature of AD, occurs in the form of intracytoplasmic vacuoles that have a central dark granule. Granulovacuolar change, which is far more severe in AD patients as compared to age-matched controls, is found almost exclusively in pyramidal neurons of the hippocampus (Ball, 1977; Ball et al., 1983; Kemper, 1984). Granulovacuolar degeneration has been associated with progressive reduction of cytoplasmic RNA and with neurons that appear to be in stages of terminal degeneration (Ball et al., 1983).

Neurochemical Changes

Considerable research effort has focused on the role of specific neurotransmitter systems in AD. The most consistent evidence for a neurotransmitter deficit in AD comes from studies of the cholinergic system. The original "cholinergic hypothesis" is attributed to Davies and Maloney (1976), who observed marked reductions in choline acetyltransferase (a biosynthetic enzymatic marker for acetylcholine) in the brains of three AD patients. Estimates of reductions in CAT activity in the cerebral cortex and hippocampal formation of AD patients range from 30 to 90% as compared to age-matched controls (Ball et al., 1983; Coyle, Price, & DeLong, 1983; Davies & Maloney, 1976; Sims & Bowen, 1983).

The nucleus basalis of Meynert, diagonal band of Broca, and medial septal nucleus constitute the major sources of cholinergic innervation for the cerebral cortex. Loss of neurons in these basal forebrain cholinergic nuclei has been implicated as the morphological counterpart to the cortical cholinergic abnormality of AD (McGeer, McGeer, Suzuki, Dolman, & Nagai, 1984; Whitehouse et al., 1982). Whitehouse and associates (1982) report a loss of neurons of up to 75% in the nucleus basalis of Meynert in AD patients and associate this selective degeneration with cortical cholinergic presynaptic abnormalities.

The degree of cholinergic reduction has been correlated with morphological changes characteristic of AD. Reductions in cortical choline acetyltransferase (CAT) activity have been found to have a significant positive correlation with the number of plaques (Perry et al., 1978; Tomlinson, 1982) and with the number and distribution of neurofibrillary tangles (Davies & Maloney, 1976). CAT activity has also been shown to correlate negatively with the severity of dementia (Perry et al., 1978). There is evidence that the degenerative nerve terminals that cluster around the central amyloid core in plaques may be degenerating presynaptic cholinergic axons, most of which arise from the cholinergic basal forebrain nuclei (Coyle et al., 1983; Struble, Cork, Whitehouse, & Price, 1982). Although there is little doubt concerning the involvement of the central cholinergic system in AD, evidence for specific disruption of other major neurotransmitter systems in AD is inconclusive, at best, to date.

Neuropeptides have recently been investigated in cases of AD. Vasopressin, cholecystokinin, vasoactive intestinal peptide, and neurotensin appear not to be affected (Davies, 1983a, 1983b; Ferrier et al., 1983; Rossor et al., 1982). On the other hand, significant reductions in somatostatin have been reported in several regions, particularly temporal and frontal cortex (Davies, 1983a; Davies, Katzman, & Terry, 1980; Ferrier et al., 1983; Rossor et al., 1982). Reports regarding substance P (SP) have not been consistent. Ferrier and associates (1983) found no reductions in SP measured in 14 brain areas, while Davies (1983b) reported SP reductions of 30 to 50%.

In summary, the cholinergic system appears to be the most viable candidate for specific neurotransmitter involvement in AD. Abnormalities of the cholinergic system are more closely related to the specific histological and clinical aspects of the AD process than those of other systems. Although other neurochemical systems (i.e., norepinephrine, serotonin, and somatostatin) have been reported as deficient in a small subset of patients, these deficiencies appear to be superimposed on more significant and characteristic cholinergic deficit.

Diagnostic Considerations

A definitive diagnosis of AD cannot be arrived at by current, routinely obtained, neurological and laboratory findings. The diagnosis of AD can be confirmed only at autopsy from histologic evidence. Hence, clinical diagnosis of AD is one of exclusion of other possible causes of dementia, including multiple infarcts, intracranial mass lesions, infection, metabolic, nutritional, and endocrine disorders, and depression. Findings from the clinical history, general physical examination, neurological examination, and ancillary diagnostic procedures are important primarily in ruling out these other possible causes. Ancillary procedures typically include blood studies, urinalysis, lumbar puncture, EEG, CT scan, electrocardiogram, and neuropsychological testing. In early stages of AD, findings on these tests are frequently normal. However, as the course progresses, abnormal EEG findings become evident and, with somewhat less frequency, CT abnormalities (atrophy and ventricular dilation) become apparent. Neurological signs may not become significant until late stages, but at that time the presence of regressive reflexes and other abnormalities are frequent.

Pseudodementia and multi-infarct dementia follow AD as the most frequently encountered causes of intellectual decline (Pirozzolo, 1982). Hachinski's Ischemic Score is useful in differentiating between AD and multiinfarct dementia (Hachinski, 1983; Hachinski et al., 1975; Rosen, Terry, Fuld, Katzman, & Peck, 1980). Patients with pseudodementia present symptoms mimicking dementia as a result of a variety of functional psychiatric disorders (e.g., depression). Clinical features have been identified to help differentiate pseudodementia from true dementia (see Wells, 1979).

A considerable error rate occurs in the clinical diagnosis of AD. Twenty percent or more of cases with the clinical diagnosis of AD have been found not to have pathological evidence for the disease (McKhann et al., 1984). Reports suggest that as many as 15% of those patients with symptoms of dementia may actually have reversible disorders, while an additional 20–25% of these cases call for specific therapeutic intervention (Wells, 1977). The need for a diligent differential diagnostic evaluation cannot be overemphasized, since an incorrect diagnosis of AD can lead to a tragic denial of potentially beneficial medical interventions with subsequently progressing dementia.

Etiology

Little is known about the causative or contributing factors associated with AD. Current theories of etiology include genetic factors, infectious agents, and toxic environmental agents (for detailed reviews, see Mortimer, 1980; Wurtman, 1985). Only the most prominent of these are briefly discussed below.

A genetic etiological component is supported by the finding of increased risk of AD among relatives of patients with AD, particularly in cases of early onset (Heston, 1983; Heston et al., 1981). Findings of a higher incidence of Down's syndrome among relatives of AD patients further strengthens the genetic hypothesis (Heston et al., 1981). Brains of virtually all individuals with Down's syndrome who survive past age 35 show neuropathological changes characteristic of AD (Epstein, 1983; Mann, Yates, & Marcyniuk, 1984a).

The possible etiological role of infectious agents in AD has also been investigated. Following the demonstration that kuru and Creutzfeldt-Jacob disease could be transmitted to primates (Gajdusek, Gibbs, & Alpers, 1966; Gibbs et al., 1968), it was suggested that AD may also be caused by a transmissible infectious agent. However, attempts to demonstrate such transmissibility have not been successful to date (Goudsmit et al., 1980; Salazar, Brown, Gajdusek, & Gibbs, 1983). Prusiner (1984a,b) has proposed that a slow infectious agent known as a "prion," which is known to cause Creutzfeldt-Jacob disease and is considered the probable agent in kuru, may be involved in the etiology of AD. Prusiner suggests that amyloid deposition in brains of AD patients may represent the accumulation of prions. Experimental efforts to demonstrate transmissibility of AD may have failed because of the inability of the particular form of prion involved in AD to replicate in the experimental animal species employed, or because the prion's incubation period may exceed the experimental animal's life span (Prusiner, 1984a,b).

Among toxic environmental agents, aluminum has been implicated as having an etiological role in AD. The aluminum hypothesis is based on the ability of aluminum to produce neurofibrillary degeneration in rabbits (Klatzo, Wisniewski, & Streicher, 1965) and on reports of increased concentrations of aluminum in neurons containing neurofibrillary degeneration in brains of AD patients (Crapper, Krishnan, & Quittkat, 1976; Perl, 1983). However, the finding that the neurofibrillary tangles produced by aluminum induction in animals differ ultrastructurally from those observed in AD challenges the aluminum hypothesis (Wurtman, 1985).

In summary, few conclusive data exist regarding the etiological factors important in AD. Why selective vulnerability of cholinergic cells should occur is not known. It is possible that more than one etiological factor is involved in the pathogenesis of this disorder. Similarly, more than one associated risk factor is likely to hasten the onset of the disease process.

Pharmacological Treatment

Although a large number of drugs have been investigated, no effective pharmacological treatment has been developed to arrest the progressive degenerative course of AD. Experimental treatments for AD have included agents such as vasodilators, psychostimulants, chelating substances, antiviral agents, neuropeptides, cholinergic agents, and nootropics (for detailed reviews, see Dysken et al., 1981; Greenwald & Davis, 1983; Pomara, Reisberg, Ferris, & Gershon, 1981).

Multiinfarct Dementia

Multiinfarct dementia (MID) is the second most frequent cause of cognitive decline in the elderly, comprising approximately 12% of all cases referred for evaluation of suspected dementia (Hutton, 1981). Consequently, a clear understanding of its neuropsychological presentation is crucial to the clinician.

The term *multiinfarct dementia* refers not to a single pathological process, but rather to a wide variety of etiological and pathophysiological subtypes, all of which produce a final common outcome of dementia secondary to multiple gross and microscopic cerebral vascular infarctions. The number of such underlying etiological and pathophysiological subtypes are numerous, and the careful diagnostic differentiation of such subtypes is essential for the determination of appropriate treatment. However, such a diagnostic process is outside the province of the neuropsychologist and will not be reviewed here; the interested reader is referred to Alexander and Geschwind (1984) and Cummings and Benson (1983) for further information.

Neuropsychologically, MID presents as a progressive decline in cognitive and emotional functioning characterized by a stuttering course and the production of focal neurological and neuropsychological signs and symptoms. The quality and severity of the dementia produced is dependent upon both the cumulative number and size of the vascular occlusions and their specific cortical or subcortical localization. The differentiation of MID and AD solely upon the basis of neuropsychological assessment results can be a difficult, if not at times impossible, task. Several studies (e.g., Perez, Gay, Taylor, & Rivera, 1975; Perez, Rivera, et al., 1975) have demonstrated that MID and AD fail to differ in their typical patterns of intellectual and memory dysfunction, the only difference between the two being quantitative, in that AD subjects, as a group, are relatively more impaired on indicators of intellectual functioning (i.e., WAIS Full-Scale, Verbal, and Performance IQ's) and memory ability (i.e., Weschler Memory Scale MQ) relative to MID subjects. When MID patients are able to be neuropsychologically differentiated from the other dementias, it is the occurrence of focal neuropsychological deficits (e.g., aphasia, apraxia, agnosia) and the concomitant sparing of other higher order cognitive processes that make the differentiation possible.

Given that MID cannot always be distinguished from the other dementias on purely neuropsychological grounds, the importance of careful medical evaluation and gathering of information concerning the patient's clinical history become apparent. The use of Hachinski's Ischemic Score (Hachinski et al., 1975; Rosen et al., 1980) can be a particularly useful instrument in documenting and defining the important factors in the patient's clinical history. Rosen and associates (1980) have documented the diagnostic utility of this instrument in distinguishing between MID and AD. Specifically, they find that MID is characterized by abrupt onset of symptomatology; stepwise deterioration of cognitive functions; history of stroke; and history or presence of hypertension, somatic complaints, emotional incontinence, focal neurological symptoms, and focal neurological signs. AD, on the other hand, typically presents with an insidious onset; smoothly progressive course; lower frequency of stroke, hypertension, neurological signs, and neurological symptoms; and fewer somatic complaints.

Parkinson's Disease

Parkinson's disease (PD) is a relatively common neurological disorder, affecting approximately 2% of the population by age 75 (Alexander & Geschwind, 1984). The primary symptoms of PD are motoric, with the cardinal triad of tremor at rest, muscular rigidity, and bradykinesia generally considered as diagnostic. Additional motor symptoms frequently include "masked facies" (a blank, expressionless stare), postural changes, slowed and shuffling gait, and dysarthria. Although once a controversial statement, it is now undisputed that dementia is also a frequent consequence of PD, occurring in approximately 50% of all cases (Boller, 1980; Mortimer, Christensen, & Webster, 1985).

Neuropathologically, PD is characterized by significant degeneration of the substantia nigra and frequent concomitant neuronal loss in the locus ceruleus, raphe nuclei, and motor nucleus of vagus. The frequent occurrence of lewy bodies (small, dense, spherical intraneuronal inclusion bodies) in the neurons of the substantia nigra is the defining neurohistological feature (Kemper, 1984). Recent studies also report degeneration of the nucleus basalis of Meynert in those PD patients experiencing dementia (e.g., Perry et al., 1985). Diffuse cortical atrophy has been reported in up to 60% of PD patients (Selby, 1968), and ventricular atrophy has been observed in 30% of such patients (Sroka, Elizan, Yahr, Burger, & Mendoza, 1981); but the relationship between such gross morphological changes and dementia in PD remains uncertain at this time.

Neurophysiologically, the motor symptoms of PD arise as a consequence of depopulation of dopaminergic cells in the substantia nigra, which in turn produces a loss of inhibitory input to the neostriatum and a subsequent unchecked excitatory effect upon motor movements (Gilroy & Meyer, 1979). The neurophysiological basis of dementia in PD remains an issue of great controversy, with multiple investigators attributing it to the above-described basal ganglia dysfunction (e.g., Albert, 1978; Stern, 1983), while others postulate co-occurring Alzheimer's disease as the causative factor (e.g., Boller, 1980; Boller, Mizutani, Roessmann, & Gambetti, 1980; Hakim & Mathieson, 1979). Dementia has been observed in PD patients lacking Alzheimer's disease neuropathology at autopsy, however; hence, it is clear that all cases of dementia in PD cannot be attributed to co-occurring Alzheimer's disease (e.g., Heston, 1980; Heilig, Knopman, Mastri, & Frey, 1985; Perry et al., 1985).

It is difficult, if not impossible, to differentiate PD from Alzheimer's disease on the basis of their neuropsychological presentations alone (Boller, 1980; Pirozzolo, 1982). Several specific neuropsychological deficits do occur quite frequently in PD, however, and awareness of such characteristics may be of heuristic, if not diagnostic, value for the clinical neuropsychologist. First, deficits in complex abstract-reasoning and set-shifting ability are often observed in PD patients (Albert, 1978; Lees & Smith, 1983; Mayeux & Stern, 1983), and such deficits manifest themselves at both the motoric and cognitive levels (Cools, Van Den Bercken, Horstink, Van Spaendonck, & Berger, 1984). Visuoperceptual and visuospatial dysfunction also occur with notable frequency in PD, manifesting themselves through impairments in judgment of visual vertical and horizontal, impaired visual discrimination abilities, defective drawing, impaired spatial orientation memory, and poor performance on WAIS Block Design and Digit Symbol subtests (Boller et al., 1984; Danta & Hilton, 1975; Pirozzolo, Hansch, Mortimer, Webster, & Kuskowski, 1982). These impairments in conceptual flexibility, set shifting, visuoperceptual abilities, and visuospatial functioning are frequently attributed to the known basal ganglia dysfunction in PD, and significant empirical support for this conclusion exists in both the animal and human neurobehavioral literature (see Stern, 1983, for a more complete review). Memory impairment, decreased verbal fluency, and impaired confrontation naming ability also occur frequently in PD, but frank aphasia, apraxia, and agnosia are unusual (Alexander & Geschwind, 1984; Matison, Mayeux, Rosen, & Fahn, 1982). Finally, depression is a common correlate of PD and may contribute significantly to the neuropsychological impairment occurring with the disease (Mayeux, Stern, Rosen, & Leventhal, 1981).

Low Base Rate Dementias

Although the most frequent causes of true dementia, Alzheimer's disease, multiinfarct processes, and Parkinson's disease are not the only such causes. A full discussion of other causes of dementia is not possible within the confines of this chapter, but a brief enumeration of these low base rate dementing disorders will be presented and the interested reader is encouraged to consult the relevent literature for a more complete understanding.

Huntington's Disease

Huntington's disease (HD) is a hereditary condition that produces severe and progressive atrophy of the caudate, putamen, and frontal cortex and frequently produces additional degeneration in other cortical areas, the corpus callosum, various thalamic nuclei, the hypothalamus, and the brainstem (Caine, Hunt, Weingartner, & Ebert, 1978; Sax et al., 1983). Onset is usually between ages 30 and 50, disease duration is approximately 10 to 15 years, and core symptoms of motoric dysfunction (chorea and athetosis), dementia, and affective changes (depression, anxiety, and, later, psychosis) occur.

The pattern and severity of neuropsychological dysfunction differ across the various stages of HD. Early cognitive changes include anterograde memory impairment, visuospatial difficulties, and motor steadiness problems (Butters, Sax, Montgomery, & Tarlow, 1978; Josiassen, Curry, & Mancall, 1983). Later-appearing neuropsychological deficits include decreased cognitive and behavioral flexibility, global intellectual decline, more global impairment of memory, and impaired verbal fluency (Butters et al., 1978; Josiassen et al., 1983). Generally, however, verbal impairment other than decreased fluency is *not* prominent in HD.

Progressive Supranuclear Palsy

Progressive supranuclear palsy (PSP) is a rare disorder of unknown etiology that affects less than 1% of all elderly *presenting* with dementia (Hynd, Pirozzolo, & Maletta, 1982). PSP is characterized by histopathology similar to that seen in PD, but with more widespread involvement of the brainstem nuclei and cerebellum, as well as third and fourth ventricle dilation (Hynd et al., 1982). Onset is usually in the fifties, with a course of 4 to 6 years. Major symptoms include opthalmoplegia (starting with impaired downgaze, then upgaze, with final involvement of all directional eye movements), falling (typically *backward*), nuchal rigidity, pseudobulbar palsy, limb rigidity, brady-kinesia, masked facies, and dysarthria. Nonspecific personality changes and sleep disturbance are also sometimes reported.

Serious question exists as to whether a true dementia occurs with PSP. Albert, Feldman, and Willis (1974) characterize PSP as a model "subcortical dementia," presenting with forgetfulness; bradyphrenia (a *slowing* of thought processes); impairment of the ability to manipulate acquired knowledge; and an absence of aphasia, apraxia, and agnosia. However, results of careful neuropsychological analysis indicate that PSP, at least in its early stages, is not a true dementia. Fundamental impairments in visual-scanning and motor response ability may well underlie the seeming impairment in intelligence and memory; responses, although slowed, are frequently accurate; and the pre-sumed cognitive decline in PSP appears to be *nonprogressive* in nature (Hynd et al., 1982; Kimura, Barnett, & Burkhart, 1981). Furthermore, when other tests of higher cognitive functioning are administered that do not require visual-scanning or motor response (e.g., WAIS-R arithmetic, auditory concept set shifting), PSP patients frequently perform in an unimpaired manner (Pirozzolo, 1982).

Normal Pressure Hydrocephalus

Normal pressure hydrocephalus (NPH) is a rare disorder producing dementia, but accurate diagnosis is extremely important since NPH is a potentially treatable disorder. Sometimes referred to as "communicating hydrocephalus," NPH is characterized by marked ventricular dilation with normal or only borderline elevated cerebrospinal fluid (CSF) pressure (Adams, Fisher, Hakim, Ojemann, & Sweet, 1965). Symptomatically, NPH presents with a characteris-tic triad of dementia, gait disturbance, and incontinence. The gait disturbance and incontinence frequently precede significant dementia, and the first indica-tion of the coming cognitive decline is frequently a *slowing* in all cognitive, motor, and speech activity (Adams, 1980). Neuropsychologically, the dementia of NPH is characterized by difficulty in planning, sequencing, monitoring and maintaining problem-solving activities, memory dysfunction, disorientation, constructional apraxia, ideational apraxia, and sometimes agnosia (Collignon, Rectem, Laterre, & Stroobandt, 1975). NPH can be differentiated from Alzheimer's disease by noting that in NPH the psychomotor retardation frequently precedes the intellectual decline, gait disturbance is an early (rather than late) symptom, language disturbances are uncommon, and CT and CSF findings are frequently abnormal.

Pick's Disease

Pick's disease is characterized by severe frontal and temporal lobe atrophy with relative sparing of the pre- and postcentral gyri. Histologically, frequent "ballooning" of neurons and the inclusion of Pick's bodies are observed. Furthermore, substantial neuronal depopulation in the nucleus basalis of Meynert has been reported, although other neuropathologic characteristics of Alzheimer's disease are lacking (Uhl, Hilt, Hedreen, Whitehouse, & Price, 1983). The neuropsychological deficits observed in Pick's disease tend to reflect the known underlying pathology, with pronounced language dysfunction (especially impaired repetition, echolalia, and auditory comprehension deficits), personality changes associated with frontal lobe dysfunction (e.g., impulsivity, apathy, disinhibition), and sometimes frank Kluver-Bucy syndrome symptoms (Cummings & Duchen, 1981; Gustafson & Nilsson, 1982; Wechsler, Verity, Rosenschein, Fried, & Scheibel, 1982). Neuropsychologically, Pick's disease contrasts with Alzheimer's disease in its early presentation of personality changes and severe language dysfunction (especially echolalia, amimia, and/or mutism), and its later onset of memory dysfunction and visuospatial and constructional deficits (Gustafson & Nilsson, 1982).

Other Dementias

Many other disorders can and do yield dementia, but they are rarely seen in the usual neuropsychological practice. These causes include Creutzfeldt-Jakob disease, hyperlipidemia, atrial myxoma, sarcoidosis, and steroid-induced dementia. Additionally, acquired immune deficiency syndrome (AIDS) frequently produces dementia, and may be an etiology of increasing prevalence in the future (Shaw et al., 1985).

Pseudodementia

Pseudodementia is an intellectual impairment in a patient with a primary psychiatric disorder (Caine, 1981). The features of the cognitive impairment observed in pseudodementia can closely resemble those produced by a true dementia; however, the neuropsychological deficits occurring in pseudodementia are *not* due to a primary neuropathological process and are reversible with appropriate treatment once the true etiology of the cognitive decline is recognized. The major causes of pseudodementia are depression, bipolar affective disorder, and, less frequently, psychosis (Caine, 1981). Given the potentially treatable nature of the disorder, it is *crucially* important that pseudodementia be accurately differentiated from the nontreatable, true dementias.

Neuropsychologically, dementia and pseudodementia are quite difficult to differentiate. Wells (1979) enumerates numerous characteristics of the clinical course and test-taking behavior of demented individuals and persons experiencing pseudodementia that help differentiate between the two processes. In brief, patients experiencing a pseudodementia frequently have a clinical history of previous psychiatric dysfunction, symptom onset that can be dated with some precision, symptoms of short duration prior to seeking professional help, rapid symptom progression, early and prominent decline in social skills, pervasive affective change; such patients frequently complain much of cognitive loss, present detailed descriptions of such loss, emphasize their disability and highlight their failures, show poor or variable test-taking motivation, give frequent "don't know" (rather than near-miss) answers, and display marked variability in performance on tasks of similar difficulty (Wells, 1979).

CONCLUSION

Dementia is a serious and frequent problem for the aged. In this chapter we have emphasized the importance of understanding normal age-related changes in cognitive functioning and stressed that these changes are clearly distinguishable from those seen in the dementias. Furthermore, we have stressed the importance of understanding the differentiating neuropsychological features of the various dementias as a fundamental prerequisite to accurate diagnosis and, when possible, treatment. It is hoped that this cursory review of the neuropsychology of normal aging and the dementias provides the reader with a foundation for further education on this topic.

REFERENCES

Adams, R. D. (1980). Altered cerebrospinal fluid dynamics in relation to dementia and aging. In L. Amaducci et al. (Eds.), *Aging of the brain and dementia* (Aging, Vol. 13) (pp. 217–225). New York: Raven Press.

Adams, R. D., Fisher, C. M., Hakim, S., Ojemann, R. D., & Sweet, W. H. (1965). Symptomatic occult hydrocephalus with "normal" cerebrospinal fluid pressure. *New England Journal of Medicine, 273,* 117–126.

Albert, M. L. (1978). Subcortical dementia. In R. Katzman, R. D. Terry, & K. L. Bick (Eds.), *Alzheimer's disease: Senile dementia and related disorders* (Aging, Vol. 7). (pp. 173–180). New York: Raven Press.

Albert, M. L. (1980). Language in normal and dementing elderly. In L. K. Obler & M. L. Albert (Eds.), *Language and communication in the elderly* (pp. 145–150). Lexington, MA: Lexington Books.

Albert, M. L. (1981). Changes in language with aging. *Seminars in Neurology, 1,* 43–46.

Albert, M. L., Feldman, R. G., & Willis, A. L. (1974). The "subcortical dementia" of progressive supranuclear palsy. *Journal of Neurology, Neurosurgery, and Psychiatry, 37,* 121–130.

Alexander, M. P., & Geschwind, N. (1984). Dementia in the elderly. In M. L. Albert (Ed.), *Clinical neurology of aging* (pp. 254–276). New York: Oxford University Press.

Ball, M. J. (1977). Neuronal loss, neurofibrillary tangles, and granulovacuolar degeneration in the hippocampus with ageing and dementia. *Acta Neuropathologica, 37,* 111–118.

Ball, M. J., Merskey, H., Fisman, M., Fyfe, I. M., Fox, H., Cape, R. D. T., Waller, S. B., & London, E. D. (1983). Hippocampal morphometry in Alzheimer dementia: Implications for neurochemical hypotheses. In R. Katzman (Ed.), *Biological aspects of Alzheimer's disease* (Banbury report 15) (pp. 45–57). Cold Spring Harbor, NY: Cold Spring Harbor Laboratory.

Baloh, R. W. (1984). Neurotology of aging: Vestibular system. In M. L. Albert (Ed.), *Clinical neurology of aging* (pp. 345–361). New York: Oxford University Press.

Baltes, P. B., & Willis, S. L. (1982). Plasticity and enhancement of intellectual functioning in old age. In F. I. M. Craik & S. Trehub (Eds.), *Aging and cognitive processes (Advances in the study of communication and affect,* Vol. 8) (pp. 353–389). New York: Plenum Press.

Bartus, R. T., Dean, R. L., Beer, B., & Lippa, A. S. (1982). The cholinergic hypothesis of geriatric memory dysfunction. *Science, 217,* 408–417.

Benton, A. L., Hamsher, K., Varney, N. R., & Spreen, O. (1983). *Contributions to neuropsychological assessment.* New York: Oxford University Press.

Birren, J. E., Woods, A. M., Williams, M. V. (1980). Behavioral slowing with age: Causes, organization, and consequences. In L. W. Poon (Ed.), *Aging in the 1980s* (pp. 293–308). Washington, DC: American Psychological Association.

Boller, F. (1980). Mental status of patients with Parkinson disease. *Journal of Clinical Neuropsychology, 2,* 157–172.

Boller, F., Mizutani, T., Roessmann, U., & Gambetti, P. (1980). Parkinson disease, dementia, and Alzheimer disease: Clinicopathological correlations. *Annals of Neurology, 7,* 329–335.

Boller, F., Passafiume, D., Keefe, N. C., Rogers, K., Morrow, L., & Kim, Y. (1984). Visuospatial impairment in Parkinson's disease: Role of perceptual and motor factors. *Archives of Neurology, 41,* 485–490.

Botwinick, J. (1977). Intellectual abilities. In J. E. Birren & K. W. Schaie (Eds.), *Handbook of the psychology of aging* (pp. 580–605). New York: Van Nostrand Reinhold.

Botwinick, J. (1984). *Aging and behavior: A comprehensive integration of research findings* (3rd ed.). New York: Springer.

Botwinick, J., & Storandt, M. (1974). *Memory related functions and age.* Springfield, IL: Charles C. Thomas.

Brizzee, K. R., Ordy, J. M., Knox, C., Jirge, S. K. (1980). Morphology and aging in the brain. In G. J. Maletta & F. J. Pirozzolo (Eds.), *The aging nervous system* (pp. 10–39). New York: Praeger.

Brody, H. (1955). Organization of the cerebral cortex. *Journal of Comparative Neurology, 102,* 511–556.

Brookshire, R. H., & Manthie, M. A. (1980). Speech and language disturbances in the elderly. In G. J. Maletta & F. J. Pirozzolo (Eds.), *The aging nervous system* (pp. 241–263). New York: Praeger.

Brun, A., & Gustafson, L. (1976). Distribution of cerebral degeneration in Alzheimer's disease. *Archiv fur Psychiatrie und Nervenkrankheiten, 223,* 15–33.

Butters, N., Sax, D., Montgomery, K., & Tarlow, S. (1978). Comparison of the neuropsychological deficits associated with early and advanced Huntington's disease. *Archives of Neurology, 35,* 585–589.

Caine, E. D. (1981). Pseudodementia: Current concepts and future directions. *Archives of General Psychiatry, 38,* 1359–1364.

Caine, E. D., Hunt, R. D., Weingartner, H., & Ebert, M. H. (1978). Huntington's dementia: Clinical and neuropsychological features. *Archives of General Psychiatry, 35,* 377–384.

Cerella, J., Poon, L. W., & Fozard, J. L. (1981). Mental rotation and age reconsidered. *Journal of Gerontology, 36,* 620–624.

Cerella, J., Poon, L. W., & Williams, D. M. (1980). Age and the complexity hypothesis. In L. W. Poon (Ed.), *Aging in the 1980s* (pp. 332–340). Washington, DC: American Psychological Association.

Cohen, D., Kennedy, G., & Eisdorfer, C. (1984). Phases of change in the patient with Alzheimer's dementia: A conceptual dimension for defining health care management. *Journal of the American Geriatrics Society, 32,* 11–15.

Cohen, M. M., & Lessell, S. (1984). Neuro-opthalmology of aging. In M. L. Albert (Ed.), *Clinical neurology of aging* (pp. 313–344). New York: Oxford University Press.

Collignon, R., Rectem, D., Laterre, E. C., & Stroobandt, G. (1975). Aspect neuropsychologique de l'hydrocephalie normopressive. *Acta Neurologica Belgica, 76,* 74–82.

Cools, A. R., Van Den Bercken, J. H. L., Horstink, M. W. I., Van Spaendonck, K. P. M., & Berger, H. J. C. (1984). Cognitive and motor shifting aptitude disorder in Parkinson's disease. *Journal of Neurology, Neurosurgery, and Psychiatry, 47,* 443–453.

Corso, J. F. (1977). Auditory perception and communication. In J. E. Birren & K. W. Schaie (Eds.), *Handbook of the psychology of aging* (pp. 535–553). New York: Van Nostrand Reinhold.

Corso, J. F. (1981). *Aging sensory systems and perception.* New York: Praeger.

Cote, L. J., & Kremzner, L. T. (1983). Biochemical changes in normal aging in human brain. In R. Mayeux & W. G. Rosen (Eds.), *The dementias* (19–30). New York: Raven Press.

Coyle, J. T., Price, D. L., & DeLong, M. R. (1983). Alzheimer's disease: A disorder of cortical cholinergic innervation. *Science, 219,* 1184–1190.

Craik, F. I. M. (1977). Age differences in human memory. In J. E. Birren & K. W. Schaie (Eds.), *Handbook of the psychology of aging* (pp. 384–420). New York: Van Nostrand Reinhold.

Craik, F. I. M. (1984). Age differences in remembering. In L. R. Squire & N. Butters (Eds.), *Neuropsychology of memory* (pp. 3–12). New York: Guilford Press.

Craik, F. I. M., & Rabinowitz, J. C. (1984). Age differences in the acquisition and use of verbal information. In H. Bouma & D. G. Bouwhuis (Eds.), *Attention and performance X: Control of language processes* (pp. 471–499). Hillsdale, NJ: Lawrence Erlbaum.

Craik, F. I. M., & Trehub, S. (Eds.). (1982). *Aging and cognitive processes (Advances in the study of communication and affect,* Vol. 8). New York: Plenum Press.

Crapper, D. R., Krishnan, S. S., & Quittkat, S. (1976). Aluminum neurofibrillary degeneration and Alzheimer's disease. *Brain, 99,* 67–80.

Cummings, J. L., & Benson, D. F. (1983). *Dementia: A clinical approach.* Boston: Butterworth.

Cummings, J. L., Benson, D. F., Hill, M. A., & Read, S. (1985). Aphasia in dementia of the Alzheimer type. *Neurology, 35,* 394–397.

Cummings, J. L., & Duchen, L. W. (1981). Kluver-Bucy syndrome in Pick disease: Clinical and pathological correlations. *Neurology, 31,* 1415–1422.

Danta, G., & Hilton, R. C. (1975). Judgment of the visual vertical and horizontal in patients with parkinsonism. *Neurology, 25,* 43–47.

Davies, P. (1983a). Neurotransmitters and neuropeptides in Alzheimer's disease. In R. Katzman (Ed.), *Biological aspects of Alzheimer's disease* (Banbury report 15) (pp. 255–261). Cold Spring Harbor, NY: Cold Spring Harbor Laboratory.

Davies, P. (1983b). An update on the neurochemistry of Alzheimer disease. In R. Mayeux & W. G. Rosen (Eds.), *The dementias (Advances in neurology,* Vol. 38). New York: Raven Press.

Davies, P., Katzman, R., & Terry, R. D. (1980). Reduced somatostatin-like immunoreactivity in cerebral cortex from cases of Alzheimer disease and Alzheimer senile dementia. *Nature, 288,* 279–280.

Davies, P., & Maloney, A. J. F. (1976). Selective loss of central cholinergic neurons in Alzheimer's disease (ltr. to ed.). *Lancet, 2,* 1403.

Dekaban, A. S., & Sadowsky, D. (1978). Changes in brain weights during the span of human life: Relation of brain weights to body heights and body weights. *Annals of Neurology, 4,* 345–356.

de Leon, M. J., Ferris, S. H., George, A. E., Reisberg, B., Christman, D. R., Kricheff, I. I., & Wolf, A. P. (1983). Computed tomography and positron emission transaxial tomography evaluations of normal aging and Alzheimer's disease. *Journal of Cerebral Blood Flow and Metabolism, 3,* 391–394.

de Leon, M. J., & George, A. E. (1983). Computed tomography studies of Alzheimer's dementia. In B. Reisberg (Ed.), *Alzheimer's disease* (pp. 258–266). New York: The Free Press.

Diagnostic and statistical manual of mental disorders (3rd ed.). (1980). Washington, DC: The American Psychiatric Association.

Dysken, M. W., Vogel, C., Davis, J. M., Lazarus, L., Lesser, J., & Hicks, R. (1981). Pharmacological agents in the elderly. In F. J. Pirozzolo & G. J. Maletta (Eds.), *Behavioral assessment and psychopharmacology* (pp. 145–177). New York: Praeger.

Engen, T. (1977). Taste and smell. In J. E. Birren & K. W. Schaie (Eds.), *Handbook of the psychology of aging* (pp. 554–561). New York: Van Nostrand Reinhold.

Epstein, C. J. (1983). Down's syndrome and Alzheimer's disease: Implications and approaches. In R. Katzman (Ed.), *Biological aspects of Alzheimer's disease* (Banbury report 15) (pp. 169–182). Cold Spring Harbor, NY: Cold Spring Harbor Laboratory.

Eslinger, P. J., & Benton, A. L. (1983). Visuoperceptual performances in aging and dementia: Clinical and theoretical implications. *Journal of Clinical Neuropsychology, 5,* 213–220.

Feier, C. D., & Gerstman, L. J. (1980). Sentence comprehension abilities throughout the life span. *Journal of Gerontology, 35,* 722–728.

Ferrier, I. N., Cross, A. J., Johnson, J. A., Roberts, G. W., Crow, T. J., Corsellis, J. A. N., Lee, Y. C., O'Shaughnessy, D., Adrian, T. E., McGregor, G. P., Baracese-Hamilton, A. J., & Bloom, S. R. (1983). Neuropeptides in Alzheimer type dementia. *Journal of the Neurological Sciences, 62,* 159–170.

Fozard, J. L., Wolf, E., Bell, B., McFarland, R. A., & Podolsky, S. (1977). Visual perception and communication. In J. E. Birren & K. W. Schaie (Eds.), *Handbook of the psychology of aging* (pp. 497–534). New York: Van Nostrand Reinhold.

Freedman, M., Knoefel, J., Naeser, M., & Levine, H. (1984). Computerized axial tomography in aging. In M. L. Albert (Ed.), *Clinical neurology of aging* (pp. 139–148). New York: Oxford University Press.

Gajdusek, D. C., Gibbs, C. J., Jr., Alpers, M. (1966). Experimental transmission of a kuru-like syndrome to chimpanzees. *Nature, 209,* 794–796.

Gibbs, C. J., Jr., Gajdusek, D. C., Asher, D. M., Alpers, M. P., Beck, E., Daniel, P. M., & Matthews, W. B. (1968). Creutzfeldt-Jakob disease (spongiform encephalopathy): Transmission to the chimpanzee. *Science, 161,* 388–389.

Gilroy, J., & Meyer, J. S. (1979). *Medical neurology* (3rd ed.). New York: Macmillan.

Goodglass, H. (1980). Naming disorders in aphasia and aging. In L. K. Obler & M. L. Albert (Eds.), *Language and communication in the elderly* (pp. 37–45). Lexington, MA: Lexington Books.

Goudsmit, J., Morrow, C. H., Asher, D. M., Yanagihara, R. T., Masters, C. L., Gibbs, C. J., & Gajdusek, D. C. (1980). Evidence for and against the transmissibility of Alzheimer's disease. *Neurology, 30,* 945–950.

Greenwald, B. S., & Davis, K. L. (1983). Experimental pharmacology of Alzheimer disease. In R. Mayeux & W. G. Rosen (Eds.), *The dementias (Advances in neurology,* Vol. 38) (pp. 87–102). New York: Raven Press.

Gustafson, L., & Nilsson, L. (1982). Differential diagnosis of presenile dementia on clinical grounds. *Acta Psychiatrica Scandinavica, 65,* 194–209.

Hachinski, V. C. (1983). Differential diagnosis of Alzheimer's dementia: Multi-infarct dementia. In B. Reisberg (Ed.), *Alzheimer's disease* (pp. 188–192). New York: The Free Press.

Hachinski, V. C., Iliff, L. D., Phil, M., Zilhka, E., Du Boulay, G. H., McAllister, V. L., Marshall, J., Russell, R. W. R., Symon, L. (1975). Cerebral blood flow in dementia. *Archives of Neurology, 32,* 632–637.

Hakim, A. M., & Mathieson, G. (1979). Dementia in Parkinson disease: A neuropathologic study. *Neurology, 29,* 1209–1214.

Hansch, E. C., Syndulko, K., Pirozzolo, F. J., Cohen, S. N., Tourtellotte, W. W., & Potvin, A. R. (1980). Electrophysiological measurement in aging and dementia. In G. J. Maletta & F. J. Pirozzolo (Eds.), *The aging nervous system* (pp. 187–210), New York: Praeger.

Hayes, D., & Jerger, J. (1984). Neurotology of aging: The auditory system. In M. L. Albert (Ed.), *Clinical neurology of aging* (pp. 362–378). New York: Oxford University Press.

Heilig, C. W., Knopman, D. S., Mastri, A. R., & Frey, W. (1985). Dementia without Alzheimer pathology. *Neurology, 35,* 762–765.

Henderson, G., Tomlinson, B. E., & Gibson, P. H. (1980). Cell counts in the human cerebral cortex in normal adults throughout life using an image analysing computer. *Journal of Neurological Sciences, 46,* 113–136.

Heston, L. L. (1980). Dementia associated with Parkinson's disease: A genetic study. *Journal of Neurology, Neurosurgery, and Psychiatry, 43,* 846–848.

Heston, L. L. (1983). Dementia of the Alzheimer's type: A perspective from family studies. In R. Katzman (Ed.), *Biological aspects of Alzheimer's disease* (Banbury report 15) (pp. 183–191). Cold Spring Harbor, NY: Cold Spring Harbor Laboratory.

Heston, L. L., Mastri, A. R., Anderson, E., & White, J. (1981). Dementia of the Alzheimer's type: Clinical genetics, natural history, and associated conditions. *Archives of General Psychiatry, 38,* 1085–1090.

Hochanadel, G., & Kaplan, E. (1984). Neuropsychology of normal aging. In M. L. Albert (Ed.), *Clinical neurology of aging* (pp. 231–244). New York: Oxford University Press.

Horn, J. L. (1982). The theory of fluid and crystallized intelligence in relation to the concepts of cognitive psychology and aging in adulthood. In F. I. M. Craik & S. Trehub (Eds.), *Aging and cognitive processes (Advances in the study of communication and affect*, Vol. 8) (pp. 237–278). New York: Plenum Press.

Horn, J. L., & Cattell, R. B. (1967). Age differences in fluid and crystallized intelligence. *Acta Psychologica, 26*, 107–129.

Hutton, J. T. (1981). Results of clinical assessment for the dementia syndrome: Implications for epidemiologic studies. In J. A. Mortimer & L. M. Schuman (Eds.), *The epidemiology of Alzheimer's disease* (pp. 62–69). New York: Oxford University Press.

Hynd, G. W., Pirozzolo, F. J., & Maletta, G. J. (1982). Progressive supranuclear palsy. *International Journal of Neuroscience, 16*, 87–98.

Iqbal, K., & Wisniewski, H. M. (1983). Neurofibrillary tangles. In B. Reisberg (Ed.), *Alzheimer's disease* (pp. 48–56). New York: The Free Press.

Josiassen, R. C., Curry, L. M., & Mancall, E. L. (1983). Development of neuropsychological deficits in Huntington's disease. *Archives of Neurology, 40*, 791–769.

Katz, R. I., & Harner, R. N. (1984). Electroencephalography in aging. In M. L. Albert (Ed.), *Clinical neurology of aging* (pp. 114–138). New York: Oxford University Press.

Katzman, R. (Ed.). (1983). *Biological aspects of Alzheimer's disease* (Banbury report 15) (p. 20). Cold Spring Harbor, NY: Cold Spring Harbor Laboratory.

Kemper, T. (1984). Neuroanatomical and neuropathological changes in normal aging and dementia. In M. L. Albert (Ed.), *Clinical neurology of aging* (pp. 9–52). New York: Oxford University Press.

Kenshalo, D. R. (1977). Age changes in touch, vibration, temperature, kinsethesis, and pain sensitivity. In J. E. Birren & K. W. Shaie (Eds.), *Handbook of the psychology of aging* (pp. 562–579). New York: Van Nostrand Reinhold.

Kimura, D., Barnett, H. J. M., & Burkhart, G. (1981). The psychological test pattern in progressive supranuclear palsy. *Neuropsychologica, 19*, 301–306.

Kirshner, H. S., Webb, W. G., Kelly, M. P., & Wells, C. E. (1984). Language disturbance: An initial symptom of cortical degeneration and dementia. *Archives of Neurology, 41*, 491–496.

Klatzo, I., Wisniewski, H., & Streicher, E. (1965). Experimental production of neurofibrillary degeneration. I. Light microscopic observations. *Journal of Neuropathology and Experimental Neurology, 24*, 187–199.

Kuhl, D. E., Metter, J., Riege, W. H., & Phelps, M. E. (1982). Effects of human aging on patterns of local cerebral glucose utilization determined by the [^{18}F] fluordeoxyglucose method. *Journal of Cerebral Blood Flow and Metabolism, 2*, 163–171.

Lees, A. J., & Smith, E. (1983). Cognitive deficits in the early stages of Parkinson's disease. *Brain, 106*, 257–270.

Mann, D. M. A., Yates, P. O., & Marcyniuk, B. (1984a). Alzheimer's presenile dementia, senile dementia of Alzheimer type and Down's syndrome in middle age form an age related continuum of pathological changes. *Neuropathology and Applied Neurobiology, 10*, 185–207.

Mann, D. M. A., Yates, P. O., & Marcyniuk, B. (1984b). A comparison of changes in the nucleus basalis and locus caeruleus in Alzheimer's disease. *Journal of Neurology, Neurosurgery, and Psychiatry, 47*, 201–203.

Matison, R., Mayeux, R., Rosen, J., & Fahn, S. (1982). "Tip-of-the-tongue" phenomenon in Parkinson disease. *Neurology, 32*, 567–570.

Mayeux, R., & Stern, Y. (1983). Intellectual dysfunction and dementia in Parkinson disease. In R. Mayeux & W. G. Rosen (Eds.), *The dementias* (pp. 211–227). New York: Raven Press.

Mayeux, R., Stern, Y., Rosen, J., & Leventhal, J. (1981). Depression, intellectual impairment, and Parkinson disease. *Neurology, 31,* 645–650.

McDuff, T., & Sumi, S. M. (1985). Subcortical degeneration in Alzheimer's disease. *Neurology, 35,* 123–126.

McGeer, P. L., McGeer, E. G., Suzuki, J., Dolman, C. E., & Nagai, T. (1984). Aging, Alzheimer's disease, and the cholinergic system of the basal forebrain. *Neurology, 34,* 741–745.

McKhann, G., Drachman, D., Folstein, M., Katzman, R., Price, D., & Stadlan, E. M. (1984). Clinical diagnosis of Alzheimer's disease: Report of the NINCDS-ADRDA work group under the auspices of Department of Health and Human Services task force on Alzheimer's disease. *Neurology, 34,* 939–944.

Meyer, J. S., & Shaw, T. G. (1984). Cerebral blood flow in aging. In M. L. Albert (Ed.), *Clinical neurology of aging* (pp. 178–196). New York: Oxford University Press.

Miller, E. (1971). On the nature of the memory disorder in presenile dementia. *Neuropsychologia, 9,* 75–81.

Morley, G. K., Haxby, J. V., & Lundgren, S. L. (1980). Memory, aging, and dementia. In G. J. Maletta & F. J. Pirozzolo (Eds.), *The aging nervous system* (pp. 211–240). New York: Praeger.

Mortimer, J. A. (1980). Epidemiological aspects of Alzheimer's disease. In F. J. Pirozzolo & G. J. Maletta (Eds.), *The aging nervous system* (pp. 307–332). New York: Praeger.

Mortimer, J. A., Christensen, K. J., & Webster, D. D. (1985). Parkinsonian dementia. In J. A. M. Frederiks (Ed.), *Neurobehavioural disorders (Handbook of clinical neurology,* Vol. 2[46]) (pp. 371–384). New York: Elsevier Science Publishing Co.

Mortimer, J. A., Pirozzolo, F. J., & Maletta G. J. (1982). Overview of the aging motor system. In J. A. Mortimer, F. J. Pirozzolo, & G. J. Maletta (Eds.), *The aging motor system* (pp. 1–6). New York: Praeger.

Mortimer, J. A., Schuman, L. M., & French, L. R. (1981). Epidemiology of dementing illness. In J. A. Mortimer & L. M. Schuman (Eds.), *The epidemiology of dementia* (pp. 3–23). New York: Oxford University Press.

Murray, M. P., Kory, R. C., & Clarkson, B. H. (1969). Walking patterns in healthy old men. *Journal of Gerontology, 24,* 169–178.

Nakano, I. & Hirano, A. (1982). Loss of large neurons of the medial septal nucleus in an autopsy case of Alzheimer's disease. *Journal of Neuropathology and Experimental Neurology, 41,* 341.

Obler, L. K. (1980). Narrative discourse style in the elderly. In L. K. Obler & M. L. Albert (Eds.), *Language and communication in the elderly* (pp. 75–90). Lexington, MA: Lexington Books.

Obler, L. K., & Albert, M. L. (1984). Language in aging. In M. L. Albert (Ed.), *Clinical neurology of aging* (pp. 245–253). New York: Oxford University Press.

Ordy, J. M., Brizzee, K. R., & Beavers, T. L. (1980). Sensory function and short-term memory in aging. In G. J. Maletta & F. J. Pirozzolo (Eds.), *The aging nervous system* (pp. 40–78). New York: Praeger.

Pedley T. A., & Miller, J. A. (1983). Clinical neurophysiology of aging and dementia. In R. Mayeux & W. G. Rosen (Eds.), *The dementias* (pp. 31–49). New York: Raven Press.

Perez, F. I., Gay, J. R. A., Taylor, R. L., & Rivera, V. M. (1975). Patterns of memory performance in the neurologically impaired aged. *The Canadian Journal of Neurological Sciences, 2,* 347–355.

Perez, F. I., Rivera, V. M., Meyer, J. S., Gay, J. R. A., Taylor, R. L., Mathew, N. T. (1975). Analysis of intellectual and cognitive performance in patients with multi-infarct dementia, vertebrobasilar insufficiency with dementia, and Alzheimer's disease. *Journal of Neurology, Neurosurgery, and Psychiatry, 38,* 533–540.

Perl, D. P. (1983). Aluminum and Alzheimer's disease: Intraneuronal x-ray spectrometry studies. In R. Katzman (Ed.), *Biological aspects of Alzheimer's disease* (Banbury report 15) (pp. 425–431). Cold Spring Harbor, NY: Cold Spring Harbor Laboratory.

Perry, E. K., Curtis, M., Dick, D. J., Candy, M., Atack, J. R., Bloxham, C. A., Blessed, G., Fairbairn, A., Tomlinson, B. E., & Perry, R. H. (1985). Cholinergic correlates of cognitive impairment in Parkinson's disease: Comparisons with Alzheimer's disease. *Journal of Neurology, Neurosurgery, and Psychiatry, 48,* 413–421.

Perry, E. K., Tomlinson, B. E., Blessed, G., Bergmann, K., Gibson, P. H., & Perry, R. H. (1978). Correlation of cholinergic abnormalities with senile plaques and mental test scores in senile dementia. *British Medical Journal, 2,* 1457–1459.

Petit, T. L. (1982). Neuroanatomical and clinical neuropsychological changes in aging and senile dementia. In F. I. M. Craik & S. Trehub (Eds.), *Aging and cognitive processes (Advances in the study of communication and affect,* Vol. 8) (pp. 1–21). New York: Plenum Press.

Pirozzolo, F. J. (1982). Neuropsychological assessment of dementia. *Neurology Clinics, 4,* 12–18.

Pirozzolo, F. J., Hansch, E. C., Mortimer, J. A., Webster, D. D., & Kuskowski, M. A. (1982). Dementia in Parkinson disease: A neuropsychological analysis. *Brain and Cognition, 1,* 71–83.

Polich, J., & Starr, A. (1984). Evoked potential in aging. In M. L. Albert (Ed.), *Clinical neurology of aging* (pp. 149–177). New York: Oxford University Press.

Pomara, N., Reisberg, B., Ferris, S. H., & Gershon, S. (1981). Drug treatment of cognitive decline. In F. J. Pirozzolo & G. J. Maletta (Eds.), *Behavioral assessment and psychopharmacology* (pp. 107–143). New York: Praeger.

Poon, L. W., Fozard, J. L., Cermak, L. S., Arenberg, D., & Thompson, L. W. (Eds.). (1980). *New directions in memory and aging.* Hillsdale, NJ: Lawrence Erlbaum.

Prusiner, S. B. (1984a). Some speculations about prions, amyloid, and Alzheimer's disease. *New England Journal of Medicine, 310,* 661–663.

Prusiner, S. B. (1984b). Prions. *Scientific American, 251,* 50–59.

Reisberg, B., Ferris, S. H., & Crook, T. (1982). Signs, symptoms, and course of age-associated cognitive decline. In S. Corkin, K. L. Davis, J. H. Growdon, E. Usdin, & R. J. Wurtman (Eds.), *Alzheimer's disease: A report of progress in research (Aging,* Vol. 19). (pp. 177–181). New York: Raven Press.

Rosen, W. G. (1980). Verbal fluency in aging and dementia. *Journal of Clinical Neuropsychology, 2,* 135–146.

Rosen, W. G., Terry, R. D., Fuld, P. A., Katzman, R., & Peck, A. (1980). Pathological verification of Ischemic Score in differentiation of dementias. *Annals of Neurology, 7,* 486–488.

Rossor, M. N., Emson, P. C., Iversen, L. L., Mountjoy, C. Q., Roth, M., Fahrenkrug, J., & Rehfeld, J. F. (1982). Neuropeptides and neurotransmitters in cerebral cortex in Alzheimer's disease. In S. Corkin, K. L. Davis, J. H. Growdon, E. Usdin, & R. J. Wurtman (Eds.), *Alzheimer's disease: A report of progress in research (Aging,* Vol. 19) (pp. 15–24). New York: Raven Press.

Roth, M. (1978). Epidemiological studies. In R. Katzman, R. D. Terry, & K. L. Bick (Eds.), *Alzheimer's disease: Senile dementia and related disorders (Aging,* Vol. 7) (pp. 337–339). New York: Raven Press.

Salazar, A. M., Brown, P., Gajdusek, D. C., & Gibbs, C. J., Jr. (1983). Relation to Creutzfeldt-Jakob disease and other unconventional virus diseases. In B. Reisberg (Ed.), *Alzheimer's disease* (pp. 311–318). New York: The Free Press.

Sanders, R. E., Murphy, M. D., Schmitt, F. A., & Walsh, K. K. (1980). Age differences in free recall rehearsal strategies. *Journal of Gerontology, 35,* 550–558.

Sax, D. S., O'Donnell, B., Butters, N., Menzer, L., Montgomery K., & Kayne, H. L. (1983). Computed tomographic, neurologic, and neuropsychological correlates of Huntington's disease. *International Journal of Neuroscience, 18,* 21–36.

Scheibel, A. B. (1981). The gerohistology of the aging human forebrain: Some structuro-functional considerations. In S. J. Enna, T. Samorajski, & B. Beer (Eds.), *Brain neurotransmitters and receptors in aging and age-related disorders (Aging,* Vol. 17) (pp. 31–41). New York: Raven Press.

Scheibel, M. E., Tomiyasu, U., & Scheibel, A. B. (1977). The aging human Betz cell. *Experimental Neurology, 56,* 598–609.

Schneck, M. K., Reisberg, B., & Ferris, S. H. (1982). An overview of current concepts of Alzheimer's disease. *American Journal of Psychiatry, 139,* 165–173.

Selby, G. (1968). Cerebral atrophy in Parkinsonism. *Journal of Neurological Sciences, 6,* 517–559.

Selkoe, D., & Kosik, K. (1984). Neurochemical changes with aging. In M. L. Albert (Ed.), *Clinical neurology of aging* (pp. 53–75). New York: Oxford University Press.

Shaw, G. M., Harper, M. E., Hahn, B. H., Epstein, L. G., Gajdusek, D. C., Price, R. W., Navia, B. A., Petito, C. K., O'Hara, C. J., Groopman, J. E., Cho, E., Oleske, J. M., Wong-Staal, F., & Gallo, R. C. (1985). HTLV-III infection in brains of children and adults with AIDS encephalopathy. *Science, 227,* 177–182.

Shefer, V. F. (1972). Absolute number of neurons and thickness of the cerebral cortex during aging, senile and vascular dementia, and Pick's and Alzheimer's diseases. *Zhurnal Nevropatologii i Psikhiatrii imeni S. S. Korsakova, 72,* 1024–1029.

Sims, N. R., & Bowen, D. M. (1983). Changes in choline acetyltransferase and in acetylcholine synthesis. In B. Reisberg (Ed.), *Alzheimer's disease* (pp. 88–92). New York: The Free Press.

Sroka, H., Elizan, T. S., Yahr, M. D., Burger, A., & Mendoza, M. R. (1981). Organic mental syndrome and confusional states in Parkinson's disease: Relationship to computerized tomographic signs of cerebral atrophy. *Archives of Neurology, 38,* 339–342.

Stern, Y. (1983). Behavior and the basal ganglia. In R. Mayeux & W. G. Rosen (Eds.), *The dementias* (pp. 195–209). New York: Raven Press.

Struble, R. G., Cork, L. C., Whitehouse, P. J., & Price, D. L. (1982). Cholinergic innervation in neuritic plaques. *Science, 216,* 413–415.

Tachibana, H., Meyer, J. S., Okayasu, H., Shaw, T. G., Kandula, P., & Rogers, R. L. (1984). Xenon contrast CT-CBF scanning of the brain differentiates normal age-related changes from multi-infarct dementia and senile dementia of the Alzheimer type. *Journal of Gerontology, 39,* 415–423.

Terry, R. D., Peck A., DeTeresa, R., Schechter, R., & Horoupian, D. S. (1981). Some morphometric aspects of the brain in senile dementia of the Alzheimer type. *Annals of Neurology, 10,* 184–192.

Tomlinson, B. E. (1982). Plaques, tangles and Alzheimer's disease. *Psychological Medicine, 12,* 449–459.

Tomlinson, B. E., Blessed, G., & Roth, M. (1968). Observations on the brains of non-demented old people. *Journal of Neurological Science, 1,* 331–356.

Uhl, G. R., Hilt, D. C., Hedreen, J. C., Whitehouse, P. J., & Price, D. L. (1983). Pick's disease (lobar sclerosis): Depletion of neurons in the nucleus basalis of Meynert. *Neurology, 33,* 1470–1473.

Wechsler, A. F., Verity, M. A., Rosenschein, S., Fried, I., & Scheibel, A. B. (1982). Pick's disease: A clinical, computed tomographic, and histologic study with Golgi impregnation observations. *Archives of Neurology, 39,* 287–290.

Weingartner, H., Kaye, W., Smallberg, S. A., Ebert, M. H., Gillin, J. C., & Sitaran, N.

(1981). Memory failures in progressive idiopathic dementia. *Journal of Abnormal Psychology, 90*, 187–196.

Welford, A. T. (1977). Motor performance. In J. E. Birren & K. W. Schaie (Eds.), *Handbook of the psychology of aging* (pp. 450–496). New York: Van Nostrand Reinhold.

Welford, A. T. (1982). Motor skills and aging. In J. A. Mortimer, F. J. Pirozzolo, & G. J. Maletta (Eds.), *The aging motor system* (pp. 152–187). New York: Praeger.

Wells, C. E. (1977). Diagnostic evaluation and treatment in dementia. In C. E. Wells (Ed.), *Dementia* (pp. 247–276). Philadelphia: F. A. Davis.

Wells, C. E. (1979). Pseudodementia. *American Journal of Psychiatry, 136*, 895–900.

Whitehouse, P. J., Price, D. L., Struble, R. G., Clark, A. W., Coyle, J. J., & DeLong, M. R. (1982). Alzheimer's disease and senile dementia: Loss of neurons in the basal forebrain. *Science, 215*, 1237–1239.

Wilcock, G. K. (1983). The temporal lobe in dementia of Alzheimer's type. *Gerontology, 29*, 320–324.

Wisniewski, H. M. (1983). Neuritic (senile) and amyloid plaques. In B. Reisberg (Ed.), *Alzheimer's disease* (pp. 57–61). New York: The Free Press.

Wong, D. F., Wagner, H. N., Jr., Dannals, R. F., Links, J. M., Frost, J. J., Ravert, H. T., Wilson, A. A., Rosenbaum, A. E., Gjedde, A., Douglass, K. H., Petronis, J. D., Folstein, M. F., Toung, J. K. T., Burns, H. D., & Kuhar, M. J. (1984). Effects of age on dopamine and serotonin receptors measured by positron tomography in the living human brain. *Science, 226*, 1393–1396.

Woollacott, M. H., Shumway-Cook, A., & Nashner, L. (1982). Postural reflexes and aging. In J. A. Mortimer, F. J. Pirozzolo, & G. J. Maletta (Eds.), *The aging motor system* (pp. 98–119). New York: Praeger.

Wright, R. E. (1982). Adult age similarities in free recall output order and strategies. *Journal of Gerontology, 37*, 76–79.

Wurtman, R. J. (1985). Alzheimer's disease. *Scientific American, 252*, 62–74.

16
Pediatric Neuropsychology

Lawrence C. Hartlage

Pediatric neuropsychology differs from adult neuropsychology on a number of dimensions. In the adult with an acquired neuropsychological dysfunction, the deficit may present as the loss of an ability that has been present in such a configuration that it is possible to identify the cortical areas involved and the likely etiology of the dysfunction. In the child, acquired dysfunction involving similar cortical areas and etiology may more likely present as an interruption of the development of subsequent abilities that depend on the integrity of the cortical areas involved. Further, although the central cortex has reached 70% of its adult mass by around age 1 (Himwich, 1970), the maturity of specific functions, such as those mediated by given frontal areas, is not reached until around adolescence, so that there may be both qualitative and quantitative differences on processing skills among children of different ages. The age at which functional cortical maturity is reached differs among children, with perhaps the greatest differences related to androgenic retarding effects on the neurological maturation of boys.

Thus pediatric neuropsychology needs to apply the principles of neuropsychological organization obtained from studies with adults with careful attention to the developmental status of the child's nervous system, which occurs at different rates and with increasingly measureable levels of skill, generally progressing from gross to fine motor, language, and higher cognitive processes. In very young children, for example, estimates of subtle central nervous system impairment or immaturity tend to depend more heavily on measures involving motor function than at later preschool ages, when language can be an important clue to such subtle problems, or at later childhood years, when higher cognitive abilities may provide more sensitive indicators of subtle dysfunction. For this reason, in order to lay the foundation for choosing which assessment approaches may be of most utility for assessing the neuropsychological status of the child at different ages, an orientation to pediatric neuropsychology needs to begin with a brief summary of the ages at which specific abilities emerge at measurable levels.

DEVELOPMENT OF MOTOR, SPEECH, AND HIGHER COGNITIVE PROCESSES

Anyone who has been fortunate enough to watch the progression of skill development in children will recognize that they are not small adults whose competencies can be addressed in the same way as can those of adults. The developing central nervous system is, from the perspective of functional organization, quite different from one that has reached maturity. To a considerable extent, the closer the child approaches the age of brain maturity, the greater the similarity of his brain to the adult brain in its functional organization. This factor necessitates the use of different sets of strategies for neuropsychological observation and measurement at different age levels. Since the very young child is most neuropsychologically remote from the adult population, from which originated most traditional neuropsychological assessment instruments, special care must be exercised in the interpretation of such instruments or downward extensions of such instruments; their implications for neuropsychological organization in children are not perfectly comparable to their implications about adults. With this in mind, a review of the sequence of neuromaturational development of abilities, which are reflected in cognitive processes measurable by psychometric procedures, may help place into context the potential need for both different conceptual approaches and measurement instruments at different age levels.

For many years it has been known that the measurement of even global cognitive functioning in very young children produces very low correlations with subsequent measures of global IQ. Researchers have reported correlations between early development scales and Stanford-Binet IQ (assessed at age 6) ranging from .13 at birth to around .50 at age 2 (Hartlage & Lucas, 1973). Subsequent research in my own laboratory, using both Bayley and Cattell developmental scales with a population of several hundred children from a high-risk neonatal intensive care unit, has produced somewhat similar findings, with correlations between early assessment scores and subsequent Stanford–Binet scores ranging from approximately .10 at birth to .53 at age 2 (Table 16.1).

Research with other developmental scales, such as the Revised Denver Developmental Screening Scale, has revealed that moderate mental handicaps and even retardation are typically not detected in the majority of young children by such procedures, suggesting that the differentiation of cognitive processing in very young children cannot be measured with sufficient precision for sophisticated neuropsychological evaluation.

**TABLE 16.1 Correlations of Early Developmental Tests
with Stanford–Binet IQ**

Test	Correlations with Binet	N	p
Apgar—1 minute	.059	102	.558
Apgar—5 minutes	.144	96	.159
Cattell DQ—6 months	.361	102	.001
Cattell DQ—12 months	.344	99	.001
Cattell DQ—24 months	.531	97	.001

The Preschool Child

By approximately age 2, the predication of subsequent mental performance has become more robust, and the differentiation of discrete abilities (e.g., verbal/nonverbal) has reached a point where some rudimentary comparison among abilities may be attempted. Standard psychometric measures of receptive language, such as the Peabody Picture Vocabulary Test, and design imitation, such as the Beery Visual Motor Integration Test, have normative data down to this age; and there are other observational and testing procedures that can be used for the development of a rough profile of different types of cognitive abilities, in addition to global measures of function. The two-year-old child can correctly identify three or four parts of his or her own body by pointing, with hair, tummy, mouth, and toes being body parts with high identification accuracy at this age. By comparing the child's receptive language on a measure such as the Peabody with performance on a task such as "Show me your hair; point to your hair; where is your hair?"—or similarly phrased questions—it is possible to relate the child's orientation toward his or her own body to the level of receptive language. For example, if the child's receptive language is found to be at or above the two-year-old level, but the child is unable to locate specific body parts at a comparable level, a hypothesis can be generated that the child can understand the task but cannot make the spatial localization needed for adequate performance. Similar comparisons of receptive versus expressive aspects of language can be made on the basis of performance on the Peabody compared with the child's ability to repeat on command such words as "kitty" or "puppy," which are commonly in the expressive repertoire of the two-year-old child.

Other nonverbal tasks that can be assigned by instruction/demonstration or by command include throwing a ball or unwrapping a piece of candy; ability to perform these tasks can be compared for verbal command vs. demonstration to develop an estimate of the child's more efficient receptive strategy. A nonverbal task that requires demonstration at this age involves imitating the drawing of a vertical line drawn by the examiner, an example of another age-appropriate visuomotor task. Finally, if there is a question of possible deprivation to an extent that could possibly depress performance on receptive language tasks, instructing the child to point to objects whose names are commonly known by two-year-old children could provide information relative to such noncultural phenomena as the child's knowledge of orientation to his or her own body parts. Objects with sufficient familiarity to children of this age as to be useful for this purpose include commands to "show me the chair," "show me the telephone," "show me the key." In the event the examiner wishes to include standardized measures of additional abilities, tasks appropriate for verbal memory can be found in the McCarthy Scales (McCarthy, 1972) for this age, as can measures of tapping sequence and puzzle solving.

It is important to keep in mind that, at this age level, considerable clinical flexibility and knowledge of developmental stages are necessary, since formal psychometric measures can be spuriously depressed by the child's attentional, motivational, and temperamental status. By a thoughtful combination of different input (e.g., command vs. demonstration) and output (e.g., saying vs. pointing), it is possible to make some preliminary comparisons of areas of relative strengths and weaknesses within the child's developmental repertoire.

By approximately age 3, the child's behavioral repertoire has increased to the point where a much wider range of behaviors can be measured. Expressive language at this age level is sufficient for the child to use complete sentences to describe a favorite toy, relate a recent happening, or talk about siblings or playmates. The recognition of pictures of familiar items or events has progressed beyond nouns, and the child can identify pictures identified as verbs, such as "cooking" and "drinking." Further, the child's reasoning will permit answers to questions such as "What flies?" or "What does a puppy (or kitty) say?" Expressive language and memory are typically sufficient for the child to repeat, on command, three digits, or to repeat, on command, simple meaningful word sequences such as "See the nice kitty." Further, the child can be given verbal instructions to either repeat or execute, such as "Give me the ball."

By comparison of the child's ability to repeat verbally versus ability to execute motorically, inferences concerning expressive language versus motor functions can be generated. Sample motor tasks that can be used with a three-year-old for such purposes include cutting paper with scissors, wiggling a thumb with hand closed, and putting on his or her own coat without help. Other motor skills may involve the ability to copy from a model such items as a horizontal line and, possibly (especially for girls), a circle. As an inquiry concerning out-of-examination behavior, three-year-olds can typically ride a tricycle with some proficiency, assuming they have had the opportunity to do so. As will be noted, children at this age do not have sufficient neurodevelopmental maturation to permit very precise comparisons of the two sides of the body on sensory or motor measures, except in cases of hemiparesis or other fairly pronounced deficits.

By age 4, however, the child should be able, with fingers spread, to touch a thumb to each finger in succession, as well as to hop on one leg, thus providing additional comparisons of right- versus left-side motor proficiency. By age approximately 4½, the child may be able to recognize by touch (as when presented under a table) such items as a block, a ball, or a crayon, thus adding an additional facet to the sensory-perceptual examination. Verbal memory is sufficient for the error-free repetition of sentences of up to seven or eight words, such as "The little boy has a big black dog"; number concepts are often sufficient for counting the fingers on one hand and are almost always adequate for spontaneous counting up to 2 or 3. Further, analogies involving questions, such as "The refrigerator is cold and the stove is _," permit assessment of concept formation using logical verbal reasoning and can add an element of higher cortical functioning involving relational thinking; this can serve as a baseline for comparison against a more perceptual type of analogy, such as presenting the child with four circles and one cross drawn on a paper and having him or her point to which one is different. Memory for verbal sequential commands can be measured by such tasks as "Take this pencil and put it on the chair, then bring me the keys lying on the chair and come sit down next to me."

Thus, between the ages of 4 and 5 the child can be assessed on a number of sensory, motor, and conceptual abilities that begin to resemble the sorts of items often assessed in formal neuropsychological evaluations, although at this age it is premature to assign to these abilities the specific localizing implications such items may have with adults.

The child of 5 years of age, especially a girl of this age, has developed many of the skills necessary for beginning a formal education. Skills include sufficient fine motor control for copying complex figures (e.g., "X") and for spontaneous drawing of human figures; asymmetry in size, detail, or line quality of the child's drawings of such figures may suggest lateralized problems relating to attentional or perceptual inefficiencies. By this age the child may be able to perform on a finger-tapping counter, especially if it has a large area for finger contact, and can be compared for recognition of X and O stimuli presented to either hand.

Formal neuropsychological assessment during most of the preschool years, then, is approached through combining various standardized assessment measures that are somewhat similar to those used in neuropsychological batteries with older persons. Since traditional neuropsychological batteries do not extend to these younger ages, and since in very young children considerably more flexibility in administration (and to some extent in scoring) is necessary, assessment in this age range is difficult to delegate to a technician. With respect to norm-referenced tests that can be used at different preschool ages for the measurement of specific types of neuropsychological functions, the reader may wish to refer to a general coverage of these measures (Hartlage & Telzrow, 1981) or to a more detailed review of specific tests (Hartlage & Telzrow, 1983).

The School-Age Child

For children more than 5 years of age, there is no difficulty in locating a variety of standardized tests that can be used for comparisons of functions dependent on cerebral hemispheric specialization or for more discrete aspects of intellectual, language perception, and motor function, both for norm-referenced assessment and for intraindividual comparisons of the relative efficiency of functions mediated by the cerebral and cerebellar hemispheres. In addition to having a repertoire of behaviors that can be assessed by a variety of measures, the child of 6 years and older is normally socialized to the point of being more task oriented and willing to work for examiner approval. As a result, children of 6 years and older can normally be assessed with some reasonably standard set of measures, in the format of a neuropsychological battery. A standard set of measures for use with the child aged 6 and older could consist of the age-appropriate Wechsler scale; an achievement scale such as the Wide Range; a measure of receptive language such as the Peabody or Ammons; a copying task such as the Beery or Bender; and measurements of rate of rapid finger oscillation, grip strength, and fingertip number writing. These measures, combined with a good developmental history and clinical observations during testing, will normally provide most data necessary for a diagnosis and intention plan; when necessary, they can be augmented by measures to assess special areas of concern in the case of a given child. These tests, representing areas generally familiar to most school and child clinical psychologists, have a two-way advantage: they communicate meaningful information to the clinical psychologists about instruments with which they feel comfortable, and these psychologists may occasionally perform them for you or already have their results available to send to you, either for baseline comparisons or to minimize your own examination time.

By late grammar school, children can be assessed in ways progressively similar to those used with adults; children aged twelve to fourteen perform in ways quite similar to adults on neuropsychological tests (Halstead, 1950).

CHOOSING AN ASSESSMENT STRATEGY

Before deciding on a specific battery of tests in which to develop expertise for neuropsychological assessment of children in a given age range, it may be of value to consider the purposes for which such assessment is most likely to be used. The specific work setting or referral network in which a given pediatric neuropsychologist practices may focus unique emphasis on the development of a high degree of expertise in a narrow area; that is, the pediatric neuropsychologist with strong neurosurgery affiliations may need very sophisticated assessment procedures for tumors or closed head injury, while a pediatric neuropsychologist who primarily sees problems involving school difficulty may need a very different assessment approach. While professionals from many specialties, such as pediatrics, child psychiatry, and mental health, may seek pediatric neuropsychological consultation, a common referral route from such sources may initially be through a pediatric neurologist. Many pediatric neurologists routinely consult with child neuropsychologists, and a brief overview of the sorts of problems with which they are most likely to seek help may provide a context in which to begin consideration of which assessment approaches may be most helpful in answering these sorts of consultation requests.

The most common problems likely to be referred by pediatric neurologists for neuropsychological evaluation of preschool children tend to involve (1) suspected mental retardation or (2) school readiness in a child who is neurologically at risk (e.g., a child who was premature, had a history of meningitis, etc.). For school-age children, frequent referral questions involve (a) evaluation of children with known neurological problems (e.g., epilepsy) who are experiencing some kind of academic or behavior problems or (b) children with a suspected learning disability but without obvious neurological disease. (For a fuller discussion, see Chapter 17, this volume.) For children of either preschool or school age, language disability could be another basis for referral. Specific issues involving head injury, a condition not uncommon among children, are addressed in Chapter 13 of this volume. Conditions frequently encountered in adult neuropsychology, such as those involving ischemic strokes, occur in children at a rate of only .63 per 100,000 (Schoenberg, Mellinger, and Schoenberg, 1978), and the referral questions associated with primary intracranial neoplasms, with an incidence of approximately 5 per 100,000 (Schoenberg, Schoenberg, and Christian, 1976), are typically addressed in referral question (2a) above.

Within this apparently restricted range of diagnostic categories, there are frequently a variety of referral questions, some of which are implicit in all diagnostic categories and some of which are especially relevant to a given diagnostic entity. The sorts of questions implicit in all categories tend to involve the effects of the disease or condition (or in some cases, its treatment) on the child. For these questions, it is necessary to have fairly broad measures of current cognitive ability and information processing, along with measures of current motor and sensory proficiency, in such a way as to allow comparisons of language and spatial functions, assess efficiencies of the two sides of the body, and provide more global measures. For such purposes, for the child aged 5 and above, such information can generally be elicited from the age-appropriate Wechsler Scales, with additional measures of receptive language, such as may be obtained from the PPVT-R (Dunn & Dunn, 1981); copying skills, such as are measured by the BVMI (Beery, 1982); motor functions, such as can be assessed with grip dynomometer and finger oscillation measures; and sensory functions, such as can be measured by the child's recognition of numbers (or symbols) written on fingertips. To compare current functions with prior levels to help assess possible effects of the disease on the child's level

of functioning, a good developmental (and possibly academic) history is necessary; if the child has been exposed to formal education, achievement testing,
such as with the WRAT (Jastak & Jastak, 1978) or PIAT (Dunn & Markwardt, 1970), can provide data that can sometimes be helpful, in conjunction
with developmental history, for generating estimates of prior levels of
functioning. Such inferences as the comparative efficiencies of receptive versus
expressive systems can be drawn from comparison of heavily receptive functions (e.g., PPVT for language function, fingertip number/symbol recognition)
to comparable functions with more expressive components, such as Wechsler
Vocabulary subtests for language functions or motor tasks such as finger
oscillation rate for measures of motor abilities.

It is important to keep in mind that most performance measures need to be
interpreted with considerable caution when used with criterion-referenced
norms. With adults, such performance measures as grip strength and rate of
rapid finger oscillation are likely to be used and interpreted only by neuropsychologists trained in their interpretation. With children there is a much greater
potential for misinterpretation: although many school psychologists and educational diagnosticians have a superficial familiarity with and access to published norms for these measures, they lack sufficient neuropsychological background to understand that their accurate interpretation depends on such
factors as the child's ability to understand and cooperate with instructions,
general maturational and intellectual level, and sex. Thus a successive subtraction strategy is especially important when interpreting children's performance
on a given criterion-referenced test.

As an illustration, the commonly used Bender Gestalt may provide a good
example. Frequently a child with a Bender performance that falls somewhat
below age expectancy may be diagnosed by school psychologists as neuropsychologically impaired (e.g., De Hirsch, 1957). A successive subtraction strategy in this case might be used by first obtaining a full scale IQ. If the child's IQ
subtests fall fairly uniformly in the same standard score range (Hartlage &
Lucas, 1971), there is clearly the possibility of a false positive error in the
inferring of specific neuropsychological impairment from a depressed Bender
score. Should the child's Bender performance fall well below IQ expectancy, a
successive subtraction strategy might involve questioning the child about
whether he noted differences between his Bender reproductions and the Bender
stimuli. An affirmative answer might help rule out a perceptual component to
this apparent perceptual-motor dysfunction; the apparent motor focus to the
deficit could then be assessed in a more comprehensive way by having the child
attempt to copy the design and by looking at motor coordination on tasks
(such as finger oscillation) that are less reliant on ideokinetic function. A
negative response may suggest more perceptually based difficulties, which can
be investigated in more depth by such procedures as motor-free visual-
perception tests (e.g., Colarusso & Hammill, 1972; Levitt & Hartlage, 1984)
and other measures more focused on purely sensory-perceptual tasks, such as

recognition of numbers written on fingertips. By putting together the sorts of information provided by these sorts of measures (or the measures provided by the comprehensive batteries described in Chapters 6 and 7, this volume), it is possible to formulate appropriate responses to the questions implicit in most categories of referrals. For more limited questions, of course, a more limited set of assessment measures may suffice, just as in more complex or comprehensive referral questions a somewhat more expanded range of assessment measures, such as are available in formal neuropsychological batteries like the Children's Luria or Reitan Indiana, may be indicated.

Perhaps because children have direct access to neuropsychologically relevent assessment sources (such as schools) to a much greater extent than do adults, neuropsychological problems in children may be well assessed, although not identified as being neuropsychological in nature. Recent research (e.g., Power, 1983; Power & Hartlage, 1984) has demonstrated that left temporal lobe dysfunction may be identified as language-learning disability on the basis of school psychological evaluation, while children with the same problems evaluated in a neurological or neurosurgical setting may present clear and unequivocal evidence of left temporal lobe dysfunction on electroencephalographic, neuroradiologic, or neurosurgical studies. One hopes that increased awareness of the neuropsychological substrates of many learning and adjustment problems in children will increasingly bring to the attention of child neuropsychologists the sorts of problems that traditionally have been handled by specialists in related disciplines.

A CASE STUDY

It may be helpful to illustrate how a successive subtraction strategy for addressing a referral question common in child neuropsychology can be implemented with a commonly used array of measurement instruments.

Mike, a white, right-handed boy aged 7 years and 3 months, was referred by his pediatrician to pediatric neurology for evaluation of a suspected learning disability. He was the older of two sons in a family in which both parents had undergraduate college degrees. The pediatrician's notes concerning developmental milestones revealed essentially normal early development. At age 5, in a playground accident, Mike had sustained a concussion involving a loss of consciousness for 3 to 5 minutes. This was followed by a generalized tonic-clonic seizure, for which he had been treated with phenobarbital. With prophylactic anticonvulsant medication, no further seizures had occurred, and his waking EEG at this time was normal. His mother had not noticed any developmental problems between the time of the injury and his entrance to first grade. Mike's first weeks of school were uneventful, with Mike described by his teacher as one of the better-behaved children in the class. After approximately 6 weeks of school, the teacher had noted that Mike did not seem to be grasping the academic concepts she was trying to teach and had mentioned this to his parents. Because of their concern about the possible sequelae of his head injury, they had requested and obtained an evaluation by the school psychologist. The school psychologist administered a WISC-R, Wide Range Achievement test, and Draw-a-Person test, scores from which are listed in Table 16.2.

The school psychologist had concluded that there was no learning disability reflected in the test scores, since there was relatively little depression of achievement scores from an expectancy based on the Full-Scale IQ of 89. However, the school psychologist felt that there was evidence of brain damage, since (1) there was a history of head injury and (2) the Performance score on the Wechsler was 20 points lower than the Verbal score. Further, since the child's Draw-a-Person was a full year below age expectancy, this combined with the depressed Performance IQ to suggest right hemisphere impairment. For these reasons the school psychologist recommended referral to a pediatric neurologist.

Pediatric neurological examination was normal. Serum anticonvulsant (barbiturate) levels taken at the time of the examination were 39 mc/ml, within the therapeutic range. A pediatric neuropsychological consultation was requested to help clarify the diagnostic picture and, it was hoped, provide some guidelines for management.

Mike's physical appearance and behavior were both unremarkable. There was no apparent asymmetry of the two sides of the body, and he did not demonstrate any unusual tendency to overuse (or neglect) one side or to be more responsive to visual or auditory stimuli presented from either side. He

TABLE 16.2 Test Results Provided by School Psychologist
(Age at Testing = 6–11)

Wechsler Intelligence Scale for Children—(R)

(a) Subtest	Raw Score	Scaled Score	Subtest	Raw Score	Scaled Score
Inf	8	11	P.C.	12	10
Sim	7	10	P.A.	6	7
Ar	5	8	B.D.	4	7
Voc	18	11	O.A.	6	6
Comp	10	10	Coa	17	5
(DS)	(5)	(7)			
VIQ=100			PIQ=80		FSIQ=89

Wide Range Achievement Test

Scale	Grade Equivalent	Standard Score
Reading	kg. 8	85
Arithmetic	kg. 5	79
Spelling	kg. 7	83
Draw-a-Person Test	Age equivalent 5–11	

was friendly and cooperative. He did not appear lethargic, although his activity level tended toward hypoactive. He did not appear to anticipate failure on any specific sorts of tasks. He responded to both praise and failure in an age-appropriate way, with no particular proclivity for either verbal or nonverbal items. His speech pattern, while not slurred in conversation, showed some difficulty with rapid enunciation of sounds like "puh-tuh-kuh." While not volunteering information, he recollected his previous examination by the school psychologist, whose name he remembered, and did not demonstrate concern or a sense of failure from either that examination or his school work. Because prior intellectual and achievement testing had been done a few months earlier, they were not repeated. Additional testing included measures of motor, sensory-perceptual, receptive language, and design-copying functional levels (see Table 16.3).

These few additional tests helped complete the diagnostic picture and clarified the most likely nature of the problem. Grip strength, which was bilaterally symmetrical and within normal limits, at first appeared to be at odds with finger oscillation rate, which was mildly depressed on the right hand and moderately depressed on the left. Sensory-perceptual functioning was bilaterally mildly depressed. Receptive language was grossly compatible with Verbal IQ score, but the Beery VMI performance was considerably better than what might have been expected from performance on the Performance IQ and the DAP. A superficial review of global test results—taking into account the apparently pathognomonic signs involved in Performance IQ being 20 points lower than Verbal IQ in a child with apparently normal pretrauma development, the impaired human figure drawing, and the greater impairment on the left hand finger oscillation—could suggest confirmation of the school psychologist's interpretation.

A closer look at the picture depicted by all the data, however, suggests quite different conclusions. The fact that grip strength was bilaterally symmetrical does not support the likelihood of long-term disuse atrophy of the left hand. While a recent condition affecting right hemisphere motor strip function could account for the depressed left hand tapping rate without necessarily showing

TABLE 16.3 Additional Test Results Obtained by Neuropsychologists

	Right Hand	Left Hand
Motor		
(a) Grip dynamometer	10.5	9.8
(b) Finger oscillation	25.0	19.5
Sensory-Perceptual		
(a) Finger-Tip Symbol Recognition	18/20	18/20
Beery VMI	Standard Score	96
Peabody Picture Vocabulary Test	Standard Score	106

up in diminished left hand strength, the presumed etiologic onset date nearly two years previous to the examinatiòn argues against this explanation. Further, the symmetrical, if depressed, finger-tip symbol recognition does not suggest the pattern expected from a closed head injury. Finally, the relatively intact VMI ability, reflected in a standard score of 96 for an individual with FSIQ of 89, does not support specific impairment of spatial-perceptual or executory function. Another indicator of relatively intact function involving receptive language comes from the PPVT: the comparability of this measure (standard score, 106) with such other measures of combined receptive and expressive language as Wechsler Vocabulary does not suggest disparity of receptive versus expressive components of language, such as is occasionally found in contre-coup profiles of impairment. With this in mind, looking again at the Wechsler subscales reveals a tendency toward poorest performance on timed measures, with fairly consistently poorer than average VIQ performance on such attentionally loaded measures as are reflected on the Digit Span and Arithmetic subtests. These findings are compatible with poorer than average performance on the timed finger oscillation task and slightly impaired performance on the attentionally dependent Finger-Tip Symbol Recognition test, although there is still some question about why the left hand tapping rate appears somewhat more impaired than the right.

However, when we consider the fact that Mike is taking barbiturate anticonvulsant medication with a serum level at the upper limits of the therapeutic range, it is possible to construct a diagnostic profile that accounts for all test findings. Addressing first the troublesome finding of greater slowing on left than right hand tapping rate, it is known that some anticonvulsant medications, especially barbiturates and nonbarbiturates with barbiturate metabolites, not only impair motor function but especially impair motor function on tasks involving the nondominant hand (e.g., Hartlage, 1981, 1984a,b) The general sedative effect would not necessarily show as impairment on functioning in preschool years, when the child can normally perform at his or her own pace. Further, the tendency for phenobarbital clearance to diminish with progressive age (Guelen, van der Kleijn, & Woudstra, 1974), with children receiving phenobarbital monotherapy showing up to a threefold reduced dosage requirement between the ages of 3 and 15 (Dodson, 1984), raises the possibility of increased effect on performance among children in this age range kept on a constant mg/kg dosage. Depressed performance on timed tasks is compatible with barbiturate effects, and the fact that (exclusive of finger oscillation measures) components of Performance IQ tend to depend on timed performance can suggest a spurious impairment of the sorts of functions mediated by the right cerebral hemisphere. In Mike's case, the two measures of visuospatial functions that do not have a timed component (BVMI and Picture Completion) are both essentially normal and compatible with his other indices of mental function. The fairly uniformly low achievement scores, while not necessarily diagnostic, are compatible with diminished attention and alertness, and this could be related to sedative effects of his medication; the hypoactive behavior observed during testing and teacher reports of good behavior could also suggest mild sedation.

In addition to helping clarify the diagnostic picture, such working through of all diagnostic findings provides important implications for intervention. Rather than attributing Mike's problems to a neuropsychological condition of presumably fixed and nonreversible etiology, this clarification of findings produced fairly specific intervention implications. By careful monitoring of his anticonvulsant levels, it was possible to lower his phenobarbital to a serum level of 18 mc/ml without the emergence of any seizures. At levels between 18 and 20 mc/ml during the remainder of his school year, he was able to be promoted to second grade. Repeat testing on the WISC-R at the end of the school year (approximately 6 months after first WISC-R evaluation) revealed no Performance IQ subtest scaled scores below 8, with PIQ at 95, VIQ at 103, and FSIQ at 100.

CONCLUSION

In many cases the pediatric neuropsychologist may be able to use data obtained from other psychologists, such as are found in school or mental health settings, with fairly minor augmentation of more neuropsychological assessment procedures, for purposes of clarifying diagnostic issues. It is crucial, however, that the pediatric neuropsychologist have a very good grounding not only in neuropsychology and child development, but also in specific aspects of other disciplines as they may relate to a given child. Examples of specific aspects of other disciplines that commonly apply to pediatric neuropsychology problems involve effects and side effects of drugs commonly used in given age groups or diagnostic populations (e.g., Hartlage & Telzrow, 1982; Hartlage, 1965); incidence by age and type of such problems as cerebral neoplasms or cerebrovascular disease (e.g. Schoenberg, Mellinger, & Schoenberg, 1978; Schoenberg, Schoenberg, & Christian, 1976); and the interaction of neuro-psychological ability and deficit patterns with educational and instructional approaches at given age levels (e.g., Hartlage, 1975, 1977, 1979; Hartlage & Hartlage, 1973). It is hoped that the diagnostic case presented will be of value both for conceptualization of the problem in light of consideration of the possible relevance of findings from other disciplines, and for working through possible interpretive hypotheses based on various permutations of test, behavioral, and developmental data.

REFERENCES

Beery, K. E. (1982). *Revised administration, scoring and teaching manual for the developmental test of visual-motor integration.* Chicago: Follett.

Colarusso, R. P., & Hammill, D. D. (1972). *Motor free visual perception test-manual.* Novato, CA: Academic Therapy Publications.

De Hirsch, K. (1957). Tests designed to discover potential reading difficulties at the six-year old level. *American Journal of Orthopsychiatry, 27,* 566–576.

Dodson, W. E. (1984). Antiepileptic drug utilization in pediatric patients. *Epilepsia, 25* (Suppl.), S132–S139.

Dunn, L. M., & Dunn, L. M. (1981). *Manual for the Peabody Picture Vocabulary Test—revised.* Circle Pines, MN: American Guidance Services.

Dunn, L. M., & Markwardt, F. C. (1970). *Peabody Individual Achievement Test.* Circle Pines, MN: American Guidance Service.

Guelen, P. J., van der Kleijn, E., & Woudstra, U. (1974). Statistical analysis of pharmacokinetic parameters in epileptic patients chronically treated with antiepileptic drugs. In H. Schuneider, D. Janz, C. Gardner-Thorpe, H. Meinardi, & A. Sherwin (Eds.), *Clinical pharmacology of antiepileptic drugs.*

Halstead, W. (1950, December 29). *Biological intelligence and the frontal lobes.* Paper presented at the Cleveland Symposium. (Halstead Papers, Box M-187; Archives of the History of Psychology; Bierce Library; University of Akron).

Hartlage, L. C. (1965). Effects of chlorpromazine on learning. *Psychological Bulletin, 64* (4), 235–245.

Hartlage, L. C. (1966). Common psychological tests applied to the assessment of brain damage. *Journal of Projective Techniques and Personality Assessment, 30* (4), 319–338.

Hartlage, L. C. (1975). Differential age correlates of reading ability. *Perceptual and Motor Skills, 41,* 968–970.

Hartlage, L. C. (1977). Maturational variables in relation to learning disability. *Child Study Journal, 7,* 1–6.

Hartlage, L. C. (1979). Management of common clinical problems. *School Related Health Care* (Ross Laboratories Monograph #9), 28–33. Columbus, OH: Ross Laboratories.

Hartlage, L. C. (1981). Neuropsychological assessment of anticonvulsant drug toxicity. *Clinical Neuropsychology, 3* (4), 20–22.

Hartlage, L. C. (1984a, August). *False positive lateralizing signs related to anticonvulsant medications.* Paper presented at the American Psychological Association annual meeting, Toronto.

Hartlage, L. C. (1984b, October). *Artifactual upper extremity asymmetries.* Paper presented at the National Academy of Neuropsychologists annual meeting, San Diego.

Hartlage, L. C., & Hartlage, P. L. (1973). Comparison of hyperlexic and dyslexic children. *Neurology, 23*(4), 236–237.

Hartlage, L. C., & Lucas, D. G. (1971). Scaled score transformations of Bender–Gestalt expectancy levels for young children. *Psychology in the Schools, 8*(1), 76–78.

Hartlage, L. C., & Lucas, D. G. (1973). *Mental development evaluation of the pediatric patient.* Springfield, IL: Charles C Thomas.

Hartlage, L. C., & Telzrow, C. F. (1981). Neuropsychological assessment of young children. *Clinical Neuropsychology, 3* (3), 41–43.

Hartlage, L. C., & Telzrow, C. F. (1982). Neuropsychological disorders in children: Effects of medication on learning and behavior. *Journal of Research and Development in Education.*

Hartlage, L. C., & Telzrow, C. F. (1983). Assessment of neurological functioning. In K. Paget & B. Bracker (Eds.), *Psychoeducational assessment of preschool and primary aged children.* New York: Grune & Straton.

Himwich, W. A. (1970). Developmental Neurobiology. Springfield, IL: Charles C Thomas.

Jastak, J. F., & Jastak, S. (1978). *WRAT manual.* Wilmington, DE: Jastak Associates, Inc.

Koppitz, E. M. ((1975). *The Bender–Gestalt test for young children* (Vol. II): *research and application 1963–1973*. New York: Grune & Stratton.

Levitt, R., & Hartlage, L. (1984, February). *Motor free block design test*. Paper presented at the International Neuropsychological Society annual meeting, Houston, TX.

McCarthy, D. (1972). *Manual for the McCarthy Scales of Children's Abilities*. New York: Psychological Corporation.

Power, J. P. (1983). *Comparison of left hemisphere damage and language learning disability in children*. Unpublished doctoral dissertation, University of Georgia: Athens, GA.

Power, J. P., & Hartlage, L. C., (1984, August). *Language learning disability and left temporal lobe damage*. Paper presented at the annual meeting of the American Psychological Association, Toronto.

Schoenberg, B. S., Mellinger, J. F., & Schoenberg, D. G. (1978). Cerebrovascular disease in infants and children: A study of incidence, clinical features, and survival. *Neurology, 28,* 763–768.

Schoenberg, B. S., Schoenberg, D. G., & Christian, B. W. (1976). The epidemiology of primary intracranial neoplasms of childhood—a population study. *Mayo Clinic Proceedings, 51,* 51–56.

Wechsler, D. (1974). *Manual, Wechsler Intelligence Scale for Children-revised*. New York: Psychological Corporation.

17
Neuropsychology of Childhood Learning Disabilities

George W. Hynd,
John E. Obrzut, Frusanna Hayes, and
Mary Gail Becker

It has long been observed that some disorders of learning in children resemble those patterns of behavior found in brain-damaged adults. Pringle Morgan in 1896 published a widely circulated report of a patient who suffered what today would be called a severe learning disability. His patient was a young adolescent boy who, although quite intelligent, had an exceptionally difficult time learning to read and write in school. He had received countless hours of instruction both in school and at home, knew most of his letters and could identify some sight words. Despite adequate abilities in mathematics, whose arithmetical signs he could read, Morgan's patient simply could not read phonetically. Familiar with Hinshelwood's (1895) description of a patient who had lost the ability to read after suffering brain injury, Morgan hypothesized that this learning-disabled, or dyslexic, adolescent suffered what was at that time termed "congenital word blindness." Kussmaul (1877) had originally used this term.

Over a period of several decades a series of reports by Bastian (1898), Hinshelwood (1900, 1902, 1909), Brunner (1905), Claiborne (1906), Foerster (1905), Jackson (1906), Stephenson (1907), and others (e.g., Fisher, 1905; Variot & Lecomte, 1906; Warburg, 1911) all contributed to a growing awareness that some developmental learning disorders, reading disorders in particular, were due to neurological factors. The prevailing notion at that time was that developmental delays in the region of the angular gyrus were responsible for the difficulty experienced in learning. While our conceptualizations as to how the brain develops and participates in the learning process have undergone considerable change since the time of Morgan (1896), the basic tenets regarding the contribution of the posterioinferior parietal region in conceptual models of reading and cognition remain (Geschwind, 1962, 1974, 1979; Hynd & Cohen, 1983; Pirozzolo, 1979; Whitaker, 1976). Some, of course, would deny the uniqueness of this region of the brain insofar as reading or learning are concerned (e.g., Von Bonin, 1962), and many educators (e.g., Smith, 1982; Spache, 1976) and psychologists (e.g., Ross, 1976; Sandoval & Haapanen, 1981) reject the neurobiological perspective as to the etiology of childhood learning disabilities. It is clear, however, that ample evidence exists as to the unique neuropsychological nature of many disorders of learning found in children, (Aaron, Baxter, & Lucenti, 1980; Gaddes, 1980, 1981; Hynd & Snow, 1984) and, as will be seen, it is the prevailing assumption that learning disabilities in children are due to central nervous system dysfunction (Hammill, Leigh, McNutt, & Larsen, 1981).

Clinical neuropsychologists are employed in many different settings and perform a broad range of services, most related to providing neuropsychological evaluations and diagnostic reports (Craig, 1979). Considering that an estimated 2 to 3% of all school-age children (and probably adults as well) suffer some form of learning disability, it is highly likely that clinical neuropsychologists will, in the course of their practice, be required to provide services to this population of patients. If one takes an estimated (and conservative) percentage figure of 3% of the population as suffering learning disabilities, multiplies it times 220,000,000 people (the estimated population of the United States), one finds that there are a possible 6,600,000 learning-disabled persons in the United States. As Duane (1979) points out, the number of children who could be classified as dyslexic alone *exceeds* the combined population of persons who are afflicted with cerebral palsy, epilepsy, or severe mental retardation. In practice, this translates into an expected incidence rate of about 20 to 30 children per 1,000. It can be concluded that this is a relatively large population of children who may need the diagnostic services of neuropsychologists who are familiar with the unique neuropsychological nature of learning disabilities, the school environment in which these children receive services, and the differences between the traditional neuropsychological evaluation and that which is usually required for these children.

It is within this context that the present chapter was prepared. Consequently, a number of relevant topics need to be addressed. First, the notion of what constitutes a learning disability will be discussed, with a focus on prevalent definitions and the existence of subtypes of learning disabilities. Second, a conceptual neuroanatomical-neurolinguistic framework for the most common learning disability (severe reading failure, or dyslexia) will be presented. Electrophysiological and neuropathological evidence will be provided in support of this conceptual neurobiological model. Finally, unique neuropsychological diagnostic-assessment needs and a conceptual framework for making educationally relevant recommendations will be discussed. From this overview, a more thorough understanding of childhood learning disabilities should emerge, and, for the neuropsychologist who may work with this population, a better understanding of how best to serve these children may be developed.

NEUROPSYCHOLOGY OF LEARNING DISABILITIES

Defining Learning Disabilities

It has been noted for approximately a hundred years that some childhood learning disorders have a neurologic etiology. While this notion was generally accepted, the children so affected rarely received appropriate individual attention in their educational environment despite the pleas of well-respected educators and psychologists (e.g., Strauss & Kephart, 1955; Strauss & Lehtinen, 1947). Part of the problem was that these children were given many different labels, including *neurologically impaired, brain injured, minimal brain dysfunction,* and *perceptually impaired.* Through the efforts of parent and teacher groups and other professional organizations, a consensus definition (McCarthy & McCarthy, 1969) as to what constituted a learning disability was developed. Kirk (1963) had originally coined the term as being potentially less damaging than other diagnostic labels currently in use. The U.S. Congress in 1975 acknowledged the right of all handicapped children to a free and appropriate education and included as handicapped all learning-disabled children. A learning disability was defined as

> . . . a disorder in one or more of the basic psychological processes involved in understanding or in using language, spoken or written, which may manifest itself in an imperfect ability to listen, think, speak, read, write, spell, or do mathematical calculations. The term includes such conditions as perceptual handicaps, brain injury, minimal brain dysfunction, dyslexia, and developmental aphasia. (*Federal Register,* 1976, p. 56977)

This definition and the accompanying regulations implied a number of important points. McCarthy (1975) pointed out that it implies that (1) these children do not learn despite adequate (average) intellectual ability, (2) a discrepancy must exist between projected levels of academic achievement and actual performance, and (3) a concept of deviation exists—in other words, that the discrepancy is so severe that some form of intervention is necessary. It might also be added that a fourth implication exists; that is, that the learning disability may be due to some form of neurological dysfunction, since it includes such conditions as dyslexia, minimal brain dysfunction, and so on.

Many state education agencies adopted this definition verbatim, and it became the standard for diagnosis. Since the concepts of discrepancy and adequate intellectual ability were so central to the definition, formulae were developed to quantify the diagnostic criteria. As Shepard (1983) noted, these formulae were seriously flawed for logical and methodological reasons, since it was assumed that all children should be achieving at or above grade level. It was also assumed that "deficits in grade equivalent units had the same meaning for all grade levels, IQ levels, and subject areas" (p. 5). A number of reviews by Shepard (1980) and others (e.g., Cone & Wilson, 1981; McLeod, 1979) attest to these conclusions.

While this definition set an important precedent legally, it was generally acknowledged as inadequate. Some took issue with the notion that it related only to children. There existed (and exists today) an effort to extend the definition (and services) to adults. Other concerns related to the inclusion of spelling disorders, the phrase "basic psychological processes," and the list of conditions (Hammill et al., 1981).

Developing A More Acceptable Definition

In an effort to address these and other concerns related to the federal definition of *learning disabilities,* representatives from six organizations formed the National Joint Committee for Learning Disabilities (NJCLD). The six organizations that participated in this effort included the American Speech-Language Hearing Association (ASHA), the Association for Children and Adults with Learning Disabilities (ACLD), the Council for Learning Disabilities (CLD), the Division for Children with Communication Disorders (DCCD), the International Reading Association (IRA), and the Orton Dyslexia Society (Hammill et al., 1981). The NJCLD defined *learning disabilities* as a

> . . . generic term that refers to a heterogeneous group of disorders manifested by significant difficulties in the acquisition and use of listening, speaking, reading, writing, reasoning or mathematical abilities. These disorders are intrinsic to the individual and *presumed to be due to central nervous system dysfunction.* Even though a learning disability may occur concomitantly with other handicapping conditions (e.g., sensory impairment, mental retardation, social and emotional disturbance) or environmental influences (e.g., cultural differences, insufficient/ inappropriate instruction, psychogenic factors), it is not the direct result of those conditions or influences. (Hammill et al., 1981, p. 336, emphasis added)

Possible Implications of the NJCLD Definition

The NJCLD definition is a considerable improvement over the one published in 1976 in the *Federal Register*. By stating that "learning disabilities is a generic term" the committee made it clear that a variety of disorders comprise "learning disabilities." Being "heterogeneous" in nature implies that many different etiologies and subtypes may exist, each uniquely different. Perhaps most importantly, the committee felt that since the term and concept of *learning disabilities* was so deeply rooted in a neurological framework it was best to state this perspective formally. According to Hammill et al. (1981), "the Committee agreed that hard evidence of organicity did not have to be present in order to diagnose a person as learning disabled, but that no person should be labelled LD unless CNS dysfunction was the suspected cause" (p. 340). Finally, the Committee felt it should be formally acknowledged that learning disabilities could occur concomitantly with other handicapping conditions. These points are indeed significant and deserve consideration.

By acknowledging the varied nature of learning disabilities, this definition makes more legitimate the study and application of the concept of learning disability subtypes. This will be considered in more detail in a following section. Suffice it to say, if clinicians can diagnose subtypes of learning disabilities, it may indeed be appropriate to do so. Clearly, however, it is the notion that learning disabilities are due to central nervous system dysfunction that stands out as most important.

If learning disabilities are presumed to be due to central nervous system dysfunction, yet the dysfunction needs only be "suspected," it would seem as if considerable problems may exist. Does this imply that no concrete evidence of the neurological basis of learning disabilities need exist? If this is indeed the case, then are clinicians left with only a severe discrepancy between achievement and potential as the primary diagnostic criteria? The four most common methods of determining a severe discrepancy include: (1) deviation from grade level, (2) expectancy formula, (3) standard-score comparison, and (4) regression analysis. All are associated with unique and significant problems (Cone & Wilson, 1981; Shepard, Smith, & Vojir, 1983). It would seem more prudent to offer some evidence as to the neurological basis of the learning disability, and it is here, perhaps, that the clinical neuropsychologist can offer much needed expertise. Certainly, as funds for the provision of services to these children become more restricted due to financial constraints in the public school setting, it is not hard to imagine that only children with diagnosed central nervous system dysfunction will be provided services. Considering the wording of the definition, this would seem very appropriate.

Some psychologists who are employed in the public school setting are trained in and use neuropsychological evaluation procedures (Hynd, Quackenbush, & Obrzut, 1980). However, these psychologists are relatively few in number and generally do not have the level of professional preparation necessary to conduct a *complete* neuropsychological evaluation. Consequently, the neuropsychologist who may work as a consultant to the schools, in a medical setting that serves school-age children, or as a private practitioner could easily provide the evidence necessary to differentiate learning problems of "presumed" neurologic etiology from those that are not. Good evidence attests to the ability of relatively simple neurologic tasks, such as finger agnosia (finger recognition) (Fletcher, Taylor, Morris, & Satz, 1982; Lindgren, 1978) or even dichotic listening (Hynd, Obrzut, Weed, & Hynd, 1979; Hynd, Cohen & Obrzut, 1983), to discriminate between children who have neurologically based disorders of learning and normal children. Other studies attest to the discriminate validity of the Halstead–Reitan Neuropsychological Battery (O'Donnell, Kurtz, & Ramanaiah, 1983; Reitan, 1974; Reitan & Boll, 1973; Selz & Reitan, 1979) and Luria–Nebraska Neuropsychological Battery-Children's Revision (Nolan, Hammeke, & Barkley, 1983; Snow, Hynd, & Hartlage, 1984) with learning-disabled children.

Finally, the definition provided by the NJCLD indicates that learning disabilities may occur with other handicapping conditions. This, of course, makes sense. However, from an educational standpoint the common practice is to treat a child as either emotionally disturbed or as learning disabled. It might well be relevant to ask educators if double tracking or the provision of services from two different special education programs is now more appropriate. While this question has more implications for educators who are concerned with providing the most cost-effective services to the most pupils, it does bear some consideration by all involved in the provision of services.

To date, most of the executive boards of the six organizations noted previously have accepted this new definition as the standard. The acceptance of this definition poses many new challenges for educators and psychologists alike. Its most significant contribution, however, is that it clearly spells out the notion that learning disabilities are due to central nervous system dysfunction and that many different subtypes exist. For the neuropsychologist, it may be suggested that it is in the domain of clinical differentiation that the greatest need exists. To treat differentially, one must first differentiate the nature of the learning disabilities. As will be seen, the approach to educational intervention for the child with neurologically based learning disabilities should be different from that for the child who does not evidence central nervous system dysfunction. This point will be elaborated in the concluding section of this chapter. Next, however, it is most appropriate to examine briefly what is known and not known about the various subtypes of learning disabilities.

Subtypes of Learning Disabilities

For many decades researchers sought to identify those cognitive processes typically deficient in children with severe learning disabilities. Most of the early research focused on deficient processes in disabled readers, since a majority of learning-disabled children experienced difficulty in reading. These children were identified, according to various investigators, as suffering deficits in perceptual processes (Lyle, 1969; Lyle & Goyen, 1968, 1975), perceptual-motor matching (Kephart, 1971), cross-modal integration (Birch & Belmont, 1964, 1965), bisensory memory (Senf, 1969; Senf & Freundl, 1971), temporal-order recall (Bakker, 1972) and, of course, cerebral dominance (Orton, 1928, 1937; Satz, Rardin, & Ross, 1971; Yeni-Komshian, Isenberg, & Goldstein, 1975; Zurif & Carson, 1970).

Each of these researchers sought to identify the cognitive, neuropsychological, or perceptual processes they believed to be deficient in children experiencing learning disabilities. However, it seemed inconsistent that one group of researchers could document one type of cognitive process as the sole cause of the learning disability while another group of researchers argued, just as strongly, that some other perceptual or cognitive process served as its foundation. The truth of the matter is, of course, that many different subtypes or subgroups of learning disabilities exist as formally recognized by the NJCLD definition. The heterogeneous nature of learning disabilities has been recognized for approximately twenty years, and much of the early evidence was provided by Kinsbourne and Warrington (1963), Boder (1971, 1973) and Mattis, French, and Rapin (1975). Their *a posteriori* studies provided convincing evidence that at least two, if not three or more, subtypes of reading disabilities existed—each with its own distinct neuropsychological pattern or profile of abilities and disabilities.

Since 1963, when Kinsbourne and Warrington published their study articulating the neuropsychological profile of verbally and spatially deficient readers, more than thirty separate studies have appeared in which subtypes of learning disabilities have been investigated (Hynd & Snow, 1984). Broadly conceived, three subtypes of reading disabilities seem to exist. One reading-disabled subgroup appears to have difficulty in auditory-linguistic processing, while a second subgroup seems to possess deficient visual-spatial skills (Pirozzolo, 1979; Watson, Goldgar, & Ryschon, 1983). A third, less well-defined subgroup seems to possess relatively few deficits but still seems unable to read normally (Satz & Morris, 1981; Watson et al., 1983). Other investigators have identified subtypes of retarded spellers (e.g., Nelson & Warrington, 1974; Sweeney & Rourke, 1978), children who are deficient in arithmetic (Rourke & Strang, 1981; Rourke & Finlayson, 1978), and dyslexics who evidence unique neurolinguistic profiles (see Hynd & Hynd, 1984, for a review). Table 17.1 provides a summary of many of the studies conducted along these lines.

Learning Disability Subtypes—Conceptual Problems

There exist many problems with the subtype literature. Perhaps most obvious is how so many investigators can identify so many different subtypes of learning disabilities? The simple matter is that most of these investigators have used either a clinical or an *a posteriori* approach in articulating the neuropsychological nature of the learning disability subtypes. Those who have used a more clinical approach (e.g., Boder, 1973; Deloche & Andreewsky, 1982) are typically restricted in terms of how well the results can be generalized by the small number of subjects employed and according to whether or not the

TABLE 17.1 Studies Investigating Subtypes of Learning Disabilities

Date	Investigator(s)	Characteristics of Subtype(s)
1963	Kinsbourne & Warrington	Verbally deficient readers Spatially deficient readers
1964	deQuirus	Auditory dyslexia Visual dyslexia
1966	Bannatyne	Neurological dyslexia Genetic dyslexia
1967	Johnson & Myklebust	Auditory dyslexia Visual dyslexia
1968	Bateman	Auditory memory subgroup Visual memory subgroup Combined type
1970	Boder	Dysphonetic dyslexia Dyseidetic dyslexia Alexic dyslexia
1970	Ingram, Mason, & Blackburn	Audiophonetic subtype Visual-spatial Combined
1971	Rourke, Young, & Flewelling	PSIQ > VSIQ PSIQ ≈ VSIQ PSIQ < VSIQ
1972	Naidoo	Reading/spelling deficits Spelling deficits only
1975	Mattis, French, & Rapin	Language disordered Articulatory and graphomotor dyscoordination Visual perceptual deficits
1977	Doehring & Hoshko	Linguistic deficits Phonological deficits Intersensory integration deficits
1977	Smith, Coleman, Dokecki, & Davis	High IQ group Low IQ group
1978	Sweeney & Rourke	Retarded spellers
1978	Rourke & Finlayson	Reading, spelling, and arithmetic deficits Reading and spelling deficient subgroup Arithmetic deficient subgroup
1979	Petrauskas & Rourke	Left temporal lobe deficits Posterior left hemisphere deficits
1979	Fisk & Rourke	Auditory-verbal processing visual sequencing and finger localization deficits Auditory-verbal processing and motor deficits Word blending, memory, and finger-tip number writing deficits
1979	Pirozzolo	Auditory-linguistic subtype Visual-spatial subtype
1980	Coltheart, Patterson, & Marshall	Deep dyslexia

TABLE 17.1 (*continued*)

Date	Investigator(s)	Characteristics of Subtype(s)
1981	Satz & Morris	Global language subtype Specific language subtype Mixed type Visual perceptual type
1981	Lyon & Watson	Language comprehension, auditory and visual memory, sound blending, and visual-spatial deficits Language comprehension, auditory-memory and visual motor integration deficits Aphasic type Expressive and receptive language deficits Visuoperceptive deficits Normal pattern with low reading achievement
1982	Deloche & Andreewsky	Surface dyslexia
1983	Sevush	Surface dyslexia Deep dyslexia Phonological dyslexia
1983	Watson, Goldgar, & Ryschon	Language disordered subtype Visual processing subtype Minimal deficits subtype

Adapted and modified from Hynd and Snow (1984), with permission.

subjects under study suffer the disability as a developmental disorder or as the result of trauma. Another approach to the study of the neuropsychological nature of subtypes of learning disabilities has employed statistical classification methods, such as Q factor analysis (e.g., Doehring & Hoshko, 1977; Doehring, Hoshko, & Bryans, 1979; Petrauskas & Rourke, 1979) or cluster analysis (Watson et al., 1983), as a means of identifying similar patterns of performance among subgroups of learning disabled children.

One obvious problem with the multivariate approach lies in the statistical properties of the tests employed to assess neuropsychological deficits. If a test is not particularly reliable, then fluctuations between scores may simply reflect the inadequacies of the test and not variance between subgroups of learning-disabled children. The *a posteriori methods* (e.g., Q factor analysis) also suffer from variations in methodological decisions. In identifying factors, does one use the Eigenvalue or Scree criteria? Also, the number of correlated or non-correlated measures administered to the learning-disabled children may well determine how many factors or clusters emerge from the data. Finally, the validity of a classification scheme needs to be addressed. Satz and Morris (1981) and Morris, Blashfield, and Satz (1981) outline a number of approaches for assessing and validating group classification schemes. Morris et al. (1981) discuss the critical nature of using internal validation procedures, including statistical measures, data manipulation measures, and graphical methods, such that the results of any particular multivariate study do not simply reflect our own biases or, perhaps even worse, the random clustering of variables.

To the clinical neuropsychologist who must work with learning-disabled children, the subtype literature could easily be interpreted as presenting such a confusing picture that no meaningful conclusions can be derived. The subtype literature is probably more important from a theoretical perspective than it is from a clinical one. It can be argued that each child probably reflects a unique clinically derived subtype, depending on the individual pattern or distribution of neurodevelopmental deficits (Hynd & Hynd, 1984; Hynd & Snow, 1984). Thus, from a clinical viewpoint it is unlikely that a particular child will exactly reflect Boder's (1973) "dysphonetic dyslexic" or Doehring and colleagues's (1979) "Type O" disabled reader. These subtypes are formulated through grouped data, thus obscuring individual profiles. Considering the evidence in favor of the neurobiological nature of learning disabilities, it makes sense for clinicians to view as the primary purpose of their evaluation the determination of whether the learning disability is due to central nervous system dysfunction. A second priority, if indeed it is due to neuropsychological deficits, is not to attempt to diagnose the particular subtype of learning disability (although probabilities would argue that the majority of learning disabled children will evidence the auditory-linguistic or language-disordered syndrome), but rather to outline clearly what that particular child's profile is like and its implications for intervention.

Since these ideas rest on the notion that reading and other particularly important cognitive processes are the result of a uniquely operating functional system or systems, the neurobiological evidence in favor of these ideas will be discussed. It is argued that the considerable variability found in the subtype literature can be explained, at least in part, by an understanding of how widely distributed and interactive are the various functional systems involved in learning. Since more is known regarding the neurobiological nature of reading disabilities or dyslexia, the following discussion will focus, as an example, on the hypothesized functional system involved in reading and in reading failure. From this discussion should emerge a clear conceptualization as to the neurological basis for one of the most common learning disabilities and an understanding as to why such a large body of evidence suggests neuropsychological deficits in almost every important cognitive or perceptual process. If, as proposed, the distribution of neurodevelopmental deficits is truly random within this functional system, then it should be possible to find many different subtypes, with each child demonstrating a uniquely different pattern even within subgroups of learning-disabled children.

NEUROBIOLOGY OF LEARNING DISABILITIES

One of the greatest problems that has plagued those interested in the neurobiological basis of childhood learning disabilities is that much of what has been known about brain function has been derived from studies of adults with known brain lesions. Simply put, what is known regarding brain function in adults may not be applicable to our understanding of how children's brains are organized. While still a concern, mounting evidence attests to the many similarities between the organizational patterns in adults' and children's brains. As Denckla (1973) has suggested, "as localization in the traditional sense is not a reasonable goal, utilization of analogies and critical differences between childhood and adult syndromes sharing similar complaints brings us closer to a clinical classification scheme" (p. 449). Recent evidence, both clinical (Aaron et al., 1980) and experimental (Duffy, Denckla, Bartels, Sandini, & Kiessling, 1980), attests to the viability of research that attempts to correlate what is known about adult brain organization with neuropsychological disorders of a developmental nature.

Since more is known about the neuroanatomical-neurolinguistic processes found in dyslexic children, the following discussion will present an overview of the neurobiological nature of this most common of learning disabilities.

The Functional System of Reading

It is a well-known fact that in the majority of cases cerebral asymmetries exist. Geschwind and Levitsky (1968) first provided good evidence that in 65% of brains the region of the left planum temporale is enlarged over the right planum temporale. Others (e.g., Falzi, Perrone, & Vignolo, 1982; Galaburda, LeMay, Kemper, & Geschwind, 1978; Galaburda, Sanides, & Geschwind, 1978) have provided further evidence in support of the notion that this degree of cerebral asymmetry is probably related to man's unique linguistic abilities (see Geschwind, 1974, 1979). Other asymmetries of potentially equal importance exist as well, supporting not only the conclusion that the right frontal and left occipital lobes are enlarged over their homologous regions (Weinberger, Luchins, Morihisa, & Wyatt, 1982), but the belief that important subcortical structures such as the thalamus (Eidelberg, & Galaburda, 1982) may also be asymmetrical. Other research has even suggested that sexual dimorphism exists in the human corpus callosum in that the female apparently has a larger splenium than the male (de Lacoste-Utamsing & Holloway, 1982).

It has long been believed that the asymmetrical nature of the cerebral cortex, especially in regard to the left temporal-parietal-occipital region is related to man's unique neurolinguistic nature (Geschwind, 1974, 1979). As Whitaker (1976) has noted,

> The picture that begins to emerge is one of a clearly distinct vocalization system in man based on a species-specific neural structure (Broca's area) and anatomic structure (the vocal tract), coupled with a significant increase in the quantity of and the information processing capacity of the homologous cerebral cortex (inferior parietal and superior temporal lobes). (p. 127)

Clearly, the unique neuroanatomical substratum that is involved in speech and language is reasonably well known. Broca's region is generally perceived as important in generating the "motor images of speech," the superior and medial temporal lobe perceives and associates linguistic material such that verbal comprehension can take place, and both Broca's and Wernicke's areas are connected by the arcuate fasciculus. While others have postulated other pathways and important cortical regions (Penfield & Roberts, 1959), few would argue as to this conceptualization.

As to the reading process, visual perception occurs in the occipital lobes, and the available evidence suggests that imageable words may be better processed in the right occipital cortex. Other evidence suggests that letter strings are processed more efficiently in the left occipital cortex. Certainly, some rudimentary understanding of written material may occur in the secondary visual association cortex. It is in the region of the angular gyrus, however, that cross-modal integration occurs.

The region of the angular gyrus, which forms the tertiary zone of the parietal, temporal, and occipital cortexes, has long been associated with reading and thus has been implicated in developmental reading disorders (Benton, 1980). As Geschwind (1974) stated, "this area may well be termed 'the association cortex' of the association cortexes" (p. 99). Thus, with input from the visual cortex via the visual association cortex, the region of the angular gyrus serves to link input with the appropriate cognitive process across modalities (e.g., visual-auditory).

It was Luria (1980), of course, who provided the conceptual framework of the functional system. Within this framework, localized basic processes, such as visual perception or expressive speech (Broca's region), all interact to provide a functional system for a given behavior (e.g., catching a ball, tapping a finger, or, in this case, a more complex cognitive activity such as reading). As noted by Luria (1980),

> If the higher mental functions are complex, organized functional systems that are social in origin, any attempt to localize them in special circumscribed areas ("centers") of the cerebral cortex is even less justifiable than the attempt to seek narrow circumscribed "centers" for biological functional systems. The modern view regarding possible localization of the higher mental functions is that they have a wide, dynamic representation throughout the cerebral cortex based on constellations of territorially scattered groups of "synchronously working ganglion cells mutually exciting one another" (Ukhtomskii, 1945). . . . We therefore

suggest that *the material basis of higher nervous processes is the brain as a whole* but that *the brain is a highly differentiated system whose parts are responsible for different aspects of the unified whole.* (Italics original, pp. 32–33)

Within this context of a functional system, the hypothesized interacting cortical zones involved in reading and reading failure are depicted in Figure 17.1. In examining this figure it is important to consider the many cognitive and related neuropsychological processes involved in reading. Within the cognitive domain one might include comprehension, verbal-semantic memory, verbal association, and so on. Within the neurolinguistic domain it seems apparent that visual perception, visual scanning and synthesis, intra- and cross-modal integration, and other abilities are included. This hypothesized model to a large extent incorporates cortical zones known to be related to these processes.

Why So Many Different Subtypes of Learning Disabilities?

If one can accept this hypothesized model of the functional system of reading it seems a reasonable conclusion that any neuroanatomical anomalies that occur in this neurological system could disrupt the functional efficiency of the system. *If the distribution of neurodevelopmental-neuroanatomical deficits is more or less random within the cortex involved in fluent reading, then each*

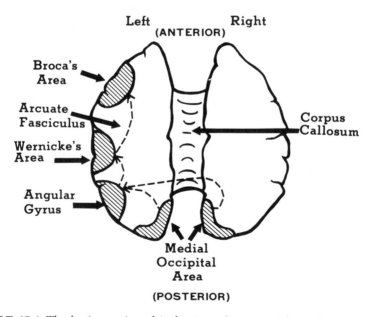

FIGURE 17.1 The brain as viewed in horizontal section. The major pathways and cortical areas thought to be involved in reading are shown.
From Hynd and Cohen (1983), with permission.

particular child will evidence a uniquely different profile of abilities and disabilities. The potential number of subtypes of reading or learning disabilities is limited only by the ability of the neuropsychological tests to differentiate efficiently the components and subcomponents involved in any particular neuropsychological or cognitive task.

It is obvious that this assertion rests on two very important assumptions. One assumption, of course, is that evidence exists as to the neuroanatomical deficits associated with disorders of learning in children. Inherent in this assertion is that the distribution of these deficits appears random. A second, equally important, assumption is that these neuroanatomical deficits are not due to brain trauma, but rather are developmental in nature. The point has been made elsewhere (Hynd & Hynd, 1984) that it is easy for psychologists to conceive of separate distributions for nearly every physical or psychological trait imaginable. However, for many it seems almost impossible to conceive of a distribution of neurological development.

Since it is so central to the perspective offered in this chapter, it is appropriate to consider the electrophysiological and cytoarchitectonic evidence attesting to the neurophysiological basis of learning disorders, in particular dyslexia.

Validation of the Neurobiological Nature of Learning Disabilities

Many techniques have been used to investigate the neurobiological nature of learning disorders. Throughout the history of such research many different psychological tasks have been used to differentiate the psychological and neurological characteristics of the learning-disabled child. One problem all of these tasks share is that they are of a highly inferential nature. Obviously, traditional neurological measures and procedures, on the other hand, have more construct validity, and much research has focused on using electroencephalographic (EEG) indices of cortical dysfunction in documenting the neurobiological nature of learning disabilities.

Electroencephalographic Evidence

Unfortunately, the EEG technique alone has not been successful in accurately diagnosing children with learning or reading disabilities. Although abnormal EEG patterns occur more frequently in children with reading problems (Ayers & Torres, 1967; Hughes, 1968; Hughes, Leander, & Ketchum, 1949; Muehl, Knott, & Benton, 1965), they also seem to be present in normal children with no educational disabilities (Bryant & Friedlander, 1965; Cohn, 1961). Pirozzolo and Hansch (1982) noted the disappointing nature of these findings and suggest there is no correlation between EEG abnormalities and the degree of reading retardation.

The brain electrical activity mapping (BEAM) procedure developed by Duffy and his associates may be a way of converting EEG and evoked potential (EP) information into a useful tool for diagnosing dyslexic children. The BEAM procedure produces a visual display, or map of regional differences, in electrical brain activity using a computer-driven color video screen (Duffy, 1981; Duffy, Burchfiel, & Lombroso, 1979; Duffy, Denckla, Bartels, & Sandini, 1980; Duffy, Denkla, Bartels, Sandini, & Kiessling, 1980). Electrical activity of dyslexic and normal children can be mapped under various conditions and compared.

Duffy and colleagues (1979) used the BEAM technique with three dyslexic adolescents who had no history of neurological difficulties. No atypical patterns were found utilizing the standard analysis of the EEG and EP data. The BEAM technique did locate significant differences in electrophysiological response to speech. The electrical activity in the brains of the three dyslexics did not show normal alpha dyssynchronization when they were required to attend to speech, which should have activated the left cerebral hemisphere. Lack of suppression of alpha activity in the left parietal lobe during a language task gives added support to the idea that the functional system, and particularly the region of the angular gyrus, is important in reading disabilities.

A later study of Duffy, Denckla, Bartels, and Sandini (1980) provided further evidence of the usefulness of the BEAM procedure in localizing the brain activity that characterizes dyslexics. Eight "dyslexic-pure" (Hughes & Denckla, 1978) males were studied. The subjects did not have a history of hyperactivity, math difficulties, motor deficits, positive neurological examinations, psychopathology, or other common behavioral symptoms often associated with the "dyslexic-plus" subject. All had normal intelligence (IQ = 94 to 114) and at least 1.5 years delay in oral reading scores from their expected potential. A well-matched control group was chosen.

EEG and EP data were collected under 10 different conditions of approximately 3 minutes each. The conditions were designed such that a linguistic task was expected to activate the left hemisphere; music or spatial stimuli was expected to activate the right hemisphere; and other tasks, such as paired visual-verbal associations, were expected to activate both cerebral hemispheres. The BEAM technique was applied, producing a color topographic map with each color representing a specific percentage index value. Normals showed more variation in state-alpha distributions than dyslexics on every state-dependent condition. The areas of greatest difference were found in the supplementary motor area (bilateral medial frontal zone), Broca's area, the left temporal region, an area roughly equivalent to Wernicke's area, and the cortex of the angular gyrus. It appears that at least four of these areas are critical to language and probably to the reading process. As Duffy, Denckla, Bartels, and Sandini (1980) stated:

> . . . so the regions that we have shown to differ electrophysically between the brains of dyslexic and normal boys appear to be among the regions normally

involved in speech and reading. Thus, dyslexia pure may represent *dysfunction within a complex and widely distributed system, not a discrete brain lesion.* (p. 417, emphasis added)

Of interest to further investigations, Duffy, Denckla, Bartels, Sandini, and Kiessling (1980) developed a classification system derived from linear discriminant analysis of their data. Of 24 total subjects (13 normals, 11 dyslexics), they were able to classify correctly 96% of the subjects, including all of the dyslexics. In cross-validating their procedures with another population, 80% to 90% success rates in classification were achieved.

Thus, within a well-defined population of dyslexics, brain electrical abnormalities appear to exist in areas of the brain known to be critical in normal language and reading ability. The advancements made by Duffy and his associates are important because they provided direct evidence that abnormal brain electrical activity is correlated with dyslexia in the regions previously identified as important.

Even though differences exist between dyslexics and normals, one cannot conclude that a neurological *deficit* is present. Snyder (1980) has suggested that the results may reflect a developmental delay rather than a deficit. This is an important point. It is only through direct observation of cortical structures that the notion of delay versus deficit can be addressed. It is in this regard that the work of Drake (1968) and Galaburda and Kemper (1979) is so critical.

Postmortem Evidence

Fortunately, children do not die from learning disabilities. Thus, the evidence as to the structural or cellular basis of learning disabilities has, until recently, been poorly documented. Drake (1968) provided the first autopsy report on a learning-disabled child, who died because of a cerebellar hemorrhage. In this brief report, an abnormal convolutional pattern existed in the parietal lobes, the corpus callosum was thinned posteriorly, and ectopic neurons were observed in the subcortical matter.

Galaburda and Kemper (1979), however, provided the first in-depth report on the cytoarchitectonic abnormalities found in a dyslexic's brain (See Figure 17.2). Their subject was a 20-year-old male with a well-documented history of severe reading problems. Both his father and brothers were slow readers, but his mother and sister were not. He died due to injuries sustained in a fall. At autopsy the brain showed no effects of trauma or gross abnormalities. In this patient, the left cerebral hemisphere was wider than the right and no neuronal loss or gliosis seemed present. Abnormalities were found in the left cerebral hemisphere. Most important in this respect was an area of polymicrogyria in the area of the planum temporale. Disordered cortical layering and dysplasia existed in various areas of the left hemisphere. A third case, reported by Galaburda, Sherman, and Geschwind (1986), revealed similar deficits, confined to the left cerebral hemisphere. Galaburda and colleagues (1986) and Sherman, Galaburda, and Geschwind (1986) hypothesize that the lateralized effect of these developmental anomalies may be due to some disturbance (possibly related to the autoimmune system) during neuronal migration.

What can be concluded from these cytoarchitectonic studies? First, it seems that solid evidence exists that some learning disabilities are due to neurodevelopmental anomalies, *not* brain damage. The effects, however, of these neurodevelopmental anomalies mimic those of brain trauma (Aaron et al., 1980). Also, and this is an important point, all three autopsy reports currently available noted neurodevelopmental anomalies in regions of the brain important to the hypothesized functional system of reading discussed earlier. However, the exact distribution of these deficits was different in each case, arguing strongly that each child will in all likelihood evidence different patterns of abilities and deficits on tests, but all will suffer some disruption of the global ability associated with reading. Thus, localization in a diagnostic sense is not a reasonable goal of neuropsychological assessment of these children.

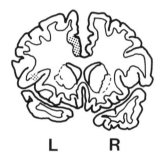
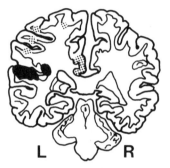
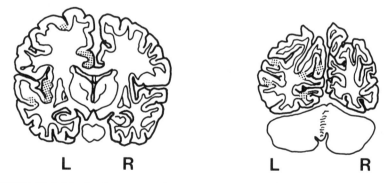

FIGURE 17.2 The brain at several coronal levels. Cross-hatching represents areas of mild cortical dysplasia in the left cingulate gyrus, rostral insula, and focally throughout the left hemisphere. Note the increased frequency of focal lesions posteriorly. Area in black represents the polymicrogyria.
From Galaburda and Kemper (1979), with permission.

Ysseldyke (1982) has observed that educational intervention is exceedingly difficult with these children if autopsy is the primary mode of diagnosis. But there do exist implications for clinicians who must attempt some formal assessment and differential diagnosis with these children.

IMPLICATIONS FOR THE NEUROPSYCHOLOGICAL ASSESSMENT OF THE LEARNING-DISABLED CHILD

It should be clear that if the neurodevelopmental deficits found in the brains of dyslexic or other learning-disabled children are random within certain parameters, then the localization of these discrete anomalies is indeed beyond the scope of any well-conceptualized neuropsychological battery. Furthermore, as argued by Gaddes (1980) and others (e.g., Hynd & Obrzut, 1981), the localization of neuropsychological deficits in the brains of learning-disabled children is, in fact, irrelevant to the treatment of these children. If this is the case, what then is the purpose of the neuropsychological evaluation of children with suspected learning disorders?

The primary purpose of conducting a complete neuropsychological evaluation of a child suspected of suffering a learning disability is to determine if the profile of abilities and disabilities is consistent with a learning disability caused by central nervous system dysfunction. If the neuropsychological evaluation reveals a significant discrepancy between intellectual potential and measured levels of academic achievement, but no neurologic deficits are evident that are consistent with a neurologically based learning disability, then, in the opinion of the authors, the child should not be diagnosed as learning disabled. However, if a discrepancy exists between potential and actual achievement and neurologic signs (e.g., finger agnosia, developmental Gerstmann syndrome, etc.) are evident, then a learning disability should be diagnosed. If one is using a standardized neuropsychological assessment battery, then it is appropriate to diagnose a learning disability when the profile is consistent with that diagnosis (see Selz, 1981).

Since most, if not all, of the readers of this volume are familiar with the three most popular standardized neuropsychological assessment batteries for use with school-age children (Luria–Nebraska Neuropsychological Battery—Children's Revision, Reitan–Indiana, and Halstead–Reitan Neuropsychological Test Battery), and since they are reviewed elsewhere in this volume (Chapters 6 and 7), they will not be discussed here. For in-depth coverage of these batteries the interested reader is referred to Selz (1981), Golden (1981), or Hynd and Snow (1984). While each of these three batteries is useful in diagnosing learning-disabled children they provide little educationally relevant information. Furthermore, these batteries, particularly the Halstead–Reitan Neuropsychological Test Battery for older children, may have many of their measures contaminated by their high correlation with intellectual ability (see Seidenberg, Giordani, Berent, & Boll, 1983).

The needs of educators for more developmentally relevant and instructionally meaningful information would suggest that the neuropsychological evaluation for the school-age child be conceptualized differently from the method commonly used with adult patients. Obrzut (1981) and Hynd and Cohen (1983) have elaborated a hierarchy of information processing, as previously discussed by Johnson and Myklebust (1967), which involves sensation, perception, memory, symbolization, and conceptualization. Within this framework one might well add motoric ability. Using this conceptual framework (depicted in Table 17.2) as an outline for the neuropsychological evaluation, the clinician would choose relevant assessment instruments from each category. In this fashion, a neuropsychological evaluation and report will reflect not only the developmental considerations so relevant in the assessment of children but will also provide sufficient information relevant to educational intervention.

Whether one uses a standardized neuropsychological assessment battery or conceptualizes the neuropsychological evaluation from the hierarchy noted above, the report must determine if the learning disability is due to central nervous system dysfunction and must provide educationally relevant recommendations. Since most clinical neuropsychologists have not had experience in working with children in school settings, the following section will provide a brief overview of educational intervention strategies for the learning-disabled child.

EDUCATIONAL INTERVENTION

The label *learning disabilities* is of little educational benefit if the assessment does not result in information needed to develop more appropriate intervention strategies for the individual. Although most children learn successfully through a variety of methods, children with underlying neurobiological deficits may respond quite differently to alternative strategies. Without knowledge of the deficit areas, the classroom teacher is forced to experiment in a trial-and-error manner or to attempt to fit the child into his or her preferred methods.

No teaching method has been demonstrated to be effective for all learning-disabled children, and given the heterogeneous nature of learning disorders it is unlikely that any strategy ever will. As Gaddes (1980) stated, "one teaching method, no matter how successful with the majority of students, will be inappropriate and even detrimental for those children constitutionally unsuited to it" (p. 298). Further, even attempts to match a child with a subtype may fail to yield the optimal strategy. While research has demonstrated that generalizations regarding subtypes are meaningful from a conceptual standpoint, the relevance of subtypes may be questionable when planning interven-

TABLE 17.2 Conceptual Hierarchy and Some Associated Tests for the Neuropsychological Assessment of the Learning-Disabled Child[a]

Sensation and Sensory Recognition

Acuity
  Visual acuity
  Auditory acuity
  Developmental and health history
Recognition
  Finger agnosia (finger localization)
  Finger-tip number writing
  Tactile form recognition test

Perception

Auditory
  Speech sounds perception test
  Seashore rhythm test
  Wepman auditory discrimination
    test
Visual
  Bender gestalt test
  Beery developmental test of
    visual-motor integration (VMI)
  Benton visual retention test
Tactile-kinesthetic
  Tactile performance test (TPT)
  Tactile form recognition

Motor

Cerebellar screening
  Tandem walking (heel-to-toe)
  Finger to nose to examiner's finger
  Tests for dysarthria
  Tests for nystagmus
  Evaluation for hypotonia
Lateral dominance-motor only
  Grip strength
  Edinburgh inventory
  Halstead–Reitan lateral dominance
    examination

Psycholinguistic

Screening measures
  Aphasia screening test
  Word fluency test
  Peabody picture vocabulary
    test—revised
Formal batteries
  Boston diagnostic aphasia
    examination

Psycholinguistic

Orzeck aphasia evaluation
Illinois test of psycholinguistic
  ability
Language asymmetries
  Dichotic listening task
  Visual half-field technique

Academic

Informal tests
  Clinical interview
    Attitudes
    Interests
    Socialization
    Self-concept
  Tests for phonetic sounds
    (nonsense words)
  Tests for vowel principles
    (nonsense words)
  Syllabication (nonsense words)
  Informal reading inventory
  Writing sample
  Try outs—diagnostic teaching
Formal batteries
  Peabody individual achievement
    test
  Learning modalities
    Mills learning methods test
    Detroit tests of learning aptitude
    Woodcock reading mastery tests
    Durrell analysis of reading
      difficulties
    Gates-McKillop reading
      diagnostic test
    Wide range achievement test
    Boder diagnostic reading-spelling
      test
Cognitive-intellectual
  Category test
  Kaufman assessment battery for
    children
  McCarthy scales of children's
    abilities
  Wechsler intelligence scale for
    children—revised
  Wechsler preschool and primary
    scales of intelligence

From Hynd and Cohen (1983), with permission.
[a]It should be emphasized that this conceptual hierarchy and the suggested assessment procedures are not meant to be all inclusive. Clinicians should use their professional expertise in designing a comprehensive and individually appropriate neuropsychological battery in keeping with each child's unique needs.

tion strategies for individuals. Oversimplification of dichotomies (e.g., successive vs. simultaneous processor or auditory vs. visual learner) may be counterproductive. Instead, each child should be analyzed individually, and recommendations should be formulated that are directly related to the profile he or she exhibits. Despite these cautions, there are some generalizations that can serve as guidelines and beginning points in this process.

Goals of Intervention

Before recommendations for intervention can be determined, the desired outcome of intervention must be established. Although this appears to be an obvious statement, it is a point that frequently produces disagreement. There is considerable controversy over the goal of intervention with disabled learners with suspected neurological impairments. Gaddes (1980) refers to the issue of whether to train the brain (indirect remediation) or teach the child what you want him to learn (direct academic remediation). Others (e.g., Hartlage & Reynolds, 1981; Kirby, 1980; Sanders, 1979) discuss whether to focus intervention efforts on remediating specific areas of deficit or exploiting strengths to circumvent those deficit areas. It is a reasonable conclusion that remediation efforts directed toward neurologically based deficits are likely to be inefficient, ineffective, and highly frustrating for the disabled learner. Hartlage and Reynolds (1981) consider attempts to improve academic performance by remediating the underlying deficit areas to be conceptually doomed to failure, as such attempts logically involve teaching to systems presumed to be dysfunctional. Additionally, in most situations by the time a child has been referred to a neuropsychologist, traditional remediation efforts have already been attempted with little success. Therefore, the remainder of this chapter is written with the assumption that the primary goal of intervention efforts will be the exploitation of an individual's relative strengths (or intact systems) in the teaching/learning environment.

Attribute Treatment Interaction

One conceptual framework that is particularly relevant to the development of remedial strategies for disabled learners is that of attribute-treatment interaction (ATI) (Kaufman & Kaufman, 1983). This concept, which attempts to integrate the study of individual differences with intervention techniques, is based on work by Cronbach (e.g., Cronbach, 1957, 1975; Cronbach & Snow, 1977). The theory was originally labeled *aptitude-treatment interaction* and dealt primarily with cognitive functioning or intelligence. Berliner and Cahen (1973) applied this line of reasoning to the study of personality and behavior, using the term *trait-treatment interaction*. Tobias (1976) espoused the use of the more general term, *attribute-treatment interaction*, thereby implying a wider range of applications. Research investigating ATI has produced inconsistent results, making it difficult to formulate a series of general ATI laws. However, several consistencies have emerged that exemplify the potential of ATI as a basis of programming for the disabled learner. Kaufman and Kaufman (1983) reviewed studies dealing with the differential effectiveness of teaching methods matched with cognitive processing strengths of learners. There is evidence that such characteristics as sequential (analytic) or simultaneous (holistic) processing (Krashen, Seliga, & Hartnett, 1973; Pask & Scott, 1972) and auditory or visual sequencing (Hartlage, 1975; Reynolds, 1981) do interact significantly with teaching methodologies. Students taught through methods matched to their relative strengths generally showed greater achievement gains than control groups. These findings further support the importance of neuropsychological information in educational programming for disabled learners. Although these results are promising, there is a need for more research involving the effectiveness of such strategies with children evidencing neurologically based learning problems.

Educational Recommendations

The heterogeneous nature of learning disabilities has been emphasized repeatedly in this chapter. Due to the complex and variable nature of individual disorders of learning, there is no single approach or comprehensive list of recommendations to offer at this point. The goal of this brief section is to aid the neuropsychologist in establishing a conceptual framework for the nature of relevant educational recommendations.

Placement Selection

The ultimate responsibility for determining the educational placement for a disabled learner in the public schools rests with a local multidisciplinary child study team, which considers all available relevant information about the child. It is likely that results of a neuropsychological evaluation would play a vital role in this decision when there is evidence of neurological deficits affecting learning. Therefore, although direct recommendations for specific placements may be inappropriate, knowledge of placement options enhances the neuropsychologist's understanding of possible intervention.

During the past two decades there has been tremendous expansion in the services offered for the learning disabled. It has been federally legislated that public schools provide services for learning-disabled children. Additionally, service must be provided to each child in the least restrictive (most nearly normal) environment feasible. Taken together, these two factors require the availability of a variety of placement options for children evidencing learning disabilities.

The most restrictive and least common placement is a segregated special school. The majority of these are private and may offer residential services.

This type of environment is usually reserved for individuals who have additional handicapping conditions, extenuating home/family circumstances, or severe deficit areas that seriously interfere with daily functioning. Even when learning disorders are relatively severe, most children can function successfully within the public schools in a less restrictive placement. Many systems have self-contained special classes available within the regular school building. These classes have a small pupil-to-teacher ratio (usually 6 to 12 students per teacher) and often are composed of children from several grade levels. The students do all academic tasks within the self-contained class but sometimes participate with other classes in nonacademic activities.

The most common service delivery model for the learning disabled is the resource room. Under this model the student is assigned to a regular classroom for the majority of both academic and nonacademic activities. The services of a learning disabilities specialist are available for limited periods (usually 1 to 3 hours per day), primarily for intervention in areas of academic deficit. The resource teacher also provides support for the regular teacher who has the learning-disabled child in class. In some cases of mild disability, the consultative or support service to the classroom teacher is sufficient to maintain progress without external intervention directly with the child. This is an example of the least restrictive service delivery model.

General Teaching Strategies

Educators are specialists in teaching methodologies, materials, and curriculum. Specific recommendation in these areas is not the function of a neuropsychological report. Instead, general statements evolving from the analysis of the individual's profile are needed. Deficit areas considered to be intrinsic to the individual should be clearly identified. This, however, is insufficient for the development of strategies, as it tells educators what *not* to do without suggesting alternatives. Equally important is the delineation of the individual's relative strengths or intact systems. It should be noted that areas of relative strength for a given individual may be average, below average, or above average, but offer the most potential for successful learning avenues for that person.

Assessment results and careful observation of the child frequently suggest ways to restructure the traditional learning environment to facilitate learning for that individual. Recommendations addressing modification of environmental and task demands are among the most effective and easiest to implement with learning-disabled students.

CONCLUSION

It has been the goal of this chapter to delineate the neurobiological nature of learning disabilities and to present clinical neuropsychologists with a perspective as to their possible role with these frequent childhood disorders. The concept of neurodevelopmental anomalies that produce similar effects as brain damage is central to the perspective offered here and thus requires that children diagnosed as learning disabled evidence some manifestation of central nervous system dysfunction. It is this point that must be addressed in providing neuropsychological services to these children and the teachers who must provide for their educational needs.

REFERENCES

Aaron, P. G., Baxter, C. F., & Lucenti, J. (1980). Developmental dyslexia and acquired dyslexia: Two sides of the same coin? *Brain and Language, 11,* 1–11.

Ayers, F. W., & Torres, F. (1967). The incidence of EEG abnormalities in a dyslexic and a control group. *Journal of Clinical Psychology, 23,* 334–336.

Bakker, D. J. (1972). *Temporal order in disturbed reading.* Rotterdam, The Netherlands: University Press.

Bannatyne, A. (1966). The etiology of dyslexia and the color phonics system. In J. Money (Ed.), *The disabled reader: Education of the dyslexic child.* Baltimore: Johns Hopkins University Press.

Bastian, H. C. (1898). *A treatise on aphasia and other speech defects.* London: H. K. Lewis.

Bateman, B. (1968). *Interpretation of the 1961 Illinois Test of Psycholinguistic Abilities.* Seattle: Special Child Publications.

Benton, A. L. (1980). Dyslexia: Evolution of a concept. *Bulletin of the Orton Society, 30,* 10–26.

Berliner, D. C., & Cahen, L. S. (1973). Trait-treatment interaction and learning. *Review of Research in Education, 1,* 58–94.

Birch, H. G., & Belmont, L. (1964). Auditory-visual integration in normal and retarded readers. *American Journal of Orthopsychiatry, 34,* 852–861.

Birch, H. G., & Belmont, L. (1965). Auditory-visual integration, intelligence, and reading ability in school children. *Perceptual and Motor Skills, 20,* 295–305.

Boder, E. (1970). Developmental dyslexia: A new diagnostic approach based on the identification of three subtypes. *Journal of School Health, 40,* 289–290.

Boder, E. (1971). Developmental dyslexia: Prevailing diagnostic concepts and a new diagnostic approach. In H. Myklebust (Ed.), *Progress in learning disabilities.* New York: Grune & Stratton.

Boder, E. (1973). Developmental dyslexia: A diagnostic screening procedure based on three characteristic patterns of reading and spelling. In B. Bateman (Ed.), *Learning disorders.* Seattle: Special Child Publications.

Brunner, W. E. (1905). Congenital word-blindness. *Ophthalmology, 1,* 189–195.

Bryant, N. D., & Friedlander, W. J. (1965). "14" and "G" in boys with specific reading disability. *Electroencephalography and Clinical Neurophysiology, 19,* 318–322.

Clairborne, J. H. (1906). Types of congenital symbol amblyopia. *Journal of the American Medical Association, 47,* 1813–1816.

Cohn, R. (1961). Delayed acquisition of reading and writing abilities in children. *Archives of Neurology, 4,* 153–164.

Coltheart, M., Patterson, K., & Marshall, J. C. (Eds.). (1980). *Deep dyslexia.* London: Routledge & Kegan Paul.

Cone, T. E., & Wilson, L. R. (1981). Quantifying a severe discrepancy: A critical analysis. *Learning Disabilities Quarterly, 4,* 359–371.

Craig, D. L. (1979). Neuropsychological assessment in public psychiatric hospitals: The current state of practice. *Clinical Neuropsychology, 1,* 1–7.

Cronbach, L. J. (1957). The two disciplines of scientific psychology. *American Psychologist, 12*, 671–684.

Cronbach, L. J. (1975). Beyond the two disciplines of scientific psychology. *American Psychologist, 30*, 116–127.

Cronbach, L. J., & Snow, R. E. (1977). *Aptitudes and instructional methods: A handbook for research on interactions*. New York: Irvington.

de Lacoste-Utamsing, C., & Holloway, R. L. (1982). Sexual dimorphism in the human corpus callosum. *Science, 216*, 1431–1432.

Deloche, G., & Andreewsky, E. (1982). Surface dyslexia: A case report and some theoretical implications to reading models. *Brain and Language, 15*, 12–31.

Denckla, M. B. (1973). Research needs in learning disabilities: A neurologist's point of view. *Journal of Learning Disabilities, 6*, 44–50.

Doehring, D. G., & Hoshko, I. M. (1977). Classification of reading problems by the Q-technique of factor analysis. *Cortex, 13*, 281–294.

Doehring, D. G., Hoshko, I. M., & Bryans, B. N. (1979). Statistical classification of children with reading problems. *Journal of Clinical Neuropsychology, 1*, 5–16.

Drake, W. E. (1968). Clinical and pathological findings in a child with a developmental learning disability. *Journal of Learning Disabilities, 1*, 486–502.

Duane, D. D. (1979). Toward a definition of dyslexia: A summary of views. *Bulletin of the Orton Society, 29*, 56–64.

Duffy, F. H. (1981). Brain electrical activity mapping (BEAM): Computerized access to complex brain function. *International Journal of Neuroscience, 13*, 55–65.

Duffy, F. H., Burchfield, J. L., & Lombroso, C. T. (1979). Brain electrical activity mapping (BEAM): A method for extending the clinical utility of EEG and evoked potential data. *Annals of Neurology, 5*, 309–321.

Duffy, F. H., Denckla, M. B., Bartels, P. H., & Sandini, G. (1980). Dyslexia: Regional differences in brain electrical activity by topographic mapping. *Annals of Neurology, 7*, 412–430.

Duffy, F. H., Denckla, M. B., Bartels, P. H., Sandini, G., & Kiessling, L. S. (1980). Dyslexia: Automated diagnosis by computerized classification of brain electrical activity. *Annals of Neurology, 7*, 421–428.

Eidelberg, D., & Galaburda, A. M. (1983). Symmetry and asymmetry in the human posterior thalamus: I. Cytoarchitectonic analysis in normal persons. *Archives of Neurology, 39*, 325–332.

Falzi, G., Perrone, P., & Vignolo, L. A. (1982). Right-left asymmetry in anterior speech region. *Archives of Neurology, 39*, 239–240.

Federal Register (1976). *Education of handicapped children and incentive grants program*. U.S. Department of Health, Education, and Welfare, *41*, 46977.

Fisher, J. H. (1905). Case of congenital word-blindness (inability to learn to read). *Ophtalmic Review, 24*, 315–318.

Fisk, J. L., & Rourke, B. P. (1979). Identification of subtypes of learning disabled children at three age levels: A neuropsychological, multivariate approach. *Journal of Clinical Neuropsychology, 1*, 289–310.

Fletcher, J. M., Taylor, H. G., Morris, R., & Satz, P. (1982). Finger recognition skills and reading achievement: A developmental neuropsychological analysis. *Journal of Consulting and Clinical Psychology, 18*, 124–132.

Foerster, R. (1905). Beitrage zur pathologie des lesens und schreibens (congenitale wort-blindheit bein einen schwachsinnigen). *Neurol. Centralbl., 24*, 235–236.

Gaddes, W. H. (1980). *Learning disabilities and brain function: A neuropsychological approach*. New York: Springer-Verlag.

Gaddes, W. H. (1981). An examination of the validity of neuropsychological knowledge in educational diagnosis and remediation. In G. W. Hynd & J. E. Obrzut

(Eds.), *Neuropsychological assessment of the school-age child: Issues and procedures.* New York: Grune & Stratton.

Galaburda, A. M., & Kemper, T. L. (1979). Cytoarchitectonic abnormalities in developmental dyslexia: A case study. *Annals of Neurology, 6,* 94–100.

Galaburda, A. M., LeMay, M., Kemper, T. L., & Geschwind, N. (1978). Right-left asymmetries in the brain. *Science, 199,* 852–856.

Galaburda, A. M., Sanides, F., & Geschwind, N. (1978). Human brain: Cytoarchitectonic left-right asymmetries in temporal speech region. *Archives of Neurology, 35,* 812.

Galaburda, A. M., Sherman, G. F., & Geschwind, N. (in press). Developmental dyslexia: Third consecutive case with cortical abnormalities. *Science.*

Geschwind, N. (1962). In J. Money (Ed.), *Reading disability.* Baltimore: Johns Hopkins University Press.

Geschwind, N. (1974). The development of the brain and the evolution of language. In N. Geschwind (Ed.), *Selected papers on language and the brain.* Dordrecht, Holland: D. Reidel Publishing Company.

Geschwind, N. (1979). Anatomical foundations of language and dominance. In C. L. Ludlow & M. E. Doran-Quine (Eds.), *The neurological bases of language disorders in children: Methods and directions for research.* Bethesda, MD: U.S. Department of Health, Education, and Welfare (NIH Publication No. 79–440).

Geschwind, N., & Levitsky, W. (1968). Human brain: Left-right asymmetries in temporal speech region. *Science, 161,* 186–187.

Golden, C. J. (1981). The Luria–Nebraska Children's Battery: Theory and initial formulation. In G. W. Hynd & J. E. Obrzut (Eds.), *Neuropsychological assessment and the school-age child: Issues and procedures* (pp. 277–302). New York: Grune & Stratton.

Hammill, D. D., Leigh, J. E., McNutt, G., & Larsen, S. C. (1981). A new definition of learning disabilities. *Learning Disability Quarterly, 4,* 336–342.

Hartlage, L. C. (1975). Neuropsychological approaches to predicting outcome of remedial educational strategies for learning disabled children. *Pediatric Psychology, 3,* 23–28.

Hartlage, L. C., & Reynolds, C. R. (1981). Neuropsychological assessment and the individualization of instruction. In G. W. Hynd & J. E. Obrzut (Eds.), *Neuropsychological assessment and the school-age child: Issues and procedures* (pp. 355–378). New York: Grune & Stratton.

Hinshelwood, J. (1895). Word-blindness and visual memory. *Lancet, 2,* 1564–1570.

Hinshelwood, J. (1900). Congenital word-blindness. *Lancet, 1,* 1506–1508.

Hinshelwood, J. (1902). Congenital word-blindness, with reports of two cases. *Ophthalmic Review, 21,* 91–99.

Hinshelwood, J. (1909). Four cases of congenital word-blindness occurring in the same family. *British Medical Journal, 2,* 1229–1232.

Hughes, J. R. (1968). Electroencephalography and learning disabilities. In H. R. Myklebust (Ed.), *Progress in learning disabilities.* New York: Grune & Stratton.

Hughes, J. R., & Denckla, M. B. (1978). Outline of a pilot study of electroencephalographic correlates of dyslexia. In A. L. Benton & D. Pearl (Eds.), *Dyslexia: An appraisal of current knowledge.* New York: Oxford University Press.

Hughes, J. R., Leander, R., & Ketchum, G. (1949). Electroencephalographic study of specific reading disabilities. *Electroencephalography and Clinical Neurophysiology, 1,* 377–378.

Hynd, G. W., & Cohen, M. (1983). *Dyslexia: Neuropsychological theory, research and clinical differentiation.* New York: Grune & Stratton.

Hynd, G. W., Cohen, M., & Obrzut, J. E. (1983). Dichotic CV testing in the diagnosis of learning disabilities in children. *Ear and Hearing, 4,* 283–287.

Hynd, G. W., & Hynd, C. R. (1984). Dyslexia: Neuroanatomical/neurolinguistic perspectives. *Reading Research Quarterly, 19,* 482–498.

Hynd, G. W., & Obrzut, J. E. (Eds.) (1981). *Neuropsychological assessment and the school-age child: Issues and procedures.* New York: Grune & Stratton.

Hynd, G. W., Obrzut, J. E., Weed, W., & Hynd, C. R. (1979). Development of cerebral dominance: Dichotic listening asymmetry in normal and learning disabled children. *Journal of Experimental and Child Psychology, 28,* 445–454.

Hynd, G. W., Quackenbush, R., & Obrzut, J. E. (1980). Training school psychologists in neuropsychological assessment: Current practices and trends. *Journal of School Psychology, 18,* 148–153.

Hynd, G. W., & Snow, J. H. (in press). Assessment of neurological and neuropsychological factors associated with severe learning disabilities. In D. J. Lazarus & S. S. Strichart (Eds.), *Psychoeducational evaluation of children with low incidence handicaps.* New York: Grune & Stratton.

Ingram, T. S., Mason, A. W., & Blackburn, I. (1970). A retrospective study of 82 children with reading disability. *Developmental Medicine and Child Neurology, 12,* 271–281.

Jackson, E. (1906). Developmental alexia (congenital and word-blindness). *American Journal of Medical Science, 131,* 843–849.

Johnson, D. J., & Myklebust, H. R. (1967). *Learning disabilities, educational principles and practices.* New York: Grune & Stratton.

Kaufman, N. L., & Kaufman, A. S. (1983). Remedial intervention in education. In G. W. Hynd (Ed.), *The school psychologist: An introduction.* Syracuse, NY: Syracuse University Press.

Kephart, N. C. (1971). *The slow learner in the classroom* (2nd ed.). Columbus, OH: Charles E. Merrill.

Kinsbourne, M., & Warrington, E. K. (1963). Developmental factors in reading and writing backwardness. *British Journal of Psychology, 54,* 145–156.

Kirby, J. R. (1980). Individual differences and cognitive processes: Instructional application and methodological difficulties. In J. R. Kirby & J. B. Biggs (Eds.), *Cognition, development, and instruction.* New York: Academic Press.

Kirk, S. A. (1963). Behavioral diagnosis and remediation of learning disabilities. In *Conference on exploration into the problems of the perceptually handicapped child.* Evanston, IL: Fund for the Perceptually Handicapped Child.

Krashen, S., Seliga, R., & Hartnett, D. (1973). Two studies in adult second language learning. *Kritikon Litterarum, 3,* 220–228.

Kussmaul, A. (1877). Disturbance of speech. *Cyclopedia of Practical Medicine, 14,* 581–875.

Lindgren, S. D. (1978). Finger localization and the prediction of reading disability. *Cortex, 14,* 87–101.

Luria, A. R. (1980). *Higher cortical functions.* New York: Basic Books.

Lyle, J. G. (1969). Reading retardation and reversal tendency: A factorial study. *Child Development, 40,* 833–843.

Lyle, J. G., & Goyen, J. (1968). Visual recognition developmental lag and stephosymbolia in reading retardation. *Journal of Abnormal Psychology, 73,* 25–29.

Lyle, J. G., & Goyen, J. (1975). Effects of speed of exposure and difficulty of discrimination on visual recognition of retarded readers. *Journal of Abnormal Psychology, 8,* 673–676.

Mattis, S., French, J. H., & Rapin, I. (1975). Dyslexia in children and young adults: Three independent neuropsychological syndromes. *Developmental Medicine and Child Neurology, 17,* 150–163.

McCarthy, J. M. (1975). Children with learning disabilities. In J. J. Gallagher (Ed.), *The application of child development research to exceptional children.* Reston, VA: The Council for Exceptional Children.

McCarthy, J. J., & McCarthy, J. F. (1969). *Learning disabilities.* Boston: Allyn & Bacon.

McLeod, J. (1979). Educational underachievement: Toward a defensible psychometric definition. *Journal of Learning Disabilities, 12,* 332–340.

Morgan, W. P. (1896). A case of congenital word-blindness. *British Medical Journal, 2,* 1378.

Morris, R., Blashfield, R., & Satz, P. (1981). Neuropsychology and cluster analysis: Potentials and problems. *Journal of Clinical Neuropsychology, 3,* 79–99.

Muehl, S., Knott, J. R., & Benton, A. L. (1965). EEG abnormality and psychological test performance in reading disability. *Cortex, 1,* 434–440.

Naidoo, S. (1972). *Specific dyslexia.* New York: Wiley.

Nelson, H. E., & Warrington, E. K. (1974). Developmental spelling retardation and its relation to other cognitive abilities. *British Journal of Psychology, 65,* 265–274.

Nolan, D. R., Hammeke, T. A., & Barkley, R. A. (1983). A comparison of the patterns of the neuropsychological performance in two groups of learning disabled children. *Journal of Clinical Child Psychology, 12,* 22–27.

Obrzut, J. E. (1981). Neuropsychological procedures with school-age children. In G. W. Hynd & J. E. Obrzut (Eds.), *Neuropsychological assessment and the school-age child: Issues and procedures* (pp. 237–276). New York: Grune & Stratton.

O'Donnell, J. P., Kurtz, J., & Ramanaiah, N. V. (1983). Neuropsychological test findings for normal, learning-disabled, and brain-damaged young adults. *Journal of Consulting and Clinical Psychology, 51,* 726–729.

Orton, S. T. (1928). Specific reading disability—strephosymbolia. *Journal of the American Medical Association, 90,* 1095–1099.

Orton, S. T. (1937). *Reading, writing, and speech problems in children.* New York: Norton.

Pask, G., & Scott, B. C. E. (1972). Learning strategies and individual competence. *International Journal of Man-Machine Studies, 4,* 217–253.

Penfield, W., & Roberts, L. (1959). *Speech and brain mechanisms.* Princeton, NJ: Princeton University Press.

Petrauskas, R., & Rourke, B. P. (1979). Identification of subgroups of retarded readers: A neuropsychological multivariate approach. *Journal of Clinical Neuropsychology, 1,* 17–37.

Pirozzolo, F. J. (1979). *The neuropsychology of developmental reading disorders.* New York: Praeger Press.

Pirozzolo, F. J., & Hansch, E. C. (1982). The neurobiology of developmental reading disorders. In R. N. Malatesha & P. G. Aaron (Eds.), *Neuropsychological and neurolinguistic aspects of reading disorders.* New York: Academic Press.

Quirus, J. de (1964). Dysplasia and dyslexia in school children. *Folia Phonetrica, 16,* 201–222.

Reitan, R. M. (1974). Psychological effects of cerebral lesions in children of early school-age. In R. M. Reitan & L. A. Davison (Eds.), *Clinical neuropsychology: Current status and applications* (pp. 53–90). Washington, DC: V. H. Winston and Sons.

Reitan, R. M., & Boll, T. J. (1973). Neuropsychological correlates of minimal brain dysfunction. *Annals of the New York Academy of Sciences, 205,* 65–88.

Reynolds, C. R. (1981). Neuropsychological assessment and the habilitation of learning: Considerations in the search for the aptitude X treatment interaction. *School Psychology Review, 10,* 343–349.

Ross, A. O. (1976). *Psychological aspects of learning disabilities and reading disorders.* New York: McGraw-Hill.

Rourke, B. P., & Finlayson, M. A. J. (1978). Neuropsychological significance of variations in patterns of academic performance: Verbal and visual-spatial abilities. *Journal of Abnormal Child Psychology, 6,* 121–133.

Rourke, B. P., & Strang, J. D. (1981). Subtypes of reading and arithmetic disabilities: A neuropsychological analysis. In M. Rutter (Ed.), *Behavioral syndromes of brain dysfunction in children.* New York: Guilford Press.

Rourke, B. P., Young, G. C., & Flewelling, R. W. (1971). The relationship between WISC verbal-performance discrepancies and selected verbal, auditory-perceptual, visual-perceptual, and problem-solving abilities in children with learning disabilities. *Journal of Clinical Psychology, 27,* 475–479.

Sanders, M. (1979). *Clinical assessment of learning problems: Model, process, and remedial planning.* Boston: Allyn and Bacon.

Sandoval, J., & Haapanen, R. M. (1981). A critical commentary on neuropsychology in the schools: Are we ready? *School Psychology Review, 10,* 381–388.

Satz, P., & Morris, R. (1981). Learning disabilities subtypes. A review. In F. J. Pirozzolo & M. C. Wittrock (Eds.), *Neuropsychological and cognitive processes in reading.* New York: Academic Press.

Satz, P., Rardin, D., & Ross, J. (1971). An evaluation of a theory of specific developmental dyslexia. *Child Development, 42,* 2009–2021.

Seidenberg, M., Giordani, B., Berent, S., & Boll, T. J. (1983). IQ level and performance on the Halstead–Reitan Neuropsychological Test Battery for Older Children. *Journal of Consulting and Clinical Psychology, 51,* 406–413.

Selz, M. (1981). Halstead–Reitan Neuropsychological Test Batteries for Children. In G. W. Hynd & J. E. Obrzut (Eds.), *Neuropsychological assessment and the school-age child: Issues and procedures* (pp.195–236). New York: Grune & Stratton.

Selz, M., & Reitan, R. M. (1979). Neuropsychological test performance of normal, learning disabled, and brain damaged older children. *Journal of Nervous and Mental Disease, 167,* 298–302.

Senf, G. M. (1969). Development of immediate memory for bisensory stimuli in normal children, and children with learning disabilities. *Developmental Psychology, 6,* 28.

Senf, G. M., & Freundl, P. C. (1971). Memory and attention factors in specific learning disabilities. *Journal of Learning Disabilities, 4,* 94–106.

Sevush, S. (1983, February). *The neurolinguistics of reading: Anatomic and neurologic correlates.* Paper presented at the annual meeting of the International Neuropsychological Society, Mexico City.

Shepard, L. (1980). An evaluation of the regression discrepancy method for identifying children with learning disabilities. *Journal of Special Education, 14,* 79–80.

Shepard, L. (1983). The role of measurement in educational policy: Lessons from the identification of learning disabilities. *Educational Measurement: Issues and Practice, 2,* 4–8.

Shepard, L. A., Smith, M. L., & Vojir, C. P. (1983). Characteristics of pupils identified as learning disabled. *American Educational Research Journal, 20,* 309–331.

Sherman, G. F., Galaburda, A. M., & Geschwind, N. (in press). "Dyslexic" abnormalities in the brain of the autoimmune mouse. *Science.*

Smith, F. N. (1982). *Understanding reading* (3rd ed.). New York: Holt, Rinehart and Winston.

Smith, M. D., Coleman, J. M., Dokecki, P. R., & Davis, E. E. (1977). Recategorized WISC-R scores of learning disabled children. *Journal of Learning Disabilities, 10,* 444–449.

Snow, J. H., Hynd, G. W., & Hartlage, L. (1984). Differences between mildly and more severely learning disabled children on the Luria–Nebraska Neuropsychological Battery—Children's Revision. *Journal of Psychoeducational Assessment, 2,* 23–28.

Snyder, R. D. (1980). Topographic mapping in childhood developmental dyslexia. *Annals of Neurology, 7,* 642–643.

Spache, G. D. (1976). *Investigating the issues of reading disabilities.* Boston: Allyn & Bacon, Inc.

Stephenson, S. (1907). Six cases of congenital word blindness affecting three generations of one family. *Ophthaloscope, 5,* 452–484.

Strauss, A. A., & Lehtinen, L. E. (1947). *Psychopathology and education of the brain-injured child* (Vol. I). New York: Grune & Stratton.

Strauss, A. A., & Kephart, N. C. (1955). *Psychopathology and education of the brain-injured child* (Vol. II). New York: Grune & Stratton.

Sweeney, J. E., & Rourke, B. A. (1978). Neuropsychological significance of phonetically accurate and phonetically inaccurate spelling errors in younger and older retarded spellers. *Brain and Language, 6,* 212–225.

Tobias, S. (1976). Achievement treatment interactions. *Review of Educational Research, 46,* 61–74.

Variot, G., & Lecomte, A. (1906). Un cas de typholexia congenitale (cecite congenitale verbale). *Bulletins et Memoires de la Societe-Medicale des Hopitaux des Paris, 23,* 995–1001.

Von Bonin, G. (1962). Anatomical asymmetries of the cerebral hemispheres. In V. B. Mountcastle (Ed.), *Interhemispheric relations and cerebral dominance.* Baltimore: Johns Hopkins University Press.

Warburg, F. (1911). Ueber die angeborene wortblindheit und die bedeatung ihrer kenntais fur den unterricht. *Z. Kinder-Forschung, 16,* 97–113.

Watson, B. U., Goldgar, D. E., & Ryschon, K. C. (1983). Subtypes of reading disability. *Journal of Clinical Neuropsychology, 5,* 377–399.

Weinberger, D. R., Luchins, D. J., Morihisa, J., & Wyatt, R. J. (1982). Asymmetrical volumes of the right and left frontal and occipital regions of the human brain. *Neurology, 11,* 97–100.

Whitaker, H. A. (1976). Neurobiology of language. In E. R. Carterette & M. P. Friedman (Eds.), *Handbook of perception* (Vol. VII). New York: Academic Press.

Yeni-Komshian, G. H., Isenberg, P., & Goldstein, H. (1975). Cerebral dominance and reading disability: Left visual-field deficit in poor readers. *Neuropsychologia, 13,* 83–94.

Ysseldyke, J. (1982, August). *Planning instructional intervention: What does the research say?* Paper presented at the annual convention of the American Psychological Association, Washington, DC.

Zurif, E. B., & Carson, G. (1970). Dyslexia in relation to cerebral dominance and temporal analysis. *Neuropsychologia, 8,* 351–361.

PART V
Emerging Areas

18
Neuropsychological Assessment and Everyday Functioning

Gordon J. Chelune and
Kurt A. Moehle

In 1970 Parsons described clinical neuropsychology as an "emerging discipline" and suggested that "all indications point to its continued growth and emphasis" (p. 3). This astute observation has certainly been borne out as clinical and theoretical advances in the field have made clinical neuropsychology one of the fastest growing specialty areas in psychology (Golden & Kuperman, 1980). Today the discipline is represented by a number of professional organizations, such as the International Neuropsychological Society, the National Academy of Neuropsychologists, the Behavioral Neuropsychology Special Interest Group of the Association for the Advancement of Behavior Therapy, and the Division of Clinical Neuropsychology (Division 40) of the American Psychological Association. Also, increasing numbers of academic and clinical training programs in neuropsychology are emerging (Lubin & Sokoloff, 1983; Noonberg & Page, 1982; Williams & Wedding, 1982). Most recently, the American Board of Professional Psychology has recognized clinical neuropsychology as a distinct and legitimate area of specialized practice.

A central factor in this growth has been the successful development of standardized assessment procedures capable of identifying and delineating the cognitive and behavioral effects associated with brain dysfunction. Although much of the early interest in neuropsychological assessment was focused solely upon making inferences regarding the organic integrity of the brain, there are now growing consumer demands for neuropsychologists to apply their knowledge of brain–behavior relationships to issues related to patients' probable

489

success in everyday tasks and activities. This shift from diagnostic to applied inferences is not only exciting, but also challenging, for neuropsychology. As noted by Miller (1980, p. 527), "one of the most important contributions of the clinical neuropsychologist, and one which has been largely neglected, is in assisting those afflicted to return to a normal, and independent as possible, way of life."

The purpose of this chapter is to examine the role of neuropsychological assessment in the prediction of everyday functioning. After examining some of the conceptual issues inherent in the shift from diagnostic assessment to prescriptive assessment, a review is presented of the growing research dealing with issues of everyday living. A heuristically derived clinical inferential model for addressing a patient's potential to carry out activities of daily living is also described. Finally, suggestions about strategies and directions for future research with respect to the neuropsychology of everyday functioning are discussed.

FROM DIAGNOSTIC TO APPLIED INFERENCES

Since neuropsychologists frequently serve as consultants to other professionals, their evaluations are tailored to answer the concerns of the professionals referring clients to them. As Cleeland (1976, p. 8) has noted, "the value of such evaluations can be measured in terms of how it influences subsequent decisions about the patient and how beneficial those decisions are for the patient." The viability, and indeed the growth, of clinical neuropsychology has been its ability to meet the changing needs of its consumers with respect to patient care. It is not surprising, therefore, to find that the emphasis of neuropsychological assessment has changed accordingly to keep abreast of expanding consumer needs.

Stages of Model Building and Assessment

In a recent paper, Rourke (1982) describes the development of clinical neuropsychology since 1945 in terms of three distinct, yet overlapping and interrelated, phases. We believe that each of these phases has had a direct impact upon the goals of the neuropsychological assessment process. In the first, or *static phase,* from 1945 through the mid-1960s, investigators were largely concerned with relating performances on standardized test procedures to the presence of well-documented cerebral lesions. The emphasis was clearly on the brain, and the approach, rooted in American academic psychology and psychometric theory, was essentially atheoretical and empirical in nature. Neuropsychological assessment during this phase served as an ancillary neurodiagnostic procedure in detecting the presence and localization of brain dysfunction. The utility of neuropsychological tests was judged in terms of their ability to yield "correct hit rates," and attention was directed toward establishing cutoff scores, impairment indices, and statistical algorithms to aid the clinician in this *diagnostic* endeavor.

In the latter part of the 1960s, neuropsychology began to take on a different emphasis. Rourke (1982, pp. 2–3) describes this shift in focus as the *cognitive phase*, characterizing it as "an attempt to understand the psychological tests and measures being employed in attempts to establish brain–behavior relationships." Attention was directed at understanding the cognitive structure of the tasks, and *task analysis* became the byword. Fueling this movement toward a cognitive perspective were a number of coalescing events. Computer technology had merged with medical neurodiagnostic practices, yielding safer and more sophisticated, noninvasive diagnostic techniques (e.g., averaged evoked potentials, computerized axial tomography) that began to supplement neuropsychological assessment for strictly diagnostic purposes. This period was also marked by the appearance of several major conceptual models of brain–behavior relationships (e.g., Luria's *Higher Cortical Functions in Man* in 1966 and Pribram's *Languages of the Brain* in 1971), and the evaluation of patients having undergone commissurotomies (split-brain surgery) by Sperry (1968) and others provided new insights into how the brain processes various kinds of information. Clinical neuropsychological assessment during this cognitive phase became increasingly *descriptive* in orientation, and the tests became not only indices of "organic integrity," but measures of "ability." The clinician's task was no longer solely to make diagnostic statements, as neurologic diagnoses were frequently already established, but rather to delineate the cognitive-behavioral deficits associated with a particular brain lesion.

Although clinical neuropsychologists are still being called upon by consumers to make diagnostic and descriptive statements, a new set of questions is beginning to be asked, requiring "an entirely new way of structuring brain–behavior relationships" (Rourke, 1982, p. 3). Patients are beginning to be referred not solely for diagnostic evaluation or even for descriptive evaluation, although neuropsychologists will continue to make valuable contributions in both of these areas. More and more consumers are asking for *prescriptive* statements: *Should John Doe return to work? For what kind of vocational rehabilitation program is Mary Smith best suited? Is the patient a good candidate for my visual-imagery training program?* The emphasis in this emerging *dynamic phase* (Rourke, 1982, p. 3) is on the individual and the "individual's approach to material-to-be-learned." Although it is probably too early to know exactly how this dynamic phase of neuropsychological model building will affect the assessment process, it does appear that issues of everyday living will be of central concern. As Heaton and Pendleton (1981, p. 807) have aptly noted: "For many patients who are known to have brain lesions that are not immediately life threatening or grossly incapacitating, the major clinical questions concern living arrangements, employability, prospects for rehabilitation and the need for specific environmental supports."

The Challenge of the Dynamic Phase

It is clear that consumer needs have shifted since the 1950s and that referral questions are increasingly becoming behavioral in nature. Concurrent with this change in focus is the tendency for clinical neuropsychologists to become involved in the evaluation process for the purpose of description and prescription *after* a neurologic diagnosis has been established. Central to the potential success of neuropsychological assessment in this emerging dynamic phase will be its ability to yield useful and valid information regarding issues for everyday living. At present it is still somewhat of an empirical question whether the same test procedures we found useful in detecting the presence and localization of cerebral lesions will be those that will enable us to make valid inferences about patients' potential success in everyday tasks and activities (Costa, 1983). In order to answer this question we feel that neuropsychology will change in three essential respects, which we will now highlight.

Assessment of Strengths and Deficits

The first development we foresee is a greater emphasis on the assessment of patients' strengths and environmental resources. It is still widely accepted that "the distinguishing characteristic of neuropsychological assessment is its emphasis on the identification and measurement of psychological deficits, for it is primarily in deficiencies of intellect, emotion, and control that brain damage is manifested behaviorally" (Lezak, 1983, p. 85). However, for neuropsychological assessment successfully to meet the needs of consumers in Rourke's (1982) "dynamic phase," a new perspective placing greater attention upon the assessment of residual strengths, as well as the identification of deficits, will have to be developed. If the goal of neuropsychological assessment is only to identify deficits, we can only make inferences about what a person cannot do. While this, of course, may be useful information, it is only part of a patient's overall clinical picture. Of equal importance, especially in terms of making inferences about a patient's potential for everyday living, is the identification of his or her strengths *and* the conditions under which these strengths can be used to compensate for deficits (Chelune, 1983a). To this end, neuropsychologists must not only be assessors of individuals but also of environments, as everyday living always represents the interaction of the person with his or her environment. This approach is already being advocated in the field of rehabilitation, where Wright and Fletcher (1982, p. 235) note that, "after all, the goal is to bring about improvement, and this requires the discovery and utilization of existing and potential resources within the person and the environment."

Expanded Clinical Assessment

The second development we feel will be important in the evolution of neuro-psychological test procedures in the dynamic phase is an expansion of the data base upon which inferences are made. In the past, when the organic status of the brain was the sole criterion on which predictions were based, the emphasis of assessment was on devising adequately diverse yet parsimonious batteries of tests that were sensitive to the integrity of the brain. As neuropsychology entered the cognitive phase, assessment procedures began to include tests that were not only sensitive to cerebral dysfunction but also sampled a broad range of human abilities (e.g., language, cognition, memory, motor functions, etc.) that could be related to the underlying neuropathologic state; the brain was still the basic criterion. However, as one attempts to address issues of everyday functioning, the environment becomes the criterion. The task of neuropsychological assessment becomes one of assessing the individual patient's *overall* pattern of strengths and weaknesses and of making inferences about how this pattern will interact with specific environmental demands that the patient is apt to encounter. To this end, neuropsychologists will need more information than can be provided by cutoff scores, impairment indices, or statistical algorithms derived from group data. Clinicians will need to synthesize their test data reflecting the patients' specific abilities with a knowledge of the patients' environmental demands and resources. Similarly, clinical neuropsychologists must take into account various moderating variables, such as the patients' motivation, psychiatric status, frustration level, and attitude toward their deficits, that could interact with patients' ability deficits to produce poorer social and vocational adjustments than would be predicted on the basis of their ability test scores alone. All in all, neuropsychological judgments about a given patient's potential success in everyday activities will require the integration of more information than that currently provided by standard "brain-sensitive" neuropsychological tests and will need to proceed on a case-by-case basis, taking into account the idiosyncracies of the patient.

New Research Methods and Strategies

With the emergence of an emphasis on issues of daily living skills, there is a fundamental shift in the basic purpose for which neuropsychological tests are being employed. As noted earlier, neuropsychological assessment is no longer being used solely to describe the organic integrity of the brain, but also to address a patient's probable success in everyday tasks and activities. As such, an entirely new empirical data base must be developed to establish the validity of neuropsychological tests for the prediction of everyday behaviors.

While early research on the prediction of everyday behavior has been encouraging (for a review, see Heaton & Pendleton, 1981), it has been somewhat simplistic in design and limited by the constraints of univariate and unidimensional statistical procedures. Multivariate methods in neuropsychology are helpful and their use is certainly on the rise (Morris & Fletcher, 1984), but many of these may prove to be less than adequate, since they generally tend to take into account only the complexity of the predictor variables and not the criterion. Consider the early study by Heaton, Chelune, and Lehman (1978) in which neuropsychological and personality variables were used to assess the likelihood of patient employment. Using a discriminant function analysis, these investigators were able to identify correctly about 84% of their subjects as employed or not employed. Although their findings are impressive, the study only examined level of performance across various predictor variables and, more importantly, treated "employment" as a unitary construct. Each patient's abilities across an aggregate of tests are multidimensional in nature and can be represented in terms of not only level of performance, but also pattern and variability of performance (cf. Skinner & Jackson, 1978). Furthermore, everyday functioning variables such as employment are also multifaceted and multidimensional in nature in that different patterns and levels of ability are necessary for different vocations. To provide the empirical data base necessary for neuropsychologists to address the complexity of issues inherent in predicting everyday functioning, researchers will need to devise equally sophisticated methods to validate the utility of neuropsychological test procedures for this purpose.

In the following sections we will briefly review some of the research that is currently emerging in this important area. We will also propose a clinical model for the evaluation of everyday functioning and will end our discussion with some comments regarding possible research strategies for the future.

EMPIRICAL RELATIONSHIPS BETWEEN NEUROPSYCHOLOGICAL MEASURES AND TASKS OF EVERYDAY FUNCTIONING

At first glance there appears to be a general paucity of research concerning the relationship between neuropsychological measures and everyday functioning criteria. This is not surprising, considering that much of clinical neuropsychology's early efforts were directed either at demonstrating the validity and reliability of its tests as neurodiagnostic instruments or at explicating the effects of various neurologic conditions. However, scattered amid this ever-growing literature are an increasing number of reports suggesting that neuropsychological assessment devices also yield information relevant for predicting the potential success of a given patient in meeting the tasks of daily living.

Until recently, measures of psychometric intelligence have been the most thoroughly evaluated class of neuropsychological assessment devices with respect to everyday functioning. In his classic volume, Matarazzo (1972) delineates a number of relationships between IQ and various everyday criteria (e.g., vocational attainment, academic achievement, and socioeconomic status). Heaton and Pendleton's (1981) excellent review of the use of neuropsychological tests to predict patients' everyday functioning also reflects the emphasis on IQ in current research; of the 40 studies reviewed, two-thirds used IQ as the primary or sole neuropsychological index. However, while Heaton and Pendleton (1981, p. 807) point out that this narrow focus may "un-

TABLE 18.1 Aspects of Everyday Living Addressed in Heaton and Pendleton's (1981) Review

Self-Care and Independent Living (24 studies)
  Degree of independent living
  Overall level of functioning
  Social adjustment
  Self-help skills
  Ward problems
Academic Achievement (3 literature reviews)
  Years of education completed
  Academic potential
  Academic performance/success
  College grades
Vocational Functioning (14 studies)
  Occupational status/prestige
  Income levels
  Vocational attainment
  Job skills
  Bench work skills
  Success in vocational training programs
  Employment status

derestimate the potential of neuropsychological methods . . . in predicting most everyday behavior," their review clearly suggests that IQ and other neuropsychological tests have at least some validity with respect to self-care and independent living, academic achievement, and vocational functioning (see Table 18.1 for a summary of the everyday functioning variables reviewed by Heaton and Pendleton, 1981).

It is not our desire to reevaluate the studies presented by Heaton and Pendleton (1981), and the interested reader is encouraged to refer to this important review for further details. With the exception of five studies, our review is independent of Heaton and Pendleton's and represents an extension of their coverage of research concerning the validity of neuropsychological tests in the prediction of everyday behavior. The following review is not exhaustive, but the studies summarized in Table 18.2 should provide the reader with an overview of the work currently being done. We have organized these studies into four general categories (employment status and vocational behavior, rehabilitation and everyday task performance, academic achievement and remediation, and life quality and emotional factors), and we will separately summarize the major findings in each.

Employment Status and Vocational Behaviors

Once adult patients have become medically stabilized and their condition considered static in terms of recovery of function, a frequent question posed to clinical neuropsychologists by consumers is whether the patients can return to

TABLE 18.2 Summary of Studies Concerning Issues of Everyday Functioning

Study	Comments
Employment Status and Vocational Behavior	
Alcorn & Nicholson (1975)	NP and personality tests used to assess the special vocational needs of the retarded
Dennerll et al. (1966)[a]	NP and WAIS scores were lower for unemployed than employed epileptics
Dikmen & Morgan (1980)[a]	NP tests related to employment occupational status among epileptics
Dodrill & Clemmons (1983)	NP tests were predictive of adequate performance in later life and separated various vocational groups
Field, Sink, & Cook (1978)	IQ used as predictor of success on timed work samples from the JEVS system
Halstead & Rennick (1962)	NP tests related to independent merit ratings given by work supervisors; correspondence was better among higher-level executives than lower-level employees
Heaton, Chelune, & Lehman (1978)	NP tests and MMPI correctly classified 85% of subjects as employed or not employed
Morris, Ryan, & Peterson (1982)	NP tests used as predictors of success or failure on the sales processing and medical services work samples of the Vocational Evaluation System among psychiatric patients
Newnan, Heaton, & Lehman (1978)[a]	NP and MMPI used to predict future employment status, income, and job skills among patients with static neurological conditions
Schwartz, Dennerll, & Lin (1968)[a]	NP and personality measures used to predict current employment status among epileptics
Townsend, Prien, & Johnson (1974)	IQ and secondary disability were predictive of performance on certain jobs in sheltered workshop for retarded
Rehabilitation and Performance on Everyday Tasks	
Abbott & Gregsen (1981)	NP variables used as predictors of relapse in alcoholics
Bolger & DuBoise (1979)	Initial cognitive functioning related to potential for successful participation and completion of a vocational rehabilitation program
Bond (1976)	Cognitive deficits following severe head injury were related to level of social functioning
Diller & Gordon (1981a)	Presents comprehensive review of interventions for cognitive deficits among brain-injured adults
Diller & Weinberg (1970)	Documents incidence of accident proneness in hemiplegic patients with neglect syndrome
Goldstein & Ruthven (1983)	Reports results of Wichita Program in which NP and IQ measures documented outcome of a 6-month sheltered workshop program
Gregson & Taylor (1977)	NP tests used to predict relapse in male alcoholics
Keenan & Brassell (1974)	Level of IQ shortly after an injury correlated with final level of recovery among aphasic patients
Levin et al. (1979)	Overall level of outcome following head injury related to cognitive deficit
O'Leary et al. (1979)	Cognitive impairment related to treatment outcome among alcoholics

TABLE 18.2 (*continued*)

Study	Comments
Sivak et al. (1981)	Performance on certain cognitive and perceptual tests related to good driving skills among brain-damaged and nonbrain-damaged patients
Walker et al. (1983)	NP performance related to measures of abstinence, employment status, and income on follow-up after an alcohol treatment program
Weinberg et al. (1982)	NP tests used as pre–post measures to evaluate effectiveness of a rehabilitation program for right hemisphere stroke patients
Young, Collins, & Hren (1983)	Training on NP measures used in remediation of perceptual deficits among left hemiplegics, leading to fewer inappropriate maneuvers and accidents while eating

Academic Performance and Remediation

Study	Comments
Aaron (1981)	Presents a neuropsychological key approach for the diagnosis and remediation of learning disabilities among children without organic brain damage
Applebaum & Tuma (1982)	WISC-R scores used as predictors of academic achievement in a clinical population
Greenwald, Harder, & Fisher (1982)	WISC scatter related to behavioral competence in high-risk children
Grunau et al. (1981)	Psychological tests and EEG variables related to academic aptitude in adolescents
Gunnison (1982)	K-ABC Simultaneous and Sequential Processing scores used to develop remedial reading strategies
Gunnison, Kaufman, & Kaufman (1982)	Sequential and simultaneous processing characteristics applied to remediation
Hale & Foltz (1982)	Pathognomonic and IQ scores used to predict academic achievement in handicapped adolescents
Hartlage & Reynolds (1981)	Discusses how neuropsychological assessment can be used to design individualized instruction plans
Kaufman & Kaufman (1983)	Presents strategies for teaching academic skills capitalizing on simultaneous and sequential processing strengths as assessed by the K-ABC
Klesges (1983)	NP tests correlated with behavioral measures of socioemotional functioning
McLeod & Greenough (1980)	Short-term memory and verbal-linguistic skills found to be important components in spelling
Morrison & Pothier (1972)	Neuropsychological analysis of deficits used to generate remedial motor training programs for retarded preschoolers
Needleman (1983)	Low-dose lead poisoning related to IQ and classroom behavior
Nolan, Hammeke, & Barkley (1983)	NP measures discriminated a group of poor readers and spellers from normals and from a group that was poor only in math
Oakland (1983)	IQ and adaptive behavior used to predict reading and math achievement scores
Peter & Spreen (1979)	Identified personality markers for children at risk for developing academic learning deficiencies

TABLE 18.2 *(continued)*

Study	Comments
Petrauskas & Rourke (1979)	Identified different subgroups of retarded readers on the basis of audio-verbal processing skills
Reitan & Boll (1973)	NP tests used to discriminate among normal, behavior-disordered, learning-disabled, and brain-injured children
Rourke (1982)	Poor social functioning associated with deficient visual-spatial abilities and math skills
Rourke & Finlayson (1978)	Analysis of verbal and visual-spatial abilities related to variations in patterns of academic performance
Rourke & Orr (1977)	Neuropsychological tests used to predict reading and spelling performances of normal and retarded readers in a 4-year follow-up study
Rourke et al. (1983)	Discusses neuropsychological assessment and remediation of brain-related deficits
Rutter (1981)	Discusses interaction of cognitive deficits and psychosocial circumstances in brain-injured children
Samuels & Anderson (1973)	Visual recognition memory found to discriminate good versus poor readers
Satz et al. (1978)	Neuropsychological data obtained in kindergarten used to predict reading disabilities in the second, fifth, and sixth grades
Strang & Rourke (1983)	Concept formation and nonverbal reasoning abilities examined among children with specific math difficulties
Sweeney & Rourke (1978)	Psycholinguistic abilities discriminated groups of poor spellers with different degrees of phonetic accuracy

Life Quality and Emotional Factors

Study	Comments
Adams, Ausman, & Diaz (1983)	NP, medical and quality of life correlates of stroke patients
Chelune, Heaton, & Lehman (1986)	Subject complaints of problems in everyday living related more to personality factors than to objective neuropsychological deficits
Flanagan (1982)	Review of quality of life measures
Jellinick, Tarkelson, & Harvey (1982)	Long-term follow-up of functional deficits and distress levels of brain-damaged patients
Kaufert (1983)	Level of functional ability related to differences in role concepts and expectancies
McSweeney et al. (1982)	Life quality of COPD patients correlated with NP summary indices of impairment
McSweeney et al. (1983)	Related NP status to quality of every day life and health among chronically ill patients
Oddy & Humphrey (1980)	Examined social recovery during year following head injury
Ross (1983)	Discusses disorders of affective language following right hemisphere lesions and their outward similarity to depression

[a]Indicates articles also reviewed in Heaton and Pendleton (1981). Abbreviations: COPD = Chronic Obstructive Pulmonary Disease; JEVS = Jewish Employment and Vocational Service; K-ABC = Kaufman Assessment Battery for Children; NP = Neuropsychological.

work, and if so, for what types of work are they best suited. Several studies presented in Table 18.2 indicate that current employment status is dependent upon level of neuropsychological functioning and that neuropsychological tests can successfully discriminate between patients who are employed and those who are unemployed (eg., Dikmen & Morgan, 1980; Heaton et al., 1978; Schwartz, Dennerll, & Lin, 1968). Furthermore, neuropsychological tests have been found to be predictive of future vocational adequacy in life (Dodrill & Clemmons, 1984) and related to eventual employment status, income, and skills required on the job (Newnan, Heaton, & Lehman, 1978). While this research suggests that neuropsychological assessment may be helpful in making general statements regarding a patient's vocational potential, it is nonetheless important to consider the demands of specific jobs. For example, in a very early study, Halstead and Rennick (1962) found that level of performance on the Halstead tests was related to merit ratings made by job supervisors, but that the relationship was much stronger among patients in high-level jobs than among those in lower-level positions. It appears that successful job performance in high-level vocations is more sensitive to cognitive changes than work performance in lower-level positions, where the job demands may be less stringent. Thus, predictions of potential vocational success based on the level of neuropsychological deficit must consider the cognitive demands of the specific occupations in question.

Consistent with the need to examine job specificity, several studies have attempted to relate neuropsychological functioning to actual success or failure on a variety of work samples. Townsend, Prien, and Johnson (1974) found that IQ and secondary disability were predictive of performance on certain jobs in a sheltered workshop for the retarded, and Field, Sink, and Cook (1978) used IQ as a predictor of success on the timed work samples from the Jewish Employment and Vocational Services (JEVS) Work Sample Battery. In a recent study, Morris, Ryan, and Peterson (1982) evaluated the utility of a number of neuropsychological measures in predicting the adequacy of performance of a heterogeneous patient sample referred for vocational evaluation on two work samples (medical services and sales processing) from the Singer Vocational Evaluation System. For both work samples, those patients failing them earned significantly lower neuropsychological scores than those passing. The Category test and Part B of the Trail-Making test from the Halstead–Reitan Battery were particularly discriminating and yielded correct classification rates between 73% and 77% for the two work samples. The actuarial use of cutoff scores from these two neuropsychological tests equaled or surpassed a neuropsychologist's blind clinical ratings based on all of the test data.

From the studies reviewed in this section, there does appear to be an empirical basis for using neuropsychological tests to make global statements regarding a patient's vocational potential. However, such general inferences must be made cautiously, since different degrees of neuropsychological deficit may be critical for different jobs (Halstead & Rennick, 1962). Research, such

as that of Morris and colleagues (1982), that attempts to relate neuropsychological performance to specific work samples with known external criterion
validity is much needed before neuropsychologists can make specific vocational predictions with much confidence.

Rehabilitation and Performance of Everyday Tasks

An area of great import and potential for clinical neuropsychology in Rourke's
(1982) dynamic phase is consultation and involvement with rehabilitation
service providers. While in the past most clinical neuropsychologists have been
content to focus on diagnostic issues and have not been closely involved in
rehabilitation planning or service (Miller, 1980), this picture has changed
dramatically in recent years. Caplan (1982, p. 362) points out that "knowledge of the mechanisms underlying cerebral function, breakdown, and recovery can provide a rational basis for designing rehabilitation programs for
brain-injured patients. Specialists in clinical neuropsychology, those who
assess the cognitive and behavioral effects of brain damage, thus have useful
diagnostic and therapeutic expertise to offer rehabilitation units." Although
"the formulation of rehabilitation programs rather than diagnoses represents
something of a challenge" (Goldstein & Ruthven, 1983, p. 161) to the clinical
neuropsychologist, there is substantial movement in this direction, as evidenced by the recent number of books and book chapters on the topic (e.g.,
Barth & Boll, 1981; Diller & Gordon, 1981b; Edelstein & Couture, 1983;
Goldstein & Ruthven, 1983; Rosenthal, Griffith, Bond, & Miller, 1983;
Trexler, 1982). An applied subspeciality within clinical neuropsychology has
even emerged, called "behavioral neuropsychology," which Horton, Wedding,
and Phay (1981, p. 60) describe as "the application of behavior therapy to the
problems of organically impaired individuals while maintaining a clinical
neuropsychological perspective to facilitate assessment, management, and
treatment."

It is beyond the scope and purpose of this chapter to attempt to review the
variety of neuropsychologically based treatment approaches (e.g., melodic
intonation, visual imagery, memory training, etc.) emerging in the rehabilitation field. The interested reader may wish to consult the review by Diller and
Gordon (1981a) for a brief summary of many of these techniques. Instead, our
focus here will be upon the use of neuropsychological tests in evaluating
potential treatment outcome and performance of everyday tasks. To be sure,
the studies presented in Table 18.2 are only a representative sample of this
growing body of literature.

Given the rising costs of medical and social services, it has become important
to target those individuals who are apt to benefit most from such services. In
this regard, neuropsychological tests have been used both as outcome measures
and as predictors of treatment outcome. Weinberg, Piasetsky, Diller, and

Gordon (1982) used a variety of verbal- and visual-cognitive tasks as pre- and postmeasures to evaluate the efficacy of a rehabilitation program "designed to establish a systematic strategy of organizing complex visual material" (p. 59) among right hemisphere stroke patients without evidence of unilateral visual-spatial neglect. The experimental group was found to show significant gains compared to the control group after one month of treatment on a subset of the visuo-cognitive tasks. Similarly, Goldstein and Ruthven (1983) report significant gains in both IQ and neuropsychological functioning among young head-injured patients after six months of participation in the Wichita Program, a sheltered workshop training program. In this latter study, it is interesting to note that the patients showed greater improvement on the neuropsychological tests than on the measure of psychometric intelligence, despite the fact that all the patients were considered to have chronic neurological conditions.

With respect to predicting eventual treatment outcome, IQ level shortly after injury has been found to correlate with final level of recovery among aphasic patients (Keenan & Brassell, 1974). Bolger and DuBoise (1979) also report that initial level of cognitive functioning is associated with potential for successful participation in and completion of a vocational rehabilitation program. Several studies have related neuropsychological functioning to treatment outcome in alcohol rehabilitation settings. Neuropsychological assessment of cognitive dysfunction among alcoholics has been found to be predictive of relapse (e.g., Abbott & Gregson, 1981; O'Leary, Donovan, Chaney, & Walker, 1979) as well as of employment status and income levels (Walker, Donovan, Kivlaham, & O'Leary, 1983).

In addition to being used as predictor and outcome measures in rehabilitation, neuropsychological assessment of patients' level of cognitive functioning may also yield valuable information regarding other aspects of daily living. Levin, Grossman, Rose, and Teasdale (1979) found that overall level of outcome following closed head injury was significantly related to cognitive deficits, and Bond (1976) reports that level of cognitive functioning following severe head injury was related to social functioning. Diller and Weinberg (1970) have documented increased rates of accident proneness among hemiplegic patients with neglect syndromes and point out that such patients are at risk when driving and operating potentially dangerous machinery. In an eminently practical study of one particular aspect of everyday functioning, Sivak, Olson, Kewman, Won, and Henson (1981) evaluated the perceptual and cognitive abilities associated with good driving skills. Although their brain-injured group as a whole obtained lower scores than the control groups on both the neuropsychological and driving measures, those patients who scored well on certain perceptual-cognitive tasks performed adequately in both closed-course and actual in-traffic driving conditions. Finally, Young, Collins, and Hren (1983) found that left hemiplegic patients who were given training on certain neuropsychological tests to remediate perceptual deficits showed improved eating behaviors and had fewer accidents when eating.

Academic Performance and Remediation

Our contention in this chapter has been that clinical neuropsychology's involvement in issues of everyday functioning is a relatively recent phenomenon. While this view is essentially accurate as a generalization, there is an area of notable exception, namely, child neuropsychology. Those practitioners who deal extensively or exclusively with child populations have long been interested in the relationship between measures of cognitive ability and academic performance, an important life activity for children. In this sense, the attempts of Binet and Simon at the turn of the century to devise a test to classify children according to their level of intellectual functioning for purposes of academic placement (Matarazzo, 1972) might well be considered neuropsychology's first foray into the realm of everyday functioning. Since that time, an extensive literature has accrued concerning the relationship between intelligence and various aspects of academic performance among normals (e.g., grades, level of attainment, etc.). We will not concern ourselves here with this body of literature, and the interested reader may wish to refer to Heaton and Pendleton's (1981) review for an overview of this area. Rather, our focus here will be upon some of the recent developments in child neuropsychology. Again, the studies presented in Table 18.2 are only illustrative of the work currently being done.

Gaddes (1981) notes that during the 1960s neuropsychological tests began to be recognized by some clinical neuropsychologists as holding "great promise for better understanding learning-disabled children," and that they began recommending the use of "neuropsychological knowledge for the diagnosis and treatment of these children" (p. 34). Gaddes further observes that over the years increasing numbers of educators, especially school psychologists, have also embraced "the rationale of using neuropsychological knowledge in their problems of diagnosis and remedial prescriptions" (p. 74). This interest has generated considerable work in the area, resulting in a number of excellent texts (e.g., Hynd & Obrzut, 1981; Kirk, 1981; Knights & Bakker, 1976; Rourke, Bakker, Fisk, & Strang, 1983; Rutter, 1983) as well as an entirely new theoretical approach to intellectual assessment (Kaufman & Kaufman, 1983).

In this rapidly expanding area, several trends can be identified. The first is that of predicting academic patterns of performance based on the assessment of cognitive functions. As one might expect, IQ, especially Verbal IQ, is a good global predictor of academic success, even among emotionally disturbed adolescents (Applebaum & Tuma, 1982). Oakland (1983) reports that inclusion of information concerning a child's level of adaptive behavior adds little to the prediction of math and reading achievement beyond that obtained by IQ alone. However, explicit neuropsychological procedures, such as a modified form of the Luria–Nebraska Battery, have been found to be better predictors of academic achievement than measures of general intelligence (Hale & Foltz, 1982). This observation is reinforced by a number of excellent longitudinal studies (e.g., Satz, Taylor, Friel, & Fletcher, 1978; Rourke & Orr, 1977). Satz and colleagues (1978) evaluated the entire white, male kindergarten population of one county's school system in Florida, using a simple battery of sensory-motor and perceptual tests, and followed these youngsters' reading achievement for six years. Using a combination of scores from tests of finger localization, alphabet recitation, and visual recognition-discrimination, Satz and his colleagues were able to identify correctly 72% of the students as severely retarded, mildly retarded, average, or superior readers at the end of six years. In a smaller, four-year longitudinal study of retarded and normal readers, Rourke and Orr (1977) demonstrated the superiority of a neuropsychological test of visual-perceptual speed and accuracy in predicting levels of reading and spelling eventually taken in the first and second grades. Taken together, these studies suggest that neuropsychological procedures can be very useful in identifying children at risk for later academic difficulty at a stage in their academic careers when remedial procedures are most efficacious (Strag, 1972).

A second line of research in child neuropsychology deals ostensibly with diagnostic issues. However, unlike diagnostic practices in traditional adult neuropsychology, the focus is upon identifying specific learning disabilities for the purpose of potential remediation. The rationale is that difficulty in any particular academic area (e.g., spelling) may have quite different neuropsychological etiologies and therefore would require different remedial approaches. In this vein, Nolan, Hammeke, and Barkley (1983) discriminated a group of poor readers and spellers from not only normals but from a group of youngsters who were poor only in arithmetic, using the Expressive Speech, Writing, and Reading subscales of a modified version of the Luria–Nebraska Battery. Visual recognition memory (Samuels & Anderson, 1973) and audio-verbal skills (Petrauskas & Rourke, 1979) have been identified as important components of oral reading skills. Children with math difficulties, but who differ with respect to reading and spelling achievement, have been found to have vastly different psycholinguistic and visual-spatial skills (Rourke & Finlayson, 1978); those who retain good automatic verbal language skills have been shown to have poor concept formation and nonverbal reasoning abilities (Strang & Rourke, 1983). Finally, subgroups of children with spelling deficiencies can be distinguished in terms of their short-term memory and psycholinguistic skills (McLeod & Greenough, 1980; Sweeney & Rourke, 1978).

Closely tied to the diagnostic process are endeavors to design remediation approaches based on neuropsychological findings and principles. Aaron (1981) has developed a neuropsychological key approach for use with "nonorganic" learning-disabled children in which diagnostic decisions are linked with specific remedial strategies. Whereas Aaron's remedial prescriptions are directed at strengthening retarded skill areas through practice of these deficient skills, others advocate attacking skill deficiencies by devising remedial strategies that capitalize upon a child's areas of strengths. For example, Gunnison (Gunnison, 1982; Gunnison, Kaufman, & Kaufman, 1982) has developed several alternative remedial strategies for teaching reading skills (e.g., decoding, comprehension, organization, etc.) that are linked to assessment of a child's simultaneous and sequential processing capabilities. The Kaufmans (Kaufman & Kaufman, 1983) have expanded these strategies in their interpretative manual for the Kaufman Assessment Battery for Children to cover not only reading, but also spelling and math. For a further discussion of how neuropsychological assessment procedures are being used to develop individual educational programs for learning-disabled children, the interested reader may wish to consult either Hartlage and Reynolds (1981) or Rourke and associates (1983).

In addition to addressing the problems of academic achievement in children, a number of investigators have begun to evaluate the relationship between neuropsychological test results and the social and behavioral functioning of children. Rourke (1982) reports that children with math problems and poor visual-spatial abilities tend to have social problems associated with a difficulty in attending to or giving nonverbal cues. He also suggests that these children are prone to overuse routine, programmatic language in social situations. Similarly, poor socioemotional adjustment has been noted among children with high intersubtest variability on the Wechsler Intelligence Scale for Children (Greenwald, Harder, & Fisher, 1982) and poor performances on various Halstead–Reitan test measures (Klesges, 1983; Strang & Rourke, 1983). Peter and Spreen (1979) have identified "personality markers" for children at risk for developing learning deficiencies; Rutter (1981) and Needleman (1983) have identified a number of common behavioral disturbances associated with childhood neurological conditions. Thus, although child neuropsychologists have been primarily interested in the assessment of ability patterns, there is a growing recognition that other social/behavioral dimensions are important to consider if one is to address "the 'whole' child and his/her important adaptive deficiencies" (Rourke et al., 1983, p. 157).

Life Quality and Emotional Factors

In this section we will examine a very important aspect of everyday living, namely life quality and emotional status. Although there is only a small body of relevant literature, changes in life quality and emotional responsivity are often concomitants of changes in neurologic/neuropsychologic status, and they can have a profound effect upon patients' overall potential to carry out tasks of daily living. If neuropsychologists are to succeed in making predictions about aspects of everyday living, these variables must be taken into account, both as moderating factors and as outcome events.

Oddy and Humphrey (1980) examined the social recovery process of head-injury patients during the year following their traumas and cite frequent problems with loneliness, social isolation, anxiety and depression, and impaired motivation. Similarly, Jellinick, Tarkelson, and Harvey (1982) report an association between functional abilities and distress levels among brain-damaged patients at long-term follow-up. Differences in functional abilities are also noted to covary with patients' role concepts and expectancies (Kaufert, 1983). In a large-scale study of nearly six hundred neuropsychological referrals, Chelune, Heaton, and Lehman (1986) found that patients' subjective reports of problems in everyday functioning were more closely related to personality variables than to their performances on an extensive battery of ability tests. These studies suggest that patients' ultimate capacity to function in the environment is apt to be multiply determined, not solely dependent upon their residual cognitive resources.

While functional factors may moderate to some degree the relationship between neuropsychological deficits and behavioral deficits in the environment, there is some evidence that neuropsychological deficits may directly affect quality of life and emotional status. Several studies report a relationship between level of neuropsychological impairment and indices of life quality (Adams, Ausman, & Diaz, 1983; McSweeny, Grant, Adams, & Prigatano, 1983; McSweeny, Grant, Heaton, Adams, & Timms, 1982). Interestingly, McSweeny and colleagues (1983) found this relationship to be true for their patient group, but not for a healthy control group. Finally, Ross (1983) summarizes recent research on disorders of affective language (aprosodias) related to right hemisphere lesions. These patients are impaired in their ability to encode and/or decode the affective aspects of language that are conveyed by paralinguistic and gestural cues. Ross points out that patients with motor aprosodia are frequently apt to be perceived by others as appearing depressed (e.g., having blunted affect, monotone voice, etc.).

CLINICAL EVALUATION OF EVERYDAY FUNCTIONING

After reviewing the studies presented in the preceding section, it may be easy to conclude that there is a sufficient (and growing) empirical data base to justify the use of neuropsychological assessment devices as valid predictors of various aspects of everyday functioning. However, it is important to keep in mind that much of what has been reported is based on group differences from fairly discrete samples with specific characteristics and is, therefore, only illustrative of the promise held by neuropsychological assessment. Practicing clinicians are well aware of the difficulties inherent in applying such group findings in the evaluation of the single case (Meehl, 1973). Each patient brings to the testing situation his or her unique constellation of strengths and deficits, premorbid history of cognitive and personality functioning, and current environmental resources and demands. Even in the realm of neurodiagnostic application, clinical neuropsychological interpretative methods have been shown to be superior to the best available actuarial algorithms (Golden, Moses, Ariel, et al., 1982; Heaton, Grant, Anthony, & Lehman, 1981). Thus, until future research can generate adequately sophisticated statistical formulae for handling the diverse idiosyncracies of individuals and their environments, predictions regarding everyday functioning in the single case will largely be based upon clinical inferential methods. In this section we will briefly outline in broad strokes the clinical approach we use in our laboratory to make inferences regarding everyday functioning (Chelune, 1983b). The reader should keep in mind that there is nothing hard and fast about our conceptual framework—it merely serves as a useful guideline.

An Expanded Clinical Data Base

Since the vast majority of our consumers refer their patients to us for evaluation of their potential for success on everyday tasks and activities, we have expanded our clinical data base in an effort to collect as much relevant information as possible within a single working day. This information can be grouped under the following headings: demographics and academic/ occupational history, medical history, patients' and relatives' reports of disability, behavioral observations, and neuropsychological and personality test data.

Demographics and Academic/Occupational History

As in most neuropsychology laboratories, we collect standard demographic information: age, sex, handedness, marital status, and level of education. However, we also inquire as to the nature of the patients' current living situations and whether there are social resources available to them. With respect to education, we ask not only about level of attainment, but also how well they did and whether they had any difficulty with particular subjects. If they left school before completing high school or during college, we attempt to determine why. Such questions allow us to obtain a better picture of their premorbid levels of functioning. Similarly, brief occupational histories can yield valuable information about patients' current employment status, job stability, vocational skills, task requirements on their current or most recent job, and amount of supervision they have generally received. This information can be especially important to consider when addressing patients' potential for future employment.

Medical History

An adequate medical history is imperative for understanding both the nature of a patient's current pattern of strengths and deficits and his or her potential physical resources and limitations for dealing with the environment. Such histories generally include questions about both perinatal and developmental difficulties, head injuries, major illnesses known to affect the brain (e.g., encephalitis, epilepsy, etc.), and periods of unconsciousness. Consideration of other nonneurologic systemic conditions, such as heart disease, chronic obstructive pulmonary disease, and diabetes, should also be included, since they can affect neuropsychological functioning and impinge upon the performance of daily activities. We have also found it useful to take a careful history of patients' use of drugs (prescribed and otherwise) and alcohol, as even occasional episodes of acute intoxification would be expected to create transient periods of much poorer functioning than would be predicted on the basis of their ability test scores alone. Similarly, notation of prior or existing psychiatric difficulties should alert the clinician to the possibility that nonorganic (emotional and/or environmental) factors would interact with ability deficits to produce lower levels of social and vocational adjustment than might otherwise be possible. Finally, some accounting of peripheral physical impairments that could affect testing and/or the performance of day-to-day activities should be made.

Patients' and Relatives' Reports of Disability

Because individuals have widely differing living and environmental demands, it is difficult to determine whether a patient's specific level of impairment in a given ability area will necessarily adversely affect his or her everyday functioning (Halstead & Rennick, 1962). While an examination of the social-vocational history may provide some useful clues, "the most convenient way of obtaining information about how patients are functioning in everyday life is to ask for their own assessments" (Heaton & Pendleton, 1981, p. 814). Lezak (1983) provides a summary of a number of self-report inventories for obtaining information regarding patient functioning. In our laboratory, we utilize two self-report inventories developed at the University of Colorado Health Sciences Center (Chelune, Heaton, & Lehman, 1986). The first, the Patient Assessment of Own Functioning Inventory, is a brief questionnaire that requires the patient to rate the frequency of difficulty encountered in various aspects of daily living. These aspects can be grouped into four general areas: memory, language and communication, sensory-motor functioning, and cognitive functioning. The second questionnaire is the Relative's Assessment of Patient Functioning Inventory, which is given to a relative of the patient to complete. The relative's form covers the same aspects of everyday functioning as the patient's and also includes additional items regarding emotional status and social behavior.

The utility of self-reports concerning disability does not necessarily lie in their ultimate validity. In many cases, we have found the patients' reports to be quite discrepant from their relatives' or from their own objective performance on neuropsychological tests. In such cases, these discrepancies provide a rich source of information concerning the patients' view of themselves and of their immediate social environment. Inferences concerning a patient's potential for everyday functioning can be quite different depending on whether the person minimizes, exaggerates, or accurately reports his or her limitations.

Behavioral Observations

Whether clinicians do their own testing or have it done by a trained neuro-psychological technician, the importance of behavioral observations cannot be overestimated. Within the context of a lengthy neuropsychological evaluation, the examiner has access to important clinical information about the patient that is not reflected in test scores (Heaton & Heaton, 1981). This information can provide a useful data base for inferring how the patient spontaneously relates to others, takes directions, responds to difficult problems and frustration, and attempts to compensate for deficits. Equally important are observations as to whether test instructions have be to be repeated or simplified, whether additional structure or praise is needed to motivate the patient, and how successful these modifications are in minimizing the patient's difficulties. Together with the patient's objective test findings, behavioral observations provide the clinician with a broad picture of how the patient will approach and deal with a variety of situations relevant to everyday functioning.

Neuropsychological and Personality Test Data

The core of any neuropsychological evaluation is, of course, the patient's neuropsychological test scores. Consistent with our view of the needs of Rourke's (1982) dynamic phase, we have expanded our testing data base in an attempt to obtain a wide-ranging picture of the patient's strengths and weaknesses. We generally include a standardized test battery (e.g., Halstead–Reitan or Luria–Nebraska Battery) as well as supplemental tests in order to generate a picture of the patient's general intelligence, academic skills, cognitive functions, attention, learning and memory, constructional skills, sensory-perceptual functions, language and communication skills, problem solving, and motor functions. In evaluating these data, we take a multidimensional perspective; that is, we consider the data in terms of overall level of performance, variability of scores, and specific patterning of abilities (cf. Skinner & Jackson, 1978).

In addition to the neuropsychological tests, we also feel that it is important to administer some form of personality test (e.g., MMPI). While such tests may be of limited neurodiagnostic value, they can be quite useful in rounding out the overall clinical picture of the patient (Chelune, Ferguson, & Moehle, 1985). However, some caution must be exercised in interpreting personality test results administered to neurologic patients. Most clinical measures of personality functioning were standardized for use among psychiatric populations, and their derived clinical descriptors may not be directly applicable to the brain-injured client. For example, we frequently observe elevated Schizophrenia (Sc) scores on the MMPI among patients with moderately impaired conceptual abilities. Clinically, such elevations seem to reflect the patients' general confusion about what is happening around them more than the presence of a psychotic thought disorder. Thus, interpretation of personality test findings must be tempered by the patient's pattern of cognitive abilities and vice versa.

Implications for Everyday Functioning

Before formulating inferences concerning a patient's potential success in everyday tasks and activities, the clinician must integrate and synthesize a great deal of information from the various data bases noted above. Despite the promising research on aspects of everyday functioning reviewed earlier, there are few, if any, actuarial formulae to date that can be used with much confidence in the individual interpretative process. The clinician must be guided by his or her own experience and intuitive skill, recognizing that the data are often overlapping and interactive.

In this section, we will outline the general steps we take in formulating inferences concerning everyday functioning. Consistent with the view of Heaton and Pendleton (1981, p. 815), the major assumption we make in this interpretative process is "that if patients show impairment of an ability in the laboratory, then they will have trouble with everyday tasks in which the same ability is required." However, we also recognize that the laboratory situation does not always take into account patients' ability creatively to use external aids and supports to minimize their deficits or to perform tasks in creative ways that do not rely on deficient skills. Likewise, we also acknowledge that the absence of impairment does not necessarily guarantee successful performance of life's daily activities.

Formulating the Case: An Overview

Before making any specific inferential statements about a patient's potential everyday functioning, it is necessary to place the data within a broad conceptual framework. We generally begin by asking ourselves whether the data are a valid reflection of the patient's basic adaptive abilities; that is, did the patient put forth adequate cooperation and effort on all the tests and were any special modifications (e.g., repetition of instructions, clarification, etc.) necessary to maximize his or her performance? The answers to these questions guide us in determining to what degree our observations of the patient's behavior and skills in the laboratory will be representative of his or her everyday functioning. In those cases where the patient is uncooperative or puts forth less than adequate effort, it is necessary to assess whether the patient is actually capable of higher levels of performance of simply attempting to mask or avoid manifesting his or her deficits.

After deciding our confidence level in the patient's data, we examine the general patterning of the data in an effort to assess how others may perceive the patient (Kaufert, 1983). Of particular concern here is whether the patient has certain strengths that might give others the impression that the patient is more intact than his or her data might suggest. Such strengths may lead others to expect more from the patient than he or she is capable of delivering. Alcoholics provide a good case in point. Chronic alcoholics frequently present a picture of intact verbal skills and psychometric intelligence, while manifesting conceptual and complex visual-spatial deficits (Chelune & Parker, 1981). Because alcoholics can maintain a good verbal facade, others are often dismayed by their poor judgment in complex situations. Of equal concern is evidence of mild deficits in areas that are central to the patient's life style. For example, a mild word-finding problem may be quite disconcerting for a teacher, and a minor tremor could be devastating for a surgeon's career. Yet, in the eyes of others, any potential abreactions that the patient may have to these "minor" deficits may appear out of proportion to what they see.

It is also useful to compare the patient's subjective reports of distress and complaints of disability to his or her objective neuropsychological test results. In this regard we ask ourselves: "Does the patient exaggerate, minimize, or accurately report his or her difficulties with respect to the test data," and "Are psychiatric factors contributing to the patient's reported difficulties?" Complaints of disability are relatively independent of neuropsychological status and more closely tied to psychiatric status (Chelune, Heaton, & Lehman, 1986). For example, patients who present with complaints of memory impairment may perform normally on formal memory tests but have indications of increased anxiety and/or depression on personality testing, suggesting that functional factors may be operating. Conversely, some patients may express little or no concern over potential deficits despite evidence of relatively severe impairment on objective measures. These individuals may be at risk for taking on problems or tasks that they are ill prepared to handle. Thus, comparisons between self-report and personality and neuropsychological data sets provide the clinician with a valuable overview of how the patient is coping and create a general context for making specific inferences and recommendations about everyday functioning.

Formulating Specific Inferences

Given an overview of a patient's global clinical picture, we are ready to begin evaluating specific areas of clinical concern. These vary considerably, depending on the given patient, the nature of the referral question, and who will be using our reports. However, over the years certain topic areas have emerged that we routinely attempt to address in our reports. We have outlined these clinical areas of concern in Table 18.3 and have provided a tentative list of associated skills we feel are necessary to function in each area. We have also provided some of the data sources from our battery that we use to guide our evaluations. The table is heuristic in nature and is provided only as a guide for generating hypotheses.

TABLE 18.3 A Tentative Guide for Clinical Interpretation of Everyday Activities

Clinical Area	Necessary Skills	Potential Tests
Behave appropriately in situations that are:		
(a) Routine and familiar	General fund of information and social common sense	WAIS Information, Comprehension, Picture Arrangement
(b) Complex and novel	Logical analysis, new concept formation, problem solving, attention	Category Test, Tactual Performance Test (TPT), Speech Sounds, Rhythm, WAIS Digit Span and Digit Symbol, Word-Finding Test
Follow detailed procedures in an adaptive fashion	Sequential thinking and cognitive flexibility	Trail-Making, Wisconsin Card Sorting Test, WAIS Picture Arrangement
Memory	Learning and recall of verbal and nonverbal materials	Immediate and delayed aspects of Story and Figure Memory Tests, TPT Memory and Location Scores
Communication Skills	Expressive and receptive language	WAIS Vocabulary, Word-Finding, Word Fluency, Aphasia Screening, Behavioral Observations
Academic Skills (a) Manage correspondence (b) Manage finances (c) Manage reading	Writing, spelling, math, reading recognition, and comprehension	Peabody Individual Achievement Test, Wide Range Achievement Test, WAIS Arithmetic, Aphasia Screening Exam
Manipulatory tasks and self-care activities	Speed, strength, fine motor coordination, tactile skills, vision	Tapping, Hand Dynamometer, Grooved Pegboard, Tactile Form Recognition, Visual Fields, Suppression Tests
Driving, use of dangerous tools and appliances	Judgment and flexibility, attention, nonverbal memory, constructional skills, right-left discrimination	Category and Trail-Making Tests, Speech Sounds and Rhythm Tests, Figure Memory, WAIS Block Design, Aphasia Screening Exam Crosses, Visual Fields
Reality orientation	Correct appraisal of potential limitations and strengths	Patient Assessment of Own Functioning Inventory, Relative's Assessment Form, MMPI, History, and Neuropsychological Test Data

The first area of concern is the patient's capacity to function appropriately in various settings. Since situations vary in their cognitive demands, we make a distinction between those that are routine and familiar to the patient and those that are more complex and novel. Depending on the individual's specific pattern of strengths and weaknesses, we attempt to describe the kinds of environments in which the patient is apt to function best and the kinds of environmental supports that he or she may need. Related to this aspect for many individuals is the question of employability. Here it is very important to consider the person's employment history and job skills.

To illustrate the kinds of inferences that might be made, consider the following case. The patient is a 53 year-old, right-handed male with a high-school education. He is married and is a boiler operator by trade; he has also been the president of his union local for the past four years. He suffered a posterior right hemisphere stroke and was hospitalized for two weeks. At discharge he manifested only mild sensorimotor deficits on the left and showed no gross visual field defects. After a short convalescence at home, he returned to his work with the union, where he was able to carry on his routine duties. Four months later he decided to resign from his union post and returned to his former job of operating a boiler. However, he quickly began to encounter difficulties on the job and was rehospitalized for further evaluation. Based on his neuropsychological evaluation, the following inferences were among those given to his neurologist:

> The patient has a good fund of general information and an average knowledge of basic social "common-sense" relationships, and he should be able to use appropriately what he knows in routine and familiar settings. However, his abilities to engage in logical analysis and new concept formation and to sustain attention to potentially relevant auditory stimuli in his environment are seriously compromised at this time. Thus, he is apt to be inaccurate quite frequently in his appraisals of complex or novel situations, particularly if they are nonverbally mediated, and he could exercise poor judgment in these situations as a result. Because of his relatively good verbal skills, he may give others the impression that he is much more intact than he actually is, when in fact he has significant difficulties with visual search and perceptual integration. He is likely to do best in relatively routine and well-structured environments that are familiar to him and well illuminated, and where there is greater emphasis placed on verbal transactions than on perceptual-motor problem solving. While he may be able to perform verbally oriented aspects of his job (e.g., handle union negotiations or even verbally instruct others how to operate a boiler), I seriously doubt he is currently able to carry out the operations of boiler maintenance without posing a significant safety risk. Although he is able to learn and retain new verbal information with normal efficiency, he is quite limited in his acquisition of new nonverbal material and tends to overlook visual details to his left. Should the patient attempt to return to work, I would strongly recommend that he limit himself to verbally oriented tasks in situations where someone else is readily available to assist him when new problems arise.

As touched upon in the above case, we also address the issues of learning and memory. Although these constructs are interrelated, it is useful to consider them separately when making inferences regarding everyday functioning. Some individuals appear to have memory problems simply because they are slow to assimilate the details of new information on its first presentation, whereas others learn new material quickly but have difficulty recalling the details of it after a few hours. In the case of the former, simple repetition or rehearsal might significantly reduce potential memory problems. However, for those individuals who actually forget (cannot retrieve) what they have learned, repetition is not apt to be of much assistance. Instead, these patients may profit from the use of external aids, such as written schedules and checklists and written notes about occasional experiences or communications that are especially important to remember in detail. It is also important to identify whether the patient's memory deficits are modality specific (e.g., verbal, visual, or psychomotor) or generalized. In the case of modality-specific deficits, the patient may be able to use his or her intact skills to compensate for or strengthen associations in the deficient modality (e.g., greater verbal analysis and coding of visual stimuli, or use of visual imagery to strengthen verbal associations). For those individuals with generalized learning and memory deficits, it may be best for them to attempt to routinize their lives (e.g., stick to familiar activities, procedures, routes, areas, etc.) as much as possible and to avoid situations that require the efficient learning and retention of new information on a regular basis.

After addressing potential learning and memory problems, we turn our attention to the patient's expressive and receptive language skills. From our observations and test data, we ask ourselves: "Can the patient understand and follow a normal rate of conversational speech?" and "Will other deficits affect these skills, and if so, what can the patient or others do to minimize potential problems?" In the case of our patient with the right hemisphere stroke, we made the following inferences:

> The patient has generally good verbal skills and expresses himself well. However, he does have some difficulty comprehending complex instructions, particularly if they are expressed in figurative or affect-laden language. In communicating with him, one would do well to limit the amount and complexity of the material presented, and use concrete and declarative statements with some redundancy.

While academic tests of reading (recognition and comprehension), spelling, and math are not especially sensitive neurodiagnostic measures among adults, they do provide important information with respect to everyday functioning. Patients with poor reading skills may need assistance when interpreting complex reading material or important correspondence. Likewise, patients who have difficulty spelling may need to rely frequently on a dictionary to look up the spelling of unfamiliar words; in more severe cases they may require help in managing their personal correspondence. Problems with math computations might be minimized by use of a mechanical pocket calculator. However, where math difficulties are coupled with general conceptual deficits, the patient may need assistance with long-range financial decisions and management of personal finances.

Finally, it is important to consider the patient's sensory-perceptual and motor abilities. Most individuals appear to be capable of performing basic self-care activities (e.g., dressing, eating, personal hygiene) with even moderate deficits in these areas. However, mild deficits, especially within the context of other difficulties, can significantly affect their performance of more demanding psychomotor tasks. For example, driving a car and using potentially dangerous machinery or tools are serious safety risks for patients with neglect syndromes and visual-perceptual deficits (Diller & Weinberg, 1970; Sivak et al., 1981).

DIRECTIONS FOR FUTURE RESEARCH

Based on our review of the research literature, it appears that many of the tests that have been shown to be useful for neurodiagnostic purposes are also helpful in addressing questions about patients' probable success in a number of everyday tasks and activities. Although this body of research is encouraging, "most of the studies have used a restricted range of test measures to predict rather gross everyday behavioral criteria in subject groups that are not very representative of the typical population of patients referred for clinical neuropsychological evaluations" (Heaton & Pendleton, 1981, p. 814). Clinical methods of interpretation such as the one we have offered may allow the clinician greater flexibility in integrating research findings within the broader context of a given patient's overall clinical picture. Still, there is a need for recommendations and decisions "that are founded increasingly upon empirical validation" (Costa, 1983, p. 7). To provide the empirical data base necessary to meet the challenges of Rourke's (1982) dynamic phase, new research paradigms and strategies are necessary. We will conclude our discussion of the neuropsychology of everyday functioning with some comments regarding possible directions for future research.

Broader Patient Representation

As noted by Heaton and Pendleton (1981), much of the research examining the relationship between neuropsychological functioning and everyday behavior has been done with select patient groups and, therefore, has limited applicability among diverse clinical populations. To increase generalizability, large-scale studies are needed that make adequate provisions for important demographic (e.g., age, sex, education), neurologic (e.g., lesion, location, chronicity), individual (e.g., motivation, personality characteristics, role expectancies), and environmental (e.g., social supports, job characteristics) variables. Such studies may not be practical within a single center, but they might be possible through multicenter collaborative research. Costa (1983) suggests that collaborative research not only has the advantage of increasing sample sizes, but also allows for simultaneous rather than sequential replication. He comments that "the power of neuropsychological researchers, as a group, to resolve rapidly certain basic questions that would take individuals, serially communicating, years to resolve, would increase. More time would become available for truly creative and innovative research" (p. 9).

Multivariate and Multidimensional Approaches

As investigators begin to use broader and more diverse patient populations in their research, more "meaningful multivariate approaches to prediction and to the identification of relevant neuropsychological constructs" (Costa, 1983, p. 9) will emerge. Even a cursory review of the research over the last decade reveals a dramatic increase in the use of multivariate procedures in neuropsychological research. Given the complexity of the relationship between neuropsychological functioning and various aspects of everyday living, use of multivariate approaches will undoubtedly be an integral part of future research in this area. However, the utility of these powerful statistical techniques will ultimately lie in the creative ability of researchers to generate clinically useful information and knowledge from them.

The studies by Newby, Hallenbeck, and Embertson-Whitely (1983) and Morris, Blashfield, and Satz (1981) serve as excellent examples of innovative applications of multivariate statistics. Newby and colleagues (1983) employed a confirmatory factor analysis method to evaluate the adequacy of four theoretical factor models for a modified version of the Halstead–Reitan Battery among a sample of 497 adult neuropsychiatric patients. Based on their analyses, the authors were able to select from among the four competing theoretical models a "structurally simple conceptual scheme of receptive, memory, cognitive, and expressive neuropsychological processes with parallel verbal and nonverbal manifestations" (p. 129) that best fit the assessment battery. Furthermore, Newby and colleagues (1983) found that they could improve upon this model by reconceptualizing some tests (e.g., Speech Sounds Perception, Trail Making) as multifactorial and by including a mental activity/arousal factor. They also note that some test measures rationally thought to load on one factor were actually more closely related to a different factor (e.g., the Location component of the Tactual Performance test was found to be more closely associated with nonverbal cognitive processes than the presumed nonverbal short-term memory factor).

While the findings of Newby and colleagues (1983) are of interest in their own right, their use of a confirmatory factor analysis also illustrates a new research methodology that may be of great potential value in developing and testing conceptual models of everyday functioning. For example, the heuristic and rationally derived guide for making inferences about various aspects of everyday behavior that we presented in Table 18.3 could be subjected to confirmatory factor analysis to determine its adequacy. Depending on its results, modifications could be made in our model and/or the tests used to measure the underlying factors until a structurally valid scheme of everyday functioning parameters was derived.

Of equal interest is the paper by Morris and colleagues (1981), which reviews cluster analytic procedures and demonstrates their potential utility by applying them to Satz and colleagues' (1978) data from the Florida Longitudinal Project. The authors describe cluster analysis as "a quasi-statistical technique which can be used on multivariate data in order to create . . . classifications" (p. 79), such as subtypes of learning disability. Whereas discriminant function analysis classifies or identifies a subject as belonging to an existing set of categories, cluster analysis generates new categories based on the statistical concept of similarity. Clusters can be formed on the basis of profile similarity or on the basis of distance measures when elevation across variables is of more interest than pattern similarity. Other procedures (e.g., Q-type factor analysis) assign subjects to clusters based on their factor loadings. Morris et al. (1981, p. 84) observe that cluster analytic techniques have been particularly useful in studies of childhood learning problems where "an objective classification of children with learning problems would help promote better prediction, remediation, and theoretical understanding of learning disabilities" (also see the section in this chapter on Academic Performance and Remediation under Empirical Relationships Between Neuropsychological Measures and Tasks of Everyday Living).

Cluster analytic techniques offer an empirical means for identifying subgroups of individuals who appear to perform similarly on some aspect of everyday behavior (e.g., reading performance) by grouping them on the basis of their neuropsychological functioning. As such, these procedures will be helpful in identifying various constellations of abilities necessary to perform a given everyday task. Unfortunately, the most commonly used methods of cluster analysis, the hierarchical methods, require a trade-off between profile pattern and elevation. Inasmuch as level and pattern are both important dimensions of neuropsychological functioning and are apt to be related to successful performance on many daily tasks and activities, research strategies that use both of these dimensions should result in more precise predictions.

A number of multidimensional strategies have been developed and could potentially be applied to everyday functioning research. Cattell has developed a measure of association called the *coefficient of profile pattern similarity* (Cattell, Eber, & Tatsuoka, 1970), which reflects not only differences in the shape of two profiles, but also the magnitude of the differences (level) between the individual elements of the profiles. The coefficient can be computed between two individuals, between two groups, or between an individual and a modal group profile. As such, the coefficient of profile pattern similarity might be used as a method for clustering individuals on the basis of both level and pattern similarity. Similarly, this procedure could be used to determine whether a given individual's neuropsychological test results more closely fit the modal profiles of individuals succeeding or failing a specific everyday activity. Also, the technique offers a means to test whether groups are significantly similar to one another if they cannot be shown to be significantly different (e.g., Chelune, Heaton, Lehman, & Robinson, 1979).

While a combined index of level and pattern of performance may be useful for certain research purposes, there are also apt to be purposes for which elevation, scatter, and profile shape should be independently treated as separate performance vectors in multidimensional space, each contributing unique information (Skinner, 1978; Skinner & Jackson, 1978). There have been a number of attempts to evaluate neuropsychological pattern differences between various groups independent of initial level differences, using a procedure called *deficit pattern analysis* (e.g., Chelune et al., 1979; Davis, DeWolf, & Gustafson, 1972; Watson, 1971). However, there have been only a few attempts to compare the relative contributions of more than one dimension at a time. Using a discriminant function procedure, Chelune and colleagues (1979) computed Mahalanobis distances for pattern and level scores to evaluate their relative contributions in the discrimination of schizophrenic and brain-damaged patients. In a related study, Lehman, Chelune, and Heaton (1979) evaluated the unique contributions of level of performance and variability (scatter) in distinguishing normal, schizophrenic, and acute and chronic brain-damaged patients. Given the complexities of attempting to predict everyday functioning, researchers might do well to examine the potential benefits of multidimensional-multivariate clustering approaches. Skinner and Jackson (1978) offer an interesting application of this approach with respect to classifying MMPI profiles.

Ecological Considerations

Just as neuropsychological research during Rourke's (1982) static phase helped dispel the myth that brain damage could be treated as a unitary construct, so also will research during the dynamic phase have to reconceptualize environmental tasks and activities as complex, multidimensional events imbedded in the immediate environmental and social context of the individual. We have previously noted the importance of such moderating variables as expectations, motivation, psychiatric factors, and environmental conditions upon an individual's functional abilities. Specific environmental activities can also be conceptualized as having contextual demands as well as skill requirements. To carry out particular tasks and activities the patient must be able to mesh his or her individual capabilities with the demands of the situation or face possible failure. In some circumstances, rehabilitative efforts may be able to provide the person with the needed skills to meet environmental demands. However, due to the nature of neurologic impairment, there are limits to such efforts. In these cases, it may be more feasible to alter the environmental demands (e.g., provide additional supervision in job environments, equip automobiles with hand controls for paraplegics, etc.). To make inferences and recommendations about patients' daily living skills, neuropsychologists need a greater knowledge of their new criterion—the environment. Research investigations that delineate the relationship between neuropsychological functioning and the multidimensional structure of environmental activities will enable clinical neuropsychologists to make more specific inferences about an individual's ability to carry out these activities.

Toward Interactional Methods

We are in agreement with the view posited by Bem and Funder (1978, p. 485) that "much of the psychologically interesting variance in behavior will be found in the interaction between the person and the situation," and that there is a "need for a common language of description for both persons and situations." Indeed, virtually all inferences about everyday functioning represent hypotheses about person–situation interactions. However, while neuropsychology has developed an extensive lexicon for describing the neuropsychological characteristics of the individual, little has been done to develop a parallel set of characteristics for describing activities of daily living, save perhaps the recent work in childhood learning disabilities. The methodology proposed by Bem and Funder (1978) appears to hold great promise for establishing an empirical base for making inferences about everyday behaviors.

Loosely translated into a neuropsychological perspective, Bem and Funder's (1978) proposal suggests that everyday situations and activities be characterized as sets of template–behavior pairs. Each template represents a neuropsychological/personality description of an idealized individual who is expected to behave in a specified way in a given setting. "The probability that a particular person will behave in a particular way in a particular situation is then postulated to be a monotonically increasing function of the match or similarity between his or her characteristics and the template associated with the corresponding behavior" (p. 486). Templates can be constructed post hoc from data, as has been done with learning disabilities (e.g., Morris et al., 1981), or they can be derived from theory as in the case of the Millon Clinical Multiaxial Inventory (Millon, 1982). In either case, the template-matching procedure results in probability statements or inferences based on an ipsative rather than normative measurement of similarity.

Bem and Funder's (1978) template-matching procedure is especially intriguing for everyday functioning research because it closely mirrors the actual clinical process of making inferences about a patient's everyday behavior. It allows one to consider both the complexities of the individual and the environment along the same dimensions, while at the same time retaining the focus on the individual. Since predictions are based on probability statements, inferences can be made on a graduated scale depending on the degree of match, avoiding the trap of all-or-none statements. Overall, the procedure appears potentially well suited for the kinds of research that will be necessary for neuropsychologists to meet the challenges of the emerging dynamic phase.

SUMMARY AND CONCLUSIONS

Neuropsychological model building has evolved through a number of phases and is currently entering a stage that will require clinical neuropsychologists to look at brain–behavior relationships in a new way. Clinicans are increasingly being asked to make statements regarding patients' potential success in everyday tasks and activities. Such requests require a shift in emphasis; the brain is no longer the primary criterion, but rather environmental activities. The change in focus requires us to examine our assessment procedures in a new light. While there is an extensive literature documenting the validity of neuropsychological tests for detecting the presence and localization of cerebral lesions, research considering aspects of everyday functioning has only recently begun to appear in the literature with much frequency.

From our review of the growing research examining the empirical relationship between neuropsychological measures and tasks of everyday living, the future appears to hold not only great promise, but also many challenges. To meet these challenges adequately, we have proposed that clinical assessment must broaden its data base and give greater attention to the identification of patients' residual strengths and the conditions under which these strengths can be maximized. In this respect, neuropsychologists must become assessors of environments as well as of individuals. Further research directed at exploring the relationship of the individual with his or her environment is needed to provide the empirical data base necessary for clinicians to make valid inferences regarding everyday behavior.

REFERENCES

Aaron, P. G. (1981). Diagnosis and remediation of learning disabilities in children: A neuropsychological key approach. In G. W. Hynd & J. E. Obrzut (Eds.), *Neuropsychological assessment and the school-age child*. New York: Grune & Stratton.

Abbott, M., & Gregson, R. (1981). Cognitive dysfunction in the prediction of relapse in alcoholics. *Journal of Studies on Alcohol, 42,* 230–243.

Adams, K. M., Ausman, J. I., & Diaz, F. (1983). *Medical, neuropsychological, and quality of life correlates of cerebral vascular disease.* Paper presented at the 91st annual meeting of the American Psychological Association, Anaheim, CA.

Alcorn, C., & Nicholson, C. (1975). A vocational battery for the educable mentally retarded and low literate. *Education and Training of the Mentally Retarded, 10,* 78–83.

Applebaum, A. S., & Tuma, J. M. (1982). The relationship of the WISC-R to academic achievement in a clinical population. *Journal of Clinical Psychology, 38,* 401–405.

Barth, J. T., & Boll, T. J. (1981). Rehabilitation and treatment of central nervous system dysfunction: A behavioral medicine perspective. In C. Prokop & L. Bradley (Eds.), *Medical psychology: A new perspective.* New York: Academic Press.

Bem, D. J., & Funder, D. C. (1978) Predicting more of the people more of the time: Assessing the personality of situations. *Psychological Review, 85,* 485–501.

Bolger, J., & DuBoise, L. (1979). *Vocational planning.* Paper presented at the Third Annual Post-Graduate Course on the Rehabilitation of the Traumatic Brain-injured Adult, Williamsburg, VA.

Bond, M. (1976). Assessment of the psychological outcome of severe head injury. *Acta Neurochirurgica, 34,* 57–70.

Caplan, B. (1982). Neuropsychology in rehabilitation: Its role in evaluation and intervention. *Archives of Physical Medicine and Rehabilitation, 63,* 362–366.

Cattell, R. B., Eber, H. W., & Tatsuoka, M. M. (1970). *Handbook for the Sixteen Personality Factor Questionnaire.* Champaign, IL: Institute for Personality and Ability Testing.

Chelune, G. J. (1983a, August). *Neuropsychological assessment: Beyond deficit testing.* Paper presented at the 91st annual convention of the American Psychological Association, Anaheim, CA.

Chelune, G. J. (1983b, August). *Neuropsychological assessment: Implications for everyday functioning.* Workshop presented for the Division 12 Postdoctoral Institutes at the 91st annual meeting of the American Psychological Association, Anaheim, CA.

Chelune, G. J., Ferguson, W., & Moehle, K. (1985). The role of standard cognitive and personality tests in neuropsychological assessment. In T. Incagnoli, G. Goldstein, & C. Golden (Eds.), *Standardized Test Batteries in Neuropsychological Assessment.* New York: Plenum Press.

Chelune, G. J., Heaton, R. K., & Lehman, R. A. (1986). Relation of neuropsychological and personality test results to patients' complaints of disability. In G. Goldstein and R. Tarter (Eds.), *Advances in Clinical Neuropsychology* (Vol. 3). New York: Plenum Press.

Chelune, G. J., Heaton, R. K., Lehman, R. A., & Robinson, A. (1979). Level versus pattern of neuropsychological performance among schizophrenic and diffusely brain-damaged patients. *Journal of Consulting and Clinical Psychology, 47,* 155–163.

Chelune, G. J., & Parker, J. B. (1981). Neuropsychological deficits associated with chronic alcohol abuse. *Clinical Psychology Review, 1,* 181–195.

Cleeland, C. S. (1976). Interferences in clinical psychology and clinical neuropsychology: Similarities and differences. *Clinical Psychologist, 29,* 8–10.

Costa, L. (1983). Clinical neuropsychology: A discipline in evolution. *Journal of Clinical Neuropsychology, 5,* 1–11.

Davis, W. E., DeWolf, A. S., & Gustafson, R. C. (1972). Intellectual deficit in process and reactive schizophrenia and brain injury. *Journal of Consulting and Clinical Psychology, 38,* 146.

Dennerll, R. D., Rodin, E. A., Gonzalez, S., Schwartz, M. L., & Lin, Y. (1966). Neurological and psychological factors related to employability of persons with epilepsy. *Epilepsia, 7,* 318–329.

Dikmen, S., & Morgan, S. F. (1980). Neuropsychological factors related to employability and occupational status in persons with epilepsy. *Journal of Nervous and Mental Disease, 168,* 236–240.

Diller, L., & Gordon, W. A. (1981a). Interventions for cognitive deficits in brain-injured adults. *Journal of Consulting and Clinical Psychology, 49,* 822–834.

Diller, L., & Gordon, W. A. (1981b). Rehabilitation and clinical neuropsychology. In S. B. Filskov & T. J. Boll (Eds.), *Handbook of clinical neuropsychology.* New York: Wiley.

Diller, L., & Weinberg, J. (1970). Accidents in hemiplegia. *Archives of Physical Medicine and Rehabilitation, 51,* 358–363.

Dodrill, C. B., & Clemmons, D. (1983). Use of neuropsychological tests to identify high school students with epilepsy who later demonstrate inadequate performances in life. *Journal of Consulting and Clinical Psychology, 52,* 520–527.

Edelstein, B. A., & Couture, E. T. (Eds.). (1983). *Behavioral assessment and rehabilitation of the traumatically brain-damaged adult.* New York: Plenum Press.

Field, T., Sink, J., & Cook, C. (1978). The effects of age, I.Q., and disability on the JEVS system. *Vocational Evaluation and Work Adjustment Bulletin, 11,* 14–22.

Flanagan, J. (1982). Measurement of quality of life: Current state of the art. *Archives of Physical Medicine and Rehabilitation, 63,* 56–59.

Gaddes, W. H. (1981). An examination of the validity of neuropsychological knowledge in educational diagnosis and retention. In G. W. Hynd & J. E. Obrzut (Eds.), *Neuropsychological assessment and the school-age child.* New York: Grune & Stratton.

Golden, C. J., & Kuperman, S. K. (1980). Training opportunities in neuropsychology at APA-approved internship settings. *Professional Psychology, 11,* 907–918.

Golden, C. J., Moses, J. A., Ariel, R. N., Wilkening, G. N., McKay, S. E., & MacInnes, W. D. (1982). Analytic techniques in the interpretation of the Luria–Nebraska Neuropsychological Battery. *Journal of Consulting and Clinical Psychology, 50,* 40–48.

Goldstein, G., & Ruthven, L. (1983). *Rehabilitation of the brain-damaged adult.* New York: Plenum Press.

Greenwald, D. F., Harder, D. W., & Fisher, L. (1982). WISC scatter and behavioral competence in high-risk children. *Journal of Clinical Psychology, 38,* 397–400.

Gregson, R. A., & Taylor, G. M. (1977). Prediction of relapse in men alcoholics. *Journal of Studies on Alcohol, 34,* 1749–1760.

Grunau, R. V. E., Purves, S. J., McBurney, A. K., & Low, M. D. (1981). Identifying academic aptitude in adolescent children by psychological testing and EEG spectral analysis. *Neuropsychologia, 19,* 79–86.

Gunnison, J. A. (1982). Remediation strategies based on the roles of simultaneous and successive processing in reading. *Journal of Educational Neuropsychology, 2,* 56–69.

Gunnison, J. A., Kaufman, N. L., & Kaufman, A. S. (1982). Sequential and simultaneous processing applied to remediation. *Academic Therapy, 17,* 297–307.

Hale, R. L., & Foltz, S. G. (1982). Prediction of academic achievement in handicapped adolescents using a modified form of the Luria–Nebraska Pathognomonic scale and WISC-R Full Scale IQ. *Clinical Neuropsychology, 4,* 99–102.

Halstead, W. C., & Rennick, P. (1962). Toward a behavioral scale for biological age. *Social and psychological aspects of aging.* New York: Columbia University Press.

Hartlage, L. C., & Reynolds, C. R. (1981). Neuropsychological assessment and the individualization of instruction. In G. W. Hynd & J. E. Obrzut (Eds.), *Neuropsychological assessment and the school-age child.* New York: Grune & Stratton.

Heaton, R. K., Chelune, G. J., & Lehman, R. A. (1978). Using neuropsychological and personality tests to assess likelihood of patient employment. *Journal of Nervous and Mental Disease, 166,* 408–416.

Heaton, R. K., Grant, I., Anthony, W. Z., & Lehman, R. A. (1981). A comparison of clinical and automated interpretation of the Halstead–Reitan Battery. *Journal of Clinical Neuropsychology, 3,* 121–141.

Heaton, R. K., & Pendleton, M. G. (1981). Use of neuropsychological tests to predict adult patients' everyday functioning. *Journal of Consulting and Clinical Psychology, 49,* 807–821.

Heaton, S. R., & Heaton, R. K. (1981). Testing the impaired patient. In S. B. Filskov & T. J. Boll (Eds.), *Handbook of clinical neuropsychology.* New York: Wiley.

Horton, A. M. N., Wedding, D., & Phay, A. (1981). Current perspectives on assessment and therapy for the brain-damaged individual. In C. Golden, S. Alcaparras, F. Strider, & B. Graber (Eds.), *Applied techniques in behavioral medicine* (pp. 59–86). New York: Grune & Stratton.

Hynd, G. W., & Obrzut, J. E. (Eds.). (1981). *Neuropsychological assessment and the school-age child.* New York: Grune & Stratton.

Jellinick, H., Tarkelson, R., & Harvey, R. (1982). Functional abilities and distress levels in brain-damaged patients at long-term follow-up. *Archives of Physical Medicine and Rehabilitation, 63,* 160–162.

Kaufert, J. M. (1983). Functional ability indices: Measurement problems in assessing their validity. *Archives of Physical Medicine and Rehabilitation, 64,* 260–267.

Kaufman, A. S., & Kaufman, N. (1983). *Kaufman Assessment Battery for Children: Interpretative manual.* Circle Pines, MN: American Guidance Service.

Keenan, J. S., & Brassell, E. G. (1974). A study of factors related to prognosis for individual aphasic patients. *Journal of Speech and Hearing Disorders, 39,* 257–269.

Kirk, U. (Ed.). (1981). *Neuropsychology of language, reading, and spelling.* New York: Academic Press.

Klesges, R. C. (1983). The relationship between neuropsychological, cognitive, and behavioral assessments of brain functioning in children. *Clinical Neuropsychology, 5,* 28–32.

Knights, R. M., & Bakker, D. J. (Eds.). (1976). *Neuropsychology of learning disorders: Theoretical approaches.* Baltimore, MD: University Park Press.

Lehman, R. A., Chelune, G. J., & Heaton, R. K. (1979). Level and variability of performance on neuropsychological tests. *Journal of Clinical Psychology, 35,* 358–363.

Levin, H. S., Grossman, R. G., Rose, J. E., & Teasdale, G. (1979). Long-term neuropsychological outcome of closed head injury. *Journal of Neurosurgery, 50,* 412–422.

Lezak, M. D. (1983). *Neuropsychological assessment* (2nd ed.). New York: Oxford University Press.

Lubin, B., & Sokoloff, R. M. (1983). An update of the survey of training and internship programs in clinical neuropsychology. *Journal of Clinical Psychology, 39,* 149–152.

Luria, A. R. (1966). *Higher cortical functions in man.* New York: Basic Books.

Matarazzo, J. D. (1972). *Wechsler's measurement and appraisal of adult intelligence* (5th ed.). Baltimore, MD: Williams & Wilkins.

McLeod, J., & Greenough, P. (1980). The importance of sequencing as an aspect of short-term memory in good and poor spellers. *Journal of Learning Disabilities, 13,* 27–33.

McSweeny, A. J., Grant, I., Adams, K. M., & Prigatano, G. (1983, February). *The relationship of neuropsychological status, quality of "everyday" life functioning and healthy and chronically ill persons.* Paper presented at the 11th annual meeting of the International Neuropsychological Society, Mexico City.

McSweeny, A. J., Grant, I., Heaton, R. K., Adams, K. M., & Timms, R. M. (1982). Life quality of patients with chronic obstructive pulmonary disease. *Archives of Internal Medicine, 42,* 473–478.

Meehl, P. E. (1973). What can the clinician do well? In P. E. Meehl, *Psychodiagnosis: Selected papers.* Minneapolis: University of Minnesota Press.

Miller, E. (1980). Psychological intervention in the management and rehabilitation of neuropsychological impairments. *Behavior Research and Therapy, 18,* 527–535.

Millon, T. (1982). *Millon Clinical Multiaxial Inventory Manual* (2nd ed.). Minneapolis, MN: National Computer Services.

Morris, J., Ryan, J. J., & Peterson, R. A. (1982). *Neuropsychological predictors of vocational behavior.* Paper presented at the 90th annual meeting of the American Psychological Association, Washington, DC.

Morris, R., Blashfield, R., & Satz, P. (1981). Neuropsychology and cluster analysis: Potentials and problems. *Journal of Clinical Neuropsychology, 3,* 79–99.

Morris, R., & Fletcher, J. (1984, February). *Multivariate methods for neuropsychology: Techniques for classification, identification, and prediction research.* Workshop presented at the 12th annual meeting of the International Neuropsychological Society, Houston, TX.

Morrison, D., & Pothier, P. (1972). Two different remedial motor training programs and the development of mentally retarded preschoolers. *American Journal of Mental Deficiency, 77,* 251–258.

Needleman, H. L. (1983). Lead at low dose and the behavior of children. *Acta Psychiatrica Scandinavia, 67* (Suppl. 303), 26–37.

Newby, R. F., Hallenbeck, C. E., & Embertson-Whitely, S. (1983). Confirmatory factor analysis of four general neuropsychological models of a modified Halstead–Reitan Battery. *Journal of Clinical Neuropsychology, 5,* 115–133.

Newnan, O. S., Heaton, R. K., & Lehman, R. A. (1978). Neuropsychological and MMPI correlates of patients' future employment characteristics. *Perceptual and Motor Skills, 46,* 635–642.

Nolan, D. R., Hammeke, T. A., & Barkley, R. A. (1983). A comparison of the patterns of neuropsychological performance in two groups of learning disabled children. *Journal of Clinical Child Psychology, 12,* 22–27.

Noonberg, A. R., & Page, H. A. (1982). Graduate neuropsychology training: A later look. *Professional Psychology, 13,* 252–257.

Oakland, T. (1983). Joint use of adaptive behavior and IQ to predict achievement. *Journal of Consulting and Clinical Psychology, 51,* 298–301.

Oddy, M., & Humphrey, M. (1980). Social recovery during the year following head injury. *Journal of Neurology, Neurosurgery and Psychiatry, 43,* 798–802.

O'Leary, M. R., Donovan, D. M., Chaney, E. F., & Walker, R. D. (1979). Cognitive impairment and treatment outcome with alcoholics: Preliminary findings. *Journal of Clinical Psychiatry, 40,* 397–398.

Parsons, O. A. (1970). Clinical neuropsychology. In C. Spielberger (Ed.), *Current topics in clinical and community psychology* (Vol. 2). New York: Academic Press.

Peter, B. M., & Spreen, O. (1979). Behavior rating and personality adjustment scales of neurologically and learning handicapped children during adolescence and early adulthood: Results of a follow-up study. *Journal of Clinical Neuropsychology, 1,* 75–91.

Petrauskas, R., & Rourke, B. P. (1979). Identification of subgroups of retarded readers: A neuropsychological multivariate approach. *Journal of Clinical Neuropsychology, 1,* 17–37.

Pribram, K. H. (1971). *Languages of the brain.* Englewood Cliffs, NJ: Prentice-Hall.

Reitan, R. M., & Boll, T. J. (1973). Neuropsychological correlates of minimal brain dysfunction. *Annals of the New York Academy of Sciences, 205,* 65–88.

Rosenthal, M., Griffith, E. R., Bond, M. R., & Miller, J. D. (Eds.). (1983). *Rehabilitation of the head-injured adult.* Philadelphia: F. A. Davis.

Ross, E. D. (1983). Right-hemisphere lesions in disorders of affective language. In A. Kertesz (Ed.), *Localization in neuropsychology.* New York: Academic Press.

Rourke, B. P. (1982). Central processing deficiencies in children: Toward a developmental neuropsychological model. *Journal of Clinical Neuropsychology, 4,* 1–18.

Rourke, B. P., Bakker, D. J., Fisk, J. L., & Strang, J. D. (1983). *Child neuropsychology.* New York: Guilford Press.

Rourke, B. P., & Finlayson, M. A. (1978). Neuropsychological significance of variations in patterns of academic performance: Verbal and visual-spatial abilities. *Journal of Abnormal Child Psychology, 6,* 121–133.

Rourke, B. P., & Orr, R. R. (1977). Prediction of the reading and spelling performances of normal and retarded readers: A four-year follow-up. *Journal of Abnormal Child Psychology, 5,* 9–20.

Rutter, M. (1981). Psychological sequelae of brain damage in children. *The American Journal of Psychiatry, 138,* 1533–1544.

Rutter, M. (Ed.). (1983). *Developmental neuropsychiatry.* New York: Guilford Press.

Samuels, S. J., & Anderson, R. H. (1973). Visual recognition memory, paired associate learning, and reading achievement. *Journal of Education, 65,* 160–167.

Satz, P., Taylor, H. G., Friel, J., & Fletcher, J. M. (1978). Some developmental and predictive precursors of reading disabilities: A six-year follow-up. In A. L. Benton and D. Pearl (Eds.), *Dyslexia: An appraisal of current knowledge.* New York: Oxford University Press.

Schwartz, M. L., Dennerll, R. D., & Lin, Y. (1968). Neuropsychological and psychosocial predictors of employability in epilepsy. *Journal of Clinical Psychology, 24,* 174–177.

Sivak, M., Olson, P. L., Kewman, D. G., Won, H., & Henson, D. L. (1981). Driving and perceptual/cognitive skills: Behavioral consequences of brain damage. *Archives of Physical Medicine and Rehabilitation, 62,* 476–483.

Skinner, H. A. (1978). Differentiating the contribution of elevation, scatter and shape in profile similarity. *Educational and Psychological Measurement, 38,* 297–308.

Skinner, H. A., & Jackson, D. N. (1978). A model of psychopathology based on an integration of MMPI actuarial systems. *Journal of Consulting and Clinical Psychology, 46,* 231–238.

Sperry, R. W. (1968). Hemisphere deconnection and unity in conscious awareness. *American Psychologist, 23,* 723–733.

Strag, G. A. (1972). Comparative behavioral ratings of parents with severe mentally retarded, special learning disability, and normal children. *Journal of Learning Disabilities, 5,* 52–56.

Strang, J. D., & Rourke, B. P. (1983). Concept formation/nonverbal reasoning abilities of children who exhibit specific academic problems with arithmetic. *Journal of Clinical Child Psychology, 12,* 33–39.

Sweeney, J. E., & Rourke, B. P. (1978). Neuropsychological significance of phonetically accurate and phonetically inaccurate spelling errors in younger and older retarded spellers. *Brain and Language, 6,* 212–225.

Townsend, J. W., Prien, E. P., & Johnson, J. T. (1974). The use of the position analysis questionnaire in selecting correlates of job performance among mentally retarded workers. *Journal of Vocational Behavior, 4,* 181–192.

Trexler, L. E. (Ed.). (1982). *Cognitive rehabilitation.* New York: Plenum Press.

Walker, R. D., Donovan, D. M., Kivlaham, D. R., & O'Leary, M. R. (1983). Length of stay, neuropsychological performance and aftercare: Influences on alcohol treatment outcome. *Journal of Consulting and Clinical Psychology, 51,* 900–911.

Watson, C. G. (1971). Separation of brain-damaged from schizophrenic patients by Halstead–Reitan pattern analysis: An unsuccessful replication. *Psychological Reports, 29,* 1343–1346.

Weinberg, J., Piasetsky, E., Diller, L., & Gordon, W. (1982). Treating perceptual organization deficits in nonneglecting RBD stroke patients. *Journal of Clinical Neuropsychology, 4,* 59–75.

Williams, J., & Wedding, D. (1982, March). *Training options in behavioral medicine and clinical neuropsychology.* Paper presented at the 28th annual meeting of the Southeastern Psychological Association, New Orleans.

Wright, B. A., & Fletcher, B. L. (1982). Uncovering hidden resources: A challenge in assessment. *Professional Psychology, 13,* 229–235.

Young, G. C., Collins, D., & Hren, M. (1983). Effect of pairing scanning training with block design training in the remediating of perceptual problems in left hemiplegics. *Journal of Clinical Neuropsychology, 5,* 201–212.

19

Forensic Issues in Neuropsychology

Erin D. Bigler

Forensic neuropsychology is an emerging subspecialty of clinical neuropsychology (Mack, 1980; McMahon, 1983; McMahon & Satz, 1981). In large part, this is attributable to the increased use of psychological testimony in legal proceedings (Blau, 1984; Shapiro, 1984; Wright, Bahn, & Rieber, 1980); but it is also related to the special role that neuropsychological testimony provides in the legal decision process regarding the extent and outcome of acquired neurologic deficits. This latter aspect is particularly relevent to clinical neuropsychology, as it is only through neuropsychological techniques that objective measures of behavioral deficits subsequent to cerebral injury can be documented.

Whether forensic neuropsychology is a specialty area or not, the practicing neuropsychologist will probably find him- or herself at some time testifying about the status of a patient. To meet this need, this chapter will overview some of the main topic areas that the neuropsychologist will need to address in the forensic evaluation of a patient, as well as preparation for testimony. Aspects of preparation will be reviewed, followed by a section reviewing the different areas of neuropsychological testimony. Case studies will be presented demonstrating the role of neuropsychological evaluation in forensic cases.

CASE PRESENTATION

The Issue of Professional Competency

Practicing psychologists are governed by state statutes that regulate the practice of psychology, as well as by the guidelines established by the American Psychological Association (1981). While the neuropsychologist must practice under the laws and statutes that govern the general licensure for the practice of psychology, the definition as to what constitutes appropriate training for one to call him- or herself a neuropsychologist is still evolving (Meier, 1981). There are current trends that are providing better definitions of competency in neuropsychology, and it is recommended that anyone who holds him- or herself out as an expert in neuropsychology should meet the minimum standards as specified by the guidelines (1984) of the International Neuropsychological Society (INS). Board certification efforts are also underway that will assist in further establishing one's competency in neuropsychology.

An objection that is frequently raised to a psychologist's competency to testify is that a psychologist is not a physician and hence can neither be an expert on nor testify concerning physical or organic illness. Vis à vis the neuropsychologist, a major flaw in this argument is that because mental functioning is dependent on physical functioning, the two are inseparable. Likewise, for the neuropsychologist who meets INS standards there will have been extensive training in the basic as well as clinical neurosciences. Also, it has been determined in federal court* (Federal Rules of Civil Procedure—Rule 35) that the psychologist is to be treated as a physician for the purposes of conducting mental examinations. Additionally, this federal rule permits licensed psychologists to perform "mental examinations"; and "since psychology is a branch of science concerned with mental operations, psychological testing is within the scope of Rule 35." Further definitional statements concerning the equality of psychologists and physicians performing mental examinations are provided by Blau (1984), DeLeon, VandenBos, and Kraut (1984), and Shapiro (1984).

Preparation

One needs to be *very* prepared to defend any aspect of one's testimony. Thus, the neuropsychologist should not make a statement unless that statement can be fully supported by the data obtained. One should be well acquainted with validity and reliability studies of all of the testing instruments used. The opposing side will usually have their own expert witnesses as consultants and, thus, they will be prepared to ask specific questions about the validity and limitations of various instruments and measures as well as about diagnostic factors. Accordingly, one should always be prepared to discuss the particular pitfalls of an examination or test procedure, although it is not recommended that this be done at the outset because it is the opposing side's responsibility and duty to discredit or devalue the testimony. To assist in such a preparation, it is a most helpful intellectual exercise to try to provide specific arguments against your own interpretation and to build a defense around these argu-

---

*Rule 35. *Massey* v. *Manitowoc Company, Inc.* v. *W. J. Sales Co., Inc.*, No. 82-2970, U.S. District Court for the Eastern District of Pennsylvania, December 6, 1983.

ments. (See Beresford, 1975; Brodsky & Robe, 1973; and Horsley & Carlova, 1983, for further review.)

It is important that the psychologist never overstate the data. If a neuropsychological deficit is truly present, it should be readily evident in the data. If very subtle or inconsistent deficits are present, it may be very difficult to give much support for such an interpretation. Such speculative interpretations should be avoided. Likewise, if one becomes overinclusive, it becomes easy for the opposing side to demonstrate flaws in the assessment. (The patient who has a mild hemiparesis, but who has good functional control of the extremity, represents such an example. It needs to be pointed out that the patient does have a paralysis and limitation in terms of some aspects of dexterity, but if one attempts to overstate the motor limitations and the implications of the underlying brain damage, then it may be very easy to refute this.) Clear and comprehensive documentation of all test results and behavioral observations is essential. Careful notetaking throughout the examination, with particular emphasis on behavioral observations during the various facets of testing, is always most helpful. Also, anecdotal information that can be given a lay interpretation is usually one of the best ways to demonstrate a particular neurologic deficit to a jury or judge. (For example, a patient with acquired alexia and agraphia as a result of cerebral trauma would not be able to read labels in a grocery store or to write a check). If a forensic case is being followed over any length of time, then the documentation becomes even more important. This is usually the situation, since most litigation is delayed 2 to 3 years following an injury, and in cases in which there is a prolonged or protracted recovery period or in which the patient is a child, it is often 5 or more years before the case is tried. In such cases, it is recommended that longitudinal follow-up testing be done every 6 to 12 months for full documentation and that a final evaluation be done just prior to testimony so that information presented under oath will be the most up-to-date information available. However, the psychologist should be cautious about presenting data from longitudinal testing. The opposing side may use the argument that if the patient is showing such steady improvement, that he or she is obviously "getting better" and may be ultimately on way to "full recovery." This argument is best handled by comparing the patient's improvement with premorbid levels of function. Likewise, if the patient does not recover premorbid ability levels, there will typically be a plateau or asymptote reached that can be clearly demonstrated by plotting out recovery of function over time based on neuropsychological test results.

The neuropsychologist can expect to defend the validity of neuropsychological testing in comparison to such measures as the standard physical neurologic exam, computerized tomography (CT), and electroencephalography (EEG), measures the opposing attorneys may argue are more "objective" and "organically sensitive." Thus, the neuropsychologist should always be prepared to respond to this question, and it is always responded to best by reviewing the research that compares these various procedures in the documentation of underlying cerebral dysfunction (see Strub & Black, 1981). An excellent article to review in this context is a recent study by Casson, Siegel, Sham, Campbell, Tarlau, and DiDomenico (1984), which compared neuropsychological testing with electroencephalography, computerized tomography, and the routine physical neurological exam in boxers. Neuropsychological testing was found to be *the* most sensitive measure of cerebral dysfunction. This is only reasonable if one assumes that the intellect is the highest expression of brain function and that neuropsychological studies are designed to detect subtle changes in cognitive functioning. Thus, even though a structural lesion may not be evident on EEG or the CT scan, a patient may still have underlying cerebral dysfunction that is only detected by neuropsychological testing. When there is good agreement between CT, EEG, and neuropsychological findings, there are obviously no difficulties in establishing the nature of the deficit.

Another frequent problem is the possible masking effects of medication. Many patients with posttraumatic or postsurgical conditions will be on medication for purposes of medical management. While some medications (neuroleptics, antidepressants, etc.) may have specific effects on certain tests (Heaton & Crowley, 1981; Tucker, Bigler, & Chelune, 1981), typically the pattern of deficits or the overall impairment is not affected by medication. Nonetheless, if the patient is on medication, it should be carefully noted and the neuropsychologist should be prepared to discuss potential medication effects on neuropsychological performance. Naturally, the neuropsychologist should not conduct detailed neuropsychological studies with a patient who is in the midst of a major medication adjustment or who is noncompliant. If these factors can be ruled out, then the overall impact of medication on the patient's test performance may be minimal, with the deficit pattern demonstrated regardless of medication effects.

Selection of Tests

There is no such thing as a forensic battery of neuropsychological tests. One should select the tests administered based upon the presenting symptoms and the history and nature of the injury or disorder. For example, with a patient who has a history of closed head injury with loss of consciousness and current complaints of memory loss, the focus should be on documenting the nature and degree of the possible memory disorder. The psychologist should also investigate the possibility of more diffuse and generalized cerebral dysfunction that may accompany closed head injury. Because of the need to answer questions concerning reliability and validity of the tests administered, one should avoid unstandardized tests or unproven tests or any tests that are controversial in nature, as these will evoke the question as to why they were used and will detract from the testimony given. Thus, the tests selected should be well standardized, researched, and documented in the neuropsychological literature.

Presentation of Testimony

If testimony is given, the neuropsychologist will be presenting technical information to a lay jury. It is always important to provide a general discussion of brain function as an opening statement. This should be given a very rudimentary and fundamental lecture format, such as that used in an introductory psychology course. It should include a brief discussion of right versus left hemispheric functioning; general brain functioning; frontal-temporal-limbic systems in control of motivation, emotion, and learning; frontal-temporal-parietal systems in language, and so forth. It is usually most helpful if much of the information can be presented visually. As will be seen in the case studies that follow, the impact of viewing the extent of structural damage in a patient, as well as the visual depiction of the patient's deficits (as in Case 1), can be much more readily appreciated than a verbal presentation alone. Also, videotaped parts of the neuropsychological examination can be played back in front of the jury. This can be extremely helpful in demonstrating particular deficits that may be present in the patient.

Deposition Versus Court Testimony

In many cases a deposition will be obtained from the neuropsychologist prior to actual court testimony. The deposition is undertaken as a fact-finding mission wherein the attorney may ask any and all questions and review whatever information is necessary. During court testimony, less information is usually presented and the questions will be more specific. In addition, in court the judge has the power to overrule, and some testimony may not be permissible. It should be noted, however, that whatever information is given in a deposition can be used in the courtroom, verbatim, if it is permissible evidence. Thus, if testimony is given in a deposition, then what is said in a subsequent court testimony should be fully congruent with what was previously stated in that deposition. Perjury applies to both the deposition and live testimony, and the law does not discriminate between the two.

FORENSIC ISSUES AND CASE STUDIES

For the practicing neuropsychologist, expert testimony mainly involves three areas:

1. *Liability* cases, in which determination of the nature, type, and cause of neurologic damages and implications for future treatment and care are needed.

2. *Disability* determination, in which the degree and permanency of neurologic deficits are the focus of evaluation and testimony.
3. *Competency* determination, in which neurologic injury or disease has affected an individual's mental abilities.

Because of the close ties between liability and disability determination, they will be discussed together; competency cases will be discussed separately. Case studies will be utilized to demonstrate these various points.

Liability and Disability

Liability and disability cases presuppose that a patient has sustained some type of injury, usually as a result of trauma or malpractice. As a result of the injury, the patient may have some type of permanent disability, which in turn may permanently affect his or her cognitive, language, motor, or perceptual functioning. Since so many of the forensic cases involving liability and disability involve some form of trauma, salient considerations in traumatic and malpractice cases will be briefly reviewed.

Trauma

The pathophysiology and neuropsychological outcome of trauma have been previously discussed in Chapter 13. Also, the publications of Bigler (1984) and Levin, Benton, and Grossman (1982) thoroughly review the recent work in this area. Although accurate national records are not specifically available, it is estimated that the incidence of significant head trauma is in the range of two to three hundred individuals per 100,000 population (Jennett & Teasdale, 1981; Levin et al., 1982). The morbidity estimates are even more difficult to verify, but Jennett and Teasdale (1981) and Levin and colleagues (1982) review studies indicating permanent neurologic sequelae in 17% to 65% of all head trauma cases. Peterson (1975) reviews other alarming statistics that suggest that on any given day about 1% of the working force is disabled because of head injury.

From the forensic standpoint, there are two major issues that need to be addressed: premorbid level of functioning and outcome. With respect to premorbid level of functioning, in most cases there was no testing prior to the injury for direct comparison. The exception may be with childhood disorders in which achievement tests had been given or intellectual assessments had been obtained by the school. If achievement scores are present, an IQ score can be approximated (Sattler, 1974). Several studies (see Reynolds & Gutkin, 1979; Wilson, Rosenbaum, & Brown, 1979) have attempted to provide a prediction formula using demographic and preinjury academic, vocational, and economic data. However, the actual clinical utility of such measures is not necessarily promising (Klesges, Sanchez, & Stanton, 1981). In this domain, it is probably best to use clinical judgment as to a presumed level of premorbid functioning, based on the patient's previous level of educational attainment, whatever standardized achievement scores may be present, the patient's vocational and work history, and social and family histories.

Additionally, by knowing current levels of intellectual functioning in individuals with acquired neurologic disorders and comparing these levels with other measures of general cognitive functioning (e.g., Raven's Coloured Matrices, Category test, Wisconsin Card Sorting test, etc.), a better estimate of the actual degree of intellectual/cognitive impairment may be obtained. Table 19.1 provides a comparison between IQ measures and Category test performance on the Halstead–Reitan Battery, which may be useful for this type of determination. The table permits the comparison of obtained and predicted Halstead Category Test (HCT) and WAIS PIQ results in neurologic patients. The clinical utility of this table is illustrated as follows: Several years ago (see Bigler, 1980), we reported a case of a 35-year-old college professor, the holder of a Ph.D., who sustained severe traumatic head injury in an automobile accident. His cognitive recovery was limited and he was not able to return to teaching because of a persistent memory disorder, despite a Full-Scale WAIS score of 134 (VIQ = 143, PIQ = 117). Although the PIQ score is substantially lower than the VIQ, it is still in the bright normal range. From Table 19.1, given his PIQ score, the predicted HCT score would be approximately 50. However, his obtained HCT score was 84. Thus, this suggests even a greater deficit in new learning than would be predicted by his level of performance on the WAIS. Similarly, the patient's predicted PIQ, based on an obtained error rate of 84 on the HCT, would be approximately 87. This latter score is more in line with the patient's actual deficits and adaptive abilities.

Clinical outcome is a difficult aspect precisely to label or rate because of the multiplicity of factors involved in recovery of function (Levin et al., 1982). The most commonly used outcome rating scale is that by Jennett and Bond (1975)—the Glasgow Outcome Scale. This rating scale indicates recovery on the basis of physical and economic dependence and social integration. The four main levels are as follows: (1) vegetative state: no evidence of psychological meaningful activity; (2) severe disability: conscious but dependent; (3) moderate disability: independent but disabled; and (4) good recovery. It should be obvious that these are very global ratings with no precise determination. However, in the courtroom this can be an adequate reference scale.

Many times there is good congruity between neurodiagnostic studies, such as EEG and CT scanning of the brain, and neuropsychological outcome. In such cases, it is quite easy to demonstrate the level of neurologic deficit, its permanency, and the behavioral sequelae. However, in mild cases of cerebral trauma it is frequently more difficult actually to document the extent of cerebral dysfunction, since EEG and CT scan of the brain may be within normal limits. In the past, there has been a consensus of opinion that many of the cognitive deficits associated with mild head injury were of a "post trau-

TABLE 19.1 HCT-IQ Predictions

Predicted HCT scores from observed PIQ scores in neurologic patients		Predicted PIQ scores from observed HCT scores in neurologic patients	
Observed PIQ	Predicted HCT	Observed HCT	Predicted PIQ
140	27	125	76
130	37	100	83
120	47	75	90
110	58	50	96
100	68	40	99
90	74	30	102
80	89	20	104
70	100	10	107
60	110		

From Cullum, Steinman, and Bigler (1984), with permission.

matic neurosis" type syndrome and did not have an organic basis (Peterson, 1975). However, there is recent incontrovertible evidence that suggests this may not be the case in a majority of patients with mild cerebral injury. These studies (Adams, Graham, Murray, & Scott, 1982; Barth, Macciocchi, Giordani, Rimel, Jane, & Boll, 1983; Gennarelli, Thibault, Adams, Graham, Thompson, & Marcincin, 1982; Noseworthy, Miller, Murray, & Regan, 1981) suggest that mild cerebral injury does result in specific cognitive deficits and that these are organically based. It is always best to follow those patients who have sustained injury for a substantial period of time with repeat testing every 6 to 12 months, since there may be recovery of function for up to 3 or 4 years posttrauma (Bigler, 1984). Thus, final conclusions about clinical outcome may not be derived for years following the actual accident or injury. If the cerebral injury occurs prior to puberty this recovery process may be extended even further.

Case Study 1 (Liability)

This 29-year-old female patient sustained an accidental gunshot wound (.22 caliber pistol) to the right orbital area, with the bullet entering in the infrafrontal area and coursing back through the parietal-occipital area. There was massive brain laceration and brain hemorrhaging, with damage essentially restricted to the right hemisphere (see CT results, Figure 19.1). She also developed a posttraumatic seizure disorder. At the time of the accident, she was an assistant section editor for a local newspaper, and although she had attended college, she did not have a college degree. There was no previous neurological history. The shooting was accidental and the gun had misfired when on safety lock. It was subsequently proven in court that the lock was defective.

Neuropsychological Findings Neuropsychological studies were consistent with generalized right hemispheric dysfunction. Hemiplegia was so profound that this patient was never able to regain ambulation. She was blind in the right eye and had a left visual field hemianopia in the left eye. Behaviorally, she displayed marked emotional lability and marked prosodic impairment. As is evident in the neuropsychological assessment, as well as the CT scan results, which depicted permanent structural damage, the patient will have permanent and lasting deficits and is totally disabled. In such a case, there is no hope for effective rehabilitation and all that can be provided is custodial care. At follow-up, although this was after the court settlement in this case, she essentially showed no change in functional ability and has required full-time nursing home placement and care.

Forensic Implications Prior to this accidental shooting, this patient was a fully intact, high-functioning individual. She was independent, living on her own and supporting herself completely. She had an extremely active and vigorous social life. She was not experiencing any emotional problems. Now the severity of her injury has rendered her totally incapacitated, and she requires constant medical supervision. This is a permanent and complete disability, and there is nothing to suggest any change in her level of function. The responsibility for this tragic accident lies directly with the gun manufacturing firm and the defective safety lock. The firm was found liable in this case and was court ordered to compensate the patient and family for lifetime medical care and therapy as well as loss of income and earning potential.

Case Study 2 (Malpractice)

This 30-year-old high-school-educated individual suffered a right anterior cerebral artery infarction as a result of the right carotid artery's being inadvertently severed during cosmetic surgery for jaw realignment. The accidental severing of the right carotid artery resulted in a "steal syndrome," in which the blood was drained away from the right hemisphere circulation. However, there was sufficient flow by the posterior communicating artery so that brain tissue supplied by the middle cerebral artery was not affected. Only the anterior cerebral artery distribution was affected, and this can be clearly seen in the CT scan (Figure 19.2), in that only the anteromedial aspects of the right hemisphere are infarcted. Neurologically, the patient developed a left hemiparesis (greater in the leg than in the arm), a frontal lobe behavioral syndrome, and dysprosodic speech.

Neuropsychological Findings The first neuropsychological evaluation of this patient took place approximately four months after the infarction. The results of testing are presented in Figure 19.2. Behaviorally, the family reported that the patient displayed rather marked emotional lability with rapid, fluctuating mood and unpredictable behavior. This, combined with decreased motivation,

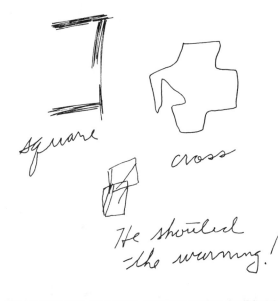

square   cross

He should
the warning!

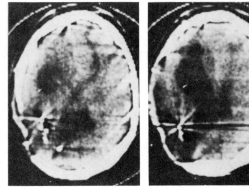

Lateral Dominance Exam

Age 29		Eye	Hand	Foot
Sex F	Right		X	X
Education 12	Left	X		
	Mixed			

Motor Examination

FOD <u>36</u>   SOGD <u>18</u>   TPT-L-d/c
FOND <u>0</u>   SOGND <u>0</u>
Left hemiplegia

Sensory-Perceptual examination
Blindness, O.D., Left hemianopsia O.S.
Tactile inattention, Left side D.S.
Auditory inattention, Left side D.S.
Left side asterognosis, dysgraphesthesia,
and finger dysgnosia

Language Evaluation
Conversational speech: Dysprosodic,
preservative
Comprehension: Mildly impaired
Repetition: WNL
Confrontation Naming: WNL
Reading: Aloud WNL
Comprehension: WNL for
material that can be read
Writing: WNL

Constructional dyspraxia
Calculations: Moderately impaired

WRAT Scores:
Reading—Grade level 8.0
Spelling—Grade level 9.3
Arithmetic—Grade level 3.0

SSRT raw score 13
Scaled score 10
SSPT errors 14/60

Memory Examination
WMS MQ = 67
LM <u>4</u>, digits <u>10</u>, VM <u>1</u>, AL <u>14</u>

Intellectual/Cognitive Examination
FSIQ = 77, PIQ = 64, FSIQ = 70
I <u>6</u>, C <u>4</u>, A <u>6</u>, S <u>6</u>, digits <u>6</u>, V <u>8</u>
DS <u>4</u>, PC <u>5</u>, BD <u>3</u>, PA <u>4</u>, OA <u>3</u>

Category Test 100 errors
Trail-Making Test
A 98 sec
B 180 sec DC 5 errors

FIGURE 19.1 Case 1. *Right:* Neuropsychological test results. *Top left:* Selected aspects of the Reitan–Indiana Aphasia Screening Test, depicting intact spelling and writing, but with a pronounced constructional dyspraxia. *Bottom left:* CT scans demonstrating generalized right hemisphere destructive effects of the trauma.

Abbreviations for all figures: FOD, Finger Oscillation, Dominant; FOND, Finger Oscillation, Nondominant; SOGD, Strength of Grip, Dominant; SOGN, Strength of Grip, Nondominant; TPT, Tactual Performance Test; O.D., Right Eye; O.S., Left Eye; DS, Suppressions with Double Simultaneous Stimulation; SSRT, Seashore Rhythm Test; SSPT, Speech Sounds Suppression Test; WNL, Within Normal Limits.

Lateral Dominance Examination

	Eye	Hand	Foot
Right	X	X	X
Left			
Mixed			

Motor Examination

FOD 39 (37)   SOGD 25 (27)   TPTD 12.0 DC 7 in (6.9)
FOND 20 (17) SOGND 15 (16) TPTND 5.0 DC 1 in (12.0 DC 3)
                             TPT both 8.9 (4.2)

Sensory-Perceptual Examination

WNL

SSRT 6 errors (9 errors)
SSPT 2 errors (3 errors)

Language Evaluation

WNL Verbal 0 Spatial 2

WRAT Results
  Reading 12.0 (11.1)
  Spelling 10.7 (9.5)
  Arithmetic 6.6 (5.6)

Memory Examination

WMS MQ = 99
LM 9 (9), D 7, F 3, R (SF, 4 R), VM 10 (8), AL 16 (8)
TPT Memory 3 (5) TPT Localization 0 (2)

Intellectual/Cognitive Functioning

VIQ = 88 (82)
  I 5 (6), D 7 (8), V 8 (7), A 10 (7), C 9 (7), S 10 (8)
PIQ = 94 (88)
  PC 10 (8), PA 9 (7), BD 9 (9), OA 8 (7), DS 9 (10)

Category Test 111 errors (116 errors)
Trail-Making Test A 40 (46) B 81/1 error (102/1 error)

MMPI

L	F	K	Hs	D	Hy	Pd	Mf	Pa	Pt	Sc	Ma	Si
43	60	42	57	71	57	55	51	70	67	84	60	70

Square cross triangle clock   SQUARE

He showed the warning

$\frac{\begin{array}{r}85\\-27\end{array}}{58}$

FIGURE 19.2 Case 2. *Right:* Neuropsychological test results. Results in parentheses are from 1 year follow-up for the same tests. Note the lateralized left side motor findings in the absence of associated sensory deficits, with essentially no change in 1 year's time. Such findings are indicative of permanent right frontal lobe damage. *Top left:* CT scans depict medial right frontal infarction (note that the CT scan is presented as if you were facing the patient, thus right is depicted on the left-hand side of the film and vice versa, along the distribution of the right anterior cerebral artery). *Bottom left:* Abbreviated Reitan–Indiana Aphasia Screening Test results obtained from the testing at 1 year follow-up.

comprised a significant management problem. Neuropsychological studies indicate residual right frontal involvement, as evidenced by the motor findings on the left side. The patient also displayed a motor dysprosodic disturbance. Problems in complex abstract reasoning were also present, as noted by the excessively elevated score on the Category test. The patient's verbal abilities were intact, except for the prosodic speech disturbance, which resulted in monotone output. The patient's MMPI studies indicated significant elevations on the Psychasthenia and Schizophrenia subscales, likely reflecting impaired mentation, excessive worry, and frustration. Follow-up studies revealed little change in this patient's status. This was despite intensive occupational therapy efforts to treat some of the functional deficits, as well as participation in a cognitive-enrichment-type program.

Forensic Implications Prior to this induced accidental vascular accident, this individual was normal in terms of cognitive, neurological, and behavioral functioning. The deficits at one year appeared to be fairly permanent, since there was little change in her follow-up neuropsychological studies even though an entire year had elapsed. She was not able to return to efficient use of some of the domestic responsibilities that she had prior to the injury. She continued to display an amotivational-type syndrome and the emotional lability characteristic of frontal involvement. There have been marked and drastic changes in this individual as a result of this accidental injury, and there is little to suggest that there will be any positive change in her future. Compensation in such a case needs to take into consideration all of these factors and their future implications.

Case Study 3 (Malpractice)

The mother of this child was incorrectly blood typed during her first pregnancy. Significant Rh incompatibility was present, but undetected because of a lab error. She subsequently became pregnant for a second time, but because of the original lab error, she did not receive a RhoGAM injection; significant complications began to develop during the latter part of the pregnancy. At seven months, amniocentesis revealed severe isoimmunization and indicated the need for prompt delivery. The delivery was by Caesarean section, and even at that point the Rh incompatibility was not known. The child had an initial Apgar score of 1, was anoxic and was not breathing, and required intubation and ventilation. She was immediately transfused and then subsequently transfused on two separate occasions within the first 24 hours of life. During the second day of life, she began displaying increased lethargy, and lumbar puncture revealed bloody cerebral spinal fluid, suggestive of intracerebral hemorrhaging. EEG was diffusely abnormal at that time. Simultaneous with this, the patient developed a right sixth and seventh cranial nerve paralysis and a right hemiplegia. No further aggressive treatment was instituted at that time, but the child did survive and gradually improved over time; she was discharged some 46 days following birth. At discharge the child displayed right hemiplegia and sixth and seventh cranial nerve palsy. Profound developmental delay was also present. The child was hypotonic. The child had a normal older female sibling. Both parents had high-school educations. There was no familial history of neurodevelopmental disorder or mental retardation.

Neuropsychological Test Results Developmental studies with this child are presented in Figure 19.3, along with the CT scan findings. This child shows persistent developmental delay in all areas, as well as permanent right-side hemiplegia and facial and ocular paresis. CT scan results reflect diffuse and generalized cerebral atrophy, greater in the left hemisphere. EEG studies were also diffusely abnormal.

Forensic Implications The child's neurologic injury would have been preventable had the mother known about her Rh incompatibility. Thus, the liability in this case lies directly with the lab that mistyped the original report. As a result of this, the child will be permanently mentally retarded and physically handicapped. Her level of retardation will likely be in the moderate-to-severe range, but this will partly depend on the type of treatment she receives during the early formative years. This child is in need of intensive and extensive occupational therapy, physical therapy, and speech and language therapy, as well as generalized pre-academic special education training. The child will also need custodial care. Intensive special education efforts need to continue with this child until the late teens or mid-twenties, depending on the progress she makes. Since she will probably have normal life expectancy, consideration has to also be given for lifetime attendant care.

Competency/Incompetency

As indicated previously, the determination of competency frequently falls within the purview of the neuropsychologist. Competency determination is usually required in cases where the patient has acquired some type of neurological disorder that renders him or her incapable of making appropriate decisions in terms of his or her best interests or in terms of the ability legally to assist counsel in criminal jurisprudence. (See also the review by the AMA task force on medicolegal problems, 1984).

Mental incompetency may be a result of any number of acquired neurologic diseases or disorders (cerebrovascular, traumatic, neoplastic, etc.), but the most frequently encountered situation involves the determination of patients' competency when they have a suspected degenerative syndrome. Two cases presented below aptly demonstrate the evaluation of competency and the important role that the neuropsychologist may play in addressing a patient's ability to continue on in his or her professional and personal affairs.

Chronological Age	Scale	Raw Score	Approximate Development Equivalent
1 year, 11 months	Mental Scale	46	4 months
	Motor Scale	26	6 months
2 years, 11 months	Mental Scale	71	6 months
	Motor Scale	39	9 months

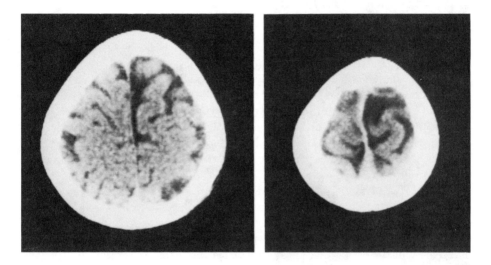

FIGURE 19.3 Case 3. *Top:* Bayley Scales of infant development results, 1 year apart. *Bottom:* CT films at 1 year, 11 months. Note the marked cortical atrophy present as evidenced by sulcal widening.

Case Study 4 (Competency)

This 50-year-old lab technician had been experiencing poor job performance and memory disturbance prior to coming in for examination. She was the senior lab technician in a hospital pathology lab and had worked at the hospital for a number of years. She had a college degree in biomedical technology. Her family described her as being a most competent and bright individual, but stated that over the past 6 to 9 months she had been showing signs of withdrawal, loss of spontaneity, emotional instability, and impaired memory. There was no history of neurologic injury or trauma.

Neuropsychologic Findings Results of neuropsychologic assessment suggest the presence of significant intellectual/cognitive decline consistent with a prob-

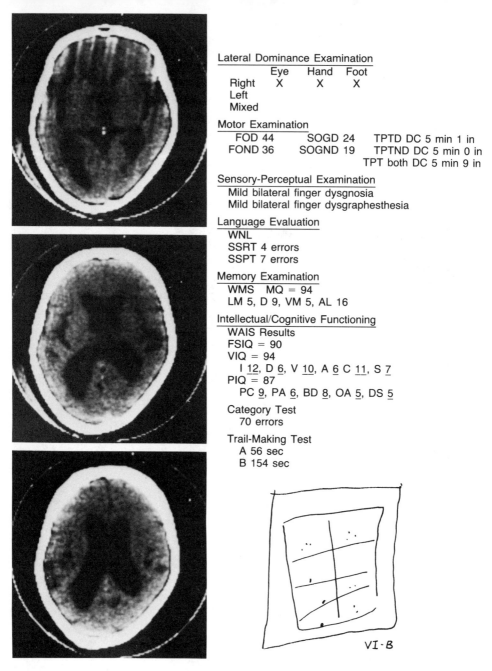

Lateral Dominance Examination

	Eye	Hand	Foot
Right	X	X	X
Left			
Mixed			

Motor Examination

FOD 44   SOGD 24   TPTD DC 5 min 1 in
FOND 36   SOGND 19   TPTND DC 5 min 0 in
                                      TPT both DC 5 min 9 in

Sensory-Perceptual Examination

Mild bilateral finger dysgnosia
Mild bilateral finger dysgraphesthesia

Language Evaluation

WNL
SSRT 4 errors
SSPT 7 errors

Memory Examination

WMS   MQ = 94
LM 5, D 9, VM 5, AL 16

Intellectual/Cognitive Functioning

WAIS Results
FSIQ = 90
VIQ = 94
    I 12, D 6, V 10, A 6 C 11, S 7
PIQ = 87
    PC 9, PA 6, BD 8, OA 5, DS 5

Category Test
70 errors

Trail-Making Test
A 56 sec
B 154 sec

VI-B

FIGURE 19.4 Case 4 *Top right:* Neuropsychological test data. For an individual with a B.S. degree in microbiology and 20 years of work in medical technology, the results reflect a significant decline in level of functioning. The results of the Visual Memory subtest (Card B) of the Wechsler Memory Scale are presented *(bottom right)* and reflect not only the visual memory deficits but also the constructional praxic deficits present (see Figure 19.5, *bottom right,* for the actual stimulus figure for Card B). *Top left:* CT scans indicate marked ventricular dilation in association with marked Sylvian fissure enlargement. These signs are indicative of generalized cerebral atrophy, particularly in frontal and temporal regions.

540

able degenerative syndrome. CT scanning reveals marked atrophy, particularly in the frontal and temporal regions (note the tremendous enlargement of the Sylvian fissures bilaterally in Figure 19.4). There was also excessive ventricular enlargement. The combination of radiographic studies and neuropsychologic testing essentially confirms the presence of degenerative syndrome, early stage.

Forensic Implications This patient had a supervisory role in a pathology lab, and this, of course, requires full and complete mental competency. In no way could this patient be allowed to return to employment in this area. In fact, it appears that she is just showing the early stages of a progressive degenerative syndrome and mental functions will only get worse. Since there is no treatment for this disorder, there is essentially no question that the patient should be relieved of her duties in terms of personal and financial affairs. The patient is also in need of some type of legal guardianship arrangement in which her best interests will be maintained as her condition deteriorates.

Case Study 5 (Competency)

Prior to his retirement, this patient was a most successful petroleum engineer. He possessed a master's degree in engineering and was instrumental in early exploration of oil in the Southwest. As a result of his successes, he became quite wealthy and was involved in numerous successful businesses. He was president and chairman-of-the-board of one of the companies that he had established. However, according to his family and business associates, he was showing signs of failing memory and impaired decision making. This was becoming quite critical, since large sums of money were involved in the various decisions that he was making. The family obtained a court order for determination of mental competency.

Neuropsychological Findings At the time of examination, this patient was 75 years of age and had no prior history of neurological injury or disorder. Neuropsychological studies reflected generally intact well-learned intellectual functions, but functions requiring new and adaptive abilities were distinctly impaired (see PIQ, Category Test, Wechsler Memory Scale results in Figure 19.5). In this case, note the wide discrepancy between the age-corrected and non-age-corrected intellectual scores. Note also the significant and pathological relationship between the measured VIQ and the patient's Category Test error score (see Table 19.1 for comparison). Even when age-corrected intellectual scores were utilized, there is a marked difference between the patient's memory quotient and Full-Scale IQ score. This is indicative of significant memory disturbance, and closer inspection of the results indicates a particular deficit with short-term memory processing. The clinical interview indicated that the patient was not necessarily depressed and that the cognitive changes were not secondary to significant emotional disturbance.

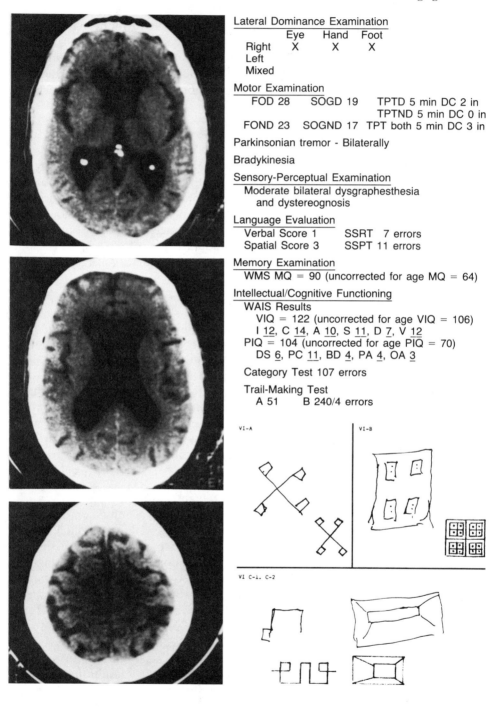

Lateral Dominance Examination

	Eye	Hand	Foot
Right	X	X	X
Left			
Mixed			

Motor Examination

FOD 28   SOGD 19   TPTD 5 min DC 2 in
                       TPTND 5 min DC 0 in
FOND 23   SOGND 17 TPT both 5 min DC 3 in

Parkinsonian tremor - Bilaterally

Bradykinesia

Sensory-Perceptual Examination
  Moderate bilateral dysgraphesthesia
    and dystereognosis

Language Evaluation
  Verbal Score 1   SSRT 7 errors
  Spatial Score 3   SSPT 11 errors

Memory Examination
  WMS MQ = 90 (uncorrected for age MQ = 64)

Intellectual/Cognitive Functioning
  WAIS Results
    VIQ = 122 (uncorrected for age VIQ = 106)
    I 12, C 14, A 10, S 11, D 7, V 12
    PIQ = 104 (uncorrected for age PIQ = 70)
    DS 6, PC 11, BD 4, PA 4, OA 3

  Category Test 107 errors

  Trail-Making Test
    A 51   B 240/4 errors

Forensic Implications This patient is displaying clear signs of early senile dementia. He is impaired in judgment, memory, and complex problem solving. He is no longer really capable of continuing with his partnership in financial affairs. Some provision should be made by the court to handle his situation with his best interests in mind, and he should not be given the opportunity to make complete and full decisions concerning his own or corporate financial affairs.

Criminal Jurisprudence

The determination of whether a patient is mentally competent to conform his or her behavior to the law has always been an area addressed by forensic psychology (Wright et al., 1980). The neuropsychologist may become involved in such forensic work when a neurologically impaired patient commits some criminal offense. For example, we were involved in the evaluation of an individual who had committed a felony theft after being released from a rehabilitation center where he had been treated for severe head injury. The head injury was the result of a rim that exploded while the patient was changing a truck tire. He sustained a decompressed skull fracture over the left frontal area, a linear skull fracture over the left frontal-parietal area, intracerebral hemorrhaging, a bifrontal-temporal contusion, and obliteration of the left orbit and eye. Neuropsychological studies clearly indicated generalized cerebral dysfunction with particular deficits in complex memory (both verbal and visual), as well as generalized deficits in all areas of cognitive functioning. Such patients often have profound deficits in impulse control. In addition, the patient was unable to recall events or assist his attorney in his defense. Obviously, as a result of this individual's traumatic organic brain syndrome, he was unable to conform his behavior to the law or assist his attorney in his defense. After neuropsychological testimony, he was considered mentally incompetent.

It appears that the neuropsychologist's forensic roles are likely to increase in proportion to our greater understanding of biological factors in psychopathol-

◄――――――――――――

FIGURE 19.5 Case 5. *Top right:* Neuropsychological test results. Note the generalized intactness of the patient's verbal intellectual abilities and the contrasting deficit in performance functioning. Particularly note the uncorrected values for age. It is not uncommon to find the demented patient with significant performance deficits with generally intact verbal intellectual functioning. However, note the marked deficit in Category Test performance and the inability to perform Trail-Making B. These findings clearly indicate the presence of marked cognitive impairment. The patient also displays deficits in a number of other areas. Note his visual memory problems on the Wechsler Memory Scale, with the entire Visual Memory examination *(bottom right)*. Note also the praxic difficulties the patient is experiencing at this time. *Left:* CT scans reflecting marked ventricular dilatation and generalized cortical atrophy. Note the distinct enlargement of the Sylvian fissures bilaterally. These results are consistent with morphologic changes seen with degenerative disorders.

ogy. For example, research is unequivocal at this time in terms of demonstrating clear organic dysfunction in some schizophrenic patients (Henn & Nasrallah, 1982). In this subgroup of schizophrenic patients, the most common neurological findings are cerebral atrophy and ventricular enlargement as determined by CT scanning of the brain and generalized cognitive deficits on neuropsychological examination (see Bigler, 1984). It is likely that these underlying organic factors will have implications in terms of a patient's competency. Similarly, research continues to unveil potential underlying organic factors in certain individuals who commit violent crimes, as well as higher incidences of organic factors in the general population of juvenile delinquents (Shanok & Lewis, 1981; Yeudall, Fromm-Auch, & Davies, 1982). These aspects may also become mitigating factors in certain competency cases that may confront the neuropsychologist.

Malingering

Regardless of whether the neuropsychologist is dealing with a liability, disability, or competency case, the possibility of patient malingering is always present, although relatively rare. The malingering patient may attempt to exaggerate, typically to increase potential compensation, or falsify an injury or attempt to falsify his or her competency (Peterson, 1975). While certain aspects of neuropsychological performance can be faked (Goebel, 1983; Heaton, Smith, Lehman, & Vogt, 1978), with the present sophistication of neurological, neuroradiological, neurophysiological, and neuropsychological tests, it would be very difficult for a patient to convincingly fake a neurological disorder.

An area where malingering is an occasional factor is in Worker's Compensation litigation cases where no objective clinical findings are present, but where the patient did sustain some type of work-related injury. Serial testing over 3- to 6-month intervals can be extremely illuminating in these cases, since the malingering patient has difficulty maintaining consistent performance from test session to test session. Similarly the type of deficits seen are inconsistent with or out of proportion to what would be expected given the type of injury sustained. The use of the Minnesota Multiphasic Personality Inventory (MMPI) can also be useful in distinguishing the patient with supratentorial (i.e., "all in his head") or functional overlay, as opposed to the patient with bona fide organic disorder (Repko & Cooper, 1983). Serial MMPI testing can also be helpful, as well as detailed item analysis of the MMPI and use of item analysis to ask specific questions of the patient.

SUMMARY

By the nature of neuropsychological practice, it is likely that every practicing clinical neuropsychologist will encounter forensic cases. Because of this, the current chapter has overviewed a variety of potential areas in forensic neuropsychology. Within this context, the chapter provides an outline of the current status of forensic neuropsychology, guidelines for evaluation and presentation of forensic cases, and a further formulation of the forensic discipline within clinical neuropsychology. As neuropsychology expands its role in the diagnosis and care of neurologic patients, it is apparent that there will be an ever-increasing role for specialization in forensic neuropsychology.

REFERENCES

Adams, J. H., Graham, D. I., Murray, L. S., & Scott, G. (1982). Diffuse axonal injury due to nonmissile head injury in humans: An analysis of 45 cases. *Annals of Neurology, 12,* 557–563.

American Medical Association Committee on Medicolegal Problems. (1984). Insanity defense in criminal trials and limitation of psychiatric testimony. *Journal of the American Medical Association, 251,* 2967–2981.

American Psychological Association. (1981). Ethical principles of psychologists. In *Directory of the American Psychological Association.* Washington, DC: American Psychological Association.

Barth, J. T., Macciocchi, S. N., Giordani, B., Rimel, R., Jane, J. A., & Boll, T. J. (1983). Neuropsychological sequelae of minor head injury. *Journal of Neurosurgery, 13,* 529–533.

Beresford, H. R. (1975). *Legal aspects of neurologic practice.* Philadelphia: Davis.

Bigler, E. D. (1980). Neuropsychological assessment and brain scan results: A case study approach. *Clinical Neuropsychology, 2,* 13–24.

Bigler, E. D. (1984). *Diagnostic clinical neuropsychology.* Austin: University of Texas Press.

Blau, T. H. (1984). *The psychologist as expert witness.* New York: Wiley.

Brodsky, S. L., & Robe, A. (1973). On becoming an expert witness: Issues of orientation and effectiveness. *Professional Psychology, 3,* 173–176.

Casson, I. R., Siegel, O., Sham, R., Campbell, E. A., Tarlau, M., & DiDomenico, A. (1984). Brain damage in modern boxers. *The Journal of the American Medical Association, 251,* 2663–2667.

Cullum, M., Steinman, D. R., & Bigler, E. D. (1984). Relationship between fluid and crystallized cognitive function using Category test and WAIS scores. *International Journal of Clinical Neuropsychology, 6,* 172–174.

DeLeon, P. H., VandenBos, G. R., & Kraut, A. G. (1984). Federal legislation recognizing psychology. *American Psychologist, 39,* 933–946.

Gennarelli, T. A., Thibault, L. E., Adams, J. H., Graham, D. I., Thompson, C. J., & Marcincin, R. P. (1982). Diffuse axonal injury and traumatic coma in the primate. *Annals of Neurology, 12,* 564–574.

Goebel, R. A. (1983). Detection of faking on the Halstead–Reitan Neuropsychological Test Battery. *Journal of Clinical Psychology, 39,* 731–742.

Heaton, R. K., & Crowley, T. J. (1981). Effects of psychiatric disorders and their somatic treatments on neuropsychological test results. In S. B. Filskov & T. J. Boll (Eds.), *Handbook of clinical neuropsychology* (pp. 481–525). New York: Wiley.

Heaton, R. K., Smith, H. H., Lehman, R., & Vogt, A. T. (1978). Prospects for faking believable deficits on neuropsychological testing. *Journal of Consulting and Clinical Psychology, 46,* 892–900.

Henn, F. A., & Nasrallah, H. A. (Eds.) (1982). *Schizophrenia as a brain disease.* New York: Oxford University Press.

Horsley, J. E., & Carlova, J. (1983). *Testifying in court.* Oradel NJ: Medical Economics Books.

International Neuropsychological Society Task Force on Education, Accreditation and Credentialing. (1984). *Newsletter 40* (Division of Clinical Neuropsychology, American Psychological Association) (Vol. 2).

Jennett, B., & Bond, M. (1975). Assessment of outcome after severe brain damage. *Lancet, 1,* 480–485.

Jennett, B., & Teasdale, G. (1981). *Management of head injuries.* Philadelphia: F. A. Davis.

Klesges, R. C., Sanchez, V. C., & Stanton, A. L. (1981). Cross validation of an adult premorbid functioning index. *Clinical Neuropsychology, 3,* 13–15.

Levin, H. S., Benton, A. L., & Grossman, R. G. (1982). *Neurobehavioral consequences of closed head injury.* New York: Oxford University Press.

Mack, J. L. (1980). The use of neuropsychological testimony in civil court proceedings. In G. Cooke (Ed.), *The role of the forensic psychologist* (pp. 212–231). Springfield, IL: Charles C. Thomas.

McMahon, E. A. (1983). Forensic issues in clinical neuropsychology. In C. J. Golden & P. J. Vicente, *Foundations of clinical neuropsychology* (pp. 310–329). New York: Plenum.

McMahon, E. A., & Satz, P. (1981). Clinical neuropsychology: Some forensic applications. In S. B. Filskov & T. J. Boll (Eds.), *Handbook of clinical neuropsychology* (pp. 686–701). New York: Wiley.

Meier, M. J. (1981). Education for competency assurance in human neuropsychology: Antecedents, models and directions. In S. Filskov & T. Boll, *Handbook of clinical neuropsychology* (pp. 754–781). New York: Wiley.

Noseworthy, J., Miller, J., Murray, T., & Regan, D. (1981). Auditory brainstem responses in postconcussion syndrome. *Archives of Neurology, 38,* 275–276.

Peterson, G. C. (1975). Organic brain syndromes associated with brain trauma. In A. M. Freedman, H. I. Kaplan, & B. J. Sadock (Eds.), *Comprehensive textbook of psychiatry* (2nd ed.). Baltimore: Williams & Wilkins.

Repko, G. R., & Cooper, R. A. (1983). A study of the average Workers Compensation case. *Journal of Clinical Psychology, 39,* 287–295.

Reynolds, C. R., & Gutkin, T. B. (1979). Predicting the premorbid intellectual status of children using demographic data. *Clinical Neuropsychology, 1,* 36–38.

Rowe, J., & Carlson, C. (1980). Brainstem auditory evoked potentials in postconcussion dizziness. *Archives of Neurology, 37,* 679–683.

Sattler, T. M. (1974). *Assessment of children's intelligence.* Philadelphia: Saunders.

Shanok, S. S., & Lewis, D. O. (1981). Medical histories of female delinquents. *Archives of General Psychiatry, 38,* 211–213.

Shapiro, D. L. (1984). *Psychological evaluation and expert testimony.* New York: Van Nostrand Reinhold.

Strub, R. L., & Black, F. W. (1981). *Organic brain syndromes.* Philadelphia: F. A. Davis.

Tucker, D. M., Bigler, E. D., & Chelune, G. J. (1981). Test–retest reliability of the Halstead–Reitan in psychotics. *Journal of Behavioral Assessment, 3,* 311–319.

Wilson, R. S., Rosenbaum, G., & Brown, G. (1979). The problem of premorbid intelligence in neuropsychological assessment. *Journal of Clinical Neuropsychology, 1,* 49–53.

Wright, F., Bahn, C., & Rieber, R. W. (1980). *Forensic psychology and psychiatry* (Vol. 347). New York: New York Academy of Sciences.

Yeudall, L. T., Fromm-Auch, D., & Davies, D. (1982). Neuropsychological impairment of persistent delinquency. *Journal of Nervous and Mental Disease, 170,* 257–265.

20

Computer Applications in Neuropsychology

Charles J. Long and
Mark Wagner

In this chapter we concern ourselves with ways in which small computer systems (microcomputers) can be employed in a clinical setting, with particular regard for neuropsychodiagnosis and cognitive rehabilitation. We make no attempt to appraise hardware, and we generally avoid discussions of specific software. We use the terms *computer* and *microcomputer* interchangeably, and in either case we are referring to an inexpensive (less than $2,000) self-contained desk-top computer system. On the question of hardware we simply advise power—all you can get, in the form of large CPU memory and at least a double floppy disc or hard disc peripheral. Fortunately, the cost of such components has declined so dramatically that a very powerful system is easily affordable. On the question of commercial software we advise caution and skepticism. Aside from statistics packages, it has been our experience that the most useful software is developed in-house.

Our discussion is necessarily rather general because, as of this writing, there is a tremendous difference between what *can be* done with computers and what is currently available. There is also a substantial difference between currently available systems and the reality of effective clinical applications. The transition from our current status will not be made rapidly. Rather, microcomputer applications will be designed, tested, and modified. Each step, it is to be hoped, will lead to efficient, cost-effective clinical applications.

Computer applications are being made in almost all areas of human endeavor, yet some areas lend themselves more readily to this technology. Neuropsychology appears to be a particularly fertile area for computer applications; however, the question remains as to how computers can best be applied and how such applications will enhance the effectiveness of neuropsychological techniques. It may be of no particular advantage to have a test available on a computer. Unless such computer applications are more effective and efficient than human administration, there is little value in changing the method of administration.

In part, the popularity of microcomputers in the clinical setting is due to the fact that they can eliminate many of the tedious daily tasks a clinician must perform. With only this application in mind, it is clear that computers have tremendous potential. Yet microcomputers also can be helpful in more complex decision-making strategies. While the potential applications of the microcomputer in the clinical setting abound, this chapter is restricted to a discussion of their role in data storage and analysis, collection (automated testing), and rehabilitation in the neuropsychologist's clinical practice.

COMPUTER APPLICATIONS IN DATA ANALYSIS

A comprehensive neuropsychological evaluation is a time-consuming enterprise that produces a large amount of data. A small computer system can be used to relieve the clinician from certain mundane, time-consuming aspects of data collection, storage, and manipulation. It can also aid in interpretation of neuropsychological test data. The first and simplest level of implementation is in storage and manipulation of neuropsychological data. The microcomputer is extremely useful and cost-effective in this capacity, and, if properly programmed, the computer can reorganize data in various ways to aid greatly in the process of data analysis. One way in which it can aid in this capacity is by transforming the test scores into more meaningful forms.

The complete Halstead–Reitan Battery, for example, yields a considerable number of test and subtest scores, which are combined in different ways in order to make diagnostic decisions. One significant problem with the traditional approach to data analysis of the Halstead–Reitan Battery is that the amount of useful data is reduced by using raw scores or cutoff scores to establish the presence of brain dysfunction. Such procedures of data reduction often do not provide data suitable for effective profile analysis of the patient's strengths and weaknesses. This problem is further compounded when the Wechsler Adult Intelligence Scale (WAIS), Wechsler Memory Scale, MMPI, and other tests are included in the battery. The problem becomes even greater when consideration is given to other variables, such as age, sex, occupation, education, and so forth. Research has clearly documented the need for age-specific norms for children (Knights, 1970; Spreen & Gaddes, 1969) and adults (Fromm-Auch & Yeudall, 1983; Moehle & Long, 1984). Without standardized age-correct test scores, the neuropsychologist is confronted with a large number of scores that are difficult to interpret as they exist and are nearly impossible to combine in meaningful ways.

Kiernan and Matthews (1976) investigated the use of standard scores as an effective method of data analysis in neuropsychology. They found that the use of average T-scores was more effective than use of the Impairment Index for older, normal subjects (over 34 years of age). Although their research indicates that traditional methods, such as the use of the Impairment Index, are better for clinical uses of the battery with younger adults, T-score conversions do provide an added source of data. The T-score conversion procedure offers a method to combine data easily in different ways and develop profiles of strengths and weaknesses.

Matthews (1977), Spreen and Gaddes (1969), and others have offered T-score conversion tables and/or age cutoffs for neuropsychological tests. The use of such tables is helpful but remains a rather slow process. Microcomputer systems offer a definite advantage in systematically converting raw-score data into standard scores and in plotting summary profiles.

The microcomputer provides data storage and standard score conversions; it can also add current data to existing files by storing medical and demographic data as well as test scores. In addition, data files can be established for groups of patients with specific lesion locations, ages, and etiologies. This type of data base can be expanded by cooperation between different neuropsychological laboratories.

As suggested previously, the microcomputer can be an excellent aid in developing and assessing decision-making strategies. Standard scores can easily be incorporated into decision-making strategies for degree of impairment, lateralization, process (i.e., chronicity), and pathology. Microcomputers have the capacity to use sophisticated statistical programs as an aid in classifying patients into various criterion groups (Knights, 1979; Swiercinsky & Warnock, 1977; Wedding, 1983). Results can then be plotted on a summary profile. This type of system can augment the efforts of the clinical neuropsychologist and thus substantially reduce the time necessary to provide diagnostic results.

Russell, Neuringer, and Goldstein (1970) developed one of the first computer programs for analyzing neuropsychological data. Their program closely followed Reitan's decision strategy model and required the examiner to provide raw scores obtained by traditional testing. The computer system then converted raw scores to ranked scores and computed an Average Impairment Rating. This Average Impairment Rating was based upon scores used in computing the Impairment Index but also included other test scores included in the battery. Analysis was accomplished by use of a successive key or decision-tree approach. Two "keys" were developed: a localization/degree of lateralization key and a process key. The localization/degree of lateralization key determined the presence or absence of brain damage and predicted lateralization. The process key was designed to determine if the brain damage was congenital, static, or acute (less than three months since onset).

A similar program was developed by Finkelstein (1976), based on seven

Halstead measures (Category; TPT Total Time; TPT Memory; TPT Location; Rhythm; Speech-Sounds Perception; and Tapping, Dominant Hand). Finkelstein's analysis also attempted to take into account intelligence, aphasia, and constructional dyspraxia. This computer analysis program was reported to rival the Russell et al. (1970) program in predicting brain dysfunction, as well as in lateralizing such dysfunction. Both systems were somewhat limited in their scope and design and generally required large computer systems for application. Furthermore, both were limited by the lack of normative data available for comparison.

While such approaches to data analysis were important in demonstrating the utility of computers and outlining various decision strategies, research has failed to support their effectiveness. Anthony, Heaton and Johnson (1980) compared both systems and found them to be of limited clinical value. Wedding (1983) evaluated the computer systems of both Russell et al. (1970) and Finkelstein (1976), as well as discriminant functions and profile matchings. He found Finkelstein's program to be unsuitable for clinical application; likewise, the lateralizing programs of Russell et al. were found to have little clinical utility. Wedding's research also indicated that the Russell et al.'s program was less accurate than the Impairment Index.

Wheeler, Burke and Reitan (1963) demonstrated that discriminant functions could classify patients with 80% accuracy with regard to presence or absence of brain damage and that the functions were superior to the Impairment Index for this task. However, Wedding (1983) found that while discriminant functions were of greater value in making more complex decisions, such as whether the dysfunction involved the left or right hemisphere or was diffuse, they were not superior to the Impairment Index for basic decisions as to the presence or absence of dysfunction.

The computer system developed in our lab attempts to address some of the questions regarding diagnostic validity outlined above. Basically, our program requires that the examiner provide raw neuropsychological test data obtained by traditional methods, as well as MMPI standard scores, demographic data, and available medical, psychological, and historical data. The computer system stores the data in a data file based upon confirmed etiology or in a general file for those cases where etiology remains unknown. It then identifies the patient's age and selects the appropriate age norms for analysis. Each test score is converted into a T-score. The presence and/or severity of cortical dysfunction is determined by first summing the standard scores of key predictive tests, which are weighed, and by then comparing this number with the patient's deviation from the normative age data. Following the determination of degree of cortical dysfunction, selective neuropsychological scores are analyzed to determine the lateralization of dysfunction based on normative data. The computer system then plots a summary profile that includes degree of cortical impairment, extent and direction of lateralization, and extent to which emotional factors deviate from the norm. Although the diagnostic conclusions are ultimately made by the neuropsychologist, the computer generates data that aid in data interpretation. Such a procedure greatly enhances the effective analyses of children and older adults by analyzing and/or displaying data according to comparisons with appropriate age norms.

A further advantage of the standard-score method is that the patient's scores can be grouped and graphically displayed across various dimensions of behavior. Thus, the individual's performance on somatosensory tasks can be grouped and displayed in a profile that is equivalent to performance on other tasks, such as motor functions, visuospatial functions, attention, language, and so forth. Such a profile can be useful in rehabilitation planning, where the patient's strengths and weaknesses are graphically displayed.

As of this writing there exists no diagnostic program adequate for clinical use. It should also be emphasized that the process of computer analysis forces the system developer to objectify and outline each stage in the decision process. Each step must be outlined and detailed, and its effectiveness evaluated. Such a process serves to clearly emphasize future research needs and provides the system developer with insights as to current strengths and weaknesses in each stage of the decision process. Thus, the microcomputer system in the neuropsychologist's office provides a method for standard-score conversions and storage. It can store data, develop and update age norms, and plot a standard-score profile of the patient's neuropsychological strengths and weaknesses.

The major diffences between the program developed in our lab and those of Russell et al., and Finkelstein is our use of standard scores. Another difference is in the fact that we do not include the Category Test. Further, our program analyzes the data and makes decisions regarding the presence and degree of brain dysfunction and degree of laterality but does not attempt to make further analyses. Instead, the standard scores are plotted according to dimensions of behavior, and further analyses are made by the neuropsychologist from the profile. An outline of the procedure and an example are presented in Appendix 20.1 and may be consulted for further reference. (See Appendices 20.1, 20.2, and 20.3.)

AUTOMATED TESTING

The use of computers to store data and to assist the trained professional in making decisions represents an application of computers that should be readily accepted by neuropsychologists. Such utilization does not change or intervene in the clinical process; thus, any strategies to aid the process are contingent upon the collection of data by traditionally accepted methods. The computer simply aids in storing and manipulating data and functions to aid the neuropsychologist in the decision-making process. Such an application is off-line and may or may not be used. Such is not the case with automated testing. This procedure can replace the trained professional and is more clearly susceptible to misuse and abuse.

Applications also vary as a function of the requirements of the test in question. True/false or multiple-choice tests are quite suitable for computer application. Other tests may be totally unsuitable, and attempts to convert a test for computer application may radically change what the test measures and invalidate available norms. Yet in other cases computer application may allow for more effective measures of certain aspects of behavior. Perhaps the greatest concern with automated testing is the potential abuse by untrained individuals or the attractiveness of excessive reliance on such procedures.

There are clearly many issues regarding automated testing that need to be carefully investigated. Cost analyses of conventional psychometrics have suggested poor time utilization (Elwood, 1972; Klingler, Johnson, & Williams, 1976). In contrast, automated testing can be much more cost-effective. Elwood (1972) reported a 50% cost reduction when an automated version of an intelligence test was compared with face-to-face administration. Similar findings have been reported with the Peabody Picture Vocabulary Test (Knights, Richardson, & McNary, 1973; Overton & Scott, 1972) and the MMPI (Pearson, Swenson, Rome, Mataya, & Brannick, 1965). In spite of such promising reports, development of automated testing has been limited, in part, by financial and technical restrictions. For example, many of the above assessment strategies used specialized automated test equipment rather than simply a microcomputer with CRT and keyboard.

Denner (1977) argued that the limited growth of automated testing was due to computer facilities' not being readily available to the typical hospital or clinic. This is clearly not the situation today. Physicians, and to a lesser extent, clinical psychologists, have realized a tremendous growth rate in the number and types of services that can be offered by the use of the computer in the clinical setting, and applications are realizing a dramatic growth. It is to be hoped that neuropsychology will focus upon the clinical efficiency of such applications and not simply view computerized automation as another method to shortcut the evaluation process.

To illustrate the potential cost-efficiency of the computer, Rizza (1981) stated that if the largest bank in California had not adopted computers to process daily transactions, every man, woman, and child in the state would have to work for the bank in order to process the volume of business it currently sustains. Because of the increasing availability of microcomputers, the potential impact for automated routine psychological testing in the clinic is enormous. It would be virtually impossible for banks to return to a noncomputer system at this point in time. In contrast, applications in neuropsychology are just beginning and it is to be hoped that caution and concern will temper developments so that future computer applications will progress in the most effective manner.

One of the obvious major assets of microcomputer-based automated testing is the more efficient utilization of the professional's time. This is particularly the case for the neuropsychologist who invests considerable time in psychometric assessment. Another advantage of automated testing is increased reliability. Standardized test presentation and scoring are insured, and unintentional examiner feedback is eliminated. Likewise, some patients are self-conscious of their performance and deficits and find the testing situation threatening. However, when left alone with the microcomputer, some patients will actually perform better because the testing situation is perceived as less threatening. Of course, the argument can easily be made that examiner feedback is essential in maintaining rapport and maximizing patient performance. To eliminate such an important factor may influence the validity of the test findings.

Finally, the value of microcomputer-based testing includes the capacity to assess dimensions of test behavior that are not easily measured. For example, response latencies and overall performance times can be easily and unobtrusively measured by the microcomputer. Such dimensions of test behavior can provide useful information for the neuropsychologist but commonly go unmeasured. It is perhaps in this area where computer applications are most attractive. There are many aspects of behavioral measurement where more effective assessment strategies are needed. Certainly, computer programs could provide a much-needed strategy for assessing vigilance, attention, and so forth.

Flowers and Leger (1981) have discussed the potential use of microcomputers in quantifying behavioral observations. These authors argued that measures of behavioral observations have been largely qualitative because of the difficulty of transforming the raw behavioral record into meaningful measures having both reliability and external validity. The microcomputer, however, offers a potential method of quantifying numerous behavioral observations; for example, a client's performance on the Halstead–Reitan Tactile Performance test. Motor, tactile, spatial, and planning strategies could be easily quantified to provide additional diagnostic information to the neuropsychologist. This area of measurement, however, has been largely ignored, possibly because of measurement complexity. Nevertheless, some researchers have been able to quantify aspects of problem-solving behavior. For example, Elithorn, Cooper, and Lennox (1979) evaluated patients' responses on a computer-presented version of the Perceptual Maze test and found that patients engaged in a preliminary search period, in tracking behavior that consisted of a series of planned sequential motor responses, and in an evaluation of their performance. These are all measures of problem-solving behavior that give clues about the client's problem-solving strategy and, ultimately, cortical functioning. The microcomputer offers a method of quantifying many dimensions of behavior easily and accurately and can aid in diagnostic accuracy.

Microcomputers can also be used to generate new neuropsychological test material. Not only are computers helpful in generating stimuli of known complexity and varying the dimensions of complexity according to specified incremental steps, but they are also helpful in generating alternate forms of a test to allow repeated testing. Matching items according to their relative complexity or randomizing items for alternate forms is easily accomplished by the computer.

Finally, the accurate determination of the patient's symptoms, medical and psychological history, and sources of stress in the home or work environment is an important but time-consuming aspect of neuropsychological evaluation. Computer interviewing offers an important adjunct to neuropsychological assessment. Computer programs can be designed for a detailed investigation of historical data. Such a program can be designed to use a keying approach, so that a computer does not simply route the patient through each and every question, but cues on the responses to specific questions in order to include or delete segments of a questionnaire. This approach to history taking offers a comprehensive and systematic strategy for investigating a patient's history and at the same time quantifies responses in such a way that these data would be available for later analysis or adjustment in the patient's performance based on the answers to various questions. History-taking programs would provide a printout of key symptoms or problem areas that the neuropsychologist could use for further exploration. This would result in a much more efficient use of time by allowing the professional to focus upon key problem areas rather than follow many dead ends.

There are significant disadvantages to automated testing procedures to be considered. This is particularly the case for many of the nonpaper-and-pencil tests that are used for neuropsychological assessment. Some of the more obvious arguments against automated testing include the potential dehumanization and negative interpersonal messages that computerized assessment may produce. The issue of cost-effectiveness of automated testing versus humanized interpersonal contact is difficult but may relate more to specific tests than to the procedure in general.

Issues that relate specifically to automated testing in neuropsychological assessment are related to limited behavioral sampling. In a comprehensive neuropsychological evaluation, behavior is sampled from various input-output modalities. However, automated testing places restrictions on both stimulus and response. For example, visual input is generally limited to a two-dimensional visual stimulus displayed on the screen of the computer terminal. Similarly, motor behavior is generally limited to simple motor responses that are collected via a keyboard or simple peripheral device (e.g., joystick). Further, open-ended verbal responses, such as those on the Comprehension subtest of the WAIS-R, are almost impossible to score with a microcomputer. Clearly, before effective neuropsychological assessment strategies can be developed for the computer, external test materials (other than the keyboard, joystick, and CRT) will need to be linked into the computer to present more varied stimuli and measure a much broader range of responses.

In summary, while the availability of low-cost microcomputers offers significant advantages over traditional testing methods, serious limitations exist at this point in time. Not only do computer systems limit the modalities of behavior sampled, but when the neuropsychologist has limited contact with the client many dimensions of behavior, such as the patient's motivation, his or her response to stress and coping style, and his or her response to feedback and/or problem-solving persistence, go unobserved and unmeasured. Thus, to the extent that the neuropsychologist is interested in observing as much of the patient's behavior as is realistically possible in order to predict day-to-day behavior, computer applications will be limited. Subtle behaviors and strategies that the patient may employ in compensating for deficits, as well as coping style and frustration tolerance, cannot be evaluated when using automated testing procedures.

While attempts at designing a total neuropsychological assessment program for the computer may be ill advised, it is clear that assessment can be significantly augmented by the judicious selection and careful documentation of specialized tests and interviewing procedures. Researchers simply must outline goals of assessment and investigate areas where computer assessment can better meet these goals than traditional behavioral assessment. Approached in this way, a computer can augment the overall program and aid in developing a more effective assessment method. Along these same lines, the more effective use of computer-administered testing for certain tests may free up the professional's time to focus upon behavioral observations during tests where the test-taking behavior (quality) is an important source of information.

COMPUTERS IN REHABILITATION

Controversy exists regarding the mechanisms involved in recovery of behavioral function (Finger, 1978). Questions about neuroregeneration, resolution of transient disturbances, functional reorganization, or behavioral compensation have yet to be answered. Both reinstitution of function theories and behavioral compensation theories exist and microcomputers have found applications in both camps.

The implications of the reinstitution philosophy in cognitive rehabilitation involve either the reteaching of lost behavioral function or stimulation of the disrupted processes in an effort to achieve maximal functioning. In both cases, the microcomputer can be used as an aid for drill and practice. Many simple drill and skill-building programs exist, or programs can easily be developed to present numerous types of material. The microcomputer is able to effectively provide extensive practice for the patient for initial learning and for building newly acquired skills. There is no shortage of computer programs available. In the area of cognitive rehabilitation, programs exist for memory, perceptual processes, eye–hand coordination, verbal exercise, concentration, and so forth (Craine & Gudeman, 1981; Lally, 1982; Lesgold, 1982; Lynch, 1982).

More sophisticated applications of microcomputers for specialized computer-aided learning packages have recently emerged and have been reviewed elsewhere (Odor, 1982; Rizza, 1981). Rizza (1981) described the use of a computer as a "learning manager" rather than simply as a drill master. Based on students' recorded performance, a computer program can be used to recommend those appropriate learning activity assignments likely to be most effective in helping the learner attain mastery of a particular skill; concurrently, it also can monitor the general effectiveness of the instructional material. An additional potential application of the computer for educational-based rehabilitation is as a learning aid. Rizza (1981) argued that the computer can be used to perform a number of specific tasks to increase the learner's ability to comprehend a subject. This approach stresses learning by discovery. Simulation programs have become available in various academic fields, such as business and engineering. An underlying theory is revealed through the learner's interaction with a conceptual model or simulation of some predetermined topic area (Odor, 1982). The potential exists to adapt this type of programming strategy to create simulation programs that are relevant for cognitive rehabilitation applications.

One advantage of microcomputer systems in cognitive rehabilitation is the presentation and monitoring of individualized instruction at reasonable costs. Computer-augmented, home-based cognitive rehabilitation programs can be designed to provide specific learning material at a pace commensurate with the learner's ability. The use of such home-based systems could serve to greatly enhance or augment time spent by the professional. Further, when programs are designed to be interesting and challenging, therapeutic time spent in cognitive rehabilitation can be enjoyable.

The behavioral compensation philosophy in cognitive rehabilitation assumes the patient compensates for a completely destroyed link in his or her behavior repertoire. This occurs when a functional link that hitherto has never participated in the disrupted functional system assumes a new role by replacing the destroyed components (Luria, 1963). Luria (1963) labeled this process *intersystemic reorganization*. The use of microcomputers as an aid to intersystemic reorganization becomes an increasingly viable option as input–output modalities become more sophisticated and as microcomputers become smaller, less expensive, and more powerful.

Rehabilitation engineers have been using microcomputers with increasing frequency to help disabled people, with an emphasis on exploiting intact functions as a means of behaviorally compensating for a particular disability. Microcomputers have helped patients compensate for physical disabilities, deafness, and dyslexia (Odor, 1982). Bach-y-Rita (1980) described a particularly interesting method of sensory substitution, whereby sight could be restored by utilizing external devices to complete a functional circuit. This was accomplished by delivering a visual image, received by a miniature TV camera, to the skin by means of a two-dimensional variable tactile stimulation matrix. Bach-y-Rita found that after sufficient training, subjects were able to "see" by utilizing the new cutaneous information.

More speculative applications involve the use of microcomputers as a personal decision-aiding system. Andriole (1982) has proposed the use of microcomputer decision aids as extensions of human problem solvers, with systems designed to be adaptive to their users, to unique problem-solving situations, and to past problem-solving experiences. An example of this type of application is the symbiotic relationship between humans and computers in lunar missions. However, the computer as a decision aid need not be limited to such esoteric applications. It may be possible to adapt microcomputers to the everyday needs of clients with limited or reduced problem-solving abilities. Andriole (1982) has argued that it should be possible to design a hardware/ software system that will interact with its human partner in a way that is consistent with specific problem-solving situational requirements. He has argued that such a system might even monitor the physiological state of the user so as to pace the interaction or repeat sequences in order to "check" the user's coherence and logic if the user is behaving unconventionally because of emotional arousal.

Weiss and Kelly (1980) have developed decision templates that free users from the model-building steps necessary to solve a decision problem. Thus, microcomputers offer a means to select, organize, format, evaluate, pace, and display information for personal decision making. This suggests that the process of objectifying decision strategies and helping the user through each step could have tremendous applications in aiding neurologically impaired patients in their recovery from and/or compensation for frontal lobe deficits. Applications of this type of computing for behavioral compensation of cognitive deficits seem very promising and essentially are limited only by the imaginations of rehabilitation engineers, computer programmers, and clinical neuropsychologists. The challenge, then, is to achieve effective interdisciplinary communication and cooperation in developing systems to serve the needs of these patients.

FUTURE DIRECTIONS AND CAUTIONS

The application of microcomputers to neuropsychology is quite new. Nonetheless, computer programs for assessment or treatment are developed daily and future applications appear limitless. Yet many of these computer systems or programs have not been adequately evaluated, and users often select programs because of novelty rather than utility. Potential users must critically appraise the evidence for the effectiveness of a program rather than the attractiveness of its graphics. Issues of reliability and validity must be thoroughly addressed.

Ultimately, the effective use of microcomputer systems will be based upon the ability of the system to provide a cost-effective method for augmenting assessment and treatment. The computer is best at performing routine, monotonous tasks rapidly and accurately. It is useful for converting, manipulating, and analyzing data in prescribed ways or routinely training a patient in basic tasks, but it is only as good as the data with which it works. Much important information in both assessment and treatment is presently, and may continue to be, qualitative. It remains for the clinician to observe, analyze, and consider this qualitative data in reaching final decisions.

Neuropsychologists interested in computer systems need to investigate carefully the decision rules employed by the system, as well as the normative data used in making those decisions. One must assess the accuracy of the system in determining brain dysfunction, in discriminating between brain dysfunction and emotional problems, and in determining the extent to which the data relate to the patient's everyday behavior. In addition, the user must ask questions with regard to specific research available supporting the program's effectiveness. Of particular importance would be the availability of research investigating the usefulness of a system by individuals other than those involved in developing the system. Finally, potential users must carefully decide what they expect the system to do and whether the computer system being investigated is capable of meeting their needs.

At present, psychologists have many fears regarding the application of computers. In particular, they are concerned about abuse of blindly analyzed data by unsophisticated users. It is clear that guidelines need to be formulated for the use of computers. If the computer is used as an adjunct to the psychologist, then existing guidelines may apply. If it is used as a substitute, then a new set of problems arise and new guidelines need to be formulated. It is to be hoped that decisions will be based upon questions of reliability and validity rather than less significant issues such as professional rivalry and territoriality.

Of particular importance is the use of computers in testing by nonpsychologists. Perhaps it is this area where guidelines are most needed for computer system vendors. While guidelines are far from settled in this area, one approach is the control of output. The MMPI can be used as a model for this discussion, since it has been available on computer and is used by a wide variety of health professionals. Unfortunately, existing systems generally provide detailed interpretations for anyone using the system. Such an application may replace the psychologist with a less reliable and less valid system. Even when the scoring and analysis system is controlled, the tests are often administered without adequate instruction.

This problem could be partially resolved by limiting the output from the system. Automated interpretation of the MMPI for nonpsychologists should be treated as screening (which it is), and the report should consider the source. A physician, for example, might be simply advised about the patient's emotional state (e.g., depressed) and the appropriateness of further psychodiagnostics or the need for psychological consultation. That information would satisfy the needs of the physician and work in the best interest of the patient. The system might even be designed so that the psychologist or psychiatrist to whom the referral was made could obtain a release form with the proper computer code in order to obtain more detailed output from the system, thereby avoiding duplication of effort.

Unfortunately, abuses of any system occur. Professionals who, due to expedience or lack of awareness, rely on an untrained person to present the tests to the patient may invalidate the testing in such a way that it is not clearly detected by the computer analysis system. Without a careful explanation as to the purpose of the test, the patient may be oversuspicious and present a distorted picture. This further reinforces the fact that the computer system is only as good as the data provided. Regardless of the type of system used, it remains for the professional to ensure that appropriate data are being obtained for analysis.

At the present time, computer applications in neuropsychology are still in the "promising speculation" stage for clinical practitioners outside the university setting. In addition, the lack of widely available software limits potential applications. However, recent developments indicate a vast potential for development of computer systems to augment both assessment and treatment of neurologically impaired patients.

REFERENCES

Andriole, S. J. (1982). The design of microcomputer-based personal decision-aiding systems. *IEEE Transactions on Systems, Man, and Cybernetics, 12,* 463–469.

Anthony, W. Z., Heaton, R. K., & Lehman, R. A. W. (1980). An attempt to cross-validate two acturial systems for neuropsychological test interpretation. *Journal of Consulting and Clinical Psychology, 48,* 317–326.

Bach-y-Rita, P. (1980). Brain plasticity as a basis for therapeutic procedures. In P. Bach-y-Rita (Ed.), *Recovery of function: Theoretical considerations for brain injury rehabilitation.* Baltimore: University Park Press.

Craine, J. F., & Gudeman, H. E. (Eds.). (1981). *The rehabilitation of brain functions: Principles, procedures and techniques of neurotraining.* Springfield, IL: Charles C. Thomas.

Denner, S. (1977). Automated psychological testing: A review. *British Journal of Social and Clinical Psychology, 16,* 175–179.

Elithorn, A., Cooper, R., & Lennox, R. (1979). Assessment of psychotropic drug effects. In J. Crooks & J. H. Stevenson (Eds.), *Drugs and the elderly.* London: Macmillan.

Elwood, D. L. (1972). Test–retest reliability and cost analyses of automated and face to face intelligence testing. *International Journal of Man-Machine Studies, 4,* 1–22.

Finger, S. (Ed.). (1978). *Recovery from brain damage: Research and theory.* New York: Plenum Press.

Finkelstein, J. H. (1976). BRAIN: A computer program for interpretation of the Halstead–Reitan Neuropsychological Test Battery. *Dissertation Abstracts International, 37,* 5349-B. (University Microfilms No. 77–8864).

Flowers, I. H., & Leger, D. W. (1981). Personal computers and behavioral observation: An introduction. *Behavior Research Methods and Instrumentation, 14,* 227–230.

Fromm-Auch, D., & Yeudall, L. T. (1983). Normative data for the Halstead–Reitan Neuropsychological Tests. *Journal of Clinical Neuropsychology, 5,* 221–238.

Kiernan, R. J., & Matthews, C. G. (1976). Impairment index versus T-score averaging in neuropsychological assessment. *Journal of Consulting and Clinical Psychology, 44, 951.*

Klingler, D. E., Johnson, J., & Williams, T. (1976). Strategies in the evaluation of an on-line computer-assisted unit for intake assessment of mental health patients. *Behavior Research Methods & Instrumentation, 8,* 95–100.

Knights, R. M. (1970). *Smoothed normative data on tests for evaluating brain damage in children.* (Research Bulletin No. 53). Ottawa: Carleton University, Department of Psychology.

Knights, R. M. (1979). Problems of criteria in diagnosis: A profile similarity approach. *Clinical Neuropsychology, 1,* 28–32.

Knights, R. M., Richardson, D. H., & McNary, L. R. (1973). Automated versus clinical administration of the Peabody Picture Vocabulary Test and the Coloured Progressive Matrices. *American Journal of Mental Deficiency, 78,* 223–225.

Lally, M. (1982). Computer-assisted handwriting instruction and visual/kinaesthetic feedback processes. *Applied Research in Mental Retardation, 3,* 397–405.

Lesgold, A. M. (1982). Computer games for the teaching of reading. *Behavior Research Methods and Instrumentation, 14,* 224–226.

Luria, A. R. (1963). *Restoration of function following brain damage* (O. L. Zanguoill, Trans.). New York: Pergamon Press.

Lynch, W. J. (1982). The use of electronic games in cognitive rehabilitation. In L. E. Trexler (Ed.), *Cognitive Rehabilitation: Conceptualization and intervention.* New York: Plenum Press.

Matthews, C. G. (1977). Adult (C.A.) 15 and older; Neuropsychological test battery. Madison, WI: Author.

Moehle, K. & Long, C. J. (1984). Neuropsychological test performance and aging: Empirical results and clinical implications. Paper presented at the meeting of the American Psychological Association, Toronto.

Odor, P. (1982). Microcomputers and disabled people. *International Journal of Man-Machine Studies, 17,* 51–58.

Overton, G. W., & Scott, K. G. (1972). Automated and manual intelligence testing: Data on parallel forms of the Peabody Picture Vocabulary Test. *American Journal of Mental Deficiency, 76,* 639–643.

Pearson, J. S., Swenson, W. M., Rome, W. P., Mataya, P., & Brannick, T. L. (1965). Development of a computer system for scoring and interpretation of Minnesota Multiphasic Personality Inventories in a medical clinic. *Annals of the New York Academy of Sciences, 126,* 682–692.

Rizza, P. J. (1981). Computer-based education (CBE): Tomorrow's traditional system. *Journal of Children in Contemporary Society, 14,* 29–42.

Russell, E. W., Neuringer, C., & Goldstein, G. (1970). *Assessment of brain damage: A neuropsychological key approach.* New York: Wiley-Interscience.

Spreen, O., & Gaddes, W. H. (1969). Developmental norms for fifteen neuropsychological tests age 6–15. *Cortex, 5,* 171–191.

Stein, D. G., Rosen, J. J., & Butters, N. (Eds.). (1974). *Plasticity and recovery of function in the central nervous system.* New York: Academic Press.

Swiercinsky, D. P., & Warnock, J. K. (1977). Comparison of the neuropsychological key and discriminant analysis approaches in predicting cerebral damage and localization. *Journal of Consulting and Clinical Psychology, 45,* 808–814.

Wagner, M. T. (1983). *Cognitive rehabilitation of brain damaged patients: An annotated bibliography.* Unpublished manuscript.

Wedding, D. (1983). Comparison of statistical and actuarial models for predicting lateralization of brain damage. *Clinical Neuropsychology, 4,* 15–20.

Wheeler, L., Burke, C., & Reitan, R. (1963). An application of discriminant functions to the problem of predicting brain damage using behavioral variables. *Perceptual and Motor Skills, 16,* 417–440.

Weiss, J. J., & Kelly, C. W. (1980). *BSCREEN and OPGEN: Two problem structuring decision aids which employ decision templates.* McLean, VA: Decision and Designs.

APPENDIX 20.1

Summary of Data Sheet Used to Record Scores During Test Administration and Input Into Microcomputer

I.D. No. (D1) _____

CORTICAL BRAIN ASSESSMENT SUMMARY

NAME (B1) _____ REFERRED BY: _____ REQUEST: _____
TEST DATE(B2) _____ OFFICE NO _____ HOSPITAL NO _____ RM _____
BIRTHDATE(B3) _____ AGE(1) _____ ED(2) _____ SEX(3)_____ RACE(4) _____

LATERAL DOMINANCE: HAND __R__   EYE __L__   FOOT __R__   DOMINANCE(6) _____3_____

PSYCHOSENSORY	(R)	(L)	LANGUAGE			CORNELL MEDICAL INDEX
Sensory Sup.			Token Test	(37)	-1	(73) 31
Tactile	0	0	Dictation	(38)	-1	
Auditory	0	0	Reading	(39)	-1	MMPI (STANDARD SCORES)
Visual	0	0	Naming	(40)	-1	L (74) 46 MF (81)145
Total	(7) 0	(14) 0	Fluency			F (75) 50 PA (82)170
Finger Recog.	(8) 4	(15) 0	Thurstone	(41)	48	K (76) 49 PT (83)166
Graphesthesia			Benton	(42)	-1	HS(77) 51 SC (84)161
Numbers	(9) 3	(16) 0	Computation	(43)	-1	D (78) 69 MA (85)140
Letters	(10) 0	(17) 0	Aphasia	(44)	7	HY(79) 76 SI (86)167
Stereognosis	(11) 0	(18) 0				PD(80) 58
Tactile Form	(12) 0	(19) 0	ATTENT./CONCENTRA.			
Auditory			Aud	(45)	-1	SUPLMENT. TEST SCORES
Speech P.	(13) 9		Vis	(46)	-1	
Rhythm		(20) 11				

			WAIS-R (ACSS)			PROFILE ANALYSIS
			*INF	(47)	7	DYSFUNCTION NORMAL
PSYCHOMOTOR	(R)	(L)	*COM	(48)	8	
Strength	(21) 28	(24) 22	ARI	(49)	7	LATERALIZING SIGNS
Sequencing			*SIM	(50)	9	
Finger-nose	___	___	DSP	(51)	7	L R
Open-close	___	___	VOC	(52)	8	
Alternation	___	___	*DYS	(53)	9	
Fist-ring	___	___	PCO	(54)	7	
Finger-thumb	___	___	*BLD	(55)	10	
Tapping-finger	___	___	*PAR	(56)	10	
Total	(22) 2	(25) 2.5	OAS	(57)	9	
Tapper	(23) 50	(26) 45	VIQ	(58)	86	
			PIQ	(59)	94	
PERCEPTUAL-MOTOR	(R)	(L)	FSIQ	(60)	89	
Trails C	(27) -1					
Trails A		(28) 17	WMS			
Trails B		(29) 80	(61)		4	SUMMARY AND CONCLUSIONS
Constructional			(62)		5	
Praxis			(63)		6	
Copy		2	(64)		6	
Command		-1	(65)		9	
B/D		-1	(66)		6	
Total		(30) 2	(67)		13	
			(68) MQ		81	
TPT	(R)	(L)				
R Hand Time	(D2) 5.8		60´ RECALL			
Blocks	(31) 10		(69) 4	-1		
L Hand Time		(D3) 4.3	(70) 6	-1		
Blocks		(32) 10	(71) 7	-1		
B Hand Time	(D4) 3.3		(72) %	-1		
Blocks	(33) 10					
Total Time	(D5) 13.4					
Total B.	(34) 30					
Memory	(35) 8					
Location		(36) 0				

APPENDIX 20.1   *(continued)*

I.D. #_____ NAME _____ TEST DATE_____
REFERRED BY _____ DIAGNOSIS_____
                                              GROUP_____

HISTORY 1 or 0   SURGERY   (113)_-1   NATURE
  EDUCATIO (87)_12   1   DEV DIS
  OCCUPATI (88)_4   DIAGNOSIS(114)_-1, (115)___, (116)___   2   TUMORS
  HIST AUD (89)_1   3   INFECT
  HIST VIS (90)_1   EEG   (117)_4, (118)_6, (119)_3   4   SEIZURE
  HIST SOMA(91)_1   55 METABOLIC
  HIST MOT (92)_0   CAT SCAN (120)_1, (121)___, (122)___   6   VASCULAR
  HIST SPE (93)_1   7   DEMYELIN
  HIS READ (94)_0   ANGIOGRAM (123)_1, (124)___, (125)___   8   TRAUMA
  HIST WRI (95)_0   9   DEG DISEASE
  HIST NUM (96)_1   CBA   (126)_4, (127)_6, (128)_3   10 AGE (OVER 70)
  HIST HA (97)_0   11 CONTROL
  HIS PAIN (98)_1   PERSONALITY(129)_2   12 EMOTION
  HIST MEM (99)_1   13XX TEMP LOBE
  HIS PERS(100)_1   SURGERY: 14 CINGULOTOMY
  HIS SEIZ(101)_0   0 = None   3 = LP   6 = RP 15 CYST
                         1 = LA   4 = RA   7 = Other 16 _____
  HIS SYNC(102)_0   2 = LT   5 = RT   17 _____
  LGTH PRO(103)_5(yr)   18 _____
  ONSET   (104)_2   PERSONALITY   13 (130)
  CARDIAC (105)_1   0 = Normal   3 = Mod.emo.adj.
  HYPERTEN(106)_0   1 = Mild distress 4 = Severe emo.
  DIABETES(107)_0   2 = Mod. distress   adj.
  CNS INFO(108)_0
  HEAD TRA(109)_0   NO DATA   = 0   NO DATA = 0   ANTERIOR   = 1
  SURGERY (110)_0   NORMAL   = 1   L > R   = 1   POSTERIOR   = 2
  CVA   (111)_0   NORMAL W/   LEFT   = 2   MIDDLE   = 3
  ALC/DRUG(112)_0   WEAKNESS = 2   R > L   = 3   POSTERIOR MIDDLE = 4
                       BORDERLINE = 3   RIGHT   = 4   ANTERIOR MIDDLE = 5
                       IMPAIRED   = 4   GENERAL. = 5
                                         BILATERAL = 6

SURGERY _____

DIAGNOSIS _____

EEG _____

CAT SCAN _____

X-RAY _____

CBA _____

PERSONALITY _____

155. COMPUTER DATA CHECK _____ DATE _____ BY _____
      1 = 1981   2 = 1982   3 = 1983   etc.

APPENDIX 20.2

Decision Strategies used in the CBA Lab Neuropsychology System

A. *Input Scores from Summary Sheet (Appendix 20.1)*
    1. Halstead Test and Subtest Scores
    2. WAIS
    3. Wechsler Memory Scale
    4. Delayed Memory
    5. Cornell and MMPI
    6. Demographic Data
    7. Medical and Psychological History
    8. Medical Test Findings

B. *Standard Score Conversion*
    1. Select and read mean and standard deviation for each test from appropriate norm file.
    2. Convert each score to a standard score.
    3. Correct scores so that impairment is reflected in the same direction.

C. *Data-Analysis to determine presence and extent of cerebral dysfunction*
    1. Compute Average Weighted T-Score
    2. Decide severity of impairment
       mild T-score > 1.15
       mod T-score > 2.01
       sev   T-score > 2.86
    3. Laterality determination
       Compute average difference T-score and determination severity.

D. *Print out Summary Sheet and Cognitive Profile*
    See Appendix 20.3.

APPENDIX 20.3

Summary Profile and Detailed Profile Plot of a Represented Case

```
   C NO. 141              Printed on 10-15-1985              18141

                   CORTICAL BRAIN ASSESSMENT LAB, PC
                     910 MADISON AVE., SUITE 609
   Charles J. Long Ph.D.                        W.L.Hutcherson M.S.
   Neuropsychologist                            Neuropsych. Examiner

                   NEUROPSYCHODIAGNOSTIC PROFILE FOR

               Left Tem   10-2-85    9-20-42  18141

        ABOVE AVERAGE          AVERAGE           IMPAIRED
    20          30       40       50       60       70       80
   ---+---------+---------+---------+---------+---------+---------+---------+-----
   PSYCHOSENSORY
   LEFT   51                  .         *       .
   RIGHT  46                  .     *           .
   PSYCHOMOTOR
   LEFT   57                  .               *  .
   RIGHT  62                  .                  .*
   PRECEP-MOTOR  46           .     *           .
   INTEGRAT   53              .           *     .
   LANGUAGE   30 *            .                 .
   VERBAL I Q  86            .                *  .
   PERF I Q   94             .           *      .
   FULL I Q   89             .               *  .
   SHORT TERM MEMORY   81    .                 .         *
   LONG TERM MEMORY   64     .                 .       *
   EMOTIONAL   76  0         .                 .      *
   ---+---------+---------+---------+---------+---------+---------+---------+-----

   MILD CEREBRAL DYSFUNCTION          AVERAGE IMP INDEX= 1.185164

   LOW AVERAGE RANGE OF INTELLIGENCE  -   FSIQ= 89 VIQ= 86 PIQ= 94

   LOW AVERAGE RANGE - SHORT TERM MEMORY       MQ= 81

   LOW AVERAGE RANGE - LONG TERM MEMORY        % RECALL= 64
                       LATERALITY PROFILE

                 LEFT HEM                    RIGHT HEM

   TEST30      20       10       0      -10      -20      -30
   ---+---------+---------+---------+---------+---------+---------+---------+-----
   SEQ 49                                   <>
   GRIP 34                  <>
   TAP 37                      <>
   IQ 30                 <>
   TPT 35                      <>
   APH 7 <>
   AUD 47                                        <>
   SN 7 <>
   A-C 31                 <>
   STM 41.5                        <>
   LTM 31.5               <>

   ---+---------+---------+---------+---------+---------+---------+---------+-----
   TOTAL LATERALITY VAL 75
   AVE LATERALITY VALUE 6.818182
   WEAKNESS WEAKLY LATERALIZED TO THE LEFT
```

APPENDIX 20.3 *(continued)*

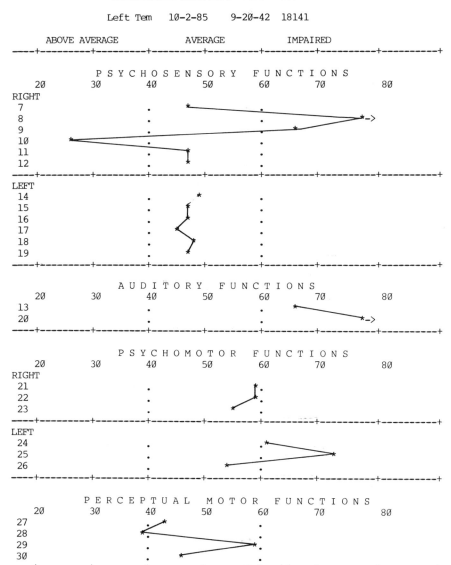

```
        C NO. 141              Printed on 10-15-1985           18141

                     CORTICAL BRAIN ASSESSMENT LAB, PC
                        910 MADISON AVE., SUITE 609
   Charles J. Long Ph.D.                           W.L.Hutcherson M.S.
   Neuropsychologist                               Neuropsych. Examiner

                     NEUROPSYCHODIAGNOSTIC PROFILE FOR

                   Left Tem   10-2-85    9-20-42  18141

           ABOVE AVERAGE            AVERAGE            IMPAIRED
   ----+---------+---------+---------+---------+---------+----------+----------+

                     P S Y C H O S E N S O R Y   F U N C T I O N S
         20        30        40        50        60        70        80
   RIGHT
      7                      .         *              .
      8                      .              .                    *->
      9                      .              .          *
     10    *                 .              .
     11                      .  *           .
     12                      .  *           .
   ----+---------+---------+---------+---------+---------+----------+----------+
   LEFT
     14                      .    *         .
     15                      . *            .
     16                      . *            .
     17                      . *            .
     18                      .  *           .
     19                      . *            .
   ----+---------+---------+---------+---------+---------+----------+----------+

                     A U D I T O R Y   F U N C T I O N S
         20        30        40        50        60        70        80
     13                      .              .    *
     20                      .              .              *->
   ----+---------+---------+---------+---------+---------+----------+----------+

                     P S Y C H O M O T O R   F U N C T I O N S
         20        30        40        50        60        70        80
   RIGHT
     21                      .              *.
     22                      .              *.
     23                      .        *     .
   ----+---------+---------+---------+---------+---------+----------+----------+
   LEFT
     24                      .              *
     25                      .              .       *
     26                      .        *     .
   ----+---------+---------+---------+---------+---------+----------+----------+

                     P E R C E P T U A L   M O T O R   F U N C T I O N S
         20        30        40        50        60        70        80
     27                      .  *           .
     28                   *   .             .
     29                      .              *
     30                      .     *        .
   ----+---------+---------+---------+---------+---------+----------+----------+
```

APPENDIX 20.3   *(continued)*

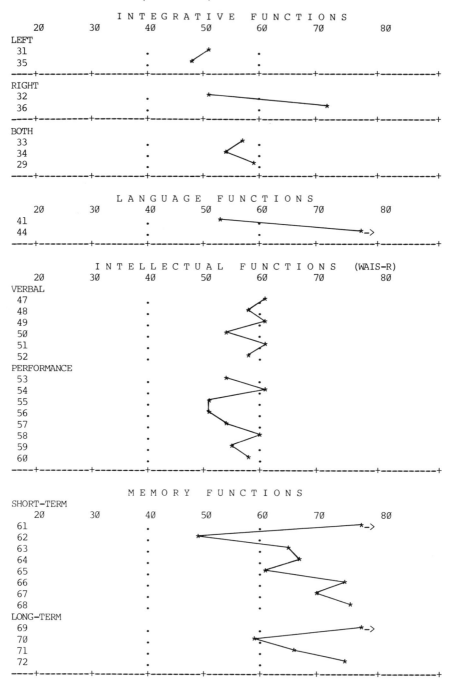

APPENDIX 20.3 *(continued)*

M M P I   P L O T

FILE NO.= 141   I.D.NO.= 18141   NAME   Left Tem TESTDATE   10-2-85 AGE   33

Index